The Theory and Practice of Philosophy

UMass Dartmouth/SEPPCE Resource Center
285 Old Westport Road
North Dartmouth, MA 02747

The Theory and Practice of Philosophy

Abraham Edel

With a new introduction by
Peter Hare
Irving Louis Horowitz

Transaction Publishers
New Brunswick (U.S.A.) and London (U.K.)

New material this edition copyright © 2009 by Transaction Publishers, New Brunswick, New Jersey. Originally published in 1946 by Harcourt, Brace and Company, Inc.

All rights reserved under International and Pan-American Copyright Conventions. No part of this book may be reproduced or transmitted in any form or by any means, electronic or mechanical, including photocopy, recording, or any information storage and retrieval system, without prior permission in writing from the publisher. All inquiries should be addressed to Transaction Publishers, Rutgers—The State University of New Jersey, 35 Berrue Circle, Piscataway, New Jersey 08854-8042. www.transactionpub.com

This book is printed on acid-free paper that meets the American National Standard for Permanence of Paper for Printed Library Materials.

Library of Congress Catalog Number: 2008019228
ISBN: 978-1-4128-0822-4
Printed in the United States of America

Library of Congress Cataloging-in-Publication Data

Edel, Abraham, 1908-
    The theory and practice of philosophy / Abraham Edel ; with a new introduction by Irving Louis Horowitz and Peter Hare.
       p. cm.
Originally published: New York : Harcourt, Brace and Co., 1946.
Includes bibliographical references and index.
ISBN 978-1-4128-0822-4 (alk. paper)
   1. Philosophy. I. Title.

BD21.E38 2008
101—dc22

2008019228

PREFACE

The objectives of an introductory course in Philosophy may be achieved in different ways—by Socratic stimulation, by exhibition of an integrated system of philosophy as example, by building on the sense of urgency in human problems and extracting their implications, by study of philosophers of the past, and, no doubt, in many other ways. No other field has a greater variety of approaches for dealing with the same fundamental problems. This diversity is seen in the introductory courses to be found at various institutions. Some stress types of philosophy, others logical or methodological materials; some take a problem approach, others an historical one; and sometimes the student is introduced to philosophy through the study of ethical and social issues.

The present book has not been cast along the lines of any one of these interests alone. This is because the writer is convinced of the fundamental interrelatedness of problems of method, metaphysics, and value. (The effectiveness of a book like Plato's *Republic,* which has probably in the past introduced more people to philosophy than any text, seems to lie in the very way in which Plato goes from one to another type of problem under the necessities of the subject-matter.) Development of a sense of method is attempted by direct exposition in Parts One and Two, and indirectly by application throughout the book. Alternative philosophic paths that men have followed are most amplified in Part Five, but they emerge also from types of leading ideas in Part One, from theories of man in Part Three, and even from issues concerning the analysis of science in Part Two. Value phases are treated in the context of whole philosophies in Part Five, in the problems of social life in Part Four, and in the attitudes that accompany different theories of man in Part Three. There is an historical element throughout, as many topics are treated developmentally and traditional philosophies frequently expounded. But this is always in the context of problems, so that stress will fall on the major objective of reflective analysis of ideas.

It ought perhaps to be added that although the book has a unitary development each part is an integral whole, complete in itself. The writer is of the belief that while the book as a whole would provide basic material for a full year course, three parts would be sufficient for a one-term course. This is rendered possible by the fact that no major objective is limited solely to one part.

At times the analysis of philosophical questions has been carried beyond the usual point for introductory students. This has been done in the belief that oversimplification is often carried too far. The writer has an underlying faith, based on fifteen years of teaching, in the capacity of students to master materials once they are interested in philosophy, and once they realize that in our modern world philosophic outlooks are not trifles but have a basic relevance to thought and action.

That philosophy has this central role, that it should be neither dissolved (as some have urged) nor set upon a pedestal apart from the pressure of human problems, is an explicit premise of the book, suggested in its title. The mammoth tasks of our world today constitute a challenge to the teacher of philosophy. He is likely to be faced increasingly with a demand for clarification on the fundamental issues of life and value. The expectation that he will provide ready-made answers is as naive as the demand for any panacea, but there is a task which is primarily his, and which cannot be turned over to any other department of human knowledge or any other branch of college activity. That is the stress on the importance of theory in matters of practice, on the need for clear and systematic understanding of the world and man within it, and on the constant role of reflection in the management of human affairs.

Although responsibility for what is presented in the book is entirely mine, it is a pleasure to acknowledge the generous contribution made to it by a considerable number of persons. I am deeply indebted to Dr. May Edel, who worked on each version of the manuscript, helping to remove many obscurities of expression and clarifying many issues, especially on the relation of philosophy and the social sciences; and to Professor Ernest Nagel of Columbia University and Professor Yervant H. Krikorian of the College of the City of New York, who read the manuscript and discussed many of its problems with me during the past few years. I am grateful to Dr. Lewis Feuer, Professor John Goheen of Queens College, Dr. William T. Jones of Pomona College, Professor Albert W. Levi of the University of Chicago, and Professor Charles Lightbody, each of whom read the entire manuscript and offered valuable suggestions and criticisms; to Professor Christopher B. Garnett, Jr. of The George Washington University, for his suggestions regarding Parts One and Two; to Dr. Helen Lewis for her advice on psychological questions at various points and especially in the problems of Chapter 8; and to Dr. Martha Wolfenstein of Hunter College for her suggestions on the treatment of art. My intellectual indebtedness to Professor Morris R. Cohen, especially in the theory of law, and that to Professor Nagel in the theory of science, will be evident from many of the analyses in the book.

A. E.

CONTENTS

PREFACE   v

INTRODUCTION TO THE TRANSACTION EDITION   xiii
Peter Hare and Irving Louis Horowitz

1   The Nature and Role of Philosophy   1

Philosophy attempts to achieve a comprehensive picture of the world . . . Philosophy is critical . . . Philosophy is concerned with understanding man . . . Philosophy is concerned with practice as well as theory

PART I   THE NATURE OF EXPLANATION   9

2   Essence and Purpose: The Teleological Approach   11

ESSENCE . . . Picture of the world in terms of essence . . . Plato's development of the approach . . . Aristotle's treatment of essence and nature . . . Estimate of essence and nature . . . PURPOSE . . . Meaning of purpose . . . Purpose applied to social groups and history . . . Teleology . . . Teleology as explanation

3   Causality and the Mechanistic Approach   28

MEANING OF CAUSE . . . THE WORLD-MACHINE . . . Does causality imply the world-machine? . . . ESTIMATE OF CAUSALITY . . . The element of temporal precedence . . . The element of regularity . . . The element of necessity

4   The Meaning of Law and the Nature of System   41

LAW . . . What is a law? . . . The meaning of probability . . . The uniformity of nature . . . SYSTEM . . . Reducing contingency . . . Types of system . . . Building a system . . . Modes of relating systems . . . The problem of novel qualities . . . Monism and pluralism . . . Explanation as systematization

PART II EMPIRICAL OR SCIENTIFIC METHOD 67

5 Science and Its Method 69

IMPORTANCE OF PROBLEMS OF METHOD TODAY . . . MAIN FEATURES OF SCIENTIFIC METHOD . . . PHILOSOPHIC ISSUES IN THE THEORY OF SCIENCE

6 The Demand for Absolute Knowledge 76

INTUITION . . . Claims for intuition . . . Estimate of intuition . . . AUTHORITY . . . Derivative type . . . Absolute or dogmatic type . . . FIRST PRINCIPLES . . . Self-evident propositions . . . Status of logical principles . . . General reinterpretation of first principles

7 Testing by Experience 93

THE MEANING OF TESTING BY EXPERIENCE . . . Pragmatic approaches . . . Positivist and operationalist analyses . . . Feeling and practice as modes of verification . . . EMPIRICAL TREATMENT OF CONCEPTS ILLUSTRATED . . . Length . . . Intelligence . . . Reality . . . Terms in social science

8 Sense-perception 108

SENSE DATA AS REFLECTION OF REALITY . . . Locke's theory . . . The meaning of correspondence . . . SENSE DATA AS ULTIMATE REALITY . . . Theory developed by Berkeley and Hume . . . HOW SCIENTIFIC METHOD USES SENSE DATA . . . Critique of ultimate data . . . Critique of building-block theory . . . Scientific method self-corrective in dealing with sensation

9 Critiques of Science 118

CLAIM THAT SCIENCE IS ABSTRACT . . . ALLEGED CONFLICT OF LOGIC AND EXPERIENCE . . . ANTINOMIES AS LIMITATION OF SCIENCE . . . Problems of space as illustration . . . Antinomies no theoretical barrier to science . . . THE SKEPTIC'S CRITICISM . . . THE METHOD OF PHILOSOPHY

10 Science, Truth, and Reality 126

SCIENCE AND TRUTH . . . Theories of truth and types of method . . . The theory of truth implicit in scientific method . . . SCIENCE

AND REALITY . . . Fact and reality . . . Does scientific method make assumptions about reality?

PART III WHAT IS A MAN? — 135

11 Man as a Twofold Being — 137

THE BODY . . . BODY AND SOUL . . . Types of soul theory . . . The group-mind theory . . . Modern vitalism . . . BODY AND MIND . . . Cartesian dualism . . . Parallelism . . . Transition to subjectivism

12 Man as Ultimately Mental — 151

BERKELEY'S THEORY OF REALITY . . . His interpretation of body . . . His theory of spirit . . . HUME'S THEORY . . . His analysis of mind . . . Critique of Hume's theory

13 Man a Machine — 157

EPIPHENOMENALISM . . . THE IDENTITY THEORY . . . MECHANISTIC THEORIES . . . Early mechanistic approaches . . . Behaviorism . . . Value attitudes conveyed by mechanism

14 A Naturalistic Account of Man — 168

THE NATURALISTIC APPROACH . . . Classical beginnings . . . Contemporary psychological approaches . . . Modes of describing human activities . . . THE STATUS OF MENTAL STATES . . . Sense-data as qualities of events . . . Alleged subjectivity of mental phenomena . . . Their alleged privacy . . . Their cognitive character . . . RELATION BETWEEN THE MENTAL AND THE PHYSICAL . . . Various meanings of explanation here relevant . . . Naturalistic analysis of body-mind relations . . . Scientific content of traditional theories . . . THE NATURALISTIC ATTITUDE . . . Roots in nature not inimical to value

15 Problems of the Self — 188

MEANING OF IDENTITY . . . THE IDENTITY OF THE INDIVIDUAL MAN . . . Physico-biological, psychological, and social categories . . . Denial of unity . . . Unity beyond experience, and the "real" self . . . Kant's theory of the self . . . Self as the systematic organization of experience . . . FIXITY AND CHANGEABILITY OF THE SELF . . . Meaning of self-expression . . . Illustrations from educational theory . . .

THE SELF AND ITS VALUES . . . The place of values in the self . . . Is egoism inherent in the self?

PART IV OF HUMAN BONDAGE AND HUMAN FREEDOM — 209

16 Values, Ends, and Means — 211

RELATION BETWEEN MEANS AND ENDS . . . EVALUATION OF MEANS AND ENDS . . . LIBERTY AND FREEDOM

17 Freedom — 217

THE ARENA OF CHOICE . . . Interpretations of will . . . Is the act of will itself caused? . . . ARGUMENTS ON FREE WILL . . . The sense of freedom and genuine alternatives . . . Alleged reductio ad absurdum of determinism . . . Do moral ideas rest on free will? . . . Philosophical naturalism and the problem of freedom . . . FREEDOM AS NEGATIVE . . . Empirical analysis of involuntary action . . . Value content of coercion, duress, provocation . . . FREEDOM AS POSITIVE . . . Freedom as an ideal of character

18 Liberty — 235

LIBERTY AS NEGATIVE AND POSITIVE . . . LIBERTY AND THE NATURAL WORLD . . . Physical factors . . . Biological factors . . . Psychological factors . . . LIBERTY AND SOCIETY . . . Social molding and social limitation . . . Search for a general principle of liberty . . . MILL'S THEORY OF LIBERTY . . . His fundamental principle . . . Application of the principle . . . Critique of Mill's theory . . . Evaluation of Mill's liberties . . . LIBERTY AS POSITIVE . . . IS LIBERTY AN END OR A MEANS?

19 Techniques of Freedom and Liberty — 264

THE CONFLICT OF DESIRES . . . The task of organization . . . The problem of absolute desires . . . VIRTUES AND SOCIAL FORMS . . . Illustration from Aristotle's analyses . . . The ethical evaluation of institutions . . . THE ROLE OF PROPERTY SYSTEMS . . . Meaning of property . . . Types of property systems . . . Principles of distribution . . . Patterns of control . . . THE ROLE OF THE STATE . . . Moralistic theories and their evaluation . . . Realistic theories and their evaluation . . . Common attitudes to the state . . . LIMITS OF RECONCILIATION AND PROBLEMS OF COERCION . . . Occasions of coercion . . . Coercion mechanisms within a society . . . War and general attitudes toward violence

20 Democracy 290

THE IDEALS OF DEMOCRACY . . . Liberty . . . Equality . . . Fraternity . . . GOVERNMENTAL PRINCIPLES OF DEMOCRACY . . . General principles . . . Government by the people . . . Faith in the people . . . DEMOCRATIC ATTITUDES . . . APPLICATIONS OF DEMOCRACY . . . DEMOCRACY AND THE FUTURE . . . Basic conditions for its stability . . . Relation of democracy and capitalism

PART V THE DIRECTION OF HUMAN AFFAIRS 311

21 Materialism and Idealism 313

PHILOSOPHIC OUTLOOK BASIC TO HUMAN AFFAIRS . . . IDEALIST AND MATERIALIST PHILOSOPHIES . . . INTERPRETATION OF SCIENCE . . . Materialism and the history of science . . . Historical relations of idealism and science . . . MATTER AND CHANGE . . . Meaning of matter . . . The relation of matter and change . . . Idealist attempts to declare matter unreal . . . Critique of Locke's conception of matter as substratum . . . Materialist view of the primacy of matter . . . SPIRIT AND THE ETERNAL . . . Types of idealism and the primacy of spirit . . . Idealist and materialist interpretations of the eternal . . . THE CONDUCT OF HUMAN LIFE . . . Where in life is philosophic outlook to be found?

22 Interpretation of Religion 337

THE PHENOMENA OF RELIGION . . . Usual features of a religion . . . Religion as a social form . . . ARGUMENTS ON THE EXISTENCE OF GOD . . . Cosmological and teleological arguments . . . Ontological, intuitional and mystical arguments . . . Moral and pragmatic arguments . . . Agnosticism, positivism, atheism . . . ATTITUDES TOWARD THE SOUL AND IMMORTALITY . . . IDEALIST INTERPRETATION OF THE ROLE OF RELIGION . . . MATERIALIST INTERPRETATION OF THE ROLE OF RELIGION . . . Santayana's analysis of religion and its values . . . Marxian socio-historical analysis

23 Interpretation of Art — 364

THE PHENOMENA AND PROBLEMS OF ART ... The problem of esthetic quality ... The nature of art creation ... The criteria of esthetic evaluation ... Ethical and social evaluation of art ... IDEALIST INTERPRETATION ... Platonic approaches ... Schopenhauer's analysis ... Hegelian theory ... Idealist answers to the four problems ... MATERIALIST INTERPRETATION ... "Naturalizing" art ... Analysis of appreciation ... Analysis of creation ... Standards of esthetic judgment ... Ethical and social relations of art

24 The Idealist Outlook on Human Affairs — 388

PLATO AND ARISTOTLE ... Plato's ethical and social theory ... The idealist strain in Aristotle's ethics ... STOICISM ... THE CHRISTIAN OUTLOOK ON GOOD AND EVIL ... The good.... The problem of evil ... KANTIAN ETHICS ... ROYCE'S PHILOSOPHY OF LOYALTY ... IDEALIST INTERPRETATION OF HISTORY ... Central ideas of the idealist synthesis ... Hegel's philosophy of history

25 The Materialist Outlook on Human Affairs — 425

MATERIALIST INTERPRETATION OF MEN'S VALUES ... The analysis of the good ... Why men have values ... Rules of right and obligation; virtues and vices ... Truthfulness as an illustration ... The individual's point of view ... MATERIALIST TREATMENT OF SOCIETY ... Individualistic forms ... Socially oriented forms ... English utilitarianism ... Historical materialism ... SOCIAL VALUES AND THE FUTURE

Suggested Readings — 461

Index — 469

INTRODUCTION TO THE TRANSACTION EDITION
ABRAHAM EDEL: THE JEWISH ARISTOTLE OF CCNY

A note on these three statements is in order. The first segment on *The Theory and Practice of Philosophy* was prepared expressly in regard to the new edition of the text. The second segment, also authored by myself, were remarks prepared for delivery for a memorial service honoring Professor Edel at the New York Society for Ethical Culture Society in New York City on October 20th, 2007. The third and final segment was prepared essentially by Professor Peter Hare of the philosophy department at the State University New York at Buffalo. He delivered this text to me a fortnight prior to his own tragic death. It was, happily, in a finished form, and is herein presented as written.

Irving Louis Horowitz

I. THE BOOK

The Theory and Practice of Philosophy came into existence during an unusual period in American society. It could be well considered the last hurrah of the good feelings that existed between the West and The Soviet Union as a result of the wartime alliance of 1941-1945. The book gave expression to the democratic impulses of naturalism—a world in which for Edel the linkage between Marx and Dewey, materialism and pragmatism formed a whole—not exactly seamless, but stitched together workably in the struggle against irrationality and ideology that Nazi Germany and Fascist Italy represented.

A strong sense of cooperation between East and West was reflected in the book by the full and deep appreciation Edel provided in detailing the idealist as well as materialist traditions in epistemology and ontology. He saw both tendencies as part of the Western tradition. And while he clearly favors the naturalistic tendencies in philosophy and its liberal potential in politics, this appreciation was more a reflection of Edel's strong commitment to the Anglo American tradition of which he was part, than any special animus toward idealism. If one can speak of World War Two in cultural terms, it was an era of good feelings among victorious allies, expressed without the harshness or polemical styles that the Bolshevik tradition had brought into being. Even official communist standard works in America such as A. Landy's *Marxism and the Democratic Tradition* reflected such generous sentiments.

Although Edel's book was a product of an era of good feelings, by the time it landed in college bookstores, that era had come to a crashing halt. Stalinism had resumed its harsh and recriminatory class warfare treatment of the Russian people. Furthermore, in the afterglow of World War Two, the Communist Third International wanted its spoils, and took its tribute through the unbridled domination of Eastern Europe from the Baltic States to Poland and Czechoslovakia. In the United States, Earl Browder was replaced by William Foster, and the notion of the popular front was replaced by demands for vigilant class struggle. One victim in such policy shifts was the notion of a democratic culture itself. In such a radically new climate of opinion, *The Theory and Practice of Philosophy* gave way to angry tracts like Harry K. Wells' *Pragmatism, Philosophy of Imperialism*.

The era of good feelings yielded to a harsh separation of radicalism from liberalism, and to a large extent, a sharp break of communism in the East from socialism in the West. The purpose of these remarks is not to summarize the history of the Cold War, but to note that books—even those designed as textbooks—have unintended consequences. This background may also help to explain why Edel's book went stone cold dead in the marketplace shortly after it was published in late 1946-47. Happily, those precious few who studied with Professor Edel, like myself, while vaguely aware of the larger goings on in the cultural wars of the time, benefited by having the book as a basic text in philosophy. His astonishingly lucid, well written, and informed text took its full title seriously—philosophy was not simply a set of theorems about the nature of the universe, but a guide to public policy and to the nature of quotidian life. His ideas helped turn my interest in philosophy from a course into a life long passion.

In a world considerably removed from wartime friendship and post-war animosities alike, we can better examine this book for what it is worth, on its own merits—and without the heavy weight of inherited prejudices and positions. It is my firm judgment that seen in this light, *The Theory and Practice of Philosophy* will be read as a masterpiece in the field—a model of how philosophy can be summarized rather than vulgarized, and a paradigm for those who can see the field as a whole. This is not to say that the world has stood still for the past sixty plus years, or that writing such a volume today would have the same contents. Indeed, much of Edel's work was developed prior to the rise of existentialism. In addition, the book only barely considers the impact of positivism. It might well be said that the continuum of idealism and materialism was shattered by such developments. But that itself is a matter for debate, one better entered into by those familiar with this book.

Indeed, when Abe and I originally discussed reprinting *The Theory and Practice of Philosophy*, I argued against its republication—to his dismay I must add. He definitely wanted the book to reappear—both as part of his legacy but also as an indication that his perspective could serve a useful purpose in charting philosophy for a new era. But if we missed republishing it as a golden anniversary tribute in 1996, we at least are not foregoing its reappearance any longer. Indeed, it might well be argued that the classical paradigm has reappeared in the present epoch. While existentialism at one end and positivism at the other still find adherents within the field and beyond, the glow of such profoundly diverse figures as Jean Paul Sartre and Rudolph Carnap have given way to reconsiderations of basic ontological judgments and logical constructs. This seems less a function of intentions, as a byproduct of a new technology—one in which issues of logical construction rather than private will seem uppermost in the minds of modern people.

So rather than view this new edition of an old text as a contribution to the history of ideas, one might better see this book as a contribution to ideas in the making of history. It is a book which, if read without precondition and prejudice, can invigorate the young to seek a life in philosophy and perhaps reinvigorate the old to recollect what has been lost in the tragic substitution of ideology for science, and reasoned discourse for unbridled irrationality. In a word, Edel was right to think that this text—written by himself, not managed by others as is now often the case—deserves a place of honor in the curriculum of our age and the reading list of books that matter whatever their vintage.

II. THE MAN

The death of Abraham Edel—born on December 6th, 1908, who died on June 22nd, 2007—filled me with a deep and lasting sadness. Not only for the loss of a special human being in his own terms, but as the final hurrah of a group of thinkers who gathered at City University of New York under the unique umbrella of Morris Raphael Cohen. In addition to being a great historian of both religions and scientific ideas, Cohen exemplified the William James epigram: that the purpose of higher education is to spot a good man when you see one. With exception of extending the word man to include women, that sentiment gave expression to the department as a whole.

I graduated from DeWitt Clinton High School in January of 1947 (in those days we actually had people complete their diplomas in both January and June, although the yearbook was issued once as in the current practice). It seemed almost axiomatic that children from poor Jewish families went from Clinton to City College. Money was not a factor, since there wasn't any. When I informed my parents that my goal was to major in philosophy, my mother cried out: "and just what do you intend to do for a living?" My father, for his part, was certain of my failure, and that I would then become a great success in his community hardware store. As matters turned out, I managed to make a living and escape the rigors of retailing as well.

My first course in philosophy as a freshman was in issues of philosophy. It was taught by a fine man, Mortimer Kadish—then a young man some years away from his leaving for Case Western Reserve. He introduced me to his own mentor, Abraham Edel, and told me point blank to take his courses and listen to him. It was advice that I heeded with relish. Over the next three years I took everything

Abe Edel taught: ethics, law, history, and a special honors program for which I wrote a paper, happily lost in space, on John Dewey's political biases as expressed in his views on educational practice. Everyone there praised the Socratic Method of M.R. Cohen—a dialogue in which received truths were challenged by rebellious youths. But that was not Abe's method. His was Aristotelian— by that I mean each course, indeed each class—began with a precise context of what came before in philosophical ideas, then followed by a close examination of the actual texts we were assigned to review. If I learned one thing from those lectures it is that context and content are united in social affairs just as theory and practice are linked in the various traditions of philosophical discourse.

This department boasted some extraordinary talents: Henry Magid in political theory, Phillip Paul Wiener in the history of western ideas, Daniel Bronstein in formal and symbolic logic, Yervant Krikorian on theory of the mind, and even the son of M.R. Cohen, Felix Cohen in legal and normative theory. It was a heady wine, probably too much so for me to properly absorb. But like all such elixirs, it was certainly too much to walk away from. All of my early effort was imbued by Abe's sense of the discipline, and applied to areas from the history of dialectical reasoning, enlightenment naturalism, and problems of war and peace. Indeed, it was Abe who introduced me to Roy Wood Sellars, with whom he cooperated on a reader in materialism, and who in turn was kind enough to support publication and write the introduction to my war and peace volume. But as I suspected, Abe knew, better than I, the field of philosophy was not a hospitable place to be in the McCarthy Years, nor for that matter, at Columbia, where I had gone for post-graduate studies. With the exception of the late, gentle Horace Friess, who frequently lectured at this very podium of the Society for Ethical Culture, Abe saw little of value in strange excursions inculcated twenty miles away from City College, and that seemed to him to have been twenty years behind in critical imagination.

But all of this says too much about myself and too little about Abe. I have broken a vow in such tributes to deceased colleagues never to speak of myself. I do so now because I would like to believe that I am the beneficiary of what made CCNY special and its philosophy department great: a spirit of fairness in discussing ideas and decency in treating students. To go to school was to capture a sense of liberation—and that Abe imparted in his gentle way of discoursing on things that matter, without recrimination, without bitterness. At the height of McCarthyism he wrote for the school paper an essay on "Struggle for the Minds of Men." It was as forthcoming a defense of classroom liberties and free speech as one dared to make. Indeed, he paid for that slender essay by being singled out by *Red Channels,* for assault by those who had little respect for scholarship or decency. It was not exactly the proudest moment of CCNY and its administration that Abe was called to account for his beliefs. Fortunately, this special humiliation went no further, although it clearly left bitter scars and a bad taste on a man who loved his college and his professional calling.

Abe did indeed hold strong views on the political life of the American nation—and that was a life long critical view. He did not disguise his radical sentiments, nor did he impose them on those who thought otherwise. We did not always agree, and as indicated in the *festschrift* that I co-edited with H.S. Thayer in Abe's honor, those differences grew sharper as the true history of Soviet Stalinism became manifest. For Abe, the political focus was on the problems of American society, for myself the center of gravity shifted to the problems of totalitarian societies the world over. I am uncertain what perspective is correct or proper or better; nor does it much matter in the course of time. My life long relationship with Abe was predicated not on ideological agreements, but on intellectual respect. Abe was, as I had occasion to say on several previous occasions, a rare combination of a Canadian background and British education, whose mature years were spent in the United States. This demographic trifecta may help to explain his constantly good manners. He was also a product of Jewish family life for whom the secular and non-religious humanist prevailed, and he possessed an unusually sophisticated blend of Aristotle, Marx, and Dewey that was uniquely his own. He picked thinkers not icons as models.

Abe also had strong views on people. He had three fine wives in his long life—big love in serial form. May was an outstanding anthropologist, Betty was equally prominent in philosophy, and Sima, who survives Abe, has been a well-respected teacher of languages. All three displayed uncommonly strong personalities and independent career tracks that, while different from him, were linked in common passions and shared broad beliefs. He imparted the same set of values to his son Matthew, who was on his way to being a first-class urban economist and Latin Americanist before a tragic early death, and his daughter Deborah, who likewise has had a professional career distinguished by philanthropic service and amazing organizational savvy.

Abe enjoyed the company of people, but in small doses and in quiet, rustic settings. He spent most summers in Croyden, New Hampshire, and in his later years, closer to home in the New Jersey shoreline. Abe had a lively and quick wit, punctuated by readily stated displeasure with foolish and venomous comment. He despaired of gossip and small talk, and very rarely spoke disparagingly of people unless provoked to do so; and even then he did so uncomfortably. From his friends and students he demanded their very best, and was not averse to speaking frankly if that best was not forthcoming. I ought to know, having being the scathing and proper object of such critique on more than one occasion. His demeanor was uniformly calm and reserved. Theatricality and histrionics were simply alien to his nature. In brief, he had strong views coupled with quiet manners. This is in contrast to the prevailing academic tendency for weak views and coarse manners.

I consider it one of the great joys of my life not only to have known and studied under Abraham Edel, but at having had the opportunity to repay my mentor in some measure by publishing just about all of his major papers and essays, and published or republished all of his main writings. As long as Transaction Publishers survives, at least under my watch, his works shall remain available. The body perishes, and the individual mind with it. What remains, as Abe well knew, is the culture, the storage of reason through the ages and its struggles with unreason. This furious dialogue links not only past with present but good and evil, right and wrong, beauty and ugliness, in the service of reason as such. The wide public realm is what philosophy is all about, and that is what Abraham Edel is all about. Abe may have had doubts concerning the very existence of the soul, but I will nonetheless close with this blessing: may his kind soul rest in eternal tranquility.

III. THE OVERVIEW*

Peter Hare

Abraham Edel was born in Pittsburgh, Pennsylvania on December 6, 1908. Raised in Yorkton, Canada with his older brother Leon who would become a biographer of Henry James, Edel studied Classics and Philosophy at McGill University, earning a BA in 1927 and an MA in 1928. He continued his education at Oxford where, as he recalled, "W.D. Ross and H.A. Prichard were lecturing in ethics, H.W.B. Joseph on Plato, and the influence of G. E. Moore and Bertrand Russell extended from Cambridge. Controversy on moral theory was high. The same was true of epistemology, where Prichard posed realistic epistemology against Harold Joachim who was defending Bradley and Bosanquet against the metaphysical realism of Cook Wilson." He received a BA in Litterae Humaniores from Oxford in 1930. In that year he moved to New York City for doctoral studies at Columbia University, and in 1931 he began teaching at City College, first as an assistant to Morris Raphael Cohen. F.J.E. Woodbridge directed his Columbia dissertation, *Aristotle's Theory of the Infinite* (1934). This monograph and two subsequent books on Aristotle were influenced by Woodbridge's interpretation of Aristotle as a philosophical naturalist. Although his dissertation concerned ancient Greek philosophy, he was much impressed by research in the social sciences at Columbia, and the teaching of Cohen at City College showed him how philosophical issues lay at the root of the disciplines of psychology, sociology, history, as well as the natural sciences.

In the 1930s City College was a special kind of environment, where radical ideas were fought over bitterly, but where the center of gravity was so different from anywhere else in America. The arguments that raged were among varieties of socialist doctrines and varieties of radical theory and not between liberalism and conservatism. Active in establishing the College Teachers Union, Edel was called before the Rapp-Coudert Committee, a New York State forerunner of HUAC

Note: This text was completed by Professor Hare, with the assistance of Professor Guy W. Stroh, only a fortnight prior to his own tragic death. No changes have been made in its presentation.

and McCarthy's Senate committee. His account of this radical movement was published as *The Struggle for Academic Democracy: Lessons from the 1938 "Revolution" in New York's City Colleges* (1990).

John Dewey was the preeminent figure in the Philosophy department during Edel's student years at Columbia. All Edel's subsequent publications can be seen as a blend of Deweyan and Aristotelian naturalisms. However, his interest was usually not in textual or historical scholarship. Rather, in the spirit of Dewey and Aristotle, Edel engaged in what he called "comparative analysis" of other philosophical viewpoints, including the various forms of analytic philosophy then dominant in the discipline. His philosophical style reflected his personality. A tolerant and modest person, his philosophical writing was never aggressive and dogmatic, as so much of the writing of his contemporaries was. Generously entering into dialogue with his opponents, he tended to interpret differences between philosophical movements as a matter of incomplete perspective rather than a question of incompatible answers.

The Theory and Practice of Philosophy (1946) was Edel's first book after the publication of his dissertation. This introductory text successfully blends several of the traditional ways of presenting philosophy to beginning students and the general reader. Writing with exceptional lucidity and fair-mindedness, he speaks to readers today as engagingly as he did shortly after World War II.

In his first large-scale work in moral philosophy, *Ethical Judgment: The Use of Science in Ethics* (1955), Edel discussed at length the problem of ethical relativism. This, he found, is not a simple problem. It has what he termed many strands or elements: that morality is a human product, that everything changes, that cultural diversity exists, that ethics depends on variable attitudes or emotions, etc. If everything in life is contingent and temporal, does this mean that ethical judgments must be arbitrary or even indeterminate? Does this mean that ethics reduces to expediency where there can be no solid or rational answers or results that can be counted on?

Edel with his naturalism was willing to forego absolute, final or a priori conclusions. If ethics is to truly apply to the world, its theories must somehow be tested by experience. Ethics, he claimed, must make use of science and like science be willing to modify its methods and correct its mistakes. This implies that ethical judgments are not arbitrary but, like those of science, they are or can be made careful and rational. Carefulness is itself both a scientific and a moral virtue, testable by its usefulness. Likewise, honesty is a value not merely in a moral sense, but also in an intellectual sense. Edel's basic point was that moral values are not special or peculiar; they permeate and are relevant to all human endeavors.

Edel's *Method in Ethical Theory* (1963) carried further his earlier studies to work out, as he said, a methodological approach for ethical theory that attempts to be both critical and comprehensive, one that will do justice to the factual as well as the normative. This raises the so-called fact-value or is-ought questions. Like the problem of ethical relativism, these issues have many strands or dimensions. He did not believe that we can evade such problems or solve them once and for all. His own extensive work over many decades was a demonstration of the need to face anew the problem of how suitable methods can be devised which can make piecemeal but not wholesale progress toward both better theories and better applications. His later essays on these problems were collected in *Exploring Fact and Value* (1980).

A Deweyan/Aristotelian ethical theory richly informed by social science and history also bore fruit in a holistic and processive philosophy of law. "[T]he law," Edel wrote, "is less a system of rules or even principles than an institution combining several processes—legislative, judicial, enforcement—in a society's effort to support a pattern of life regarded as desirable and to meet the indefinite variety of problems that arise in its life. Hence law is throughout saturated with values, values that can be seen in the ethical terms of the good, the right, responsibilities, significant attitudes (virtues), and obligations."

Perhaps more deeply and extensively than any American philosopher of the twentieth century, Edel's philosophical work involved the social sciences. *Anthropology and Ethics* (1959), co-authored with anthropologist May Mandelbaum Edel, was an attempt to compare moral systems in cultures worldwide. His subsequent publications in the philosophy of the social sciences were brought together in *Analyzing Concepts in Social Science* (1979).

In some respects, Edel's most original contribution to the tradition of pragmatic naturalism can be found in his treatment of categories and concepts. At the very beginnings of pragmatism, William James stressed that concepts are teleological instruments, and Dewey famously endorsed a functional view of logic, but none of this work was given a hearing by philosophers practicing "conceptual analysis" in the middle of the twentieth century. Having studied closely what analytic philosophers had to say about categories and concepts Edel, in his books on Aristotle, an article on categories in *The Review of Metaphysics,* and numerous essays on concepts in social science and ethics, presented a detailed methodology of conceptual analysis that demonstrated the wealth of resources pragmatic naturalism has to offer.

After teaching at City College from 1931 to 1973 and from 1970 to 1973 at the CUNY Graduate Center, he retired to become a research professor at the University of Pennsylvania. He held visiting appointments at Columbia University, University of California at Berkeley, Swarthmore College, and Case Western Reserve University among others. He was an associate at the National Humanities Center (1978-79); senior fellow at the Center for Dewey Studies (1981-82); recipient of the Butler Silver Medal from Columbia University (1959); and a Guggenheim Fellow (1944-45). He served as vice president of the Eastern Division of the American Philosophical Association (1972-73); president of the American Society of Value Inquiry (1984); and president of the American Section of the International Association of Philosophy of Law and Social Philosophy (1973-75). In 1995 he received the Herbert W. Schneider Award for contributions to the understanding and development of American philosophy from the Society for the Advancement of American philosophy.

In the 1980s Edel gave much attention to the burgeoning field of applied ethics and published *Critique of Applied Ethics: Reflections and Recommendations* (1994) with Elizabeth Flower and Finbarr W. O'Connor. In 1987 Edel was honored by a volume titled *Ethics, Science and Democracy: The Philosophy of Abraham Edel*, edited by Irving Louis Horowitz and H. S. Thayer. Edel's last book was a return to Dewey—*Ethical Theory and Social Change: The Evolution of John Dewey's Ethics, 1908-1932* (2001). Abraham Edel died on June 22, 2007 in New York City.

Chapter 1 THE NATURE AND ROLE OF PHILOSOPHY

The word "Philosophy" means the love of wisdom. Any man, therefore, who seeks understanding is in spirit a philosopher. The philosopher may work in many fields. He may concern himself with problems of human conduct, with the assumptions that underlie religious or scientific beliefs, with the tools and methods of thinking, or with issues that arise in any field of human activity. The things he is seeking to understand may range in complexity from the nature of the universe to the meaning of the word "the." The conclusions he reaches may have world-shaking significance or they may have merely passing importance to a small sect. There are all kinds of philosophies and all kinds of philosophers, but they all have this in common: their inquiry is reflective and they aim at fundamental understanding.

The more significant a problem is—the more it is a problem to which mankind must have an answer—the more likely it is to attract the attention of the greatest philosophers over the longest period. It is not surprising, then, that in the long history of philosophy since its origin in ancient Greece philosophers have displayed certain major concerns. Perhaps a summary of these concerns will serve as our best introduction to the theory and practice of philosophy.

PHILOSOPHY ATTEMPTS TO ACHIEVE A COMPREHENSIVE PICTURE OF THE WORLD

From the days when the philosophers of ancient Greece were asking: "What is the nature of all that is?" philosophy has been seeking to provide a consistent and complete account of the world in which men live. Philosophers such as Plato, Aristotle, Thomas Aquinas, Spinoza, Kant, and Hegel [1] have erected philosophical systems which fascinate the minds of men by their very completeness. Such systems seek to state the principles of all knowledge; they establish a pattern for the universe; they distinguish between what is eternal and what is changing; they explain the relationship

[1] Birth and death dates will be found under the listing of the individual's name in the index.

between matter and mind; they plot the curve of all history; they discover the basic trends of human conduct. In short, they seek a universal order which accounts for everything.

The meaning of order. This notion of order is a familiar one to man. He sees the sun rise and set with regularity. He watches the seasons follow each other in unvarying succession. He discovers changeless properties in the objects around him: water is wet, the oak yields acorns, and only acorns produce oaks. In his own life he passes, in turn, through childhood, youth, and age. And as he sees each generation facing the problems of its predecessor, he is aware of a pattern in the behavior of men. Not without reason he finds himself tempted by the saying of Ecclesiastes, "there is nothing new under the sun," as a philosophical conclusion about all existence.

There is nothing remarkable, then, in man's search for order. If there were no order, if things always behaved in different and surprising ways, man would live—if he lived at all—in complete bewilderment. Experience could teach him nothing, since it had nothing to teach. He could make no plans; he could draw no conclusions. The world would simply be meaningless to him.

Ancient Greek attempts to find a universal order. The desire to establish a universal order is a dominant characteristic of the earliest Greek philosophy. What, asked the Greeks, is that nature which is common to everything? Thales answered that everything is water in some form. Other philosophers suggested air, or fire, and sought to show how this common element could take different forms. Some philosophers suggested that all things were composed of four elements—earth, air, fire, and water. In the fifth century B.C. Democritus elaborated the atomic theory which asserted that everything was ultimately composed of small particles or atoms and the different properties of things depended on different combinations of atoms of varying size and shape. Thus was begun the tradition that explains the universe in physical terms. That this tradition could be established with so little aid from experimental evidence is a triumph of the philosophical imagination.

The answer of Democritus to the question of the ultimate nature of the reality of the world was only one of many answers provided by the Greeks and elaborated on by their successors. Popular philosophers have compared the world to a symphony whose tones blend in perfect harmony; to a perfect mechanism which, like a clock, once wound continues to run; to an animal whose parts work together as an integrated whole; or to the chance arrangements of a hail-storm.

Natural and supernatural orders. Such explanations as that given by Democritus set up an order which is natural rather than supernatural. They take man into account but they do not emphasize his role in the scheme of things. Religious philosophers, on the other hand, explain the order of the universe in terms of some supernatural source or creator. They also explain the order in terms of man's relation to that supernatural source. The Christian tradition, for example, sees the totality of human history as beginning with God's creation of the world and culminating in salvation.

Metaphysics. The creation of general systems is known as *speculative* philosophy; as a branch of philosophy it is called *metaphysics*. As we survey the variety of such systems in the course of history we cannot resist the suggestion that many of them have been, to a great extent, landscape and portrait paintings—the landscape of man's surroundings as the sciences of the day understood them, and the portrait of the human heart as the culture of the period had fashioned it. Later philosophers examine these pictures for hints useful in developing their own systems. Historians study the pictures for other reasons. They are looking for the social background and intellectual traditions which contributed to the painting and for the influences that the pictures have had in molding new beliefs and practices.

Despite the fate of successive systems of philosophy, it is undeniable that there has been an accumulation of wisdom in their very succession. If we pay attention less to the individual systems than to the broad traditions in which they fall, the growth of maturity stands out rather than the localisms of each period. Analyses have become more refined and alternatives clearer. Differences among fundamental philosophic outlooks remain as sharp as ever, but the points and grounds of difference have emerged more definitely. Men need not therefore despair because they still strive to form a better conception of the world in which they live.

PHILOSOPHY IS CRITICAL

In the search after wisdom it is not enough to discover the facts. Man wants to know how these facts are to be used. He also wants to know what methods he should employ to discover and use new facts. Thus the philosopher examines critically the fundamental notions and assumptions of any field of inquiry. He wants to know what they mean, on what grounds they are selected, and to what end they are employed.

Critical philosophy at work in special fields. Take the work of the scientist. He discovers laws; but what is a law? It used to be said that science looked for causes. What is the relation between a cause and a law? What methods of thought does the scientist employ? Which methods are most reliable? What is the relation between theory and experiment in his work? These questions have to be answered if the work of the scientist is to be efficient.

Let us look at the legal domain. It is a principle of many systems of law that private property should be protected. But what is private property?

Why should it be protected? These are questions which the lawyer would not find himself raising in his regular practice; yet the welfare of society may depend on their being answered. Beneath such questions are certain assumptions. The critical philosopher is the busybody who examines those assumptions and, if necessary, calls attention to their weaknesses.

In this fashion critical philosophy has a role to play in any field of study. This does not mean that the philosopher sets himself above the specialist in each field. The latter may himself do whatever philosophical work is to be done. But when he does he is a philosopher as well as a specialist.

Socrates as a critical philosopher. The Greek philosopher, Socrates, was the first to make critical philosophy a specialized pursuit. Socrates thought of himself as the gadfly on the body politic of Athens. He conceived it his task to buzz around and discover the assumptions of men's beliefs and the implicit principles of their conduct. He paid special attention to morals and kept asking military men what they meant by courage, religious specialists what after all was piety, teachers of virtue whether moral instruction was really possible, politicians what was justice, and so forth. As he explains, men came to consider him a nuisance, for he revealed their fundamental ignorance by getting them repeatedly to contradict themselves. Eventually he was put to death on charges of impiety.[2]

Logic and epistemology. Invariably investigations of this sort raise general problems. From asking what particular terms mean in special fields, philosophers came to raise the problem of the nature of meaning in general. From examining particular methods of inquiry they came to ask about the nature of knowledge and the reliability of men's ways of acquiring it. Thus were developed two extensive branches of philosophy—*logic,* which provides the standards of correct thinking, and *epistemology,* which performs a critical analysis of knowledge and its objects.

PHILOSOPHY IS CONCERNED WITH UNDERSTANDING MAN

Although man is but a small part of the whole universe a great share of philosophizing is inevitably man-centered. We want to know who we are, what our relation is to our world, what we *can* do in it, and what we *should* do in it. Philosophers, therefore, have long been concerned with the nature of mind and personality, with the ways in which we can know ourselves, and with the character of human institutions. They ask whether man acts freely or by constraint, and whether men can change the course of history.

[2] See Plato's *Apology.* But philosophers need not flatter themselves that abstract philosophy alone had stirred the passions of men so deeply. It is clear that political philosophy and political motives were involved as well. See below, pp. 296-97, 392.

The field of ethics. The attempt to give a comprehensive account of man's role in the world and of what he ought to strive for, is the part of philosophizing traditionally known as *ethics*. It considers everything in terms of value, of what is good. It surveys man's conduct and institutions and bids him fashion them in accordance with the criteria that it establishes. Sometimes it issues sharp commands, sometimes merely invitations. Always, however, it is concerned with helping man to live in accordance with a rational pattern of conduct.

PHILOSOPHY IS CONCERNED WITH PRACTICE AS WELL AS THEORY

So far we have spoken of philosophy in terms of understanding, whether it be understanding of the world at large or the character of knowledge or man and his values. From another point of view philosophy may be seen as an approach to practice. Every philosophy indicates certain beliefs or attitudes with which men accepting it will face the world. Similarly every man's practice has an implicit philosophy, whether or not he likes it, or even knows it.

System in human conduct. A man's conduct may often exhibit greater system than he realizes. There is an order in the way he treats his fellows, selects his pleasures, and maintains his beliefs. Even in dealing with material things we express different outlooks. In building a trustworthy boat a Pacific Islander thinks the magic spells he utters are as important as the quality of the wood or the workmanship; he treats things as expressing the will of commanding spirits. Modern men, too, sometimes take a superstitious attitude towards their tools and materials. Hence the philosopher may perform a useful service by revealing the assumptions that lie behind men's actions and attitudes.

Relations between theory and practice. Now, while every philosophy constitutes a guide to practice and every form of practice may be expressed as a philosophical outlook, the relations between theory and practice are by no means simple. The expressed philosophy of a given group or individual may not always correspond to that evident in its practice. Instead of clarifying and harmonizing beliefs and attitudes, a theoretical framework may in fact serve some quite different purpose. It may be a means of justifying the beliefs or attitudes in terms currently respectable. It may even serve as a screen to obscure the real character of behavior, or as an instrument to convince or convert others to a particular attitude, or as a flag to arouse emotion.

This point must serve as a warning concerning much that is to follow. The history of written or expressed philosophies in our western culture is not the mere unfolding of seeds of reflection planted by the ancient Greek philosophers. Men have eaten, worked, prayed, farmed, conspired, traveled, and philosophized, and their various activities have not gone on in separate compartments. Philosophical speculation has affected other kinds of activity and has been affected by them. Thus the philosophical problems and answers of the Greeks influenced the form of Christianity; they gave a bent to schools of science and were in turn shaped by scientific developments; they were utilized by various movements as flags under which to march; often they clarified men's aims. Again, they were refashioned by scientific developments, and given different interpretations under varying social conditions. This does not mean that a history of philosophical problems cannot be written, but that such an account is selective. It selects from the interwoven pattern of philosophical speculation only those strands which have reference to its interests. Only the greatest philosophical systems get into the standard books on the history of philosophy. Many that were philosophically very fragile, but emotionally powerful, operated widely in their own day and then were gone.

In this introduction to philosophy our interest is not primarily historical. Some problems and formulations will have to be torn from the context of their origin, for our concern is with their validity today and their usefulness for the student who sets out to analyze his own practice and to start formulating an adequate theory.

Need for clear philosophizing today. There is special need today for clear philosophizing precisely because we recognize so clearly that social attitudes are not stable. We are not living in a world in which men, secure in their attitudes, can dismiss theoretical philosophy as impressive, lofty, but impractical. The attitudes themselves are changing in all fields—economic, political, social, and even scientific. Instead of asking merely, "In the light of our values what path should we take?" men find today that the fundamental values themselves have been challenged. Sweeping changes must come from the war and the post-war reconstruction. In fighting for their values, men have been driven to clarify them; and these restated values will in turn point the way to further construction. Thus the necessity of reorganizing our world has forced us to recognize the practical value of philosophy. Events have made us critical. We are living in a time when philosophy counts.

In this situation every man must be a philosopher. He must find out what he really stands for. He must put his beliefs and attitudes into a crucible to be acted on by critical reflection. Thus to philosophize is to take the risk of emerging other than one began. And to establish the habit of philosophy will render a man more sensitive to values, more discerning of worth as distinguished from appearances or instrumentalities, and more constantly aware of the implications of his conduct.

Order of problems to be raised. In the present book the problems of philosophy will be raised in the following order. We shall first, in Part One, ask "What is explanation?" and examine its nature so as to gain an understanding of the ideas, concepts, and methods that may be employed in formulating a comprehensive picture of our world. We shall find that the methods themselves to some extent limit or determine the kinds of pictures we get. Thus in discussing explanation we are not doing something merely preparatory, but are already engaged in philosophic construction. The variety of concepts and methods proposed will itself give us an initial glimpse of the major types of philosophic structures that men have devised.

In Part Two we shall ask "How does science explain things?" We shall examine the character of scientific method, its reliability in constructing an account of our world, and its relation to rival methods and approaches.

In Part Three we shall use the tools fashioned in Parts One and Two in order to examine man himself. We shall ask "What is man?" and study the various answers that have been given by different philosophies.

Part Four will discuss the question "What can we do?" in order to throw light upon the possible scope of human life and activity. We will discover the bonds that hamper man and we will look for the freedom he may hope to achieve.

As we study the questions raised in these four parts, the points of view and the methods and conclusions of different philosophies will become increasingly clear. We shall then be ready to ask in Part Five "What are the choices before us?" There we shall seek what philosophy has to offer us as a guide to a wise life by contrasting two major views—idealism and materialism—and examining their application in various fields of human endeavor.

Part One

THE NATURE OF EXPLANATION

Chapter 2 ESSENCE AND PURPOSE: THE TELEOLOGICAL APPROACH

In ordinary life, when we ask for the explanation of some thing or happening, we may have one or more of several questions in mind. Compare the following:
1. What's that thing with the knobs in front? It's a radio.
2. What's that noise? It's thunder.
3. Why did he fall down? To avoid being hit.
4. Why did he fall down? He stepped in a hole.
5. Why did the creek freeze? Water freezes at 0° Centigrade.
6. Why did he lose his job? With the end of the European war there were cutbacks in munitions production and a period was required in that industry for retooling and reconversion to peace-time production.

In each case the question constitutes a request for an explanation of some thing or happening. The first two answer by giving a more specific account of what the thing is, by stating its nature or *essence*. The third states a *purpose*. The fourth presents a *cause*. The fifth explains by giving a *law* to which the things in question are subject. The sixth tries to give a *systematic* picture of the whole situation to which the event belongs.

In ordinary life these different senses of explanation are not thought to be incompatible. They may even seem to overlap, and certainly to supplement one another. The thing with the knobs in front, for example, has an essence, is intended for a special purpose, is constructed by definite causal methods, obeys the laws of electricity, and fits into physical, economic, and esthetic systems. On the other hand, in particular cases such as the fall of the man, the two different senses of explanation appear to be in competition, and only one of the two answers can be correct. Clearly, the analysis of the five concepts of explanation is no simple task. An understanding of their meaning, their relations, and their utility as tools for building a comprehensive view of our world, requires careful philosophic treatment. This is confirmed by the role these concepts have played in the different philosophies of western thought. The major philosophies of ancient Greece were chiefly concerned with the essence of things. Early western religious philosophers concentrated on purpose. The popular contrast of the religious and scientific approaches to the world sees them as a conflict of purposive and causal explanation. Modern science finds a system of laws to be its most satisfactory interpretation of explanation.

Since in Part One we are dealing with the nature of explanation, let us begin our study by seeing what philosophers have meant by the essence and purpose of things. Then, in subsequent chapters, we will study the explanations they have given in terms of cause, law, and system.

Essence

PICTURE OF THE WORLD IN TERMS OF ESSENCE

We say that the name *John Williams* is a proper noun because it refers to a particular individual, while the word *man* is a common noun because it refers to no particular man but to the whole class of men. Similarly such words as "this pencil that I hold in my hand," "that table over there in the corner," "the brown on the surface of that table," and "the time I fell off the roof and broke my collar bone" refer to particular objects, qualities, or occurrences. We do not call such phrases proper nouns, but, inasmuch as they refer to specific experiences, they perform the same function as proper nouns. On the other hand, words like "pencil," "table," "brown," and "accident" point only to those characteristics that are common to all pencils, tables, brown-colored objects, and accidents.

From this simple beginning we can go on to examine a whole way of looking at our familiar world which at first may seem strange. It is the special outlook which the essence philosophies of ancient Greece fashioned when they began to analyze the phenomena of existence and knowledge. Let us trace this development, attempting to put ourselves as much as possible in their frame of mind.

Particulars and universals. The distinction between proper nouns and common nouns that you are familiar with in grammar is represented in philosophy by the terms *particular* and *universal*. John Williams and this pencil I hold in my hand are particular objects, or simply particulars. Man and pencil, on the other hand, are universals. The particulars are the existent things, events, qualities of our world. They are to be found at definite places at definite times. A universal, however, has not the same kind of existence. You never see or touch a universal; it is not in time or space at all. Your mind grasps it when it understands the definition of the common term that designates the universal. Thus you grasp the universal circle when you learn that "a circle is the locus of a point that moves in a plane equidistant from a given point." But what you can draw or see are particular circles of different diameters, each of which approximately fits the definition.

Can we know particulars? If we try to give an account of a particular we find that for the most part we simply heap up descriptive terms in sufficient number to distinguish it from other particulars. This pencil is brown, six inches long, wooden, and so forth. Each of these terms, however, refers to a universal. What we really know about the particular, therefore, is that it is a meeting-place, so to speak, of a large number of universals which it exemplifies. Universals thus seem to be the stuff of which knowledge is made.

Are particulars real? From the point of view of a philosophy that is trying to explain things in terms of their essences, the universals are more important than particulars. Such philosophies, in fact, often question the reality of the particular. Which, for example, is the real circle? Is it the crude drawing on the blackboard which the geometry teacher uses to explain a theorem in Euclid? Even if it were carefully constructed it would still be imperfect, since no circle drawn by human hands can be perfect. Or is the real circle the ideal one grasped by the mind, of which the truths of Euclid really hold? When the world is viewed in this perspective, the particular is felt to be an imperfect representation of the universal, approximating to it, but never achieving equal reality.

The ordinary perspective is thus completely reversed. Ordinarily we tend to regard common nouns as merely devices in thought and discourse to achieve generality in describing existent things. We are inclined to call the world of things with which we come in contact through our senses the real world. In the perspective of the essence philosophies this world becomes regarded as essentially a representation of the ideal world which is the world of universals. The ideal is real, the existent an imperfect copy. Such an explanation of reality includes a moral touch, since all particulars are seen as striving towards an ever closer approximation of the ideal which they represent. This drive towards perfection becomes an inherent property of all existence.

Things have essences. The particular as we have described it illustrates innumerable universals; there is one for every property that it has. Which among these universals constitute its *essence*? Clearly, it is assumed in the essence approach that some are peculiarly appropriate to it. They are the ones that constitute its nature, the reality or perfection at which it is aiming. They are the ones that we specify in giving an answer to the question "What is it?" In fact the Greek term for essence employed by Aristotle is very revealing: it is simply an expression formed of the definite article and the question "What is it?," namely "the-what-it-is." You and I share a common essence, that of humanity, just as all circles share circularity. That is what we really are—human beings—and all differences are incidental.

PLATO'S DEVELOPMENT OF THE APPROACH

Such a philosophical approach was first developed systematically by the ancient philosopher Plato, the disciple of Socrates. Socrates had concentrated attention on definition, especially of moral notions, such as justice, wisdom, courage, piety, beauty. He had taught that their essence could not be confined to any particular example. It was a good lesson in logic; a definition, as that of the circle showed us, does give a universal account.

Universals eternal, particulars changing. Plato paid special attention to a feature of the essence approach which we have not yet mentioned. Since the particular is in time and space, it will have a history and be capable of change. Plato, in fact, accepted the view that the material world is constantly changing. The universal, on the other hand, is not in time and space. Therefore Plato regards it as eternal and unchanging. This contrast between the changing and the eternal is coupled with that between the senses and the intellect. We meet the material world through our senses. But we do not learn of the ideal world through our senses. The ideal is never seen by our eyes or felt by our hands. We know of it and its existence only through our minds, and Plato attributed the failure of those who do not grasp the reality of universals to lack of intelligence. Thus, when one of his hearers argued that he was able to perceive horses but not horseness—the universal quality of being a horse—Plato replied, "That is because you have eyes but no intelligence."

The Platonic Ideas. These universals which were the essence of things Plato called *Ideas*. You must not confuse Plato's Ideas with the meaning we give to that word when we spell it with a small letter. For Plato thought of Ideas as having an existence independent of our minds. The intellect perceived Ideas, but it did not create them. The ideal circle, for example, was not a product of man's imagination. It existed before the minds of men perceived it. It was not the result of experience with particular circles. It was rather the eternal reality that men were trying to reproduce in the circles they fashioned.

Since our knowledge of Ideas could not have come to us through our senses, Plato argued that we must have had this knowledge implanted in us, and we must be recalling the Idea from some previous existence. The distractions and imperfections of our physical existence, he thought, prevent the intellect from achieving a complete grasp of the Ideas for which it strives. It is only when death has liberated the soul from the tyranny and weakness of the body that pure and complete knowledge of the universals is possible to man.[1]

[1] For the ethical and social outlook associated with this Platonic approach, see below, p. 389 ff.

The world as a copy of Ideas. Plato was fond of speaking in myths, and sometimes it is hard to tell whether he means literally what he is saying. But there is no doubt that he looked upon the universe as a system of eternal Ideas, upon existence as a vague, shadowy, unreal copy or imitation of these Ideas, and upon the vocation of man as primarily the care of the soul and the cultivation of the intellect. There is a touch of Platonism in the common view that science discovers what the world is *really* like, whereas ordinarily we are concerned merely with its transitory appearances.

ARISTOTLE'S TREATMENT OF ESSENCE AND NATURE

In the work of Aristotle, the notion of essence is given a more logical character. Aristotle distinguishes between the essence of a thing (stated in the definition, which gives an account of what it is), a property of a thing (a necessary aspect of it, found in all members of the class and deducible from the definition), and an accident of a thing (any other attribute, not necessarily found in every member of the class.) Thus a man's rational animality is his essence (man being defined as a rational animal), his capacity for laughter is a property because only rational beings are capable of laughter, and his whiteness or blackness is an accident. Similarly to be a plane figure bounded by three straight lines is the essence of a triangle, to have an angle-sum of two right angles a property, and to have an area of three square feet an accident.

How essences become known. In Aristotle's system the essence of anything is learned by a process of intuitive induction (not the modern sense of induction) which consists in leading on the soul by giving it specimen after specimen until it intuitively perceives the universal quality in all the specimens. This is the process by which, for example, a formula arises in the mathematician's mind as he looks at a series of numbers, or the idea of a man becomes fixed with growing experience in the mind of the child. In the same way the metaphysician, seeing that a statue is made out of bronze, a house out of timber, an argument out of premises, forms the general idea that every thing has a matter in the sense of the material out of which it is made. The process is not different in outline from that by which the universal is grasped in Plato's theory. The contact of the mind with the essence is direct and immediate.

Once the essence is grasped, according to Aristotle, the mind has a fixed and certain starting-point for knowledge. In each science the statements giving the essence of the things being investigated constitute the fundamental definitions, axioms, and postulates from which the science is derived. The properties are deduced from the essence; e.g., that a triangle has an angle-sum of 180 degrees is deduced from the definition of a triangle as a plane figure bounded by three straight lines, together with the axioms and postulates of Euclid which tell us the essence of planes and lines. The accidents are learned in sense-perception; for example, by hearing him play, one learns that a certain man happens to be a musician.

Essences immanent in things. For a thing to have a certain essence is, however, not an accident. The essence is what that thing *really* is, that is, its continued identity or being, its *nature*. It is interesting at this point to note the difference of stress in Plato's and Aristotle's approach. Plato's interest is centered almost wholly on the network of Ideas that he takes to constitute reality. The material, changing world is an unreal or formless flux. Things are a kind of shadow cast on the flux by those universals which we say it illustrates. Aristotle shows a greater interest in mapping the specific characters of the existent or sense-perceived world. For him the Ideas are essences inherent in things.[2] He views every form of existence as containing within it a definite plan which guides its development and controls its subsequent activities. The acorn grows into an oak and acts like an oak in accordance with the pattern that was *immanent* in the acorn. Similarly the pattern inherent in the human embryo from conception controls the development of that embryo into a man, and determines the pattern of manhood. In short all things are what they are because of the pattern that is their essence. It guides the growth and activity of the thing just as the idea or inspiration in the mind of the sculptor guides his chisel strokes. Nature works unconsciously just as the artist works consciously.

Natural form and natural behavior. For Aristotle such an explanation did not rule out exceptions. The relative heights of men and oaks do not vary, yet within the class oaks and the class men variations of height exist. Some oaks grow taller than others; some men are giants, others dwarfs. Such variations may exist in all fields without destroying the belief that things have a natural form towards which they will develop. The natural form of any species is the form that members *generally* take. Aristotle recognized that "disturbing factors" may sometimes operate to thwart the development towards that natural form. Thus an acorn may never develop into an oak because it was eaten by a pig. The pig, then, is the disturbing factor that

[2] This difference between the attitude of Plato and Aristotle to universals or Ideas has sometimes been magnified into an opposition of philosophic systems. Thus in Rafael's painting *The School of Athens* Plato points up to the heavens, Aristotle down to earth. The medieval controversy on the question whether universals were *before* (prior, transcendental to) things or *in* things developed this antithesis. The difference may be illustrated by the term "formula." The Platonic sense is illustrated by a formula in chemistry, the Aristotelian sense by the use of the term for a baby's special food. Similarly the term "prescription" indicates in Platonic fashion the doctor's recommendation, in Aristotelian the parcel called for at the drug store.

prevented the acorn from achieving its natural destiny. Similarly, says Aristotle, it is natural for men to be right-handed, but it is possible to train them to be ambidextrous. Such training would be a disturbing factor that prevented the development of the immanent pattern of right-handedness in men. The natural pattern, however, is that behavior or development which proceeds from an immanent design when there is no interference.

ESTIMATE OF ESSENCE AND NATURE

The theories of Plato and Aristotle illustrate the conception of explanation as the discovery of essences. They thereby illustrate the perspective which views things in the world as the embodiment of essences. As we have seen, they introduce a number of fundamental cleavages in our understanding of the world. Universals are sharply distinguished from particulars, the intellect from the senses, the eternal from the changing, the fixed nature of things from their accidental properties. The ideal of science which developed from their work was that of a logical system in which knowledge was derived by deduction from first principles. The estimate of these different elements is a complex philosophical task. Each of them will be considered in detail below in connection with the special field involved.[3]

General critique. In general, there was a scientific stress in the view that explanation is fundamentally the discovery of essence. It provided an impetus to the search for order. The philosophies of Plato and Aristotle had this scientific bent. Plato's stress on the Ideas encouraged the examination of types of order and thus the growth of logic and mathematics. Aristotle, with closer attention to the forms of existence, developed logic as a tool for science and devoted himself especially to biology. At the same time, however, the stress on essence as directly grasped by the mind involved a general dogmatism, an unreadiness to re-examine first principles once they were elaborated. Deduction from first principles was substituted for fresh observation of existence. In ethical and social theory the approach in terms of essence likewise tended toward dogmatism. For it viewed the world as a system of fixed forms. Order was exalted, the unchanging and the eternal became major goals, and human nature and destiny were seen as fixed.

Logical critique of the natural. If we turn to the modern logical criticism of these notions of essence and natural pattern, we find that it is precisely

---

[3] For the problem of universals as it appears in the theory of first principles, see Chapter 6; for the relation of intellect and senses, Chapter 7; for the underlying theory of man involved, Chapter 11; for the eternal and the changing, Chapter 21; for the consequences of fixed natures on the treatment of human affairs, Chapter 24.

their arbitrary and dogmatic tendency that is challenged. This can be seen in a simple example. Suppose you have concluded that a certain man is naturally foolish. Everything he does foolishly you consider natural; everything he does well you call luck. Someone else may decide that this man is naturally clever, and call anything he does badly an accident. In other words, what is thought natural may depend to a considerable extent on the point of view with which one begins.

Even in biology the idea of a "natural" pattern inherent in a living organism has to be accepted cautiously. To the modern biologist an organism is a complex result of a process of growth, and variations of the environment at any stage may profoundly affect the subsequent development of the organism. For example, certain cave-dwelling fish are blind and unpigmented. When born in the caves their offspring share these characteristics. It would be easy to conclude, therefore, that such fish are "naturally" blind and unpigmented. But if the same fish are allowed to breed in the sunlight, they bear pigmented offspring which can see. These, in turn, are capable of producing either type, depending on the environment in which they breed. Both patterns, therefore, are equally natural, and it is the environment that determines which of the two shall be developed.

The same thing is true of man's inheritance. One physical and social environment may be favorable to the development of one set of traits, while a quite different environment will encourage a different set. Insofar as both sets can and do occur they are natural. But we must not forget that both are changeable and that what is significant is the conditions of their occurrence or change.

Modern science thus minimizes the inevitability that clings to the term "natural" both in Aristotelian and in common usage. In its own work it substitutes for a natural pattern a description of conditions and of their invariable or general resultant. By doing so science allows for a greater appreciation of the possibility of varying classifications for various purposes. The so-called "natural" classifications of biologists, for example, are devised to show not merely what characteristics in the animal world go together, but also what kinds of animals are historically or genetically related. In such a classification the fact that whales live in the ocean is not central. But when the biologist is concerned with other problems, habitation may be central, and whales grouped with other sea-dwellers.

Logical critique of essence. The notion of essence is subject to similar analysis. It too has relative utility in modern life. We point to something and ask, "What is it?" We expect an answer such as "It's a table," or "It's a tree." The answer "It's wood" might not satisfy us. We would feel like replying, "I don't want to know what it's made of; I want to know what it *is*." When we ask what a thing is, we are really asking how that thing is classified, and the kind of classification we have in mind is indicated by the context of the question. Thus where a chemist, asked "What is it?", might answer, "Carbon," a jeweler would say, "A diamond." Each classifies it according to his prevailing interest in it. If we do not share that interest we must be careful to rule it out in our question. If we ask the jeweler, "What is it in terms of its chemical composition?" he will understand what kind of answer we want, and he, too, will reply, "It's carbon." The search for an essence—i.e., the question "What is it?"—seems therefore to be simply a request for starting-points from which we may derive the kind of information in which we have implicitly expressed an interest.

This kind of analysis is reinforced by the explorations of anthropologists among different peoples. It is discovered that the actual classification of everyday phenomena may differ considerably. Thus Franz Boas notes that among the Eskimo there is no single concept of "snow," but rather diverse ones for snow on the ground, falling snow, drifting snow, and a snowdrift.[4] Among ourselves there was no single word to include ice and snow, dew, frost, water, and steam, until the chemist unified them as H_2O. The differences were obviously more important than the similarity from a practical point of view, just as in the case of snow among the Eskimo.

The apparent arbitrariness revealed by this analysis indicates simply that there may be a variety of interests. It is to be noted, however, that once the interest in a given investigation is made explicit the arbitrariness disappears. What will be discovered as the "essence" thereafter depends on the facts, that is, the properties and relations of the materials under investigation.

It is well to note that from a broad point of view those traits that Aristotle called "accidents" also contribute to our understanding of things or terms. It certainly increases our understanding of man to know that some men under certain stimuli will engage in warfare, that under other conditions some men will pray, endure, rebel, invent, and philosophize. That these are customarily treated as "accidents" rather than "properties" is a result of classifying in terms of the more stable "biological" traits.

It follows that the general problem of distinguishing essences is ultimately the problem of determining the relative value of different systems of classification. The essence of a thing may then be viewed as those traits by virtue of which it may most fruitfully be classified. And from the point of view of modern science the fruitfulness of a classification is judged by its contribution to the development of systematic knowledge.

[4] Handbook of American Indian Languages. Bulletin 40, Bureau of American Ethnology, 1911, Part 1, p. 25.

Purpose

MEANING OF PURPOSE

Ordinary meaning. The ordinary notion of purpose is clear enough. A man has a purpose when there is some end or goal toward which he is consciously directing his efforts. We cannot always judge his purpose conclusively from his actions, but we are often ready to guess at it. We may judge that a certain young lawyer is working in support of a political candidate because he wishes to further certain principles for which the candidate stands, while we suspect another of "jumping on the bandwagon" to serve the interests of his career. While we may not be certain, we do generally assume that the man himself knows—though he may not admit—his purpose.

This idea of purpose is fairly useful in ordinary life in accounting for men's behavior. In human affairs when people ask for an explanation of some happening they frequently are thinking of the purposes of the people involved. Thus if I ask why A is going to college when it involves such a strain on his health (suppose he also works eight hours a day to earn a living), the answer may very well be that he wants to become a doctor. But if I ask why B failed his examination the answer will probably not be in terms of purpose. In short, purpose is a term useful for relating some human events as means to ends or goals.

Extended meanings. Though the concept of purpose, in this sense, is useful in describing man's conduct, it is obviously limited to human behavior, and indeed, to that small portion of man's behavior that is conscious. There is, however, another and more extended meaning of purpose which drops out the element of conscious awareness. The Freudian psychologists have adopted one such view. They have advanced the theory that no human action is without a purpose. What we laugh at, what we dream, the slips of the tongue we make, may be expressive of unconscious purpose, being indicative of repressed wishes and desires.

A still more extended view is found in animal psychology. For a time it was thought that the term "purpose" could not be fruitfully employed with reference to animals because of its anthropomorphic associations. Recently, however, it has been reintroduced with new caution, with no special implication of awareness, and simply as a systematic description of a sequence of animal behavior in which there is a pattern of developing activity which ends in the achievement of a goal. Thus we may speak of the behavior of the cat scratching at the door in order to get out without being guilty of anthropomorphism. For the cat's behavior is purposive in the larger sense of fitting into a system of activity which results in its getting the door open. More technically, animal psychologists speak of purpose as a drive to get to or from a given type of goal-object. Purposive behavior involves persistence and learning power with respect to achieving the goal.[5]

Such extended uses of the concept of purpose are found in other domains as well. For example, it is often said that when the body is ill, it has getting well as its goal. For automatic processes go on within the body—such as the activity of white blood corpuscles—which have as their end result the body's restoration to health. Again, purpose has been ascribed to the various organs of the body, instead of to the body as a whole: the purpose of the eye being to see, of the ear to hear, and so forth. The ancient physician Galen in fact thought that every part of an animal served some end, and was perfectly adapted in structure to that end. An amusing illustration of such an account of the body's constitution is Plato's explanation (in the *Timaeus*) of why we have bowels. By preventing the food from passing quickly through the body, they save us from perpetual eating and drinking and thus render possible philosophy and art!

"Final cause" in Aristotelian theory. A widely extended view of purpose is found in the Aristotelian theory of the nature of things.[6] This theory is often called a doctrine of "final causation," the final cause being the end or goal which is immanent in the thing.[7] In the natural world, Aristotle believed that each of the elements (earth, air, fire, water) composing sublunar bodies possessed an inherent nature which expressed its purpose, and he thought of these natures as tendencies toward a definite place. According to him, the element earth tends to reach the center of the world, and water, air, and fire in due order tend toward the places around it.[8] Within the system of Aristotelian physics the fact that an object falls is therefore interpreted as an earthly "striving" within it, rather than as a result of gravitational forces. It is perhaps needless to dwell on the fact that Aristotle's use of purpose as an explanatory category in physics did not lead to a fruitful development of this science.

Apart from a theory like that of Aristotle, the only sense in which an inorganic thing may be said to have a purpose is that the object is used regularly by men with this purpose (e.g., a spade is used to dig) or has a constant part in something to which a purpose is thus assigned (e.g., the carbu-

[5] Cf. E. C. Tolman, *Purposive Behavior in Animals and Men*, Century, 1932.
[6] See above, p. 15 ff.
[7] The original Aristotelian term for "final cause" means literally "the-for-the-sake-of-what," which is just making a noun out of the question "What's it for?" There are traces of such use of "cause" even in our language, e.g., to fight for a cause, a lost cause.
[8] The fifth element was that of which the heavens were composed, and its natural motion was circular.

retor in an automobile). In such a context the purpose is really ascribed to men and so involves no special problem.

PURPOSE APPLIED TO SOCIAL GROUPS AND HISTORY

So far we have been considering purpose as a concept for explaining the behavior of living things and inorganic nature. We must recognize, however, that an attempt has also been made to apply purpose to social groups, nations, and to history as a whole. Thus we say that a bridge club has a purpose—that of enabling people to play bridge conveniently. Actually many of its members may have as their purpose social contacts rather than playing the game. The legislature is said to have a purpose in passing a statute. But in practice the measure as passed may itself be a resultant of numerous conflicting purposes on the part of legislators and bear little relation to any one set of original intentions.

A nation's purpose. To speak of a nation's purpose is correspondingly more difficult. At particular times there may be sufficient unity in a nation to make reference to its purpose intelligible. During a war, for example, there is a great unity of effort and many phases of life may be geared to a single end. But when reference is to a nation's history, such unity of purpose is more difficult to establish. The statement that America's purpose has been the development and preservation of democratic institutions could probably be given a meaning in terms of the continuous purposive behavior of dominant elements among successive generations of Americans. Such a meaning of purpose is quite definite, and its particular application is to be established by historical research. It does not depart too far from the primary meaning of "purpose." It does not equate purpose with mere order of development, thereby automatically declaring every trend in a nation's history to be purposive. Nor does it turn the nation into a kind of super-being having purposes of its own irrespective of the aims of individual men within it.

Purpose in history. Sometimes, when men speak of the purpose of a nation as such, and no longer refer to the behavior and attitudes of its people, they may be thinking of its achievements in the development of world civilization. From this view purpose may be assigned to the whole of history, and particular peoples become the agents, at particular points, of this purpose. Thus the philosopher Hegel held that history was the realization of the idea of freedom. This tendency towards freedom becomes unfolded in the course of events and determines the general outline of what is to be. He concluded that everything that happens would, on philosophical inspection, be found to be necessary. Similarly some of the theologically-minded evolutionists saw the history of the world as the achievement of a vast plan to culminate in man's development.

TELEOLOGY

When the notion of purpose is broadened to provide a perspective in which the world at large may be viewed, the result is the "teleological" approach. The term "teleology" (the Greek *telos* means an end or goal) designates the belief that the world has a purpose. It may mean that everything in the world has its purpose, or that the world as a whole has a single or unified purpose. For example, many primitive peoples have believed that every existent thing has its indwelling spirit; while western peoples have come largely to hold to monotheism, a belief in a single divine power which provides a destiny for the world. It is convenient to distinguish two kinds of teleology: the purpose may be something dwelling in the world, as in the Aristotelian and Hegelian notions; or it may belong to some deity outside of this natural world. The former is called *immanent,* the latter *transcendental* teleology.

Transcendental and immanent teleologies. The most familiar example of transcendental teleology is the Christian doctrine. God created the world, and since the deity has will, the term purpose is used in precisely the same sense as when men attribute purpose to one another. The purpose of the world is to provide a place in which man, exercising his freedom, will become prepared for his role in the life hereafter. However, if God is assumed to have stamped a purpose on things, species, or peoples, then the purpose is God's, and only derivatively that of the thing, species, or people, just as the purpose of an automobile is primarily man's rather than the engine's.

In transcendental teleology the notion of purpose is used in its original sense as involving awareness of a goal and conscious action to achieve it. This form of teleology usually entails belief in the existence of a God who has the purpose and who carries it out. Immanent teleology, however, uses the notion of purpose in its very widest or most extended sense. A kind of directional striving, somehow analogous to what goes on in human beings, is imparted to all existence. Sometimes this view is the vestige of a theological approach which has lost its personal God whose purpose would be more readily intelligible. It is hard to see how such a view can mean anything more than regularity in behavior or the possession of fixed properties. Such a view of purpose without its being anybody's purpose makes the word lose its specific meaning, unless there is implied some theory of a super-individual soul or type of being, whose purposes this trend exhibits. But this turns again toward transcendental teleology.[9]

The universe ultimately spiritual. Two major consequences seem to flow from the teleological approach, whether it be immanent or transcendental.

---

[9] For such a view of the group-soul, see below, p. 141 ff.

The first tendency is to regard the universe as in some sense ultimately *spiritual* in character. For purpose in its primary sense expresses man's mental activity. It embodies goal-seeking and it involves intelligent adaptation of means to ends; hence even where purpose is believed to occur without awareness it is taken to share to some degree in these qualities. If the world be thus regarded as somehow ultimately spiritual it is in that sense akin to man. It is, therefore, truly his home and friendly to him.

The universe fundamentally moral. The second tendency, somewhat converging with the first, is to regard the universe as fundamentally moral. For the notion of purpose is associated in men's minds with the good, since men feel that the objects of their striving constitute their good. Most teleological theories have thus taken the purpose they find in the world's development to be good and to provide a standard for human conduct. The picture of the world in the western religious tradition is a teleological one. The moral attitudes associated with teleology will therefore be discussed more fully in connection with the treatment of religion.[10]

TELEOLOGY AS EXPLANATION

After this brief survey of the meanings and applications of "purpose" and of the type of philosophic outlook in which it is embodied, we are ready to consider the question of its validity. In what sense, if any, is the revelation of purpose in special fields and in the world at large the answer to our search for explanation?

Clearly the revelation of purpose constitutes explanation when the inquiry concerns purpose. This is seen in the assertions of what is often called "naive" teleology, where the implied standard is man: it rains so that the crops will grow, so that man will have enough to eat; the sun shines to provide man with light and warmth. Such a teleological explanation is transparent and no confusion arises so long as it is taken to be merely an answer to the question "What is it good for?" and is not presumed to carry any causal implication. However, a real issue arises when the revelation of purpose lays claim to constitute the explanation of the existence or origin of things and of their mode of behavior. For here it seems to deal with questions which ordinarily fall in the province of causality.

Teleological account of change. In order to explain how things originate and develop the teleological explanation must provide an account of how change is initiated which will not simply appeal to the impact of one object upon another as causality does. It must be an explanation in terms of the unique character of purpose. Now we have seen that purpose involves a goal which *attracts* a man, thereby setting him in motion. It does not push

---

[10] Chapter 24 below.

him, nor exert any literal force on him, but somehow the goal without moving and simply by being what it is generates striving in him. Often the goal is something to be created; it does not yet exist; it is an ideal or spiritual object. Nevertheless, as the object of desire, it draws men while itself unmoving. This is the sense in which, in religious theory, God, immaterial and outside of the realm of change, is sometimes said to initiate motion within the world. This teleological account of motion is often contrasted with the "mechanistic" account in which motion is imparted by contact as in the striking of one billiard-ball against another. The contrast between the mechanical and teleological explanations is sometimes described as that of *push* versus *pull*.

Along these lines a teleological approach explains action within the human, biological, and physical realms. The actions of men arise in the attraction of ideals upon them, not in the influence of various factors in their environment. The reason some plants turn of themselves towards a source of light is not that certain chemical changes occur within them but that they strive to secure light. There is a sun and it shines because it has a definite role to achieve in the plan of the cosmos, or because it was created so that there should be light and warmth.

We can best estimate the claim of teleology to constitute explanation, by seeing what success this approach has had in the various fields of human knowledge.

Teleology in the sciences. In the medieval world scheme the teleological conception prevailed in all fields. Since then science has gradually eliminated the notion of purpose as an element in the scientific account of things. Astronomy and physics first let it go, though Kepler who himself played a large part in the process still believed that angels moved the planets.[11] To explain the movements of heavenly and earthly bodies came to mean an account in terms of physical laws. By Newton's time the world as pictured by the physicist was a huge machine, and although God might be responsible for the whole and for its laws, divine interference in its detailed operations was deemed rare. The philosopher Descartes was ready to regard everything but intellectual activity as explicable on mechanistic principles, not excepting the behavior of animals. Thus he surrendered teleology as an explanatory principle for the world of nature, but retained it for the realm of mind. Descartes' dream of a universal mechanics, applicable to organic as well as inorganic things, was slow to be realized, but its develop-

[11] He noted that the distance of the planets was not proportional to their time of revolution around the central sun, the motion of outer planets being too slow. In his attempt to explain the facts, he debated whether the moving intelligence of the outer planets was weaker, or whether the central intelligence residing in the sun and moving the planets around it had a weaker effect on the outer planets because of their greater distance.

ment received a powerful stimulus from Darwin's achievements in biology.

The advance of science did not respect Descartes' sharp boundary-line between the physical and the mental. Modern developments in psychology tend to dispense with teleological explanation. The development of physiological psychology has led some to a theory of mind which defines the mental in terms of observable bodily behavior. Even the psychological uses of "purpose" to which we referred above—in the Freudian theory and in animal psychology—are not regarded generally as teleological in character. Although Freudian psychology is liberal in its use of the language of purpose, it is really interested in showing that an individual behaves in the way he does because, given a certain equipment of initial drives, he is affected in definite ways by his early experiences. In short, though the term "purpose" is used to describe a sequence of behavior or of conscious experience, the existence of such purpose is subject to scientific explanation which is not itself teleological.

The same distinction is important in the social sciences and in history. Most of the phenomena in these fields, consisting of human activity, are purposive in character. It does not follow, however, that *explanation* of these purposive phenomena need itself be purposive or teleological. In general the advance of the social sciences has brought a keen recognition of the role of physical, economic, traditional, and even chance factors in the flux of human events. Historical and social events can thus be seen as complex wholes, in the explanation of which men acting purposively are merely one factor.

Nevertheless in the psychological and social sciences and in history the view that genuine explanation is teleological has far from disappeared. The reason is that the sharp separation of the physical and the mental—the realm of nature and the realm of spirit—is a widely prevalent philosophical conception.

The teleological approach to the study of man utilizes this division of matter and mind, or body and soul. It rejects the belief that man is a physical object comparable to the rest of the natural world. Instead it distinguishes between those characteristics of men that are physical and those that are spiritual or mental. This problem of what man is and what is the relation between body and soul will be more fully explored in Part Three.

Teleology and the world as a whole. The progressive elimination of teleological explanation from many of the sciences has led some philosophers to abandon the attempt to pit it against other types of explanation, such as causal. They recognize that science thrives on approaches other than the teleological. Hence they look to religion and morals for a field of application for teleology. In short, the teleological outlook is maintained as a perspective on the world as a whole and the orientation of conduct within it, while it is abandoned for the explanation of particular events in the world.

According to this view the formation of the solar system, the development of organic life, the evolution of man, the processes of social change are all to be scientifically explored; and to explain them means to find the causes which brought them about. But the *meaning* of the world and the *meaning* of life are to be found not in showing causal origins but in a revelation of purpose, role, and destiny.

This view, like Descartes' sharp distinction of mind from matter, hopes by surrendering a great part of the territory of teleology to remain undisputed master of the rest. From the point of view of a transcendental teleology it retreats too far. From the point of view of the opponents of teleology, far from appeasing, it invites further inroads.

As Santayana has pointed out, there is no objection, until experience provides one, to trying out any notion to form a conception of the world. I might even try to explain the world in terms of personal omnipotence. But I would soon learn that things did not go just as I willed them. So, too, there is nothing illegitimate in trying out the approach of transcendental purpose.[12] Whether it can succeed or not depends on the evidence we find in the world for the existence of God and for God having a purpose. These questions will be discussed later.[13]

If teleology be excluded from the explanation of anything *in* the world, the conflict we have been examining remains in the attempt to retain it in religion and morals. Do religion and morals in any genuine sense explain the world at large and human life by ascribing purpose to them? Or do they simply give expression to human hopes, fears, and purposes, that have grown up in men's struggles with their environment and with one another during the course of history? These contrasting or antithetical analyses of religion and morals—one idealist and religious, the other naturalistic or materialistic—together with their differing attitudes on the world and human life will be explored in Part Five.

---

[12] The conception of immanent purpose cannot be tried out in this way, for it points to nothing unique for which evidence can be sought. For this view robs purpose of its specific meaning and merely equates it with order.

[13] The problem of method to be employed in dealing with evidence will be discussed in Part Two. The problem of the nature and existence of God will be discussed in Chapter 22.

Chapter 3 CAUSALITY AND THE MECHANISTIC APPROACH

In many of the affairs of ordinary life we explain an event by stating its cause. We say that the spring floods were caused by melting snow. We assume that had the snow not melted the floods would not have occurred. Thus we assume that there is a connection between the first event and the second, and we say that the first event brought about or determined the second. When such a relationship exists between two events we call the first event the *cause* and the subsequent event the *effect*.

Meaning of cause

The difference between an explanation in terms of cause and one in terms of purpose is well illustrated by an old story of Democritus, the father of the atomic theory.[1] A respectable citizen of the town in which Democritus lived had been killed by a tortoise suddenly falling from the heavens upon his head. How explain this unusual event? Someone nearby had seen an eagle hovering overhead. Now the eagle was the bird of Zeus, king of the gods. Hence rumor began to attach a purposive significance to this event. Why should this have happened under divine auspices unless some grave offense warranted it? Had the man been lax in his civic duties? Or what scandal would examination of his life unearth? If such a scandal had been discovered many, no doubt, would have felt his death explained in terms of a moral governance of the world, human presumption in challenging its rules, and divine vengeance dramatically staged.

Democritus, however, was committed by his philosophy to a causal approach. The explanation of an event lay in the occurrence of antecedent events, but the connections were not moral and purposive. A thing moved because motion was imparted to it by impact from something else in motion. And since all events (such as the crushing of the man's skull by the tortoise) are types of motion, the Case of the Falling Tortoise would be solved by finding causal connections. Democritus proved to be a very successful detective. He revealed that eagles are very fond of tortoise meat,

[1] Recounted in A. D. Winspear, *The Genesis of Plato's Thought*, Dryden Press, 1940, p. 150.

CAUSALITY AND THE MECHANISTIC APPROACH

and that in order to crack the hard shell, they drop the tortoises down on rocks. The missing link was a simple one—the man was bald and his head shone like a rock from a distance. So, far from exhibiting the wrath of Zeus, the case exhibited the fallibility of an eagle's judgment.

Use of cause in different fields. The notion of causality exhibited in this illustration is a familiar one and seems very simple. Actually, however, the idea of *cause* is ambiguous and involves several elements, not all of which are present in all uses of the term. Let us look briefly at a number of examples of the way the term is used in different fields.

Ordinary life. We explain Johnny's stomach-ache by finding that he ate green apples. Or we say that this piece of wood fell apart because the man brought his ax down with full force upon it. Indeed, our very use of transitive verbs becomes almost equivalent to causal assertion. To say "I did it" means in effect "I brought it about" or "I was the cause of its happening." Thus when a person lights a match and an explosion follows, we say that *he* caused the explosion.

History. The historian explaining the First World War looks for causes in the behavior of groups of men in various countries, in their needs, biases, and aims. Thus he points to German imperialist economic expansion and rivalry of Germany with England, nationalist movements in the Balkans, personal ambition of monarchs, the assassination of an archduke, and so forth.

Law. The lawyer in considering a grade crossing railway accident may ascribe the causal activity not to the engineer who guided the mighty power of the engine, but to the car-driver who neglected to "stop, look, and listen."

Social sciences. Social scientists investigating the causes of crime may engage in different kinds of studies. They may map typical attitudes, motives, and stimuli found in criminal activity in a given society. Or they may point to factors—such as slums and maladjustment—that were operating in the lives of men before they engaged in criminal activity.

Physical sciences. The engineer may ascribe the fall of a bridge to the previous undermining of its foundations or to a mistake in the original calculation of stress. The physicist, asked for the cause of the balancing of two weights in opposite pans, would probably answer in terms of the general formula that the product of weight and distance from the fulcrum is the same on each side. (He does not say that the cause of these two weights balancing is that he put them in the pans, though in a sense this is true.) The biologist finds that evolutionary changes in the past are the cause of the present characteristics of a species. The physiological psychologist finds the cause of hunger in the contraction of the walls of the stomach.

Elements of causality and the machine idea. The idea of explanation as the discovery of causes would seem, then, to involve one or more of the following elements:

(a) The cause is an event *preceding* the effect. Thus the eagle dropping the tortoise came before the impact of the tortoise on the skull; Johnny ate the green apples before his stomach-ache occurred.

(b) The cause in its occurrence illustrates some *regularity* in the operations of nature. This regularity may be expressed as a *generalization:* "Eagles are fond of tortoise's meat" and "Eagles drop tortoises on rocks"; "When heat is applied to gunpowder an explosion occurs"; "Hunger is felt when there are contractions of the stomach walls."

(c) The connection between the cause and effect is somehow *necessary* so that the result is *determined* when the cause takes place. Thus anyone learning of the faulty calculation would be able to predict that the bridge would collapse under certain loads.

These three elements—temporal precedence, regularity, necessity—may be recognized in the operation of a bicycle. First, if you press the pedal the wheel revolves (first the cause, then the effect). Second, the mode of operation is always regular (always when you turn the handlebars to the left the front wheel is inclined to the left and the rear wheel follows it). Third, each step in the operation of a bicycle necessarily brings about subsequent steps. The machine being what it is, certain actions inevitably produce predictable consequences. Such illustrations from the operation of machines are so typical of causal explanations that the causal approach has come to be regarded as a *mechanistic approach.*

The world-machine

From a technique for analyzing particular happenings the mechanistic approach readily became a way of interpreting the world as a whole. It grew with the development of modern science and with the decline of teleology, especially during the 17th and 18th centuries. The world came to be regarded as a huge machine whose mode of operation could be completely described if our knowledge of physics were perfect. Thus if one could know the position, velocity, and mass of all the particles in the universe at any time, and the laws governing the behavior of the particles, he could predict any subsequent state of the universe.

This interpretation of the world as a machine was a grandiose conception that brought everything within the possibility of human understanding. With such an interpretation no phase of existence was exempted from scientific investigation. Since all events in the world were the results of other events, nothing in the world was accidental or arbitrary. Every event had its place in the scheme of things, a scheme provided not by teleology but by physics, and science had only to keep searching for more and more knowl-

CAUSALITY AND THE MECHANISTIC APPROACH 31

edge about the world-machine in order to provide a more and more complete explanation of its working.

The effect of this view on human attitudes was twofold. The teleological philosophers accused the mechanistic philosophers of reducing the world to blind chance, of analyzing it on the analogy of the random movements of billiard balls pushing each other about. The mechanistic philosophers replied that such movements appeared random only because the teleologists looked for purpose; from the causal point of view they were examples of strict law. The opponents of mechanism shuddered at the idea of man being himself a machine whose action was completely determined on a cosmic scale. They thought such fatalism would produce a sense of futility, a belief that men have no intrinsic worth or dignity, and thus a tendency to use others as instruments for any purpose one might have. The mechanists emphasized instead the possibility of controlling human action and of fashioning a new people by changing their environment. They pointed out that to feel oneself part of a world-machine need not cause one to be depressed at being a cog; he might instead be exalted with a sense of unity with the totality of things.[2]

DOES CAUSALITY IMPLY THE WORLD-MACHINE?

Before examining the validity of the causal approach to explanation, it would seem desirable to decide whether the theory that every event has a cause really necessitates the world-machine idea. The argument from the ideal observer is certainly question-begging. This argument says, "If anyone had full knowledge, then he would be able to predict everything." But what is meant by *full knowledge?* If it means knowledge sufficient to predict everything, then the argument is a tautology asserting that if one were able to predict everything he would be able to predict everything. On the other hand, if full knowledge means knowing everything capable of being known, it still remains to be asked whether everything in the world is even theoretically completely knowable. If because of the nature of knowledge, there are some aspects of the universe not amenable to knowledge, then knowledge might be complete in the sense that it covered everything knowable, but still not be a sufficient basis for predicting everything. (To ask how we know about an unknowable world, of course, would be an embarrassing question.[3]) Again, some philosophers have claimed that the act of knowing consists in isolating a segment from the continuous process

[2] The attitudes and problems of conduct involved in the conflict of these approaches will be discussed below. See Chapters 13, 14, 22.

[3] Some philosophies, such as Herbert Spencer's, have, however, made the unknowable an integral part of their system.

which is the universe, so that no matter how much knowledge a theoretically all-powerful mind might acquire it could never reach the end. This would be like bisecting a finite straight line continuously in an attempt to exhaust it; the very nature of the process makes it theoretically incapable of completion. It is not a practical difficulty of a finite mind, but a really endless process. A finite mind would tire in the process; even an omnipotent mind would not be able to complete it, though it would be able to go on forever.

On either of these alternatives the world would not be a completely determined system despite the fact that for every knowable event there would be a discoverable cause. These conceptions are not offered here as necessarily acceptable on further reflection, but the very fact that there are conceivable alternatives to the world-machine idea shows that this idea is not inevitably entailed by the simple belief in causation.

Estimate of causality

As a matter of fact, the very foundations of the world-machine idea have been undermined in modern philosophy. The machine analogy itself is not an adequate account of explanation, however well it may account for certain types of relations. Let us then re-examine the three elements we found in the idea of causality.

THE ELEMENT OF TEMPORAL PRECEDENCE

Although generalizations offered by scientists as refinements of the causal approach do not require the cause to precede the effect,[4] causal explanations generally assume that the cause occurs before the effect. The cause may occur immediately before the effect, as it does in the case of chopping wood, or there may be an interval between the time of the cause and the time of the effect, as when Johnny eats green apples and gets sick hours later.

Problem of time lapse. When there is a time gap between cause and effect something may occur to interfere with the sequence. Thus Johnny may take an emetic and so escape the expected stomach-ache. Such illustrations have provoked the suggestion that the idea of cause should be extended to include every factor of the total situation in whose absence the effect would

---

[4] For example, formulae in mechanics which state the relationship between different elements of the same situation, as a formula describing the comparative weight and distance on both sides of the balance. On the other hand, there may be formulae of the form "If A at time t_1 then B at time t_2," where t_2 is subsequent to t_1.

not occur. Some philosophers think that such an extension would defeat the whole notion of cause; for, they say, if you follow this procedure you will have to end up with a complete cross-section of the world However, this does not necessarily follow. The attempt to include all *relevant* factors need not cover the *whole* world: it may merely increase the extent of the cause, as in Johnny's case by including as part of the cause the bodily changes that occurred between his eating of the apples and the beginning of his illness. Cause and effect would then be regarded as a continuous process. If anything occurred to stop the effect's happening the cause would in fact not have been completed.

Problem of continuity of cause and effect. Where the cause runs into the effect to such an extent that any distinction between the end of the cause and the beginning of the effect is purely nominal, there is a tendency for the analysis to extend the cause into the effect itself. Not the man bringing down the ax, it will be said, is the real cause of the wood falling apart, but the force of the ax on the wood. But the force of the ax on the wood is a phase of the event whose correlative phase is the wood falling apart. The question of causality is thus transformed into this: under what conditions of pressure does wood of such-and-such a kind fall apart?

Causality and control. This transformation represents an important shift in interest in the search for causes. In ordinary life our dominant interest is the practical one of control—both determination and prevention—of specific happenings. Thus we look at points in the continuous flow of events at which control is possible. That the cause precedes the effect means simply that we look to the past to explain a given event. And we do this because the present in which we are acting bears a like relation to the future events which we desire or dread—for the present will be the past of the future. Thus we may say the man lighting a match caused the explosion because the prevention of explosions is best controlled at that point, and because the gunpowder was taken for granted as present. A man throwing dynamite into a fire would not say ordinarily that the fire caused the explosion. The search for causes is thus a search for means by which we may control the occurrence or non-occurrence of subsequent events.

We cannot, however, merely look to the past—we look to the *habits* of the past. Accordingly the search for causes tends to pass into a study of the regularities that occur in the operations of nature. When this becomes sufficiently refined, the interest in temporal successions becomes subordinate. The elements spoken of as cause and effect may be, as we have seen, joint elements in a single situation. Or the language of "cause" may give place to that of "law." Nevertheless the power of control is increased, not diminished. To know the law of the lever is to have a means of reckoning, in specific temporal situations, what force applied at what distance from the fulcrum will raise any given weight. Causality in the temporal sense may not be evident in the law of the lever but it is evident in the operations of the derrick which are based upon it.

THE ELEMENT OF REGULARITY

In recognizing that the search for causes carries one into a study of the habits of the past, we have pointed to the fact that any discovery of a cause is taken to be a discovery of some regularity in the operations of nature. This is obvious in the work of the physical scientist. The character of the historian's work, however, as well as some types of ordinary usage, sometimes suggests that causality may be a relation between individual events. Usually, when historians discuss the causes of the Great War they are concerned with a particular set of events preceding the war and having some relation to it. But they do not assume that these need be the same kind of events that caused the Thirty Years' War or the Hittite invasion of Egypt. Occasionally historians appeal to a doctrine called the *plurality of causes:* the same kind of event can be caused by alternative sets of causes. Hence the emphasis on generalization seems to most historians inappropriate to their study.

General statements needed to connect singular events. There are, however, many statements in ordinary discourse which appear to deal with singular events but really refer to groups or classes of events. For example "John is of average height" seems to state a certain quality of John. But more accurately it refers to his position in a group, with other members of which he is being compared. Similarly if B strikes A after A shouts toward a group containing B and his friends, can we say that A's utterance caused B's striking? Where does the connection lie between these singular events? We can assert a connection only if we find some quality which A's utterance possesses (suppose it is insulting) and some quality which B possesses (suppose he is a "fighting Irishman") and some relation of qualities of that sort (e.g., "Irishmen fight on being insulted" or "Irishmen have a strong sense of honor, and leap readily into action when they are roused.") If no general statement appears in the analysis, we shall have no way of connecting the qualities to claim a causal relationship.[5]

[5] Of course the terms appearing in the generalization need not be the ones appearing in the original statement of causal relation. The insistence on a generalization somewhere in the analysis does not compel us to assert "All persons who make an utterance are struck by those to whom they make them," nor even "All who utter insults are struck by those to whom they utter them." Sometimes, however, our knowledge is insufficient to permit extended analysis, and the analysis of the assertion of causality may yield a generalization employing the same terms as the original assertion.

When we assert a causal relation between two events solely on the observation that one preceded the other, we run the risk of committing the fallacy of *post hoc ergo propter hoc,* the fallacy of assuming that because B followed A, B was caused by A.[6] Therefore we feel safer about asserting causality when our analysis of the situation of which A and B are factors and our accepted theory of the subject-matter allow us to deduce that B *must* follow A, or our experience with such situations tells us that B generally follows A. In short, we can assert causation more confidently when our observation of temporal precedence is supported by our awareness of necessity or of recurrence.

The analysis of unique events. Now in historical investigation events are frequently unique. Clearly we cannot expect generalizations of the form "All Napoleons," nor should we be too hopeful even of generalizations about all wars or all dictators. But by describing events in great detail and paying attention to their more elementary components we may be able to find appropriate generalizations to relate them. Thus a particular war, unique though it is, will be seen as a pattern of the interaction of groups which have certain types of aims and resources. In such fashion the unique event admits of causal analysis. The generalizations on the basis of which such judgments of historical causation are made usually come from common experience and the social sciences. They need not be universal assertions, but may pertain to what happens for the most part.

Necessary and sufficient conditions. The difficulties of finding causes in historical investigation may also be resolved by recognizing certain logical distinctions which aid in the analysis of causation. Such distinctions are (a) necessary condition, (b) sufficient condition, and (c) necessary *and* sufficient condition. To have food is a necessary condition for continuing to philosophize. But it is not a sufficient condition, for one may have food and still not engage in philosophy. On the other hand, taking a sleeping powder is a sufficient condition for falling asleep, but not a necessary condition. The necessary and sufficient conditions of any phenomenon are those conditions under which it will occur, and in the absence of any of which it will not occur. Thus in the case of some civil service posts, to be among the top three persons on the list of candidates who passed the examination is a necessary condition for appointment; to be among the top three and receive the unanimous approval of the commission is a sufficient but not a necessary condition; while to be among the top three and receive a majority vote is a necessary *and* sufficient condition.[7]

---

[6] E.g., a man may attribute spraining his ankle to his having broken a mirror two days ago.

[7] These distinctions may be stated readily in logical terms. Given the statement "If A is B, then C is D" we may then assert: (a) The truth of "A is B" is a sufficient condition for the truth of "C is D." (Obviously if the antecedent of this

Now in most of the natural sciences the implicit definition of "cause" is that of *necessary and sufficient* conditions, that is, the discovery of the conditions under which, and only under which the given phenomenon occurs. This is seen both in the operations of the sciences and in many analyses of methods for discovering causes. Thus John Stuart Mill's "methods of induction" state in effect that to find a cause you have to look for the factors that are present when the effect is present, absent when the effect is absent, and vary as the effect varies.[8]

On the other hand history, together with a great part of the social sciences, has had to be content with looking for causes in the sense of sufficient conditions. In this sense it is quite possible that there should be a *plurality of causes* for any given event. For example, if the sun shines John will be happy; if he learns this news, John will be happy. But such a plurality of causes does not prevent the discovery of generalizations, even though they be multiple, about the manifold types of conditions under each of which men are happy. Nor can the historian or social scientist be denied the right to go on even further and look for necessary *and* sufficient conditions in his field, although he may be skeptical of success.

THE ELEMENT OF NECESSITY

The last question we shall consider in analyzing the notion of cause is the nature of the claim that the occurrence of the cause *necessitates* the occurrence of the effect. The idea of a necessary connection of cause and effect is a most complicated one. Where the idea of temporal precedence is dominant in the analysis of causation necessity has sometimes been taken to mean the "push" of one thing upon another by direct contact. This was especially true where the approach in terms of causality was directed against the teleological approach. This pressure involving a direction of energy was

hypothetical statement is true the consequent will be true.) (b) The truth of "C is D" is a necessary condition for the truth of "A is B." (If the consequent is false then the antecedent must be false.) (c) Suppose in addition we are given "If C is D, then A is B." Then we may assert that the truth of "A is B" is a necessary and sufficient condition for the truth of "C is D." Thus the fact that a number is divisible by 10 is a sufficient condition for its being divisible by 5, a necessary condition for its being divisible by 30, and a necessary and sufficient condition for its being divisible by 2 and by 5. Thus briefly, "p is a sufficient condition for q" says the same as "If p, then q," "p is a necessary condition for q" as "if q, then p," and "p is a necessary and sufficient condition for q" as "if p then q, and if q then p."

[8] For a discussion of Mill's methods, see M. R. Cohen and E. Nagel, *An Introduction to Logic and Scientific Method,* Harcourt, Brace, 1934, Chapter 13.

CAUSALITY AND THE MECHANISTIC APPROACH 37

compulsive and compulsion entails necessity. Necessity was thus thought to be a discoverable character in the operations of nature.[9]

Ordinary usage no doubt also conveys in the notion of cause the idea of a force exercised upon an object so as to compel an alteration. Here, as has been frequently pointed out, the fact of causation is conceived as analogous to the exertion of will and energy in human activity. Such a conception is thoroughly anthropomorphic.

Hume's analysis of necessity in causation. The most emphatic attempt to get rid of this anthropomorphism was made by the philosopher David Hume in his famous analysis of causation.[10] Hume belonged to a line of philosophers who held stoutly that all knowledge begins in experience and that in the case of every meaningful idea it must be possible to point to the experiences or observations from which it was derived. From this point of view he asked for the meaning of such assertions as that A is the cause of B (e.g., touching a lighted match to the gunpowder caused the explosion). The analysis yields: (1) Observation of A, (2) observation of B, (3) observation of succession of B to A, (4) idea of necessary connection between the occurrence of A and the occurrence of B. The first three are observations; since they are experienced, they involve no problem. But the fourth is an *idea*. What are the experiences or observation from which this idea of *necessary* succession is derived? What do we mean by saying this takes place *necessarily* instead of simply that it takes place? Common-sense seems to suggest that the necessity, like succession, lies in things or events. But if so, argues Hume, it must be observable and it is not. On the other hand, there is a necessity which lies purely in the relation of ideas, such as two plus two equals four. But, instances of this cannot be conceived to be otherwise, whereas we can conceive of B not occurring after A occurs even where we firmly believe it will happen. Causation refers to experience and not merely to the relation of ideas; and the relation of experiences must be itself a matter of experience.

Hume's conclusion was that the necessity involved in asserting that A causes B is psychological or subjective. We find that wherever anything like A occurs something like B will occur. From our observation of the repeated occurrence of B after A we have developed the habit of associating the two and as a result when A occurs we feel a mental compulsion to anticipate B. It is our subjective observation of this compulsion which yields the idea of necessary connection. To assert causation is therefore to assert unvarying

---

[9] It is interesting to note that the Newtonian system, which gave such an impetus to the world-machine idea, in its theory of gravitation departed from the notion that causal action involves direct push; for gravity involves action at a distance, a fact that displeased both Newton and his contemporaries.

[10] *A Treatise of Human Nature*, Book I, Part III.

sequence together with a psychological feeling about that sequence. For the sake of reference we shall call this the view that necessity is *psychological*.

The major difficulty with Hume's analysis is not that it cannot be consistently employed, but that it does not seem to be what people intend when they say that the occurrence of one event necessitates another. Of course there may be no clear meaning in ordinary usage, but before adopting this conclusion it is appropriate to see what other notion of necessity there may be. For after all, cause is a concept employed in scientific investigation, that is, in the attempt to get an objective and stable account of the world, not a recording of variable and fleeting impressions.

The meaning of logical necessity. The chief alternative conception of necessity is that of the logician. For the logician necessity is a relation between evidence and conclusion such that given the evidence the conclusion follows by the laws of logic. To take a simple example, given "All men are mortal," and "All kings are men," it follows necessarily (i.e., by the laws of logic) that "all kings are mortal." This derivation of conclusion from evidence is called *deduction*. Many logicians hold that there is no necessity other than that of deduction. Though they may disagree about the analysis of the nature of logical laws, they hold that all necessity is logical necessity.

On this view, when we say of something that it *must* take place, how does it differ from saying that it *will* take place? To say that something *must* take place means that we are prepared to offer evidence from which it follows logically that the event will occur. The "must" is the logical connection of our evidence and our prediction. The same holds for the assertion that a past or present event occurs necessarily. The evidence together with the conclusion following from it may be said to form a little "system."

Such necessity is of course relative, not absolute. For the system contains in its evidence—as we have seen every statement of causality involves—at least one general statement in addition to particular or singular assertions. Thus the statement that the lighting of a match caused a particular explosion involved certain generalizations about the chemical relation between gunpowder and heat as well as particular assertions about the lighting of a particular match at a definite time and place. The general statement itself rests on evidence of particular happenings whose character can ultimately be established only by experience. Thus Hume was right in asserting that no knowledge of fact was absolute.[11] But this need not mean that the element of necessity in the analysis of cause is psychological rather than logical.

Is there necessity in nature? There are many philosophers who attack such analysis on the grounds that, when carried thus far, it results in ruling necessity out of nature. Actually it need not do so unless we are using the

---

[11] For a discussion of the process of clarifying or establishing matters of fact and its ultimately tentative character, see below, Chapters 5 and 8.

word "necessity" to designate some concrete object in nature. If necessity be understood as a complex relationship between events, the analysis in no way abolishes it.

This can be clarified by other examples. Take, for instance, the term "night." What does it mean? It does not mean darkness, else we could turn day into night merely by pulling down close-fitting dark shades. "Night" is the name we give to the situation in which the earth's rotation regularly cuts off the sun's light from a portion of the earth so that beings with eyes find it dark. But have we ruled night out of nature when we have thus analyzed its meaning? Clearly not. The truth is that the term indicates a complex of *related events* and cannot be made to correspond to any single part of the complex or to one relation in it.

Another example can be seen by analysis of "difference" in nature. We may test for difference in length between two sticks by placing them next to one another. All we find is one stick projecting beyond the other. But where is difference in length? "Difference in length" is a term employed to indicate just this fact and a host of other facts, such as that the one stick will fit into a space into which the other will not. It is a term referring to an aggregate of possible consequences, and what we mean by saying that there are differences of length in nature is that these consequences are discovered to hold in experience. What we mean by difference in nature is that differences of length, weight, color, and so forth, are discoverable.

The meaning of necessity is most dramatically brought home to us when processes, whose continuation might be anticipated, in fact do not continue if certain conditions are not met. Thus I discover necessity in nature if I try walking across the room and through a closed door, or if I make all the plans and carry out all the initial activities for an automobile journey but run out of gasoline. Such an experience convinces us that necessary conditions do exist, without which expected results will not take place.

More generally, what we mean by saying that there is necessity in the world is that a system of logically related generalizations about the world stands the test of experience. The growth of the sciences therefore constitutes the evidence of necessity in nature, and each of the sciences is descriptive of necessities in its domain. Thus the laws of physics tell us of the necessities of physical objects in the world and their reactions. Causation, then, does refer to the facts of nature, and the analysis of events in terms of causation is not subjective. It is objective in the sense that anyone performing the analysis in a designated way should find the same set of objective happenings pointed to or predicted.

In the light of the analysis of causality given above we can see why explanation has so often been identified with the search for causes. For all events occur in time, and the relation of events in time and the control of subsequent events by the molding of prior events is the domain of causality proper. In this domain, as we saw, meaning was readily given to its three elements of temporal priority, regularity, and necessity. But in advanced sciences the temporal aspect recedes into the background and the emphasis on generalization or law and system becomes central. In the next chapter we shall analyze these wider conceptions.

Chapter 4 THE MEANING OF LAW AND THE NATURE OF SYSTEM

A system of laws is the central notion in the modern scientist's picture of the world. To explain an event means to show it as a special application of part of such a system. The various notions we have been discussing are all looked upon as special instances of this fundamental idea. To ask for the essence of a thing or event is to ask for the system of classification in which it falls from the point of view of a revealed interest.[1] A thing's purpose is its place in the system of men's aims, conduct, or welfare. Its cause is a set of prior events to which it is related in a discoverable system. As is apparent from these formulations, the critique of the notions of essence, purpose, and cause in the preceding chapters has been carried out in terms of the point of view presented in this chapter.

It has often been denied that scientific procedures constitute explanation. Science, it is said, describes but does not *explain*. It deals with the *how* but not the *why*. But if we ask what after all is the difference between explanation and description we reach no ultimate distinction. We press a switch and the lights go on. This is description. To explain the phenomenon we describe further—the connections of wires, the generating plant, etc. To explain these we describe further—the operation of the generating plant, the electrical properties of matter. Explanation is therefore *systematic* description of order as against isolated description of order. The distinction between description and explanation is one between fragmentary knowledge and systematic knowledge.

This point of view will become clearer if we analyze the notions of law and system more carefully and examine the way in which they are applied.

Law

WHAT IS A LAW?

Consider the following statements:

"A body at rest remains at rest, and a body in motion continues to move at constant speed along a straight line, unless the body is acted upon in either case by an unbalanced force."

[1] See above, pp. 18-19.

"The volume of a confined body of gas varies inversely as the absolute pressure, provided the temperature remains unchanged."

"Water is composed of two parts of hydrogen to one part of oxygen (by volume)."

"Haemophilia behaves in human heredity as a sex-linked Mendelian recessive."

"When a man looks steadily at a red surface and then closes his eyes, he sees a patch of green."

"Bad money drives out good money."

Laws as statements. Such statements (and innumerable others) are called *laws* of one or another science. Roughly speaking, a law is a generalization, the formulation of a discoverable regularity or uniformity. In this sense a law is a statement about the world for which considerable evidence has been gathered. The types of statements that may be called laws as against those that are descriptions of single events or sets of events is a detailed question of logic into which we cannot here enter. Some have insisted that the term "law" be restricted to universal statements, so that a single exception would disprove a law. Others have extended the term and spoken of "statistical laws" which describe what happens not universally but in a definite proportion of cases. Again, some feel that "proper" laws have no temporal reference; they should state what happens to all bodies at all times, all men in all societies, and so forth. Others would permit the use of the term "law" for generalizations about specifically historical material, such as the regularities found in the behavior of a particular society, or even perhaps the "laws of the Nile," e.g., that the Nile overflows its banks at a particular season every year.

From a philosophical point of view there is clearly little importance in the attempt to set precise limits to the application of the term "law." It is important instead to distinguish between different logical forms of statements (universal, statistical, singular, and numerous complex forms) and to prescribe the kind of evidence that would be required for statements asserted in each form. It is also important to recognize that the attempt to state laws is part of the general effort to attain systematic knowledge. In the remainder of this chapter the term "law," unless otherwise indicated, will denote primarily the universal type.

Laws as uniformities. A certain mystic quality has often been associated with the notion of law. This character cannot be intended for the *statement* as such. We must therefore distinguish between a law as a form or type of statement and a law as a uniformity or regularity described or designated by such statements. It is clear that the awesome attitude refers to uniformities or regularities and only derivatively to the statements in which they are expressed. Hence the attitudes directed toward law are really concerned with the problems of order, permanence, and change in the world to which men belong and which they explore.

Various philosophies have modeled their ideas of law in their own image. The teleological approach sought to read laws as expressive of some law-giver, and hence as evidence for a divine being. The same garb of eternity, immutability, and ideality worn by essences in ancient philosophy was used by some to clothe the concept of law in the development of science. The defenders of a world-machine organized on causal principles added to law the idea of necessity which, as we have seen, was inherent in their conception of cause. But from the point of view which regards explanation as the development of a system of laws, law may readily shed these attributes.

Scientific law does not imply a law-giver. A scientific law does not imply a law-giver any more than it implies a potential law-breaker. When we speak of human law, legal law, or moral law, we are speaking of law in a very different sense. There is a punishment for the violation of legal laws imposed by a recognized public authority. But no punishment can descend on the violator of a scientific law, for the simple reason that no one can violate it. You are not breaking the law of gravitation by going up in a balloon, but merely exemplifying its operation under special circumstances and in connection with other physical principles. If you find a genuine exception to a universal statement then the statement is false, hence not a law; if the law is a statistical one, exceptions are expected, hence are not violations. The belief in miracles, so prevalent at one time, implied that the deity set aside the usual procedures of things on special occasions in order to achieve a higher purpose. Many scientists—Newton among them—have thought themselves to be discovering the laws set down by a divine law-giver. But clearly this assumption is not inherent in the notion of law.[2]

Scientific laws not immutable. Nor is there anything fixed or immutable about scientific laws. The appearance of eternity and ideality in scientific laws is due both to the mode of setting them forth in universal statements and to the exigencies of any scientific analysis. Laws are frequently stated in ideal terms for ideal sets of conditions. This is done in order to study one phase isolated from a complex situation. Thus the law of the lever—that the products of weight and distance on each side of the fulcrum are equal—is stated for a perfectly rigid body. The laws of motion are stated under ideal conditions of the absence of friction, and the coefficient of friction is separately assigned as a fixed property of the material. The eternal and ideal character of the laws thus comes from abstraction, and the temporal and material element reappears whenever the laws are applied to any existent situation.

---

[2] In effect it is equivalent to the argument from design; see below, p. 344 ff.

Actually, it is perfectly meaningful to speak of laws themselves as changing. Such change can have a number of different senses:

(1) A law may be said to change because it is discovered to be false. What on the basis of fragementary evidence may be thought to be a law (e.g., "All educated people are broad-minded") may turn out not to be generally true, and thus not a law at all.

(2) A law may be said to change when it is refined. Refinement consists in supplying qualifications concerning the conditions under which the law operates when these conditions have been too widely stated. Thus "The volume of gas varies inversely as the pressure" is refined to "The volume of a gas varies inversely as the pressure, provided the temperature remains constant." Such refinement is a change in the law if by a law we mean a universal statement for which there is considerable evidence.

(3) A law may be said to change because the conditions under which it is applicable or exemplified have ceased to exist. In the same sense a new law may emerge for the first time. This is no doubt true of many biological laws and of all social laws; they could not have been exemplified before there were human beings or societies in existence. To take a simple case, Gresham's law that bad money drives out good money obviously could not have held before there was some form of money, and would cease to hold if all forms of money disappeared, or even if there were extremely rigid control of economic transactions.

In this third sense, however, when it is said that the law changes because of changed conditions, there is the shift we noted above in the meaning of the term "law." In the first two senses what was changed was the formulation or statement, since the law was false or proved not to be accurate in all details. In the third case the law in the sense of the statement may remain true; if the conditions presumed by it recur, it may once again be confirmed. What has changed is not properly called the law, but the uniformity or regularity or trend in the physical or social field which the law designated.

This distinction likewise shows what is at stake in the claims for eternal and immutable laws governing nature, man, and society. It is not the statements whose immutability is insisted on, but the regularities to which they refer. Hence this conception of law postulates fixity in the world, fixity in the nature of man, and permanence of his institutions. And while the notion of men abolishing or changing scientific laws in the sense of making true statements untrue is patently absurd, the notion of men changing trends, regularities, or uniformities, in the physical conditions on the surface of the earth and in the social conditions of their life, is far from absurd. For here knowledge is power.

Scientific laws not absolute. Again, the notion of law need not possess the qualities of absoluteness and necessity in the sense in which they were asserted in the mechanistic idea of causality. We have already seen that the necessity which appears in the analysis of causation is logical necessity. Now logical necessity depends upon logical form. The assertion "If all little boys who eat green apples get a stomach-ache, and Johnny is a little boy who has eaten green apples, then Johnny will get a stomach-ache" is logically necessary since it illustrates a special form of syllogism. But the statement "All little boys who eat green apples get a stomach-ache," even if we suppose it true and a scientific law, is not thereby logically necessary. For its truth depends on physiological evidence, not logical form.[3]

Laws distinguished from definitions and analytic statements. In part, perhaps, the attribute of necessity has been affixed to the notion of law by a confusion of assertions which are laws with other types which are not laws. For example, definitions which merely state a resolution about the use of a term—e.g., Euclid's definition of "triangle" as a plane figure bounded by three straight lines—are neither true nor false and require no testing. Yet once the resolution is adopted there seems to be some necessity in the fact that you will not get a triangle that is not a plane figure bounded by three straight lines. Clearly it is simply a case of living up to the agreement to use one term as short-hand for a longer term. Such a statement is called a *nominal definition*.

Again there is a common type of statement which bears the color of necessity (in the sense that we cannot conceive of denying it) with which there may be a tendency to assimilate scientific laws. These are *analytic statements*. Kant described an analytic statement as one the meaning of whose subject included the idea of the predicate, so that it stated nothing new. Examples of analytic statement are: "A black cat is black," "Murder is wrong" (if by "murder" is meant wrong deliberate killing), "Every effect has a cause" (since by an effect is meant the result of causal action), "If you follow the circumference of a closed figure you get back to where you started." Kant's mode of expression, while not the best, is most easily grasped at this stage of our investigations. It makes clear that since an analytic statement says nothing new it requires no testing in experience. We shall have occasion later to examine more carefully the nature of such assertions in connection with mathematical statements.

As opposed to analytic statements we have *empirical statements;* e.g., "I am now writing," "There are eleven words on each line," "This has been the rainiest summer on record," "Water expands on freezing." The truth or falsity of an empirical statement depends upon the results we get in testing it in experience; it is not, therefore, necessary. Scientific laws are of this empirical type.

[3] See above, p. 38. For the way in which laws are established, see below, Chapter 5.

THE MEANING OF PROBABILITY

The historical association of scientific law with the world-machine idea, and its view that every event is completely determined, was largely responsible for the restriction of the notion of law to universal statements and the disparagement of judgments of probability. In its early days, probability theory itself accepted such a view. Probability was not knowledge of the objective world; it was a measure not of the situation but of our ignorance or belief.

The subjective theory. Consider, for example, the classical probability situation. I am about to toss a coin. Assuming that both alternatives are equally likely, and therefore that there is one favorable (heads) out of two equally possible alternatives, I judge that the probability of getting heads in my forthcoming toss is $\frac{1}{2}$. The subjective theory argues that $\frac{1}{2}$ is a measure of my confidence or belief that the desired end—heads—will come about. I can only half count on it. An all-knowing mind, however, would be able to predict accurately the result of my toss. It could estimate the tension of my fingers, the energy about to be expended, the relation of the position of the coin to external forces like draughts, vibrations, everything, in short, relevant to the result. On a world-machine theory, such a mind could know it all as it lay there to be known; nature would show itself as it really is, without chance or probability and with every event fully determined.

The frequency theory. Opposed to this theory was an *objective* interpretation. Its advocates escaped the difficulties of the world-determinism assumption by taking the judgment of probability to refer to classes of events, not the single event such as the forthcoming result on this next toss of the coin. When we say "the probability of getting heads in the next toss is $\frac{1}{2}$," we are saying in effect "the frequency with which we get heads in tossing coins of this sort is $\frac{1}{2}$," i.e., we get heads about half the time.[4]

Now clearly it will not matter, in this view, whether world determinism holds or not. If it does, probability examines how often events are *determined* to turn out in one of an alternative number of ways. If it does not, probability refers to how often events *happen* to turn out in one of an alternative number of ways. The objective frequency theory is favored today as the analysis of most scientific uses of the term "probability," although the subjective theory gives a pretty accurate account of some of our everyday guesses and hunches.

Since probability on the objective theory refers only to the behavior of groups, no statements or discoveries of probability can be directly applied to

---

[4] We cannot here go into the complicated problems of the modes of reckoning or representing results. This leads into the techniques of probability and statistics.

particular individuals. A knowledge of the suicide rate in a particular region will not tell us whether a designated individual is going to commit suicide. Other information and generalizations might enable us to make such a prediction—data, for example, on his psychological condition. That is to say, our description of group behavior in the language of probability does not preclude the discovery of other laws applicable to the action of individuals in the group. On the other hand, no such discovery is guaranteed; the events involved may be unique or too complex for our analysis and manipulation.

Probability and indeterminacy. The reaction against the universal determinism of the world-machine idea has carried some theorists to an opposite extreme in their denial of the subjective theory of probability. They go on, in seeking to adopt an objective interpretation, to the conclusion that since probability refers to groups only, and since in some fields our knowledge appears to be limited to judgments of probability, the individual occurrence is therefore truly indeterminate. Thus they attempt to introduce a genuine indeterminacy into nature itself. A considerable controversy has arisen in connection with such an interpretation of some of the findings of sub-atomic physics.[5] When the smoke of controversy clears it will probably be evident that these physical results have to a very great extent been employed as a flag in a philosophic battle, with scant respect for their scientific meaning.

Nevertheless the analysis of probability which the controversy has stimulated has been fruitful in releasing the notion of law from the absolutism of the world-machine philosophy. As a result it has become possible to recognize that laws and probability judgments are in no sense contradictory modes of describing events in the world. Laws are statements of what happens in every case; probability judgments state what happens with a certain frequency. So far from being in conflict, the one appears to be the limiting case of the other. Or better still the term "law" itself may be extended, with "universal" and "statistical" as sub-types.

Finally, it is important to avoid confusion in applying the notion of probability to a law itself. We may distinguish probability *in* the law from the probability *of* the law. The former means that the law itself is a statement about groups, as in the case of statistical laws. The latter refers to the fact that the evidence for any law is never completely gathered. This is obvious since a law may refer to *all* possible members of a class which may have an indefinite number. Thus it is loosely said that every law is itself only prob-

---

[5] Stated in Heisenberg's principle of indeterminacy—that it is impossible at any instant to determine both the position and speed of an electron. For a discussion of this problem, see Hans Reichenbach, *Atom and Cosmos*, Macmillan, 1933, Chapter 18; also Philipp Frank, *Interpretations and Misinterpretations of Modern Physics*, Paris, 1938, and "Determinism and Indeterminism in Modern Physics," in *Between Physics and Philosophy*, Harvard, 1941.

able, the contrast intended being between "probable" and "proven true." The way in which a law is tested will be examined in the subsequent account of scientific method.

THE UNIFORMITY OF NATURE

So far we have been concerned largely with the meaning of law and the interpretations given of it by various types of philosophy. We turn next to the question of application of the concept of law to the world of events. Have we any guarantee that it is applicable, that our world is such that laws are to be discovered? In general, this has been called the problem of the Uniformity of Nature. Some such assumption is found in each of the philosophies we have touched. In a teleological theory this assumption takes the form of a belief in the constancy of God's purpose. In an essence philosophy it appears as a belief in the intelligibility or determinateness of the world. In the language of causation it is sometimes expressed as "same cause, same effect." In what sense, then, does this general kind of order characterize our world?

Suppose we have discovered by the best available means that when a, b, and c are given, p will occur. We express this as a law or assert more roughly that a, b, and c constitute the cause of p. Now suppose we find a fresh case in which a, b, and c are present but p does not occur. Does this shake our confidence in the principle of the uniformity of nature? No, rather we suspect that we were wrong in saying that "If a, b, and c, then p" is a law. There must be some d present in the cases where p occurred and absent when p did not occur. For example if we assert, "Given a lit match touched to gunpowder, there will be an explosion," and on some occasion the result fails to follow, we examine the gunpowder, find it wet, and state as our law, "Given a lit match touched to *dry* gunpowder there will be an explosion."

In this way we constantly refine laws which do not meet the test; such failures do not make us question the principle. In short we are setting up as a condition of something being a cause that it should always produce the same effect. Hence the principle of the uniformity of nature is really defining what we mean by a cause and what we are hoping to find. In other words it says that we are looking for laws of a universal type; if any proposed law does not hold we will go on refining it or suggesting another rather than give up the search. The principle of the uniformity of nature is, therefore, equivalent to a confident prediction that there are uniformities to be found, so that laws may be asserted.

Laws and levels. What ground have we for this belief that there are uniformities to be found in this world? If we consider this question seriously it turns out to be ambiguous. If the assertion that there are uniformities in nature means that there is at least one uniformity, it is correct, since there have been laws established in physics and chemistry at least. And if it means that wherever you look you will find a uniformity, again it is correct because some physical laws refer to all material bodies, and in every existing situation there is a material body. But if the principle means that everywhere you look and *on any level of analysis or investigation,* you will find uniformities, the answer is that we do not know. If we do not find any uniformities in a particular investigation, it may be because we have been unable to discover them or because the events in question on that level have no repeatable phases or are unique. The implications of this reply may best be illustrated by an extensive analogy.

Consider, for example, the following sets of numbers (A and B). Each number is analogous to an event and each set to a succession of events. The whole example constitutes an analogy to the work of the scientist in looking for laws, and is deliberately over-simplified. It must not be concluded that the scientist works with such scanty data, or that he jumps to such hasty conclusions.

A. 1, 2, 5, 4, 2, 5, 7, 9, 2, 5, . . .
B. 1, 2, 5, 2, 7, 4, 6, 9, . . .

Obviously, we need a language and a technique with which to describe and analyze the events in question. In this case we can use arithmetic, which gives us a set of terms, a set of rules for analyzing and operating on them, and information about some of their properties; e.g., that some are odd and some are even numbers.

The discovery of laws on a given level. What "laws" can we assert of each set of events? From A it might appear that whenever a 2 occurs, a 5 will follow immediately. (This is the technique we use when we assert as laws such observed sequences as: the market value of munition stocks rises with a war scare, every revolution has to face the threat of a counter-revolution.) In B we find no similar recurrences. If we begin with our information gleaned from A as a preconception, our attention is fastened upon 2, 5, 2. But the fact that the second 2 is followed by 7 leads us to reject the hypothesis that every 2 is followed immediately by a 5. Of course, hypotheses concerning B may be offered for future testing. There are an indefinite number possible: every 1 will be followed by a 2; every 6 will be followed by a 9; when a 2 appears before a 5 another 2 will follow the 5; when the second of any two successive numbers is 3 greater than the first (as in 2, 5, 2) the first will be repeated after the second (this would be tested by the next new number, which will be 6 if this hypothesis is correct); and so forth.

Set A thus illustrates phenomena on a given level in which a law has been discovered, and set B phenomena on the same level in which no law has appeared although numerous hypotheses are suggested. In the case of A it is interesting to note that although there is no simple numerical law describing the succession of *numbers,* there is a spatial law describing the succession of *numerals.* The distance between any two successive numerals is greater than the distance between the earlier numeral and its predecessor. It is a sobering reflection that the kind of uniformity which is discoverable in a succession of events may be quite unlike the kind of uniformity we were looking for or that we have been used to. Thus we now think that historians who wrote of periods in terms of the moral characters of monarchs were concentrating on the wrong thing; we expect more satisfactory explanations from those who turned to economic phenomena. To the spatial order discovered in A we may compare the attempt of Spencer to assert a law for all development, namely that any later stage is more complex than any earlier one.[6]

Higher level laws and the relation of levels. If we group the numbers in B in couples we get

B. (1, 2,) (5, 2,) (7, 4,) (6, 9,), . . .

and if we add each couple we get

3,   7,   11,   15, . . .

which is obviously a series in which every number is greater by 4 than the preceding one. Let us speak of the more complex manipulation as dealing with the "higher level." For just as each of the items on this higher level is some complex of those on the lower level, so each of the items in the biological, psychological, and social sciences may be regarded as a complex of those on the preceding level, beginning with the physical.

Our analogy reveals that laws may be discovered on a higher level and yet none be discovered on a lower one. The converse is, of course, also often true; laws may be discovered on a lower level, but not on the higher. As we have seen above, we may gain statistical knowledge about groups on the basis of which group results can be predicted, although the reaction of a designated individual is not; and on the other hand we may know laws concerning all the chemical elements without knowing the laws of a complex

---

[6] This was taken up by many disciples who sought to find laws of evolution for the special fields: of religion (e.g., from animism to monotheism), social organization (e.g., from promiscuity to the monogamous family), art (e.g., from realism to symbolism), and so forth. A teleological touch was added in the conception that the existent forms were the best, since they were the latest. Social scientists have for the most part abandoned such evolutionary schemes for separate institutions or fields of human activity, or for inherent development within individual peoples; they concentrate rather on discovering the order of social development in the history of mankind and the globe as a whole.

organism. We may state this conclusion generally in terms of the various sciences. The fact that there are laws of physics, chemistry, biology, does not guarantee laws of psychology and the social sciences. Conversely, laws of economics and sociology do not guarantee laws of individual psychology; nor, for that matter, do laws of mechanics, dealing with large-scale or macroscopic bodies, guarantee laws of sub-atomic phenomena.

Predictability and the relation of levels. Where laws are discovered on a given level, successful prediction of phenomena becomes increasingly possible. It is not guaranteed, since prediction in every case requires additional knowledge which may not be available. Thus we cannot predict actual speed of an object through a medium simply because we know the laws of motion; we must also know the laws of friction and the character of the medium.

Sometimes prediction is possible from laws on a different level. Our higher level law concerning couples in set B enables us to predict on the lower level; we can predict the second member of a couple if we know the first member and the total of the preceding couple. Conversely, even if events in a domain appear to be unique, we may sometimes predict by means of a lower level law. For example, if we consider the set of phenomena described by such terms as "a dull day," "depressing weather," "fair and warmer," we may not be able to make such predictions as "after every dull day comes a bright one." But by analyzing the set in terms of winds, barometric pressure, and temperature conditions, we may be able to achieve a considerable measure of predictability about the phenomena we call weather.

There is a difference of great theoretical importance between the two examples just given. In set B, the higher level is secured by known arithmetical operations (addition) on the elements of the lower level. The higher level, we can tell in advance, will consist of numbers also; and since we know the properties of numbers we can predict what character its elements will have, even before the higher level is, so to speak, created. In the case of the weather, the situation is quite different. The amount of moisture in the air is an element in the lower level; the psychological feeling of oppressiveness is an element in the higher level. We could not predict the latter from the former until we had first discovered the trans-level relationship that told us what conditions of relative humidity a man finds oppressive. Once the relationship between the levels is known, we can of course predict from a knowledge of lower level events on any given occasion what the psychological effect is likely to be.[7] It is important to note that the inability to predict the higher level qualities from the lower level qualities alone is not removed by a more systematic explanation of the oppressiveness, e.g., that when the atmosphere is saturated in warm weather perspiration cannot evaporate and

[7] For the mode of establishing trans-level laws, see the account of steps in building up a system, p. 57 ff. below.

the desired cooling effect cannot take place. For the higher level qualities are already implied in speaking of warm weather and the desired cooling effect; if the description were purely physical and physiological we would be told nothing about psychological qualities of oppressiveness.

Law and the sciences of man. Where no uniformity is found we should not hasten to conclude that none exists. It may be that the material is too complicated for our present methods of investigation. We may not have refined our units sufficiently or we may be looking in the wrong direction.

This problem arises especially in the social sciences where, in addition to a too ready despair, certain preconceptions often stand in the way of continued effort. Some, for example, deny the applicability of the conception of law to the behavior of men. Law, they say, may be of use in dealing with physical nature, but when it comes to man, one deals with entirely different material, the human spirit and its more spontaneous expression. Hence other methods must be applied and the artist's brush must supplement the descriptive sciences. The analysis of this position depends upon the analysis of man's nature and his relation to the world. This whole problem shall be our special concern in Part Three. Here it is enough to point out that the difficulties in studying man and society need not necessarily flow from any special nature of man, but simply from the complexity of the material and the diversity of factors involved in it.

There may, it is true, be fewer uniformities in human events than in physical ones; they may be less universal and so require description in terms of statistics, probabilities, rough classifications, and even broad guesses. But just because there do happen to be regularities of a comparatively simple type in the physical world, and because as a result we tend to associate simplicity with the inorganic world, we should not, on failing to find comparable uniformities in human affairs, believe it to be a sign of the special cosmic status of man. If we are more attentive to nature we find sufficient complexity even in the purely physical realm. Try to plot the motions of a particle in a whirlpool and find a simple formula to describe them!

Another reason for the comparative lack of success in the sciences of man is a weakness stemming from the human heart, which makes men look for the results they desire and reject any views which run counter to their wishes. Those especially who cherish specific forms of institutional life—economic, familial, religious, educational—are loath to allow the truth of any discoveries whose consequences are opposed to their special interests. Many will not believe an account, however scientific, which concludes that no inborn racial differences in capacity and intelligence have been demonstrated; and organized religions have frequently resisted medical views of birth control. Such problems no longer beset the physical sciences, although they do occur in biology. Questions of race and of eugenics have given rise to much pseudoscience. When we think that the interference of values with the development of science is limited to the social sciences it is well to reflect on the history of superstition in medicine, on the long life of alchemy and astrology, and on controversies about evolution.

How laws reduce contingency. In any field in which uniformities have been discovered and laws asserted, systematic knowledge is increased. Single events occurring in that field need no longer be regarded as isolated, as *just happening,* or, to use a more technical philosophical term for the same thing, *as contingent.* When we begin the scientific investigation of a field it may be that most of the facts we know about it are unrelated or contingent. The object of scientific inquiry is to discover relations and further facts such that contingency will be reduced. For example, it happens that this pen falls when unsupported; it also happens that this stone falls when unsupported. Now if we accept the general statement that all bodies fall when unsupported, the fall of this pen is no longer seen as contingent, as just happening. Rather, given the general statement, and the statement that this pen is a material object, then that this pen falls when unsupported follows logically and is in that sense *necessary.* Of course that all bodies fall when unsupported is still contingent, and so is the fact that this existent is a pen. Similarly, if we plot the path of Mars and find it is an ellipse, that conclusion is contingent. But if we plot the orbits of the other planets and assert the law that all planets move in an ellipse with the sun as one of the foci, then the statement about the motion of Mars is no longer contingent. The motion of Mars is in accordance with the law describing the motion of all planets. Thus the discovery of a law is a way in which contingency is diminished.

Laws are thus the first results of an effort to gain a systematic understanding of a field. In order to trace the process beyond this point and more minutely, we turn to the idea of system itself.

System

The systematic theory of the most advanced sciences is a very impressive achievement, so impressive indeed that the beginning student is apt to be overwhelmed by it and to look on it as something beyond the understanding of ordinary mortals. It is better, therefore, in considering the nature of system, to start not with the end product but with the effort of *systematizing.* This is an effort carried out by men along numerous fronts. It is an uneven advance showing different stages of progress in different fields. When we view this whole picture we get a clearer understanding of the unity of the whole endeavor and of the continuity between ordinary knowledge and refined theory.

REDUCING CONTINGENCY

Roughly speaking, systematization is the process of reducing contingency in giving an account of a particular field. We have already seen the way in which laws perform this function. This process is carried further in scientific work by the attempt to reduce the contingency of the laws themselves. This involves relating them to one another by means of other general statements. For example, in the illustrations given above the statements "All bodies fall when unsupported" and "All planets move in elliptical orbits" were contingent. There was no relationship between them. But when we study Newton's principle of gravitation we see that both statements follow from the more general statement that we call the law of gravity given the mass and position of the bodies in question. Thus the law of the motion of falling bodies and the law of the motion of planets cease to be contingent.

The analysis will be clearer if we take a relatively simple example. "Ice floats on water" and "Water expands on freezing" are two general statements which may be learned independently by separate series of observations. But if we define the density of a substance as weight per unit volume and accept the general statement that a substance (liquid or solid) of lesser density will float on a liquid of greater density, then we may deduce from the fact that water expands on freezing, that the density of ice is less than the density of water, hence that ice floats on water.

The attempt to discover logical relations among statements usually involves the addition of other statements, thus broadening the material under consideration. Scientific work in any field aims at the most extensive systematizing possible, hence at a minimum of contingency. Clearly contingency cannot be entirely eliminated. The most general ultimate laws in any system will be contingent since they are not themselves deduced from anything else; and the fact that certain existent material satisfies the conditions (e.g., that this existent happens to be water or a planet or atoms occupying this position at this moment) will also be contingent.

The mechanistic ideal of complete determinism in the world supposed contingency reduced to the barest minimum. It desired one universal law and, in addition, the contingent assertion of the position, mass, and velocity of every particle at one instant.[8] Given this starting point, with the whole world treated as embodying a single determinate system, the result would be complete predictability. Clearly this is not the present state of science. Systematizing has gone on in many different regions and the result has been a great number of separate systems. How far the process of systematizing can continue depends upon the way in which the various systems may themselves

[8] See above, p. 30.

be related. A survey of this whole problem therefore entails an examination of the meaning or nature of a system, the way in which a system is constructed, the way in which systems may be related, and the limits of such relationships.

TYPES OF SYSTEM

The term "system" is very widely used. People speak of a mathematical system, of the capitalist system, and of introducing system into one's daily life. In short it has come to be synonymous with any type of order. But there is a fundamental difference between a type of order which is actually discoverable in what exists and a type of order which might exist but does not. A Utopia describes a merely *possible* system, but capitalism is an *actual* system. Usually the context of our remarks will make clear whether we are speaking of a merely possible order or an existent order.

Possible systems. Within possible systems two subtypes may be distinguished—logical and experiential. A system is logically possible if it is internally consistent, that is, if it violates no law of logic. Thus the syllogism about what happens to little boys who eat green apples was logically consistent. A system is experientially possible if it is in conflict with no law of established science. Thus we can draw up systems as pictures of the world of the future, as such imaginative writers as Jules Verne and H. G. Wells have done.

Interpreted and uninterpreted systems. There are still further degrees of abstraction from the existent. We may develop a possible system about Utopian behavior as follows: "If this globe were a Utopia, men would love one another; if men loved one another there would be no war; therefore, if this globe were a Utopia there would be no war." This, however, still talks of men and war; in short, the terms still refer to specific characters of existent things. Suppose now we were to write: "If A is B, then C is D; if C is D, then E is F; therefore, if A is B, then E is F." We have now something of the same form, but have eliminated direct reference to characteristics of existent things. We have therefore a formal system, or as we shall call it, an *uninterpreted system*. There are an indefinite number of ways in which we can interpret it by assigning different values to the variables in the formal system; for example, "If John has the measles, his sister will be kept home from school; if his sister is kept home from school, her friends will miss her; therefore, if John has the measles, his sister's friends will miss her."

As we have seen above, an interpreted system may describe a possible state of affairs or an actual (existent) state. We have, therefore, distinguished three uses of the term "system":

(i) An uninterpreted or formal system;

(ii) An interpreted system describing a merely possible state of affairs;
(iii) An interpreted system describing an actual or existent state of affairs. (Of course, an actual state of affairs is also *possible,* since otherwise it could not exist.)

Sometimes we cannot tell from the statement of a system which it is. Of course if there are a's and c's in it, it is probably uninterpreted. But if it has words in it which we do not understand it is as good as uninterpreted unless a definite meaning is assigned the terms, a meaning enabling us to identify what is being talked about. For example, "The fly chick's a hepcat" is apparently an uninterpreted statement, but there are initiates for whom it has a clear interpretation.

Again, when a statement or system of statements is interpreted, we may not be able to tell without investigation whether it refers to a merely possible or actual state of affairs. For example "All men think themselves superior to women" describes a possible state of affairs, but if any men do not share in this vanity, then it does not describe an actual state of affairs. In short, when an interpreted statement is true it describes an actual state of affairs, when it is false, merely a possible state of affairs.

In the language of truth and falsity the meaning of "uninterpreted" would be this: A statement is uninterpreted if at least one of its terms is without interpretation. An uninterpreted statement is neither true nor false, but may be used to generate true or false statements by substituting different interpretations for its uninterpreted term. For example from "x is a man" we may generate the false statement "this pen is a man," or the true statement "I am a man."[9] Sciences aim at interpreted systems whose statements are true or describe actual states of affairs in the world. Mathematics in its purest form aims to devise systems of completely uninterpreted statements. Logicians sometimes speak of pure and applied mathematics to distinguish the uninterpreted from the interpreted systems. Applied mathematics in this sense, is science (if it describes actual states of affairs).[10]

Logic and the ideal type of system. Formally, a system consists of definitions and initial statements, from which other statements are derived as *consequences.* In the ideal type of system the consequences follow by the rules of logic alone. The logicians have elaborated these rules most carefully and in fact have formulated logic itself in systematic fashion. We cannot

---

[9] What we have called an uninterpreted statement logicians ordinarily call a propositional or sentential function. This is defined as any assertion containing one or more variables from which may be generated statements whose truth or falsity depends on the values substituted for the variables.

[10] This distinction is not the same as the ordinary distinction of pure and applied science. The latter differentiates theoretical scientific work (which itself may be applied mathematics) from the utilization of theory for some type of practical engineering.

enter upon this field here, but it is sufficient to illustrate some cases of consequences following logically. Let S_1, S_2, etc., be statements. From "if S_1, then S_2," and "if S_2, then S_3" there follows necessarily "if S_1, then S_3." Again from "if S_1, then S_2" and "S_1 is true" there follows necessarily "S_2 is true."

Now not all studies are able to achieve results that can take such an ideally systematic form. Mathematics does, since its task is precisely the building of systems. Among the empirical sciences physics has achieved a high degree of systematization. The extent of such achievement diminishes rapidly as we climb the roster of science towards those dealing more exclusively with human material. But the drive toward system is there, and its results are varieties of approximation.

BUILDING A SYSTEM

There are various degrees of success in the process of building up a system. One may take the first steps and merely establish terms for the identification of events, such as, in physics, "pressure of a gas." Or one may find general statements relating those terms, as, for example, when pressure is related to volume. The discovery of systematic relations between the laws or general statements—as in the kinetic theory of gases—is a more advanced step in this process. That there are identifiable terms does not guarantee the discovery of laws, nor does the discovery of the latter guarantee further systematization.

Identification of terms. Take, for example, a set of events or phenomena about the explanation of which there is uncertainty—slips in speech and reading. We have here a clearly identifiable phenomenon, viz., the utterance differs from what most people and the same individuals on other occasions would express and what the individual intended to express. From the point of view of initiating a study it is sufficient that the identification be clear enough to designate a large body of events as examples, even though the classification of some of these may later need revision.

Search for laws and the location of field. Given the terms, the old difficulties which we examined above in our numerical analogies of the search for laws, arise in full force. Are mistakes in speech unique events, whose common character is accidental? In short, is our classifying them together and designating them by a single term analogous to the creation of a class of all things precisely 5 ft. 3 in. in length, whether human, stick, or pile of earth? Or if they are not in this sense contingent events, of what sort is the order to be discovered? In his *Psychopathology of Everyday Life* [11] Freud refers to the hypothesis of Meringer and Mayer who hoped to find linguistic rules

[11] Chapter V, "Mistakes in Speech," in *The Basic Writings of Sigmund Freud*, Modern Library, 1938.

and a definite psychic mechanism "whereby the sounds of a word, of a sentence, and even the words themselves, would be associated and connected with one another in a quite peculiar manner." Meringer and Mayer dealt with the qualities of the sound and the effects of these qualities. Freud looks in a quite different direction, to the intruding and disturbing effect of "something *outside* of the intended speech. The disturbing element is either a single unconscious thought, which comes to light through the speech blunder and can only be brought to consciousness through a searching analysis or it is a more general psychic motive, which directs itself against the entire speech."

Other alternatives can be imagined. For example, one might conceivably construct an explanation that speech mistakes result whenever certain similar physiological situations recur.[12] Without considering the adequacy of these three hypotheses we may notice the directions in which they point. The first one would try to systematize mistakes in speech within a study of phonetics and sound effects, the second within the psychology of repressed wishes, the third within the framework of physiological study. Thus we would have a linguistic, a psychological, and a physiological explanation of speech mistakes.

Suppose that instead of accepting any of these explanations we tried to explain mistakes by setting up a science of "errorology." We would then look for generalizations relating speech mistakes with mistakes in arithmetic, fallacies in thinking, and errors in all fields. Suppose we succeeded in establishing a generalization for mistakes in speech and separate generalizations for mistakes in reading and in arithmetic. We would then have three contingent laws, and whether a system of "errorology" could be established would depend on our discovering a generalization that removed the contingency of our three laws by making them merely special cases of a more general law.

Further systematization. This more general statement might of course be in psychological terms or in physiological terms, in which case errors would turn out to be psychologically or physiologically explicable. Or again the general statement might contain terms purely from the "science" of "errorology." In that case it would continue to be a relatively independent system. If, however, no more general statements were established and separate laws of arithmetical error and speech error were not independently related to different psychologic or physiologic laws we would have a field of "errorology" in which there were terms and laws, but no higher degree of system. Many fields are in precisely this position, e.g., religious, artistic, intellectual, and moral phenomena, concerning which some have even doubted the existence of general statements.

[12] This is suggested by analogy to the kinds of utterances that occur in *aphasia*.

MODES OF RELATING SYSTEMS

Our example has brought us to the next problem in understanding the nature of system: the different ways in which two systems may be related. Obviously the first step is the relation of terms, that is, establishing some formula of translation between the terms of the first system (S) and those of the second (Z). This can be done in at least two ways, by *equating the terms* (direct translation), and by *empirically relating them*.

Equating terms. If the terms are equated, that is, directly translated, then one term gives up its independent designation. For example, some philosophers who had used a term like "good" for many years in personal and social life, decided on reflection that all they really meant by it was "the object of their desire." Thus when they said that philosophy was a good activity they meant that it was an activity which they desired to carry on. On such a view "good" was equated with "desired," and thus a term in the study of morals was translated into a term in psychology. Frequently one term may be translated into another without loss of meaning, and sometimes with genuine clarification, for the second term may include more information. Thus "speed" is replaced by "distance/time."

Empirical relation of terms. The second mode of relating terms in two systems is empirical. Each term retains its independent identification, but it is found that wherever anything can be identified as t in one system it can also be identified as r in the other. This is really an empirical trans-level law relating t and r. For example, let t be a term designating a sound of a particular pitch and r a special frequency of air waves. It is found that whenever anything can be designated as the pitch t, it can also be designated as the frequency r. Hence t has been empirically related to r. Such relation may be one-way or reciprocal. In this case it is one-way: the presence of something that can be designated as r does not indicate that it can be designated as t, since in addition to the air-waves there must be an organism present to have the sensation which we call sound of a certain pitch.

Direct translation and empirical relation are two quite different modes of relating terms of different systems. The important thing is that the empirical relation of terms does not abolish the independent designation of each. "Hotter than" continues to have an independent psychological meaning even though empirically related to "producing a greater lengthening of the mercury in an inserted thermometer" and to "greater energy of its constituent molecules."

Deducing laws. Relating the terms of two systems is only the first step in "unifying" the systems, and it does not guarantee the next. There may be a relation of t_1, t_2, t_3 of one system with r_1, r_2, r_3 of the other respectively, but this does not enable us to deduce laws relating t_1, t_2, t_3 from those relating r_1, r_2, r_3. For example we may empirically relate the terms "red," "blue," and "green," in the sense explained above, with particular ranges of light-waves. Thus t_1 (red) may be empirically related to r_1 (waves of length between such-and-such limits), and so for t_2 and r_2, t_3 and r_3. Again there may be laws in visual terms relating t_1 and t_2, such as those of color afterimages. And there may be laws of the interference of light-waves connecting r_1 and r_2. But we are not now able to deduce the laws of our perception system from those of the physical system, even though the terms of each are empirically related. Such a prospect is of course theoretically possible, and might come about with increasing knowledge.

Unification of systems and boundaries between systems. Complete unification of systems occurs when the laws of one system are deducible from those of another, or when both are seen to be special cases or sub-systems of a third system. Thus it is often said that chemistry has been reduced to physics. But in fact it is not the case that 19th century chemistry has been reduced to 19th century physics; it is rather that new terms have been introduced into physics and new laws discovered so that both 19th century physics and a great part of 19th century chemistry fit into this new system. It is conceivable that physiology may become unified with physics and chemistry, and parts of psychology (e.g., the psychology of perception) be integrated with a system of physiology and physics.

In short, it is futile at any one time to regard the boundaries of systems of knowledge (such as the sciences) as if they were eternal divisions or phases of existence. Any body of identifiable events may be investigated for whatever order is discoverable in it. Further knowledge may dissect or unify a particular science and "combine" it with or "reduce" it to others in the sense of the relation of systems which we have so briefly discussed.

THE PROBLEM OF NOVEL QUALITIES

This analysis of the modes of relating systems throws considerable light on the old philosophic controversy concerning the appearance of novel qualities in the evolution of the globe. Under the influence of the world-machine idea and the belief in world determinism [13] it has sometimes been said that nothing novel can appear in the world because everything is theoretically predictable on the basis of the laws of the universe and its state at any given time. Thus it is implied that a sufficiently detailed physical account of the universe at some time in the past would have been sufficient for predicting the appearance of life, the development of consciousness, and the character of society. Opponents of this position insist on the occurrence of genuine novelty, unforeseen before its occurrence. Each higher level—biological, psy-

---

[13] See above, p. 30 ff.

chological, and social phenomena respectively—is therefore sometimes said to have inexplicable "emergent" qualities.[14]

The meaning of "novelty." In approaching the question from the point of view of relating the various systems of knowledge—physics and chemistry, biology, psychology, social science—we are not, of course, considering the historical perspective at all. For we begin with terms designating phenomena on all levels, and are therefore seeking systematic relationships among qualities that already exist. Properly speaking, "novelty" refers to the first appearance of a phenomenon in the evolution of the universe. It is *prime novelty*, such as the first appearance of life or of consciousness. It must be carefully distinguished from such notions as "having a special character"; life, wherever it appears, has a special character as contrasted with its milieu, but on this globe it is no longer novel. Similarly, every time we light a match, a special quality appears in the situation; but it is no longer new.

Incompatibility of prime novelty and predictability. A truly novel quality cannot be predicted prior to its first occurrence. Prediction means deducing from premises (either accepted or offered as hypotheses) the proposition that a certain event of specified quality will occur. On logical grounds no term can appear in the conclusion which did not appear in the premises. I cannot predict that John will visit me on Sunday unless "John" appears somewhere in the evidence, as in "All my friends who live in New York will visit me on Sunday, and John is one of my friends who lives in New York." It follows that to predict the first appearance of a quality (such as life, or some specific quality in a new combination of familiar elements) at a definite time on the globe, on the basis of a physical description of the universe, will involve among the evidence some statement to the effect that there is such a quality (life) when there is such-and-such a pattern of physical elements. But this is, as we have seen, a trans-level *empirical* law. It must, being empirical, rest on experience. Therefore, the phenomenon cannot be occurring for the first time if it is really predictable in advance. The world-determinist in his statement of the case against genuine novelty is obscuring the fact that his "laws of the universe" if they are to enable him to predict from the physical description of the universe at any time, must include trans-level laws relating every possible quality to physical conditions. His theoretically all-knowing mind robs the universe of novelty only by having *experienced in advance* all the qualities that can ever appear.

If this argument is correct, it shows that the world-determinist's basis for the denial of genuine novelty is insufficient. The argument does not, however, assert the existence of novelty in the world. It simply explicates the consequences of a given meaning for the idea. Nor does it support the defenders of genuine novelty in their argument that novel qualities are inex-

[14] For the vitalistic view, which resorts to an explanation of novel qualities in terms of some unique purposive factor, see below, p. 143 ff.

plicable. These questions—the explanation of novelty and its existence—require separate analysis.

The explanation of the novel. Once a novel quality has appeared, there is no reason why we cannot attempt to explain it. If we are successful we can then predict its subsequent occurrence. Such explanation involves, as we have seen, an empirical relation of this quality to others, and this does not mean somehow eliminating it. Our analysis has shown that there is no theoretical obstacle to attempting to build up and unify systems, but there is equally no theoretical guarantee that this can be accomplished.

A novel quality need not, therefore, remain a mysterious appearance on the face of the globe. In Part Three we shall consider in detail the various attempts to explain mental phenomena in relation to physical phenomena.

The existence of novelty. The question of the existence and degree of novelty is, therefore, an empirical one. The growing success of explanation has enabled us, to a considerable extent, to trace continuities, and to suspect many where they have not yet been found. These do not remove novelty from the total event, but enmesh it in a network of relations that make knowledge and even future prediction possible. Thus, to revert to the previous example of humidity and the feeling of oppressiveness,[15] we might very well predict now that certain describable physical weather conditions not yet encountered would produce psychological disturbances, but be unable to imagine the qualitative character of the experience. Perhaps the best analogy is that of a man blind from birth who is about to gain sight. Suppose he has a thorough knowledge of the physics of light and of the physiology of vision. Certain terms in his knowledge, however, remain empirically uninterpreted. He may know, as Locke tells us a blind man responded to a vivid description, that scarlet is like the blare of a trumpet; and he may have the relations among colors ordered in his anticipation. But there is a remainder of qualitative experience that is yet to be his, which he cannot anticipate.

In individual life, there is much that has such novelty, old as it may be in the history of the world. Perhaps more than we think is novel even from a world perspective. As Walter Pater so eloquently pointed out [16] we cease through the burdens and routines of life to be aware of the unique and let the richness of the world slip by unattended. But a world-historical view provides by far the most dramatic procession of novelty. It reveals the development of different forms of existence throughout the ages, manifesting novel qualities that appear for the first time at definite points in the process of evolution.

To deny the existence of novelty is therefore to gainsay the evidence of science, history, and human experience. Yet to recognize its existence in no

---

[15] See above, p. 51.
[16] In the epilogue to *The Renaissance*.

way impedes the endeavor to achieve an explanation of any and every phenomenon, and to secure the widest unification of human knowledge.

MONISM AND PLURALISM

In the light of these discussions we may return to the problem raised earlier of how far we can expect a unification of all systems of human knowledge. The desire for complete unity has led some to the conviction that ultimately not merely all known systems but all knowable systems can be unified into a single all-comprehensive system. Such a position is generally called *monism*. The belief that there are several systems and these incapable of unification, with only contingent relations, is called *pluralism*. Within each of these positions further distinctions may be made. Thus the *monistic* theory may be intended to assert a monism of *stuff* or a monism of *change*. The first would be the claim that the world is made of a single stuff or material; in effect it is the assertion that the system of physics has universal application, and that any event can be analyzed to yield electrons and protons. The second is the view that every change however small results in a change in everything else, however imperceptible. Move your little finger and you stir the distant stars. There is a logical monism which is parallel to this last position; it claims that all truths are so related that one of them could not be false without every other being false. In other terms, if any event in the world were different from what it is, everything else would have to be different.

Illustration from a special field. An analogy from a more special domain may aid in clarifying the difference between monism and pluralism as approaches to analysis. For example, in the field of cultural and social activity one finds the same issues. There have been social philosophers who have tried to reduce every kind of activity to the same type. Thus everything a person does has been called pleasure-seeking, self-assertion, economic activity, or self-preservation. In short all activity is analyzed in terms of "motives" and one motive is found prevalent whatever the appearance of others. This is parallel to the monism of stuff, e.g., that when you are praying or making love or philosophizing you are fundamentally engaged in preserving yourself. Again, comparable to the monism of change is the view that all elements of social and cultural activity are intimately related so that a change in one (e.g., in the mode of production as Marx believed, or even in the style of music as Plato asserted) would eventually cause an alteration in all the other branches of social and cultural activity.

The problem ultimately empirical. Now just as in such special fields the issue between opposing positions has to be resolved empirically, so the issue between monism and pluralism at large is ultimately empirical. In the case of the basic material of the universe the evidence clearly favors the monism of stuff, and physicists are constantly probing further into the nature of the fundamental matter out of which this universe is constructed. In the case of change the evidence, though less decisive, would appear to be against extreme monism and extreme pluralism. In a general sense, of course, things are interrelated. But we cannot say on scientific grounds that a change in anything would produce a change in everything; nor is there evidence for the existence of something whose change would affect absolutely nothing else.[17] Science constantly seeks the specific relations of given changes to some other changes against a stable background or under conditions that are otherwise constant.

Monism and pluralism as attitudes. Finally, concerning the relation of systems of knowledge, neither monism nor pluralism is theoretically impossible, and only the future expansion of knowledge itself can bring clearer insight into how the conflict of these two positions may be resolved. In this context, monism and pluralism may be interpreted rather as attitudes than as doctrines—monism as a confident program for the unification of all science, and pluralism as a type of skepticism. The monist is encouraged by every growth in knowledge and in the interrelation of sciences. In his zeal he likes to think of contingency as mere ignorance of connections that really exist. The pluralist, on the other hand, points to increasing and novel discovery and the numerous contingencies in the relations of systems as evidence that ultimate unification is an idle fancy.

EXPLANATION AS SYSTEMATIZATION

A system of laws, in the sense in which these terms have been explained in this chapter, is the answer of the scientist to the demand for a picture of the world. As we saw above, this was implicit in most of the other concepts employed to build world-views. But these assimilated the idea of system to the special model of a particular field or interest. Even when the notion of system has been freed from the teleological and mechanistic interpretations, it is important to exercise continual caution in order to avoid its subjection to some fresh model. Thus a system is not "organic" just because its parts hold together and it grows. Nor is the systematic order found in any field somehow "mental" just because a system of statements is the product of human thought and experience. But one can look for system or connected order in terms of any of the interests or fields to which men have sought to assimilate the general idea. Thus classification (or discovering essences) is a special type of systematizing. One can look for system among men's pur-

[17] For a fuller discussion of this problem, see Abraham Edel, "Monism and Pluralism," in *The Journal of Philosophy*, Oct. 11, 1934.

poses, in the domain of temporal and causal relations, in the field of organic phenomena, in the realm of the mental, and so forth. To establish a system in any domain is to map the order discovered, to find what "determinism" can be asserted of it, to see what predictability there is for phenomena within that domain.

A liberating approach. The view that explanation is a search for system is thus a liberating approach. It prevents us from reading the world in any *one* model, and from imposing the characteristics of one activity or field upon another. It leaves the way open for the discovery of fresh types of phenomena and fresh types of relations. It is, therefore, peculiarly appropriate to the scientific enterprise of free inquiry.

Philosophy uses the same conception. This approach is equally appropriate to the process of philosophizing which attempts to be at the same time critical and comprehensive. Philosophy does not require a distinctive meaning for explanation. It meets with no difficulties in regarding systematizing as explaining. And if philosophy is sometimes called upon to explain a system itself, it only means that it is being asked to fashion a *wider* system. It is not being asked to produce a meaning beyond meaning or a truth beyond truth.

The remaining parts of this book will clarify and develop the use of the notion of system in philosophy in attempting to get a systematic picture first of the process of scientific inquiry, next of man and his capabilities, and then of men's outlook on the world and human affairs.

Part Two

EMPIRICAL OR SCIENTIFIC METHOD

Chapter 5   SCIENCE AND ITS METHOD

Importance of problems of method today

It is a common remark that the growth of science has changed our world. Not only has it given us devices for controlling our environment and many aspects of our own lives, but it has also prompted alterations in our institutions, values, and ways of thinking. Man's growing reliance upon the methods and findings of science has brought it into sharp conflict with traditional beliefs and vested interests in various fields of life. The story of the early struggles of scientists against dogma, superstition, and inertia is too well known to the reader to require repetition. Nor are such struggles over. In Nazi and fascist theory and practice the world has been facing a systematic and streamlined attack upon the liberal scientific tradition. That its efficient war-machine employed the results of physical science and its continuous propaganda rested upon elaborate psychological study does not belie this view. For theoretical physics was abandoned or perverted, biology made a support for an absurd race-theory and a political encouragement of race hatred, and the social sciences and history rewritten to exalt the leader or the state. And for the general atmosphere of freedom of inquiry upon which scientific progress has rested there was substituted a strict regimentation not merely for the fighting of wars but for the glorification of war.

But attacks upon science have also been found in those countries which are the traditional home of the liberal outlook. Some of these attacks have taken practical forms—for example, there were attempts during the thirties to blame the depression on the productivity of scientific invention and to call for a moratorium on scientific research. More common is the attempt to limit the method of science to the physical world, leaving the domain of social institutions to tradition as against experiment, to feelings of right and wrong as against scientific study of human welfare. The reliance on scientific method, the value we place upon it, and the scope we allow it, constitute a significant part of our world outlook. In some ways it is even a critical part, for it is closely related to our conception of the nature of truth. In this part of our study we shall examine the reliability of scientific method as a tool for understanding our world and directing action in it. We shall first consider briefly the character of empirical or scientific method, and then at greater length probe for any assumptions on which the method rests. Controversies have centered about such assumptions; and to understand them we shall have to examine proposed alternatives to scientific method as a reliable way of attaining truth. We shall also need to examine the conception of truth itself.

Main features of scientific method

Any full characterization of the empirical or scientific method would require a whole treatise in logic. Here only its most general features can be indicated. For the most part they will seem very familiar. This is because in sound practical everyday investigation we really do proceed scientifically, though not, of course, all of us or all the time.

Formulating the problem. When difficulties arise in some practical or theoretical situation, the situation itself takes the form of a problem to be solved. We ask a question and in doing so we are already formulating the problem, though not always precisely. We use terms and ideas with which we are already familiar, and we fix upon one or more points in a situation whose character we already take for granted. Thus if I ask, "Were you at the theater last night?" I assume that there was a performance, that there was an audience and ask simply whether you were a member of it. If I ask, "Did you see him at the theater last night?" my formulation is less precise. I may be assuming that both you and he were there and be asking whether your eyes fastened upon him; or I may may be assuming that you were there and asking whether he was there and seen by you. Sometimes the problem may appear merely as a felt difficulty; when my car stops I may ask simply, "What is wrong?" But even this implicitly formulates the question as one of explaining the cessation of motion in terms of the character of one of the parts of the machine.

The way we formulate a problem is exceedingly important, because it determines the general direction our inquiry will take. Thus, as we have seen in Part One, to ask for a purpose is often to look to an end that is to come, while to ask for a cause directs inquiry back in time. Not all inquiry appears to seek an explanation. Some directs the search towards a date (when?), or a place (where?), or a person to be designated (who?), or simply describes a state of affairs and asks whether it is so. But in the wider sense of "explanation" in which it means setting the event or fact in some system, even these are explanatory. For to give the date of an event is to place it in an ordered system of time; and likewise for the rest. The very formulation of a problem indicates the type of system in which we hope to find an answer.

Getting the hypothesis. When a problem has been formulated and an investigation is required the next step is to get an idea for solving the problem; the more good ideas the better, since the correct solution is then more likely to be among them. This is technically called offering a hypothesis, i.e., a suggestion as to how the question may be answered. That a particular man in a particular situation facing a particular problem gets a particular idea, is, of course, itself an event in nature, and one might ask for its explanation. Logic cannot give this explanation; it is essentially a problem for the psychologist to investigate. To learn how we get ideas we need to know how associations occur in a man's mind, and how different ones occur to different people. Questions of the role of intelligence and of previous background would be important too. The inquiry would thus involve the social scientist and intellectual historian as well as the psychologist. We could well study the whole fascinating field of the rise, growth, acceptance, and sometimes the decline of major hypotheses.

Elaborating the hypothesis. Once hypotheses have been formulated the next task is to develop their implications. Starting with each hypothesis we combine it with other knowledge which we take for granted in that context, and *logically* deduce the consequences. Thus to test the hypothesis "All philosophers are fond of music" we may couple it with the further information "The author of this book is a philosopher." This yields the consequence "The author of this book is fond of music," whose truth we may test in experience. If it is incorrect, our hypothesis must be wrong. The consequences thus tell us what to look for, thereby furnishing material for testing the correctness of the hypothesis.

There seems to be no rule for the selection of the relevant other knowledge with which to combine the hypothesis. This too is a matter of intelligence and background. But there are very definite rules for the discovery of the consequences. These when systematized are the laws of logic. This part of scientific method is very important. For if it is neglected, then even if our experiments turn out happily we shall not be sure that they are at all relevant to the hypothesis we are testing. Thus since "You are enjoying reading this" is not deducible from "the sun is shining," its truth or falsity cannot be used as experimental evidence for or against the statement "the sun is shining." Neither will the correct prediction of a war prove that man is naturally pugnacious, nor correct estimate of fluctuations on the stock market that a man has a lucky star.

Sometimes the hypothesis itself follows logically from knowledge previously established. In that case we are able to prove or deduce the hypothesis so that further investigation of it by developing its implications may be unnecessary.

Testing by observation. The next task is the experimental or observational testing of the hypothesis by seeing whether the predicted consequences do in fact occur. Experiment and observation do not differ essentially; in an experiment we arrange material so as to be able to make observations under controlled conditions. The observations ultimately rest upon selected sense-perceptions; e.g., in testing whether A and B are the same weight, they are put in opposite pans of the balance-scale, and we look to see if the tip of the pointer coincides with a center mark; in testing whether that book is the one you are looking for, you look to see the shape of marks (i.e., the letters) on the title.

Estimating the extent of verification. The final step is to figure out what has been established. This is by no means a simple task. Briefly, our hope is either to reject or confirm the hypothesis we are testing. Now if the observation predicted did not occur, we will have reason to reject the hypothesis, unless we believe something went wrong in the experiment or begin to suspect part of the information which we coupled with the hypothesis in order to get the conclusion. Thus Galileo had the hypothesis that the sun had spots and when one looked through the telescope one would make the observation he predicted. The Aristotelian professors, however, were so unempirically minded that they refused to look through the telescope, convinced that the sun, on their theory made of celestial substance, could have no spots. But they were not unaware that an observation *alone* could not prove or refute the theory, that science does not consist *merely,* as some have since preached, in collecting and arranging observations. The refusal of his colleagues to look through Galileo's telescope could mean that they *granted* his observation, but questioned one of his other assumptions, namely, that the telescope did not distort. For if the hypothesis that the sun has no spots is correct, and if the telescope does not distort, then logically no spots will be observed through it. But spots are observed. Therefore, either the sun has spots or the telescope distorts. The former must be conceded only if the latter is taken to be false. The controversy shifted, therefore, to the reliability of the telescope; they claimed that since it was not made of celestial substance it would distort while Galileo argued that our eyes also were not made of celestial substance and yet showed no spots.

Holding to a dominant hypothesis against some fresh startling observation must not too readily be interpreted as dogmatism. It is to be distinguished carefully from an unreadiness to investigate assumptions or a habit of invoking a saving hypothesis which cannot be tested, e.g., the magician's hypothesis invoked whenever he fails, that some more powerful magician is at work. Such general hypotheses hinder rather than promote scientific advance.

If the observation turns out as predicted, it tends to confirm the hypothesis. It does not prove it, since the same observation might have been predicted on the basis of other hypotheses. An hypothesis therefore becomes established only to the degree that its rivals are rejected, while it is confirmed by correct predictions, preferably in diverse fields of observation. Its status is always at the mercy of a more powerful hypothesis which may come on the scene, make all its predictions and others which it could not make or which it could make only with the aid of subsidiary hypotheses invented to fill the gaps. In such a case the more powerful hypothesis is accepted as logically simpler. Sometimes the field is divided by two contenders and at that time choice between them is impossible. Sometimes both cover the field equally well, so that choice between them is arbitrary. The aim in all this is to achieve as wide a *system* as possible, to provide a general theory logically connecting the various hypotheses that have been confirmed. This is a complicated problem for which scientific method has had to work out explicit techniques. The results, too, can never be absolutely certain, and are at most only *probable*. The meaning of probability and techniques for estimating it are likewise matters of careful logical analysis.[1]

Scientific method and science. The reader will recognize, whether he has previously done scientific work or not, that this is a method commonly used in ordinary life, and in fact in any practical situation. Suppose my car makes all the proper noises, but the engine does not start. It does not then seem to be a serious matter, but the suggestion occurs that the gasoline is not properly ignited. Then either the gasoline is not reaching the carburetor properly or the ignition is not taking place. If it's the gasoline, the tank may be empty. If not, then perhaps the feed-pipe is clogged. I remove it and pump air through it, but nothing emerges except air. I screw it back on and the car still refuses to start. It must therefore be the ignition. I reconnect a wire which I find to be loose and, on trying the starter, am happy to see the car start. In this process, the formulation of the problem, the hypothesis, other assumed information, elaboration by deduction, testing of consequences, rejection of one hypothesis and verification of the other, can all readily be identified.

The account we have been giving might be said to be of empirical method generally. If a distinction is to be made between this and scientific method as such it can only be in the increased precision and elaboration of techniques of the latter. Scientific method is not limited to the acquisition and development of the bodies of knowledge called "sciences," although these are the best illustrations of its operation. A detective in following up a clue, the judge in deciding a case, the historian in reconstructing the events of a certain day, all may employ empirical or scientific method. In the ordinary sense of the term "science," however, their results do not constitute a science. For in addition to the use of scientific method, we commonly think of a science as comprising a system of laws. Scientific knowledge differs from common knowledge in scope, degree of refinement and systematic organi-

---

[1] For a good fuller account see Cohen and Nagel, *An Introduction to Logic and Scientific Method*, Harcourt, Brace, 1934, Part 2.

zation. As a matter of fact, however, the term "science" has become to a great extent honorific, that is, a term of praise, so that students in some fields resent the withholding of the title from their subjects. In the social field, for example, some speak of "social sciences," others of "social studies." Such tea-pot tempests represent in part a struggle for a share in the prestige of science. There is, however, a sound basis for the wider usage. It does not restrict the kind of results to be aimed at and allows greater flexibility. New fields of inquiry can then feel free to develop their own forms without fear of ostracism from the fraternity of science.

Philosophic issues in the theory of science

Although empirical method is the core of all reflective treatment of our environment, alternative methods of procedure have received philosophical formulation. They are not intended to replace it entirely; it is usually granted priority in ordinary life, or for practical purposes. But they are offered to supplement it and to take precedence in cases of conflict. These alternative methods, as well as the various conceptions of truth involved, may best be studied by examining a number of special problems raised by the various steps of the scientific process just discussed.

Are first principles needed? Scientific method, as we have described it, operates in a situation already formulated as a problem. In this formulation there are assumptions, and again in deducing the consequences of a hypothesis, the hypothesis is combined with other knowledge. Where do these assumptions and this other knowledge come from? If they also rest upon evidence secured by scientific method, and the evidence similarly on other evidence, and that again on other evidence, and so on, do we never come to an end? Aristotle long ago argued that if we did not reach absolute starting-points, first principles or self-evident axioms which require no scientific proof,[2] we would be in a dilemma. If the search for evidence is to go on endlessly we can never be sure of our evidence and thus can never be sure of the truth of what we are seeking to establish. Or if the search for evidence is not to go on endlessly, but yet does not terminate in principles established in some non-scientific fashion, it can only be circular, and our whole procedure illogical. This claim that scientific method, if it is to prove reliable, involves some appeal to a method other and firmer than itself, requires careful consideration.

The role of experience and sensation. Again, the method as described above assumes that the consequences deduced from hypotheses point to ex-

[2] By scientific proof Aristotle meant logical demonstration, but the argument has the same weight for scientific method as we have described it.

periments or observations, in short that they end up with perceptible differences. This has seemed to many to be an undue stress on sensation. Why should sense-perception be preferred to intellectual insight, or, for that matter, to feeling, as an avenue to knowledge? All of these are human activities. When I think, do I not also grasp truth? In my finer feelings, do I not also sense something of what the world around me is like? In any case, what right has science to assume that sense-perception is trustworthy?

Truth and reality. A further question is raised by the last step in the method—figuring out what has been established. For this is to estimate what truth has been discovered and how much of reality has been disclosed. What conception of truth is entailed in the method of science? What assumptions, if any, does it make about nature, about truth, about reality? Or are these questions beyond its scope, and is there a philosophic method superior to the scientific?

The analysis of these questions in the chapters that follow will give us a systematic picture of scientific inquiry in respect to the interrelation of its various elements and its relations to the world in which it is employed.

Chapter 6   THE DEMAND FOR ABSOLUTE KNOWLEDGE

The view that some knowledge is direct, immediate, and absolute, with no need for the laborious enterprise of scientific inquiry with its tentative results, has been a persistent one since Aristotle's day. It has assumed various leading forms. One is the claim that there is a type of insight which is *intuitive* and brings an immediate inner conviction of its certainty. A second is the assertion that *authority* is the best guide for the solution of problems and the establishment of beliefs. A third appears in the analysis of science itself. This view holds that there are innate or intuitive *first principles* upon which each science rests. A study of these three claims will make clear the issues involved in the conflict of scientific method and its traditional rivals.

Intuition

CLAIMS FOR INTUITION

Many people have believed in the existence of intuitive insight, that is, a kind of direct grasping of the truth. When a man has such insight it is accompanied by a certainty of its correctness. Sometimes he is unable to give reasons for an intuitive assertion, but if he does the reasons are secondary. He feels that he has grasped the truth, and often he trusts his vision more than the evidence he may thereafter muster to justify it to others. A doctor's diagnosis on slender symptoms, a first impression startlingly confirmed, a sense of foreboding actually followed by disaster, a flash of inspiration unraveling a complex problem, a conviction of right, "the still small voice" of conscience, a vision of destiny, even ordinary hunches—all these add their weight to the belief in intuition.

No doubt many people act on their "intuitions." Practical problems are frequently so complex that people cut the Gordian knot by acting on impulse. This is not necessarily random. The impulse represents the accumulation of habit and experience and its very force and feeling of rightness probably rest on the weight of history behind it. The same is true of the specialist's hunch, grounded in initial skill and intelligent practice.

Intuition is a much quicker procedure than scientific investigation. The latter is tedious, never complete, and it yields only probable results. Intuition, on the other hand, has been valued as bringing not *belief* but certainty. This formulation takes the emphasis away from the objective situation to be investigated and throws it on the attitude of the person who is seeking knowledge. A correct attitude becomes the guarantee that its object is truth.

There have been numerous philosophic elaborations of these views. Sometimes an insight theory is rationalistic, claiming direct knowledge of first principles from which the sciences may make deductions. There is said to be an "adequation" of the intellect and its object like a light suddenly focussing on an object so that it becomes luminous and clear. Sometimes it is more concerned with the emotional qualities of the experience. In the rare moments when a man is engaged in a task concentrating and liberating all his energies (e.g., artistic creation, philosophic speculation, or falling in love) he may be said to become one with the object of his interest and lose all sense of self in his absorption. This is the experience which the mystics have made much of, as the transcendence of the self's finiteness and its merging with the boundless or infinite self. In the past this attitude has been largely a religious one, keeping on speaking terms with ordinary empirical procedures, to which it conceded the domain of appearances, while it claimed reference to an underlying reality.[1] Its recommendations were usually some form of virtuous life, often ascetic practices, until the body should be disciplined and rid of worldly desires.

ESTIMATE OF INTUITION

When the intuitionist endeavors to apply his method seriously in the domain of the sciences his scope is severely limited. Many of the first principles which have been stated as intuitively certain have been discarded in the advance of the sciences; equally possible alternatives have been stated for others. "Nature makes no leaps" has suffered as much as "Nature does nothing in vain." The postulates of non-Euclidean geometry hold as dignified a position as those of Euclidean geometry. Theological assumptions are no more evident to theologians than their contradictories are to atheists. Moral rules are notoriously open to challenge by those of other peoples and other cultures. Staid legal maxims like "No one can convey a greater estate than he has" become suspect where possession is as good as title in conveying ownership to a third party. The character of all such axioms, and to what extent they are presuppositions of special sciences, we shall examine below. Even

---

[1] Cf., the argument of Plotinus that Reality is One and therefore the understanding, involving always the *duality* of the understander and the understood, could never attain a knowledge of the One. See below, p. 141.

without that analysis of the nature of axioms it is clear from their historical fate that intuition is not a reliable way of establishing unquestionable first principles for the sciences.

Intuitionism as irrationalism. Sometimes to say that a belief is intuitive merely indicates that one is unwilling to put it to the test. This is clear in much of the widespread contemporary movement against reason and empirical method. This movement is a social and economic phenomenon. It is rooted in a rejection of the social changes demanded by an empirical treatment of social institutions and cultural habits. In this reaction, best seen in Nazi ideology, the exaltation of intuitionism has been exemplified in such phrases as "thinking with the blood." It is carried into domains hitherto conceded to empirical method. Thus in biology it claims that individuals of different races can be recognized, irrespective of physical traits, by a kind of rational insight.[2] Even different types of mathematics are said to bear obvious racial marks. In America the use of intuition as a barrier to investigation may be illustrated from those who insist on the segregation of Negro blood donated for transfusion; they *feel* that it is a different kind of blood in spite of the unanimous scientific judgment that it is not.

Social role of intuitionism. Although contrary intuitions can readily be found on almost any subject there is no intuitive way of deciding between them. Reliance on intuition as ultimate or absolute leads, therefore, to arbitrariness and dogmatism. It is interesting to note that intuitionism in its various forms has sometimes been attacked as the intellectual mainstay of absolute or arbitrary power. Jeremy Bentham, seeking a sweeping reform in English morals and law, labeled the modes of defense of the entrenched system as the *arbitrary* principle.[3] John Stuart Mill describes the reading of Bentham's book as a turning point in his mental history. "What thus impressed me was the chapter in which Bentham passed judgment on the common modes of reasoning in morals and legislation, deduced from phrases like 'law of nature,' 'right reason,' 'the moral sense,' 'natural rectitude' and the like, and characterized them as dogmatism in disguise, imposing its sentiments upon others under cover of sounding expressions which convey no reason for the sentiment, but set up the sentiment as its own reason."[4]

Intuitionism is sometimes, on the other hand, seen as a theory covering a revolt from established authority. Thus the view that personal conscience as enlightened by the indwelling presence of the Holy Spirit is a valid criterion for personal conduct met with wide religious opposition. It is inconsistent

---

[2] E.g., S. Houston Chamberlain, one of the predecessors of the movement, argued for a "rational" anthropology; he found Dante's face characteristically Teutonic and insisted that Paul and Jesus could only have been Aryans, not Jews.

[3] *The Theory of Legislation*, ed. by C. K. Ogden, Harcourt, Brace, 1931, pp. 6-10.

[4] *Autobiography*, Chapter 3.

with Catholic doctrine and was also attacked as anarchic and immoral by Luther, Calvin, English bishops, and Scotch presbyters.[5]

Causal analysis of intuitive state. Since the test for intuition lies in the state of mind, it becomes relevant to inquire into the causes of such states of mind or dispositions. Such an inquiry may be carried out in terms of physiology, psychology, or the social sciences. Physiologists have shown that states similar to those of the mystic may be engendered by special drugs, or may be concomitant with special types of illness. In psychological terms beliefs to which a man holds may often be seen as attempts to justify his conduct to himself; thus the tenacity with which a belief is held may indicate merely an unreadiness to abandon a specific line of conduct. In terms of social analysis, the tenacity of beliefs may likewise be seen as a function of the role they play in supporting and justifying systems of conduct, so that there is no direct relation between tenacity and truth. All these causal analyses of intuitive states do not, of course, necessarily imply the falsity of the views asserted in such states, but they do indicate that independent verification is required.

Role of insight. The psychological features upon which the intuitionist's claim is based are, of course, very marked phenomena. Premonitions and divinations do occur, most frequently among men of wide experience in the field in question; and the verification may seem secondary because it comes later and simply fulfills the expectation. (When it fails to verify we all too easily forget it!) Intuiting the pattern of a succession of events, whether it be diagnosing an illness, solving a mystery, getting a formula, or making some invention, is an impressive happening, both to the agent and to the observer. Even when we are given an hypothesis, insight is required to suggest what deductions to make from it. There is no gainsaying either the pervasiveness or the indispensability of insight, nor is its spontaneous nature to be rejected. The important point to notice is this very pervasiveness, that the occurrence of *all* hypotheses, true and false alike, of *all* implications, whether they really follow or not, the making of *all* diagnoses right or wrong, is a matter of intuition and insight. The character and basis in intelligence and experience of this psychological phenomenon has yet to be thoroughly explored. In more common terms it is the use of the *imagination,* a kind of playing with the materials of sensation and feeling and with ideas, and a construction of fresh patterns not bound by previously formulated rules. When imagination becomes trained and harnessed we have understanding; when it is permitted to develop of itself we have fantasy,

---

[5] John Dewey, "The Motivation of Hobbes' Political Philosophy," *Columbia Studies in the History of Ideas,* Vol. I, Columbia Press, 1918, p. 96. For the role of intuitionism in Cromwell's thought, see A. D. Lindsay, *The Essentials of Democracy,* Univ. of Pennsylvania Press, 1929, Lecture 1.

whether its material be ideas or sensations.[6] But if our concern is truth, its insights are *proposals for testing,* not revelations.

We may therefore conclude that an account of the nature of truth as the object of intuition, finding its test in the act of intuition, is fundamentally an exaggeration of one phase of scientific method, that which we termed above "getting the hypothesis."

Authority

A second form taken by the demand for absolute knowledge is the appeal to authority. The concept of authority is a broad one. In its minimum meaning a belief is said to be held on authority when it is accepted unquestioningly because it is asserted by some source, whether person or book or tradition or organization. It involves an attitude of trust on the part of the one who accepts the belief; and no reasons or evidence are required of the authority.

There are two quite distinct types of authority. They may be distinguished as relative or derivative, and absolute or dogmatic. The difference lies in the source of knowledge in the authority.

DERIVATIVE TYPE

Role in science. In the relative or derivative type, knowledge is acquired through experience and the use of scientific method. In this sense authority plays a role in all scientific inquiry, for in every investigation there are some statements taken for granted. A single scientist does not deal with all fields. He builds upon the results of other scientists. He also trusts that the specifications according to which his instruments were to be constructed have been faithfully followed. He may even leave some of his observations to an assistant or collaborator.[7]

Such scientific acceptance of another's work rests, however, on the trust that this work was itself performed by using scientific method. Hence there is nothing intrinsically *private* about the authority's knowledge. Every step on which there was reliance is *public*—the instruments can be checked, the assumptions outside of the field of work can be tested again. In fact, a scientist may himself go into another field to examine why its implications are

---

[6] This contrast is beautifully elaborated in Santayana's essay on "Understanding, Imagination and Mysticism," in his *Interpretations of Poetry and Religion,* Scribner's, 1900.

[7] There have been cases in which over-zealous assistants have distorted results in order to prove a thesis.

not consonant with his own results. More than ever, science today demands mutual good faith, co-operative division of labor, and completely public avenues for going over its results.

Cautions in reliance on authority. In practical matters reliance on expert authority is, of course, unavoidable—even desirable, since no one has time to master all fields. But its use must be strictly qualified in a number of ways.

For one thing, the degree of reliance should vary according to the degree of general agreement or established empirical knowledge in the field in question. Thus authorities in physics or medicine should win readier acceptance than authorities in the disputed domains of politics. The conflict of authorities in a field will itself be indicative of the unsettled state of that field. In case of conflict, however, the assumptions on which authority rests ought themselves to be considered. For example, two doctors who disagree settle the problem by discussing not the respective merits of the universities from which they graduated, but the evidence for their respective diagnoses—perhaps eventually by an exploratory operation.

Great care should also be taken against relying on a person as an authority in one field because he is an acknowledged authority in another field. The provincialism of many scientists has been accentuated by the specialization that has characterized our intellectual life. When some of them transfer their thoughts to other domains like religion, philosophy, and politics, they frequently relax the rigorous logical standards appropriate to their scientific labors. Business advertising in our society adds to the confusion of authorities, by turning actresses into authorities on tooth-paste.

ABSOLUTE OR DOGMATIC TYPE

The second type of authority—absolute or dogmatic—is marked by an insistence on the *intrinsically private* and *inaccessible* character of the authority's source of knowledge. Thus the authority's pronouncements, if they are accepted, must be accepted without investigation or demand for any evidence to support them. In this sense of authority, scientific method is in spirit anti-authoritarian. As a result science has not had smooth relations with religions that treat certain persons or even books (e.g., the Bible, the Koran, etc.) as absolutely authoritative, or with dictators who renounce science and claim for themselves some higher direct personal knowledge.

Its metaphysical bases. Absolute authority usually rests on some theory of how the world works. The person designated as the authority is usually credited with some special type of inner illumination, or certain of his judgments (as in the Pope's judgments on faith and morals) are held to be directly controlled by a divine power. In some idealist philosophies the "great man" in any age has a sense of destiny, if he is fully conscious of his role. He feels himself freed by the magnitude of his task from adherence to ordinary rules of conduct and holds himself responsible only to himself and his insight. The Nazi theory of absolute leadership, with all authority emanating from the leader and everyone responsible ultimately to him, has systematized this approach for political purposes.

Attitudes encouraged by it. The attitudes that absolute authority encourages are, of course, dogmatic in character. In religious absolutism there has been the view that heresy is the most fatal of vices, since it corrupts a man at his very source. Political absolutism may be illustrated by a statement of Goebbels, Minister of Propaganda in Nazi Germany, uttered in the spring of 1934: "Since we National Socialists are convinced that we are right, we cannot tolerate anybody who contends that he is right. For if he, too, is right, he must be a National Socialist, or if he is not a National Socialist, then he is simply not right." [8]

From the point of view of those who follow authority, the central attitude is a readiness to believe without question and in practical affairs a readiness to obey without question. Sometimes this demands complete self-surrender. Ignatius Loyola, the founder of the Jesuit order, writes recommending obedience as the backbone of his order:

"I ought on entering religion, and thereafter, to place myself entirely in the hands of God, and of him who takes His place by His authority. I ought to desire that my Superior should oblige me to give up my own judgment, and conquer my own mind. I ought to set up no difference between one Superior and another, . . . but recognize them all as equal before God, whose place they fill. For if I distinguish persons, I weaken the spirit of obedience. In the hands of my Superior, I must be a soft wax, a thing, from which he is to require whatever pleases him, be it to write or receive letters, to speak or not to speak to such a person, or the like; and I must put all my fervor in executing zealously and exactly what I am ordered. I must consider myself as a corpse which has neither intelligence nor will; be like a mass of matter which without resistance lets itself be placed wherever it may please any one; like a stick in the hand of an old man, who uses it according to his needs and places it where it suits him. So must I be under the hands of the Order, to serve it in the way it judges most useful." [9]

Authoritarianism in modern life. Although the attitudes here illustrated are extreme ones, they enable us to single out authoritarian elements in a complex outlook. Authoritarianism has receded somewhat in our intellectual

[8] Quoted in F. M. Marx, *Government in the Third Reich*, rev. ed., McGraw-Hill, 1937, p. 113.
[9] As rendered by William James, in his *Varieties of Religious Experience*, Longmans, Green, 1925, pp. 313-14. Quoted by permission of Mr. Henry James.

life, partly through the clash of authorities, and more importantly because of the advance of science. But it has maintained its hold to a very great extent in our social and moral life. It is encouraged by many institutional forms even in democratic countries. Thus the organization of our business life has been largely autocratic, and our educational institutions and moral training have followed a similar authoritative pattern. In fascist countries authoritarianism was encouraged and the leadership principle elevated into the basic principle of all political and social relations. The analysis of the social utilization of the method of authority will be considered in some detail later in connection with the analysis of freedom and democracy.[10]

First principles

Our account of empirical method showed that in deducing the consequences of any hypothesis there are always some assumed propositions which are not put to the test in that context. These may themselves be made the subject-matter of investigation, but this will in turn involve assuming other propositions. As we noted above, this raises a number of serious questions. Is this to go on forever, or does one ultimately come to some propositions accepted without evidence and without testing? If so, on what basis are these accepted?

SELF-EVIDENT PROPOSITIONS

The Aristotelians and later the so-called Rationalists denied the possibility of the "infinite regress" or endless chain of premises. If we are to have knowledge they felt this process must terminate in self-evident premises of which we have intuitive knowledge. The ideal science stated its self-evident principles or axioms and then demonstrated deductively the properties of the domain in question. Thus men have sought self-evident premises in theology, psychology, ethics, natural science, mathematics, and law.

Strictly speaking, a self-evident proposition or statement is one whose truth or falsity is immediately apparent once its terms are understood. This is not guaranteed to everyone, but to the awakened intelligence. Experience is required to awaken the mind, or to suggest the meanings, but once the meaning of the statement is grasped there is no need of experience to *prove* or *establish* the truth or falsity.

---

[10] For J. S. Mill's classic defense of freedom of thought and speech against authoritarian claims, see below, p. 249. For the contrast of authoritarian and democratic principles, see Chapter 20.

Illustration from moral theory. The argument for the existence of such statements may be illustrated from the field of morals. It goes as follows:

To understand a term is to break up the idea it denotes into its parts. Since this cannot go on forever the analysis will eventually reach simple unanalyzable ideas. *Right* and *wrong* are of this kind. They are suggested in experience, it is true, but after a while most people come to apprehend their meaning directly. You can thus engage in moral discourse with people and help one another clarify insights as to what acts are right and what wrong. You will come to see, by analyzing and apprehending the meaning of murder, killing, and cruelty, that they are wrong, and of preserving life, truth-telling, and helping others that they are right. This does not mean that in some actual situation you may not recommend killing to avoid a greater wrong. That will always be a difficult question to decide because the application of moral truths depends upon special circumstances. But the ideas themselves are clear and distinct, and the rightness or wrongness of the acts is indubitable. If anyone disagrees and if you have no ground for suspecting his sincerity, you must look first for a misunderstanding. He may, for example, have a strange way of expressing piety or affection, as when, according to Herodotus, among some Scythian tribes children killed their parents in the prime of life in order that they might not, in the hereafter, have an eternally weak and decrepit form. The parents, we are told, appreciated this favor immensely. If, however, you eliminate differences of belief and information, and still the disagreement persists, you can only call the other man morally blind or perverse. You may, of course, then look for the causes of his blindness—and attempt to learn by what neglect or wicked practices he lost or failed to acquire the vision of rightness.

The substantial agreement upon the content of the values here involved should not blind us to the method offered to establish them. The appropriateness of analyzing fundamental moral concepts is denied and the need for evidence rejected. An empirical approach would insist on both these elements. Thus in the case of "Murder is wrong" it would press for a definition of "murder" as distinguished from "killing," and point to the fact that killing in war is not regarded as murder. The analysis would probably reveal that by murder is meant "the unlawful killing of a human being with malice aforethought." And if the notion of the "unlawful" be analyzed in moral terms (rather than as simply an arbitrary state prohibition), it turns out to entail the idea of wrong conduct. The self-evident character of the rule that murder is wrong thus comes from the tautology that a certain type of wrong killing is wrong.

On the other hand, such an analysis does not hold of the rule that killing is wrong. Here the situation is more complicated. For although some types of killing are regarded as right (in war defending one's country), even in such cases there is agreement that the result would be better accomplished, if it could be, without killing. An empirical approach would therefore insist on an analysis of "right"—for example, as "conducive to the general good"— and a further analysis of "good," and would claim that when the analysis is completed the wrongness of killing could be established on the basis of human experience as evidence.[11]

Mathematical axioms. Although the resort to first principles has been frequent in morals, its historical stronghold has been in mathematics, where the axioms or postulates in any system are assumed without proof as the starting-points for deduction. Even nowadays philosophers pressed to maintain a proposition in morals or politics which they take to be self-evidently true will appeal to the fact that axioms in mathematics have this status, and so why should not their own assertion? Accordingly we can best analyze the problems involved by rushing boldly into the citadel and asking "Are axioms in mathematics self-evidently true?"

Take as an illustration the assertion "Things equal to the same thing are equal to one another." No one in fact seriously doubts that this will be found on examination to be true in every case. The assurance with which it is held as a truth applicable to our world seems to render almost trifling the argument that we know it only because we have found it to hold in countless cases. There is indeed an obvious difference between the axiom and the assertion that the sun rises every day. We can conceive of the latter not happening, whereas we cannot even conceive of the former not being so. If we find two things equal to the same thing and not equal to one another we begin instead to suspect that they are in fact not really equal to the same thing.

However, there is something unfair in this procedure. If things said to be equal to the same thing are found equal to one another it is taken as showing the truth of the axiom. If they are not found equal to one another it is taken not as disproving the axiom but merely as an error in the original statement of their equality. Perhaps it is best to recognize that confirming instances are also unnecessary. The statement is not an empirical statement at all, but rather an *a priori* statement (in the sense of logically, though not historically, prior to experience).

The nature of this axiom will become clearer if we compare it to two statements that are definitely empirical: (a) weights that balance the same weight balance one another, (b) sounds that sound the same as the same sound, sound the same as one another. The first is tested by seeing the position at which the pointer comes to rest when weights are placed in opposite

---

[11] For a discussion of the empirical treatment of ethical terms, see below, p. 425 ff. For an extended illustration of such analysis of ethical rules, see the discussion of truthfulness, p. 434 ff.

pans of a scale that is in good condition (judged by independent standards). In the second the test of sounding the same is that the two sounds are indistinguishable to the same human ear when struck together. Since it is the same ear, the problem of greater acuity is irrelevant. Of these two empirical statements, the first turns out to be true when tested. The second, however, is false since there will be some sounds M and N which are indistinguishable from P and yet distinguishable from one another. The physical reason is obvious—the interval between P and each of M and N is too small for our ears, whereas that between M and N is great enough.

The general axiom "Things equal to the same thing are equal to one another" guarantees the truth of neither of our two empirical statements. Each requires to be tested empirically. Because the first is true, we may appropriately call weights equal or unequal. Because the second is false such language is inappropriate for sounds. The general axiom thus functions in effect as a definition or convention concerning the application of terms. To call it true is equivalent merely to saying that that is how we have agreed to use the term equality.[12]

Arithmetical statements. Similar controversies have occurred in the history of philosophy concerning assertions about number. Thus $2 + 2 = 4$ has been taken to be a necessary self-evident truth which no experience could possibly refute and which, moreover, tells us something about the structure of our world. In the Platonic language discussed above [13] it states the relation between forms or essences of twoness and fourness. Modern logicians readily grant that it is not an empirical statement. Nor does its acceptance guarantee the truth of such a true empirical statement as "Two plates placed on top of two plates yield four plates," and certainly not of such a false empirical statement as "Two drops of mercury placed on top of two drops of mercury yield four drops of mercury." But instead of regarding it as a self-evident truth about the structure of our world they take it to be an analytical (i.e., tautological) statement.[14] For $2 + 2$ turns out on analysis to be asserting the same thing as 4. The analytic character of the assertion that $2 + 2 = 4$ may be roughly indicated in mathematical language as follows: Given the definitions of 2, 3 and 4 as respectively $1 + 1$, $2 + 1$, $3 + 1$, and a rule concerning parentheses to the effect that $a + (b + c) = (a + b) + c = a + b + c$, then $2 + 2 = 4$ is equivalent by substitution to:

[12] More precisely stated, the general principle in question would be a theorem in a system based on a fundamental postulate which defined equality. For such a system, see Alfred Tarski, *Introduction to Logic*, Oxford Press, 1941, pp. 55-58. Tarski defines equality or identity by means of the formula: $x = y$, if and only if, x has every property which y has, and y has every property which x has. The law we are considering is proved as a theorem: If $x = y$ and $z = y$, then $x = z$.
[13] Pp. 12-15.
[14] For a definition of "analytical" see above, p. 45.

$(1+1)+(1+1) = 3+1$, which is equivalent to

$1+1+1+1 = (2+1)+1$, which is equivalent to

$1+1+1+1 = (1+1)+1+1$, which is equivalent to

$1+1+1+1 = 1+1+1+1$.

Geometric postulates. In addition to analyzing alleged self-evident truths as conventional *definitions* and *analytic statements,* contemporary logical theory finds some of them to be uninterpreted statements or *propositional functions*. Such assertions contain variables and are neither true nor false in themselves. Problems of truth or falsity arise when definite values are substituted for the variables.[15]

This analysis is used especially of postulates of geometry. For example, the Euclidean postulate that a straight line can be drawn from any point to any point, seems naively to be self-evidently true of our world, and was long so regarded. It seems to picture a necessary character or structural property of the space of our world, and its truth to be grasped directly and intuitively. The term "straight line" is presumed to be understood directly, or perhaps from the familiar definition as "the shortest distance between two points." Many properties of straight lines are established thereafter in Euclidean geometry, by deduction from the postulates and axioms.

Difficulties arise in this view, however, if we take seriously the idea of "shortest distance between two points." In any actual situation the shortest distance between two points is a function of the character of the domain in which the points occur and the task at hand. Thus if the problem is one of getting somewhere and there is a mountain in the way, the shortest distance may be around the base. If the problem is one of measuring, then the shortest distance cannot be determined before designating the instruments to be used and performing the measurements. Of course, we can speculate in advance about the possible character the domain may turn out to have, hence what the shortest distance between two points will be like. If it is anything like what Euclid talks about in his geometry then it will of course have the properties he demonstrates of *any straight line that satisfies what he postulates about straight lines*. However, if the domain turns out to be like the surface of a sphere, the shortest distance between two points will be the arc of a great circle in which both points fall. Many things Euclid says about straight lines will not hold in this domain.

The modern conclusion of such an analysis is that the term "straight line" in the postulate that a straight line can be drawn from any point to any point is best treated as an uninterpreted term, which has a different value according to the mode of measurement proposed for the shortest distance be-

---

[15] See above, p. 56, where the assertion "*x* is a man" was offered as an example.

tween two points.[16] And in fact, a logical rewriting of Euclid as a system of pure mathematics replaces such terms by abstract logical symbols. Thus the character of the postulate as a propositional function, itself neither true nor false, emerges clearly. If, however, the term "straight line" is kept, then the postulate can only be regarded as a *partial definition* of the term, telling us one of the conditions assigned by Euclid which anything must satisfy in order to earn the designation "straight line." In this case, if nothing in existence turned out to satisfy his postulate, we should have to conclude that there are no such straight lines in our world. The decision would be empirical, since existence cannot be determined by convention.

This account may be generalized to cover most mathematical systems. They consist of definitions and postulates whose logical consequences are elaborated as theorems. Both the basic assertions and the theorems are usually propositional functions and so no question of their truth can really arise. If, however, interpretations are given to the terms in the basic assertions and the theorems, indicating some experimental or observational procedures, the general hypotheses (i.e., the axioms and postulates interpreted) may be tested empirically. Thus systems of pure mathematics are for the most part uninterpreted systems or systems of propositional functions; systems of applied mathematics are propositions about existence, together with their consequences.

STATUS OF LOGICAL PRINCIPLES

The examples we have taken of alleged self-evident first principles have, up to this point, come largely from mathematics. It is important to consider how this analysis would apply in the theory of logic. For logic, as a discipline treating of rules of necessary inference, constitutes an important part of empirical or scientific method. We have seen its role in deducing the consequences of hypotheses and deciding what has been established by observations, and its place in the ideal of system at which the advanced sciences aim. What assumptions about the world does scientific method make in employing logic? Does it assume that our world is a logical world and has a logical structure? Or what else is the ultimate status of logical principles?

A number of contrasting theories have developed concerning this difficult and complex question of the status of logic. They fall regularly into two groups, one taking logical rules to be descriptions of general features of the world, the other taking them to be analyses of our procedure in dealing with the world.

[16] For further discussion of this problem, see below, p. 121 ff.

THE DEMAND FOR ABSOLUTE KNOWLEDGE

Traditional laws of logic. In traditional logic there were three important principles: *identity* (A is A), *contradiction* (A cannot be both B and not B at the same time in the same respect), *excluded middle* (A is either B or not B). Since modern logicians have reformulated logical rules as a system, these principles, once considered ultimate, may sometimes appear as theorems deduced from other postulates.[17] They may, however, be kept in mind as illustrations for what follows.

Are logical rules descriptive? If logical rules are descriptive, they must be hypotheses of tremendous scope, finding verification in any and every human experience. The objection usually offered against this view is to exhibit a circle in its claims. Empirical hypotheses should be able to be tested. Such testing, as we have seen, consists of making deductions from the hypothesis terminating in predictions about experience. But if we do this in the case of logical rules, would we not be assuming these very rules in making *logical* deductions, and thus using the point to be established as something taken for granted? Furthermore, an empirical hypothesis should indicate a type of observation which, if it actually were found, would act as evidence against the hypothesis. Can we formulate such an experiment that would really test a logical rule? Accordingly it has often been held that if logical rules are to be taken as descriptive of general features of the world they must simply be discovered in some intuitive fashion. Aristotle held such a theory of logical principles.[18] He further tried to show that anyone who denied their truth would be reduced to silence, since he would otherwise constantly be contradicting himself, and even if he kept silent his actions would show that he regarded things as having a determinate character, since he behaved towards them in specific ways. This form of the view is still very prevalent, and many philosophers speak, as a consequence, of the *logical structure of nature*.

Are logical rules laws of thought, not of things? The view that logical rules characterize our methods rather than existence also has several forms. One formulation has been "Logical principles are laws of thought, not of things." This offered many difficulties. If logical rules are laws of our thinking, then they are part of the subject matter of psychology, and are descriptive in character. But in fact people do at times think illogically. These principles would then have to be treated as *normative*, i.e., as furnishing *rules* of *correct* thinking. This raises such questions as "Are they forms of thought to which we are bound, regardless of whether they accurately reveal the structure of things?" or "Can we change them?" or "How can we keep on thinking them so persistently if they are not true?" and so forth.

---

[17] See, for example, Lewis and Langford, *Symbolic Logic*, Century, 1932, or Russell and Whitehead, *Principia Mathematica*, 2nd ed., Cambridge Press, 1925-27.

[18] *Metaphysics*, Book IV.

Are logical rules instrumental or conventional? Now recently a clearer form of this view has been expounded. By some of the pragmatists (especially Dewey) logical rules have been considered pervasive instruments of very wide applicability, developed by man for reflection and intelligent action. Some of the logical positivists (especially Carnap) consider logical rules to be rules of language, that is, conventional rules according to which sentences may be formed and translated into other sentences.

In both of these formulations the question of the "truth" of logical rules becomes irrelevant. They have an historical explanation, but are not propositions about existence. They belong either to languages that have gradually developed (English, Sanskrit, etc.) or to special languages devised for a special field (systems of mathematics, as applied in physics) or they may characterize all languages. They can be estimated for their convenience, for their utility, and for the resulting power of organizing our experience.

Central issues. The chief objection urged by the descriptive theory against the instrumentalist view is that it leaves unexplained the success of logic as an instrument in scientific work. Why should its rules be so useful if they do not bear some type of relation to the structure or organization of the world of which the propositions of science are true?

The controversy between opposing views is being considerably altered by the developments of modern formal logic. It is quite possible that, as distinctions are made in the meaning and types of logic, it will be entirely resolved by recognizing a sound core in each of the opposing views. The parallel controversy concerning the nature of mathematics—whether its propositions are analytic or empirical—was resolved, as we have seen, by distinguishing between pure and applied mathematics, the former analytic, the latter empirical.

An analogous process is taking place in logic. Logical forms have been elaborated in highly abstract calculi, rather than in the language of things used in the traditional laws. Thus instead of the rule "A cannot be both B and not B at the same time in the same respect" we get a set of symbols which, interpreted for statements, yields the result that "a statement cannot be both true and false." Now this is clearly a definition of "statement" and can therefore be treated as conventional. Similarly, the law of the excluded middle becomes "A statement is either true or false." We can, for that matter, construct a system in which the language of truth and falsity is replaced by, let us say, three terms—"true," "false," "undetermined"—or even by five terms—"highly probable," "fairly probable," "undetermined," "fairly improbable," "highly improbable." The rules of such systems will differ considerably from those of the two-valued truth system. Some philosophers have held that some among such systems may prove more serviceable for scientific purposes than the traditional logic. Clearly the various types of systems as thus elaborated may best be viewed as conventional in character and constituting possible instruments for organizing bodies of knowledge.

On the other hand, it appears equally possible to press the inquiry concerning the kinds of existence to which a body of knowledge thus organized may *successfully* apply. Instead of formalizing the traditional laws, one might seek to translate them into definite assertions about the world. Thus the law of identity (A is A) would be replaced with the *material* proposition that there are constancies in the world; or the law of contradiction with the proposition that there are distinct properties among things in the world. The status of such propositions would be similar to that of principles like the Uniformity of Nature discussed above,[19] and in comparable fashion they would require more refined formulation. They would maintain an empirical reference, even though their generality made verification very indirect, that is, through the success of science in establishing certain types of results.[20]

In the light of the two quite different inquiries just distinguished the problem of the status of logical rules demands no single answer. There is no objection in traditional or popular usage to embracing both inquiries within the field of logic broadly conceived. Both may be given free scope, one to provide increasingly refined forms, the other to sketch leading ideas, based upon the history and results of the sciences.

GENERAL REINTERPRETATION OF FIRST PRINCIPLES

The general philosophical shift involved in the reinterpretation of first principles is thus clear in all fields. Instead of thinking of them as ultimate absolute truths revealing an unchanging structure of our world and unchanging bases of the physical universe and social life, a careful distinction is made among them in terms of their mode of functioning. Some turn out to be matter-of-fact assumptions; these may themselves be tested and in fact are tested in part by the consequences which they aid in producing. Others turn out to be analytic statements, definitions, propositional func-

[19] P. 48 ff.
[20] See below, p. 131 ff. For example, the Law of the Excluded Middle, which has sometimes been questioned from this material point of view, would in effect be asserting that things in the world are such as to admit of an ideal type of classification such that no "twilight zones" would be found containing specimens to be classified or falling equally well in opposing classes. This is a proposition about the patterns of similarities and differences of things in the world; its verification, because it is so broad, can only come from the general character of the results of science as it progresses. By and large, in many fields the case against this proposition is a strong one. It must be repeated, however, that it concerns the material proposition, and does not affect the use within certain domains of a system of logic in which a statement is assigned only one or the other of the two values of truth and falsity.

tions. These are estimated as forms and instruments for their utility in organizing the scientific enterprise.

In both respects the rejection of the demand for absolute knowledge, so far from weakening the basis of science, renders it much stronger. For the view that our knowledge of matters-of-fact is probable, not absolute, does not mean that the method of science yields an inferior brand of knowledge. On the contrary, progress in knowledge becomes increasingly possible, and the experimental attitude is carried not merely into matters of detail but into every phase of the search for knowledge. The growing body of factual information becomes wider, more stable and more reliable, and modes of organizing it become increasingly more refined. Even in the mathematical side of scientific work, the denial of absolute first principles has meant a liberating development of alternative systems, and the role of theory in science has been enhanced, not crushed, as a result. While the stress on first principles may have seemed to glorify the role of abstract thought in assigning to it the immediate and absolute revelation of the world in which we live, the rejection of this view does not mean the degradation of thought. It is not robbed of a role but assigned a more dynamic one.

Chapter 7 TESTING BY EXPERIENCE

The meaning of testing by experience

The motto inscribed on the banner of modern science has been "Test by experience." This was the salient point in the warfare of scientific method with systems resting on self-evident first principles, and with the whole intuitive approach. It is the point stressed in popular controversy. And the role of experience is indeed pivotal in the scientific process. It provides the basis on which, as we have seen, hypotheses are confirmed or rejected. The insistence, therefore, that no hypothesis is intelligible unless it is translatable into definite consequences in experience is fundamental to scientific method. It must have *testable consequences,* i.e., its logical consequences must state *possible observations.*

On such an empirical approach understanding consists not in fixing an intellectual gaze upon an illuminated object, but in anticipating the happenings in the world that are being pointed to in discourse. We are not minds separate from a world of matter, capable of surveying it all, extracting pure meanings and discovering indubitable truths. Instead, thinking is to be regarded as a tool which has grown to tremendous proportions and provided for man a pervasive means of successful adjustment to his environment. It has, like all functions, its intrinsic joys, and has developed ends in which it finds expression. But the meaning of a term lies in its reference to events in our common world.

PRAGMATIC APPROACHES

The general approach is well illustrated in some of the earlier analyses of the pragmatic philosophy.[1] Charles Peirce, the father of pragmatism, enunciated the principle that the meaning of any idea was the discoverable differences it pointed to.[2] William James took up the notion and developed it,

---

[1] There are several varieties of pragmatism which are fairly distinct. The general approach to meaning is similar, but differences arise immediately thereafter.

[2] "How to Make Our Ideas Clear," in *Chance, Love and Logic,* ed. by M. R. Cohen, Harcourt, Brace, 1923.

at times picturesquely. In a lecture on *What Pragmatism Means*,[3] he gave the now famous example of the squirrel, the man, and the tree. A squirrel runs around on the trunk of a tree, and a man runs around the tree in order to catch sight of the squirrel. Although the man makes complete circles he is foiled by the swiftness of the squirrel which always keeps the tree between itself and the man. Does the man run around the squirrel? The answer, explains James, "depends upon what you *practically mean* by 'going round' the squirrel." If it means passing from north of him to east, to south, to west of him, and then to north again, then the man does go round the squirrel. If first in front of him, then on the right, then behind, then on his left, and finally in front again, then the man does not go round the squirrel because the latter keeps his belly turned towards the man all the time and his back turned away. The issue here is not merely a verbal one, indicating two meanings of "go round." The point is that each of those meanings has a separate mode of practical identification. James accordingly describes the pragmatic method as the attempt "to interpret each notion by tracing its respective practical consequences. What difference would it practically make to anyone if this notion rather than that notion were true? If no practical difference whatever can be traced, then the alternatives mean practically the same thing, and all dispute is idle."[4] And in support James quotes a letter from the chemist Ostwald in which the latter says, "I am accustomed to put questions to my classes in this way: In what respects would the world be different if this alternative or that were true? If I can find nothing that would become different then the alternative has no sense."[5]

In these contexts *practical* means simply that the marks suggested by the term are sufficiently precise so that one is able to *work* with the term, to proceed towards some identification in the actual world. The consequences are, broadly speaking, observable. For many purposes analysis need be carried no further. We may agree, for example, that a man running is a phenomenon observable by using our eyes. So long as no problems arise from using this observation for the science we may be trying to build up, or the purpose we have in mind, there is no need for greater refinement. Even complex situations like "The audience was spellbound" might be observed impressionistically with a high degree of agreement. There remains the possibility of noting actual consequences in sense-perception by which such an identification itself could be tested, and which probably served for its recognition.

[3] *Pragmatism*, Longmans, Green, 1928, Lecture 2.
[4] *Ibid.*, p. 45.
[5] *Ibid.*, p. 48.

POSITIVIST AND OPERATIONALIST ANALYSES

The most refined development of this approach among contemporary schools is to be found in the logical positivists who stress especially the element of sense-perception in a theory of meaning. Proceeding from an intensive examination of scientific method they have regarded words as programs for research and experimentation, indicating situations in which some experiment may be tried and some kinds of perceptions anticipated. Thus if I say "This is an apple," you may anticipate that if you look you will see a roundish object, two or three inches in diameter, yellow-greenish or with some red surface; if you bite it, you will note a familiar texture and taste; if you cut it open and let it stand, the cut surface will rust; if you analyze it chemically you will get certain results; and you can predict a host of other similar consequences. If many of these anticipations are not fulfilled you will decide that it is not really an apple. The countless ways in which you might go about testing the truth of the statement "This is an apple" make up the meaning of the statement.

Their theory of meaning. In the light of this analysis some have defined the meaning of a statement as its *mode of verification*. Bridgman in his book *The Logic of Modern Physics*[6] has advocated a similar position under the name of *operationalism;* the concept or idea, on his formulation, is identical with the set of operations by which it is applied.

Such approaches have been employed to rule out as nonsense a considerable body of traditional questions. By nonsense was meant assertions or questions which violated some logical rule or combined words in a way contrary to the implicit rules of the language (for example, "How many pounds of sense did he talk?"), or which otherwise employed terms in such a way that no testable consequences—no mode of verification or operational interpretation—was possible. From this point of view an attack was directed against such questions as "Is there a sound in the room when there is nobody there and an object falls?" Since the term "sound" refers in this context to a sensation that a person has when he is present, there is no way of posing the question empirically. Some of the positivists also directed their approach at theological and ethical statements. For example, they argued that statements about your duty are really just exhortations or commands ("It is your duty to do this" is more appropriately simply "Do this"); hence to speak of ethical statements which are true or false is to talk nonsense.[7]

Narrow operationalism. This approach might, of course, narrow considerably the scope of meaningful assertion. An extreme case is seen in Bridg-

[6] Macmillan, 1928.
[7] For a criticism of this approach in ethics, see below, pp. 428-29.

man's argument (in his book *The Intelligent Individual and Society* [8]) that the intelligent individual finds *his own death* meaningless since there is no way in which he himself could verify the fact that he was dead. Obviously this takes the notion of "mode of verification" to refer to operations performed by the individual concerned. It is important therefore to distinguish between a narrower and a broader operationalist approach, indicative of two directions in which this method of analysis may be carried.

On the narrower approach the view that the meaning of a statement is the way in which it would be tested is pressed literally. Since the meaning of a statement is ordinarily "what it talks about," it is taken for granted that all discourse is ultimately about human operations and sensations. Thus all we can know about is the activity of men. It is difficult to see on such a position what meaning there could be to scientific assertions about what happened in the physical world before man came into existence and there was sensation, or about what the earth would be like if human beings all perished because of an excessive drop in temperature. The narrower operationalist approach must therefore regard all knowledge as descriptions of complexes of operations or sensations, and is sometimes led to describe reality as itself a flux of sensations.

Broad operationalism. The broader operationalism begins by taking the "mode of verification" to refer not to accomplished verification or to the operations of any given man, but to the way in which a statement might be tested and turn out true or false. Thus the statement "It will rain at 12 noon a year from today" should be meaningful on this criterion. If it is, so would be the statement that it will rain a century from now. Similarly, even a statement like "There are mountains on the other side of the moon" is meaningful, even though we shall probably never be able to observe whether it is true. For we can state the conditions required and the observations to be made for the statement to be true or false; e.g., we know what we would expect to see if we got round the moon, or what markings a photograph would have to show, if we could get one, in order to confirm the hypothesis.[9] Similarly, statements about the past are meaningful; for they have consequences in present memories, in present records, and in present effects.

If this liberalization of the operational criterion be carried out completely, "mode of verification" and "operational interpretation" come to designate *not some actions or observations that might be performed by an observer,* but *events in the world that are not intrinsically incapable of observation.* A statement is meaningful not merely when it refers to such events but also when it has consequences referring to such events even if what it talks about

---

[8] Macmillan, 1938, pp. 168-69.

[9] It is interesting to note that a few years before the spectroscope was invented Auguste Comte, the founder of the original Positivist school, said that the chemical composition of the heavenly bodies would remain unknowable to men.

may not be humanly observable. Thus statements about the earth before there was life cannot be declared to be meaningless. The broader operational approach becomes identical with an empirical attitude which simply underscores the character of verification in scientific method, the role of sensation within that process, and which refuses to allow statements that claim immunity to scientific scrutiny.[10]

FEELING AND PRACTICE AS MODES OF VERIFICATION

Such an attitude has met with considerable opposition from those who wish to speak of truth in domains to which they do not think scientific method applicable or in which they find its results unpalatable. There have been attempts to limit the results of science by calling them *merely scientific* truth, with the implication that other domains have a truth of their own and methods of their own. Thus some speak of poetic verification and poetic truth, religious verification and religious truth, and likewise for morals and practical life. Where this does not represent an anti-empirical trend, as in mysticism and the stress on intuition, it is a serious attempt to broaden the notion of testing in experience by recognizing that experience after all includes not merely perceiving, but also thinking, feeling, and doing.

James's extension of the pragmatic approach. William James's treatment of religion is a good example of such efforts. Keenly interested in problems of religion and morals, but dissatisfied with their traditional foundations he sought to approach them empirically. In accomplishing this he found himself extending the criteria of meaning and getting rid of the traditionally objective character of truth. Where testing in sense-perception would not achieve the results he wanted he came to rely on testing in feeling and doing.

The ambiguity of the term *practical* readily permitted this extension of the criteria of meaning. "Practical consequences" could mean not merely "observable consequences" but also "useful consequences." And the truth of an idea or assertion would lie in those consequences *working out satisfactorily*. This notion might indicate, with convenient ambiguity, that the observations anticipated were actually secured, or that the results satisfied the person concerned—that is, made him happier. The pragmatists stressed the utilitarian role of ideas as plans leading to action; they condemned the purely contemplative interpretation of knowledge and treated sense-perception itself as a stimulus to action rather than as an entry to knowledge. James

[10] If this liberalization be not carried out completely then operationalism remains restricted and "subjectivistic." How much of the stir created by this approach in contemporary philosophy has been due to its more restricted form, how much to its scientific stress need not here be discussed.

spoke of the "cash-value" of ideas, and truth was sometimes defined as the expedient in the way of belief. The distinction was not always carefully drawn between the consequences of a proposition and the consequences of *holding* that proposition, so that your feeling happier by holding it might seem to be part of its satisfactory working out and hence point to its truth.

The identification of truth with what is expedient or even good to believe, tends to make truth a matter of personal preference.[11] For judgments of goodness are traditionally variable, differing from individual to individual, and more so from group to group. Thus for James *true* came to mean *true for someone,* so that I may speak of what is true for me but not for you, true for modern men but not for medieval men, true for France but not for Germany, and so on.

James's theory of religious truth. This approach was especially applied by James to those fields in which verification by sense-perception is difficult or remote. Thus in his *Varieties of Religious Experience* he interpreted God as a reservoir of spiritual strength upon which people may draw in moral or emotional crises. As empirical evidence he marshaled the accounts of people who had undergone such stresses and emerged in sudden conversion into a serenity of spirit considerably enriching their lives. These feeling-consequences are the test of the divine existence. Again, in his essay on *The Will to Believe,*[12] he built a faith-ladder with rungs from "It is fit to be true," "It would be well if it were true," "It may be true," to "It ought to be true," "It must be true," "It shall be true for me." In religious matters, he argued, if we remain skeptical, waiting for proof, we lose just as much as if we had disbelieved. For during the lapsed interval we have none of the happiness which conviction brings. Hence we ought to give way to our will to believe and accept some things as true for us.

At times James even used the argument in more mundane matters, seeing the will to believe as creative, at least in the realm of action. Thus my believing that I can jump a ditch which is at the limit of my jumping capacity may be the very element which, in giving me confidence, renders true the proposition that I can jump it. Faith in someone's honesty may keep him on the narrow path. Such examples can readily be discovered from the domain of action. And, after all, the pragmatists were essentially interested in action, in human beings and their thinking as part of their adjustment to an environment which at the same time they were changing.

[11] This treatment of truth as personal gave rise to a storm of controversy concerning the philosophy of pragmatism. The enthusiasm of the movement and its practical flavor were derided. It was called an expression of American haste and practicality, making a virtue out of the endless pursuit of the means, yielding to the chaotic planlessness of competing individualism, substituting confident belief for the rigorous search for truth.

[12] In *The Will to Believe and Other Essays in Popular Philosophy,* Longmans, Green, 1912.

Clearly, James was attempting to extend the domain of testing in experience by calling attention to the feeling and activity components of experience and urging their claims in addition to sense-perception. In one sense he was right—*a priori* any mode of identification may qualify as *observable*, whether it be feeling, sense-perception, or even intellectual insight finding a place for itself in an empirical framework. But the choice among them is not an *a priori* matter. It depends upon which proves successful—for the purposes of truth—in building up a body of common and stable knowledge, public in its mode of verification and yielding consequences on which agreement is possible. These empirical considerations, after long and critical human investigation, point to sense-perception as crucial for at least two reasons: feeling and practical activity do not successfully meet the needs we have indicated, whereas sense-perception does, and, more generally, sense-perception is required in the very identification of feelings and activities.

Objections to feeling as mode of verification. The traditional reference to *conscience* as the still small voice telling us what is wrong is a good example of an attempt to use a kind of feeling for testing moral statements in experience. The difficulty with employing conscience as a test is the discovered variability of its verdicts in the same person. Socrates, who had a refined ethical sense, sharpened by a life of discourse, spoke of a divine sign which guided his conduct; but the best it would do was to make him feel uncomfortable when he was about to do something wrong. The feeling phenomenon of conscience is a resultant of complex beliefs and attitudes.[13] Its voice has to be supplemented by reflection, habituated to differential instead of gross reaction and sometimes retrained in the light of rational considerations. The same difficulties are evident in other realms where the feeling-response is employed as test; for example, in esthetic reactions and judgments of beauty. It follows that although feelings could possibly be the basis of verification, they have not always the constancy and sharper identifiability which would make them widely useful as termini in verification. Where they are thus used it is largely because the inquiry itself directly concerns feelings, as in parts of esthetics and ethics.[14]

Objections to practice as mode of verification. Practical activity has even less claim than feeling to a role as mode of verification. The exigencies of action are often pressing, but action may be decisive without requiring unreserved mental commitment to a belief on which we are compelled to act. It is enough to recognize it as more probable if the evidence points to it, and as a chance bet or a hope, if the preponderance of evidence is equally balanced between it and another hypothesis. The will to believe, on the other

---

[13] The Freudians in the theory of the *super-ego* have explored the mechanism intensively.

[14] For the role of feelings in religion, esthetics, and ethics, see below, Chapters 22, 23, 24, 25.

hand, may prove dangerous in tempting us to overlook contrary evidence and in prompting us to suspend investigation.

Men do, it is true, speak loosely of testing a belief by acting on it. Especially in the case of large-scale social hypotheses it is sometimes said that the way to test the truth of a social program is to throw yourself whole-heartedly into working for it. What is meant in such cases is probably that engaging in such activities puts one in a position in which modes of verification become more accessible. Or perhaps there are values involved which cannot be tested without tentative action along their lines, just as the quality of a food cannot be tested without tasting.

Ultimate resort to sense-perception. In general, when we wish to identify a feeling or an activity we find ourselves resorting to sense-perception. We may not always need to carry the analysis far in ordinary life, but in any scientific work, as both the psychologist and the physicist have discovered, more precise modes of identification become necessary. Carefully discriminated elements of sense-perception become the signs which best serve the purposes of scientific inquiry. What this reliance upon sense-perception entails will be discussed in the next chapter.

Empirical treatment of concepts illustrated

Because of the complexities of the issues discussed and their importance to scientific procedure, it is worth while illustrating the practical effect of a consciously empirical stress in various fields. For this purpose we may select several concepts which play an important role in one or another study and trace the consequences of an empirical as against an intuitive treatment.

LENGTH

In the physical sciences the empirical approach has achieved greatest precision. As an illustration of the treatment of concepts we may take Bridgman's discussion of *length*.[15]

Our ordinary understanding of the term "length" is intuitive. For the most part we feel that we have an intellectual grasp of its meaning, and we translate it into something like "the distance between the extreme points of a thing," or think of the "ideal line which has length but no breadth," or of "the shortest distance between two points," or of "the first dimension

---

[15] P. W. Bridgman, *The Logic of Modern Physics*, Macmillan, 1928, Chapter 1. Our reference is to the broad character of the approach, not to the detailed construction which narrows unduly the scope of empiricism.

of space." The result is, as an analysis of the operations of measuring length shows, that we treat as one phenomena which may prove empirically distinct.

Length is ordinarily measured by applying the standard measuring-rod to the object to be measured and counting the number of applications required to complete it. But for very large objects this is too great a task. Hence the surveyor's methods and instruments are employed. But in this process, a base line is measured in the ordinary way, then a distant point sighted and the angles measured. The ensuing calcuiation of distance involves the Euclidean assumption that the sum of the angles of a triangle (two of whose sides in this case are rays of light) is 180 degrees. Now if we had no method of comparing the results of the two measurements we should simply have to say that there were two kinds of length—tactile and visual, and that in one domain we found it convenient to use one, in another, the other. Different names could be given to them if we found people confusing them. One would be used in carpentry, the other in large scale boundary mapping. In fact, however, we can check the results of one method of measuring length by the other, and such attempts have yielded a correspondence. The result is that we can employ either method indifferently and say that they are both ways of measuring the same length. This treatment is entirely empirical, and so would require continued investigation before it could be extended. Thus where light-rays constitute sides of a triangle, there is adequate ground for believing that the angle-sum will exceed 180 degrees if the triangle is sufficiently large, so that the practical coincidence of the two kinds of length may depend upon our dealing on the whole with relatively small-scale magnitudes.

INTELLIGENCE

Intuitive idea of intelligence. Probably we all would say we have some notion of the meaning of intelligence. We intuit it, it might be said, judging intelligence from chance remarks, an appropriate smile, or studious questions, or after long hours of discussion, or by witnessing a person's actions in some complicated and pressing situation. It seems both a kind of wisdom and of ingenuity, as well as the spark which differentiates endurance or courage from obstinacy, modesty from self-abasement, temperateness from dullness. It seems to penetrate with a kind of native cosmopolitanism into any field and, though the form in which it issues differs according to education, to be beholden to no training. Skill is not intelligence, but the product of intelligence, a ready hand, and an attentive spirit. Intelligence even admits of degrees of variation. One man may be reckoned more intelligent than another, though he would probably not be said to be exactly twice or three times as intelligent. Again if we meet a man a second time and find him now less intelligent than he used to seem, we would attribute the mistake to ourselves, not to him. We must have been deceived either by some special spark, or by a confusion on our part of intelligence with some specialized aptitude or with knowledge of some special subject-matter; for intelligence as ordinarily conceived of is unitary and it is native. Only if we learned of some tremendous change in his life, whether physical operation or mental shock, might we grant an alteration, and say according to the case, that a man has become dulled or some hindrance to the blossoming of his intelligence has been removed.

Intelligence tests. Such is the intuitive idea of intelligence. In ordinary life we may retain it only by ignoring the mistaken judgments of individuals to which it often leads us. This is more readily done because ordinary judgments are based on limited experience of persons, so that when we are mistaken we feel no inadequacy in our concept but only in the extent of our experience. Situations arise, however, in which more precise methods are required. Psychologists have accordingly attempted to devise a more objective measure for the quality which we roughly appraise with so much subjective variation. Devised to meet practical needs, the intelligence test has had its greatest success in that sphere. The tests have become numerous and diverse. Some test for problem-solving ability in many domains; others include direct tests of information and understanding. Some have attempted to avoid language entirely. Fairly high statistical correlations of these results with such standards as school performance have been established for many of them. But a great many pitfalls still surround them. Such factors as experience, varying attitudes toward the testing situation, and relative emphasis on speed and accuracy have shown that they are in no sense measures of native qualities; while the variations between the results of different tests and the varying performances which may yield like scores on individual tests, show that they are not, at least in any simple sense, measures of a unit quality of performance.

View of narrow operationalism. Psychologists have treated the intelligence test with varying degrees of respect. But granting them even an ideal success, the question of what they measure still remains. Is intelligence merely what tests test, or do we refer to something beyond by which their adequacy can be determined? In reaction against intuitionism many have swung to the former view. From such a position it follows that where there are several tests yielding different results there are several different "intelligences." Should these be empirically related and effectively correlated with other forms of testing such as classification by expert judges, the result would earn the title to intelligence itself. And if physiological measures appeared to coincide with this result, they might be referred to also as giving the meaning of intelligence, just as one calls the results of various measures the "length" of the object.

Critique of narrow operationalist view. Unfortunately, this result seems to achieve clarification at the expense of the very interest which guides the inquiry—to "discover the nature of" or "explain" intelligence. It is not, however, necessary to accept such a formulation in order to avoid intuitionism. Such a restricted operationalism fails to take account of the entire method of science. We can clarify this point by an analogy. Hot is a quality of sensation as intelligence is of performance. Now we know that varying lengths of a mercury thermometer correspond with variations in cutaneous sensations of heat. While we are ready to accept the thermometer as a measure of heat, we do not accept it as its meaning. For we mean a great deal more by "heat" than either this measure or even the sensory quality. We recognize the mercury column as a better measure because it makes finer distinctions than we can feel. We credit these distinctions, because they are associated with other consequences which we consider relevant. For example, the patient whose temperature has gone down by thermometer readings has a better appetite and feels stronger.

Now if this is all we know, heat is simply a complex set of unknown conditions, many of whose consequences we can itemize. This is roughly parallel to the situation in current psychology with respect to intelligence—except that the measures themselves have not the predictive accuracy of the thermometer. But a further step has been achieved in relation to heat. A theoretical account of the nature of heat has been developed in terms of the energy of the molecules. Taken together with certain systematic knowledge about mercury, the sensory properties of the skin, and so forth, this yields an explanation of the various phenomena whose interrelation had previously been merely contingent. It seems appropriate to refer to this systematic account as the *meaning* of heat.

Need for systematic unification. So too in the case of intelligence we cannot be content even with a set of tests yielding high correlations. A systematic account is necessary for explanation, an account which would give a meaning to the term. It is important to note that such an account need not be a physiological or physical one, though such may be an ultimate hope. It may be possible to analyze the factors upon which a systematic theory could be based in *psychological* terms.

Intelligence thus turns out to designate neither a concept capable of direct intuitive grasping, nor merely the result of a definite set of operations (tests or measures). It has a double reference, one prior to systematic investigation, the other subsequent. In the first place it refers to a quality of men's activity or performance. In the second place it refers to the results of the psychological investigation of this material, and to the factors which will be pointed to in the theory that ultimately clarifies or unifies the material

These results happen, unfortunately, to be inadequate at present for a full and systematic account of the meaning or nature of intelligence. Whether the outcome will be a single theory exhibiting a unified character in the initial material or whether they will show that material to be an amalgamation of diverse and distinguishable elements, is itself to be discovered only by the exercise of the method of science.

REALITY

"Real" motion. An interesting and philosophically very important example of the empirical approach is the empirical analysis of such terms as *real, really, reality*. They occur in many fields. For example, if observer on planet A says planet B is moving and observer on planet B says planet A is moving, we might feel tempted to ask "Which is *really* moving?" And if we assume that the term "really" has a meaning because we understand it in many contexts and so feel we have achieved an insight into it, we may decide that the question cannot be answered, because only relative motion can be known. Thus if an observer on planet C agrees with the observer on B, then the observer on A will no doubt accuse them both of moving. The result is that we might feel inclined to say that which one is really moving remains a mystery, that we are limited to phenomena and will never know the reality. On the other hand, we may recognize that the statements "A is really moving" and "B is really moving" are uninterpreted, and so neither true nor false, and that to get propositions we require some interpretation of "really" which in fact turns out to be an assumed fixed point of reference. Thus roughly speaking we may say that motion means relative motion.

"Real" shape. Clarification of the meaning of "reality" is particularly important in the theory of knowledge or epistemology, which investigates how we attain to knowledge, by what criteria we can test that we in fact have knowledge, and what is meant by truth. We may choose only one of its problems, the search for the "real" thing perceived. For example, I look at a penny, and hold it up before my eyes in different positions at different angles. The shape I perceive varies from one position to another, consisting for the most part of a variety of ellipses. Nevertheless, most of us would say that the penny is really round. What do we mean by the assertion "This penny is really round," or "The real shape of this penny is round"?

If we assume that each of these words has a meaning which can be directly grasped, and that we already know it, we shall find the question a most difficult one to answer. For on what ground can we give a privileged status to the one appearance (roundness) as compared to the various elliptical shapes? From an empirical approach this special problem disappears, although many others in the theory of perception undoubtedly remain. The empirical approach simply insists that interpretation be offered for the term "real." Otherwise we might as well substitute x and say "The x shape of this penny is round." Some standard of "reality" must be offered to give us an interpreted statement. "The real shape" will be defined either as what is beheld when the object is held directly in the line of vision and perpendicular to it, or as what can be correlated with the shape as discovered by touch and measurement. The real shape of the penny thus defined is an empirical question, and for most pennies is found to be approximately round. That there is some such tacit assumption about the meaning of "real" is clear if we turn the tables and argue that the *real* shape of a penny held at an acute angle to the line of vision is elliptical. For if it then appeared perfectly round we should begin to suspect that something was wrong. Here "real" obviously means "visual shape appropriate to that position" and any disagreement with this usage compels one to render explicit some other meaning assumed instead.[16]

TERMS IN SOCIAL SCIENCE

The problems raised above occur to a proportionately greater extent in the social sciences, because the material is both human and familiar, and so it is assumed that we know what the terms refer to. But it is obvious that we do not always mean the same things by such terms as government, state, class, religion, law, not to speak of more difficult notions such as justice, social order, value, security, or more general notions such as determinism or social causation.

Meaning of "the state." The state, for example, means to the jurist a territory under some sovereign authority. For the sociologist it is a form of social order, sometimes one actually found, sometimes one which he thinks is developing. To the moralist it may be a pattern of order, which people ought to live under, so that he will speak of a country only partially achieving statehood. So too the state has been defined as a harmony of classes, as an instrument of the dominant class to keep the subordinate classes in submission, and so forth.

From the point of view of an empirical approach, there is no sanctity to a term. When its different interpretations are distinguished it may be found that different writers while using the same term are really talking of quite different things. This is especially evident when it is found that some are painting a picture of their heart's desire under the guise of defining the term *state*, while others are trying to describe the way men actually behave to-

---

[16] For a fuller discussion of the concept of reality, see Chapter 10.

wards one another.[17] There is usually, however, some common set of problems to which the various theories may be related.

Meaning of "constitution." The use of the term "constitution" is a good example in American society. On an intuitionist theory one might feel content to accept one of the following definitions which are among those quoted by H. L. McBain in his book *The Living Constitution:*[18] "A constitution is a fundamental law or basis of government . . . established by the people in their original capacity" (Justice Joseph Story). "A form of government, delineated by the mighty hand of the people, in which certain first principles of fundamental laws are established" (Justice Paterson, 1795). ". . . Those of its rules or laws which determine the form of its government and the respective rights and duties of it toward the citizens and of the citizen toward the government" (Bryce).

McBain on the basis of such an inspection recommends abandoning any attempt to define the term in general. "Everybody knows in a general way what a constitution is even though he may not be able to fuse the sense of his concept into impregnable words" (p. 10). In spite of this remark, his whole attitude is a good example of the empirical approach. He refers in the case of the American constitution, to the document drafted in 1787, its ratification and amendments, the growth of custom, practices of political parties, the action or inaction on special kinds of matters of Congress and President and Judiciary. Then he examines such properties as flexibility in American government. The net result is the conception of a constitution as the set of most general rules, procedures and limits of operation *discoverable over a specified period of time* in the actual goings-on of government officials, such as Presidents, legislatures and courts. Now while this makes the discovery of America's present constitution a difficult empirical task, it is far from rendering it meaningless. And while apparently reading off from a document and understanding its words would be less laborious, the actual practical difficulties in guiding one's conduct by this second method would be quite great. Such recourse has always involved appeal to the spirit of the constitution, and this is but a name for what one thinks it ought to mean, or what one has found it to have meant in history.

Legal usage and meanings of terms. Not merely in the analysis of general terms, but in dealing with the more specific decisions of practice, the emphasis on observable consequences serves to bring greater precision and more experimental attitudes into social life. The intuitive approach on the other hand fosters or expresses a tendency to rest content with vague meanings. This is especially apparent in such disciplines as the law, where the decision of the meaning of a term frequently represents the decision as to how the case will go. Where a "sympathetic strike" is forbidden by law, is

[17] See below, p. 277 ff.
[18] Workers Education Bureau Press, 1927.

the strike of typesetters in aid of reporters in the same newspaper a sympathetic strike? Would it be such if they are separate craft unions, but not if they formed one industrial union? The decision of meaning may be equivalent to settling the men's wages for a period of years. What constitutes "due process," "interstate commerce," "monopoly," "fraud," "freedom of speech"? Disputes about meanings of terms in such contexts turn out to be not arguments about intellectual insights, but in larger cases different programs for the direction of American life.

We may conclude that in the scientific program testing by experience is not an anti-theoretical approach, but a fruitful method of imparting precision to theoretical concepts and an essential part of determining the truth of an hypothesis. It is also clear that the conception of experience itself is a broad one, but that where refinement is required the reference is ultimately to sense-perception. We therefore turn next to this phase of scientific method.

Chapter 8   SENSE-PERCEPTION

In the preceding chapter we examined the meaning and importance of the notion of testing by experience. We have seen that to test by experience is ultimately to look for the consequences of our beliefs in sense-perception rather than in feeling or intellectual insight or action as such. Granted, then, that sense-perception does play this critical role in verification, it may now be asked what right science has to assume that sense-perception is trustworthy. This is a problem that has often been raised. To Plato, as we saw above, sensation was obviously untrustworthy. Its objects are constantly changing. Does science, in fact, rest on shifting sands? Or does sense-perception give us truth? Are there elementary sensations directly given, directly corresponding to the qualities of things and so indubitable? We shall examine three views concerning the reliability and ultimacy of sense-perception:

(1) That elementary sensations correspond to the qualities of things and so give us truth directly.

(2) That sensations have nothing to correspond to and are themselves the building blocks out of which things as we know them are constructed.

(3) That scientific method does not need to assume a general reliability of sensations, but can investigate this reliability, and can test the reliability of specific sensations as it tests any other facts.

Sense data as reflection of reality

Some have argued that there are ultimate data of sense corresponding directly and infallibly to qualities of existence. In having these ultimate sensations you are grasping in immediate perception representations of features of the world. Out of them you construct your knowledge of the world. Because of their simplicity they cannot go wrong, although, in combining them to form complex ideas, errors may arise.

LOCKE'S THEORY

A theory of this sort (generally called a correspondence theory) is best illustrated in the views of John Locke, one of the fathers of the British empirical tradition in psychology. Locke began with the assertion that all ideas arise from sensation and reflection. Simple sensations are derived through the various senses (for example, colors, sounds, shapes, smells), and there are internal copies of these, such as memories and images. And again there are internal observations of our processes in getting these ideas, for example, of our thinking or perceiving. Complex ideas are formed from the simple ones under rules of association. What is our idea of a rose, asks Locke, but a name for certain sensations of color, shape, number, smell, which constantly recur together? The most abstract ideas have this basis. Knowledge rests on agreement or disagreement of ideas, and is based on the correspondence of ideas (sensations) with the qualities of things. Thus our ideas of hard and soft disagree with one another; and our idea of a rose agrees with our present sensations of color and shape. The simple idea (sensation) of round corresponds to the quality round. A more complex analysis would be required to show what corresponds to the assertion "This table is round."

Now in Locke's scheme, apart from problems of the relation of things and minds,[1] there is one fatal difficulty. The simple ideas (or simple sensations) are supposed to correspond to qualities of things. But how can we know that there is genuine correspondence if our knowledge is limited to or consists wholly of ideas (sensations)? We have to have some access to the object other than through ideas in order to know whether there is really a correspondence. In short, the notion of correspondence of ideas and qualities as Locke uses it has legitimate application only if there is direct insight into the qualities of things. But if there is, we do not need copies to give us truth; if there is not we cannot perform the comparison. Locke seems, in fact, to rely more on the notion of agreement of complex ideas with simple sensations. The notion of correspondence seems superfluous embroidery on the fact that the simple sensations are taken on trust, that is, not further questioned in seeking to establish the truth of a statement.

THE MEANING OF CORRESPONDENCE

The notion of correspondence is thus a very complicated one. Even if we abandon the type of absolute correspondence of ideas and qualities desired by Locke, as an inadequate basis for a theory of knowledge, there remain several different meanings which correspondence may have in terms of the

[1] See below, p. 148.

procedure of science or in terms of specific psychological theories to which men have adhered. We may survey these meanings briefly.

(a) The "correspondence" of perception to reality may mean that we perceive the world around us by a specific psychological process—namely, by receiving a kind of camera-photograph impression on our minds. This "impression" is *direct,* i.e., it is a mirror-like reflection of the things in the world. Such an analogy underlies Locke's whole treatment. This view is founded on mistaken psychological notions; our eyes are not camera-plates nor is vision our only important sense. Nor does sensation come only in a passive "looking" or reception. It involves active participation in the surrounding world. This is perhaps clearer if we pay attention to kinesthetic, tactile and auditory experience and do not model an account largely on visual perception alone.

(b) The "correspondence" of perception to reality may mean that we perceive the world by compounding "elements of sensation," i.e., red, soft, smooth, and so forth. These elements of sensation are of equal importance and are compounded (added) together to form our perception of things. This notion is also based on an inadequate psychology of perception. Instead we are learning that simple "elements of sensation" are abstractions from experience rather than basic to it, and that perception of the world is an *organized* process involving whole things and their backgrounds in dynamic relationship. To abstract simple visual color-elements is a special task to which the painter must carefully school himself.

(c) To say that our perceptions "correspond" to reality may mean that they change with changes in the stimulation sent to our sense-organs by the physical energies in the world. This is, of course, commonly accepted. Locke included in his account the causal action of physical things on our sense-organs. Correspondence in this sense is established by correlating the data of physics with the data of psychology. It does not, however, answer the question of how faithfully sense-perception "corresponds" to reality.

(d) Our perceptions may be said to "correspond" to reality in the sense that, under most conditions, they represent pretty faithfully the main outlines of whatever aspects of the world around us we happen to be viewing at the time. This is a statement based upon the empirical findings of the psychology of perception and refers to the fact that man (and other animals) is able under most conditions to perceive accurately many aspects of the world in which he functions. For example, psychological experiments show us that man perceives with considerable accuracy the correct size of an object [2] (under ordinary conditions, where distance is also visible) even though the size of the retinal area excited by that object may be varied rather widely. The same constancy or accuracy in perceiving the physical characteristics of the object is found for brightness, shape, color. Thus a bright object keeps

---

[2] The correct size is here judged by results on standard measurements.

most of its perceptual brightness even though it is seen in low illumination—even though, in other words, the physical intensity of retinal stimulation corresponds more closely to darkness.

In this sense, man's perceptions correspond rather stably to the characteristics of objects as determined by physical measurements, instead of changing indiscriminately with every change in sense-organ stimulation. Man perceives an organized pattern—objects in surroundings—which corresponds to the organization found in his wider perceptual experience and established in terms of the inquiry of physics. But it should be clearly understood that in this meaning of the term "correspondence," no single one of our perceptual experiences inevitably "reflects" reality. The relation of any one of our perceptual experiences to reality is a question for empirical psychological study and is not of determining importance for our theory of knowledge. We gain our knowledge of the world by checking and weighing our perceptual experiences against each other. In fact, we often learn about the world precisely from our "mistaken" sense-perceptions.

(e) In terms of an analysis of scientific method, another meaning can be given to the "correspondence" of idea and fact. We confirm the belief that this is a rose by noting that on observation we see the color red, and a certain number and arrangement of petals, that we smell its fragrance, and that other operations get other specified results. The so-called simple sensations of Locke will then be the *relatively* ultimate perceptual experiences in terms of which *verification* takes place. The correspondence lies in the agreement of actual observation with anticipated observation. On such an analysis, however, Locke's psychological theory of ideas is irrelevant. For the account turns out to report not the way in which knowledge arises from sensation, but the way in which sense-perception functions in scientific method. To make truth consist in the correspondence of ideas of the mind to qualities of objects, is an exaggeration and misinterpretation of one phase (the observational phase) of scientific method.

Sense data as ultimate reality

Locke himself prepared the way for an alternative view that sensations have nothing to correspond to or reveal and are themselves the building blocks out of which things are constructed. For Locke did not hold that all simple ideas (images, sensations) correspond to qualities. Ideas of shape, size, number, etc., correspond to primary qualities, but others such as color, sound, sweetness, pain, etc., are spoken of only by courtesy as referring to secondary qualities. Secondary qualities are not qualities of things. They are powers that the things possess in virtue of their primary qualities, which affect the perceiving organism so as to produce sensations and ideas of color, pain, and so forth.

It is not hard to understand the drift of Locke's thought. Conceiving the world in terms of the scientific discoveries culminating in Newton's work he thought of objects as possessing in themselves all those qualities of size, shape, number, motion which entered into the physicist's account. That was the world outside, the objective world of nature. But man's experience contains much more—there are pleasures and pains, colors and sounds, smells and tastes. How do these get into the world? Man's body is part of nature and comes in contact with things and their primary qualities. It is in this contact that the secondary qualities arise. Surely on reflection no one can believe that pain lies in the object. It, at least, must be an effect produced in the mind. And is the sweetness in the sugar? Rather the particles of sugar by their shape or motion produce alterations on the tongue and palate culminating in a sensation of sweetness in the mind. So, too, sound and color in themselves are mere movements.

THEORY DEVELOPED BY BERKELEY AND HUME

Clearly Locke's use of correspondence for simple qualities went only halfway. George Berkeley thought that even this was too far. In his *Principles of Human Knowledge* and his *Three Dialogues between Hylas and Philonous*, he applied to primary qualities Locke's arguments against the objectivity of secondary qualities. He argued that they reveal the same relativity, and the same dependence on the perceiving subject. The "same" distance may be great or small, the "same" time drags or speeds away, and so forth. All qualities are of one type and if some are secondary, so are all. Hence we can dispense with matter, which Locke had postulated as a substratum, a something I-know-not-what which must be presumed to support qualities because they could not stand by themselves. The mind is sufficient support for secondary qualities and hence for all qualities. The world, then, consists of spirits or minds and their ideas, and all knowledge is built out of ideas as original elements. This type of view has been called *subjective idealism*.

Berkeley treated sensations as original data, having nothing behind them. They are themselves the expression of spirit. David Hume, who continued Berkeley's work as Berkeley had continued Locke's, used the same arguments as Berkeley had used against matter to dispose of our knowledge of mind or spirit. It is, he said, simply postulated as a substratum for ideas, and we have no more knowledge of it than we do of matter. Our knowledge is limited to sensations and consists in manipulating them and our ideas, which copy them according to laws of association. Hume did not speak of the sensations as ultimate reality, because taking a skeptical attitude he thought we could not get beyond sensation to find out what the world was really like. But sensations remain in his system the building blocks of knowledge.

Whereas the Berkeley-Hume tradition had begun in the investigation of the origins of knowledge, a similar view with regard to the character of sensation was developed in the *positivist* tradition on the basis of an analysis of science. It is clearly seen in the view of Ernst Mach that reality consists of the flux of sensations and that scientific hypotheses are conventions, convenient though fictional, to order the material of sensation. Some of the recent positivists likewise have spoken of atomic facts, which are facts of sensation like brown-here-now, in which the analysis of knowledge terminates and which are directly verifiable.

How scientific method uses sense data

The third view is that scientific method while it assigns an important role to sensation does not need to assume its general reliability, but can instead investigate it, and it can test the reliability of any specific perception roughly in the same way as it tests any other assertion. This view would deny the indubitable and directly cognitive character of each single simple sensation maintained in the correspondence theory and the role of sensations as atomic elements urged in the building-block theory.

CRITIQUE OF ULTIMATE DATA

It is true that in any one experiment the terminus of testing is some designated perception upon which there is agreement. But this need not be treated as indubitable knowledge. In fact, it is not when there is a disagreement. The disputed sensation is then itself made the subject-matter of fresh experiment. Suppose in weighing an object on a balance-scale two observers differ as to whether the scale's pointer actually coincides with the mark indicating balance. They may then try the object on another scale in which a bell rings when the weight is balanced. Assuming both scales to be correct, the bell's ringing would show that the man who did not observe the coincidence was wrong. If we differ on two colors we may investigate questions of wave-length, or test our observation in terms of some other visual agreement. For example, if I regard A as pink and B as blue, whereas someone else sees them as the same color, we may test by making different predictions. Thus I would say that if a designated (red) glass were held up and looked through, A and B would appear the same color but not the same shade. The other party to the dispute would predict a complete similarity. We would thus be able to settle our disagreement—provided of course that we agreed upon this fresh observation.[3]

If no single sense-perception need be an indubitable datum for the testing process, but can always in turn be tested in other experiments in terms of other sense-perceptions, it follows that scientific method does not presuppose that any simple sensation gives us a direct revelation of reality. Of course the process at any time comes to an end when people agree in their perceptions. And in fact scientific method would yield no common results if there were not such agreement empirically discovered. We would then each have to exercise the method in a solitary world of our own, if indeed we could continue to exist. But the agreement *is* empirically discovered, and though there could be no science without it, the discovery that there actually is science is an empirical discovery.

This does not, of course, mean that *mere* agreement guarantees truth in sense-perception. There are phenomena which, it has been found, men all see alike. The straight stick partly in water looks bent, and there are many other optical illusions which psychologists have explored. The perception remains the same, but in the light of further experience is shown to be illusory. The agreement on any sense-perception is tentative, like agreement on any hypothesis. It rests on a whole system of established knowledge.

CRITIQUE OF BUILDING-BLOCK THEORY

This argument from the actual character of scientific method does not appear to touch the second position, the building-block theory. In fact it may appear to strengthen it. For if I regard A as pink and B as blue whereas someone else sees both as the same color, science finds no contradiction. It accepts both sets of data. Though only one of us makes successful predictions about a later perception there is no doubt that originally we saw the colors differently. So a man may feel hot in a chilly room when he has a fever, and be wrong if he says "The room is hot." But he is entirely correct if he says "I am hot." For he is telling us not about something outside, but what he sees by direct inspection of his own state of consciousness. So that finally, it appears that this is all science ultimately tells me about, and what I call the world is an organized complex of my own states of consciousness.

Some forms of this view have especially important consequences in the social sciences. It is argued that whatever the case in the physical sciences, in the social studies at least we deal with human material, and being human we can look directly into our consciousness. We can therefore immediately understand terms referring to our conscious acts and directly verify asser-

[3] For a discussion of the role of such agreement see Norman Campbell, *What Is Science*, p. 27.

tions about them. The result has been an unwillingness to explore scientifically terms denoting feelings and attitudes. Social generalizations accordingly are frequently stated in terms fundamentally vague.

Uncertainty in statements about one's consciousness. Against this whole type of view we may argue that there can be just as much uncertainty and error in statements about one's consciousness as in statements about the "outside" world. From the Socratic stress on the difficulties of following the Delphic maxim "Know thyself" to the Freudian insistence that the significance of our motives in our own living may be quite different from what we consciously conceive them to be, there is a long tradition that recognizes the fallibility of men's judgments about their conscious reactions.

The presence of uncertainty in recognizing as well as reporting phenomena of consciousness is of course clearer in what we call feeling than it is in sensation. The child may not be sure whether he is hungry or has a stomach-ache. I may be uncertain whether *I really* want chocolate now, and when it is given me, may say on one occasion that I have changed my mind, but on another that I really did not want it after all, but only thought that I did. Mr. A may think he hates Miss B, only to discover that it was profound affection.

The same is possible, though it occurs to a lesser degree, with sense-perceptions. I may imagine or even see a color and be uncertain whether it is an exact match of another. Now if I am shown two patches of color under the same conditions and one moment I find them the same and the next moment somewhat different, it is likely that I do not know the character of my sensation or have not built up a standard by precise comparison of past experiences. And the fact of such uncertainty indicates that even where certainty exists there may be a mistake.

This line of criticism suggests that although we know the character of our conscious states the greater part of the time, and with such a high degree of probability that it would be folly to question them, especially in the case of sensation, nevertheless the status of this knowledge is not immediate certification of truth by direct inspection, but empirical information gathered just as knowledge of objects is gathered. In fact there are many assertions about our world of everyday experience (such as that the sun rises every day) which it would be equal folly to question.

Relation of concepts and percepts. The above analysis applies not merely to reporting our conscious states, but to recognizing them at all. The very experience of red-here-now with its explicit recognition of redness, implies a comparison of present experience with past and future experience, and so an element of interpretation. Kant expressed this view when he pointed out, in his *Critique of Pure Reason,* that percepts without concepts are blind, concepts without percepts empty. Otherwise red-here-now is simply an exclamation in experience, like "Uh!" "My!" When I say that I see red I am not merely reporting *an* experience but saying that it has some quality. Otherwise, clearly, my experience is unrecognizable and inexpressible, even to myself.

If the experience is thus inexpressible and essentially non-conceptual it cannot very well serve as a building-block of knowledge. If it is expressible, there is already knowledge embodied in it. In the latter case sensations turn out to be not directly known ultimate elements of knowledge but a special type of events in experience which need knowledge to be intelligible; their recognition requires and is capable of empirical testing.[4]

The same considerations apply against the view that scientific method is ultimately concerned with ordering sensations or atomic facts, using hypotheses as convenient devices. For if knowledge cannot ultimately be analyzed, even theoretically, into sensory building-blocks, the role of hypotheses and of general ideas is more essential. An ideally complete process of verification is not simply a resolution of the hypothesis or theory into a complex of sensations or atomic facts to be looked for in experience. Rather, the process involves careful selection of some elements of sensation because they are pointed to by the hypothesis *together with* the system of knowledge in which it falls.[5] Scientific method therefore involves what may be called a *polarity* of ideas and sensations.[6]

SCIENTIFIC METHOD SELF-CORRECTIVE IN DEALING WITH SENSATION

It follows from our discussion that there is no *general* problem of the reliability of sensation. Any specific propositions about sensations may be tested. That theoretically the testing need never come to an end points to the circular character of the scientific method which, far from being a vicious circle, becomes as a consequence *self-corrective,* and by sacrificing any claims to absolute certainty on matters of fact, can yield increasingly greater probability, and refine both its ideas and its modes of observation and experiment. The question "Is sensation ultimately reliable?" treated from the point of view of an empirical theory becomes either a form to be filled for each particular observation by inquiring whether it will stand indefinitely continued testing, or a general question which involves an inquiry as to

---

[4] It is important to note that this view does not say that what is perceived or the content of experience varies as a function of knowledge and past experience. Whether certain visual characters, for example, are constant for all men of whatever past experience, or whether none are, is a question for empirical psychology to resolve.

[5] See above, p. 71 ff.

[6] We have a polarity when the two entities involved cannot be conceived of without reference to one another. For an account of the concept of reality implicit in scientific method, see Chapter 10.

whether any other method has proved more reliable than empirical method in building up a system of knowledge. If any other interpretation is to be given to the question, such as "Is the picture given of the world by empirical method including the use of observation, a *true* picture of the *real* world?" then an analysis of *truth* and *reality* is needed. If, however, the question merely indicates that eventually some of the results of our sciences may be far different from what they are now, to that extent it is true but it makes no significant contribution to the theory of sensation.

Chapter 9   CRITIQUES OF SCIENCE

Up to this point we have dealt largely with the elements of scientific method. Problems are also sometimes raised as to the validity of the method as a whole in framing a comprehensive account of the world. We shall consider the implications of these criticisms in this chapter. Sometimes such attacks on science are launched in the interests of a skeptical philosophy, sometimes to further the adoption of one of the alternative methods we have examined. The critique of science has taken a variety of forms. Science has been attacked as a whole as falsifying reality. Or logic, one phase of the scientific method, has been set against observation or experience, the other phase. It is then asserted that logic sets problems which contradict experience and its insights directly, or itself offers contradictions which experience cannot resolve.

Claim that science is abstract

One such critique claims that science analyzes, breaks up into parts, is abstract. There must be some other method which synthesizes, grasps things as wholes, is concrete. The scientist deals with abstract phases of things; but the artist, for example, tries to see things whole. Hence the artist's vision (or the religious man's or the mystic's) gets to the core of things. Scientific knowledge is like trying to know a town by looking at photographs from all points of view, instead of by taking a walk through it. So with the reality of things—we must get at it by a mature, direct, or intuitive experience, a kind of empathy. Common sense may add that an ounce of experience is worth a pound of description.[1]

But does such experience always give the best account? The general at headquarters knows the war better than the private at one corner of a far-flung front. A tourist's walk through a town surely yields a more superficial knowledge than is acquired from a study of the history of the town, its industries, composition of its population, and so forth. It is true that direct experience on top of all of this renders knowledge clearer as well as more in-

[1] A critique similar to this is presented by Henri Bergson, e.g., in his *An Introduction to Metaphysics,* tr. by T. E. Hulme, Putnam's, 1912.

tense. But any experience is concerned with limited phases of existence. In fact no human activity deals with the totality of its environment. The "whole vision" of the painter is concerned with the visible rather than the chemical; weighing neglects the psychological properties of the man who is weighed; love is proverbially blind and feeling has no concern with electronic properties. This does not belie the fact that actual experience frequently puts us in a better position for testing, and at the same time stimulates hypotheses. But mere experience is as we saw above simply a "blind" event, like other events in nature.

Alleged conflict of logic and experience

A second critique of science points to the contradiction of logic and experience. It is said, for example, that logic shows reality to be static while experience discerns directly that reality is dynamic. This critique frequently invokes the arguments of the ancient Greek philosopher Zeno, who aimed to prove that motion is self-contradictory, that is, incompatible with logic.

Zeno's paradoxes. The arguments themselves are extremely simple and surprisingly stubborn. Their substance may be stated in the following synthetic example: You cannot get out of the room you are in, because if you have gone half the distance to the door, $X/2$, you still have to cover half the remainder, that is $X/4$, then half the remainder, $X/8$, and so on ad infinitum. Since you cannot cover an infinite number of intervals in a finite time you cannot get out of the door. In fact, you cannot move at all, since the same problem arises about covering the first step. Again even if you are finally outside the door you have not moved; for at any moment in the time which you say it took you to cover the distance, you were at some point. Since at every moment you were in some spot, when were you in motion?

Zeno trusted his logic and was ready to accept the conclusion that experience gives us an illusory account and that motion is unreal. In fact his whole purpose in advancing these arguments was to bolster the position of his teacher Parmenides, who claimed that all change is appearance and reality is One, Boundless, Eternal. Those, like Bergson, who invoke the arguments as a critique of logic, conclude instead that they prove logic incapable of grasping the dynamic nature of reality. In either case one phase of scientific method is set against the other and a choice is forced between them.

Logical answers to Zeno. The use of such arguments assumes too hastily that logical analysis cannot unravel them. The logical answers to Zeno's paradoxes have taken various forms. The most precise are the analyses of the infinite by modern mathematicians.[2] But it will be sufficient to show the character of a logical solution if we give the earliest explicit reply to Zeno, which we find in the *Physics* of Aristotle. Aristotle in effect accuses Zeno of using "infinite" in an ambiguous way. The paradox consists, he says, in the necessity of covering an infinite number of intervals in a finite time. But the time may likewise be divided infinitely. Thus if Zeno says we have an infinite number of intervals to cover (by division) we have likewise an infinite time (by division) in which to cover them. If it is a finite distance, then we cover it in a finite time. It is obviously erroneous to correlate one type of analysis for distance with a different type of analysis for time.

In a similar fashion we can see that there is no genuine paradox in a moving body being at just one point at any particular moment. This does not mean that it is *at rest* at the point. Within a point there is neither rest nor motion. But if the body were *at the same point at two different moments* then it would have been at rest (if it were also at the same point at any moment between those two moments). Conversely, a test for the motion of a body is that for any two moments of time, however close, the body is at different points in space (except for recrossing of points, as in circular motion). Therefore if Zeno had included the element of difference of points of location, so far from contradicting motion he would have given one of its consequences. It is by no means the only one; there are visual consequences, tactile ones, consequences involving force, possible effects on obstructions and countless others. Bergson is right in saying that the cinematograph effect of motion—the roll of film showing discrete positions—is not the whole of motion. It is but one consequence among an indefinite set; but no more does any single intuition or feeling of movement embrace them all.

The example of Zeno's paradoxes may be taken as confirmation of the view that any purely logical analysis which purports to contradict empirical facts is either bad logic, or employs ambiguous terms. But if science in using logic does not falsify existence, it is a mistake to think that a scientific description must be in the same state of flux as the existence of which it is an account.

Antinomies as limitation of science

A third type of critique of science is the view that there are problems which neither logical reasoning nor any possible experience can solve, and which thus lie beyond the scope of scientific method. Kant, for example,

---

[2] For a summary of these solutions to Zeno's paradoxes, see Bertrand Russell, *Our Knowledge of the External World*, Norton, 1929, Lectures 6, 7.

insisted in his *Critique of Pure Reason* that our empirical knowledge is limited to phenomena. Reason cannot solve the problem of reality behind phenomena. When reason begins to consider such questions as whether the world is finite or infinite, whether time had a beginning or no beginning, whether there was or was not a first cause, it can make an equally good case for both. These paradoxes Kant called antinomies.

Such objections can be met by showing that the antinomies are capable of statement as questions to be empirically resolved. This may be exemplified by treatment of one selected problem. For this purpose we may deal with the questions concerning the meaning and nature of *space,* and especially the question whether it is finite or infinite.

PROBLEMS OF SPACE AS ILLUSTRATION

Space as we ordinarily conceive it (what philosophers have called *conceptual space*) turns out on careful examination to be an elaboration in imagination of the properties described by Euclidean geometry. Conceptual space is presumed to be infinitely extended; a Euclidean straight line may be endlessly produced. Any part of conceptual space is infinitely divisible; a Euclidean straight line is divisible at any point, nor for any given point is there any point next to it, since between them lies a line and so the possibility of endless division. Conceptual space has three dimensions—up and down, forward and backward, right and left; Euclidean plane geometry has length and breadth, and solid geometry adds height.

The question "What is conceptual space?" may therefore aptly be answered "What Euclidean geometry describes." This makes it necessary to re-examine the question of what, after all, Euclidean geometry does describe or represent. In answering this question we find a great distinction between the intuitionist or Platonic approach to mathematics and the empirical approach. We may suggest that the antinomies only arise in the context of the Platonic approach. Let us elaborate each alternative.

The Platonic approach. If we think as Plato did that geometry has been uncovering part of the structure of the world we will say that the product, namely Space, is a huge emptiness, having the structural properties that Euclidean geometry describes. Bodies may fit into or *occupy* this space, but the space itself is somehow independent of the existent things in it. This is the Newtonian conception of absolute space: "Absolute space, by virtue of its own nature and without reference to any external object, always remains the same and is immovable."[3] As a preface to the definitions Newton

[3] Cf. his account of absolute time: "Absolute, True, and Mathematical Time, of itself and from its own nature flows equably without regard to anything external, and by another name is called Duration." (From the Scholium of Bk. I of Newton's *Principia*.)

writes: "I do not define Time, Space, Place or Motion, as being well known to all. Only I must observe that the vulgar conceive those qualities under no other notions but from the relation they bear to sensible objects. And thence arise certain prejudices for the removing of which, it will be convenient to distinguish them into Absolute and Relative, True and Apparent, Mathematical and Common."

The underlying belief is that absolute space is discovered by the intellect. This is clearly in the Platonic tradition. What is discovered by the intellect is not a mental figment, but the very reality of the world. Conceptual space is objective space—the real space.

The Kantian theory of space. Kant, while developing an entirely different theory of space, adhered unwaveringly to this intuitionist approach. He does not doubt for a moment that fundamental geometrical terms and assertions refer to profound and direct insights into the structure of space, and that their consequences accordingly hold with absolute certainty of phenomena in space. But he is impressed with knowledge so secured and is mystified by the fact that long mathematical operations issue in results that *must* hold of our world, never questioning that they do hold. Kant accordingly asks how it can be that our intuitions of the properties of space have such a binding effect upon phenomena. It seems to him that we are not so much apprehending reality as laying down the law for it. His solution is that space and time are among the forms which our minds bring as a framework for the ordering of the material of sensation. As for the paradoxes of space and time, e.g., that space can hardly be conceived as coming to an end, nor again as actually infinite—these as we have seen, he holds to be insoluble by reason.

Aristotle's analysis. It is clarifying to examine an early attempt at a more empirical analysis of space, time and motion. Aristotle, without holding an empirical approach to meaning, developed what is in fact an empircal meaning for space and time. He does not speak much of space, but rather of place, and not of place abstractly but of the places of things. The place of anything, he decides, is the innermost boundary of whatever contains it, and the dimensions are analyses of such relations of bodies. The world as a whole has no place since it is not contained in anything else. The implication is that space would be just an abstract name for the place-relations of bodies.[4] Or else it might be the idea of a void or empty space which Aristotle treats as the ideal limit of a process of rarefaction; he denies, however, the existence of a void.

[4] His analysis of time follows similar procedure. Time is the number of motion or change in respect of the before-after relation, i.e., time is literally the number of *times* some specified process has occurred, that is its relation to some standard process. Ultimately Aristotle's standard is the uniform motion of the heavenly bodies.

Aristotle obviously could not hold to the infinite extension of space on his theory, and as he did not believe there was infinite body, he had to hold to a finite world. Later commentators discuss common objections to this view. If the world is finite, what happens when a man moves up to the edge and tries to stick out his hand? Either he is stopped, and so there is matter beyond, or he succeeds, in which case there is space beyond, whereupon he moves farther into the beyond and tries sticking out his hand again. On the Aristotelian position one could escape between the horns of this dilemma by reference to his theory of matter. Aristotle believed, as we have seen, in the traditional four elements—earth at the center of the world, then water, air and fire in turn. And above them was the *quinta essentia* or fifth substance of a pure heavenly kind. Now each element had its appropriate or natural motion, that of earth being down, water downish, air uppish, and fire up, while the fifth element engaged in circular motion. Thus a human hand could not in the first place get up there, and in the second place, if we overlook this and allow it to, when you try to stick it out it will go in a circle. Hence it will never have to stop, nor will its not stopping prove the world infinite.

An empirical treatment of space. In modern times our methods are more refined, and so we send rays of light to perform the task. On an empirical approach questions of the nature of space would, therefore, have to be formulated in the following way: the terms appearing in Euclidean geometry must be given an interpretation by means of experimental or observational procedure. Then any questions may prove practically insoluble, but are no longer antinomies in the Kantian sense. Thus "straight line" may be interpreted as the path of a ray of light, and the question whether space is finite would now mean whether a ray of light sent off in one direction is ever actually visible from the opposite direction, whether the angle sum of celestial triangles is more than 180°, and so forth. The suggestion made by some modern astronomers that we see in one direction the back of some stars whose front we see in the opposite direction would thus be one type of evidence for the proposition that space is finite.[5]

Any other questions about space would have to be treated in the same fashion. Thus the infinite divisibility of space might be investigated by specifying some operation for the term "division of a line" and some existent for the term line. Otherwise one may go on in fantasy, performing acts of division. Psychological studies of minima visibilia, or thresholds of vision, in

---

[5] The findings of modern astro-physics do in fact entail the rejection of Euclidean geometry as an account of the space of our large-scale world in which rays of light are offered as interpretation of the term "straight line." Of course some other interpretation might be offered for which Euclidean geometry would hold for a specified domain. Thus it is applicable to any small portion of the earth's surface although from a wider point of view the straight line employed (e.g., metal rod) is seen to be bent with the curvature of the earth's surface.

fact are testing the proposition of indefinite divisibility by a visual interpretation of line, e.g., as a band of color. If there prove to be a minimum length after which nothing is visible then of course for this interpretation space is not infinitely divisible. What philosophers have called *perceptual space* as distinguished from *conceptual space* is simply the results of an interpretation of the terms of geometry by visual material. The discrepancies of perceptual and conceptual space amount to the recognition that many of the statements of Euclidean geometry do not hold when interpreted in terms of perceptual qualities.

The implication of these procedures is clearly that Euclidean geometry is a system of pure mathematics, that is, of propositional functions, an uninterpreted system. It is not the elaboration of direct insights into the meaning of space, as it was believed to be for so many centuries. The development of non-Euclidean geometries [6] finally established its character, as did its rewriting in such a fashion as to eliminate the reference to points, lines, and so forth, and to substitute purely abstract symbols.

ANTINOMIES NO THEORETICAL BARRIER TO SCIENCE

The discussion of space has shown the way in which the distinction between an uninterpreted and an interpreted system may be utilized to clarify the antinomies. To say, as Kant did, that reason could prove both sides of the question of the infinity of space turns out to mean nothing more than that differing systems of geometry are capable of logical construction. It ceases to assert a contradiction if no one of them is regarded *a priori* as holding for our world. Such contradictions do prove the power of logic to lay bare possible structures for subsequent experience to explore and decide among. So, far from working to cross purposes, reason and experience form a happy couple when the true function of each is recognized.

The skeptic's criticism

We may note, in concluding, one more traditional critique of science —that of the skeptic. Insofar as skepticism declares the world to be falsified by science, its basis has been discussed at the outset of this chapter. Insofar as it declares the world to be essentially unknowable, it must assume the burden of clarifying its own conception of the truth or reality which it denies we can know. It can do this only by relinquishing its skepticism for

[6] I.e., systems which substituted a contradictory or contrary postulate for one of the Euclidean postulates (the "parallel postulate") and discovered that the results were equally consistent systems.

some positive metaphysical position. Otherwise it is merely a reflection on the limitations of human knowledge. Thus it can say with Protagoras, "Man is the measure of all things," dwell on the flux of the world, recite the long history of human error, and lament the fallibility of man's few senses.

Scientific method can readily admit this part of the skeptic's claims. There is much that will probably not be known, not because it is inherently unknowable, but because it is practically unapproachable, because it is too complex, too difficult to manipulate in any system of mathematics as yet developed, or because the evidence is unavailable and inaccessible. Likewise much that we reckon as known may require revision in the light of further discoveries. A skeptical spirit remains a critical guardian against dogmatism and a sobering influence against arrogance, but a hardened skepticism brings despair and an inability to act decisively.

The method of philosophy

Finally we may ask whether philosophy has a unique method of its own, or relies on the logico-empirical method of science. Much of philosophizing is simply using the tools of logic for the critical clarification of common beliefs and fundamental notions in all fields. From this point of view its scope and purpose, not its method, distinguish philosophy from science. A great part of philosophy is likewise empirical. It involves organizing whatever material from the sciences and history may be relevant for the formulation on our part of a unified attitude towards the world at large and towards men and ourselves. Here again it is not method that is distinctive but purpose. Philosophy is not the product of a special supra-scientific method, but the greatest philosophy has a breadth of vision which is the expression of a wide and mature learning and a comprehensiveness of purpose.

If this is the case, can we now say that scientific method is the path to truth and reality in ordinary life, in science, and in philosophy? This final step brings us to the analysis of the concepts of truth and reality as they are implicit in scientific method.

Chapter 10   SCIENCE, TRUTH, AND REALITY

In the previous chapter we defended the method of science against attacks which accused it of misrepresenting reality or being unable to disclose it. If the argument has been correct, the method of science, with its combination of logical and experiential elements, remains the most reliable way of framing an account of our world. There remains still the task of analyzing the conceptions of truth and reality implicit in the method. For what, it may be asked, is the point of seeking a reliable method if it is not to discover truth and disclose reality? What is the point of a discussion of knowledge if it is not knowledge of what is true and what is real?

The concepts of truth and reality are sometimes used interchangeably; we speak, for example, of discovering the truth about an event or discovering what really happened. But there is a distinction between them which may be simply stated. Truth characterizes opinion—statements are true or false—whereas reality is a name for existence and its characters. Reality is what a true statement talks about.

Science and truth

THEORIES OF TRUTH AND TYPES OF METHOD

Every conception of truth rests basically on some notion of a method by which the truth is to be reached. In intuitionist theory, as we saw above, the truth is an account of the structure of the world, and the way to attain it lies ultimately in direct intellectual grasping or illumination. Another type of theory finds truth to lie in the correspondence of our ideas to the qualities of existence. Locke's position discussed above,[1] is of this type. The method it employs for attaining truth is primarily the use of the senses which are receptive to impressions from objects and record them faithfully; thereafter the activity of mind enters in noting the agreement and disagreement of the ideas that have arisen.

Another type of theory has stressed in its account of truth, the element of *coherence*. Truth is thus said to have an organic character. Now "coherence"

[1] P. 109.

means literally "sticking together," and so truth becomes that body of judgments or propositions that stick together well. At any time a proposition will be called true if it introduces greater coherence into the body of accepted knowledge than would its contradictory. This view claims that no proposition is wholly true or wholly false, since it always coheres with some propositions and may be discrepant with others. There are degrees of truth. This is not skepticism, resting on an inability to decide, but the definite assertion that if truth means coherence, only the whole system can in any proper sense be said to constitute truth. On a coherence theory truth is not so much attained as developed, and the method involved in this process is the activity of mind judging and discriminating, separating coherence from discrepancy and noting the growing system.

The pragmatist approach as elaborated by William James stressed the notion of working satisfactorily as the central element in the analysis of truth. Hence the method of estimating the truth of an idea is essentially evaluative —judging from the point of view of long-range human interests what is good in the way of belief.[2]

THE THEORY OF TRUTH IMPLICIT IN SCIENTIFIC METHOD

Scientific method likewise has a conception of truth which is based upon its method. "The truth" is that body or system of propositions which an ideally successful science would assert. A true account is one reached by the process of objective verification which we have already analyzed. Since this verification is never completed, to assert that a proposition is true means to predict its continued verification, its permanent presence within the body of accepted knowledge.[3] The notion of truth thus functions as an ideal of science, indicating the direction in which it strives and the conditions its assertions must continue to fulfill.

Other methods stress selected phases of scientific method. When the methods implicit in these various theories of the nature of truth are compared with scientific method, each can readily be interpreted as concentration on some selected phase of the scientific process. Thus, as we have seen in our critique of intuition, that method made an avenue to truth out of the element of insight whose importance in scientific method lies in the *suggestion,* not the *validation,* of hypotheses.[4] Similarly, the correspondence theory fas-

[2] See above, p. 97.

[3] Compare the definition given by Charles Peirce, the father of modern pragmatism, in "How to Make Our Ideas Clear," in *Chance, Love and Logic,* ed. by M. R. Cohen, Harcourt, Brace, 1923, pp. 56-7: "The opinion which is fated to be ultimately agreed to by all who investigate, is what we mean by the truth, and the object represented in this opinion is the real."

[4] P. 79.

tens on the appeal to sense-experience and the correspondence of actual observation to anticipated observation. This is indeed a critical phase of scientific method. It is the point at which, when a problem has been formulated and the implications of various hypotheses ascertained, a question may be put to nature with a genuine possibility of a "no" answer as well as a "yes." Again, the coherence theory, if "coherence" is more than a metaphor, stresses the logical or mathematical aspects of scientific method, the fact that observation is guided by theory and that conclusions depend to a large extent on what other assumptions are to be found in the body of accepted knowledge. The correspondence and coherence theories thus stress the observational and logical phases respectively of the method of science, each theory tending to minimize the role of the opposing phase. The pragmatic theory concentrates on the general character of the purposes for which scientific method is employed—its role in solving problems and its application in orienting belief. Science on the other hand formulates its criterion of truth in terms of the method of science as a whole.

The attributes which common usage ascribes to truth are preserved in this conception. Thus truth is ordinarily regarded as *eternal, objective* and *universal*. The pragmatic conception of truth as enunciated by William James made it changing, subjective, and localized, almost private. It seemed to have little in common with what men strive for in the search for truth.

Eternal character of truth. Truth is indeed *eternal*. But the notion of eternity must itself be operationally regarded.[5] To speak of truth as eternal is not necessarily to locate it outside of the changing world. It means instead that continued testing of the proposition's consequences will continually confirm it. Eternal truth is an ideal of stable results on endless testing. Since such completion is impossible, it is sometimes said that truths come and go, or truth changes, or all truth is relative and not absolute, or that truths are relative, truth absolute. Whatever the merit of such formulations, certainly refinement and revision are often required in the generalizations men make.[6] And even singular statements about a fact sometimes turn out to be insufficiently precise in the light of a change in the technique of verifying such assertions, as, for example, in the finer calibration of measuring instruments. Nevertheless there is sufficient evidence for many assertions men make—both of individual events and about the general behavior of things—to warrant calling them true. That is, we may expect that further search for evidence would add to an already extended or impressive confirmation.

Objective character of truth. Truth is also *objective*. But this need not mean that it is an ideal realm spread out like a road to be traveled. It requires that the meaning of truth be such as to be independent of any par-

[5] For an analysis of "eternal" from opposing points of view, see below, pp. 331-33.
[6] Cf. the discussion of laws changing, above, pp. 43-44.

ticular set of verifications, or of reference to any single individual whose "private" truth it should be. Now our analysis shows that an assertion such as "This proposition (p) is true" means that p has consequences capable of verification and that the testing of consequences of p will yield favorable results. None of this depends upon any person's arbitrary choice; nor does the fact that a particular person's perception is involved in his testing render it arbitrary or subjective, for he cannot choose what he will observe. That the meaning of "This proposition (p) is true" has an objective character guarantees the objective character of truth.

Universal character of truth. Again, truth is *universal*. Though it be the truth about an event in which only one person could participate or which only one person could in fact verify, it is still intelligible to ask whether it is true that the experience was *of a certain sort*. This is, in effect, asking for a *universal* of which it is a special case. That truth is universal means simply that the conditions for verification can be stated without reference to any one individual, though in fact it may be the case that only one individual (or no one) satisfied those conditions.

What men expect of knowledge. Truth as we have described it thus possesses the traditional attributes of eternity, objectivity, and universality. The only difference is that these concepts are themselves interpreted in terms of the process of scientific inquiry and the aims men in fact expect science to fulfill. Thus such attributes as eternity, objectivity, and universality express, perhaps in a rather figurative fashion, what men expect of knowledge—that it will actually relieve doubt, that it will be dependable, that prediction on its basis will not go too far astray, that action on its basis will render possible a greater degree of control and the satisfaction of human needs, that agreement among men will be widened and not contracted, and so forth. It is this insight which was so faithfully rendered by Charles Peirce when he phrased his inquiry as the search for the most reliable way of resolving doubt and defined truth in terms of the ultimate outcome of investigation.

Now if truth is to be marked by such characteristics and is to be understood in the context of such aims, it follows that our choice of a method for defining truth is not itself arbitrary. The method is an expression of man's fortunate achievement over many ages in maintaining himself, altering his surroundings to suit his needs, and adjusting himself to changes in his environment. Truth at any time is constituted by the body of results achieved by the method. Method becomes refined as it is tested on results of long standing, and refined method leads to alteration in the body of results. Although the form of scientific or empirical method is constant, any part of it, any of its guiding conceptions, may very well undergo change. In short no portion of the method, no corner of the results should be made a fetish. The reciprocal interaction of methods and results allows for progressive correction suitable to a world in which change is so pervasive a feature.

Science and reality

FACT AND REALITY

The intimate relation of the concepts of truth and reality can be seen readily from the ordinary uses of the term "fact." Thus it is said that the proposition "the rose is in bloom" is true if *it is a fact that* or *it really is the case that* the rose is in bloom. This is taken to mean that there exist *facts* which may be accurately or inaccurately reported.

The meaning of "fact." The notion of *fact* seems a clear one. Surely it is the purpose of science to discover the facts. We test our hypotheses by marshaling the facts and the facts determine the truth of the hypotheses. Difficulties begin to arise, however, as soon as we seek to locate the fact that the rose is now in bloom. The rose will wither, but will the fact that it bloomed here on this day pass away? The event is in time, but the fact is eternal. Does the moving series of events grind out an eternal network of facts which then await the historian's discerning eye? Is it also the case that particular propositions report particular facts, general propositions general facts, affirmative and negative propositions affirmative and negative facts? Then what of true and false propositions? There cannot be false facts; hence true and false must refer to correspondence and non-correspondence of proposition and fact. The common view brings us back to an even more difficult form of the correspondence theory than the one we examined above.

Such an approach to the nature of reality is, in effect, committing a fallacy akin to *reification,* making existent things or entities out of what are abstractions or processes or events. It is as if we were to look in existence for the song which may be sung over and over again, and not be content with the pattern of notes on the page, the cultural habits of training in singing, or the sound waves set up in performing. The fact is like the notes and the singing schools and the sound waves, or like the ideal of the series of songs sung correctly. It need not be something leading a shadowy timeless existence between the two.

Two senses of "fact" can then be distinguished. The distinction can readily be seen in two familiar usages: "It is a fact that . . ." and "Look at the facts." One refers to the accuracy or truth of a statement, the other to the events referred to by the statement. While the first sense corresponds to what we mean by "truth," the second corresponds to what we mean by "reality." In scientific method results are facts in the first sense of the term, and they are presumed to "tell the truth" about facts in the second sense. And "telling the truth" about them means that the results spoken of will continue to be confirmed in any subsequent investigation.

The meaning of "reality." Reality, according to the conception of it implicit in the method of science, is thus disclosed by the outcome of science or represented in the true opinions that are the results of successful science. But it is objective and self-existent. As Charles Peirce has phrased it, the real is "that whose characters are independent of what anybody may think them to be."[7]

Such an account of reality is not far distant from the ordinary conception. Reality is simply the world of things that exist and events that take place, and the qualities, characteristics, and relations that they have to one another. Now if the method of science is indeed the most reliable, the characters of things will be best described in terms of the results the method achieves. This is expressed in the ordinary assertion that science tells us what our world is really like. But in the sense of reality in which it refers to existence and events, all of our life is a "contact" with and a "sharing" of reality. All of the process of scientific inquiry as a human activity is therefore part of reality, and the reference to existence may be seen explicitly in its various steps.

DOES SCIENTIFIC METHOD MAKE ASSUMPTIONS ABOUT REALITY?

These relations between scientific method and reality are sometimes expressed as *assumptions* of scientific method. This formulation, employing "assumption" in the sense of "taken for granted prior to empirical determination," tempts one to raise the further question of the grounds on which such assumptions can be made. This throws the way wide open for some other method—faith or insight—to establish itself by laying the foundations for scientific method. It is therefore important to examine more precisely the specific relation of scientific method to such presumed assumptions. The problem may be sketched briefly by considering three separate questions:

(a) Does scientific method assume that there is a reality to be disclosed?
(b) Does scientific method assume that reality has a particular character?
(c) Does scientific method assume that the results reached by its use "represent" reality?

Does scientific method assume that there is a reality to be disclosed? There is a reference to reality at many points in scientific method. In the first place, scientific method is a mode of procedure or a way of reflection and doing by men. It therefore presupposes men engaged in some inquiry and puzzled by some problem. What they find to be a problem, and the manner in which they approach it, is related to their way of life and to the special emphases of their culture. Some applications of scientific method also require complicated instruments and involve a society of men at a certain level of wealth and industrial production and with certain liberties.

[7] *Op. cit.,* p. 53.

Furthermore, even the individual's utilization of the method involves a reference to existence at almost every stage in the problem. His formulation of the problem entails a language, which is a social product. His selection of a hypothesis and his deduction of consequences implies the acquisition of previous knowledge. To experiment he must handle materials, and he needs sense-organs in order to make observations.

The reference to reality is therefore constant in the operation of scientific method. Reality can hardly be thought of as an assumption of the method; it is not a mere statement whose truth is taken for granted prior to investigation. Remove the reference and there is no problem, no investigator, no phenomena, no observation, no possible answer.

Such reference to reality throughout need not however presuppose any particular type of reality. Fellow-men, the subject-matter which gave rise to the problem, materials handled, sense-organs, and so forth, may be matter or mind or ideas or things or anything else that has been offered as an all-embracing characteristic of the world. The investigation of the character of reality is thus a separate problem.

Does scientific method assume that reality has a particular character? Do the sciences, in their investigations of nature, take for granted that nature is knowable or relatively simple in its operations? It is true that any exercise of scientific method employs some guiding idea, such as looking for the causes of phenomena, looking for laws, or for an account of what occurred. (Some of these notions we have examined in Part One.) But this does not imply any assumption about the world; these guiding ideas rather define the type of inquiry and the kinds of relations to be looked for. If, for example, empirical method is being used to look for causes, it is not necessary to assume *a priori* that every event has a cause. As we saw, this may be offered as a general hypothesis, and the notion of *cause* defined. The rest is an empirical question of the degree to which causes of specific phenomena can in fact be discovered. The character of assumption seems to cling to such broad notions because they apply so widely, and there is always hope for future discovery beyond discoverable present limits. This implies that reality is not chaotic; if it were, scientific method could not be applied. But the discovery that scientific method can be applied is itself an empirical discovery, not merely an assumption. What we have said of *cause* holds equally of the intelligibility of the world. If we define the notion carefully we may then seek to discover whether the world is knowable. Likewise the assumption that nature operates simply means that formulae of a certain type will provide adequate explanations. This again is to be discovered empirically.

The question of the character of reality is thus to be decided by the outcome of scientific inquiry not by the fact of its occurrence. Whether there is an answer to an inquiry cannot be determined in advance. The question is always the empirical one of whether there is a specific answer to a specific question formulated in a certain way.

Does scientific method assume that the results reached by its use "represent" reality? In this question the term "reality" is not being used to refer to things or events as such, not to mere existence which just is, but to the *characters* of existence. For to represent means to show what existence is like, to exhibit its properties. Now the question whether the results of science represent reality in this sense of the term only arises when the method has been successful in producing results. And to say that results have been achieved is already to imply that true opinions have been asserted and have maintained themselves. This means that the criteria of knowledge we have discussed above—dependability, systematic predictability, greater degree of possible control, greater degree of lasting agreement, and so forth—have been satisfied. Hence the only issue that seems still to be involved in the general questions whether the results of science represent reality is whether these criteria are themselves arbitrary or whether we have any reason to believe that reality (the character of existence) satisfies them, so that the scientific results which satisfy them also disclose reality.

Once the question is formulated in this fashion, the answer is likewise apparent. The central point is the meaning of "character" in the phrase "character of existence."[8] If we ask ourselves what, after all, we understand by the term, it becomes apparent that the criteria actually explicate our meaning. To say that things or events have characters is to imply that their behavior, their qualities, their relations, actually exhibit some order, hence that we can depend on things, predict successfully about them, gain greater control over them, widen the area of agreement, achieve stable scientific results, and so forth. The opposite of character is chaos. Once this meaning of "character" is clearly understood, the question whether the results of science represent reality is transformed into the question whether existence in fact has a character or whether it is chaotic. The answer, as we have suggested above, is an empirical one. To say that the results of science represent reality is

[8] The inquiry takes a quite different form if the question concerns itself primarily with the meaning of "representation." Several senses may be distinguished: e.g., the appearance in a mirror represents a person or object because it has observable properties in common with it; the speedometer reading represents the speed of the car, but in a very different sense; an arrow represents the direction in which it points, and words represent objects by common convention; one thing may represent another because it is an effect of it or simply because it is associated with it. Further analysis would deal with the types of terms and constructions employed in scientific work to see which had a direct empirical interpretation, which an indirect one, and which were in some sense purely instrumental. It would be necessary to analyze the use of "models" in scientific work and the role of mathematical operations and formulae, and so forth. Clearly Ohm's law "represents" reality in a sense far different from a mirror image.

thus equivalent to the assertion that in the long history of mankind the method of science has provided the most reliable and systematic account of the dependable features of our world, and that this world has been shown thereby to have dependable features. These discoveries can be made side by side precisely because our criteria of knowledge are identical with our meaning of the "character of existence."

Attempts to introduce a wedge for some non-empirical method in the very framework of science by making a mystery out of the relation of the results of science to reality usually rest on a vague or ambiguous sense of the terms with which we have been dealing. They may fail to distinguish the two senses of "reality"—as existence and as character of existence. Hence they may be reducing reality to a bare x, an unknown by definition, and thus be left with the puzzle how the unknown can be known by science.[9] Or they may misunderstand the nature of meaning, and ask how we know that reality has a given meaning, or if we answer that we are defining the term "reality," they may ask what right we have to legislate a meaning for reality. Actually, however, we have done nothing of the sort. We have simply analyzed the meaning of the term "character of existence" which is one of the senses we find the term "reality" to have in men's usage. But the question whether existence did or did not have a character as so defined was not settled by legislation, by definition, or by verbal operations of any sort. The ultimate test lies in the growth of the sciences and the progress of human knowledge.

[9] It is possible that some of the difficulties raised in this problem may concern the utterly different question of the relation of "properties" or "qualities" and "things" or "events." This is the metaphysical issue of the categories by which our world is to be analyzed, not of the relation of the results of science to existence. Some discussion of the problem of categories will be found below, p. 325 ff.

Part Three

WHAT IS A MAN?

Chapter 11 MAN AS A TWOFOLD BEING

In Parts One and Two we have examined various concepts of explanation and methods proposed for achieving an understanding of our world. In the present part we shall apply these analyses to man himself, in order that understanding may begin at home; for a comprehensive picture of the nature of man is an essential part of any well-rounded philosophy. It provides a fundamental orientation for the estimation of what man can do in this world as well as what he can know and how he may best direct his energies.

The body

Of the various concepts in terms of which man has sought to describe himself—body, soul, mind, self—it is well to begin with the body. For there is considerable agreement on its character.

The career of the body. Man's body is clearly part of the natural world. It moves in that world, comes into contact with other objects in it, exercises itself upon these objects and reacts to them. It is immediately dependent on innumerable phases of its environment. Much is known of the body's chemical composition and cell structure, its complex organs and their mode of functioning. Man's body has not the stability of a rock or an oak, but it frequently manages to satisfy its needs sufficiently to maintain a precarious equilibrium for the greater part of a century. During its life-time it is a constant locus of activity, internal as well as external, of growth and decline, elimination of waste and continual replenishment. Breathing is the plainest mark of its physical reciprocity with the surrounding world, just as from the point of view of perpetuation of the species sexual activity is often regarded as the most dramatic. Upon the breakdown of the body, which is called death, the body eventually loses its complex structure and returns to the dust. It is philosophically helpful, if somewhat disturbing, to compare the body not to a stone but to the flame of a candle, which is constantly fed, constantly in process, but maintains a certain form while the candle and the oxygen last and there are no interfering draughts. Such a conception views the body more as activity than as substance, more as event than as thing.

Our knowledge of the body. There is much about the body which we do not yet know. The operations of the brain, the nervous system, the subtle changes that take place within the body, contain a story whose details are still to be unfolded. There are some types of illness for which no organic basis has been found, and there are many normal activities whose specific bodily basis is unclear.

We do know something about the history of the body. Biologists have long since developed and increasingly confirmed a theory of organic evolution which traces the development of animal forms from lowly unicellular beginnings aeons ago through stages of development represented still today in modified form in the varied types of lower animal life. Man himself, they tell us, first appeared on the earth perhaps a million years ago, in a form closely resembling the ape-like ancestry from which he and his gorilla and chimpanzee cousins are sprung. Modern man, with his amazingly expanded and complex brain, his fully erect posture and child-like, light-boned face, is the baby of creation. *Homo sapiens*—the wise species of man, as we so flatteringly call him—has lived in Europe a mere 25,000 years, and the first traces of him thus far found elsewhere are but little older. Embryologists, biochemists, and biophysicists tell us an increasingly detailed story of how life begins and grows for each individual. They are expanding the familiar account of bodily growth with an exciting tale of the many physical and chemical factors which serve to control and direct it. And science is turning to careful research into some of the mysteries of life itself, creating organic syntheses in the laboratory, and exploring the nature of elusive viruses which may prove to represent a transition between the inert and the living.

Do the higher functions require a special explanation? Such a picture of the body seems, however, to describe only a very small part of what man actually is. What about his thinking, feeling, willing? Do music, religion, science and philosophy have natural causes and solve material problems? Certainly they are not usual animal activities. How are we to understand this aspect of man and human living? Are mental and spiritual phenomena a separate part of man, with an independent existence and career? What is the relation of man's mind and spirit to the body which lives and moves and breathes in such familiar fashion? If we are to understand man's position in the universe and learn how we are to treat him and his ways, both to deal with our fellows and to know, control, and develop ourselves, we must find answers to these questions.

The theory which has long dominated the western philosophic tradition and has had important consequences in the way men regard themselves, their world, their knowledge, and their conduct, has seen man as a twofold being, whose soul or mind is of an essence quite distinct from that which constitutes his body. The various vital and mental phenomena distinguishing the living man are taken to be wholly or in part "due to the operation within him of something which is of a nature different from that of the body, an animating principle generally, but not necessarily or always, conceived as an immaterial or individual being or soul."[1]

So pervasive is the dualistic approach that even attempts to override it have started from and been colored by it. Such attempts have sought for the most part to reduce man to one of the two elements of the dualistic approach, to view him as a purely bodily or a purely mental or spiritual being. Only in modern naturalistic or materialistic approaches has thinking about the nature of man been fully emancipated from the dualistic tradition. This has meant a re-examination of man's nature in its entirety as part of the natural world and a reconsideration of thinking and feeling, willing, hoping, and striving as phenomena to be explored on their own right and explained in natural terms.

Body and soul

The most familiar dualistic position is one of the longest and most widely held philosophic traditions. It conceives of man as primarily a soul temporarily lodged in the body. There are varying conceptions of the relations between the body and the soul. The body may be regarded as a prison in which the soul is lodged. It may be a material vehicle provided for the use of the immaterial soul in steering its way around the natural world. It may be a slave to do the bidding of the soul. In any case the body is transitory and merely instrumental; the soul is what we "really" are.

In such an account all the activities of man which are customarily called "higher" belong to the soul. The soul is responsible for all thinking, willing, and feeling. It is the initial source of all movement. Though it may use bodily instrumentalities, activity is primarily to be characterized as the soul's.

TYPES OF SOUL THEORY

There have, of course, been numerous and varied interpretations of the nature of such body-encumbered souls. The most familiar tradition, found in the Christian doctrine, conceives the soul as a single, indivisible unit, immaterial and eternal and immortal. On the other hand some great thinkers have held that each of us is but a fragment of a world-soul, temporarily separated from its parent being and striving to return to it. The Buddhist concept of Nirvana embodies such an approach.

[1] William McDougall, *Body and Mind, A History and Defense of Animism*, 6th ed., Methuen, 1923, p. viii.

Sometimes there are held to be several entities instead of one soul; one, for example, may be the vital principle which gives life to the body, and another the entirely body-free spirit or mind which is concerned only with the highest functions. Plutarch believed in two entities, reason and soul; reason was as superior to soul as soul to body. Both left the body together on its death and a second death took place later in which reason was separated from soul.[2] Plato and Aristotle discussed at length the various parts of the soul and their inter-relations.

Types of theories of the indwelling soul may be illustrated by a brief consideration of the Platonic view, the Christian doctrine, and the world-soul theory.

The Platonic concept. In Platonic theory the nature of the soul is primarily intellectual. Its real home is the eternal. While it is tied to the body, it tries to free itself by sharing in the Ideas, the eternal objects of knowledge.[3] Bodily contacts provide the stimuli which gradually awaken the slumbering soul. Sensation is the crutch it leans on till it rises to independent contemplation of the eternal. The more the body's passions are stilled, the more active the mind can be. In this sense Plato (in the *Phaedo*) paradoxically calls the true philosopher a lover of death. Since complete knowledge cannot be achieved by the soul embodied, the true philosopher must yearn for the eventual freeing of the soul. Death is regarded as a release from bondage. The soul existed prior to its embodiment—in fact knowledge during life is really recollection—and will continue after the death of the body.

The soul, striving towards the eternal, is in Plato's system the master of the body. True happiness lies in the welfare of the soul. Hence the cultivation of the soul is man's prime object in this life. Disparagement of the body does not, however, lead to its neglect. Great attention is paid to the body's training in order that proper habits may be developed to serve as instruments for the soul.

The Christian conception. In the Christian conception each soul is individual and constitutes a complete and unitary being. It will not perish on the body's death but will continue eternally as an individual entity. As in the Platonic view, care of the soul is man's primary concern. In the medieval outlook the world revolved around man as a center. It was a stage on which he enacted a dramatic role and by his actions brought eternal happiness or eternal damnation to his immortal soul.

[2] Many primitive peoples have similar beliefs. In dealing with the concept of the soul in the western tradition it is important to remember that the concept itself is not an original contribution of Greek philosophy, but part of a wide religious heritage. For a discussion of soul theories among primitive people in many parts of the world and of theories of their origin, see Ruth Benedict, "Religion," in Boas and others, *General Anthropology,* Heath, 1938, and A. A. Goldenweiser, *Early Civilization,* Knopf, 1922, Part III.

[3] See above, p. 14.

The dominant note in the medieval synthesis was the eternal. The cost of all conduct was reckoned in terms of its eternal consequences. Disputes about the origin of the soul (whether created by God for each child at birth or generated from the parental souls) and difficulties about bodily resurrection, although presenting genuine problems in the attempt to elaborate a consistent theory, occupied a secondary place by comparison with the essential moral content in the Catholic doctrine of Heaven and Hell.

Just as in this view the rewards and punishments for man's worldly conduct were everlasting, so the proper content of his values was the eternal. The less a man clung to the things of this life, the more virtuous he was, the more scope he gave to the exercise of the soul. An occasional result of this disparagement of the body was the elaboration of asceticism and the humiliation of the body. Bodily functions—sex primarily—were declared evils and were made the objects of intense restraint. Since the body was seen as an impediment to the soul—whether as a prison or a source of temptation—the breach was widened between nature (in the sense of the material world) and spirit. Not only was spirit the source of all value but nature was the enemy of spirit and value.

The conception of the soul as an individual entity in Christian doctrine sometimes gave support to individualism in ethical theory. In the first place every man was held to have worth as an individual irrespective of his powers and accomplishments. This conception of the dignity of man is seen today, for example, in the Catholic Church's formally enunciated opposition to the doctrine of superior and inferior races which would make a man's worth dependent on his race. In the second place, every man's decisions were held to be his own. He was reckoned responsible for them; hence the stress on conscience and the horror of sin. Religious individualism was also influential in the development of democratic political theory.

The world-soul theory. The world-soul theory—the view of the individual soul as a fragment of a world soul—often takes a mystical form. The soul is said to have been separated in some way from the original unity; its whole effort is a striving to return once more to that larger soul of which it is a part. The body is either a temporary alien residence or an expression of the world soul at a lower level than individual souls. In such a view the entire material world is sometimes declared to be an expression of soul. In any case man's nature is essentially incomplete. Our finite nature is said to be the source of all imperfection so that true salvation lies in the loss of selfhood, the complete blending of the individual with the greater all-embracing spirit. As we suggested in the discussion of Intuition [4] this view is modeled upon those intense human experiences during the course of which consciousness of self disappears. In the individualistic western tradition this theory has

---

[4] See above, p. 77.

been less popular than in the Orient. In the Hindu belief, for example, the object of all life's striving is Nirvana: a state of self-effacement and cessation of desire in which a man, having disciplined his body to complete self-control, achieves unity with the Source of all Being and complete dissolution of the individual self.

THE GROUP-MIND THEORY

In the western tradition we do find occasional views that the individual self is incomplete and gains some completion in a larger self—a sort of communal soul of which the individual is a part. These doctrines share some of the mysticism of the world-soul view, although sometimes their language suggests that the notion of the communal soul is largely metaphoric. Thus it is said that the individual is merely a molecule in the body of the state, or that every group has a personality of its own, that there is a kind of objective mind or communal purpose. The organic analogy in politics—that the state is like an organism—really implies and sometimes states such a view. Men are called upon to recognize their incompleteness and to admit that there may be duties and sacrifices destructive of personal interests—as well as social restriction of personal liberties—which nevertheless represent their *real universal* as distant from their *apparent personal* interests.

Ethical and social usages. It is interesting to note some of the ethical and social usages that have been associated with group-mind theories. In some types of idealist theory [5] a group-mind approach embodies an attempt to break through an egoistic or possibly cynical individualism and give a character of reality to the object of loyalties. In fascist philosophy, group-personality theory represents an attempt to dislodge liberal individualism and justify the state's insistence on absolute obedience from its citizens. The theory that every group has a personality has, however, also been used to establish independent rights against state control. Thus in American legal history the claim that a corporation is a person was in effect a demand for the right to sue in federal courts under the 14th amendment and a means (through the protection of the due-process clause) to prevent states from interfering with the undertakings of corporations. In Laski's earlier work on sovereignty, on the other hand, the theory of group personality was a cry against the centralized authority of the state and a plea for free play for trade unions, etc.[6]

The nature of group-phenomena. The theory of group personality is at its strongest when attacking its individualist antithesis. Society, it is said, cannot

---

[5] E.g., that of Royce. See below, pp. 411-16.

[6] Harold J. Laski, *Authority in the Modern State,* Yale University Press, 1927, and *The Foundations of Sovereignty,* Yale University Press, 1931.

be merely a collection of individuals. How can language, morals, law be merely the work of indviduals as such? No man ever invented English—it was the work of the English people as a whole. Similarly we have duties to the community, and we pledge allegiance to the state. Thus "community" and "state" are not abstractions; they have some concrete personality which has a reality of its own. The same holds for particular groups. An ardent alumnus recognizes his loyalty to his college as something greater than loyalty to a particular set of other individuals. Sociologists have frequently described how men in a mob behave differently from the way in which each would behave were he acting alone. Some have phrased this as the "mob-spirit" gripping them and have meant it literally. The theory asserts the existence of what is essentially a soul, with many of the properties and causal powers which are attributed to the individual soul in the western religious tradition.

We must of course recognize that the organization of men living in groups need not have the properties that individuals would have living alone. But to speak of a group-mind is to talk about ghosts. It is no mystery but an obvious fact that men living together stimulate and affect each other. The interaction of men over a long period in which many minute changes occur and grow into great differences can well explain the growth of distinct languages, religions, legal institutions, and moral systems. Certainly there should be no more wonder at sharp differences and developed group characteristics in the social realm than biologists now feel for such phenomena in the animal world.

The examples given above of both the individual soul theories and the collective soul theories are simply a few illustrations from the vast store of men's beliefs that the body is only a temporary dwelling for a more enduring spirit. By and large these beliefs have been tied in with the religious outlook. But the theory of the soul as a separate principle necessary to explain life has also been found within the scientific framework. Modern Vitalism is the best example of a view that seeks to restore to the soul or some similar entity or principle the functions of which the western scientific tradition has increasingly robbed it.

MODERN VITALISM

Vitalism as a philosophical theory is in many respects similar to the indwelling soul theories. It claims that the phenomena of life, when carefully studied, are seen to be of a special kind, and cannot be reduced in a process of explanation to physical and chemical phenomena. The latter are characterized by machine-like regularity. Press the appropriate lever and the wheels begin to turn. Mix the correct quantities of hydrogen and oxygen under proper conditions, and the outcome is water. Living phenomena, on the other hand, reveal not only greater complexity but also novelty and spontaneity. The behavior of living things is often unpredictable. You cannot tell what a man is going to say to you next in conversation, much less what will be the outcome when he sets to philosophizing. People working, planning, falling in love, learning are not just machines going through their paces. Novelty and unpredictability are not merely characteristic of higher human creativity but run through all phenomena of life.

These features express something more than chance combinations. There is a *purposive* character to life. Its processes involve fitting means into patterns of activity which achieve ends. Living things are *organic,* with the parts working together toward the harmonious operation of the whole. This is manifested in the division of labor in the growing individual organism. It is found in the way the body undergoes all sorts of minute changes to fit it for typical situations—for example, in resisting disease, or when a man's anger mounts. This is a complex *adjustment,* not mechanical action. It is revealed most clearly in the phenomena of consciousness, but is not, of course, limited to that domain.

According to Vitalism, this *adaptive* or *purposive* nature of life is a fresh principle not to be found in mechanical explanation. In its contemporary forms Vitalism has to a large extent been on the defensive. Faced with the growth of mechanistic explanation which was enhanced by the prestige of science, it took refuge in the domains which mechanism had scarcely entered. In stressing the inadequacy of mechanical explanation, Vitalists deny that the failures of mechanism are due merely to lack of present knowledge. They affirm the need for recognizing a positive principle which shall guarantee the independent character of vital and mental phenomena. Writers like McDougall carry the analysis of the purposive principle throughout the whole range of living creatures down to elementary organisms. Bergson speaks of the *élan vital* as characterizing all life (and ultimately constituting reality in general). Driesch uses the term "entelechy" to designate the purposive principle.

Objections to Vitalism. The usual objections to Vitalism are of two sorts. One rests on a faith in the ultimate success of causal explanation in physicochemical terms. It points to the growth of the physical and biological sciences, and to the way in which biophysics and biochemistry are attacking the hitherto unclear borderlines of the physical and the vital. The second objection rests on logical grounds. It claims that even if we grant the qualities pointed to by the Vitalists—adjustment, novelty, and so forth—the conclusion is merely that we require *fresh categories of description.* It does not mean that some separate entity must be assumed as a carrier for those qualities, or some vague principle as an independent reality. Thus even if fresh categories such as *purpose* prove requisite for biology, psychology, or sociology, they need not be construed in dualistic fashion.

We may illustrate this latter answer to the Vitalist by E. B. Holt's treatment of the physiology of wishes.[7] He uses the example of a hypothetical organism endowed with two eye-spots and two fins. When light hits the left spot the right fin is set in motion and the organism veers towards the left. As a result the light will hit the right spot too and the left fin will begin to move. The path of motion with both fins in action will be in a straight line in a forward direction. This is a mechanistic picture in terms of cause. It describes behavior in terms of the succession and combination of elementary interactions within the organism as a response to stimuli impinging upon it. On the other hand, Holt points out, an account of the same behavior could be phrased in purposive terms as *motion toward the light*. Such an account describes behavior in terms of the whole organism and as a response to some object or fact of the environment.

In this and comparable analyses, the sharp distinction between the mechanical and the purposive—so often drawn as a contrast between the *push* in causality and the *pull* or *attraction* in purpose—is translated into a difference of modes of describing behavior in familiar scientific terms. On such an analysis—if it is consistently carried out and supplemented by a theory of thinking in order to be applicable to human purpose—the ground for ascribing a distinct principle to the purposive disappears, even though in some contexts the purposive description may prove the more useful.[8] Such a solution in terms of merely varying modes of description is, of course, an extreme one. In the criticism of mechanistic theories and in the account of a naturalistic theory in subsequent chapters we shall see that it is possible to achieve the same result against the Vitalistic contention while making greater allowance for qualitative differences in different forms of behavior. Nevertheless the possibility of the extreme position shows that dualism is not logically required by the facts of novelty.[9]

Body and mind

The approach we have just examined, which was concerned with the discovery of man's real nature in his soul, personal or group, or in the special character of vital phenomena, represents only one of the two major strands in the dualistic tradition. Another dualistic approach focuses attention more on the phenomena of consciousness or the mental side of man, and phrases its dualism in terms of body and *mind* rather than body and

[7] *The Freudian Wish and Its Place in Ethics,* Holt, 1915, Chapter II.
[8] See below, pp. 183-85.
[9] See also the analysis of novel qualities, above, p. 60 ff.

soul. The pattern of such analysis was set in the 17th century, especially in the philosophy of Descartes, and this is the framework within which philosophical dualism has since then largely operated.

The difference between the two formulations is of historical significance. The body played a very subordinate part in the conception of man offered by the soul theories—at most it held a junior partnership in the understanding of the human being. With the growth of scientific knowledge about nature, however, it rapidly worked its way up and threatened to dominate the enterprise of explaining man. The formulation of the problem of man's nature as that of the relation of body and mind thus represents a sharp line drawn to limit the growth of mechanism. But at the same time this formulation was a retreat; for it involved surrendering those vital phenomena which were not conscious (and which the soul theory had interpreted as part of the activity of soul) to the domain of the body. So vast was this new territory that from the point of view of the history of science Descartes was advancing, not retarding, mechanism.

CARTESIAN DUALISM

The Cartesian view (that of Descartes) held that mind and matter are both *substances* ("a thing which exists in such a way as to stand in need of nothing beyond itself in order to its existence"[10]). Literally speaking, Descartes points out, God is the only substance; both mind and body are created substances, but they are both substances in the same sense, hence of equal standing. The essense of matter is spatial extension, while the essence of mind is thought.[11] Matter is inert, mind is dynamic; matter is spatial, mind does not occupy space; matter requires to be set in motion, mind is spontaneous. Among living things much can be explained in mechanical or physical terms. Animals, for example, Descartes takes to be automata, and their apparent passions merely mechanical transformations. In man, however, thought enters and mechanical explanation can no longer suffice, for this is something whose essence is entirely different.

Descartes' interactionism. Having decided that man is a twofold being, Descartes had next to see how the two substances get along together in a single man. Here his approach is very similar to the ordinary view of the relation of body and mind. Each of them he held to be capable of affecting the other. (This is called an *interaction* theory.) Mental phenomena may

[10] Descartes, *The Principles of Philosophy*, trans. by John Veitch, Everyman's Library, Part I, §LI.

[11] "By the word thought, I understand all that which so takes place in us that we of ourselves are immediately conscious of it; and, accordingly, not only to understand, to will, to imagine, but even to perceive, are here the same as to think." *Op. cit.*, Part I, §IX.

have physical consequences and physical phenomena may have mental consequences. This may be represented diagrammatically as follows (where mental events are placed above the line and physical events below):

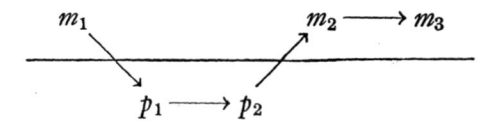

$$m_1 \searrow \qquad m_2 \rightarrow m_3$$
$$\underline{\qquad\qquad\qquad\qquad\qquad\qquad}$$
$$\qquad \searrow \quad \nearrow$$
$$\qquad p_1 \rightarrow p_2$$

For example, my desire to write this chapter (m_1—mental phenomenon) causes me to get up very early (p_1—physical movement) which in turn places my body in the chill morning air, affecting its condition (p_2—physical phenomenon) which in turn dampens my spirits (m_3—mental phenomenon), which in turn leads me to think of using this example (m_3—mental phenomenon).

Objections to interactionism. The usual objections to an interactionist theory arise from its underlying dualism. If mind and body are entirely different substances how can they affect one another? To bring about physical effects the mental cause must add energy to the physical. Does this entail abandoning the belief in the law of conservation of energy according to which the sum total of physical energy in the world is constant? Again, there must be some meeting-point in causation. But how can the immaterial meet the material? If in space, it ceases to be immaterial. If not in space then how can the material be involved, whether to affect or be affected?

Descartes' attempt to overcome this difficulty was to specify a point in the body where mind and body meet; he suggested the pineal gland as the point where the mind exercised itself upon the brain and nervous system and in turn was influenced by the body! Such a solution, however, merely transferred the general problem to the pineal gland, making it a question of the relation of the mind to this part of the body.

The Occasionalist retreat. In their attempt to overcome this difficulty some of Descartes' followers frankly recognized that the question of mind-body relation becomes a miracle on Descartes' dualistic premise. Now a miracle is literally the work of God and, in the theory which they developed, God's intervention is required to bring about the appropriate physical or mental phenomenon when a phenomenon of different type has preceded it in apparent causal relation. (Some even went so far as to deny that the physical could act on the physical without God's efficient causation.) God's intervention is alone causal on this view, and the apparent cause is really only the *occasion* of the apparent effect. Hence the doctrine was called *Occasionalism*.[12]

---

[12] This view was advocated by Malebranche, Geulincx, and other followers of Descartes.

Locke finds no difficulty in interactionism. On the other hand, John Locke finds no problem involved in the interaction of mind and body. Like Descartes, Locke treats spirit and matter as ultimately disparate substances on an equal footing. Just as matter is a *substratum* we assume for the sensible qualities that affect us from without, so spirit is a substratum for the internal operations of thinking, knowing, willing, and so forth—a kind of pin-cushion to hold them up.[13] These substances serve the double function of *supporting* the properties or ideas which are said to inhere in them, and providing a constant identity for the thing or self as the properties or ideas change. Locke is emphatic on the point that we know as much—or rather as little—about spirit as we do about matter.[14] "So that, in short, the idea we have of spirit, compared with the idea we have of body, stands thus: The substance of spirit is unknown to us; and so is the substance of body equally unknown to us. Two primary qualities or properties of body, viz., solid coherent parts and impulse, we have distinct clear ideas of: so likewise we know and have distinct clear ideas of two primary qualities or properties of spirit, viz., thinking, and a power of action; i.e., a power of beginning or stopping several thoughts or motions."

Locke therefore thinks that the production of motion by spirit is no more mysterious than the production of motion by impulse among bodies. Less so, Locke says, because the mind every day gives us ideas of an active power of moving of bodies; whereas two bodies placed next to one another at rest never give us an idea of the power of one to move the other. How both physical impulse and mental power of initiating motion operate to produce a result, we have no idea, says Locke, and he appears content with that. Locke's is thus a thorough dualism, whose impartiality as between matter and spirit rests upon having reduced all the problems of their nature and relation to an equal state of ignorance.

PARALLELISM

A possible alternative, if the Cartesian premise of the separate nature of mind and body was not to be abandoned, was simply to surrender the interaction of mind and body. The theory called *Parallelism* takes this step. Diagrammatically we may represent it thus:

$$\frac{m_1 \longrightarrow m_2 \longrightarrow m_3 \longrightarrow}{p_1 \longrightarrow p_2 \longrightarrow p_3 \longrightarrow}$$

[13] This analogy is suggested by Bertrand Russell, *Religion and Science*, Holt, 1935, Chapter 5.
[14] *An Essay Concerning the Human Understanding*, Book II, Chapter 23, §30.

As compared to interactionism it contains a marked shift of emphasis. Its concern is no longer with the temporal succession of different-level phenomena—e.g., m_1 (a man's anger) causes p_2 (his striking someone else)—but with their *concomitance,* that is, the way in which phenomena on different levels go together. Thus m_1 (a man's anger) causes m_2 (the purposive mental element in his aiming and exerting will in striking), but p_1 (the physical conditions of anger—increased blood-pressure, contraction of muscles, etc.,—occurring together with m_1) causes p_2 (the physical striking-activity occurring together with m_2). From this point of view the theory contains a concealed mechanistic premise—that for every identifiable mental phenomenon there is a unique physical concomitant.

The obvious difficulty with a parallelistic theory is, of course, why there should be so precise a parallelism at all. Why should the succession of bodily phenomena and mental phenomena go side by side? The analogy of two clocks keeping the same time is often employed to illustrate the view, and some have held to the consequence of the analogy—that body and mind were "set" together in some divine pre-established harmony. Others, like Spinoza, abandoned the theory of two substances and treated the mental and physical as two attributes of a single substance. The parallelism nevertheless remained for the attributes.

TRANSITION TO SUBJECTIVISM

A still different development took its origin from the theory of knowledge that Descartes associated with his theory of mind. It is important to note this line of thought because it was soon to subvert entirely the foundations of Cartesian dualism.

When Descartes began to examine men's standard equipment of ideas to see which were trustworthy, he found that few of them were beyond doubt. He accordingly made doubt a principle of reflection to see if anything would withstand it. An interesting account of his progress is found in his *Meditations* in which he gradually strips away all presumed truths which rest upon perception (because perception sometimes yields illusions), all mathematical propositions (because he has thought others in error although they believed they had perfect knowledge, so that he too might be mistaken), and all religious assertions. Finally he even supposes for the sake of argument that instead of a benign deity watching over the world, some demon is busily engaged in constant successful attempts to deceive man. What knowledge then remains? Descartes finds that there is still knowledge of his own existence as a thinking being. For if he is being deceived at least there is a *he* who is being deceived. That is how he reaches his fundamental tenet "I think, therefore I am." And by an examination of this indubitable proposition he hopes to find the criteria of knowledge. The conclusion he reaches is that when ideas are so clear and distinct that they cannot be doubted by the scrupulously inquiring mind, they give us genuine knowledge. His previous difficulties, he concludes, came from lack of restraint in affirming to be clear what was not so; for example, when it was clear that he had an idea of the stars he should have affirmed no more than that he had the idea, not that the stars existed. By employing this criterion and by reasoning from the data that it yields Descartes establishes the existence of God.[15] Adding to this the proposition that God is not a deceiver he rapidly restores the knowledge of the world which he had stripped away.

But the problems he had raised were not so easily disposed of. He had questioned the existence of the world of matter—the external world—and the truth of human perceptions. Only his mind had remained undoubted. This stamped the pattern of a great deal of subsequent epistemological inquiry. Mind had been severed from the world: how could it be reunited in knowledge? How do *I* (taken for granted) gain knowledge that is reliable of the existence and character of a world outside me? And with such a formulation there soon developed a theory that there is no "outside" world. To this view and the conception of man it implied, we turn in the next chapter.

[15] For this argument, see below, pp. 347-48.

Chapter 12 MAN AS ULTIMATELY MENTAL

Berkeley's theory of reality

"Some truths there are," says Berkeley,[1] "so near and obvious to the mind, that a man need only open his eyes to see them. Such I take this important one to be, to wit, that all the choir of heaven and furniture of the earth, in a word all those bodies which compose the mighty frame of the world, have not any subsistence without a mind, that their *being* (esse) is to be perceived or known; that consequently so long as they are not actually perceived by me, or do not exist in my mind or that of any other *created spirit,* they must either have no existence at all, *or else subsist in the mind of some eternal spirit....*"

This is indeed a startling thesis. The whole world that appears to a man to be external to him is really in some sense constructed out of his consciousness—his sensations, feelings, images, etc. All these Berkeley calls *ideas,* not in the Platonic sense of universals, but in the sense of particular impressions. In fact Berkeley attacks the view that there are universal or abstract ideas and regards a universal as a sort of blurred image, like the one we would get by imagining a triangle which was neither scalene, isosceles, nor equilateral. Man is thus ultimately a mind or spirit, engaged in having ideas, and out of these as building-blocks he fashions a picture which he calls his knowledge of things and their behavior. If there were no mind there would be no ideas, hence no things.[2]

---

[1] George Berkeley, *Principles of Human Knowledge,* VI.

[2] In Lewis Carroll's *Through the Looking-Glass,* Chapter 4, Alice is warned by Tweedledum and Tweedledee not to wake the Red King:

"He's dreaming now," said Tweedledee: "and what do you think he's dreaming about?"

Alice said, "Nobody can guess that."

"Why, about *you!*" Tweedledee exclaimed, clapping his hands triumphantly. "And if he left off dreaming about you, where do you suppose you'd be?"

"Where I am now, of course," said Alice.

"Not you!" Tweedledee retorted contemptuously. "You'd be nowhere. Why, you're only a sort of thing in his dream!"

"If that there King was to wake," added Tweedledum, "you'd go out—bang!—just like a candle!"

HIS INTERPRETATION OF BODY

But what of man's body? Even if he is a spirit or mind, is not his body part of an external world? No, is Berkeley's answer. Like all other things in the world what we call the body is merely a collection of our ideas and memories. For, after all, a man's experience of his body rests upon observation, and observation is merely having ideas in definite order and combinations. Even the most refined knowledge of anatomy and physiology is ultimately nothing more. Nor is Berkeley perturbed by the obvious objection that ideas or sensations themselves depend upon the body and its sense-organs. This simply means for him that one set of ideas is conjoined with another in experience (that is, in the activity of a mind). The one set we call sensations, the other in a more roundabout way, the observation of physical conditions.

General denial of matter. Berkeley's denial of the existence of an external body is part of his general denial of the existence of matter. This view of his embodied a belief that the notion of matter served no useful theoretical purpose, and was in addition an obnoxious conception. Berkeley is quite frank about his reason for wanting to disprove the existence of matter: "How great a friend material substance hath been to atheists in all ages, were needless to relate. All their monstrous systems have so visible and necessary a dependence on it, that when this corner-stone is once removed, the whole fabric cannot choose but fall to the ground; insomuch that it is no longer worth while to bestow a particular consideration on the absurdities of every wretched sect of atheists." [3]

His critique of Locke's dualism. Berkeley sought to establish his position by a critique of Locke's dualism. Locke distinguishes between primary and secondary qualities. Primary qualities—extension, figure, motion, rest, solidity, number—inhere in material substance; secondary qualities such as sounds, colors, tastes and the like, are merely powers arising from these primary qualities, powers which enable things to cause certain ideas in our minds.[4] Berkeley argues that if secondary qualities do not resemble anything existing without the mind, the same must be true of all alleged primary qualities. The relativity of temperature to the state of the hand that feels it is admittedly ground for considering hot and cold secondary qualities. Why should not the relativity of shape to the eye at different positions likewise be a reason for declaring figure secondary? Similarly with the relativity of motion and rest; and so forth. Berkeley refuses to distinguish between qualities and ideas. He concludes that both are subjective, being de-

[3] *Principles of Human Knowledge*, XCII.
[4] For a fuller exposition of Locke's position, see Chapter 8 above.

pendent on a perceiving mind. The very relation of resemblance that Locke sought between ideas and qualities is found meaningless. An idea, says Berkeley, can be like nothing else than another idea.

Berkeley states several grounds for his objection to the notion of matter. In the first place we have no clear idea of it; Locke had himself admitted it was vague. Again, matter had been invoked by Locke as a support for qualities; but if all so-called qualities are really ideas, then a material substance in which they may inhere is clearly unnecessary. Furthermore, no intelligible account can be given of the way in which matter can act upon spirit to cause ideas; defenders of matter themselves find it incomprehensible. Berkeley therefore brands matter as a meaningless and useless concept, and concludes that the contents of the world (ideas) are produced by mind or spirit, the single substance of the universe. The world as Berkeley pictures it thus consists of minds and their ideas.

Not strict solipsism. Berkeley's view up to the point to which we have expounded it, threatens to reduce the whole world to facts of consciousness in *my* mind. The stress is on the first person. Not *your* mind, because the only evidence I can have for your existence is my observation of you, and these observations, like everything else, can be analyzed as a complex of my ideas. Such a position, to which Berkeley's theory seems to point, is called *Solipsism*.

But Berkeley was not really interested in a metaphysical egoism which would crowd the world into his own ego. He wanted to eliminate material substance but leave the contents of the world the same. People would continue to be many, not conglomerations of his ideas; there would still be bread to eat, but it would have a spiritual flavor.

HIS THEORY OF SPIRIT

God as source of ideas. Berkeley's insistence that all knowledge consists of associations of ideas and that all ideas are mental realities is not therefore the end of his account. He goes on to explain that we find in our experience two kinds of ideas. One set is flickering, less vivid, inconstant—these are the images we conjure up when, as we say, our eyes are shut; they are the work of *our own* minds. The second set is stable, vivid, constant; we cannot choose what ideas we shall have on opening our eyes. They are, therefore, not the work of our minds, but since they are mental in character, differing only in degree from the ideas we conjure up, they must be the work of an infinitely greater Mind, which we call God. The world as we ordinarily know it consists therefore of ideas existing in God's mind. Things are God's constant perceptions, and thus abide even when we do not perceive them. An objective reference is thus given to knowledge, and a reality provided in place of the "external" world which science may describe. Thus laws of nature which scientists discover are simply God's habits in having ideas.[5] On the relation of our individual minds and the infinite Mind which is God, Berkeley throws little light. In fact he spends more energy disposing of matter than in establishing a clear conception of spirit.

How the mind knows itself. The core of Berkeley's radical treatment of man thus lies in his denial that the body has other than a spiritual reality. A man's body is a complex of ideas in God's mind. A man's mind is what he essentially is—a spiritual substance. Berkeley had some difficulty with the question of how the mind knows itself. For he had argued that all knowledge consists of ideas and the mind knows only ideas. Must the mind, then, itself be an idea? Moreover, Berkeley had maintained that ideas are inactive and that their existence consists only in being perceived, whereas spirit is essentially active and its existence consists in perceiving and thinking. Must spirit then remain essentially unknowable? If so, how would we know of its existence? Berkeley resorted to the view that although we have no idea of spirit we have a *notion* of it—presumably because we are spirits. Thus we are not wholly ignorant of what we are.

Hume's theory

HIS ANALYSIS OF MIND

Hume, seizing upon these points, offered the same critique of spiritual substance that Berkeley had given of material substance. Spirit, Hume asserts, is as gratuitous an assumption as a substratum for ideas as matter was for qualities. Ideas (or "impressions," as Hume generally spoke of them, reserving the term "ideas" for the copies of impressions which we have in memory and imagination) congregate according to laws of their own. Nor is a spiritual substance needed to provide an identity of the self. Man is a bundle of perceptions; any unity of experience, any personal identity, is due to a clustering of experience by association according to contiguity, resemblance, and causation. "The mind is a kind of theater, where several perceptions successively make their appearance; pass, repass, glide away, and mingle in an infinite variety of pictures and situations. There is properly no *simplicity* in it at one time, nor *identity* in different, whatever natural pro-

[5] Thus there is science since God's habits show sufficient regularity. There would be no science if they appeared arbitrary or even if they were so complex that our minds could not grasp a repeatable pattern. For example if God made it a rule to imprint continuously variegated impressions so that recurrence of an impression was spaced by exactly 1000 years, then science would be a divine prerogative, not a human one.

pension we may have to imagine that simplicity and identity. The comparison of the theater must not mislead us. They are the successive perceptions only, that constitute the mind; nor have we the most distant notion of the place where these scenes are represented, or of the materials of which it is composed." [6]

Man a chain of impressions and ideas. Man emerges from Hume's analysis as nothing but a chain of impressions and ideas. He is not a mind in Berkeley's sense, because spiritual substance has been dispensed with. Nor is he a body, because Hume follows Berkeley in the elimination of matter and in regarding things as clusters of impressions. But since impressions and ideas retain even in Hume the flavor of the *mental,* it is appropriate to classify Hume among those who analyze man as ultimately mental.

Why we cannot look beyond impressions. Hume's reasons for refusing to allow a man to look beyond impressions either for a body or a spirit are, of course, more general than their application to man alone would indicate. They are ingrained in his theory which is so constructed that a search beyond impressions and their order becomes meaningless. There can, for example, be no question of *correspondence* between impressions and an outside reality, because our impressions are direct experience, not *representative* of anything else. Nor can one on Hume's theory look beyond experience (in the sense of impressions) for some reality to serve as the *cause* of experience, nor with this intent ask *why* there should be habitual association of ideas or recurrence of impressions. For on Hume's own analysis of causation,[7] to ask for a cause is to look for other impressions with which the particular phenomenon is habitually associated. Hence no such inquiry can, without becoming meaningless, look for a reality beyond experience. Finally, if one were to surrender any attempt to find a reality beyond, but insist that there must be something, even though we cannot know its character, Hume would regard the known existence of an *unknowable* as a meaningless idea.

CRITIQUE OF HUME'S THEORY

Hume's views have had great influence in both philosophical and scientific circles. It is not, however, the subjectivistic elements in his position (which are due to the historical circumstances of its derviation through Locke and Berkeley) but his general empirical standpoint which has proved most attractive. He has eliminated Berkeley's spiritual substance; he does not renew Locke's distinction of primary and secondary qualities. Why then must experience be construed to be *mentalistic* in character? If what he calls impressions are not tied up with a mind, there is no reason to think of them

---

[6] David Hume, *A Treatise of Human Nature,* Book I, Part IV, §6.
[7] See above, p. 37 ff.

in other than neutral terms—as simply qualities or phenomena in this world, some groups of which would be called bodies, other groups selves.[8]

Thus while Berkeley's subjective idealism remains one of the clearest expositions of man as ultimately a mental phenomenon, Hume's account when carried to a conclusion strictly in its own terms readily sheds its mentalistic garb. In the one, man is viewed as entirely spirit and its operations; in the other, he becomes, like everything else of which one may speak, a complex of events whose difference from other complexes is to be found in distinguishable experience.

[8] Bertrand Russell, in many ways a philosophical descendant of Hume, at times adopts a position of this kind. Russell maintains that the concept of substance is due to the linguistic habit of having a subject capable of association with different predicates. The common subject is transformed from a grammatical construction into a substance in which the attributes are then said to inhere. Russell regards a thing as merely the assemblage of its attributes and as having no more self-identity than there is constancy in this assemblage. (*Religion and Science,* Holt, 1935, Chapter 5.)

Chapter 13   MAN A MACHINE

Not all views have found it necessary to grant a primary or independent character to the sentient and affective qualities in man. The attempt to fit man into a natural framework which would require no separate world of spirit is an old one. In some of its versions the problems are formulated in terms which derive from dualistic conceptions. In such views mental phenomena may be treated as unique in kind, but their status is reduced in importance. In other forms their very existence is denied. A comprehensive naturalism, however, has reformulated these issues completely. It is concerned with understanding the entire nature of man, his mental and emotional as well as physical qualities, as part of the natural world. We shall consider first some of the materialist developments from dualistic theories, and then some independent formulations.

Epiphenomenalism

One of the materialistic views most clearly stemming from a dualistic position is called epiphenomenalism. In this view the separate identity of mental and physical phenomena is maintained, but the status of the mental is reduced in importance. Physical phenomena (physical, chemical, physiological) are to be studied and understood in terms of familiar cause and effect sequences. Corresponding to some physical conditions or occurrences in the human organism and caused by them are mental phenomena. These are merely a kind of by-product, which affect neither the physical situation nor each other. Thomas Huxley compared mental phenomena to the whistle of the locomotive which arises as the steam-pressure reaches a certain point. To think that the mental determines the physical is like believing that the sound of the whistle determines the motion of the wheels. Santayana likewise has spoken of the soul as "But the last bubble of a long fermentation in the world," and has compared human ideas and feelings to the music of the waterfall.

The theory reflects clearly the fact that there is much going on in our bodies of which we are little aware, that even in our mental life much arises and disappears without any conscious control. This view seems to be supported by the many arbitrary elements in our desires. It is less well supported by those phenomena of planning and reflecting and willing which issue in definite courses of action on our part.

Uncertain status of the mental event. The status of the mental event is itself somewhat ambiguous in epiphenomenalism. It may be taken as a very weak kind of physical event, or else as essentially non-physical. If it retains its independent existence as essentially different in kind from the physical event which it accompanies, epiphenomenalism remains a shadowy type of dualism. It fails to meet any of the difficulties of that position.[1]

An epiphenomenalist position may instead maintain that the mental event, the shadowy by-product of physical events, is itself a happening in the same domain. On such a materialist view it is difficult to see how the causal efficacy of mental events can be ruled out *a priori*. A disparaging view of subtle phenomena is understandable in an age when mechanics is the outstanding physical science; it is not appropriate to the age of the photo-electric cell, of the aeroplane guided by radio, and of laboratory exploration of atomic structure.

Effect on values. In either form epiphenomenalism, minimizing as it does the element of conscious control in human life, is particularly disastrous to values. For values are associated with the domain of the mental, whose importance is here reduced virtually to the vanishing point. The feeling of drift and helplessness which this engenders is in many ways similar to that arising from other mechanistic views which we will examine later. It is interesting to note the social analogue to this epiphenomenalist feeling of helplessness—the view common to many historical theories of the 19th century that the individual (as a conscious person making plans in the light of his understanding) has little control in the processes of social development.[2] Man can do nothing to change his social environment. He can at most anticipate a direction of change and line up with it, or simply wait for it to come.

The identity theory

Another view, which like epiphenomenalism shows clearly the traces of a dualistic origin, holds mental and physical events to be different views of the same thing or different aspects of the same phenomenon. This approach was suggested in Descartes' assertion that God is the only ultimate substance and mind and body his equal creations. It appears in Spinoza's treatment of

---

[1] Compare especially p. 147.
[2] See William James' bitter attack on the theory in "Great Men and Their Environment," in *Selected Papers on Philosophy*, Dutton, 1917.

thought and extension as different attributes of one substance.[3] In modern formulations this has taken a more materialistic turn. There is a single kind of substance or happening. Studied externally by the methods of physical science this substance is seen as bodily phenomena. Seen internally by those biological organisms capable of such introspection, it appears as what we call mental phenomena. In a figurative sense, mind is but an internal view of the brain. The external view is public, the internal one personal and private. Thus, in drawing a sharp distinction between scientific observation and introspection, the *identity theory* replaces the dualism of substance with a dualism of method.

Problems solved by the theory. This theory circumvents many of the problems of dualism. We do not need to worry about the expenditure of energy in connection with the mental phenomenon; the energy expenditure of the whole event is one and the same and no problem is raised by looking at it from different points of view. Nor are we troubled by the problem of the causal interaction of the mental and the physical. For it is indifferent whether we speak of a mental event, m_1, causing a subsequent physical event or whether we cite p_1, the physical equivalent of m_1 as the cause, since p_1 and m_1 refer to different views of the same event. H. S. Jennings, who advocates the identity theory, brings out this point forcibly in his book *The Universe and Life*[4] by an appeal to the criteria of scientific method. Since m_1 and p_1 are experimentally inseparable (we cannot eliminate m_1 and still see if p_1 is followed by p_2, or eliminates p_1 and see if m_1 is followed by p_2), it is scientifically indifferent whether we say the mental causes the physical or the physical causes the physical.

Again, by reinstating the mental as one of the two views of the same substance the identity theory may eliminate the helplessness associated with the epiphenomenalist view. Whatever be the degree of control a man has in our world, it is really his, and is not to be disparaged by saying that it is due to the strength of his body and the state of his nerves instead of to his firm will and clear thought. For we are viewing the same thing in two different ways.

Dualism of method a fundamental weakness. In spite of these conveniences the identity theory has been attacked as offering a merely verbal solution. Is not some further account of the *relation* of inner and outer view required, when the results of the views are so disparate? Again, to what precisely does the inner view refer? How do we identify a mental phenomenon as distinct from a physical phenomenon? Actually it is difficult to maintain such distinctions with any rigidity, even where they are to be regarded as only points of view. Descriptions of the mental in the history of philosophy

---

[3] See above, p. 149.
[4] Yale University Press, 1933, pp. 43-46.

have been wide enough to include everything we know. At its minimum the mental includes feelings, sensations, and thoughts. But do we not require reference to observed qualities and sensations to identify the falling of a stone? And, on the other hand, do we not identify sounds in part by such physical properties as location and direction, thoughts by their objects? And is not even the character of a sensation tested by reference to parts of the body—or else why is it nonsense to think of feeling hungry in the finger-tips? Even so clearly "mental" a phenomenon as imagination or memory is readily described as conjuring up an image *when the eyes are shut* or as *restoring the vision when the object is absent*. In short, the identification of what is called physical requires a reference to what is called mental, and conversely the identification of what is called mental requires a reference to what is called physical. A careful study of the role of sensation in knowledge and a scientific study of the character of sensation thus play havoc with the fundamental distinction of the identity theory.

Mechanistic theories

The materialistic approaches to the analysis of mind examined above stem from the dualistic formulation of the problems they sought to examine. Their attempt has been to explain the status of mind—conceived of as distinctly as in the dualistic tradition—in a world of materialist causation. There are, however, other materialist accounts developed in the context of the materialist tradition. We shall turn first to the most outright mechanistic theories, and in the next chapter examine the more mature naturalistic accounts.

The mechanistic theory in its application to problems of the nature of man embraces a number of separable elements. There is the belief in a bodily basis for all mental qualities, and a confidence in the possibility of discovering laws. These elements are common to all forms of materialism. In addition the mechanistic conception of man has two features peculiar to it. One is the belief in the primacy of physics, i.e., that an account of man in terms of physics will ultimately yield a more comprehensive system of human activity than is possible on any other basis (biological, psychological, or social). This often leads to the view that sense-qualities are somehow illusory or unreal. The second feature is the more specialized belief in the machine-like character of man. This means, in effect, that the laws sought for his behavior will be of a special form modeled largely on those of mechanics. They will deal with more or less simple or elementary units and express relations in terms of the interaction of such units.

EARLY MECHANISTIC APPROACHES

Democritus. Among the Greeks, Democritus developed what was almost a full-fledged mechanism. His universe consists of atoms in space. All events in nature are to be interpreted as varying aggregates of differently shaped atoms moving in space. A man is thus a mass of atoms—what roughly we call the body. Since vital and mental phenomena are clearly very subtle, Democritus attributes them to the atoms that are most active and most capable of rapid motion throughout the body. These are the round smooth type. Mind, for Democritus, is thus simply a special material, and sensation and thought are merely its activities under stimulation from outer movements. What is sour, for example, is atomically angular, minute, thin, thereby readily penetrating; what is sweet is atomically rounded and not too small, and gentle in its action; and similarly for other sense qualities. All these qualities—all those other than shape, size, and number, which characterize atoms—are appearance, not reality. "By convention color exists, by convention bitter, by convention sweet, but in reality atoms and the void."

Hobbes. Among modern philosophers Thomas Hobbes was most influential in the development of mechanistic materialism. In his *Leviathan* he attempts to found the whole of our knowledge on natural science. The 17th century was a period when the growth of physical science was beginning to inspire individual philosophers, and it is this branch of science by which Hobbes was chiefly impressed. Everything, he says, is motion, and different qualities represent changes in motion. "All which qualities called Sensible, are in the object that causeth them, but so many several motions of the matter, by which it presseth our organs diversely. Neither in us that are pressed, are they any thing else, but divers motions; (for motion, produceth nothing but motion.) But their apparance to us is Fancy, the same waking, that dreaming."[5] Imagination is "nothing but *decaying sense.*" Small beginnings of motion within the body of man, before they appear in visible actions are called Endeavor; when endeavor is directed towards something which causes it, it is called Appetite or Desire. Pleasure is really nothing but a kind of motion about the heart. In short, says Hobbes, every mental phenomenon is *really* only a physical phenomenon—some form of motion.

Hobbes carries into ethics the formal outlines of his mechanistic physics. Man is a gross complex of motions, seeking to preserve and extend itself. The approach is egoistic; all obligations arise ultimately from this self-interested activity of individuals. Men in general have "a perpetual and restless desire of power after power, that ceaseth only in death." Men compete for riches, honor, power, but they fear death, poverty, and other calamities. The

---
[5] Hobbes, *Leviathan,* Part I, Chapter

state is an efficient way of establishing and maintaining peace. The surrender of all rights in return is on the whole worth while. However, a man being led to his death by the sovereign is released from allegiance; for then he has nothing to gain by retaining any obligation. Hobbes' egoism was the center of controversy in English ethical theory for several centuries thereafter.

La Mettrie. The mechanical materialist interpretation of man was further developed by the French materialist philosophers of the 18th century. For example, La Mettrie in a small book frankly entitled *Man a Machine*[6] states the position bluntly: "Man is not molded from a costlier clay; nature has used but one dough, and has merely varied the leaven." "The soul is therefore but an empty word, of which no one has any idea, and which an enlightened man should use only to signify the part in us that thinks." ". . . man is but an animal, or a collection of springs which wind each other up. . . ." On questions of morals La Mettrie thought that we derive our good qualities ultimately from nature. There is so much pleasure in virtue that it is sufficient punishment not to have been born virtuous. Preeminent advantages come from one's organism, secondary ones from education.

BEHAVIORISM

Among modern psychological schools *behaviorism* has inherited the mechanistic approach. It has attempted to write a psychology entirely in physicalist terms. In practice, since it is not in a position to carry on psychological experiments in the language of electrons and protons, its general bent issues in a more modest insistence that the terms of psychology refer to observable behavior. This behavior may be described in the ordinary language of things and activities, e.g., "there is a loud noise," "the baby begins to cry," and so on. What the more extreme behaviorists rule out is such mentalistic expressions as "I am thinking," "I am feeling angry." In each case they would insist upon the description of behavior, the report of observable activity, such as "*X* is pacing up and down the room frowning; there are discoverable incipient movements of the larynx," and "*X's* blood-pressure has gone up, his face reddens." Consciousness is thus treated as if for scientific purposes it did not exist.

Difficulties in its use of observable behavior. That there is an inconsistency in such a treatment, we saw above in discussing the relation of the internal and external views on the identity theory. The behaviorist speaks of observable behavior and ultimately seeks to achieve descriptions in terms of the language of physics. But how can one describe observable behavior without

---

[6] Trans. by M. W. Calkins, Open Court, 1912.

reference to qualities of color, sound, and so forth, which are just the same in type as the sort of introspective material that the behaviorist seeks to shun? The behaviorist's selection among these qualities is not really guided by any coherent criteria of "real" existence. It expresses the belief that some qualities (those discovered introspectively) are less controllable in the light of science and ought therefore to be ignored. This reflects the fundamental mechanist thesis that there are specific physical conditions for all these qualities, and that when they are discovered the physical account will yield a more comprehensive picture of human behavior than is possible on any other basis.

Such assumptions must, however, be recognized as largely programs for future research and a hope of future discovery, not a description of the present state of successful psychological inquiry. For in some fields more distinctions may be drawn and more scientific work carried on by including rather than excluding introspective material. Thus, in the study of the emotions, the bodily conditions discovered up to date yield no measurable distinctions adequate to explain observable behavior differences, but the subject may be able to report quite subtle distinctions which do correspond to them. For example, he may distinguish the anger which is resentment, that which is outraged dignity, and that which is primarily envy. And even if his distinctions turn out sometimes to be erroneous in the light of a psychiatric reinterpretation of the facts, they have at least made available data by which such an analysis is furthered.

Several types of arguments have been directed against the behavioristic thesis. Some are valid in opposing a specific behavioristic formula; others seek to overthrow the entire mechanistic hope of a "physics" of man, or deny the legitimacy of determinism in human affairs.[7]

Objection from variable responses. It is claimed, for example, that variable responses to the same physical stimulus disprove the theory; for example, the responses of Arab and Christian to a dish of pork, or of a man who knows no French and of one who does to the same telegram written in French. The same material stimulus has caused different behavioral manifestations. What then has become of the mechanical causation?

This, however, is a misunderstanding of even the most extreme behaviorist positions. These represent a mechanistic approach sufficiently sophisticated to have no difficulty with such a problem. A man brought up to loathe pork as food is presumably different in important physical details (for example, grouping of centers in cerebral cortex) from one who does not exhibit this reaction. And a man who knows French has certain auditory and linguistic habits (presumably based on discoverable physical differences developed in him) which the other man has not. Clearly the effect of physical impacts

[7] This last approach, resting on a theory of free will, will be discussed below, Chapter 17.

will depend upon the object struck as well as the striking object. Even in the case of two billiard balls, if each is hit in turn by the same ball sent in the same way, the resultant motion will be different if one of them was at rest when struck and the other in motion. The same pressure of a finger in the same way on the same kind of switch may in one case ring a bell, in a second light a bulb, in a third cause an explosion, in a fourth launch a battleship, and in a fifth do nothing at all. How much more likely are such subtle mechanisms as men to respond differently under the same external stimulus?

Can behaviorism construct a theory of knowledge? Behaviorism has also been charged with rendering knowledge impossible and therefore negating itself as a theory. This claim is sometimes cast as ridicule: if the behaviorist's theory is true, he is himself a machine and not responsible for his irresponsible chatter. Unfortunately if the theory's truth be granted, the same may be said of the objector. The more serious argument points to difficulties in the formulation of the theory, and declares it an impossible task to construct a theory of knowledge within its framework. This, however, is a challenge which the behaviorist can take up. For the mechanistic approach renders impossible only the theory of knowledge that has been common in the dualistic tradition. In mechanistic theory knowledge is analyzed as one type of effect of environment on the body, or more properly, one mode of interaction of the body and its surroundings. Whether it is expressed in Hobbes' terms of the meeting of internal and external motions, or in Pavlov's language of conditioned reflex, or in any other categories of body-environment interaction, the fundamental idea is the same. Analyzing the nature of knowledge involves the double task of discovering the causes and character of bodily processes, events, patterns that are identified as knowing, and estimating their reliability. Whatever the success of such an account, it is at least not *a priori* inconsistent.[8]

Contemporary critique of behaviorism. A contemporary scientific reckoning with behaviorism cannot be a simple one, for it must pass judgment on the multiple thesis of mechanism. Briefly it may be sketched as follows:

(1) There is dominant agreement on the mechanistic stipulation of a physical basis for sensory qualities.

(2) There is little agreement on the mechanistic hope that a type of physics can replace psychology and social science in the study of man. Insofar as this is merely a hope of future discovery, it is left for future empirical investigation. Insofar as it was in early behaviorism a disparagement of lines of research not conforming to the criterion of strict (easy) observability, it is now recognized as an undue restriction on fruitful psychological inquiry.

---

[8] Such a behaviorist theory of knowledge and truth could be formulated along lines similar to the pragmatic operationalism discussed above, pp. 95-96.

(3) There is general scientific agreement on the mechanistic search for laws of human activity, insofar as this means the search for systematic explanation, and the use of determinism as a principle of inquiry.

(4) There is wide disagreement in psychological theory with the specific types of laws that contemporary behaviorism offers. This is, of course, a technical question of the evidence for specific psychological hypotheses, and does not concern us here. But it is the point on which in present-day psychological investigation the controversy between behaviorism and other approaches is most pronounced. Broadly speaking, the inadequacy of behavioristic hypotheses is felt to lie in their adherence to the guiding machine idea, and their consequent insistence on dealing with simple, elementary units and simple forms of laws. Thus laws of perceiving and remembering are stated (in the tradition of Locke and Hume) as a function primarily of the number, contiguity and recency of experiences. If I experience A-B-C-D together a sufficient number of times, then A-B-C-D will be perceived thereafter as a group and A alone will lead to the recall of B-C-D. This is especially true if the experience A-B-C-D is followed by pleasure. While these laws have had some limited success in predicting perception and recall of meaningless material, they have been seriously challenged with respect to meaningful material. The chief difficulties seem to lie on the one hand in the neglect of organizations of the perceived material, which depend on factors other than chance contiguity and frequency, and on the other hand the failure to take adequate account of the organism, which plays a dynamic rather than merely passive role in perception and recall.

VALUE ATTITUDES CONVEYED BY MECHANISM

Mechanism, particularly in the form of rigid behaviorism, has sometimes led to a profound pessimism. For it has stressed the purely physical roots in man, ruling out almost entirely the whole realm of consciousness in which inhere most of the values upon which our way of life has been built. Joseph Wood Krutch has expressed this dejection in a book which epitomized an attitude prevalent in the 1920's.[9]

Krutch's pessimism. The essence of Krutch's position is that not merely particular values have been lost, but that the very meaning of value has disappeared. Values are illusions with which, unfortunately, we moderns are no longer able to fool ourselves. We are no longer children and there is, also, no Santa Claus. Past generations exalted love, felt the impersonal value of scientific search for truth, appreciated the genuine tragedy which can be written if man is conceived of as a noble being. Among us, however, Krutch says, religion has no hold. Love is being increasingly explored on the physi-

---

[9] *The Modern Temper*, Harcourt, Brace, 1929.

cal side, and threatens to be revealed as a purely glandular reaction. Science set out to conquer ignorance and make man comfortable in the world but has instead brought fresh evils. Man is now revealed as but a speck of dust in a vast cosmos and to such there is no dignity. In *Romeo and Juliet,* though the hero and heroine perished, love itself triumphed and to an audience of the past showed its ultimate worth in the universe. But none of man's doings now bear the stamp of worth. Science, the villain of the piece, set out to establish values, but ended by discovering their—and its own—illusory character.

This type of pessimism insofar as it is philosophically grounded is not a necessary consequence of mechanism. It stems rather from a kind of residual dualism. It sees man as a puppet buffeted about by physico-biological forces, and finds no place for beauty, truth, and goodness, all the nobler objects of human striving. For these, it has assumed with the dualists, are all identified with mind or spirit, and science has seemed to declare that there is no such realm of being.

Human control of human destiny. That values can have a real place in a real universe becomes clear in a more comprehensive naturalism to which we will turn in the next chapter. But even a materialism which takes the mechanistic position of orthodox behaviorism need not give way to despair. On the contrary, the essential element in the behaviorist faith is the belief that man's nature can come to be fully understood in scientific terms. And this faith is accompanied by a dream of human power in human affairs, a dream that man, discovering the principles of human behavior, may learn not only to predict but to control his destiny. This hope is strengthened by the belief in the predominant malleability of man.[10]

The claim for the malleability of man issues in two quite different moral directions depending upon the ends with which it is conjoined. On the one hand it offers the possibility of control *over* men. Propaganda as a technique for making people believe what you want them to has become sufficiently refined and sufficiently powerful to constitute a serious threat in evil hands. Its use by the Nazis rested on a thorough contempt for men and the view that the greater the lie the more readily it could be put over. The attitudes of the German youth brought up under Nazi domination remain a serious problem of the post-war world. In his imaginative novel *Brave New World*[11] Aldous Huxley paints the picture of an extreme situation in which with complete control over the production of human beings, grade C men are brought into existence to do the work of the world. They are conditioned to dislike the good things of life—for example, as children they are

[10] For example, John B. Watson, leading exponent of behaviorism, has claimed that with sufficient care any normal child can be made into any desired type of person.
[11] Doubleday, Doran, 1932.

shown beautiful flowers and given electric shocks as they reach for them—and to find delight only in the use of a particular drug with which their labors are rewarded. This of course is a fictional account, but it bears a disturbing resemblance to a great part of the lives of men.

On the other hand, the malleability of men offers possibilities of tremendous development for the good. When men become conscious of the possibility of change they may strive to direct development in the light of their ideals. The instruments that operate in propaganda lie at hand also for education. Men may remake not merely their surroundings, but even themselves, to embody their highest aspirations. The only problem is to discover and evaluate those aspirations. This task is better carried out in the framework presented in the next chapter than it can be under a rigid mechanistic behaviorism.

Chapter 14 A NATURALISTIC ACCOUNT OF MAN

The naturalistic approach

Modern naturalistic theories of man proceed from a more mature conception of matter than is found in the mechanistic theories—a conception enriched by all the sciences, and not formulated entirely in terms of physics.[1] Such a naturalistic approach relies on the method and criteria of science in its account of the mental as of all else in nature. Its essential core is the stress upon man as dynamic, participating in events and reacting with and to his environment. Mind is understood in terms of activities or events and their qualities.

CLASSICAL BEGINNINGS

The beginning of such an approach is found in classical philosophy. In Aristotle mind is to body as "axness" or cutting power is to the ax, that is an organization which enables it to achieve the active fruition of its possibilities. If the eye were an animal, says Aristotle, eyesight would be its soul.[2] This is somewhat ambiguous; it might mean seeing as an activity, or the organization in virtue of which seeing is able to take place. Aristotle definitely means the latter. He frequently draws the distinction between having knowledge and using knowledge—between knowing a language, for example, and the act of speaking and reading it. The former he calls a "first actualization," the latter a "second actualization." The former is constant in a man who knows the language; the latter is intermittent. Now a man has his soul when he is asleep as well as when he is awake. The soul is therefore a first actualization of a natural, organized body. It is a way in which the body is organized so as to be capable of the manifold activities that constitute life. It is interesting to note that such a theory gave little scope for a belief in personal immortality. Aristotle in fact held that only the active reason which operates in man and is impersonal is eternal.

Aristotle's examination of the soul becomes, in effect, an inquiry into the

---

[1] For a discussion of this conception see below, pp. 322-23.
[2] *De Anima* 412b.

different functions of organic life—nutrition, growth, reproduction, movement, sensation, imagination, thought. His analysis of each function calls attention to what is relevant both in the body and in the environment for the occurrence of the phenomenon in question. For example, in the case of vision, when the eye and the object of vision establish certain relations in existence there is a going-on in which they are joint participants. This happening, analyzed as an attribute of the eye, is called seeing; as a property of the object it is called color; and with respect to the general medium it is called light. Similarly on his view when you have a special movement of an object in air (e.g., motion of a bell) and an activity of the receptive ear, the co-operative situation is one of hearing-and-sounding. His conception of "mental phenomena" is definitely not that of a spectator self receiving copies of an external world, but more that of a member of the community of nature participating in the joint production of nature's qualities.[3]

CONTEMPORARY PSYCHOLOGICAL APPROACHES

Such an approach is common in contemporary psychological theory. Woodworth, for example, defines psychology as "the science of the activities of the individual" and adds, "The word 'activity' is used here in a very broad sense. It includes not only motor activities like walking and speaking, but also cognitive (knowledge-getting) activities like seeing, hearing, remembering and thinking, and emotional activities like laughing and crying, and feeling happy or sad."[4] Earlier,[5] Woodworth had suggested that most of the nouns in psychology are properly verbs or adverbs; only one noun—the organism—is needed as subject of the verbs. Thought is a verb, and intelligence an adverb. Mind is to be understood in terms of the organism's activity-relations with its environment. Thinking, sensing, feeling, and so forth, are natural events in the world. These activities may be explored scientifically in order to determine the conditions and occasions under which they occur or take specific forms.

It is clear why, from this point of view, an internal examination of the body is insufficient for an account of mind. No dissection of the body reveals the mind, any more than a cross-section of the ax will reveal its cutting. We may, when we are told that the metal is hard and the angle between its sides very acute, call it "sharp" in anticipation of its performance in contact with things in the environment. So too we may think of mind as a *potentiality* of the organism even when it is not engaged in mental activ-

[3] For a discussion of the conception of soul in Aristotle's ethical theory, see below, pp. 392-96.
[4] R. S. Woodworth, *Psychology*, 4th ed., Holt, 1940, p. 3.
[5] In an earlier edition of the same book.

ity. But as cutting is a special activity of the materials we call an ax when it is associated with timber in a certain way, so mental phenomena are highly specialized activities of a very complex organism in various types of contact with particular features of the world about it.

MODES OF DESCRIBING HUMAN ACTIVITIES

So far we have located merely the *genus* of mind, that is, the domain of a man's activities. To complete the outline of a naturalistic theory we must distinguish among these activities and ask which class of them or phase of them constitutes the mental. This commits us to the task of examining the principles on which the description and classification of human activities rest. How adequate is the traditional distinction among physical, vital, mental, and social activities or phenomena?

Various phases rather than distinct activities. It is important to recognize at the outset that in many cases in which we make such distinctions we do not have in mind different activities but different phases of a single going-on. Thus we speak of the social meaning of a movement of the hand, and call it waving good-bye. The distinction between the physical, vital, mental, and social seems in such cases to be simply one of different descriptions of the activity of the individual in the light of different relations into which he enters with the rest of the world around him. And each description may be formulated in terms of the distinctive equipment (concepts, methods, and results) of the relevant science—physics and chemistry, biology, psychology, social science.

Ordinary discourse recognizes that a happening studied by different sciences or described in different sets of terms may nonetheless be one event. Take for example the simple happening of "throwing a baseball." It is obvious that this may generate or be part of innumerable studies. It has its physical aspect which we may illustrate by the gross movements of the body in terms of leverage, momentum, spin, and so forth; its biological aspect in the muscular tensions and relaxations and concomitant or directive physiological changes—metabolism, energy consumption, breathing, circulation adjustments; its psychological aspect in motor-habits, types of stimuli responded to, effort of will and perceptions and desires involved in playing and aiming; its social aspect not merely in the history of the ball and the occasions of throwing it, but in the very style of throwing.

Levels not sharply distinguished in ordinary discourse. Furthermore, if we may speak of the four aspects as levels of analysis ordinary discourse often employs one set of terms for several different levels, leaving it to context to indicate which phase is being specially stressed. When a man reports that on a specific occasion on which he got into a fight his "blood boiled," he may be indicating that he felt angry and insulted, or that he felt a definite irregular internal pounding, or that a test of his blood-pressure and adrenal secretions on that occasion would have yielded unusually high results.

Again, ordinary discourse has no compunctions in going from one level to another in search of explanations. Thus the judge will look to the insult and the prevailing sense of honor (social) to explain the defendant's reported anger (mental) which issued in the assault (physical). The doctor will not hesitate to advise the man to avoid discussion of politics (social) to keep his blood-pressure down (physical).

"A purely physical activity." In the light of this analysis we must reinterpret such expressions as "a purely physical (biological, psychological) activity." Such a designation is really negative. What it asserts is that there is no fruitful study of the activity in the terms and techniques of a higher level than the one specified. That is, a purely psychological activity is not one that has no physical or biological aspect—all human activities have—but one which has no social phase. Similarly a purely biological activity has no psychological or social phase. The extent of such activities is probably less than most people imagine. Thus cell growth and division is probably a purely biological activity of man, but digestion has its psychological, even its social, side, as medicine has come to recognize. Thus ulcers are widely considered to have a "psychogenic" origin. Again, clenching the fist in anger is not merely a psychological response but one with social conditions. For among other peoples with other habits we may find very different gestures in anger, such as incipient spear-throwing. On the other hand, according to the tenets of the contemporary school of Gestalt psychology, there are some perceptual configurations which are purely psychological facts, independent of social patterning.

Distinction between levels and the relation of sciences. The question of the adequacy of the distinction between physical, vital, mental, and social activities is thus translated into the question of the usefulness of the distinction between the physical, biological, psychological, and social sciences. And once it is thus formulated it is well to recall that there is an increasing number of borderline sciences—biophysics, physiological psychology, biochemistry, etc.—and that the boundaries of a field change as the methods of its science improve and as relations are discovered which bring fresh phenomena within its scope. Attempts to delimit a field permanently whether by characterizing the properties of a phenomenon or by insisting on a single method, only serve to thwart scientific growth.[6] The limitation of psychology to introspective materials and its expansion in overriding this limitation

---

[6] See above, Chapter 4, esp. pp. 59-60 and p. 63 ff.

is only one illustration. Within the social sciences themselves the attempt to make a sharp separation of economic, political, and religious phenomena led to efforts to systematize each separately. Some institutions were classified as economic, others as political, and the development of each traced in its own terms. Many modern social scientists have pointed out that this failed to recognize that the same social event may be at the same time political, economic, and religious. Thus a political party may be based on a unifying economic interest; a wedding may have its religious, economic, and even political significance. Similarly the explanation of a political event may lie in its economic content, or the choice of a philosophic system may rest in part on an esthetic interest.

On the other hand the scientific approach does not logically exclude the possibility of a classification with sharp divisions that continues unaltered indefinitely. For the stability of the classification is an empirical question and so cannot be settled *a priori*. The history of science does, however, seem to warrant the assertion that any sharp delimitation made at a time of rapid growth in a science is likely to need further revision.

Sharp cleavages not warranted. We may conclude, therefore, that the absolute separateness of the classification of human activities which occurs in some of the theories we have examined is something added to the facts of experience by the theories and not an established datum to which they may appeal for confirmation. Especially is this true of the attempt to assume separate substances to which the classes of activities are assigned, whether it be in the extreme form of four stuffs—physical phenomena as properties or workings of *matter,* essential vital phenomena of *soul,* mental phenomena of *mind,* social phenomena of a *group-mind,* or the more usual dualism of body and mind or body and soul.

In the light of the lessons to be gathered from the history of science and the history of conceptions of mind, a naturalistic approach is unready permanently to isolate one phase of the activity-relations of the organism with its environment and label it as mental, reserving to it some special method of inquiry. Certainly in the light of the development of modern psychology there remains little ground for identifying the mental solely with the contents of introspection. Broadly speaking we may identify the mental with the phases of human activity studied in contemporary psychology and social science, as distinguished from those studied in biology and physics. Thus evaluative or purposive behavior, and perception, knowledge, self-consciousness would be included. But even such a distinction may have overlapping segments or come to have them. The fact is that the naturalistic approach dispenses with much of the drive for making a sharp distinction; with a recognition of the elementary state of our knowledge, interest centers rather on learning as much as we can about as many phases of man as possible.

But if the mental ceases to be sharply differentiated as a category of existence and is instead understood to be a loosely grouped set of human activities, what happens to the "content" of these activities? What becomes of thoughts, ideas, feelings? And what is the relation of the various phases of human activity which we study by different procedures? In what sense, if any, does a naturalistic approach maintain that the mental can be *reduced* to or *explained* by the physical? We have seen that such questions loomed large in the various approaches we have examined. How does naturalism answer them?

The status of mental states

The description of mental phenomena on a naturalistic approach as certain *activities* of the organism in relation to its environment, and the identification of those activities as the phases of human activity studied by psychology and the social sciences, accounts for one aspect of the traditional meaning of "thoughts," "sensations," "feelings," and other such notions embraced under the usual idea of mental phenomena. There is, however, another aspect of the traditional meaning which should now be rendered more explicit. This second aspect concerns itself not with the activities but the "content" of those activities—not with thinking, sensing, feeling, but with thoughts or concepts, sensations or sense-data, feelings or emotions. For purposes of simplifying the account we may omit here the discussion of thought, which would involve the problem of symbolization, and deal only with the simpler problem of sense-data like "this-particular-green-here-now" or feelings like "hot-here-now," "angry-here-now."

SENSE-DATA AS QUALITIES OF EVENTS

On a naturalistic approach sense-data will be treated not as "contents of a mind" but as *qualities of the process or activity or event*. The idea of events having qualities is really a familiar one. Take, for example, an ordinary billiard-ball moving across the surface of a table. We may think of the ball as a thing and its size, shape, motion, texture, weight as its qualities or attributes, its distance from the table edge and the direction of its motion as some of its relations to other things. On the other hand, we may think of its motion and weight as goings-on rather than as qualities; direction and speed can be taken as qualities of its motion, while its particular texture is a quality of situations of contact with other things. Furthermore, the whole billiard-ball may itself be thought of as an aggregate of rapidly moving particles, in which case its very shape and size are dynamic properties of the aggregate or total event.

In a similar fashion the sensation "green" which I have when I look at a picture on the wall is not something suddenly filed in my mind while the activity of sensing goes on in my body. What I refer to by the term "green" is a quality of brain-nerve-body-environment process. The nature of this process constitutes a subject-matter for extensive scientific exploration; but the sense in which green is a quality of that process is analogous to the sense in which its size, shape, texture, etc., are qualities of the moving billiard-ball and speed a quality of its motion.

It may be objected to this account of green that color-sensations can be produced by pressure on my eyeball and that therefore the sensation as quality is somehow internal to me. All this proves, however, is that the environmental factor in a certain process may be altered without a comparable change in the kind of quality. For the pressure replaces the picture and the light-waves in the process. Experience enables us to distinguish between such occurrences. As a result we can test to find out whether we are "really seeing something." For seeing is something that goes on in the room, or in the vicinity, rather than simply in the eye or in the brain.

Mental phenomena part of the natural world. Such a naturalistic interpretation restores so-called mental phenomena to a place in the natural world. They are not to be regarded as private insights without place in the external world, but as qualities that occur under definite natural conditions, just as any quality of any sort occurs only under its own "proper" specific conditions.

Such incorporation of man into nature—to use Woodbridge's formulation—changes our conception of nature as it does of man. Nature ceases to be the colorless, odorless, soundless place of traditional Lockean dualism. It becomes a matrix in which all sorts of qualities occur under specific conditions. Thus, as Woodbridge says in formulating a naturalism of this sort, "Man himself discloses the kind of nature in which atoms can exist fully as much as atoms disclose the kind of nature in which man can exist. . . . The question why and how man lives, how and why he walks and thinks, is, in principle, the same sort of question as why and how the atoms move. This does not mean that the movement of atoms is the thinking of man, or that thinking is some curious addition to motion, but that both motion and thinking are a co-working with nature under controlling laws." [7]

If nature be regarded through the eyes of a mechanical materialist as consisting of atoms, a naturalistic approach warns that we must not underesti-

---

[7] Reprinted from Woodbridge, *Nature and Mind* (p. 255), by permission of Columbia University Press.

mate what atoms can accomplish. Atoms are seen to be capable of a great many things when they "aggregate" or organize appropriately. The richness of nature and life which the mechanical materialist disparaged, a more mature materialism thus restores. Or, if a temporal perspective be taken, there is a recognition that the qualities of groups may be novel as compared to the qualities of their constituents taken individually.[8] Thus the vital and mental and even the social may be regarded as different levels of evolution in which new qualities have appeared.

Three important objections arise to this incorporation of mental phenomena into nature. It is said that such an approach overrides the acknowledged *subjectivity* of mental phenomena, that it robs them of their *privacy,* and that it deprives them of their *cognitive* character, rendering knowledge of the world impossible by making the sensations merely qualities of occurrences instead of reports about the world.

ALLEGED SUBJECTIVITY OF MENTAL PHENOMENA

It is said that mental phenomena are *subjective,* physical phenomena *objective,* and the incorporation of man into nature threatens to eliminate the difference. A naturalistic approach does indeed deny the sharp distinction which a dualistic theory makes between the subjective and the objective, but it substitutes distinctions of its own. Thus I may distinguish between those happenings and qualities which would not take place without the presence of my organism, those which would not take place without some organism like mine present, and those which could take place without any such organism.

Happenings requiring my organism. Clearly all my mental phenomena are included in the first class, but so are my physical activities and their qualities, such as my wearing gloves or my swimming well or quickly.

Happenings requiring some organism. Again, there is no doubt that a great many of the qualities I call sensory require some kind of organism in order to occur; it need not, however, be mine. Thus when I say that such qualities occur in nature—e.g., that the sense-quality "yellow" characterizes a happening in the next room—I am referring to a happening which involves a certain picture in that room, the light-waves there, and the organisms of some friends who are visiting me. I do not imply that this sense-quality occurs when there are no organisms present. But the same point can be made of many phenomena which all would consider purely physical. The particular qualities of the Australian crawl as a form of swimming could not take

---

[8] See above, p. 60 ff.

place without a human body; other kinds of swimming (the dog-paddle, for example) may occur with other animals, but not *without* any animal.

Happenings requiring no organism. The third class is that of happenings and qualities which take place without the presence of any organism. Such a class is involved in the commonly accepted belief that the physical universe existed before man or other animals, that events are constantly happening in which organisms have no part, and in the view that knowledge in some sense or other discloses the character of the universe in which we dwell.

It may then very well be asked how we *know* that these events occur and have qualities of their own. This fundamental limitation, that all my knowledge is after all *my* knowledge—hence already involves my organism in the process—has been called the ego-centric predicament. It is true that there is a fundamental relativity, but this must not be construed as if it were the plight of a solitary mind limited to scanning uncertain copies of an external world otherwise unknown. From a naturalistic point of view, my basis of knowledge is the whole career of my body in the world. In the course of my life I develop a language to talk about that experience. I study isolated phases of it; in effect, I prepare maps for possible use in finding my way in domains of existence that I have not yet traveled. When I engage in discourse with others I am issuing and receiving invitations to further experience in a more extended field of existence. And insofar as the maps I have prepared prove useful and accurate they help to verify the understanding that I have developed of the world in which I live.

Demand for a description of the world without organisms. But what, it will then be asked, would the world be like if there were no organisms? This is a tricky question, for it is not satisfied with a straight-forward answer. Making use of symbols developed from experience, we could give the evolutionary account of astronomic history and its picture of pre-organic conditions; or we could describe what would happen to houses, untilled fields, etc., if all life suddenly ended, or—to be even more imaginative—what one would find if all but he perished and he slumbered for a stated period. But such answers would probably not satisfy the questioner. For the answers are in the terms of possible experience and he is asking for an answer apart from experience. This means that I cannot perform any tests. It is like asking me how many leaves there are on a tree, but refusing to let me count them. I am to answer, but may not speak or make any other intelligible sign. My failure to answer is then construed as ignorance. For what the questioner really wants is an account without symbols.

However, he has no more right to expect such knowing without symbols than cutting without a knife or other sharp instrument. Nor can he expect to be told how long something is, without allowing a reference to a measuring-rod and a system of measurement. Can he expect to be told what something would look like if there were no looking? It is reasonable to ask what color-qualities we would be conscious of if our eyes were otherwise constructed, but not if we had no eyes. The dog hears things we cannot, and many subtle reactions are perceived by us in animal and plant life which we do not understand. Because my body occupies only a small part of actually observed space, and because I have experienced the extension, often novel, of my experience, and because I am impressed with the immensity of human ignorance as compared to human knowledge, I find meaningful but not alarming the assertion that this world has many events and qualities that men do not know and that do not require the presence of an organism. And any reasonable humility requires such a conclusion.

THEIR ALLEGED PRIVACY

The second objection to treating mental phenomena as simply a special class of qualities in the natural world—those occurring with highly organized bodies such as ours—is the claim that qualities in the natural world are public, but mental phenomena are essentially private. Naturalism denies such essential privacy. It must therefore give a reasonable reply to the traditional query: How can I know someone else's mind?

There are two aspects to this question. One is whether I see the same quality as another observer; e.g., do you see the same green as I do in looking at the grass? The second is whether I can know your mental state; e.g., a tooth-ache. Clearly the two questions are the same if the green that you see is treated as a sensation in your mind.

Do you and I see the same green? Such questions are beset with all the ambiguities of the term "mental"; they therefore require analysis before an answer is attempted. In the first place, then, what is meant by asking whether you and I see the same green? If the question asks whether the same type of light wave is impinging on your retina as on mine, this can be physically investigated. If it asks whether the two qualities—that occurring on your looking at the grass and that occurring on my looking at the grass—are of the same type, then difficult as the investigation is and difficult as it is to get a reliable answer at the present stage of scientific work, we may doubt whether the question really presents a theoretical quandary—that is, if it is treated as a serious empirical question. On the basis of current knowledge of vision I may compare your retina and mine to see if they are alike in relevant respects. On the assumption that a quality occurs under determinate conditions I may seek to establish whether our respective conditions are comparable. I might also make deductions from the hypothesis that we see the same green to more subtle tests concerning what we would see in other color-situations.[9] Certainly we have little difficulty in distinguishing the color-blind from those of normal vision.

Can I know your tooth-ache? The problem of my knowing your tooth-ache is not very different. I can learn about it from your facial behavior, your verbal report, and other so-called "external" conduct. Of course it is an advantage to have had such a pain myself so that I may appreciate yours by *empathy* (i.e., *feeling* oneself *into* someone's situation). But it will continue to be said that I do not know your tooth-ache; I know only its external conditions and my *own* feeling in similar conditions.

In one sense this objection is empirically grounded. Individual differences are great enough in gross activities—are they not likely to be even greater in more subtle activities? Will not differences in our sensitivity, general attitudes, as well as the sheer complexity of the situation and the difficulties of devising ways of testing make it impossible for me actually to know your tooth-ache? These are indeed tremendous practical difficulties and it is probable that there will be a wide margin of error in my conjecture about the quality of your tooth-ache. But this is not a theoretical impossibility. It is no different in type from my inability to discover whether Napoleon had the same thing for breakfast on January 12 and February 12, 1803.

On the other hand, we may very much doubt whether the objection is intended to rest on empirical grounds. It will probably be claimed that even if I were able to perform *all conceivable tests* and knew everything *about* your tooth-ache, there would be no guarantee that I had knowledge of its inner quality. This claim assumes the very point at issue, an inner core of privacy in the character of the quality which is accessible *by definition* only to the person concerned. The basis of the claim seems to be a confusion between the actual "having" of a quality and "knowing" its character. Of course I cannot know your tooth-ache if that entails that I should also *have its pain*. I may wear your glove, but I cannot do your wearing of it.

THEIR COGNITIVE CHARACTER

The third objection to the reincorporation of mental phenomena into nature raises the question of the meaning of truth. If sense-data and thoughts are simply qualities of events in which the organism participates, then it is said they do not bring us any news of the world. They simply happen. They tell us about themselves, but are not reports of anything beyond themselves. Without representing anything beyond themselves how can they give man knowledge of a world about him?

This objection rests on dualistic premises. It assumes that a report about the natural world cannot itself be part of the natural world, hence that

---

[9] For an illustration, see above, p. 113.

sense-data if cognitive must be somehow non-natural. On a naturalistic theory of mind this problem disappears. There is no inherent difficulty in one element of nature symbolizing, pointing to, or otherwise representing other parts of nature. To realize the cognitive character of sense-data it is only necessary to recall the role of sensation in scientific method.[10]

With the restoration of man to the natural world—long overdue since Darwin—these problems, generated by a dualistic approach, disappear. The question of the sources of knowledge becomes primarily a problem for empirical psychology and sociology. It calls for the psychological study of perception, the study of linguistic structures and symbolism, and analysis of ways of thinking. The question of the relation of knowledge to reality becomes (as raised in Part Two) a question of the relative reliability of various methods of resolving doubt; from a naturalistic point of view it entails the analysis of logic and scientific method, together with an account of men's problems, instruments and ends and the history of the success of science, and the philosophic analysis of such concepts as reality, substance, and quality (to be discussed below).

Relation between the mental and the physical

Apart from the question of the nature of mental states, the chief issues which give rise to difficulties in both dualistic and mechanistic theories concerned the relation between the mental and the physical. We shall now look at the account which a naturalistic approach may give of these issues. In general, it recognizes all efforts to *reduce* a phenomenon, whether mental or physical, to the other type, and all efforts to trace the *cause* of a phenomenon—whether on its own level or on another—as attempts to *explain* the phenomenon. We shall accordingly summarize briefly several relevant meanings of "explanation," [11] and apply them to the special problem of the relation of the mental and the physical. In each particular case, the kind of explanation that is being sought will have to be judged from the context of inquiry.

VARIOUS MEANINGS OF EXPLANATION HERE RELEVANT

(a) To explain a phenomenon may mean to describe it more fully. Thus the vital phenomenon of *eating* may be explained by describing the process of moving one's hand, opening the mouth, putting the food in, salivating, chewing, swallowing, and then indicating the path of the food down the

[10] See above, Chapter 8.
[11] Cf. the account of building up a system in Chapter 4 above.

esophagus and into the stomach, and the operation of the organs concerned. This would involve translating the term of ordinary discourse ("eating") into the language of physics and biology. Suppose now that such terms as "chewing" were translated into "bringing so-and-so much pressure to bear in such-and-such a fashion" and similarly that the path through the esophagus and in the stomach was described in terms of physico-chemical reactions in spatio-temporal regions; then, awkward as the result might be for ordinary discourse, it would have provided a physico-chemical account of eating. "Eating" would thus have been *reduced* to physico-chemical processes.

In this sense, which we called above *translation of terms,* the term "eating" would be equated with its translation. There would be no separate phenomenon of eating distinct from the processes described. Any other connotation of the term would probably be due to associated ideas, such as that we eat to provide for continuation of the body; this might be translated into the physical outcome of the processes into which eating was translated. As so defined eating could be properly said by the mechanist to be *merely a physico-chemical process.*

(b) The type of explanation of a phenomenon which is called *reduction* has also been used to cover the *empirical relation* of phenomena *on different levels.* Thus the sensation of "sweet" may be correlated with the process of stimulating certain nerve-endings. Such correlation of sensation and physiologic processes differs from the translation described above in the separate identifiability of the terms. One term describes a *quality,* the other a *physical process* found invariantly related to it. Each can be independently detected. A statement of such a correlation is a law relating terms on different levels. When this is achieved the sensation may be said to be explained by or reduced to the physical process.

(c) The usual sense of explanation is the *discovery of a cause,* that is, indication of some other occurrence, from the assertion of whose existence, together with one or more accepted general statements or laws, the occurrence of the phenomenon in question can be deduced. Thus, when a man who has forgotten to drain an outside water-pipe discovers that there has been freezing temperature, he can predict that the pipe will probably have burst, since he knows that water expands when it freezes. The empirical relation of terms described in (b) is a special case of this use of explanation. That is, given the occurrence of the specific physiological process in Mr. X and the correlation statement there indicated I can deduce that Mr. X is now having the sensation of sweet.

(d) A fourth process sometimes intended by explaining is the *relating of laws.* Thus in Newtonian physics the laws of planetary movement are derived from the principle of gravitation. In a parallel fashion Pavlov has attempted to associate psychological findings about the conduction and inhibi-

A NATURALISTIC ACCOUNT OF MAN

tion of conditioned reflexes with physiological laws about the interrelations of nerve impulses.

In general, in this sense explanation consists in *incorporation into a wider system of laws*. It is important to note that the relation of terms as described in (b) does not necessitate or entail the relation of laws, and on the other hand that the incorporation of a law in the wider system on another level does not destroy the law so "reduced." [12]

NATURALISTIC ANALYSIS OF BODY-MIND RELATIONS

We may now turn to the question of the relation between the mental and the physical on a naturalistic approach. In what sense is the mental "reduced" to the physical? In what sense does the mental "cause" the physical or the physical the mental? The following is a composite illustration of the way these problems may be analyzed. For the sake of brevity, and also because some of the interrelations are programs for investigation rather than established results, the account here given is partly hypothetical and deliberately oversimplified.

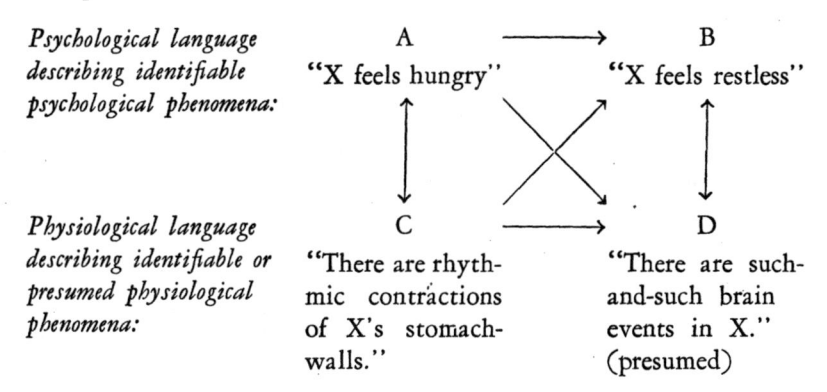

	A	B
Psychological language describing identifiable psychological phenomena:	"X feels hungry"	"X feels restless"
Physiological language describing identifiable or presumed physiological phenomena:	C "There are rhythmic contractions of X's stomach-walls."	D "There are such-and-such brain events in X." (presumed)

(with arrows: A → B, C → D, A ↔ C, B ↔ D, and diagonal crosses A↔D, B↔C)

We may read a number of laws from this diagram:

(1) *If A, then C, and conversely.* (When X feels hungry there are rhythmic contractions of his stomach walls, and vice versa.) [13] This is a trans-level psycho-physiological law stating a reciprocal relation. A is thus "reduced" to C or "explained" by C or "caused" by C.

(2) *If A, then B.* (If X is hungry, he feels restless.) This is an intra-level psychological law. It holds for some persons; let us assume it to hold generally, for purposes of illustration.

---
[12] See Chapter 4, pp. 59-60.
[13] This proposition does not, in fact, hold invariably, but this is here disregarded for the sake of simplicity.

(3) From these two laws we may derive: *If C, then B.* (If there are rhythmic contractions of his stomach-walls, X feels restless.) This is a trans-level physio-psychological law. B is thus "caused" by C—a "mental" by a "physical" phenomenon.

(4) Suppose now that the psychological phenomenon of restlessness, B, were reduced to physiological phenomena, D, in the same way as hunger was to stomach contractions, C. This would give us the law *If B, then D, and conversely.* (If X feels restless, certain brain events take place and vice versa.)

(5) As a result of all this, we could derive a law from 3 and 4: *If C, then D.* (If X has stomach contractions, certain brain events take place.)

(6) And from (2) and (4) we may derive *If A then D* (If X is hungry, certain brain events take place), which is a trans-level psycho-physiological law. D is thus "caused" by A—a "physical" by a "mental" phenomenon.

Mechanist and dualist misinterpretations of reduction and explanation. If all these laws are achieved, the scientist may find that he has no more need of referring to the psychological phenomena A and B in his work, since each of them has been "reduced" and the law relating them is deducible from the law relating C and D. He may even go so far as to redefine hunger and restlessness in physiological language. This, however, while it may eliminate hunger and restlessness from psychology, does not eliminate them from human experience. For the reduction of A to C and B to D is an *empirical relation across levels,* not a translation. Thus the mechanist, when he says that red is *merely* a certain wave-length, or, as Hobbes did, that pleasure is a movement about the heart, is erroneously overriding this distinction. Where the phenomenon on one level has been identified *by a different procedure* from that to which it is reduced, and not merely by a different verbal symbol, it cannot be validly conjured away.

The dualist is making the converse mistake when he argues that physical conditions cannot *explain* the mental or the mental be reduced to the physical. Clearly C explains A in the above diagram, and A is reduced to C, in one sense of these terms. The dualist is thus regarding all explanation and reduction as if they were equivalent to complete translation. He is right in thinking that physical conditions cannot explain *away* the mental. But not all explanation—and certainly not the most valuable—is of that sort.

Trans-level causation and the language of interactionism. Again it will be noted in the diagram that there are cases of both the physical causing the mental ("If C, then B") and the mental causing the physical ("If A, then D"). Such formulations rest on the meaning of causality, described in Chapter 3, as an invariant relation between phenomena. Thus there is no valid reason for disallowing the language of interactionism on a naturalistic approach.[14] If Mr. X finds that whenever he has discussed politics for ten

---

[14] For a similar result on the Identity theory see above, p. 159.

minutes his blood-pressure has gone up, nothing is to be gained by refusing to call it causality. The language of interactionism is constantly employed in ordinary life and in the description of personal history. We describe people's actions in physical terms, and we do not know enough to talk of their thoughts and purposes by means of empirically related physical terms. Even if we knew enough, it is doubtful whether we should find it practicable to speak in completely physical terms since they would probably be extremely complicated.

Again, to refuse to use the language of interactionism where it yields fruitful scientific results—even while hoping further investigation will supplant it—is to hinder possible scientific advance. The Freudian analysis of such physical states as hysterical blindness in terms of suppressed desires, guilt feeling, and the whole mentalistic equipment of Freudian psychology, is a case of such fruitful trans-level usage.

The aim of the sciences in searching for causes is, however, not merely to find invariant relations—that is the first step—but to incorporate these into a wider system. It is at this point that the chief scientific objections to the language of interactionism have arisen. It is frequently held that to interpolate mentalistic language in the description of physiological processes, except as a symbol for undiscovered physiological conditions, would foster mythology. Such objections rest upon the past successes of reduction in the sense described above, and the hope of continuing such systematic reinterpretation into the more refined units and more general scope of the physical sciences. They express a desire to guide scientific work in the directions that have proved most fruitful in many fields. But this does not mean that mentalistic language for practical use and even in earlier scientific stages is in some sense "misrepresenting reality."

For a naturalistic theory of mind, therefore, both causality and reduction are concepts or methods utilized at certain stages in building up the sciences that study human activity. Their use calls neither for a dualistic theory of two substances, nor for a mechanistic denial of the qualities of events called sense-data. The causality of the mental does not mean anything like the radiation of energy from "disembodied" qualities, nor does the reduction of the mental mean the "evaporation" of qualities.

SCIENTIFIC CONTENT OF TRADITIONAL THEORIES

On a naturalistic theory of mind one may scan previous theories for their scientific content. Most may be viewed as different answers about the possibility of systematic study of the various activities of man. They reflect different interests in the analysis of man's nature or different stages in the growth of scientific knowledge about man, or different programs for the future path of science, or several of these.[15]

Dualistic theories. Thus viewed, the various forms of dualism and mechanism and even some forms of soul theory [16] embody claims concerning the relations of the various levels of phenomena and thus of the sciences. Reinterpreted in the more technical language suggested above, Vitalism with its description of the novel character of organization and purpose in living phenomena embodies the claim that the laws of biology will not be explained by laws of physics. Dualism in its Cartesian forms insists, in effect, that the terms and laws of psychology cannot be reduced to those of physiology. Parallelism represents a combination of two elements: it makes a dogma of the hope that every mental phenomenon may be found to have a unique physical concomitant, and at the same time demands entirely separate sciences of psychology and physiology.

The dualism that is predominant in Locke is less that of matter and spirit than that of primary and secondary qualities—what is objective and physical on the one hand, and what is subjective and mental on the other. This clearly represents the stage that scientific growth had reached in Locke's day. Its confidence in current physical science leads it to regard the qualities physics studies as all there is to nature. The rest are thus thrust out of nature and assigned to mind.

Mechanistic theories. The mechanistic theories in general represent the premature hopes and exaggerated claims of scientific work. The dogmatic character they often possess is in part a function of reaction to dualistic claims. Their reduction of sensory qualities to the status of illusion represents a refusal to grant the status of reality to anything with which science is not yet able to cope. Epiphenomenalism, assigning an uncertain place to sensory qualities and denying their efficacy, embodies a twofold attitude—confidence in the reduction of psychological to physiological phenomena and an overhasty rejection of the possibility of developing psychology in its own terms.

The Identity theory, with its claim that mental and physical are two views of the same substance, may be seen as representing an attempt to give the materials of introspective psychology a place within the framework of science, while maintaining the advantages of mechanism. Its chief danger is

---

[15] This is, of course, a limited perspective looking merely for the elements in the various theories that are of value in outlining the program of the sciences. In other contexts, such as social and intellectual history, a naturalistic approach would examine the same theories for what they reveal of the different needs and interests of men in various periods which often led them to support theories they found instrumentally valuable.

[16] For the role of the soul concept as *explanatory* of natural phenomena in astronomy, physics, medicine, etc., see A. D. White's classic work, *A History of the Warfare of Science with Theology in Christendom*, Appleton, 1925.

that it creates within science itself an unwarranted dualism of method—introspection or direct internal inspection on the one hand, and outer examination on the other hand. As we have several times noted, this does not faithfully represent the way in which we identify either set of phenomena.

The outright mechanistic theories combine at the same time the widest ambitions of science with a restriction of its scope. The latter comes from ruling out as illusory the terms of all sciences not yet well developed. The former is revealed in the hope that every phenomenon will eventually be "reduced" to a physical phenomenon.

Group-mind theory. The scientific content in the group-mind theories, especially in such concepts as social organism and super-organic, is an effort to maintain the independence of the social sciences. Social phenomena are to be identified in their own terms in relation to groups and studied in those terms. Politics should not be reduced to the personal psychology or behavior of the ruler, nor should it be assumed that economic laws are merely deductions from the presumed psychological laws of an economic man. In general, the appeal to social substance, social wills, or the spirit of an age has embodied a protest against undue reductionism in social science.

Need for empirical resolution. From the naturalistic point of view from which this survey has been made, the various claims embodied in the different theories may be divorced from their special origins and seen as theoretically possible alternatives within a naturalistic framework. The issues with respect to the relation of the sciences must then await empirical resolution. Meanwhile the conflicting hypotheses function as programs for investigation resting on the history and mapping the prospects of the various sciences. Naturalistic theory, regarding the subject-matter of study as events and qualities in a natural world, is committed neither to an absolute unity nor to an ultimate plurality. It can press the search for unity without overriding present differences, and it can insist on qualitative disparities without abandoning the search for fresh directions in which unity may be found. In fact naturalism rests its claims for its perspective on mind and body on the wide scope that it provides and the initiative that it encourages in the study of man and nature.

The naturalistic attitude

In the preceding chapter we examined the ambivalent position in which men found themselves when their values and attitudes were based on traditional dualism and their faith in science seemed to point to mechanism. The world in general then appeared as a hostile residence for a residual mind that doubted its own reality. The type of naturalistic theory now suggested views the world as neither hostile nor specially prepared for man. Empirical investigation has shown the ultimately precarious and limited conditions under which mind flourishes. Nevertheless it also reveals the opportunities for modeling, within those limits, more favorable conditions.

ROOTS IN NATURE NOT INIMICAL TO VALUE

Central in such an attitude is the recognition that values have roots and that the flower is not the less beautiful because it springs from the soil and will one day return there. Thus we may reckon with the values which Krutch found disappearing.[17] Love is no less worth-while because it is a quality of human beings; it need not issue from a disembodied spirit to be precious. Truth is no less worth-while because it is a light that guides a plodding army of men, instead of an absolute revelation; the army is one in which mankind might all joyfully enlist. And insofar as the dignity of man is concerned, the part of the self-made man has always seemed more admirable than that of the pampered child of creation. If the present lot of mankind is a pitiable one it need not follow that men's values are illusory, but only that they have not been achieved. This very plight should summon the best energies of men to work out a harmony of their ways and lay a groundwork for the richest flowering of their common garden.

Santayana's naturalistic interpretation of religious virtues. A naturalistic approach need not deprive man of a sense of exaltation in contemplating the cosmos and his part in it. One set of such attitudes is suggested by Santayana in his reinterpretation of the traditional religious virtues of piety, spirituality, and charity.

Piety, says Santayana, is loyalty to the sources of one's being. In addition to local manifestations in devotion to such objects as parents and country, there is *cosmic* piety in relation to the universe at large. This is a feeling of one's ultimate kinship with all that is. "Great is this organism of mud and fire; terrible this vast, painful, glorious experiment. Why should we not look on the universe with piety? Is it not our substance? Are we made of other clay? All our possibilities lie from eternity hidden in its bosom. It is the dispenser of all our joys. We may address it without superstitious terrors; it is not wicked. It follows its own habits abstractly; it can be trusted to be true to its word. Society is not impossible between it and us, and since it is the source of all our energies, the home of all our happiness, shall we not cling to it and praise it, seeing that it vegetates so grandly and so sadly, and that it is not to blame for what, doubtless, it never knew that it

---

[17] See above, pp. 165-66.

did? Where there is such infinite and laborious potency there is room for every hope."[18]

Spirituality is living in the presence of the ideal. It involves a development of purposes and an organization of one's life in the light of the things one finds most worth while. It is "an inward aim and fixity in affection that knows what to take and what to leave in a world over which it diffuses something of its own peace."[19] Realizing that all ideals have a natural basis, the spiritual man neither hopes to transcend all human purposes in mystic feeling, nor seeks fanatically to steer life into some narrow channel.

Charity is the name Santayana gives to the attitude accompanying the realization that, given other conditions of life, other natural and social bases, other ideals arise. For ethical and social standards are seen not as absolute and self-determining, but as qualities of life springing up under specific conditions. Charity therefore involves a liberality to alternative modes of life without surrendering one's own ways. A life lived in line with these virtues is firmly rooted, generates organizing purposes and allows differences.

These attitudes constitute only one of a variety of sets that may be associated with the type of theory of mind expounded above.[20] They serve to illustrate the fact that the denial of mind separate from nature does not necessarily generate regret or disillusion.

[18] From George Santayana, *Reason in Religion*, pp. 191-92. By permission of Charles Scribner's Sons, publishers.
[19] *Ibid.*, p. 194.
[20] Further examination of naturalistic attitudes to values will be found in Chapters 22, 23, 25.

Chapter 15 PROBLEMS OF THE SELF

Our consideration of the question "What is a man?" led to an outline of the naturalistic theory in the preceding chapter. Its answer consisted in an account of the body viewed in constant and dynamic interaction with the world about it (as seen from the standpoint of *all* the sciences), and a study of the qualities that occur in this career. Thus a meaning was given to mind and its relation to body. In the present chapter we shall turn more specifically to the indefinite article in the question and ask "What is *a* man?" We shall consider a number of problems that arise about the individual or the *self*, that which is designated when I speak of "I" or of "myself."

The first of these problems concerns the meaning of identity and the sense in which we can speak of *particular* or *individual* selves. Is there any *unity* in the three-score years and ten that constitute the career of a body? What is there to hold together the experience of an infant, a child, a man through the middle years and into old age, that we should think of him—or he should remember himself—as *one* person?

The second problem concerns the *fixity* or *changeability* of the self. Is there a definite and constant core to the self, which men designate when they seek *self-expression* or *self-realization*? The answer to this question obviously rests upon the prior determination of what constitutes the unity of a self. And the result reached is of tremendous consequence for the theory of education, insofar as education has as one of its major objectives the development of the self and the molding of personality.

The third problem concerns the consequences of the naturalistic conception for moral theory. Specifically, the question arises whether the self as pictured in the naturalistic account provides a standard of valuation or a source of values. It is by no means a mere pun to ask if the self because it is a self is committed to *self*ishness; whether I because I am an *ego* must therefore in some fundamental sense be an *ego*ist.

In its formulation and solution of such problems a naturalistic conception of man lays the basis for its theory of what man can achieve and what directions his energies should take.

Meaning of identity

Before we can discuss the problem of the identity of the self, certain aspects of identity in general require exploration. In theory identity can be defined very simply. According to what the logicians call Leibniz's law, "x is identical to y" means "x has every property that y has and y has every property that x has." For purposes of application a number of further qualifications are required. Let us consider these, using as an illustration "The pen with which I am now writing is identical with the one I used yesterday."

Preliminary identification of existents. The existents in question have first to be identified in some preliminary way. In the present case it is assumed that we are talking about what was in my right hand at certain times yesterday and was instrumental in my making identifiable marks on certain papers, and likewise what is in the same hand today again making marks on papers. There is, in short, an identifying context for the two existents that are being called identical. It is worth noting that this entails reference to other objects and may even assume their identity over a period of time.

Testing for a given property. We must know how to test for x's having a given property and for y's having it. In other words we must know how to offer evidence that a given existent fits a given description. (The testing is carried out in regular scientific fashion by the processes of verification.) Thus we should be able to test whether what I had in my hand yesterday was in fact a pen, whether it was black, six inches long, etc.; and the same tests can be carried out for what is in my hand today. When two existents thus tested turn out to have the same property they are said to be of the same *kind* in that respect.[1] In traditional philosophic terminology they are said to be instances of one *universal*.

Selecting relevant properties. In any particular inquiry concerning identity there must be some limit to the number of properties considered relevant. The person raising the question of identity has in mind some context of kinds or properties or descriptions which fits both existents indicated by the preliminary description. He cannot have *all possible* properties in mind, because there is already (in the case of the pen) a difference in time; furthermore, the amount of ink inside varies, the point gets more worn, and so

---

[1] It is worth noting that to test whether the two existents are of the same kind itself presupposes that the two *tests* are of the same kind. This is assumed in that context but can itself be independently tested. That the need for such assumptions in applying the method of science does not imply a vicious circularity was shown in the discussion of science above (Chapters 7, 10). To want absolute identity without a standard in the given context is like refusing to use any standard in measurement but insisting on an answer in yards.

forth. What is more, unless all change has ceased in the world about it, its relations to other things must have varied, e.g., distance from other objects.

The set of properties relevant in any given case of a judgment of identity depends upon the purpose of the inquiry and is usually implied by an unexpressed criterion of importance. Thus in the present example when a person asks if it is the same *pen* I used yesterday, our familiarity with the definition of a fountain-pen will prevent us from answering, "No, it has differently colored ink today." Again, if the cap of the pen were lost in the interval we should still answer that it was the same pen. The change would not be judged of sufficient importance to interfere with the identity.

Absolute identity, relative identity, and self-identity. It follows that absolute identity would be asserted in a case in which *all conceivable properties that were not precluded as irrelevant* were taken to be present in the entities judged identical. Most of the time we are content with an approximation—when a *limited* set of properties taken to be important for the purposes at hand are found to be present. We may call this relative identity.

When we speak of the self-identity of an object over a span of time, however, we do not intend to limit ourselves to two times t_1 and t_2. For we can conceive of the possibility that the pen was destroyed and a fresh one substituted for it which, at a given time, had every relevant detectable property of the first one, but had not engaged in the same previous activities. This difficulty shows that no account of identity is complete without pointing to the element of continuity. (Or, if we wish to keep the previous account, we must point out that we mean by the properties of the object at time t_2 its *historical* properties as well.) Thus when we speak of complete self-identity we do not mean merely that all intended properties or descriptions fitting the designated context or existent at time t_1 also fit the designated context or existent at time t_2, but that it is possible to designate existential contexts for *any* time t_n between t_1 and t_2 which all the intended properties or descriptions will fit. This historical continuity is perhaps the dominant element in distinguishing *self-identity* from *same kind*.

Nevertheless, historical continuity has its empirical limits, since the interval between t_1 and a selected t_n can become so small that two successive observations could not be made so close together. There is no guarantee that the so-called identical object could not disappear or be withdrawn and be replaced. This happens not merely in the magician's tricks where the hand is quicker than the eye, but is involved in the fact that our vision of anything depends on successive energy quanta coming from it. This does not, however, of itself lend any basis to fantasies sometimes proposed according to which the identity of an object is denied, and it is said to be constantly destroyed and recreated without our noticing it. For just as identity required an empirical interpretation, so also do concepts like vanishing, destroying, and recreating in contexts of this type.

The identity of the individual man

If we turn to the special case of the human being, it appears that an inquiry into the identity of the self may be carried out on different levels and for different purposes.

PHYSICO-BIOLOGICAL, PSYCHOLOGICAL, AND SOCIAL CATEGORIES

There is in the first place the problem of the self-identity of the body, that is, whether the body is identical over a span of time. This is an inquiry in terms of physics and biology. We discover that a particular body has a relative identity—a continuity of historical process combined with some constancy of form. By the constancy of form we mean not merely the observable and recognizable features more or less maintained by a man during the course of his life, but also those subtler constancies within the brain and nervous system which are the bases of habit, character, memory, and association.

The identity provided by the body as a physico-biologic organism is sufficient for many human purposes. Proper names attach to a man as a particular body. The individual upon which legal punishment is inflicted is identified by the body. For most causal relations the individual engaging in the action is located by the position and role of his body.

In the second place there is the problem of self-identity as explored in terms of psychological and social categories. Our individual reflections upon ourselves are usually in such terms. The body often seems to take a background place in such self-identification and the emphasis tends to be upon conscious experience. Here is my mental biography hour after hour. What reason have I to regard this "stream of consciousness," as it has been called, as constituting one identical self? Is it simply because I find this succession of qualities clustering around the identical body which is mine? Or is there any unity in that set of psychological experiences that make up my "mental" career?

Attempts to answer this question fall roughly into three types:

(a) denial that there is any unity other than that provided by the body;

(b) an attempt to find unity of the self in something beyond experience, or in some "true" self or "real" self;

(c) an attempt to find unity in some systematic organization of experiences themselves.

DENIAL OF UNITY

On this view conscious experience is regarded as possessing little or no unity or order, but rather as a heap of relatively unique events. The basis of such an approach varies. Sometimes it rests on an underlying mechanism which regards consciousness as the feeble product of biologic forces, flickering and discontinuous. On this view, there is no unity in a particular man's life other than that discoverable in the career of his body as a physical phenomenon illustrating physical law.

Sometimes, however, the denial of unity rests on the very richness of psychological experience. My conscious experience, it is said, is really so rich, so complex, that only verbal habits prevent me from seeing how different a self I am from hour to hour.

Both these views regard the varying experiences of a man as relatively unique events, exhibiting no discoverable order, and hence possessing no unity.[2] Such positions are of course theoretically possible, but they are certainly premature. The growth of the psychologic and the social sciences may provide the tools by which an individual can discover the unity of his psychological experience, just as the physical sciences provide the tools by which the judgment of identity for a particular body has been rendered more precise.

UNITY BEYOND EXPERIENCE, AND THE "REAL" SELF

There are many philosophic theories, samples of which we shall examine, which attempt to find a unity beyond experience, to discover or establish a "real" self. The theories of soul and mind, discussed in Chapter 11, are the most prominent of these. It is worth while, even at the risk of some repetition, to consider these approaches from our present point of departure. In this context the problem to be solved is that of the unity of experience—what makes an "I" out of all that a man does and undergoes. The characteristic mark of these theories is their attempt to transcend experience in finding this unity. To do this, they generally fasten on some phase of experience, some part of its content, and find it to be a special or superior brand. This special character becomes the arrow that points beyond. To achieve some knowledge, or inkling, at least, of the real "I" all that is necessary is to follow this direction, according to the rules of the philosophic system engaged in the inquiry.

Ordinary use of concept of real self. Ordinary language encourages such an approach, distinguishing somehow between those actions that constitute

---

[2] Such a view constitutes a kind of "nominalism"; see below, p. 347.

what I "really" am, and those "alien" to my "true" self. A man will say of sudden desires, especially if he is ashamed of them, that they "don't really represent me." He considers them chance elements alien to his real self. The familiar distinction between "freely choosing" and "being carried away" further supports this dichotomy. Occasionally a man may find himself acting and feeling differently in quite different contexts, and may ask himself, "Which is really me?" Psychologists report cases of split personality, in which a man has two quite different personalities, at least one of which does not know of the other's existence.

When different experiences seem each to bear the stamp of genuineness while they occur, how is one to decide between them? Am I fundamentally the cool reflective person who soberly reckons costs, or the impulsive reckless person of other occasions? In the first mood I deprecate the second as hasty; in the second, I scorn the first as petty. Am I the individual who stands aside and surveys alternatives in terms of personal consequences, or am I most true to myself when I identify myself with some wider set of ideals that reveal their truly representative character by the exaltation they produce in me? And when psychologists tell me of repressed desires am I to regard these as real elements of my self seeking expression or as not really of my self because I have in fact suppressed them?

Plato on "real" pleasures in the self. Plato's account of the nature of pleasure in Book IX of his *Republic* is an interesting illustration of this attempt to distinguish, within experience, a "superior" or "real" brand from an "inferior" or "unreal" brand. It is especially worth examining because it shows transparently the way in which such distinctions already presuppose a whole philosophy, including a conception of a self with determinate characteristics. Plato's analysis of pleasure occurs in a context in which he is trying to show that the good man is far happier than the tyrant. Bodily pleasures, he points out, have their origin in the cycle of depletion and repletion. It is as in the case of health: when a man is healthy he takes health for granted without finding special pleasure in it, but when he is sick, recovery is a pleasure. There are three states of feeling—pleasure, an intermediate state of rest, and pain. So-called bodily pleasures (e.g., of food and sex) are transitions from pain to rest; they appear to be in the domain of pleasure but are not. Plato compares the three states to regions of absolute space. In going from down to middle one thinks he is going into the up, but ends in the middle without reaching the real up.

Clearly Plato is fashioning an instrument to be used against the man who defends his activity by the joy he takes in it. This is not necessarily real joy, Plato would say: he may just be laboring under an illusion. The ordinary man in his pursuit of pleasure is just like the sick man and in no position to judge. Who, then, is to judge? Plato finds three types of pleasures or pseudo-pleasures corresponding to the parts of the soul—pleasures of intellect, of ambition, and of bodily desires. Now the man of ambition has tasted bodily pleasures and declares in favor of ambition. The man who favors bodily pleasures has tasted only those. But who has tasted all three? Only the philosopher. Hence he is the best judge. Now which does he favor? Certainly the intellectual pleasures. Therefore they are the best.

Plato never envisages the possibility that a man might prefer other pleasures than the intellectual after tasting all three. His whole approach here implies the metaphysics on which he operates—the identification of reality with the eternal—and the rest of his views concerning the relative reality of different pleasures follows almost deductively. A generous interpretation of his account—which enables him to tell a man that he is really not being pleased when the man himself feels that he is—would take it to express a passionate preference for intellectual activity. A less generous account would find Plato here forging an instrument for rule by the "philosopher" over the common man, on the basis of a presumed higher knowledge.

A second argument for the greater reality of intellectual pleasures is that they are concerned with the eternal. The pleasures of the body are concerned with the flux of existence and so are least valuable. Pleasures of sight and smell occupy a kind of middle position. They are superior to bodily pleasures for they do not come in the context of departing pain. But they are transitory and do not admit of the genuine growth that knowledge does; hence Plato regards them as less real than the intellectual pleasures. This argument clearly rests on the assumption, basic in all of Plato's thinking, that the eternal is more real than the changing.

We may note that Plato's conception of the self, as we have seen elsewhere,[3] was based on the same phase of human activity as that exalted in his theory of pleasure—intellectual experience, with its timeless objects of understanding. The real self, according to Plato, is akin to the eternal and unchanging for which it yearns. It involves a soul actively striving for the eternal and finding a unity or intelligibility provided by the system of Ideas which it is seeking to grasp.

"Real" self based on special feeling. The mystical tradition finds the clearest indication of the true self in mystic or ecstatic experiences in which all sense of self disappears.[4] From this a man may learn the fragmentary character of his finite self and at the same time grasp something of the ultimate world-unity to which he belongs, and to which he may return. With the exception of such mystical philosophies, the philosophic interpretation which finds the identity of the individual man in some true or real self beyond experience has tended to look to intellectual or conscious experience as a basis for its claims.

[3] See above, p. 140.
[4] See above, p. 141.

KANT'S THEORY OF THE SELF

Kant's view of the self is a very complex one carefully worked out, because he was cognizant of all the difficulties involved in trying to establish the existence of an entity beyond experience on the basis of evidence within experience. Kant takes his point of departure from Hume's philosophy in which knowledge is merely an association of impressions and the self a name for an association of experiences. Kant agrees with Hume that the discovery of the self in experience is an empirical matter, just as is the discovery of objects. But experience itself, Kant claims, has two components. There are the materials of sensation, which seem to be provided from without. But there are also such forms as space and time and the various categories of causality, substance, reality, possibility. These forms in which experience is ordered Kant regards as provided from within.

The existence of these forms becomes for Kant the basic evidence for the operation of mind. Furthermore, since they are not *added* in conscious experience, but are revealed by philosophic analysis as a constitutive part of the phenomena which are our experience, mind has a hand in the very creation of the world of phenomena. It is not something that learns a ready-made or external world but cooperates in the very fashioning of phenomena. The world of phenomena is regarded by Kant as a joint product of mind which provides the forms and things-in-themselves which provide the content of sensation.

Thus although Kant regards the self of psychology as an empirical self and part of the phenomenal world, he thinks that the critical analysis of experience points to a real or "noumenal" or transcendental self beyond, which yet conditions the forms of all experience. It is not pictured in experience, but appears as an "I think" accompanying all experience and tying it together. Thus every little bit of experience is not felt as an isolated event, but related within what Kant so formidably calls a "synthetic unity of apperception." In Kant's *Critique of Pure Reason* this self appears merely as the indicated source of order and unity in experience; in the *Critique of Practical Reason* it is pointed to as the source of moral law.

It is interesting to compare Kant's conception with that of Descartes. Descartes in his "Cogito, ergo sum" (I think, therefore I am),[5] had attempted to find a unity and identity for the self in a substance or stuff underlying the thinking activity which he took to be unique. Kant criticized Descartes' assertion as "really a tautology since the *cogito (sum cogitans)*[6] asserts my existence immediately."[7] Nevertheless both views are similar in

---

[5] See above, p. 149.
[6] Literally "I think (I am thinking)."
[7] *Critique of Pure Reason*, translation by N. Kemp Smith, Macmillan, 1929, p. 337.

their effect. Descartes postulates a self for the thinking phase of human experience. Kant concentrates on more refined phases of experience—the ordering of the materials of sensation and the sharp feelings of duty; and his net result is to point to a self that does these jobs, although any attempt to gain an experiential knowledge of that self—or a rational knowledge for that matter—is given up.[8]

Developments from the Kantian conception. In the development of German idealist philosophy from Kant through Fichte to Hegel, the Kantian distinction between the transcendental self and things-in-themselves was questioned, and the ultimate source of all phenomena was eventually taken to be Spirit or Self. In the Hegelian picture this appears as Absolute Spirit which reveals itself in nature and in the development of social institutions. As such it expresses for each of us what we really are. The upshot is that any man can best follow his true self by identifying himself with the social system of which he is a part. Thus Hegel insists in his *Philosophy of Right* that the murderer who is to die has himself willed his own punishment; for that is the law of the state which embodies the reality of that man's will. If he tries to escape, presumably these bodily movements do not represent what he "really" wills. Such claims for absolute obedience in the name of a state that presents itself as a man's real will or as the highest good of his true self are also found in fascist philosophies.

In general, the attempt to find a real or a true self beyond experience represents in each case the consequences of an assumed special metaphysical account of reality. Reality is first defined implicitly either as the eternal or the whole or the rational or the universal; thereafter the real self is identified by that part of experience which shares in or points to this selected property. Apart from such metaphysical assumptions, when it is said that the individual should give preference to the promptings of this self, the approach we are considering turns out in effect to be a disguised mode of evaluation. Plato values the eternal more highly than the ephemeral; Kant the universal and absolute more than the special and the relative; and Hegel the state more than the individual. In this fashion such theories function as *evaluations of* or *exhortations to* specific fields of human activity.

SELF AS THE SYSTEMATIC ORGANIZATION OF EXPERIENCE

The third type of approach does not deny the unity of the self nor seek it in some self beyond experience. As explored in terms of psychological and social categories, a particular self, it holds, is a name for a systematic

---

[8] For Kant's use of the self in moral theory, see below, p. 407 ff.; for his arguments concerning the immortality of the soul, see p. 355.

organization of experiences and activities associated in the career of a particular body.

Hume's treatment of self-identity was, as we have seen, of this type. He began by collapsing the "I" into many series of discrete experiences, and then met the question of how experiences hang together with an account of laws of association according to which impressions cluster. His analysis was, of course, carried out in terms of the restricted introspective psychology of his day; a contemporary statement would correlate introspective materials with behavioral description, psychoanalytic accounts and sociological or cultural analysis—in short, it would use every available technique for providing a systematic picture of a given self.

Personality the unity of the particular self. The particular self thus viewed is to be identified by its special pattern of habitual responses, characteristic drives, specific desires, and so forth. The particular self is the totality of the activities and qualities associated in the career of that particular body, seen in the perspective of their special organization. The unity of that self—what we may call its personality—is the pattern discoverable in those activities, their dynamic organization, as psychologists sometimes call it. The description of a man's personality is thus an account systematizing his psychological and social activities or experiences.[9]

Self-knowledge and the role of memory. This process of coming to know the unity of a particular self is, of course, one in which we all engage, both unreflectively and reflectively, and both with respect to ourselves and to others. Every man has a sense of himself through the pattern of conscious experience that he has gradually pieced together. All his experience comes to be felt by him as the extension of a dynamic core of already organized experiences by already established modes of experiencing and associating—the whole of which he calls his self. This is the sense of "It's I" which Kant described as the "I-think." It is a discoverable empirical phenomenon, any part of whose content we may hope to study in scientific fashion.

The basic psychological process in this construction is, of course, that of memory. Memory is involved in the very apprehension of things about us by which a partial experience is rounded out into a familiar object. Memory is involved in the understanding of a sentence; for it holds the earlier parts until the entire thought comes into view. And memory is intimately involved in the sense of self; for without the continuity it provides to experience the

---

[9] Some psychologists stress the element of uniqueness in a definition of personality, treating it as that which distinguishes one man from others. It is difficult, however, to see why uniqueness should be integral to the definition of personality any more than it should be to the definition of height. That the personality of individuals varies—just as that the height of individuals varies—is an empirically discoverable fact. That some may be the same is possible *a priori*, and is probably also a fact.

self as conscious experience would be literally born anew at every successive moment.[10]

If a man were asked what evidence he had that a sound just heard in the room was *his* utterance, not someone else's with similar voice, his reply would indicate some of the criteria of self involved in that kind of case. For example, he would say that he had not only felt the vibrations in his mouth and throat, but that he could recollect having the intention of making the statement, and so forth. Of course if he was a *very* absent-minded professor he might not be sure whether it had been he who spoke! Similar questions arise with respect to the relation of a man's memory and imagination—that is, how he distinguishes remembered from imagined experiences.

In the growth of the self, a man's knowledge of himself becomes more than the mere sense that he *is,* and is extended to knowing something about what *sort* he is. This is the Socratic concept in the injunction, "Know thyself." Through reactions in conduct—both by introspection and by observation of one's behavior—there comes a growing recognition of the pattern of the self. The surprised exclamation of the two-year-old pointing to her leg and saying "Mama, it's me" is succeeded by the often disappointed sigh of the grown-up when he says, "So that's what I'm like!" Similarly, a man's outline of another's self arises through judgment and interpretation of observed behavior.

Social character of the self. It is important to note the social character of the self at every stage of its development. That many of its characteristics, directions of growth, and opportunities of expression come from the social milieu in which the person moves is so obvious that it is sometimes overlooked.[11] That the child's character is molded by his elders about him is also obvious, at least to every parent. But even these formulations speak of the individual as acquiring habits and characteristics and therefore suggest the existence of a self *prior* to its acquisitions, however much affected by them. There is a profounder sense in which the self is sometimes said to be social, which refers to the very genesis of selfhood. This self which a man comes to know as his "inmost being" comes to maturity with the growth of thought in the man. Thought is a kind of inner discourse, and discourse is the utilization of a language that can arise only in a social group. The fundamental fact which allows for the growth of the self is thus the

---

[10] Henri Bergson has explored intensively the phenomena of memory especially on their introspective side. For him, mind is consciousness and consciousness signifies primarily memory. From its analysis he seeks to develop a theory of mind in which the brain is rather the instrument of consciousness than the latter an effect or operation of the brain. Cf. Bergson's *Matter and Memory* (translated by N. M. Paul and W. S. Palmer), Macmillan, 1929; also his *Mind-Energy* (translated by H. Wildon-Carr), Macmillan, 1921, Essay II.

[11] See below, p. 242 ff.

fact of communication, not merely in the verbal sense, but in co-operative activities of men within a society.[12]

The study of the self. Since the unity of a particular self is, on this approach, to be empirically discovered, there is no *a priori* guarantee of a single pattern. Men's personalities thus constitute phenomena for the exploration of the psychological and social sciences. There is a theoretical possibility of multiple types, and experience certainly knows many forms. The unity of some men's selves appears to lie in their social values, and they behave very much as the group-mind theory would have men behave. The unity of others seems to lie in cold reason coupled with set values. Some men may have a minimum of unity and almost resemble the self of discrete experiences bound in random associations, which is one extreme form of Hume's picture. Certainly some have two alternating unities, although these can sometimes be resolved into one by psychological treatment. Such descriptions of the unity of a self are, of course, largely impressionistic. The possibility of the occurrence of different types of unity and their explanations, the degree to which there are elements common to all selves, the extent of social patterning of the typical self in a community, are all issues to be explored by the empirical sciences of psychology and of society. Similarly, psychology is theoretically in the best position to decide what conceptual framework to employ; for example, whether to allow such concepts as "dual self" or whether to assert a dynamic unity even in a sharp dichotomy of behavior; similarly whether to allow isolated acts of behavior not in line with the systematic personality of a man to be regarded as "chance deviants" or whether, as is more generally held today, to interpret even such responses (on some theory of the dynamics of personality) as integral to the systematic unity of the self. Again, no *a priori* decision can determine whether the unity of a given self can best be established by using the concepts of psychoanalysis, social psychology, the every-day language of morals and character-development, or the concepts of sociology and anthropology in the description of cultural values, or some fresh theory of personality. Nor need we expect that the concepts now in use will continue to be employed throughout the progress of the psychological and social sciences.

Fixity and changeability of the self

The account given above of the self and its unity in no way determines the degrees of fixity to be found in the self. This becomes entirely a question for empirical investigation. Only a well-developed physiological,

[12] For an evolutionary view of the self as social, stressing these features, see G. H. Mead, *Mind, Self and Society*, University of Chicago Press, 1934.

psychological, and social science will be able to tell us what physiological, psychological, and social factors, if any, are common to all selves, what are peculiar to individual selves on the basis of heredity or early environment, and how much at present regarded as "natural" expression is really a function of chance circumstances. Insofar as attitudes are concerned, social scientists have long recognized that these are a function of early influence and social surroundings. The realization that attitudes are susceptible of change is becoming widespread today. The attempt to treat attitudes as by and large the expression of inborn tendencies in the self is recognized to have represented insufficient knowledge of determinants.

On the question of the limits and determinants of human action there will be further comment in Part Four. At this point, however, the clarification which is rendered possible by the kind of analysis of the self which we have worked out above may be illustrated from an analysis of such concepts as self-expression, self-realization, and self-development. In their application to educational theory these notions crystallize sharply the issues of fixity and change in the self.

MEANING OF SELF-EXPRESSION

What can be meant when I am told to "express myself" or "fulfill my self"? In one sense—since on an empirical approach all a man's activities have equal reality though not equal importance—everything I do is part of my self and develops it, strengthening some tendencies, weakening others, sowing seeds in relation to my surroundings whose fruits are unforeseen.

Clearly the meaning of self-expression will vary according to the type of context in which it is employed. Where the reference is to an integrated adult personality it means pursuing the lines of conduct that have generally characterized it (as distinct from deviant trends) or that could stem from its previous habits; or else pursuing those lines of conduct successfully (some standard of success being implied), rather than in a slipshod manner. In such a context when the individual is told to be "true to yourself" or simply to "be yourself" or where he wonders whether certain actions really represent him, there is an implied reference to an already established personality, to an order that already exists. The individual may not be completely aware of that order, and may thus formulate his task in Socratic fashion as one of learning to know himself. And this, as Socrates repeatedly stressed, is no easy matter.

Where there is not yet an integrated adult personality, where the plan of the self is not manifest or is believed not to be sufficiently stabilized, the concept of *self-realization* emerges as more definitely evaluative, more clearly hortatory. To call for self-realization in that context is either to urge a specific line of development in conduct and personality (as in the real and social self theories) or to have formed a hypothesis about some line of development *appropriate to that individual* and urge its acceptance. In its most general form it may be equivalent to the advice to make a system of the self—where system and its fruits constitute the values. For the individual appealing to himself, the task is one of self-molding rather than self-knowledge.

Self-knowledge and self-molding. It is not suggested that these two tasks—knowing oneself and molding oneself—are to be regarded as altogether distinct. Since it is probable that no individual is completely set, the process of knowing oneself is at the same time a kind of stabilizing or crystallizing of the self. Similarly, molding oneself involves at least implicit acceptance of certain values that are identified with the self, hence at least a partial self-knowledge. These values, in acting as the basis of choice, serve as pivots around which the form of the self may be redirected. Such processes take place continuously throughout a man's life. In all of them, whether a man is being told to express himself or to realize himself—and certainly when he is asked to change himself—the evaluative element is dominant.

ILLUSTRATIONS FROM EDUCATIONAL THEORY

Some of the problems involved in these conceptions may be illustrated on a large scale from controversies that have gone on in American educational theory for the past two decades. Some exponents of progressive education have worked on the assumption that the differential potentialities of children will develop of their own accord if they are not repressed into narrowly standardized molds but given free scope, with rich materials available. To what extent does the individual have within himself the basis of spontaneous development or decision? How much external determination of direction is necessary or desirable?

Some molding of attitudes unavoidable. So wide a question ought not to expect a single answer. At least the answer might not be the same for some skills as for some attitudes, for early years as for college life. Take the concrete situation of a teacher who finds six-year-old A about to take paints away from six-year-old B. In what does giving free scope to the child here consist? If the teacher takes the stand that B should be left undisturbed in possession of the paints because they are his, he is strengthening property rights. If he gives the paints to A because A shows greater abilities, he is developing a principle of the rights of ability. If he simply stops the impending fight and gives A other paints, the effect may be to cultivate paternalism and pressure-techniques. If he insists on the children "arguing" their claims, he is hoping to instill rationality or at least discourse as a technique. Finally if he pretends not to notice or goes out of the room the effect is to strengthen force as a technique. In short, doing anything or doing nothing in such a situation is objectively strengthening certain tendencies or stimulating others. A choice must thus be made about the desirable direction of the self. But this does not mean that the choice is arbitrary or that we start with empty selves. For the whole problem arises within a matrix of the children's needs and social needs which set limits to the choice of alternatives and make some better than others.

The problem of indoctrination at the college level. It will be of interest to the reader to apply this discussion of self-expression to the problem of indoctrination in colleges. The question here is generally phrased in terms of the teacher's avoiding the imposition of his own attitudes and values on his students. On the one side it is said that a teacher should be neutral; it is not his business to indoctrinate but only to present all aspects of a question for the consideration of his students. On the other side it is argued that neutrality is a fiction, that a teacher cannot help expressing and communicating attitudes and values. The very aim of presenting all sides of a question is itself an attempt to develop a fundamental rational or critical attitude, while failure to take a stand indoctrinates either indecision or the teacher's own unrealized preferences. It would be better, on such a view, for him to render his own assumptions explicit for critical student consideration.

This problem reaches very deeply into teaching methods. Does the instructor teach as if he were presenting a series of portraits for mere contemplation, or as if he were fashioning tools for conduct? The traditional aloofness of academic men from pressing problems (political, economic, social) of the day is no doubt expressed in the former attitude. Insofar as this is inculcated in students, potential social leadership may be lost.

A complete answer to the question of fashioning attitudes in colleges requires a fuller analysis of the aims of a college in the community. What attitudes capable of intensification in college life are socially indispensable? What attitudes does the pursuit of knowledge require in order to endure as a stable goal? Certainly there is no room for inculcation of scientific hypotheses on emotional grounds. Nor should avoidance of indoctrination mean treating all hypotheses as if they were free and equal in spite of experience. If the suggestions of "irrationality" and "inducing belief by unfair means" are removed from the problem, what remains is fundamentally the question of molding the direction of the self, the idea of control versus drift, *not* control versus free development.

This has become especially clear in the problems of education for democracy. The challenge of fascism in the thirties and the gigantic struggle against it in the forties have made men more conscious of the foundations of their own beliefs and attitudes. We can no longer assume that a democratic outlook or character springs up of its own accord irrespective of social conditions and educational influences. To cultivate democratic ways is no more imposition than to cultivate habits of bodily health or cleanliness. The problem of assessing our educational system at all levels to establish a genuinely democratic outlook is therefore a particularly pressing one.

The philosophic foundations of the whole problem of fashioning attitudes clearly involve three factors: a knowledge of the determinants of the self, an analysis of the meaning of freedom, and an investigation of the criteria of what is socially desirable. Each of these will be discussed below.[13]

The self and its values

A man's activities are best identified by the directions of his striving. The objects of his striving, that which he is seeking to attain, we call his goals or ends or values. When they are very broad—or perhaps remote—they are sometimes called ideals. When they are classified for a given man we often speak of them as his conception of the good. Our final problem in this chapter is to see the place of values in the account of the self as given above.

THE PLACE OF VALUES IN THE SELF

A man's goals delimit rather than limit his activities. They tell us what he is up to, what he wants or is trying to do. In this sense an account of a particular man's goals is a picture of his *self*. To know the pattern of a man's values realistically analyzed is to know what he is like. As we saw above, the unity of a given self lies in the systematic organization of the experiences of a particular body. A systematic account of a man's values is simply one way of describing that unity. It constitutes a description of the self in action by analyzing the course of its motion.

To the extent that a man's values change, the pattern of his self must be recognized to be undergoing change. Such change may be slow or rapid, conscious or only partly conscious. To trace the continuities and map the constant and changing aspects during a given period is the task of personal or group history. To discover the causes of these changes and constancies is the task of social science. It must treat constancy as something to be explained just as it regards change as a problem. The discovery of these causes would show at the same time what the determinants of the self have been,

---

[13] Chapters 17, 18, 25.

what the direction of further striving is likely to be, and what limitations are likely to operate in further conduct.[14]

It follows that values are not extraneous to the self as pictured above, not factors which somehow set a self in motion from without, but genuine constitutive elements of the self, in the sense of directions of its movement. Hence no self is without values. To ask, "If I had no values what would I choose?" is to talk nonsense.

The analysis of fixity and changeability of the self thus likewise applies to values. The discovery of constancy and variability in the values of a man or group is therefore recognized as a question of empirical science and history, not to be determined by *a priori* postulation of a fixed self and its fixed nature.

In order that the path may be clear for an empirical study of values, it is important to recognize not merely that the self cannot be determined without empirical knowledge of the contents of the self, but also that no specific values are ingrained or determined by the fact that it is a self. This latter point is difficult to establish, for it runs counter to the common view that all men are naturally selfish. Although selfishness has often been condemned as a vice, it is as often exalted as the universal basis of a realistic morality. The analysis of the self given above enables us to reformulate the traditional controversy of the inherent selfishness of men so as to admit of an intelligible solution.

IS EGOISM INHERENT IN THE SELF?

A man is said to be *egoistic* or *selfish* if he acts on the principle of pursuing *his own* interests, *altruistic* or *unselfish* if he reckons the interests *of others*. Philosophical egoism has generally involved one or both of two theses: (a) all men *in fact* pursue their own interests; (b) men *should* pursue their own interests. The first of these is generally called *psychological egoism*, the second *ethical egoism*.

Psychological egoism. The view that all men in fact pursue their own interests is sometimes held on *a priori* grounds, sometimes on empirical grounds. When *a priori*, it means that altruism is meaningless or impossible. It is argued, for example, that the man who inconveniences himself to help others is really finding greater pleasure in helping others; else why would he do it? Altruism is thus simply egoism which happens to find its expression in directions that serve others.

The objection to this *a priori* argument is that it is trivial or merely verbal. Since no empirical fact—e.g., martyrdom or giving up one's life to save someone else—could possibly disprove it, it is merely a mode of speech, an-

---
[14] For a fuller account of naturalistic theories of value, see below, Chapter 25.

other way of talking about empirical facts. Instead of saying that a man is an altruist because he inconveniences himself to help others, we must simply say that he finds his egoistic satisfactions in helping others. Thus, in effect, we eliminate the term "altruism" and make "egoistic conduct" synonymous with "conduct." The result is that by destroying the meaning of altruism the *a priori* argument destroys all specific meaning for egoism.

An empirical approach to psychological egoism. An empirical argument for psychological egoism would not maintain that unselfish conduct is inconceivable. It would claim that unselfish conduct never or rarely occurs. This would entail specifying empirical tests to decide whether conduct is selfish or unselfish. It is impossible for actions themselves to be so classified irrespective of motivation. For example, a man helps a second man in the presence of a third. Is this to be interpreted as aiding a fellow-man or impressing a third person? Wider knowledge would be required of the actual circumstances in order to find the answer. Similar tests might be made with the same man in other, varying situations. Results of such observations could be correlated with his introspective reports. Thus it might be decided whether aiding others in distress is the sort of thing he does spontaneously without regrets, or with a firm sense of his own righteousness, or in the hope of building up a credit account of good will, and so forth. It is on the basis of such observations that we do in fact judge other people's character.

Selfishness defined in terms of such empirical testing would be a state of character—a set of general attitudes, motives, and desires. For example, action intended by a man to secure his own increased wealth, prestige, power, without regard for its effects on others, might be called selfish; likewise action with concomitant concentration on the sort of spectacle he was making.[15] Selfishness would be as definite a state of character as individualism, self-reliance, competitiveness, co-operativeness, and misanthropy.

Egoistic character-traits are social products. Now our scientific knowledge of character traits suggests their malleability: they are functions of the preferred pattern which a society and its institutions cultivate. Thus in our own urban life young people learn quickly to regard wealth and success as prizes worth striving for and to measure other things by the wealth and success they bring. People learn to be competitive; business life forces them to regard others as rivals, and the assurance that "business is business" makes them unsparing in their competition. The attitude becomes widely implanted. It is not enough to keep up with the Joneses; you have to go them one better. It is not enough to do excellently; you must win out over the rest. In short, the self-centeredness that seems so widespread as to be natural

---

[15] For the use of such a distinction in psychological experiment, see Helen Block Lewis, "An Experimental Study of the Role of the Ego in Work," *Journal of Experimental Psychology*, Vol. 34 (1944), Nos. 2 and 3.

is a carefully cultivated character-trait having its roots deep in the functioning of our dominant institutions.

Is egoism somehow "more natural"? The defender of the egoist thesis will grant that men can be trained to forget themselves and to act for the benefit of others. In fact, part of the task in war is to persuade people to be ready to give up their lives, if necessary, for goals like honor, country, and democracy that they would scarcely regard as egoistic. But the philosophical egoist will look upon such people as if they were overcome by excitement or as laboring under some "idealistic" delusions. In short it will be implied that altruism is an artificially induced state, egoism a natural one.

The metaphysics of such an approach was discussed above in connection with the concepts of essence and nature.[16] Insofar as the approach claims to be an empirical one it must rely on the evidence of psychology and the social sciences. The attempt to establish native, primitive or inherent human traits does not today meet with much favor in those sciences. Most of the specific traits discoverable in the self turn out to depend on the culture and institutions of a people. Thus a readiness to give up one's life on a serious issue is probably no more nor less inherent than to devote constant attention to clinging to it under any and all circumstances. History and anthropology show us tremendous variety of specific goals. Although these may be understood as special forms of expression of fundamental drives or dependable motives, the latter themselves are so wide as to determine in themselves neither selfishness nor unselfishness. Drives, such as hunger or the demand for affection, provide a motor-power, but they can be the base of either predatory or co-operative social forms.

A more mature psychology does not look to inherent traits to determine specific patterns of motives or conduct. Viewing conduct as issuing from the constant interaction of men with their physical and social environment, it can reckon the factors that incline individuals and societies to one or the other type of character. It can go further, and offer judgments about which type provides greater satisfaction of basic drives in the long run. In such an estimate, factors like initial outgoing tendencies in the child, the constitution of our world such that some co-operation of men is required to meet our basic needs, and the lessons of historical experience in social organization, all become relevant. And in the light of the outcome some modes of action may be viewed as fundamentally warping rather than expressing basic drives. But such judgments are essentially ethical. They state what is better for man. Hence they concern the claims of ethical rather than psychological egoism.

Psychological egoism, empirically interpreted, thus finds little support in scientific findings. The possibility remains, of course, that it may describe ac-

---

[16] Chapter 2, above.

curately certain limited regions of human conduct. For example, it may be true that personal pain can become so great that social ideals will crumble, or that personal hunger can in extremes drive men to all sorts of things they would not usually do. But such limited assertions bear little resemblance to the sweeping claims of universal egoism.

Ethical egoism. The view that men *should* pursue their own interests, translated into the empirical terms we have considered, means merely that a certain type of character is recommended as desirable. The question then arises as to why this particular type of character should be so valued. Self-seeking men may be useful for the rapid development of a continent which is sparsely settled, though one may wonder why communally-minded men would not be better. But what ground is there for making an absolute value out of this special type of character? Clearly none. Once the prop of inevitability is gone—when we realize that men are not bound by nature to such a character—ethical egoism must justify itself by showing that a community of self-seeking men is today most capable of achieving the life that we regard as good. It must justify itself against other and competing types, for example, against the co-operatively-minded type which might appear more appropriate to a highly integrated modern community.

The problem of the desirable kind of character for men is one to which there will be frequent reference in subsequent parts of this book. It is sufficient for the present to have suggested that selfishness or egoism refers not to an inherent property of the self but to one type of character of the self to which there are alternatives. Man is inherently self-seeking only in the sense that every self embodies seeking or striving. This is a description of the self which gives it no ready-made goals. The way is thus clear for a careful examination of the conditions upon which the self and its striving depend and the forms they may take.

Part Four

OF HUMAN BONDAGE
AND HUMAN FREEDOM

Chapter 16 VALUES, ENDS, AND MEANS

Nothing is more striking in the world around us than the extent and depth of human bondage. And nothing is more stirring than the hope of human freedom. When we considered the problem of the nature of man, we saw that we could regard ourselves as part of the natural world, responsive to forces operating within and about us. We learned, however, that this did not make us passive bodies buffeted by these forces, for we in our turn influence them. In fact, we found that one of the most distinctive features of ourselves as selves was this character of striving, seeking to mold our environment and to gain control of our futures and our destiny. It is therefore appropriate now to examine the extent to which we can realistically do this. What are the limitations that operate to check man? To what extent is liberation from these limitations possible? The theme of the present study may therefore appropriately be phrased as "What can we do?"

In such a study the starting-point is inevitably human values. If men had no values there could be, strictly speaking, no limitation of their activity. If I am standing still you cannot stop me from going, unless you mean that *if* I were to go in a certain direction I would be stopped. Even if I move in a straight line from A to B where I am stopped, this has not limited my motion unless you assume impulse towards further motion in the same direction. Hence if there are no strivings, no directive tendencies, there is no possible bondage. If there is no *possible* bondage, there is no meaning to liberty or freedom. This should not, however, be taken to mean that *actual* bondage is a prerequisite of liberty or freedom.

That men have values means only that men's strivings have direction, that they so orient their conduct as to try to achieve their aims. If to wish were to achieve, if to dream were to possess, then there would be no problem of effort nor of choice. Effort is necessary when there are difficulties in the way, and choice arises when there are alternate paths to a proposed goal or alternative goals bidding for human striving. Even this oversimplifies the actual situations that men face. For goals do not lie ready to be seized at the end of paths ready to be trodden. The achievement of a goal is only figuratively an act of reaching; it is realistically an act of creating. Between the first beginnings of action within a man which constitute the phenomena of choice and the happy attainment of his aims lie the tasks that constitute the means. That values have this cost is the ultimate source of human bondage. What philosophers have analyzed as the problem of means and ends is in effect a cost-accounting system of human values.

Relation between means and ends

The relation between means and ends is a fundamental problem in ethical theory. Formally an end is something we aim at, something we choose for its own sake. A means is something we choose because of the results it will yield. If I go for a walk because it is good for my health, then my walking is a means to health. If I go because I like walking, then it is an end. If for both reasons, it is both means and end. Thus the distinction comes to coincide with the distinction between what is regarded as good in itself (the end) and what is regarded as instrumentally good, or good for something beyond it (the means).

No fixed ends. Dewey's writings have been particularly effective in American ethical theory in destroying the sharp dichotomy so often set up between means and ends.[1] He opposes especially the idea that there are fixed goals for man whether these be in some sense "natural" or "instinctive" or otherwise predetermined. He views ends as arising in problem-situations. When men face difficulties and find themselves involved in problems which they must solve, they set up aims as proposed resolutions. Hunger is a problem-situation, but the end which is sought on a particular occasion may be a medium rare steak with French fried potatoes. This is as true of the major goals that motivate men in living as of the small ones that arise from day to day. In this analysis ends are in a sense also means, since, in addition to their satisfying "terminal" character, they act as pivots for reconstructing the situation. They can therefore also be evaluated as instruments.

Complexity of interrelation. Historical study as well as ordinary observation confirms the view that the interrelation of means and ends is a complex one. What one individual or group treats as an end (political power, for example), another may treat as a means (power in order to acquire use-values). In fact what one individual or group treats at one time as an end it may treat as a means at another time, and what is treated as a means at one time may become an end at another. When Aunt Polly wanted the fence whitewashed, Tom Sawyer's work was her intended means. When Tom's friends saw him taking apparent joy in the task it rapidly became an end for them. Their end proved a means for Tom not only to secure leisure, but also to obtain a small fortune of odds and ends charged for the privilege of doing his whitewashing. So, too, a man may set out on a business career

---

[1] See especially John Dewey, *Human Nature and Conduct*, Modern Library, 1930.

to make his "pile" with the hope of retiring early to "enjoy life," but by the time he is ready to retire, may find his joys to lie wholly within his business activities. Like habits, values cannot be summoned up at will, nor their realization in conduct indefinitely postponed.

It is equally common for some ends upon their achievement to recede into means for further ends. Leisure is often valued highly in a busy life, but scarcely is it achieved when a man looks about him for new fields of activity, like Alexander sighing for more kingdoms to conquer. This phenomenon of achieved goals turning into mere resting-points for further goal-seeking sometimes gives rise to familiar laments on the vanity of all desire. Again, fresh ends may emerge in the process of pursuing a goal and may become sufficiently impelling to cause the abandonment of the initial objective. Thus a keen student of literature, reading Plato for his literary qualities, may become fired by the philosophic problems there presented and completely shift the focus of his interest and activity. It frequently happens too that the attempted solution of one problem generates fresh and more interesting problems. Thus workmen seeking to remove a grievance may be led into unionization and ultimately into an interest in the structure of their society's economic life.

From these considerations it is clear that ends and means cannot be sharply separated in any problem, that to embark on the means toward a given end may be a genuine adventure, and that the complexity of life combines with the plasticity of human material to make the outcome of large-scale social enterprises difficult to anticipate. Nevertheless, in any given context at a given time, ends and means must be distinguished irrespective of possible subsequent change. For the ends in that context mark the direction of striving and the means are elements which might be altered or, if possible, dispensed with. In practice we rarely have a pure means, unless it be pure drudgery. Rarely, too, do we have pure ends that fit into no wider context to be achieved. Most activities are both ends and means—but in different respects.

Evaluation of means and ends

We do not ordinarily evaluate means simply in terms of *whether* they will achieve a proposed goal, but also *how well* they will do so. When we analyze what we mean by this we find that it involves comparing the original goal with ends implicit in the means. Take an extremely simple example. I want to get to a particular place. The subway is the obvious means of getting there. Now I may decide to sacrifice the *speed* of the subway trip for the *sunshine* of some other means of getting there. Or, if the subway is the only means available, I may decide that it is so unpleasant that I give up my proposed visit. That is, the value of the original goal is not fixed merely by its attractiveness in isolation, which may have been the ground for setting it up originally as a goal-to-be-achieved. The goal may itself be re-evaluated in terms of the values implicit in the means necessary to achieve it.

There is still another set of considerations which enters in rational choice thoroughly carried out. The end must also be estimated in terms of the values in the predicted *consequences* of its achievement. In a sense this involves seeing it as a means toward further ends. It is not enough that I want something and can get it; I must consider the effects of my having it upon my life and that of others. Conduct is often a type of installment buying with a part of the costs to be borne after purchase and consumption.

The judgment of efficiency. Weighing relevant factors may be a very complex problem when the field of consideration is a broad one. Can we, for example, judge the economic value of a particular factory purely in terms of its "efficiency" in production, that is, maximum production at minimum cost? Comparative productivity can, no doubt, be measured in quantitative terms, for we can assume a standard quality for the commodity. Difficulties will arise, however, in comparison with a shop producing handmade products, for here questions other than speed and cost—such as judgments of value between a hand-made suit and a standardized factory suit—will have to be made.

Great difficulty is encountered even in stating cost of production in purely monetary terms in order to compare two establishments. For example, monetary costs will be lower if there are no laws compelling the payment of compensation for industrial accidents, if workmen are not given vacations with pay, or if they are worked harder and then dismissed when worn out. Costs of the factory are considerably increased if we reckon in the effects of its price policies on other parts of the nation's economy, the unemployment re-relief given to workmen it drops, the old-age assistance given by the state to those employees whom it may discard, the differential cost to consumers arising from tariffs protecting that enterprise, and so forth. Thus the estimate of the cost of production—even in monetary terms—turns out to involve an evaluation of the factors in the economic operations of the society to be included or excluded in the reckoning. It is correspondingly more difficult to treat the reckoning of cost as a non-evaluative procedure if we raise the further question of the human happiness or suffering incident to the operations of the enterprise.

Evaluation of the end does not destroy its character. The end is then itself evaluated in terms of the means and in terms of the consequences to which it leads. But this does not destroy its character as an end. For, as we have seen, we do not evaluate the end in terms of the means as such but in terms of the values and disvalues embodied in or advanced by the means, and similarly we do not evaluate the end by its consequences as such but in terms of the values and disvalues embodied in its consequences. Thus, throughout, the process of choice between alternative courses of conduct involves continual choosing between proposed ends or values.

Does the end justify the means? In the light of this analysis, the old controversy of whether the end justifies the means disappears as a general question. Asking it generally would be asking whether the purchase is worth the price. Obviously this depends on what is purchased, what is paid, and what the consequences will be of the purchase and of the payment. Some things, although desirable, may not be worth buying at any current price, or any possible price. For some things it may be worth paying almost any price. Similarly, some ends justify some means, and some do not.

The real core of the usual denial that the end justifies the means is the correct but unanalyzed demand that the means themselves be evaluated. As we have seen in our examples, in everyday practice and single choices the adult individual does just this. The point usually intended in the general assertion is to call attention to the need for examining even more distant and less obvious consequences, especially the probable effects on the character of the agent. The use of lawless means, it is said, tends to breed lawlessness, of warlike means a violent character, and so forth.

On the other hand the assertion that the end justifies the means has as its core the recognition that some ends require infliction of pain, and yet cannot lightly be given up. Pulling teeth does not make a villain of the dentist, however much it may hurt. In some cases one end may be regarded as of such paramount importance that all other ends pale to comparative insignificance. Thus in many a European country under Nazi subjection men were compelled to use any and every device and they readily made sacrifices of all sorts in order to further their national liberation. For they realized that without such liberation most of the values to which they held would be permanently out of reach. Clearly questions of the justification of means and ends have to be considered concretely in the light of ends held and means available, in order that the evaluation may be of the total activity and its consequences.

Liberty and freedom

This analysis of values, means, and ends is fundamental to the consideration of human bondage and human freedom. Our purpose is not at this point to give a philosophical analysis of the nature of values; this important question will be dealt with in Part Five in the context of whole systematic philosophies. Nor is our concern here with the sociological description of men's concrete values. Our purpose is rather to see the way in which values function in men's lives, and how out of the attempts to achieve them arises the ideal of liberation from human bondage and the potent and stirring ideals of liberty and freedom.

Our analysis in the chapters that follow will be organized around these two concepts of *liberty* and *freedom*. In spite of frequent interchange of terms the problems of liberty and freedom have been fairly distinct in traditional philosophy. Freedom in this usage concerns the early beginnings of action within a man, his *choosing* or *willing*. Liberty concerns the fate of his action once it gets under way—the factors that thwart it or bring it to a successful completion. A prisoner in a Nazi concentration camp has no liberty. But there may be unquenchable personal freedom in his dedication to the ideals for which he has been imprisoned. Nor is this freedom an empty one because its result in action seems so remote. In many cases the very strength of this will has been the source of the dauntless vigilance and practical determination which issued in eventual escape.

The question of liberty is usually treated as a question of social ethics; that of freedom has been dominantly a question of metaphysics centering around problems of choice and will and entailing important ethical consequences.[2] The relation, as we shall see, is however a much more intimate one than this dichotomy would lead us to expect.

[2] Although the two terms, "liberty" and "freedom," are often used as synonyms, we shall try to keep them apart in the present discussion. The adjective "free," however, seems indispensable to avoid the cumbersome "at liberty to" or the really awkward "at liberty from." Context will show whether the term refers to liberty or freedom.

Chapter 17 FREEDOM

The arena of choice

In dealing with the problem of freedom our context is a narrow one. We do not reckon with social and economic forces, groups of men, historic movements. Instead we focus attention on the individual. As we noted above, the problem of freedom has traditionally concerned the way in which action gets started in the individual. When we ask whether a man is free we are not thinking of his success or failure in carrying out a plan, but of his very adoption of the plan, that is, of his act of *choosing* or *willing* to embark upon it. Is man's choice free or is it determined by some play of external or internal forces? This question has troubled men both in observing the actions of others and in observing the course of their own lives. Are we pulled on strings, or do we jump in response to some internal mechanism? Or is choice or will a genuine assertion of ourselves?

Choice is a kind of administrative hearing going on in the courtroom of the self. The witnesses are heard, and the lawyers argue. They report, predict, express hopes and forebodings. An occasional witness mumbles with inarticulate feeling; he is not understood but there is a sense that he represents powerful interests who threaten revolt if they do not have their way. The hearing is ended. Sometimes a specific decision is reached. In any case action begins. But where is the judge? Is there a judge at all? Or was the force of every argument, the momentum of every desire, the strength of every fear, automatically registered and weighed, so that the scales of their own accord tipped in one direction or another? The drama of choice is indeed a puzzling one.

INTERPRETATIONS OF WILL

Since willing is an activity of the self or within the self, all the diverse interpretations of mind and self have been brought to bear upon its analysis. On a soul theory [1] willing is a purely spiritual exertion which may affect matter but is not governed by physical laws. In a dualistic theory that

[1] See above, p. 139.

sharply separates the mental from the physical, willing designates the activity of mind as setting itself—and, in some dualistic theories, the body—into motion. On a mechanistic approach willing is a name for that point in the balancing of bodily forces in which, so to speak, the scales are tilted in one definite direction. On a naturalistic theory a man willing is an event in the natural world which has determinate conditions for its occurrence, and the feeling of effort involved in it is the unique quality of that sort of event. It is in the historical conflict of such theories that the problem of the freedom of the will may be rendered intelligible.

Before proceeding to that problem, however, a few initial points require clarification: (1) the "reality" of the will; (2) the importance of the will; (3) whether willing has any causal efficacy. Such issues will serve to locate and isolate the problem of freedom itself.

The reality of will. The reality of the act of willing as a phenomenon or event occurring in the world is generally unquestioned. The only exception arises when a metaphysical mechanism is assumed which, by defining the real as the physical, can give no status other than the vague or illusory to non-physical qualities. Even there the attempt is rather to explain the will in physical terms than simply to dismiss it. Thus Hobbes says, "In *Deliberation* the last Appetite, or Aversion, immediately adhering to the action, or to the omission thereof, is that we call the Will; the Act (not the faculty,) of *Willing.*" And appetite and aversion are themselves reduced to small beginnings of motion within the body of man.[2]

The importance of will. The importance of the phenomenon of willing is obvious. As the starting-point of conduct in man it is the focus of attention for all who hope to guide or fashion conduct. If a man steps on your toes in a crowded subway you do not necessarily *attribute* the act to him, although the foot upon your toes is his. But if you learn that he *intended* this —that is, he willed it, foreseeing this occurrence as a result of his conduct— you assign an entirely different significance to the event. This importance ascribed to willing does not depend on any specific interpretation; it will be explained in different ways by different theories. Even theories most hostile to the conception of free will would regard the fact that the act was intended as *indicative* of the state of the agent; it need not imply that the act was done freely, but merely that it issued from some disposition or attitude or habit of action; hence a willed act is a clue to the kind of behavior you may continue to expect from a man, whereas an accidental act may have no such import.

Causal efficacy of the act of will. On the question of whether willing has any causal efficacy there is more disagreement. This question is clearly part of the general problem of the efficacy of the mental, discussed above.[3] Soul

[2] *Leviathan*, Part I, Chapter 6. See above, p. 161.
[3] Chapters 11, 13, 14. See especially p. 157 ff.

theories and dualistic theories generally affirm the causality of willing. Mechanistic theories deny it, assigning the efficacy to the physical or physiological bases of the act of willing. Naturalistic theories grant the efficacy of willing when it is interpreted as an event in the natural world. The act of will (described in psychological terms) is regarded as a real cause or partial cause in the affairs of men. As in any causal situation one may therefore say that if the will had been differently directed the result would probably have been different.

IS THE ACT OF WILL ITSELF CAUSED?

Whether an act of willing is itself caused is the crucial point of controversy. To look for a cause, it will be recalled, is to look for a system of laws such that, given a prior state of affairs, a subsequent state can be predicted.[4] On mechanistic and naturalistic theories there is no reason to make an exception of acts of willing among the phenomena of this world; hence these psychological phenomena are explored in an attempt to relate them to other psychological phenomena and also to relate phenomena on the psychological level to those on biological, physical, and social levels. The actual discovery of regularities in men's reactions and the elaboration of systematic explanation has been sufficiently successful to justify the assertion that causality does operate in human affairs. At the present time the results are certainly sufficient to disprove the view that there is no causality in psychological phenomena. But they are far from sufficient to show that there is complete causality, that is, that there are discoverable laws on the basis of which all psychological phenomena can be predicted. Nor can we tell whether such laws, if achievable, would ultimately be in psychological or physiological or physical terms.

At the same time the belief on other grounds that man is part of the world of nature (for example, his evolutionary descent) strengthens the view that even the initiation of inexplicable conduct on his part is not an instance of uncaused behavior but rather the appearance of novel qualities in highly complex conditions. In short, although novel qualities may be a consequence on a free-will theory they are also a possible consequence on a causality theory.[5]

[4] See above, Chapter 3.
[5] This whole problem of the relation of causality, novelty, complexity, and the possibility of discovering laws and systematizing them into a complete determinism, is not peculiar to the study of mental phenomena. It is a problem in any domain of investigation. We have no complete determinism for many physical phenomena either. A fuller analysis of what this problem entails was carried out in Chapter 4; see especially p. 60 ff.

The denial that acts of willing have causes is to be found among many soul theories and dualistic theories, and the core of this denial is a rejection of determinism in psychological phenomena, hence in human affairs. Willing is taken to be an act expressive of a self whose essence is thought; or, according to some, the teleological or purposive direction of energy is itself the essence of the self. The self is thus the true judge rendering the verdict in choice. Willing stamps purpose on conduct. It has a spontaneity that is characteristic of mind; in contrast external causality characterizes the operations of matter.

Traditional meaning of "free will." This denial of determinism in human affairs and assertion of a spontaneous quality in willing is precisely what many philosophers have intended by *freedom* of the will. Their claim takes many forms. In some it is almost a contention that the act of willing is a capricious or whimsical element in conduct which renders it unpredictable. They refuse to analyze the act itself even in the psychological language of a conflict of motives or reaction to habit or the relation of thought and desire. The act of will thus retains a mysterious character; it is said to be an uncaused cause in the determination of conduct. Such a view welcomes the scientific discovery of unpredictability in quantum mechanics,[6] interpreting it as a revelation of indeterminism or arbitrariness in the fundamental texture of matter.

Types of free will and theories of the self. Other defenders of free will allow for partial determination of the will, or rather admit of influences on it which do not interfere with its essential spontaneity. The picture varies according to the conception of the self involved. Where the self is widely conceived as including all the elements of consciousness, there is usually a belief in limited freedom only, since the passions clearly operate under earthly influences. Where the self is identified with reason alone, the will may be regarded as completely free. If it then exercises its fredom it can subdue the passions. Sometimes—and this is a concession to nature—when it is half-asleep the appetites may win and the action will be called involuntary. But the self may also will its surrender to passion, and in so doing it may will what is evil. Kant's theory of freedom is a shadowy image of this conflict, no doubt because the self he speaks of is only a faint suggestion of the older traditional soul. Kant believes freedom means *self-determination*: one's actions do not arise from the desires but from a sense of duty or respect for the rational laws of the real self.[7] In all these concepts—as in many others—the degree of freedom ascribed to the self in its willing varies. Where factors related causally to the natural world are encompassed within the self, freedom diminishes; where the self is narrowed to those human op-

---
[6] See above, p. 47.
[7] For Kant's conception of the self, see above, pp. 195-96; for his conception of duty, see below, pp. 407-11.

erations that appear most independent of the natural world, freedom is regarded as greater.

The case for "metaphysical freedom" outlined. Such theories of free will are often said to advocate "metaphysical freedom." Much of the controversy that has gone on in the history of philosophy concerning the freedom of the will has taken the form of affirmation or denial of such metaphysical freedom. Its defenders have rested their case on three types of argument. They have claimed that such a concept is required to explain the ordinary consciousness of freedom in the act of willing. They have sought to show that absurdities result from the application of determinism to human affairs. And they have attempted to base their case on moral grounds, urging that many specifically human phenomena such as praise and blame, fault and responsibility, and other concepts essential to morals, education, and legal theory, become inexplicable if freedom of the will is denied. On the other side, determinists, mechanists and naturalists, whatever the differences among them, have rested largely on the causal conception of the world and the claim that man is no exception to the natural order. Relying on the growing evidence of the sciences, they have attempted to offer an explanation of the phenomena to which the defenders of free will pointed, in order to show that these phenomena could be explained without a resort to free will.

In the remainder of this chapter we shall examine some of the arguments utilized in the controversy and estimate their significance; and thereafter we shall examine the theory of freedom from the point of view of the naturalistic concept of mind and the self elaborated in Part Three.[8]

Arguments on free will

THE SENSE OF FREEDOM AND GENUINE ALTERNATIVES

The defenders of free will assert that a man's ordinary consciousness in the act of willing involves a sense of freedom, of dealing with *real* or *genuine alternatives*. He feels that it was genuinely possible for him to have chosen another alternative rather than the course of action upon which he embarked, even if all external causes operating upon him had remained the same. On a determinist position, if the act of will itself is caused, a man could not have acted in any other way than he did act. Hence the sense of dealing with real alternatives in the process of willing seems to argue against the prior determination of the will and for its free or spontaneous character.

A determinist position need not, however, regard this sense of freedom or of dealing with real alternatives as illusory. It may instead explore it as a

---
[8] Chapters 14 and 15.

quality occurring in the complex act of initiation of conduct, and seek to delineate its character. Thus there might be a distinction drawn between the feeling of freedom and the sense of real alternatives, and a separate account offered of each.

From the point of view of a psychological determinism the feeling of freedom many indicate the congeniality of the act to the person, the sense of its being in line with his general character or the dominant core of his self. The mechanism whereby he came to act this way may be unknown to him. For example, it may mean that the cultural prohibitions which were directed upon the person have been internalized so that their operation is felt as his own will. There need thus be no contradiction between the feeling of freedom and the fact of determinism.

The sense of genuine alternatives seems to have a rather different meaning. Its essential point is the recognition that a man could have acted differently if he had so willed it. Therefore it proves (if the sense be not deceitful) that if the act of willing had been different the resulting conduct would have been different. This establishes the character of the act of willing, psychologically described, as a true cause of conduct. (The form of language in which it is expressed is typical of any causal situation: if factor x had been differently directed, the result would have been different.) But the genuineness of the alternatives proves nothing more. It does not indicate any sense in which the act of willing itself is free or whether it is caused. The sense of dealing with genuine alternatives as distinct from the feeling of freedom thus concerns the question of whether the act of will has effects, rather than whether it has causes. It proves nothing one way or the other about freedom of the will in choosing.

It should be noted that even from a free will point of view it is inadvisable to regard the sense of genuine alternatives as a necessary element. For it is often absent in what men commonly regard as the highest acts of freedom. Many an underground worker caught by the Nazis preferred death to betraying his co-workers, feeling he had no genuine alternative. Religious martyrs have faced torture and death, rejecting disavowal of their beliefs as impossible. Heroes in the war, too, have said that their acts of great bravery were undertaken as "the only possible thing to do."

ALLEGED REDUCTIO AD ABSURDUM OF DETERMINISM

The second type of argument for freedom of the will takes the form of a *reductio ad absurdum* of determinism in the context of action. It is an attempt to show that the consequences of complete determinism in choice are untenable, hence that some other factor must be invoked to explain the direction of choice. Suppose, goes an old argument, that a donkey is standing between two bundles of hay, exactly equidistant from both, so that (by hypothesis) the factors inclining it to one bale exactly equal the factors inclining it to the other. The logical consequence is that it should starve to death.[9] If man were an automaton, similar consequences could be expected. Now such a situation is nonsense. Therefore man is free.

Determinism can accept the allegedly absurd result. The determinist need not, however, accept this argument as a *reductio ad absurdum* of his denial of free will. For he may be quite ready to agree with the logical consequence pointed out—that if exactly equal factors inclined a man in two opposite directions he would be able to do neither. The determinist might go on to add that experimental work on dogs shows the result is not improbable, much less nonsensical. Pavlov, in his famous experiments, conditioned a dog to salivate on seeing a circular spot of light and to inhibit salivation on seeing an elliptical spot of light. When these habits were firmly implanted, he widened the elliptical spot until it was difficult to tell whether it was ellipse or circle. Both salivatory and inhibitory responses on the part of the dog could not coexist, and—to put it anthropomorphically—the poor dog had a "nervous breakdown." Although we cannot pass too readily from results in the case of dogs to an inference about man, it is clear that men too may suffer from indecision or conflicting desire-systems. For minor situations of this sort we have developed methods of decision ranging from tossing a coin or acting on impulse to rational exploration of consequences; and on many matters ambivalence may cause little strain. But if the strain or clash is great enough, men too may break down.

DO MORAL IDEAS REST ON FREE WILL?

Perhaps the most formidable defense of free will is the third claim mentioned above, that a great many basic ideas fundamental to the management of human affairs will lose their meaning if we deny free will. What meaning is there, it is asked, to praise and blame, sin and repentance, conscience and remorse, fault and responsibility, to punishment, even to an ordinary appeal to reason, if man's actions are not in some sense his own and free? If he cannot help what he is doing, if he is the victim of circumstances, why should we treat him as we do in all these relevant respects? This argument rests, of course, on the assumption that these phenomena make sense. It is quite possible for the opponent of free will to deny them, but they have played such a large part in education, morals, and law that he is more likely to reinterpret the phenomena to show that there are hypotheses other than free will on which they equally well make sense. Since the conse-

[9] This kind of argument arose in a 14th century controversy on the relation of will and intellect. It is attributed to Buridan or to his opponents in the argument.

quences of such reinterpretation are tremendously important in the various fields of practice, it is worth tracing them in some detail.

Praise and blame. The defender of free will argues that if a man did not freely will an action then he does not merit praise or blame for it. When Aristotle discussed the question of voluntary and involuntary action, he remained content with the conclusion that men's bad deeds were in the same boat as their good deeds insofar as freedom was concerned. Presumably he felt that men would not surrender praise; they merely argued that all actions were involuntary in order to escape blame. Hence putting both on the same level sufficed for morals.

Dewey [10] applies the instrumentalist approach most effectively to the solution of this problem. The difficulty with the traditional view of praise and blame is that it takes a retrospective rather than a prospective view. Praise and blame are primarily sanctions. They are used to develop and strengthen admirable habits and to discourage and weaken actions disapproved of. They are thus stimuli for the future, rather than payment for past conduct. We start using them on children even before they understand the nature of their actions. By praising and blaming we train them to discern features which they will later come to regard with approbation and disapprobation. An act does not therefore have to have been done freely to be praised or blamed. Not freedom of the will but plastic materials of character are the requisites. Hence neither idiots nor incorrigible persons are worth blaming except for the sake of those who listen. Similarly it is a work of supererogation to praise a saint.

The developmental bases of praise and blame—how they secure a foothold in the child—is a matter of present psychological investigation. One hypothesis connects this process with the child's need for warmth and affection. Praise would be a satisfaction of these requirements under readily recognizable conditions. Blame would be a withdrawal of their satisfaction. Whatever the precise psychological explanation, it is clear that the efficacy of praise and blame, so far from requiring the existence of free will, need not even require the existence of will.

Sin, repentance, conscience, remorse. These are theological and moral concepts that appear to require the existence of a free will. Otherwise, why should a man feel that he has sinned? Why should a man repent or feel conscience-stricken or remorseful over his actions if he had not been free in choosing them?

Insofar as the question concerns feelings, the opponent of metaphysical freedom would answer that the problem is one for psychology, the social sciences, and history. Fundamentally these feelings are different patternings of grief or sorrow at the consequences of one's actions, which assume dif-

---

[10] In *Human Nature and Conduct*, Modern Library, 1930.

ferent qualities according to the context in which they function. In many societies this sorrow appears as guilt-feeling, and the four concepts here listed represent different degrees or patterns of such feeling. The psychological and cultural bases of guilt-feeling are no doubt extremely complex. In psychoanalytic theory, for example, it represents a recoil from the expression of repressed or censored desires; the pattern of both the dominant self and the repressed desires is determined by factors in the individual's early history along the lines of the psychoanalytic theory of man's dynamic organization. Some have even suggested that it may serve as compensatory self-punishment which enables one comfortably to express repressed desires—a kind of psychological sale of indulgences. But the role of the feeling and its varieties is by no means simply a psychological question. The significance of the sense of sin, for example, is social and historical and is intimately bound up with the institutions and beliefs of western religion.

In general, these types of feeling, once they are made the subject of careful scrutiny, turn out to be complex phenomena which may not even possess a unitary character. For example, conscience in its negative phase as the "pangs of conscience" appears to be a simple type of guilt feeling. After the event it is remorse; before a man acts it is the "still small voice" that warns. But as a positive impressionistic grasping of the moral import of a course of conduct it is more a kind of synthetic judgment. And as such it may or may not have anything in common with the negative phase.

The opponent of free will thus need not deny the qualitative character of the various complex phenomena to which we have pointed. But he finds their significance in the way in which they function psychologically, socially, and historically in the individual's life; and this points rather to a search for a causal mechanism in a theory of the growth of personality than it does to metaphysical freedom.

Fault, responsibility, and punishment. The concept of fault implies that a particular deed is assigned to a person as his responsibility, and in juristic theory punishment or payment of reparation for damage done is often meted out on this basis. What is to happen to this web of legal theory if there is no "genuine" freedom, hence no "genuine" responsibility?

The theory of punishment shows most clearly the conflict of views. The free will theory has been used traditionally to justify punishment. If a man freely willed the criminal action, let the punishment be the return for his act; for he could, had he been so minded, have refrained. The denial of free will has brought a more careful attention to the conditions that make criminals—slums and poverty, distorted personalities, disturbed childhood, and so forth. Reformatory and deterrence theories of punishment have arisen to supplement and even replace the free will retribution emphasis. Thus, it is argued, punishment should be a process of curing in which constraint or pain should serve merely a corrective function. Modern prison reformers have paid attention to prison conditions, teaching prisoners useful occupations, trying to make socially co-operative persons out of them. The deterrence theory gives the kind of analysis of punishment which we offered of blame above. The suffering is inflicted to deter men from criminal action. It affects the offender directly and others by example. Bentham, who adhered to a deterrence theory, said the appearance of punishment should be as imposing as possible, its reality just adequate to deter the criminal. If it were possible, he would have liked, in cases of men condemned to death, to send them secretly off to the colonies to start life anew while the public, impressed by the apparent punishment, restrained itself from similar offenses. It is worth noting that from a wider social point of view these theories do not adequately resolve the problem of preventing crime, since they do not tackle the reform and prevention of the social conditions that generate crime itself.

The partisans of freedom of the will have been very much enraged at the reformatory theory. Hegel thought it robbed a man of his dignity by making the action seem less his doing than something done to him. Nietzsche somewhere suggests that crime should be treated on the model of treason, where a man in full possession of his senses freely rebels against an order.

There are many other theories of the nature of crime and the grounds for punishment which a complete ethical investigation would examine. But enough has been said to indicate that the phenomena of punishment even with little alteration are capable of reinterpretation without assuming the freedom of the will.

Fault and the theory of torts. The use of the concept of fault in the theory of torts (legal action for redress of private wrongs) constitutes another interesting chapter in the history of free will theory. In the 19th century the maxim of no liability without fault became dominant, expressing the general philosophy that legal obligations arise from the action of men's free wills.[11] Intentional aggression fell simply within this framework. Negligence, however, had to be reinterpreted as an indirect expression of intention or will. For example, if a physician was negligent and was legally liable for damages, it was in theory because of defective early preparation, presumably his willing to do other things rather than prepare himself properly. If a parent was liable for a child's torts up to a certain age it was likewise for not having properly trained the child; in fact in some legal systems the parent could accept the burden of proof and avoid responsibility by showing he had done everything that could be reasonably expected of a parent in the way of education and example.

Existent forms of vicarious liability (for example, where a man was held responsible for the acts of his servant) taxed the theory to its utmost. The

---

[11] For a brief survey of this trend, see Roscoe Pound, *An Introduction to the Philosophy of the Law*, Yale University Press, 1922, Chapter IV.

theory demanded narrowing such liability to cases in which some connection could be proved or conjectured: where you were at fault in the selection of your servant, where he was acting directly on your orders or had the "accident" in the course of your business. Social necessities, especially in large-scale industry, demanded broadening the theory to cover accidents occurring in the course of employment even if they could not be traced to inadequate safety devices. The question of workmen's compensation was fought around such issues. On the one side it was argued that in accidents where nobody was at fault the loss should lie where it happens to fall; to hold the employer liable is to take money out of his pocket, just because it is deeper, without due cause; even if he is better able to pay, that is no reason why he should be compelled to do so; you might as well assess a stranger who happened to have money.

On the other side the argument began with the lesser ability of the employee to stand the cost; it hesitatingly suggested fictions, like the implied agreement of the employer to restore the employee to himself in good condition on the cessation of service. Gradually, however, it was realized that the inadequacy lay in connecting liability with fault and free will. It was seen that there might be other bases for responsibility than a man's freely willing something or even implicitly willing it. Thus there emerged a cost of production theory (aided by the discoverable statistical regularity of accidents in industry and the techniques of insurance): accidents that are no one's fault can be considered part of the cost of producing the commodity; they are the human wear and tear which we seek to minimize but which like depreciation of machinery should be borne by the industry; whether it then comes from a diminution of the employer's profits or an increase in price is a separate question. An industry that cannot stand its human costs (it has even been argued that these might include old-age pensions, sickness insurance, and unemployment insurance) either requires a government subsidy if it is socially important, or has no right to exist.

More recently, the broadening of concepts of social security, as for example in the Beveridge plan in England or in comparable American projects, has carried the theory of responsibility even beyond the cost of production idea. Health is regarded ultimately as a national responsibility to be carried out through insurance systems, health benefits, provision for health education, preventative care, medical training and research, and a host of similar measures. What remains of the earlier problem of responsibility is largely a question of how the costs of the enterprise are to be distributed, e.g., by employer-employee-government contributions or by the general tax fund.

Thus it is possible in modern legal theory—and from the point of view of present-day values it is even desirable—to drop willing of wrong as the uniquely necessary basis of liability and to analyze the question of liability or responsibility in other ethical terms, such as the social goals to be achieved and the means to be employed for achieving them. The same type of reinterpretation fits the treatment of negligence. Negligence on my part need not imply any deliberate carelessness willed in my past; it simply means a failure on my part to conform to a standard which it is socially desirable to enforce upon people in my position or situation. Thus the obligations of parents, teachers, public carriers, employers, employees, and so on, may be worked out in terms of a theory of social ethics, and negligence will mean a failure to conform to these standards.

Importance of will not minimized. The above analysis of fault, responsibility, and punishment shows that these concepts of legal and moral theory do not require freedom of the will in order to be meaningful. In fact, as we have seen, in many applications of these concepts even the notion of an act of will is not required as a basis for affixing liability. Liability may be ascribed in order to fashion men's wills for future action; a great part of law exhibits this educative strand among its functions. Nevertheless our analysis should not be taken to minimize the importance of the act of will—as distinguished from the claim of its metaphysical freedom—in moral and legal theory. Attention was called to the importance of *intention* early in the chapter. For legal and moral theory its significance lies in the indications it gives of the character and attitudes of a person. Intentional evil indicates a socially more dangerous person than accidental evil; and intentional good shows a stable moral character. Hence whether an act was willed or not is often the basis for distinctions in the legal and moral treatment of the person concerned. For example, intention is sometimes important in distinguishing different degrees of murder. And in some questions of damages, intention may be the decisive factor; thus a man driving a car in the normal course of events may go through a puddle and splash me with mud without being liable, if he has not been careless; but a man who intentionally comes close to the sidewalk to spatter me may be liable for a single drop.

The appeal to reason. "But surely," it will be said, "the ordinary appeal to reason shows that will or choice is free." "No," says the mechanist, "it is analogous to tinkering with levers and buttons trying to get a machine to go in a certain direction." One may differ with both these views. The appeal to reason does presuppose communication, with its own special qualities; it does presuppose men who are reasonable, whose thinking follows logical channels. But this need not entail freedom of the will in the metaphysical sense. In fact, if there were complete freedom, unpredictable and therefore capricious in effect, the argument might be pressed that there could be no appeal to reason; an irrational result might just as readily be expected.

The defense of metaphysical freedom rests on a substantival or *dualistic* theory concerning mind and, thus, reason. The opponent of such free will prefers to speak of reason as a quality of human behavior. A reasonable man is one whose decisions and actions manifest an order in their direction; they represent an equilibrium of forces rather than the drive of isolated component forces. The mastery of reason over desire is not the domination of a master over his slaves, but the organized strength of a stably organized system of desires over one or two aberrant desires. Such a balance is perhaps not something with which a man is initially endowed. It is hammered out over the course of his years; it is at best a precarious balance, frequently disturbed. Its specific pattern is a social product. The result bears the stamp of the society, and in its most ideal forms (and this is a value-judgment) we call it reason. In Part Two, we suggested that the techniques and principles of reason in its operations with experience constitute the most reliable way men have found for approaching, understanding and rendering an account of their world.

PHILOSOPHICAL NATURALISM AND THE PROBLEM OF FREEDOM

The analysis given of the various arguments for metaphysical freedom of the will shows that they fail to establish its existence as necessary. We are led, therefore, to the conclusion suggested earlier that metaphysical freedom of the will is not so much an interpretation dictated by a study of human action as it is a theory emanating from an underlying philosophical dualism.

Rejection of metaphysical freedom does not imply world-determinism. It is also important to note that the rejection of metaphysical freedom, implying as it does that human will and choices have causes, does not mean necessarily accepting a mechanistic determinism in which man becomes a completely determined puppet. This theory emanates from an assumed conception of man as a machine and a failure to distinguish between causality and the world-machine approach.[12] And just as the naturalistic conception of man differed from the mechanistic, so a naturalistic theory of freedom cannot be equated with the assertion of a world-determinism. We therefore turn next to a naturalistic approach to see how a modern philosophical materialism may deal with the concept of freedom.

Why naturalism needs a concept of freedom. A number of points stand out on reflection concerning the approach of philosophical naturalism to the problem of freedom. In the first place it cannot admit of metaphysical freedom, since it regards an act of willing as a natural event having its determinate conditions and controls which science may explore and attempt to systematize.

In the second place, naturalism shares the tremendous interest which dualism has in the phenomenon of will. As the above discussion implied, it takes the ultimate interest of the moral sciences—morals, law, education—to lie in

[12] For the former see Chapter 13; for the latter, Chapter 3.

encouraging the pursuit of desirable lines of conduct and the avoidance of undesirable lines. Hence, choice or will, which is often the initiation or starting-point of conduct, should be the special object of attention in the moral sciences, since by rendering will deliberate we may make conduct more susceptible to human control and prediction.

In the third place, it may readily be seen from an inspection of the moral sciences that there are many concepts in which some notion of freedom is implicit. Among these are *voluntary* and *involuntary, coercion, constraint, duress,* and so forth. In the writings of legal and moral philosophers we find attempts to give these concepts an empirical interpretation. Again there are various conceptions of the "free man" offered by philosophers. A naturalistic approach is therefore faced with the alternative of abandoning the whole concept of freedom and translating these usages into other terms, or working out a consistent empirical interpretation of freedom.

An empirical interpretation of freedom of the will. The notion of freedom can prove fruitful if we replace the idea of absolute or metaphysical freedom of the will with an empirical study of typical factors in choice or will which thwart a desirable issue, and types of attitudes or traits of character that yield or encourage desirable lines of choice. The former constitutes a conception of freedom as negative, the latter freedom as positive. As we shall see in the next chapter, such an approach is likewise fruitful in the analysis of liberty. But whereas freedom concerns the restraints and necessary attitudes for what is desirable in the localized context of choosing or deciding, liberty concerns restraints upon and necessary conditions for what is desirable of achievements in life as a whole.

Freedom as negative

EMPIRICAL ANALYSIS OF INVOLUNTARY ACTION

The conception of freedom as negative is probably the dominant one in the ordinary use of the terms "voluntary" and "involuntary." The meaning of these terms varies somewhat in different contexts. "Voluntary" is commonly used to distinguish psychological phenomena of choice and subsequent conduct (such as deciding to climb down a hill and doing so, or looking for something) from purely physical or physiological reactions on the part of a man (such as falling down the hill when pushed, or the reflex action of blinking when there is a rapid movement in front of the eyes). In such contexts the term "involuntary," when used of the action of falling or blinking, means presumably either that there is no willing involved or that even if you will your hardest in the opposite direction the result will be the same.

Voluntary and involuntary choice. In other cases, however, the distinction of voluntary and involuntary is made *within the context of choice*. A man is asked for his money at the point of a gun; or he is offered an unpleasant job at next to no pay, when he and his family are starving. He foresees what will happen to him if he refuses in the first case, or to his family in the second case. Such foresight of results operates within the very act of choosing so that those choices do not take place, much as he would otherwise desire to say no to the robber or to refuse the job. The dramatis personae in this episode are not "outside" forces with which a completed will-act contends successfully or hopelessly—as would be the case if the man chose to resist the robber and gave battle. Rather they are motives, fears and hopes, desires and purposes. Even those external forces which would hinder or aid his liberty of action become translated in the process into knowledge, foresight of consequences, anticipation, foreboding. If the choice is carried out deliberately and explicitly it involves an imaginative rehearsal of possible dramas that might thereafter be enacted in conduct.

How involuntary choice is judged. In such contexts we may call the choice itself involuntary if we find operative in it factors that are either universally or commonly irresistible, and which we do not regard as desirable. A man may say that he acted against his will, identifying his will with the desirable line that, but for such restraints, he would have followed. He may say that he acted under *coercion* or *duress*. "Voluntary" thus characterizes choice in which such restraining or coercive or hard-trying factors are absent. It is interesting to note that a philosopher like Aristotle, who had actual practice in mind, turned first to an account of "involuntary" and then defined "voluntary" by contrast as, in effect, choice that is not involuntary or unfree.[13] Aristotle lists special types of ignorance and coercion as grounds for declaring the choice involuntary. Bentham, on the other hand, discusses contracts that ought to be reckoned void without even using the conception of involuntary agreement on the part of one of the parties.[14] Instead he lists particular causes for the invalidation of exchanges, such as concealment, fraud, coercion, erroneous idea of value or of legal obligation. Many of these function in the same way as would criteria of involuntary agreement; but Bentham justifies their use directly in terms of the injury that enforcing the bargain would bring to the individual or to the public.

---

[13] "The voluntary would seem to be that of which the moving principle is in the agent himself, he being aware of the particular circumstances of the action." (*Nicomachean Ethics*, W. D. Ross translation, Book III, 1. Most of the chapter is concerned with an attempt to work out testable criteria for the involuntary; for example, in asking whether ignorance was really operative in choice, Aristotle suggests using subsequent remorse as a test.)

[14] *Theory of Legislation*, ed. by C. K. Ogden, Harcourt, Brace, 1931. Principles of the Civil Code. Part II. Chapter 2.

VALUE CONTENT OF COERCION, DURESS, PROVOCATION

The content of such concepts as coercion and duress is clearly shown, even on historical grounds alone, to be a matter of social evaluation. We do not generally consider that a man's action in abiding by the law is coerced by the threat of punishment, even though he may have been held back only by that fear. For we think it entirely appropriate that such restraints operate. When a man hands over his money at the point of a gun, he is thought to be coerced, even though an occasional stoic may risk death in a scuffle instead. But if a man threatened with a gun did something very dishonorable (e.g., killed a friend when so ordered) we would probably consider his action voluntary because we do not think even threats of death should lead one to act in that way.

The idea of provocation exhibits similar variation in the way it is applied. Values enter into the delimiting of provocation, the judgment that a man was drawn into action, so that his action was less than voluntary. Again, in the making of a contract—where choice is supposed to be voluntary— American courts long refused to recognize economic needs as coercive. Thus legislation limiting the working-hours of women was declared contrary to the constitutional guarantee of the women's freedom of contract rather than understood as alleviating coercive influences in their choice. Many other measures to eliminate discriminatory conditions of employment (long hours, payment in scrip, "yellow dog" contracts, that is, contracts stipulating that the employee shall not join a union) for a long time met a similar fate. Only in recent years has the view prevailed that a man in desperate economic condition is not in a position to choose freely; however, this view is still vigorously and successfully resisted in many fields.

As a negative concept, freedom is therefore an indirect vehicle for social value judgments concerning the kinds of restraints people in a given society find effective but undesirable. In this sense the concept of freedom requires constant refinement in terms of social conditions and men's goals.

Freedom as positive

FREEDOM AS AN IDEAL OF CHARACTER

The concept of freedom may readily be transformed from the negative idea of absence of undesirable restraints in choice to the presence of traits of character that issue in or encourage desirable lines of choice. The content of freedom as positive is then social in origin and reference. The ideals of character which it embodies will differ with what a given society or group takes to be the desirable direction of choice.

Such a conception of freedom is, of course, quite different from the original idea of freedom of the will with which we began. Yet the gap between that dualistic conception and this naturalistic conception is bridged in application. For dualistic theory does not end its account of freedom of the will by asserting it, but often goes on to state the conditions which render its exercise difficult. This involves an account of the strength of the passions which hamper its true expression, and so leads to an account of the states of character which make possible its ready exercise. On a naturalistic interpretation, this is the point at which dualism approaches a realistic empirical theory of freedom.

Types of "free man" proposed. There have been many types of "free man" proposed as ideals. There is the self-reliant type whose freedom means independence in action. There is also Russell's free man who scorns power and the hostile flux of nature and remains loyal to his ideals of truth, beauty, and goodness.[15] His freedom clearly consists in not being bound by ordinary desires and attractions. There is also the disinterested man praised by Krutch, who has freed himself from taking the impelling power of his own values seriously and is sufficiently aloof to watch himself as an actor with a spectator's sense of unreality.[16] Then there is the anarchic ideal—the man who can follow every impulse, free from regret. There is the dutiful man, who tramples every passion under foot in stern devotion to a reason that is free from worldly bondage. There is the man who is not bound by the routines of habit, who, in Pater's words, "burns with a hard gem-like flame," savoring the fullness of each novel situation. There are probably as many conceptions of the free man as there have been general attitudes struggling for recognition or temperaments demanding their rights in the selection of values.

The integrated man. One type of ideal on a different plane of generality has been the conception of the integrated man, dear to the hearts of both philosophers and psychologists. He is the type in which there is a minimum of repression of impulse, not because he has subdued and successfully enslaved parts of his nature but because he has achieved their harmonious development. He suffers no conflict of appetite and reason because his desires have become stably organized according to the system that is reason. Similarly there is no conflict of principles and practice, because his principles are his guides to practice and his habits of thought are not idle fancy but starting-points of conduct. He is sensitive to differences and there is variety in his aims; yet his life is more than a succession of goals. He knows himself

[15] "A Free Man's Worship," in *Mysticism and Logic*, Longmans, 1925.
[16] Compare Krutch's account of values, above, pp. 165-66.

and the direction of his aims and can estimate clearly the situations under which they can effectively be realized. He is critical without being destructive and has initiative without being merely volatile. The aims of others are constituent elements of the pattern of his values. In short, his integration is not merely within himself, but with his physical and social environment. The details of such a picture of the free man vary considerably, but in outline he is the Socratic wise man, the Aristotelian man of practical wisdom, or the Spinozistic free man.

Such a man is in the fullest sense free. For he is self-reliant, independent in spirit, most able to control the instrumentalities of living. His character is attuned to the more general features of human problems and so is not limited to the habits of one set of conditions; he shows a greater adaptability to change. In a simple society his love of freedom may mean individual independence, but in a complex society it need not mean unco-operativeness. Instead it can spell an unreadiness to rely on mere authority, an explorative restlessness in social forms to meet novel social situations, and, above all, a ready leadership in progressive social mastery over nature.

Such freedom a social product. In all these senses positive freedom is not something *given* to man, with which he is natively endowed. It is the product of careful nurture in well-ordered society. Some men more nearly approximate the ideal than others, but if the ideal is actually to be attained in a specific society, sanctions and influences will have to be so arranged as to guide men in that direction. In short, the problem of clarifying a positive conception of freedom is the problem of the direction of an educational system and the ideals of desirable character which it embodies. It is the problem of all human institutions insofar as their role is educative and they fashion the men and women of the community.

Chapter 18 LIBERTY

The concept of liberty has had a varied role in the course of human history. The profound differences in attitude towards it are illustrated by such cries as "Give me liberty or give me death," and "O Liberty, what crimes are committed in thy name." The Declaration of Independence states that people are entitled to life, liberty, and the pursuit of happiness. Mussolini repeatedly said that men were tired of liberty. What do men mean, argue about, fight about, when they declare liberty their object?

Liberty as negative and positive

For the most part the idea of liberty is a negative one—removal of obstacles or felt restraints. Yet, as we have seen, the very idea of restraint or limitation implies a direction of striving, hence a positive goal upon which men have their eyes as they struggle to remove restraints upon them. Thus emerges a positive conception of liberty which is constantly implicit in the negative idea. To distinguish the negative and positive concepts of liberty is to distinguish emphases in the single process of men's striving for their goals. The distinction is, however, not without importance.

The negative aspect. The negative aspect of liberty—the removal of restraint—is found on historical analysis to be basic to the earlier stages of most revolutionary struggles in the name of liberty. The motor power of the movement comes from the very strength of the evils under which multitudes of men are suffering. Slave revolts conceive of the liberty at which they aim as the abolition of the hardships and indignities of servitude. The English Civil War of 1642-1646 was, for many, a fight for liberty from arbitrary crown taxation. The American War of Independence was provoked by arbitrary English taxation. The French Revolution aimed at liberty from a host of feudal and semi-feudal restrictions. The Communist Manifesto calls upon workers of the world to unite—"You have nothing to lose but your chains."

In every age men have found special obstacles in the way of the satisfaction of their needs. These obstacles may have been rigors of physical environment for some—farmers on difficult soil, for instance—or social arrangements which brought suffering or strain or hindered the hope of gain. The removal of such obstacles formed the specific content of struggles for liberty.

One general question arises immediately. Can men be objectively unfree without knowing it? This issue may take trivial or serious forms. It may be nonsense to debate whether the ancient Greeks lacked certain liberties because they did not know the radio. But the 19th century faced a perfectly serious issue in debates on the extension of free public education. Workmen, it was said, were not deprived of liberty in not being given an education, since they had no conception of what they were missing. Smoking by the fireside at night (or drinking beer in the corner tavern), they would not miss the delights of luxurious tastes whose cultivation would only embarrass them because of their limited means. Clearly the difference between the trivial and the tremendously serious issues of this type is one of degree.

The positive aspect. The positive aspect of liberty refers to the conditions and opportunities which make it possible to achieve desired goals. Such goals—implicit or explicit—may vary from "to be let live" or "three square meals a day" to the dream of exercising tyrannical power. We find, however, that an individual's goals tend to represent those current in the group or class or society to which he belongs. At different times there are differences in the content of men's goals, and corresponding differences in the conditions necessary for achieving them. Most historical struggles for liberty have been waged by coalitions of groups with varying aims. For example, in the French Revolution the peasant wanted to till his soil unburdened by forced levies, uninterrupted by the corvée; the poor of Paris wanted bread and work; the middle class whose victory shaped the historical character of the revolution wanted the freedom to buy and sell in the open market, a "business government," a share in political power and the principle of a "career open to talents." The Russian peasant in 1917 cared little about the promise of socialism; he was interested primarily in land-ownership free from Tsarist burdens.

The same is true of positive liberty in contemporary American life. To the sharecropper liberty means some land of his own without payments that deplete his livelihood. To the Negro liberty means primarily an equal chance at a job and the right to live as anyone else does. The Liberty League, organized during the first term of Franklin D. Roosevelt's presidency, meant by liberty removal of restrictions imposed by the federal government—for example, upon the issuance of securities, upon traditional practices in crushing labor union organization. But many whom these measures aided saw them as charters of liberty providing the possibility of a living wage and safe investment.

In the remainder of this chapter we shall examine problems of liberty, both negatively and positively formulated, as they arise in the physical, biological, psychological, and social realms of human life.

Liberty and the natural world

From the point of view of human hopes, the natural world—which is itself the matrix in which those hopes are born—sets many a limitation and provides many an opportunity. Whatever nature does not allow to be changed—whether it be a mountain or hereditary characteristics in a human body—becomes an obstacle when it thwarts the satisfaction of human needs. But when it provides the necessities of human existence and achievement—the blanket of air around this planet, for example—it is a source of positive liberty in the opportunities that it affords. Limitations on human activity and opportunity for human activity are the features of the natural world to be explored. In this section we shall illustrate these from the physical constitution of the world and the biological and psychological constitution of man. The problems of the social world will be dealt with subsequently in greater detail.

PHYSICAL FACTORS

The natural environment—geographic, climatic, mineralogical, plant and animal surroundings—constitutes an interacting milieu for what men do. Man can use only the plant and animal resources that he finds available, but these are sufficiently extensive, when cultivated, to support a very large population on the surface of the earth. When skillfully utilized fertile plains have been a source of wealth and leisure. Bodies of water are obstacles to be crossed, but they also contain fish and aid transportation. Indeed the seats of many intermittent or continuous civilizations have been contiguous to bodies of navigable water. Mountains have proved barriers both to social intercourse and to invading armies. Minerals, lumber, oil have played their role where knowledge was adequate to use them; and where a civilization comes to depend greatly upon them—as a mechanized country on oil—their loss is a source of upheaval. Modern wars have been fought for natural resources.

Theories stressing physical factors in history. The full picture of nature as object of human use, as source of human opportunities, as stimulus to human fancy, as the reef on which many a plan has crashed, almost coincides with the history of man. Some theories have even taken the role of physical factors in history to be ultimately determinative of what man does. Buckle,[1] for example, believed that nature had a prime role in the earlier history of mankind, mental habits in the later history, in fact that soil, climate, and

---

[1] *History of Civilization in England,* 3rd ed., London, 1861, Chapter 2.

the general aspect of nature made earlier civilizations what they were. Fertile soil led to easy existence, large population, leisure class, knowledge. High mountains, huge plains, swollen torrents overwhelmed the imagination and generated weird Hindu gods, whereas moderate landscape begot Greek anthropomorphism. Ellsworth Huntington [2] ascribes all great civilizations to a certain type of climate. Feuerbach in his youth produced the famous aphorism "Der Mensch ist was er isst" (Man is what he eats) and sought to find a food which would sustain the working-class cheaply and give them the requisite health ingredients for revolutionary power; his choice was beans.

Their neglect of social element. While the phases of nature which such theories stress are often critical for human welfare, they are not in any simple sense determinative. The theories disregard the role of such social elements as technical knowledge, interest, and economic organization. Historical and cultural factors alone can explain man's selective utilization of nature and the varied activities found in similar natural settings.

It is primarily to knowledge and the social organization requisite for applying it that we must look in seeking the elements that liberate men from restrictions of the natural environment and turn those limitations into opportunity. The advantages that technological advance has brought in communications, travel, building, clothing, variety and preservation of food, regulation of temperatures, and a thousand and one sundry details of living are too well known to require recounting. Such advances have lifted burdens from men and women in factory, farm, and kitchen, thus adding to the sum of liberty. They have also provided sufficient possibilities of abundance to eliminate war and human want, given requisite social arrangements, and so created the opportunity for widespread achievement of many human goals.

BIOLOGICAL FACTORS

Biological limitations are inherent in the limitations of the human body. The body can do many things, but many are ruled out from its ready accomplishment. We can walk but not fly; the pace of swimming and running is limited; so are the weights we can lift. We cannot dispense with food; we have been unable to eliminate fatigue or the need for sleep.

Liberating effect of technology and medical science. Technology has, however, liberated man from many of these limitations, thereby adding to the scope and range of bodily activity. Telephone, radio, and television give us, so to speak, long-distance voices, ears, and eyes—as writing and dating systems long ago gave us accurate extended memory. The automobile provides figuratively extended legs, and the aeroplane literal wings. Lighting doubles

[2] *Civilization and Climate,* 3rd ed., Yale, 1924.

the time of possible vision, derricks give the hands greater strength than any man's arm ever possessed. In the same class are all the devices which aid defective organs—eye-glasses, so common that we forget we wear them, artificial teeth, auditory aids,[3] artificial limbs, and so forth.

Medical science has also been a great liberator of men from specific biological limitations. It has diminished the incidence of disease, reduced the infant-mortality rate, diagnosed many diseases at an earlier and curable stage, wiped out the causes of some types of illness, and lengthened the span of life. The distribution of many of these benefits—as of technological benefits—remains limited for socio-economic reasons, but the potentialities of tremendous increases of liberty are there. Similarly birth-control techniques are liberating, for they make it possible to plan the number and spacing of childbirths for a woman, and indirectly regulate population growth.

Biological needs the basis of many values. Biological needs—food, sex, shelter, warmth—by their imperative character and the large share their satisfaction occupies in human endeavor, constitute severe limitations on the possible scope of human activity. At the same time, however, they are the very source of many of the purposes and aims of men for which liberty is desired, and sometimes generate the most stirring of human ideals. The body, in general, is thus more than a limitation or an opportunity. It is the basis of the strivings which make liberty meaningful.

The role of heredity. Nevertheless, the body is not always a finished instrument for the achievement of the goals which arise from its strivings. Bodily skills may be developed insofar as the body is flexible. There are limits, however, to what can be done with a particular body. Different individuals appear to differ considerably in capacities and aptitudes, and one of the sources of these differences lies in characteristics believed to be hereditary.

Heredity is a general term covering the biological transmission of characteristics from parent to offspring. Much controversy has been waged around the relative roles of heredity and environment in producing the characteristics of men. In fact heredity and environment have been separated with a sharpness comparable to the traditional distinction of matter and mind. Modern science has been pushing back the boundaries of heredity and revealing the extent and pervasiveness of environmental influence. This has a liberating effect on men's attitudes, bringing character and personality and even physical traits within the range of human control. Thus, for example, crime and juvenile delinquency become social problems rather than marks of inherent criminality and inherent wickedness; and in personal life too

---

[3] Attitudes toward some of these devices show interesting traces of the "essence" or "nature" philosophy. Some people feel ashamed of sensory defects, and avoid using auditory devices, for example, as if wearing these had a certain "unnatural" quality which they would rather not confess. A more naturalistic approach to bodily needs and defects is becoming the consequence of technological benefits.

bad habits become less a ground for resignation to what a person "is made like" than for active endeavor toward change. Biologists and psychologists are ceasing to think of heredity and environment as separately operating "factors"; the physical self is seen as a dynamic product of continuous interaction from the very moment of conception. Embryological studies of prenatal environment extend the search for such interactions, refusing to allow an appeal to heredity to cover ignorance concerning determinants.

Eugenics. The dream of eugenics—the liberation of an improved future stock from the faulty traits of present specimens—is an old one. One element in it—selective mating to produce better offspring—is an old technique in animal husbandry. Plato suggested its application to men and women—choosing the good warrior, and presumably the philosopher as his ideal type. But we do not even now know enough about the hereditary transmission of detailed characteristics to do more than warn against some special cases of mating—such as of two persons from families with haemophilia.

A second element in eugenics—sterilization of the so-called "unfit"—has been enacted in many legal codes. However, many of the definitions of "unfit"—habitual criminals, for example—refer to social characteristics acquired as a result of environment and not to inherited characteristics. Thus sterilization becomes simply a penalty, like prison or death, for certain repeated offenses, and may mean cutting off potentially excellent rather than inferior offspring.[4]

PSYCHOLOGICAL FACTORS

Psychological limitations are of two sorts—those characterizing man at large and those arising from personal history.

Human nature and instinct theory. Human nature is commonly held to have definite and unchangeable directions, determined by fundamental instincts. Among the traits which have been regarded as instincts are self-assertion, food-seeking, mating, acquisitiveness. Instinct theory has often been used in an attempt to limit the variability of human institutions. It is argued, for instance, that war is inevitable because men are naturally self-assertive, that private property is rendered necessary by the acquisitive instinct, that the family is the only possible adequate form for control of mating and child-raising because of the parental instinct.

The special concept of instinct has been analyzed by psychologists from psychological, anthropological, and physiological points of view, and however legitimate it may be as a category for the study of man's makeup, its use to limit social forms has been found unwarranted. Some have substi-

[4] For an account and analysis of sterilization laws and biological information on eugenics, see J. B. S. Haldane, *Heredity and Politics*, Norton, 1938.

tuted for it the notion of "dependable motives," which avoids assuming any *inherent* character in complex human behavior. Klineberg, for example, uses as criteria of dependability "the existence of continuity between a particular form of behavior and that of other biological species, particularly the anthropoid apes," "the discovery of a biochemical or physiological basis for any specific activity," "the discovery of a form of behavior common to all human societies in spite of the variations in their culture."[5] As thus interpreted the limits of psychological variability are found to be considerably wider than is commonly believed. Far from being true, the old adage "You can't change human nature" turns out to deny a fundamental human process.

Sensory and motor reactions. In the domain of sensory and motor reactions contemporary psychology in conjunction with applied physical science has devoted considerable study to ways of relieving strains, both natural strains and those incident to the special conditions of modern living. Securing the best type of artificial light, minimizing irritating and excessive noise in cities, diminishing fatigue by optimum conditions in factories are only some of the numerous respects in which knowledge for the increase of liberty is increasingly available. It is important to note that such increase of liberty involves curtailing certain individual liberties, such as the freedom to honk automobile horns at any time of night and to work factory employees at any speed. It also involves extensive expenditure for the application of the research. The utilization of these potentialities of liberation is therefore a complex social question.

Personal history and psychological aids. Personal history—which we called the second source of psychological limitations—is a name for the experiences that shape a particular man. These open for some men possibilities not open to all and close for some possibilities that others achieve. A great part of this experience consists in conscious acquisition of information, skills, habits of judgment and so forth, which have a positive effect in that they enable us to accomplish desired results. A great part consists of habits and tastes imposed upon us by the conscious action of others, as in our childhood training. But of much that goes on within and about us we are not conscious, and even when we observe results we may be in no position to estimate or interpret them. Psychoanalysis has directed special attention to the mechanisms by which emotions and desires are set in motion in early years, and has shown how they operate unrecognized in the development of personality. Many of the later obstacles in a man's activity—as well as unexpected strength—may come from such sources. Liberation from oppressive and socially disorganizing states of emotion and feeling is the goal of psychoanalytic and psychiatric techniques.

Again, differential personal histories in a complex society produce serious problems of general orientation among the young and adolescent. Vocational

[5] Otto Klineberg, *Social Psychology*, Holt, 1940, p. 61.

and other types of professional guidance can help discover the direction of a person's abilities and turn him toward channels for their satisfactory exercise. It thus may liberate people from the restrictive results of misplaced efforts. On the other hand, there is the potential danger of regimentation. This double possibility—like the use of a drug to cure or kill—is inherent in most valuable techniques.

Liberty and society

SOCIAL MOLDING AND SOCIAL LIMITATION

The society of which he is a part both molds and limits the character of the individual's activities. That a man acquires the language he uses from the social tradition and training of his group is transparently clear. The same is true, in varying degrees, of economic institutions, political forms, kinship structure and family arrangements, religious usages, philosophic problems, technical skills, motor habits, sense of beauty, discriminations of right and wrong, prejudices, and, it might almost be said, the greatest part of the specific character of men's responses. The investigations of social psychologists suggest that even perception, which might be thought to be purely physiological, involves in the subject's interpretation selective elements imparted by social tradition. Emotional behavior is also profoundly affected by social conditioning; this is shown by the variety among different peoples in the occasions and grounds and forms of expression of anger and jealousy, sorrow and love.

In addition to the elements common to the individuals in any society, many differential characteristics are social in origin. For a society—a complex one especially—is not necessarily a single unified group. There are differences in status and role for different individuals, and there may be class differences, regional differences, occupational differences, and so forth. Each of these may come to be conjoined with a cluster of habits, attitudes and values, which make them seem almost of a different world. In the United States, a southern Negro share-cropper, a northern automobile worker, a college professor in a large city, a New York "playboy," a western lumberman, a California banker live different kinds of lives. Each may find it difficult to see beyond his own ways. It is important to note that even the forms of dissent within a society are social products, expressive of the type of conditions that give rise to them, as for example the flocking of "bohemians" to Greenwich Village in the nineteen-twenties.

The common remark that man is a social animal has therefore a very profound meaning. A man's self is social in origin, social in the aims and attitudes that it develops,—even where these turn out to be of the most self-centered or egoistic type—social in the influences that play upon it and hinder its development or exercise, and social in the very goals for which it strives.

Economic limitations. From the point of view of the individual's activities, economic factors are the social elements providing the most serious limitations. The grinding effects of poverty upon men's lives and the distress it brings to lives compelled to focus on the narrow limits of the search for daily bread have been often described and more widely felt. Nothing short of a Great Plague compares in its consequences with widespread near-starvation and insecurity. Most historians and social scientists agree that an economic background is involved in all social, political, religious, or moral upheavals; opinion differs merely in assigning relative importance to economic determinants in particular historical movements.

Nevertheless, economic factors are not always expressed by men as social limitations. In a great part of the history of our own society, for example, poverty was viewed as a personal failing; it was attributed to lack of initiative or effort or to bad luck. This attribution was itself a socially standardized response. For a long time the dominant economic science made the workings of the economic system appear as part of the natural order, hence not amenable to human control.

Political limitations. On the other hand, political limitations on men's activity have always been clearly recognized. In part this is because the application of political sanctions constitutes the most dramatic form of interference of man with man. The action of police and soldiers in the name of the sovereign power, the presence of prisons, the assessment of taxes, the formulation of laws, and the judgment of courts cannot fail to impress men directly. Furthermore the particular development of western countries focused attention on the state at a time when it hindered the economic growth of the commercial classes. To curb the arbitrary tyranny of the king and the entrenched landed aristocracy became a prime necessity.

The natural rights conception of liberty—"that all men are endowed by their Creator with certain unalienable Rights"—was an expression of this need. This view grew into a comprehensive philosophy of human rights, telling the individual the fields which no sovereign power might rightfully invade. In the Declaration of Independence these rights include "life, liberty and the pursuit of happiness." The French Declaration of the Rights of Man lists among his rights liberty, property, security, and resistance to oppression. In the American Bill of Rights there is clear indication that the old evils are fresh in memory. It is well to be reminded today of the dangers which men feared from government in the early days of the republic, and to see how constant and living such dangers have remained throughout the world. The following comprise the American Bill of Rights:

ARTICLE I: Congress shall make no law respecting an establishment of religion, or prohibiting the free exercise thereof; or abridging the freedom of speech, or of the press; or the right of the people peaceably to assemble, and to petition the government for a redress of grievances.

ARTICLE II: A well regulated militia, being necessary to the security of a free State, the right of the people to keep and bear arms, shall not be infringed.

ARTICLE III: No soldier shall, in time of peace be quartered in any house, without the consent of the owner, nor in time of war, but in a manner to be prescribed by law.

ARTICLE IV: The right of the people to be secure in their persons, houses, papers, and effects, against unreasonable searches and seizures, shall not be violated, and no warrants shall issue, but upon probable cause, supported by oath or affirmation, and particularly describing the place to be searched, and the persons or things to be seized.

ARTICLE V: No person shall be held to answer for a capital, or otherwise infamous crime, unless on a presentment or indictment of a grand jury, except in cases arising in the land or naval forces, or in the militia, when in actual service in time of war or public danger; nor shall any person be subject for the same offense to be twice put in jeopardy of life or limb; nor shall be compelled in any criminal case to be a witness against himself, nor be deprived of life, liberty, or property, without due process of law; nor shall private property be taken for public use without just compensation.

ARTICLE VI: In all criminal prosecutions, the accused shall enjoy the right to a speedy and public trial, by an impartial jury of the State and district wherein the crime shall have been committed, which district shall have been previously ascertained by law, and to be informed of the nature and cause of the accusation; to be confronted with the witnesses against him; to have compulsory process for obtaining witnesses in his favor, and to have the assistance of counsel for his defense.

ARTICLE VII: In suits at common law, where the value in controversy shall exceed twenty dollars, the right of trial by jury shall be preserved, and no fact tried by a jury shall be otherwise re-examined in any court of the United States, than according to the rules of the common law.

ARTICLE VIII: Excessive bail shall not be required, nor excessive fines imposed, nor cruel and unusual punishments inflicted.

ARTICLE IX: The enumeration in the Constitution of certain rights shall not be construed to deny or disparage others retained by the people.

ARTICLE X: The powers not delegated to the United States by the Constitution, nor prohibited by it to the States, are reserved to the States respectively, or to the people.

Other restraints. In addition to the economic and political limitations, there are manifold other pressures, social, moral, and religious, which may be felt by man as restraints upon his action. The opinion of his fellow-men, the promptings of duty, and the fear of divine wrath are powerful sanctions in most men's lives.

SEARCH FOR A GENERAL PRINCIPLE OF LIBERTY

The various restraints imposed by society on human action have led men to seek a formula by which the individual may understand what he may rightfully do. Such a formula would constitute a principle of general social liberty. Many candidates have appeared. For example: Liberty consists in doing as you please irrespective of effect on others. Liberty consists in following momentary impulses. Liberty consists in doing what is not against social interest. Liberty consists in following reason. Liberty consists in doing what you wish provided it does not infringe on someone else's like liberty. For the most part such formulae do not set goals for men's striving—except perhaps where pleasure or development of individual differences is the implicit aim—nor do they point to the positive conditions requisite for the achievement of goals. Their purport is essentially negative: they tell the individual what restraints on his will he may legitimately disregard and upon which he should reckon. Thus they reflect the dominant tendency in the modern world up to recent times to construe liberty simply as the removal of restraint.

The last of the examples given above—liberty consists in doing what you wish provided it does not infringe on someone else's like liberty—is the principle offered by John Stuart Mill in his essay *On Liberty,* stated from the point of view of the individual. It is worth considering his account in some detail, not only because it reveals the way in which such principles function and the difficulties of a single-principle formulation, but because of its historical importance in providing the present-day liberal framework of approach to such questions.

Mill's theory of liberty

John Stuart Mill's theory of liberty constitutes an impressive systematization of the negative aspect of social liberty. That is, his formulation of the issue is in terms of liberty *from* definite restraints rather than opportunity to accomplish definite goals. Mill poses the general problem as "the nature and limits of the power which can be legitimately exercised by society over the individual." In earlier days, says Mill, summarizing western political development, the restraints upon the individual came chiefly from political rulers, so that liberty consisted in setting limits to the ruler's power over the community. This was done first by obtaining recognition of political rights for the subjects, second by constitutional checks. Later, however, men attempted to make the ruling power itself emanate from the ruled. At this point, says Mill, arose the conception that when the rulers were identified with the ruled the limitations on government required against older rulers were no longer necessary. But such self-government, Mill finds, turns out to be "not the government of each by himself, but of each by all the rest." Hence precautions are needed for the protection of a minority which the majority may desire to oppress. In short, the tyranny of the majority is itself a possibility to be guarded against. Such tyranny need not be exercised through government; in fact its thorough-going character is largely due to the way it can operate through non-political everyday sanctions in wiping out dissent and hindering development of opposing opinion.

HIS FUNDAMENTAL PRINCIPLE

"The object of this Essay,"[6] Mill says clearly, "is to assert one very simple principle, as entitled to govern absolutely the dealings of society with the individual in the way of compulsion and control, whether the means used be physical force in the form of legal penalties, or the moral coercion of public opinion. That principle is, that the sole end for which mankind are warranted, individually or collectively, in interfering with the liberty of action of any of their number, is self-protection. That the only purpose for which power can be rightfully exercised over any member of a civilized community, against his will, is to prevent harm to others. His own good, either physical or moral, is not a sufficient warrant. He cannot rightfully be compelled to do or forbear because it will be better for him to do so, because it will make him happier, because, in the opinions of others, to do so would be wise, or even right. These are good reasons for remonstrating with him, or reasoning with him, or persuading him, or entreating him, but not for compelling him, or visiting him with any evil in case he do otherwise. To justify that, the conduct from which it is desired to deter him must be calculated to produce evil to someone else. The only part of the conduct of anyone, for which he is amenable to society, is that which concerns others. In the part which merely concerns himself, his independence is, of right, absolute. Over himself, over his own body and mind, the individual is sovereign."

Initial reservations. Mill points out that his principle applies only to "human beings in the maturity of their faculties," that is, where questions may be settled by free and equal rational discussion and men may be persuaded and convinced about their own improvement. Thus children are excluded from the operation of the principle, and Mill gives rather a blank check to

[6] J. S. Mill, *On Liberty*, Chapter I.

rulers in what he calls backward states of society. He limits despotism in dealing with barbarians, however, by insisting that the end be their improvement and the means be justified by actually effecting the end. He also assumes somewhat over-hastily that most countries of western Europe are, in his sense, civilized.

Positive values aimed at. Mill is thus interested in pushing back the borders of social restraint; he is seeking to remove those hindrances to man's activity which in a general historical survey he has found typical, important, and dominant. It is in this sense that we described his position as a systematized general theory of negative social liberty. He does not stop at this point but goes on to state explicitly the *values* in human activity which would be advanced by removing such restraints. In the third chapter of his essay he selects especially such factors as individuality, individual spontaneity, diversity. These are the ends which he thinks his system of liberty would serve. There was a time when spontaneity and individuality were in excess and a hindrance to social development. But in his own day he finds the danger is precisely the opposite: ape-like imitation will replace conscious choice, to do what everybody else does will become a dominant value, individuality will be worn down into conformity instead of being cultivated. Mill appears to regard individuality and spontaneous choice not only as ends worth while in themselves but also as means. For he assumes that only by the encouragement of originality will progress be possible.[7]

The principle as criterion. Mill's principle may be regarded as a general criterion offered to legislators, educators, and to all citizens in their conduct towards others, to be invoked when they are about to frame laws or exercise other social pressures against any activity of an individual or group. Different types of liberty, e.g., economic liberty, civil liberties (of speech, thought, and so forth), liberty of press, of religion, of movement, of vocation, are simply the application of the formula to the relevant fields of activity. From the point of view of the individual or group concerned in the activity, the principle acts as a kind of charter of liberty with a warning as to where they may expect to be restrained. It says, in effect, "You are at liberty to do what you please, free from restraint on the part of others, provided that your activity does not harm others."

How is a principle to be tested? Mill's formula is, as we have noted, one of several possible principles. Mill himself was warring against the principle that a majority has a right to lay down rules for individuals on the basis of its likes and dislikes, so that any kind of individual conduct *displeasing* to society could be banned.

[7] In his *Autobiography* (Chapter 7) Mill speaks of the central truth of his *Liberty* as "the importance, to man and society, of a large variety in types of character, and of giving full freedom to human nature to expand itself in innumerable and conflicting directions."

This possible variety of formulae for liberty raises the question of how one is to decide between them. To do this the formulae must be considered in a context of possible conduct, so that their functioning may be envisaged. They may then turn out to operate in several different ways. They may, in the first place, turn out to be arbitrary definitions of the term "liberty," which simply tell us how Mill and others use the term. Secondly, they may function to state or describe systems taken to be ideal—worthy ends in themselves. As such they are pictures offered to attract us, to arouse our admiration, respect, or whatever ethical attitudes we may find appropriate to ends. Such usage will be considered below in relation to positive liberty. In the third place— and this is probably the most common—the formulae may be offered as reliable instruments or means to ends on which we are presumed to agree. For example, Mill holds to the end of the greatest happiness of the greatest number.[3] He is implying that it will be best achieved by allowing every man to make his own decisions about himself insofar as others are not affected thereby. Mill is against the paternalism of some men deciding what is better for an individual when he himself disagrees. In the long run the world will be better off (that is, more men more happy) if you are permitted to go to perdition in your own way rather than to heaven in mine.

Clearly Mill's thoroughgoing individualism must be tested by long-range observation (or experiment) to decide whether it is productive of greater human happiness than some other formula. If another formula proved itself empirically more reliable, his would have to yield. Similarly, if the goal is individual happiness, the principle "Follow momentary impulse" would have to be tested empirically to see whether even on the egoistic criterion it succeeded in bringing greater happiness than an alternative principle introducing more long-range calculation. In all these cases the formulae are offered as reliable means to indicated or suggested or sometimes merely implicit ends.

APPLICATION OF THE PRINCIPLE

In applying his theory Mill consistently places the burden of proof on those—whether individual or government or majority—who urge interference with what a man wishes to do. A man has economic liberty, political liberty, liberty of thought, speech, action in any direction he may desire, subject only to someone else's justifiable complaint of interference with his liberties. The state acts on the kind of questions on which experience has shown that complaints will arise. We have here the makings of the nothing-but-policeman theory of the state which took its harshest form in Herbert Spencer's political theory.

But not even every hurt felt by another at my conduct is sufficient ground for repressing me. Mill says: "There are many who consider as an injury to themselves any conduct which they have a distaste for, and resent it as an outrage to their feelings; as a religious bigot, when charged with disregarding the religious feelings of others, has been known to retort that they disregard his feelings, by persisting in their abominable worship or creed."[8]

On such a ground Mill argues against laws prohibiting drinking. If you can show that a man is spending on drink the money required by his family and so hurting them, it is not an infringement of individual liberty to prohibit his drinking. But otherwise the choice of whether or not to drink is any man's own. On the other hand, Mill recognizes offenses against decency as ground for restraint; further, many actions not in themselves condemnable are objectionable if publicly done. Divisions among what is merely distasteful to the narrow-minded, what is a violation of good manners, and what is positively injurious to others are not entirely clear. Nor does Mill provide a criterion for measuring differences in degree, if the difference be just one of degree.

Liberty of thought and discussion. Mill's arguments on liberty of thought and discussion—a major application of his view—give classic expression to liberal values. He calls for absolute liberty in these respects. To silence expression of opinion is to rob posterity; the opinion under attack may, after all, be true, and to suppress it is, therefore, an unwarranted assumption of infallibility. It is one thing to act on high probabilities—because action is necessary—and quite another to suppress an opposing view because one's own appears probably true. Nor should suppression take place on grounds of utility; for the usefulness of a belief is itself only another belief which also requires free and open discussion. The history of the way in which many true beliefs have been pilloried is itself sufficient to give pause to those about to suppress an opinion. Mill does not believe that truth always triumphs over persecution. Furthermore, no truth we possess is complete. Its best chance of becoming fuller truth lies in conflict with opposing opinions.

On the other hand, even where the opinion one is tempted to suppress is clearly false, it does not follow that its suppression is right. Its expression can serve to make us conscious of the reasons for the views we ourselves hold, so that we shall not be holding to unreasoning belief. For truth is best discovered in the conflict of reasoned opinion. Finally, if contrary opinions are suppressed, beliefs will not merely be unreasoned in the minds of most men, but will actually come to be held as dogmas and opinion will tend to become sectarian.

Liberty of action in different spheres. Mill recognizes that the same reasons which make liberty of thought and discussion so valuable point to liberty of action. We need not follow his detailed account of liberties of worship, trade, contract, marriage, and so forth. A few illustrations of his atti-

---

[8] *On Liberty,* Chapter IV.

tude to government undertakings as limiting such liberties are, however, especially interesting. He thinks that the government should require a good education for every child and if necessary pay for it, but he is opposed to having the whole or a large part of the education of the people in the hands of the state, lest it mold people uniformly to suit the predominant power in the government. He thinks laws which forbid marriage unless the parties show they have the means of supporting a family do not exceed the legitimate powers of the state, but he leaves open the question of the expediency of such laws. He even looks with alarm on a situation in which the best talent of a country is likely to be drawn into civil service, since this would tend to give rise to a dominant bureaucracy. As a practical principle he urges the widest decentralization of power consistent with efficiency, but he also urges that information be gathered from a central source, since correlation of knowledge is necessary for its rapid advance.

CRITIQUE OF MILL'S THEORY

Individualistic vs. social framework. Mill's framework is thoroughly individualistic. To justify the state's compelling an individual to act against his own desire it is necessary to show that other people would otherwise be harmed. It is not enough that the vast majority will gain by such action. The only resort this leaves in practice is to persuade the recalcitrant individual that he too will gain. Suppose (as has indeed happened) that a man refuses to allow government inspectors to vaccinate his cows on the ground that the milk from them is used only on his farm by himself, his family, and their willing employees. By strict application of Mill's principle, the state would be infringing his liberty by enforcing vaccination, unless it can prove that somehow other people would be hurt. Similarly, if a man who sends his children to private schools is taxed for the support of public schools, the state must justify such taxation by showing that he also benefits through his workers being educated or the crime rate lowered by widespread education.

A social framework would shift the burden of proof in cases in which the great social value of a measure has been established. The individual would have to show that his claim for exemption rests on substantial ground, that individuality is somehow genuinely interfered with, not merely by state action *per se,* but by the thwarting of specific aims. Otherwise, even such state grounds as the cost of admitting exceptions (either through expense of hearings or because of the opening wedge for fraud) would be sufficient to outweigh a claim resting on whim. Just as Mill does not believe that mere dislike of another's activity is sufficient cause to warrant infringement of his liberty, so a social approach would not allow mere dislike of state action to hinder the accomplishment of socially valuable objectives.

Even where the individualistic and the social approach agree on particular steps, the framework of justification is different. Mill's principle of individual liberty, with its insistence that the sole rightful basis of governmental compulsion is to prevent harm to others, seems to act almost as a screen which hides his general happiness principle and hinders the direct formulation of social policy in terms of general welfare. A social framework need not neglect the aims underlying Mill's formulation—his evaluation of initiative, originality, diversity, and their importance to progress. Such values could be placed high on a list including others such as security, public health, and public education, and a scheme of legitimate liberties could be worked out embracing all the values listed, not merely the selected first group.

Coercing a man for his own good. Such a social approach would sometimes be faced with the problem of coercing an individual for his own long-range good. It is important to note, therefore, that Mill does not successfully solve this question. He is rightly wary of the possibilities of abuse in such a conception, but we may wonder whether such coercion is really excluded even on his own approach. There are cases, such as melancholia after childbirth, in which restraint may be required against the person's present judgment of her own welfare. Is a man, after due deliberation, at liberty to commit suicide, especially if we suspect that an enforced regimen of some sort will cure him of the desire? Similar problems arise in matters of drink, and, on a smaller scale, in many less dramatic situations in which a man feels tempted to act as his brother's keeper.[9]

Clearly there can be no general answer to such questions. Each situation must be analyzed separately and attention paid to the probable outcome for good or ill. While the individualistic stress is a salutary warning not to ride rough-shod over a person's values, it fails to recognize the malleability of the self, of which Mill in other contexts was perfectly aware. Perhaps Mill's provision noted above, that his individualism is meant only for the finished individual, the complete adult, covers such cases. If it does, an important source of control over men lies in those who are to judge who is adult. Perhaps Mill's approach should be refashioned to state that the only warrantable use of pressure on a person for his own good is when it is highly probable that he will thank you for it afterwards; and even then one must not trust too much one's own judgment about the probabilities nor develop busybody habits. Perhaps increased knowledge of the determinants of personal feelings and desires would make possible more mature judgments in such matters, as seems to be the case in medical questions where health is the value agreed on. Otherwise the most satisfactory way to mold another person's

---

[9] Mill even contends that a man may be forcibly prevented from exposing himself to a danger, and not merely warned, when he is "in some state of excitement or absorption incompatible with the full use of the reflecting faculty" (*Liberty*, Chapter V.).

character would seem to be by slow stages, with his voluntary co-operation at each step.

Weakness in Mill's conception of the individual. Such criticisms point to a fundamental weakness in Mill's conception of the individual—his treatment of a man as an isolated atom rather than as predominantly a product of his society. Mill fails to appreciate sufficiently the role of the interaction of men in molding their selves and thus establishing the very interests and desires whose satisfaction constitutes happiness. Once this fact is recognized, large-scale remolding of men's character through socially established means becomes possible. Thus an individual's present character loses the privileged position which Mill's treatment had given it.

EVALUATION OF MILL'S LIBERTIES

We may also look to the lessons of experience since Mill's day. We must remember that Mill was not predicting that the particular liberties he championed would conquer, but that a system in which they prevailed would be one in which men would be happier in the long run. From this point of view, while some of these liberties have proved a precious heritage which men have been ready to defend with their lives, it cannot be said that Mill's specific approach provides a fruitful contemporary formulation of the problem. For it is doubtful whether the values which he was striving to secure can be widely maintained by a system operating according to his indications.

Mill's shifting views on economic liberty. The crux of the matter has been, of course, what is commonly called economic liberty and the rights of private property. On this question Mill's attitude changed considerably. At first, he tells us in his *Autobiography*,[10] he saw no further than the old school of political economists. "Private property, as now understood, and inheritance, appeared to me, as to them, the *dernier mot* of legislation: and I looked no further than to mitigating the inequalities consequent on these institutions, by getting rid of primogeniture and entails." But eventually, he says, "our ideal of ultimate improvement went far beyond Democracy, and would class us decidedly under the general designation of Socialists." In his *Principles of Political Economy* he distinguished between the laws of the production of wealth, as real laws of nature dependent on the properties of objects, and the modes of distribution which are socially determined, hence changeable. In his essay *On Liberty* (Chapter 5) his treatment of economics is brief but revealing. In the first place he recognizes that the pursuit of one man's good may bring injury to others, but denies that disappointed competitors have any legal or moral right to immunity from such suffering unless there has been fraud, treachery, or force. Mill thus appears to support competition

---

[10] Chapter 7.

upon which business rests. But immediately after he says that trade is a social act. Thus at one blow he removes it from the protection of his liberty principle, except insofar as all restraint *qua* restraint is an evil. Nevertheless, he takes for granted that "both the cheapness and the good quality of commodities are most effectually provided for by leaving the producers and sellers perfectly free, under the sole check of equal freedom to the buyers for supplying themselves elsewhere," and asserts that this view "rests on grounds different from, though equally solid with, the principle of individual liberty."

Traditional formulation of economic liberty. It is not surprising therefore that the tradition of popular economics has continued to regard economic liberty in the simple terms of the right, unhindered by any governmental check, to buy what one chooses, sell what one chooses, and to compete in buying and selling. Mill's conception of liberty as directed against governmental and popular control of the individual has been reflected in dominant attitudes more than his more subtle reservations.

Economic liberty in this sense is possessed by very few people today. I may be at liberty to sell my labor for a "living wage," but if no one is ready to buy it at that price, my liberty has little meaning. This has been the lot of a great part of the people for a great part of the time. The concentration of economic power has given those in control of large corporations the liberty to make decisions of tremendous scope in which the masses of men have been able to do little but acquiesce.[11] In such a situation the language of economic liberty is inappropriate. If it is retained it leads to such formulations as "I am at liberty to set myself up as a steel manufacturer, but that liberty is not worth much to me," "Most men's economic liberty is worth little or nothing, whereas some men's economic liberty is worth almost everything," "A man is at perfect liberty to eat—for no one will stop him if he begins—even though he happens to have no food," or Anatole France's famous comment, "The law in its majesty gives liberty to rich and poor alike to sleep under bridges and beg for bread."

Such formulations are still frequently found. Thus the attempt of men to invoke governmental aid in maintaining the minimum conditions of life is called an abandonment of liberty in favor of security. Now whatever Mill's own sentiments might have been had he envisaged contemporary society, the essentially negative character of his principle of liberty makes his concepts ready instruments for these common formulations. For his principle is, in effect, addressed to governments and people telling them not to interfere. If they so withhold interference, the person from whom they keep their hands has liberty. But it is not clear today as it was perhaps in the days of the rising power of the industrial class that government restrictions constitute the greatest real check on general personal liberty. It is therefore much

[11] For the question of control in property-ownership, see below, pp. 276-77.

more realistic, today, to abandon Mill's concepts and redefine our terms by restating most men's values in the domain of economic activity, reassessing the obstacles that stand in their way and redefining economic liberty in terms of the minimizing or removing of those obstacles.

Redefinition of economic liberty. The National Labor Relations Act provides a good illustration of the point at issue. Because of the encouragement it gives to labor unions, and because unionism often means the restriction of certain powers of the employer—such as the right to dismiss arbitrarily, or to work his employees long hours—the NLRA has been attacked as curtailing economic liberty. Using the older formulation, its defenders may agree but claim that economic liberty must give way in part to social interests. Abandoning the older formulation, it becomes possible to say that the National Labor Relations Act increases rather than diminishes economic liberty. For the growth of labor unions points in the direction of equalizing bargaining power and so gives workers in their organizations a greater share of economic liberty.

This reformulation involves abandoning Mill's concept and carrying out afresh the kind of analysis he was making in his own time. Economic liberty is thus redefined in terms of the dominant values of most men in their economic activity. Their aim is to get jobs in order to support themselves and their families. Hence the typical obstacles to their achievement of such aims become the center of attention, and the removal of such obstacles is called the achievement of economic liberty. Mill found government restriction to be the major obstacle. In this view he was carrying on what had become the traditional view of the commercial and industrial middle class. Today the obstacles to men's economic aims come from other sources—e.g., limited production, insufficient bargaining power of employees, lack of general planning. Hence steps taken, often by government, to increase production and enable workers to join unions without fear are liberating rather than restrictive. They ought more properly to be regarded as additions to economic liberty.

Political and civil liberties. Political and civil liberties embrace a host of activities which on Mill's formula would be guaranteed against interference: the right to do as you please in voting, petitioning, forming political associations, thinking, speaking, writing, assembly—all the activities of representative government and mature citizenship.

In the western world, before the outbreak of the Second World War, it had become fashionable in many circles to decry parliamentary government as inefficient and to regard civil liberties as self-contradictory in allowing the expression of opposition to these very liberties. In many cases the attack on parliamentary government represented deliberate or incipient fascist attitudes. In others, however, it was merely a hasty generalization from the failure of many governments to cope with economic problems which crushed a large part of their populations. The intensity of the struggle against fascism and nazism on a world-wide front has to some extent clarified these issues. It is important, therefore, both for an understanding of the past and for the problems of the future, to ask whether the condemnation of political liberty as organized inefficiency really represented lessons of experience.

Justification of political liberty. This condemnation of political liberty rested on the oversimplified theory that because there were clashes of interest between parliamentary groups representing clashes of interest within the country, and because these clashes often rendered decisive action on economic issues difficult, therefore centralized and more authoritative control would be in the public interest. It was, in effect, the old cry for authority on the naive assumption that an authoritative rule would represent no interest and therefore everybody's interest.

As against this view of political liberties and their expression in representative government, two explanations of parliamentary troubles have been current. One points to economic difficulties and depressions. The other goes even further and suggests that attacks on representative institutions increased as men sought through those institutions to extend social gains and distribute more widely the economic advantages of modern industry. In short, this view claims that political liberties disappeared just because they threatened to be successful in overcoming entrenched interests of dominant economic groups.[12]

Justification of civil liberties. A similar defense has been made of the self-consistency of civil liberties. For instance, there is no inconsistency in allowing liberty of speech and writing even though they present extremist positions of a fantastic character. In fact the danger lies in not allowing it; for the suppression of the civil liberties of an extremist group has usually been followed by suppression of intermediate groups, then of all liberal opinion, until finally all political liberties disappear. In addition to Mill's argument traced above, it is clear that fantastic doctrines feed only on the despair of large multitudes of men.[13] Counter-propaganda can always be released in much greater volume by governmental authority or majority opinion organizations. (Whether it will be is a complex question of social relations.) The growth of the minority view is therefore indicative of serious social dislocations, usually economic, rather than of too much liberty of expression. Suppression of minority civil liberties is therefore useless; attention should more properly be directed to elimination of the evils which are the source of the trouble. Mill presents this view in insisting that not merely should there be no crusade against the Mormons in their own territory, but

[12] For further discussion of these issues concerning political processes, see the account of the state (Chapter 19) and of democracy (Chapter 20) below.

[13] For a discussion of this question, see Hadley Cantril, *The Psychology of Social Movements*, J. Wiley and Sons, 1941.

that even outside their territory their teachers should not be silenced: "If civilization has got the better of barbarism when barbarism had the world to itself, it is too much to profess to be afraid lest barbarism, after having been fairly got under, should revive and conquer civilization. A civilization that can thus succumb to its vanquished enemy, must first have become so degenerate, that neither its appointed priests and teachers, nor anybody else, has the capacity, or will take the trouble, to stand up for it."[14]

Limitations on freedom of speech are, of course, necessary where there is immediate demonstrable danger. Justice Holmes pointed out that freedom of speech does not allow a man to shout "fire" in a crowded theater. Nor can it allow an employer to threaten his employees prior to a Labor Board election. Again, during the course of a war, freedom of speech does not include the right to broadcast information valuable to the enemy, nor to spread false rumors which stir up strife and weaken morale in a center producing military supplies. Such acts as these would usually be punishable as sedition. It is important, of course, that such concepts as *sedition, license,* and *libel* be employed in an explicit and not a vague fashion, with the burden of proof resting on those who make accusations. Otherwise they can readily be extended to cover all opposition to those who may happen to be in the seat of authority. The importance of freedom of speech in the modern world, however, can be judged from the fact that President Roosevelt included it among the Four Freedoms which he enunciated on January 6, 1941, as principles underlying the war against nazism and fascism.

Religious liberty. Of all the liberties Mill dealt with, religious liberty has perhaps fared best. Persons are rarely attacked nowadays for religious opinions as such. This may be a result of the decreasing importance of formal religion in modern life. Certainly intolerance as such has not abated; it has merely shifted ground, now stressing race, social status, and heterodox political opinion. Where religious liberties do conflict with other interests there has been restriction. The Supreme Court of the United States at one point denied the liberty of a child attending a public school to refrain from saluting the flag because of religious scruples;[15] it found such refusal dangerous to the foundations of national sentiment. Yet genuine conscientious objectors on religious grounds have been exempted from front-line war service. Where moral views held on religious grounds are concerned, conflict has been sharper. There is still today in the United States considerable censorship of movies and literature engendered by direction action of religious groups. A problem of this sort was posed in 1940 in New York in the objections raised by religious groups to the appointment of Bertrand Russell to a professorship at the College of the City of New York.

[14] *On Liberty,* Chapter 4.
[15] In the Gobitis case; the court, however, reversed itself in a later case.

Although religious liberty is threatened by any attempts to penalize persons for their religious views, the value of the liberty itself is widely conceded. Thus freedom of religion was included among the Four Freedoms. The general interpretation of religious liberty has, however, tended to limit it to non-interference with any man's religious belief and worship. To carry this liberty to a logical conclusion would entail admission of the right to disbelieve in any religion and to follow no form of religious worship. At present religious liberty sometimes becomes a liberalism within the family of religions which offers a united hostility, involving numerous social penalties, against those whose convictions lead them outside the circle of religions.

Liberty as positive

The critique of Mill at various points has shown the need for a reformulation of the concept of social liberty in order to render it positive and set it in relation to the goals of men in society. This involves estimating social forms and social techniques in the light of the *opportunities* they actually provide for the achievement of men's goals. Liberty becomes a name for a state of affairs, a set of techniques and rules of operation which allow men to attain what they conceive to be the good life. Liberty is thus construed as a positive instrument or means making for the good.

Illustrations of liberating social techniques may be taken from many different fields. Writing and increase of literacy have opened tremendous possibilities. Division of labor has increased efficiency and thus productivity. The principle of insurance—death, old age, unemployment, illness, fire, accident—by distributing cost widely in the form of premium payments, enables men to cope with unexpected or untimely suffering and even regularly anticipated evils. Co-operation increases manyfold the return on individual effort, whether it be in such simple tasks as two men lifting a log or the complex procedures of joint stock corporations in which capital is pooled or the gigantic undertakings of a government enterprise. Formal schools develop habits that serve as useful tools, and educational theory, broadly conceived, sharpens the instruments for the fashioning of character and personality.

Role of standardization. Underlying all organization and therefore tremendously important in keeping the complex system of life and society functioning smoothly is the phenomenon of standardization. Paradoxical as this may seem, standardization is an essential element in positive liberty. The number-system, for example, is a standardized set of symbols capable of very wide application. Units of measurement, weight, exchange-value (whether monetary or not) are basic in an industrial society. Standardized equipment, tools, and machinery-parts are essential to large-scale rapid production. Standardized legal documents, standardized contracts in special fields, standardized procedures and responses in specialized situations all aid the rapidity of transactions. Nor does standardization in any field mean, necessarily, reduction to drab uniformity. Often the finer the elements with which it deals, the wider the variety of possible combinations. In many cases also any loss in variety is compensated for by reduced cost and increased production. Again there are contexts in which lack of standardization means confusion (e.g., hundreds of brands for the housewife to pick among) and enforced standardization (such as simple grading of tinned products according to quality) brings rapidly improved and better informed selection.

The roots of standardization are, of course, very deep in human life, for standardization is ultimately only another name—from the point of view of the individual participant—for habit formation coupled with conscious realization of the purpose and role of the habit. It is important at this point, therefore, to note the fallacy in the view that speaks of all social regulation, including all conventions, as curtailment of liberty. Social conventions are important for economy of time and effort. The standardized type of greeting exchanged by persons in passing one another in the street, avoids the need for framing language suited to one another's mood at the particular moment. Nor does this convention interfere with a more intimate meeting of personalities if the participants so desire. It is true that some conventions become ridiculous or even engender rather than remove social friction. This proves merely that a change of those conventions is desirable, not that convention as such should be abolished.

Pressed to the extreme, a view that regards all convention and standardization as *ipso facto* evil would be driven to consider all habits as restraints on what might have been possible differences, hence as obstacles to liberty, liberty being defined as the absence of *all* restraint. This view is open to objection on both empirical and logical grounds. Experience shows that in many cases to substitute conscious for habitual conduct is to breed confusion. The story of the centipede that crawled happily along until asked which foot it used first, whereupon it became practically paralyzed, is a familiar one. The logical difficulty in the view is its conception of the self. Habits are necessary to the formation of a self that has values. Hence no habits, no self, no values, and thus no meaning to restraint or to freedom. To talk of liberty under such conditions is nonsense. The view is therefore an exaggeration of the perfectly sound proposition that some habits require alteration in the light of the values a man may hold.

Economic bases of positive liberty. Attention to the economic basis of the individual's life is, of course, fundamental to a positive conception of social liberty. This is by no means a novel consideration. In Aristotle's *Politics* we find the view that property is necessary for men's liberty and that men should be neither too rich nor too poor. Jefferson's view was not fundamentally dissimilar. He put his trust in the small farmer and in widely diffused land-holdings. He believed that American liberty rested on the absence of sharp wealth distinctions and feared that it would end if commerce and industry developed and if people were crowded into cities. The realization of the need for economic security and independence was coupled with a reliance on reason and education and a deep faith in the common people.

A positive theory of liberty of this sort today would have to revise its content in the light of present conditions and present goals. Jefferson feared trade; we should have to fear unemployment or any arrangement whereby large masses of men live precariously. Hence prime emphasis would lie on a job, or the right to work. This may be viewed in either negative or positive terms. The French phrases make clear such a distinction: the negative right against being kept from one's work is called the *droit du travail* (right of work); there is also the *droit au travail* (right to work), the positive right to have a job. The French Provisional Government of 1848 proclaimed this latter right during its brief existence. The constitution of the U.S.S.R. embodies it, and provides for a number of other positive liberties, such as the right to rest and leisure, the right to maintenance in old age and sickness, and the right to education.[16] The Four Freedoms include freedom from want, and the Atlantic Charter of August 14, 1941, speaks of "the fullest collaboration between all nations in the economic field with the object of securing, for all, improved labor standards, economic adjustment and social security."

The growing strength of the idea in the United States that full employment should be guaranteed as a matter of national policy is a mature expression of this trend. The Economic Bill of Rights, embodied in Franklin D. Roosevelt's message to Congress in January 1944, articulates this approach in full outline:

"The right to a useful and remunerative job in the industries or shops or farms or mines of the nation;

"The right to earn enough to provide adequate food and clothing and recreation;

"The right of every farmer to raise and sell his products at a return which will give him and his family a decent living;

"The right of every business man, large and small, to trade in an atmosphere of freedom from unfair competition and domination by monopolies at home or abroad;

"The right of every family to a decent home;

"The right to adequate medical care and the opportunity to achieve and enjoy good health;

---

[16] *Constitution of the U.S.S.R.*, American Russian Institute, New York, Chapter X.

"The right to adequate protection from the economic fears of old age, sickness, accident and unemployment;

"The right to a good education."

Positive political liberty. In the traditional realm of politics, positive liberty lies in a form of organization by which decisions on social policy are made by the widest possible group. Aristotle stated this simply, juxtaposing this sense of liberty with a wider one, when he wrote:[17] "One principle of liberty is for all to rule and be ruled in turn. Another is that a man should live as he likes." Today democracy with its constituent ideals may most properly be said to embody a concept of positive political liberty. This concept will be discussed in detail in Chapter 20.

Health and Education. Political rights and economic security are, however, only the first basic conditions for leading the kind of life men want today and for which sufficient natural and social resources are available. The inclusion of health and education in the Economic Bill of Rights reflects the fact that economic security as well as political democracy now require a well-rounded conception of positive liberty. Health is not only a basic instrument for successful living, but an indispensable element in a productive economy. Hence the empirically discoverable conditions requisite for it, such as vacations, moderate hours of labor, parks and athletic facilities in cities, available medical service, maternity services, and the various recognized forms of social insurance belong in a positive conception of liberty. Similarly, education is not only a key to many treasures of the good life, but an indispensable requirement of a complex highly industrialized society. That every man should know something of the nature and findings of the sciences is as necessary today as the "three R's" were when the right to learn them was struggled for. Equally necessary is definite provision for the advancement of the sciences and of human knowledge in general. So essential has such advancement proved for all phases of modern civilization that no arrangement in which the fate of scientific research and the spread of scientific knowledge depend on chance or on the fluctuations of the business market or on the expediencies of political groups can be said to constitute a state of positive liberty for mankind. In such provision, freedom of speech and expression is only a starting-point. What is also required is definite maintenance for the scientific enterprise in an organized democratic fashion and provision for application of its socially valuable findings.

The way in which one can hardly touch any of the separate rights, whether economic or political, without being led into a comprehensive formulation of positive liberty, is well illustrated in an analysis of the Four Freedoms issued by the Office of War Information in August 1942 on the anniversary of the signing of the Atlantic Charter. Thus, in considering the

[17] *Politics* 1317b.

positive conditions implied in the effort to guarantee freedom of speech, the statement says:

"The first condition is that the individual have something to say. Literacy is a prerequisite of free speech, and gives it point. Denied education, denied information, suppressed or enslaved, people grow sluggish; their opinions are hardly worth the high privilege of release. Similarly, those who live in terror or in destitution, even though no specific control is placed upon their speech, are as good as gagged.

"Another condition necessary for free speech is that the people have access to the means of uttering it—to newspapers, to the radio, the public forum. When power or capital are concentrated, when the press is too closely the property of narrow interests, then freedom suffers. There is no freedom, either, unless facts are within reach, unless information is made available. And a final condition of free speech is that there be no penalties attached to the spread of information and to the expression of opinion, whether those penalties be applied by the Government or by any private interests whatsoever."

A detailed conception of positive liberty clearly requires a fuller exploration of social ethics. This would entail an examination of men's goals and the systems of organization by which they may best be furthered. This includes a study of methods of economic, political, and cultural organization, and a critical estimate of the institutions of society regarded as means. In Chapters 19 and 20 some of the problems thus raised will be approached through consideration of the techniques for reconciling aims, and in particular of democracy as the systematic pursuit of liberty.

Is liberty an end or a means?

We turn finally to the question of the extent to which positive liberty is held by men as an end, and the extent to which it should be so held. That it is a very useful means can be accepted without question, but this does not, of course, preclude its possible character as an end.

Liberty for liberty's sake. Do we want liberty for liberty's sake? Clearly we do not mean to deny that we want the benefits to which it is instrumental. We mean rather that quite apart from or in addition to these benefits, we should want or choose it as an end. So much is this the case that, for many men, possessing liberties is a desired end even when there is no intention of using them. Take, for example, freedom of movement. It is good to know that if I had the fare I could go for a trip to California without asking the permission of any government official or securing a passport. A man who never bothers to vote may still feel that his right to vote is a precious possession. It is difficult in both these cases to dissociate any possible value-element from the realization of the evils that men have suffered where movement and expression of political will were restricted. The element of joy in the possession of the right is perhaps more akin to the feeling of security in looking out of the window at passers-by hurrying in the rain than it is to the positive pleasure of watching a sunset or listening to music. Nevertheless, pending the more careful scientific investigation of such general attitudes, we must not rule out the possibility that devotion to certain liberties may have the character of choice of ends. For comparative anthropological and historical study shows that almost any human pursuit may come, under special conditions, to play the role of an end in human life. Certainly liberty has had an inspiring history as an ideal to which men have devoted their energies and their lives.

Should positive liberty be held as an end? Turning to the ethical question, to what extent *should* positive liberty be held as an end? If we take positive liberty as the provision of the necessary conditions for living what men deem a good life, then some of these conditions are clearly so important in the structure of our lives that their incorporation as ends must naturally occur. Such ends help vitalize men's energies by the devotion they bring forth, as do any great goals that stir men out of themselves. And in turn the fruits of these liberties would be best protected when the liberties themselves were incorporated as ends.

Caution is required, however, on such an approach. If liberties have been construed too narrowly in terms of the conditions necessitated by one age they may remain entrenched, even when conditions have changed, just because they have been treated as ends. The economic liberty of laissez-faire is a good historical illustration and is still sometimes spoken of as the be-all and end-all of social life, in spite of the disorganization that planlessness brings in a complex industrial order. On a smaller scale free trade and the gold standard—however appropriate as means to human ends at some periods—have sometimes had undue devotion as goals in themselves. Even widely established liberties may require occasional temporary eclipse in critical situations, and if they have become incorporated as ends this will be increasingly difficult. Yet this very treatment of liberties as ends may prevent a temporary eclipse becoming permanent.

We may wonder, in completing this examination, whether greater clarity would not be engendered by abandoning the language of liberty and freedom and substituting that of goals and means to achieve them, including among these, desirable ways of living, principles of social policy, approved types of character, and so forth. It may come to pass, at some future time, that such linguistic revision will be desirable. At present it hardly seems so. For the use of concepts, after all, is relative to the problems that men face.

We may, therefore, expect the emphasis on liberty and freedom to diminish only to the extent that physical and social obstacles diminish. Among these, two major struggles face men. The first is to achieve a greater knowledge of the self; that is, to widen the bounds of physiology, psychology, and the social sciences. The second is to achieve a greater mastery of social control in order that men may develop institutions in which their positive aims shall be more fully realized. And these two problems coincide broadly with the domains of freedom and liberty respectively.

Chapter 19 TECHNIQUES OF FREEDOM AND LIBERTY

To describe adequately the techniques of freedom and liberty would be to map the whole domain of industrial and social technology. This, in effect, would be to write, from a special perspective, the entire history of mankind. Nothing so pretentious is the subject-matter of this chapter. We shall instead follow a single thread. Our point of view continues to be the fate of values in the welter of means that human life requires. Nothing is more obvious, nothing more pervasive than the clash of values, the conflict of aims within a man and among men. This does not mean that strife is the core of human living. It means rather that human living is essentially selective and that it involves from its very beginning a process of integration or harmonization without which its continued being would be difficult and its well-being certainly impossible. The conflict we observe so widely occurs within a growing context of agreement. Unresolved social problems, which threaten our whole existence in the wars they generate, represent needs of men for the satisfaction of which a solution must be found. A solution is wanted which will breed harmony instead of conflict, perpetuate peace instead of prompt to war, and supplant want with abundance.

In the present chapter we shall begin with the clash of desires within any given individual, go on to the wider problem of conflict among individuals and between groups, and end with the philosophic issues involved in situations of open and irreconcilable conflict. In a very general way, we shall see that virtues and institutions may be studied as modes of harmonizing the aims of men. And among institutions we shall examine especially the role of property systems and of states with their instruments of legislation, judicial decision, and administration.

The conflict of desires

THE TASK OF ORGANIZATION

Conflict of desires is inevitable within an individual, for life is short, a human being's time and energy are limited, and he can do only one thing at a time. As Santayana says, "That life which once seemed to spread out infinitely before us is narrowed to one mortal career. We learn that in morals the infinite is a chimera, and that in accomplishing anything definite a man renounces everything else. He sails henceforth for one point of the compass."[1] Within this basic limitation how can the clash of desires be minimized? How can a man develop a pattern in which there will be harmonious fulfillment of his wants?

This is, of course, the whole task of organization of the self, a task begun for the baby from its very first moments by its nurse or mother, carried on in the family and in the many social relationships which constitute the milieu of the growing child and the field of operations for the adult. The actual efforts of men may not, of course, be devoted specifically to this goal, and even in the case of the parents the conscious aim is too often merely to secure conformity to traditional ways. The resulting pattern of the self is usually one which contains discrepant and conflicting elements. This intensifies the problem of reconciliation on a conscious level.

Treating conflicting desires. In principle the issues raised by this problem may be examined in the simple case of the clash of two desires. We may take as an illustration of such analysis the discussion of E. B. Holt in his book *The Freudian Wish*. Holt uses the wish as a starting-point, translating Freudian into almost behavioristic language. A wish is *"a course of action which some mechanism of the body is set to carry out, whether it actually does so or does not."*[2] A wish not carried out but repressed frequently becomes a malignant force in its effect upon other wishes and their mode of expression. The wolf, so to speak, dresses in sheep's clothing and its relations with the other sheep become far from amicable. Holt takes the simple case of the baby reaching out to touch the glittering fire.[3] The mother stops its hand and the baby becomes conditioned to fire plus mother as an occasion for failing to satisfy a wish. Suppose, however, the facts about fire were themselves allowed to operate as a sanction in conduct. Let the baby's hand be allowed to go slowly toward the fire until the heat takes effect and makes the baby withdraw its hand of its own accord. Now there has been no repressed desire; the child will behave properly in relation to fire, without being unduly attracted by it and without coming to feel his parent as a barrier to his expression of desires.

This example is simple not merely because the facts are so clear, but also because—a phase of the matter Holt does not adequately stress—the desire not to be burned is fairly uniformly agreed upon. A more complicated illustration that he offers shows the problem of wish-conflict in a much more difficult situation.

[1] *Reason in Society*, Scribner's, 1905, p. 35.
[2] E. B. Holt, *The Freudian Wish*, Holt, 1915, pp. 3-4.
[3] *Ibid.*, pp. 101-107.

A country girl, brought up in pious fashion to abhor the theater, comes to the city and finds going to the theater practically a condition of having friends.[4] What is she to do? Several courses of action are open to her, according to Holt. The first is suppression; she may suppress completely either the desire to stay away or the desire to go. In the one case, Holt suggests she will almost inevitably overthrow not merely this point in her parents' training, but all the rest as well, and probably drift into immorality. In the other case, she will have no friends and drift into a desolate spinsterhood. Another course of action Holt calls dissociation; first she represses one wish, then the other. Periods of indulgence in the theater might be followed by periods of remorse and abstention. This is clearly an unhealthy state. The alternative which Holt recommends he calls discrimination.[5] Neither wish is cast away, but each affects the form of expression of the other. The girl probes behind the bidding of her parents and realizes that their abhorrence of the theater was based on its presumed immorality. She gives expression to one of her wishes by accepting this ground. She gives expression to the other wish by going to the theater. The discrimination arises in choosing the kinds of plays which satisfy her parents' (and now her own) basically moral intention. There is no repression, no dissociation, and the conflict is over.

Reason and the systematization of desires. The process of discrimination thus described is clearly equivalent to the working of reason. It begins, in fact, by asking for *reasons* instead of treating each desire as absolute. It distinguishes between the substantial core of a desire and its special form, and thus renders possible retention of the essence by alteration of the form. The same is true in giving any reason for a command. If I say "Do X" there is nothing but obedience and disobedience between which you may choose. If I add, however, "because Y" you may now try to show me that X is not perhaps the best way to get Y, or that Y may not be worth getting. And it may be possible for us to reach a common agreement on values and on the judgments of means. Thus we might decide upon Z to be done instead of X.

The technique of discrimination is thus equivalent to making a system out of our desires in the light of fuller knowledge instead of treating them as absolute imperatives. It is the same process that moral philosophers have sometimes called "harmonizing" one's desires. Of course the occasions on

---

[4] E. B. Holt, *The Freudian Wish,* Holt, 1915, pp. 118-124.

[5] The description here given of discrimination is the writer's elaboration of Holt's statement that "It consists in a full play of *both* the involved sets of tendencies, whereby they *meet* each other, and a line of conduct emerges which is dictated by *both* sets of motives together, and which embodies all that was not downright antagonistic in the two" (p. 122). In applying this to the present example Holt appeals without analysis to the fact that the theater is partly good and partly bad.

which one salvages a substantial part are the more successful ones. There is a whole range of possible results with varying degrees of expression from full harmony through compromise or acceptance with regrets to a toleration that verges on rebellion. In any case no one desire is treated initially as absolute. A process of harmonizing is attempted on the hypothesis that in the face of the whole mass of desires found in the self, no one desire will be able to maintain dogmatic claims without some concessions. This is recognized in ordinary life in the remark that time heals all wounds. It is not the mere passing of time but the variety of pressures and interests that grow from a man's contact with his physical and social environment which accomplishes this.

THE PROBLEM OF ABSOLUTE DESIRES

Where an absolute desire or an unalterable passion does arise, it is by definition not amenable to discrimination, and must therefore either find expression as such or be repressed as a whole. It may still be possible, however, for the dissident aim to be supplanted by another. This is particularly likely to be achieved through outside intervention.[6]

Ethical advice. Ethical advice may represent a genuine understanding of what someone else's own aims "really" are, which he is himself misinterpreting. The least we can do in such a case is to offer our view as an hypothesis to the man concerned. Differing in degree from this is the case of our knowing what the man himself will want if he only tries it or takes certain steps. In its simplest form this is seen in matters of taste, e.g., if the old adage is true about having to taste a dozen olives to like them, or in the formation of drug-habits, or in getting out of sluggish physical habits by exercising. In such cases the process of growing into a new value is a genuine one which we may induce a man to undergo, just as when the new value is evil we are ready to spend energy inducing a man to avoid it. This process is sometimes called "appealing from Philip drunk to Philip sober" after the old story of the man who thus impressed Philip of Macedon when the latter was sentencing him to death in a drunken mood, and thereby saved his life.

The process of inducing a man to try a new value may vary from enticement to pressure. Sometimes instead of growing into the new value he may renounce the dissident one as he becomes aware of its incompatibility with a wider system he adheres to. To urge this, is, as we have seen, to "appeal to reason."

Such process educative. In all these cases we have either a clarification of the means, or of the man's own ends, or a growing acceptance of the new

[6] See also above, p. 251.

value or a renunciation on his own part. The processes by which such agreement is ultimately brought about are *educative* in character. Broadly they consist in building upon attitudes and values which the person or group already has and turning this dominant structure against the dissident desires. In this process attitudes and values may themselves become broadened and refashioned.

Virtues and social forms

ILLUSTRATION FROM ARISTOTLE'S ANALYSES

Virtues or approved states of character likewise function as techniques for resolving conflict and harmonizing desires. Aristotle's discussion of the virtues in his *Nicomachean Ethics* illustrates this phase well. He begins the account of each particular virtue by indicating the materials of feeling or behavior which are to be fitted, harmonized, or patterned. If this work is *properly* accomplished we have a virtue.

Courage. Take courage, for example. We find that men at times show fear, at times confidence. These are feelings or emotions to be organized in such a way that their satisfaction or expression will enhance the rest of life rather than obstruct it. To repress confidence and always to be afraid would produce the vice of timidity. To repress fear and always to be confident would produce the vice of rashness. Between the two lies the mean—according to Aristotle the general mark of a virtue—and this is *courage*. The courageous man knows when, how, what, why to fear and similarly to be confident. That is, while a man's various acts take place separately, and at different times, they follow from an integrated character, from a habit of discrimination, from a knowledge of himself and his desires and the appropriate conditions of their expression. Of course many subsidiary judgments of fact and of value are required in deciding what is appropriate.

Liberality. A similar analysis of *liberality,* which Aristotle offers, deals with more specifically social materials. Always to give, never to take, produces a prodigal; the reverse a miser. The virtue resulting in a harmonious correlation of giving and taking is *liberality*. The liberal man knows how, when, what, why, to whom, from whom, how much to give and take, and does it in a gracious way, not by constant calculation.

General and particular elements in the virtues. Aristotle's account deals only with the broadest role of virtues in individual and social life. So viewed the more general virtues—courage, wisdom, self-restraint, justice, humility—are really broad habits of energetic action, discrimination, caution and deliberate weighing, realization of limitations, which are indispensable components of any successful ordering of one's desires and activities. But the degrees of emphasis, the map of the domain of their application, the attitudes implicit in their exercise, vary so widely from age to age or culture to culture that frequently only a kind of broad analogy holds together diverse instances of these virtues. The courage of the warrior is quite unlike the boldness of the investor, and the honor of a medieval knight responsive to elaborate codes differs from that of a business man scrupulous in paying his debts or from the honor that a matron or a maid must protect.

THE ETHICAL EVALUATION OF INSTITUTIONS

From the individual's point of view, social forms—institutions, customs, rules, and even beliefs—may be examined as proposed techniques for fulfilling aims and avoiding possible conflict both within himself and in relation to others. A bank, a church, a college, a factory, a family, a meal, traffic rules—all involve objects of a determinate character inviting human activity of a certain kind, and they have determinate consequences in subsequent behavior. A system of traffic regulation reconciles the desire for speed on the part of the driver with his and the pedestrian's interest in safety. The regular evening meal satisfies a person's desire for food, often for food in certain proportions; it may at the same time be beautifully served thus tending his esthetic needs; by occurring at a regular time, it furthers the planned expression of other impulses at other times; and in addition it may satisfy the desire for companionship or the feelings of family unity. The typical family itself provides economic protection for the wife, care of his daily wants for the husband, affection, security, and experience for the children, a vicarious immortality for the parents, and so forth. Many traditional beliefs function to provide mental and emotional security. And so on through the whole range of social forms.

Ethical criteria and their application. From an ethical point of view, therefore, social forms may be evaluated by the extent to which they fulfill men's needs and do it in such fashion as to enhance (or stand least in the way of) the fulfillment of other needs. This is not a simple task, since, as conditions change, the role of social forms may alter, and some, valuable in one age, may be harmful in another. The traffic laws of horse-and-buggy days would work havoc if applied in the contemporary city. Similarly judicial review of administrative decisions—a useful check on possibly arbitrary administrative action—may hinder the development of necessary detailed regulation where complicated and expert administrative agencies have grown up as a novel institution. Again, the use of a specific social form may generate fresh needs to be reckoned with. Thus war, corporate enterprise, consumer co-operation, advertising, installment buying were not isolated developments, but where they occurred they in turn produced all sorts of changes in needs, expectations, and desires. The survey of needs at any one time and the evaluation of social forms can thus never be absolute and complete for all time.

The role of property systems

Among the social forms in the modern world, the two that play the most important part in determining the fulfillment of people's aims and in setting the pattern of conflict or reconciliation of men's efforts are property and the state. We shall therefore examine each of these in turn and indicate the types of problems that they raise.

MEANING OF PROPERTY

A property system ensures the conditions under which a man shall be protected in the use of consumable goods and of the various instruments required for the activities of life. It provides the type of security that will exist and the types of long-range planning that will be possible, and the degree of control that some men will have over other men's lives.

Traditionally, property has been conceived of as things owned; this has been expressed legally as a bundle or cluster of rights over the objects in question. These rights include use, consumption, sale, transfer, and so forth. Little analysis is required, however, to recognize that property is fundamentally a legal concept, that without law there would be merely physical possession and power of control, and that to understand the nature of property we must look to the point at which legal machinery may come into play.

Thus viewed, property in our society is seen to be a legal device whereby the force of the state is available under certain conditions for the protection of men against interference with their pursuit of specific aims. If I have clear title to a piece of land I can grow a garden or build a home, and invoke the power of the state (for prevention or restitution) against anyone who tries to appropriate my vegetables or establish an unbidden residence. If I have bonds, securities, or similar paper assets, I am in effect promised certain monetary returns; I can call on the state to aid me in getting these returns and in some cases to protect my interests if the enterprise on which they rest is collapsing. The conditions of such procedure are quite definitely patterned, although very complex.

Since it is widely known what the state will do, it is for the most part unnecessary for the state actually to interfere. A system of property becomes one of the most solidly embedded of social institutions; respect for its bases and principles is fortified by utility, education, and occasional dramatic enforcement, and in complex societies by the existence of a police and prison

TECHNIQUES OF FREEDOM AND LIBERTY

system. The interplay of multiple interests and fears is well illustrated in a passage in John Steinbeck's *The Grapes of Wrath* in which the tenants are dispossessed from the land:

> Sure, cried the tenant men, but it's our land. We measured it and broke it up. We were born on it, and we got killed on it, died on it. Even if it's no good, it's still ours. That's what makes it ours—being born on it, working it, dying on it. That makes ownership, not a paper with numbers on it.
> We're sorry. It's not us. It's the monster. The bank isn't like a man. . . .
>
> The tenants cried, Grampa killed Indians, Pa killed snakes for the land. Maybe we can kill banks—they're worse than Indians and snakes. Maybe we got to fight to keep our land like Pa and Grampa did.
> And now the owner men grew angry. You'll have to go.
> But it's ours, the tenant men cried. We—
> No. The bank, the monster owns it. You'll have to go.
> We'll get our guns, like Grampa when the Indians came. What then?
> Well—first the sheriff, and then the troops. You'll be stealing if you try to stay, you'll be murderers if you kill to stay. The monster isn't men, but it can make men do what it wants.
> But if we go, where'll we go? How'll we go? We got no money.
> We're sorry, said the owner men. The bank, the fifty-thousand-acre owner can't be responsible. You're on land that isn't yours. . . .[7]

In this forceful illustration we see at once the ultimately legal character of property-ownership, the fact that it involves control over things and people, the fact that it relies ultimately where necessary on the armed force of the state, and the fact that it determines eventually the distribution of the necessities as well as the luxuries of life. As a social form property is thus a *pattern of distribution and control,* and a particular system of property stands out as a set of rules according to which the use of things and the control of land and industry and thereby of the livelihood of men are determined.

TYPES OF PROPERTY SYSTEMS

There are different kinds of property systems loosely tagged as "private property," "state socialism," "communism," and so forth, and within and between these there is much room for variety. In the United States, as in most western countries, private property is the prevalent system. Goods, land, factories, patents, and copyrights may be owned by individuals or groups and may, for the most part, be devoted to the use, enjoyment, or profit of the owner. The chief contrasting type of property system existent today is that

---

[7] From John Steinbeck, *The Grapes of Wrath,* pp. 45-46. By permission of the Viking Press, Inc., publishers.

of the Soviet Union in which land, natural resources, and implements of production are either state property or property of collective farms and co-operative associations; personal property exists in the form of income from work, savings, dwelling-house and domestic articles and objects of personal use, and also small private farms based on personal labor.

Complexity and variety within each type. Each contrasting type of property system includes so many kinds of rules that numerous significant varieties are possible. In the case of private property, there are, for example, the rules of inheritance: the system will be different in its effects if all land passes on to the eldest son, or in equal shares to all children; if entailment is allowed or forbidden. There are the rules of association: whether holding-companies are permissible, whether groupings with intent to monopolize are forbidden. There is the effect of taxation: whether inheritance taxes reach 75 per cent, or whether large enterprises (e.g., chain stores) are specially taxed. There is the regulation of industry: whether prices are controlled, whether unions are free to strike or wages are, in effect, dictated; whether profits in some fields are limited to six per cent. There are all the fields controlled by government—post office, water systems, railroad systems in some countries, and so forth. And there are the various types of producer and consumer co-operatives, upon whose extension many people pin their hopes for a stabilized system of private property to satisfy human needs. A picture of all such factors is required to see how distribution of the products of land and industry is routed, and how control of industry is patterned.

No type of property "natural." In the light of such complexity it is clear that no system of property is "natural" in the sense that all others are artificial. There is nothing more artificial in a government's taking over any industry than there is in its imposing a tariff to aid an industry. Much of the talk in the '30's about the government "keeping out of business" failed to recognize not merely the large share that government has long had in the operations of our economic system, but, even more, the essential role of legal rules and the state in the actual existence of a property system at all. The assumption that private property is a natural condition which would exist without a recognized system of social control is likewise mistaken. Anthropologists have found that even where we have no state of our type there may be all sorts of patterns of distribution, control, and reciprocal obligations, maintained by varied customary and religious sanctions. In short all types of property systems are equally natural or equally artificial. They are sets of rules socially produced in the history of a society, often open to constant revision in details of structure.

From the point of view of the fulfillment of men's aims and the techniques of freedom and liberty, our principal concern is with two major features of property systems—the patterns of distribution and of control which they embody.

PRINCIPLES OF DISTRIBUTION

Principles of distribution are the rules and formulae according to which the material goods of a society are apportioned. Such rules are implicit in many important practical decisions. For example, when an income tax is used instead of a poll tax it is presumably on the principle of "contribution in proportion to ability to pay." Where a poll tax is employed the principle is "every man counts as one." If a factory pays its employees by the hour it is "equal pay for equal length of work," if on a piece-work system it is "equal pay for equal quantity of work."

Traditional principles of the laissez-faire approach. In spite of the use of varied principles within a single society, a property system as a whole is generally characterized by its broad utilization of a specific principle. The traditional laissez-faire approach in a framework of private property insisted that every man should get whatever share he could himself manage to secure. This meant distribution according to a principle of strength with an element of chance. Under this system workers most often get a subsistence wage except where strong unions develop. Consumers are charged all that the traffic will bear, more when there is monopoly, less when there is great competition, or the gains of rapid technological development are partly passed on. Owner-managers get great profits when strong, small ones when weak; sometimes they go bankrupt. In modern corporations the investor has lost power, as the losses of the depression clearly showed; management control has gained in strength. Berle and Means in their well-known book *The Modern Corporation and Private Property*[8] point out that profit served a double function in the traditional logic of property—reward for management and for risk in investment. There has been rather complete separation of control and ownership in modern corporations, and most stockholders tend merely to give money and draw interest. Hence the outcome of the traditional view would be that investors receive a more limited reward—just enough to keep investment going—and that the reward for control be increased. Noting this logical outcome, Berle and Means point instead to a new conception of property, which would embrace the interests of workers and consumers as well as those of investors and management, and assign to each interest a portion of the income of business enterprise on a basis of public policy.

Recent changes and proposals. Such proposals for the alteration of principles of distribution in our society appear to stem from two causes. One is the tremendous change in the character of property control, to be considered shortly. The other is the actual failure of the laissez-faire principle to justify the claim that it would yield a continuously productive and expand-

[8] Commerce Clearing House, Inc., 1932.

ing industrial machine with the increasing spread of its benefits. The years before the war were marked by a growing concentration of wealth in a very small percentage of the total population and by widespread increase of unemployment. Full productive capacity was not used, and technological improvements were actually withheld.[9]

This failure to keep production at an increasing level and to spread a higher standard of living intensified interest in alternative principles and opened the door to recommendations for revision. Many of these took the form of political movements which gained temporary followings. Some of these plans focused on currency and its rapid circulation, e.g., the Social Credit scheme and the Townsend plan. Others aimed at utilization of unused equipment by means of state aid, as in Upton Sinclair's End-Poverty-in-California plan. Still others aimed directly at increasing production under technical leadership, brushing aside all other questions. Of these Technocracy was the most dramatic, involving as it did the idea of a ruling class of scientists with absolute authority. The tremendous increase in production during the war and the example of an economy functioning at full blast have given impetus to demands for government guarantees of full employment.

In actual practice, revisions in the United States up to the present have chiefly taken the form of increased taxation to correct the most urgent shortcomings by relief and government spending, some devices to regulate the conditions of investment, wider scope for unionization to increase the bargaining strength of labor, and sporadic attempts at price regulation and regulation of monopoly control. During the war price ceilings and wage ceilings were added but only as emergency measures. Proposed post-war measures do not constitute radical departures from the traditional principles of distribution. More adequate social security and extension of the principle of the TVA to many parts of the country are in the tradition that has been developing, while programs for full employment are being geared to private enterprise, government stepping in only where private initiative fails to create jobs.

Fascism made no fundamental change. Fascist and socialist theories have set forth more sweeping programs for the solution of these economic problems. However, most observers agree that in those countries where social and economic crisis led to fascism there was no fundamental change in the distribution principles of the property system.[10] A strong state machine accel-

---

[9] Material on these points will be found in various government reports, e.g., *Technological Trends and National Policy*, National Resources Committee, 1937; *Investigation of Concentration of Economic Power*, Temporary National Economic Committee, 1941.

[10] For a recent analysis, see Maxine Y. Sweezy, *The Structure of the Nazi Economy*, Harvard University Press, 1941.

erated the development of monopoly control of industry. It utilized the entire labor supply by turning the productive force of the people into war preparation. But it wiped out labor standards and considerably reduced the standard of living.

Socialist and communist principles of distribution. Socialist principles of distribution vary from "To every man the produce of his labor (or according to his abilities)" and "equality of pay for all," to the communist hope of "From each according to his ability, to each according to his need." In the U.S.S.R. the instrumental character of principles of distribution stands out clearly, and there has been conscious shifting of principles where different instrumentalities were found necessary. Thus, when it was found necessary to stimulate increased production, a principle of fixed pay was abandoned in many fields for a principle of pay according to work done. On communist theory the U.S.S.R. is now realizing the socialist principles "He who does not work, neither shall he eat" and "From each according to his ability, to each according to his work." [11] When production shall have been sufficiently increased and security achieved in a world-socialism, the theory goes on, and when the habits of socialist co-operation have grown, the socialist principle of reward according to labor will not be needed to make men work according to their ability, and the communist principle of distribution—to each according to his needs—will then be applied.

Criteria for evaluation of principles. From the point of view of our present consideration—a property system as a technique for satisfying human needs and minimizing conflict of aims—such principles of distribution as have been enumerated are to be evaluated by the degree to which their employment leads to wider satisfaction of needs, minimizes heavy burdens, increases total production, advances technology, and in general, in the sense indicated in the previous chapters, increases men's concrete liberties. It is important in such an evaluation to stress those factors that make for increased production, since principles of distribution become a less critical issue where there is abundance. Thus, for example, it is commonly agreed that every man in any large American city may have all the water he needs. The possibility of general economic abundance has been made a genuine one for the first time in the history of mankind by the advance of scientific knowledge and large-scale industry. To the extent that abundance is achieved the crucial problems of distribution will be less those of partition of scarce goods and more those of division of work to be done and of opportunities for special kinds of self-development.

[11] Article 12 of the 1936 Soviet Constitution.

PATTERNS OF CONTROL

The pattern of control which a property system entails is of fundamental importance. For one thing, it determines the actual distribution. It may be decided that I am to be paid according to labor or according to need; but the amount I receive ultimately rests with those who have the power to decide how much I have accomplished or what my needs are.

Control in American society. The complex character of our industrial society places tremendous power in the hands of those who are in control of property. They are in a position to dictate the extent of production and to channelize distribution. In addition to this control over men's lives, they determine the character of the products of industry—the clothes we wear, the food we eat, the movies we see, the kind of education we get, the wider influences that play upon us and fashion us.

In America, the greater part of the corporate wealth is controlled by a small part of the stock-holders who own a very small percentage of the shares but who are able to perpetuate their control through the legal machinery of the corporation by which their successors are selected. The shareholders at large have little to say in the management of the enterprise—and the outside public nothing.[12] Thus we get, in effect, large financial principalities with self-perpetuating governors. Such a property-structure differs radically from the classical conception of private property, in which each man owns and manages his small business. It is still, however, a system of private property—in fact even more private in the concentration of its control. Such a property-structure is really analogous to a political form; captains of industry have often been compared to feudal barons.

From the point of view of control, the whole domain of small business and small-scale farming plays a subordinate role. The welfare of these groups is largely affected by the decisions of corporate policy and their effect on purchasing power. The American property-structure does, however, allow for considerable exercise of governmental power chiefly through taxation. Public services and undertakings thereby supported determine to some extent the character of distribution. The action of government on such questions therefore provides a channel for democratic elements in our control-structure.

Control in fascist society. In fascist theory control emanates from the leader and can extend to any phase of property he finds necessary. In Germany owners in various fields were given state appointment to act as sub-leaders for their fields, thus recognizing the political character of their control. The

---

[12] See Berle and Means, *The Modern Corporation and Private Property*. Also TNEC report, esp. Nos. 21, 26 and report of the Executive Secretary.

path of responsibility is upward to the leader and the path of policy-determination downward from above.

Control in socialist society. In socialist theory all the methods of political life are available for property control—election of representatives by workers in an industry, appointment by elected government officials, and so forth. Responsibility would be to the executive and legislative organs of the people themselves, and the determination of fundamental policies would lie with the same agencies.[13]

Political character of property systems. In general, the differences between property systems in respect to control can perhaps best be defined in political terms. They may be described as monarchical, oligarchic, democratic, and so forth, although the political character of the property system does not always turn out to be the same as the political character of the state in which it exists. In examining control in a property system we may fruitfully ask how controlling officers are selected, to whom they are responsible, and how fundamental policies which affect people's lives are decided. Since such questions in the theory of property merge with traditional problems of political theory, any further evaluation of them will coincide with the consideration of democracy in Chapter 20.

The role of the state

The state includes perhaps the most specialized instruments men have devised for the wide-scale resolution and prevention of conflict of aims. Definite legislation—whatever the form of government—is a technique capable of adjusting behavior to changing conditions. In this respect—disregarding the content and looking at it purely as technique—it is vastly superior to mere customary regulation. Administration can be a skilled attempt to carry broad decisions into practice in the light of special conditions. Courts and the system of law on which they are based not only decide conflicts between disputants, but also thereby establish guides for future conduct. Furthermore a well organized modern state has numerous service-agencies providing for spread of information (e.g., on standards for consumers' goods, or care of children), mediation of disputes, conservation of natural resources, flood-control, aid in meeting special disasters, and so forth. In fact most of the tasks of government and its network of agencies and civil service can be studied as specialized techniques for performing socially important tasks and meeting socially important needs.

[13] For a discussion of the agencies employed in the economic life of the U.S.S.R., see Sidney and Beatrice Webb, *Soviet Communism: A New Civilization,* Scribner's, 1938.

Conflicting descriptions of the state. Nevertheless the theory of the state has been the center of considerable philosophical controversy. Descriptions of the state have been as varied as: a partnership of men, a union of families aiming at the good life, an organization to achieve the universal external conditions of social order, the social will organized and expressed, a synthesis of classes, a mediator between different classes, a hodge-podge of pressures, a defender of propertied classes, a mode of robbery. Clearly the account of the state is a meeting-place of important ethical and social questions revealing different conceptions of the way in which societies operate and different plans which men have for its operation.

Some philosophers have regarded the state as the culmination of a society's purposes, the all-embracing whole into which men's lives fit and to whose pattern their destiny belongs. Hegel's glorification of the state is the standard instance of this type.[14] A more empirical approach sees the state as a pattern of authority and obedience habitual in a given country, strengthened by systematically organized coercive power and resting where challenged on army, police, and penal instruments.

Moralistic and realistic theories distinguished. Concerning such a pattern, we may ask: How is it used? How should it be used? Most theories of the state reflect an interest in one or the other of these two problems. Some constitute blue-prints for a desirable use of the authority pattern; others attempt to describe how it has been used in the past or to predict how it will be used —either in a particular country or in most countries with organized states. The former we shall call *moralistic* or *idealistic* theories, the latter *descriptive* or *realistic* theories.

MORALISTIC THEORIES AND THEIR EVALUATION

The moralistic theories sometimes appear frankly as Utopias, but more often as statements of *purposes* toward which it is presumed men are striving both in exercising and in obeying authority. Plato fashioned a picture of the state in which everyone was set by the governing philosophers at what he was best suited to do.[15] Thomas More, Francis Bacon, Edward Bellamy, and numerous others have painted schemes upon which their hearts were set, with perhaps more than secret hopes that they would some day come to pass. Aristotle pictured the state as a union of families for the common good, but the numerous slaves in Greek communities would probably not have recognized this description. Even theories that speak of the state as a specialized instrument to accomplish what it has historically been found that it can *best* do, are often moralistic in type; analysis of the "best" usu-

[14] See below, pp. 422-23.
[15] See below, p. 390.

ally reveals a special direction in which it is being urged that men turn their society. Perhaps the majority of theories of the state are disguised pictures of a social order that is being advised or defended. That is why moralistic theories of the state serve so admirably as weapons in social conflicts. Mussolini's account of the state as a synthesis of classes, for example, glossed over the genuine problems of unequal distribution of the fruits of an industrial civilization.

Mode of evaluation illustrated. A moralistic theory can be evaluated, like any other ideal, by its consistency, practicability, suitability for the purposes for which it is recommended, attractiveness, and so forth. Take, for example, the theory that the state is organized to reconcile different social interests. Men in modern society, it is said, are workers, consumers, and investors. These interests are often in conflict: higher wages, for example, raise prices, and higher profits lower wages. The government's function is to protect and reconcile all these interests. Clearly its legal system protects various interests; its service-systems promote common interests; let it further see that consumers purchase at fair prices commodities of good quality, that workers work under fair conditions at fair wages, that investors invest with reasonable security and get a fair return. Such a theory guided many supporters of the New Deal in its earlier days, and was used to defend control of investments, freedom of organization for labor, and price regulation by industries.

The evaluation of such a theory poses many questions. Are these interests compatible or can reasonable profit be made only at the expense of labor or consumer? How is fairness to be decided? Is it practicable to give the government all the powers required by such a conception? What guarantees the fairness of government rather than its acting as a vehicle for one set of interests? Are any of the interests themselves undesirable? (For example, some might ask why there should be investment by individuals.) And in general what will be the effect on the concrete positive liberties of men of granting recognition to these interests and employing the instrumentalities requisite to safeguard them? The thorough evaluation of a moralistic theory requires a thorough clarification not merely of means and consequences but even of the ends or goals implicit in the theory.

REALISTIC THEORIES AND THEIR EVALUATION

Realistic theories of the state are, of course, different historical descriptions of the uses to which authority and organized coercion are alleged to have been put. Here the chief views have been what we may call the liberal theory and the class theory.

The liberal theory. The liberal theory (exemplified by men like Charles Beard, Roscoe Pound, A. F. Bentley, M. R. Cohen) holds that the pattern of state action expresses a hodge-podge of miscellaneous pressures. Laws are thus constant compromises or treaties of peace between warring groups.[16] But the groups are constantly shifting for different purposes, and economic groups, temperance groups, farmers, shippers, skilled labor, unskilled labor, consumers, religious groups, do not fall into any single alignment that would explain the course of state action. Similarly individuals shift from context to context, and no single group wholly absorbs a given man.

There are many illustrations of this approach in the Beards' *The Rise of American Civilization*. For example, they say of the American railroads,[17] "With their rates fixed by state and federal commissions, acting always under the eagle eyes of shippers, and with their wage schedules prescribed by trade unions, railroad companies found it impossible to increase freight and passenger charges at will to meet the rising costs of operation or to cut wages at their pleasure for the purpose of enhancing profits by reducing expenses. So, through political action in one sphere and direct labor action in another a large and important class of American property owners suffered a substantial diminution in their incomes for the benefit of wage-earners, travelers, and shippers. In other words, by a gradual and peaceful operation was effected a transfer of economic goods greater in value than the rights shifted from the French nobility to the peasantry by the national assembly on the night of the famous fourth of August, 1789. Reputable American historians now recorded in their books that the theory of the public interest was being substituted for the older doctrine of *laissez faire*. Apparently it pleased everybody except the holders of railway securities."

The class theory. The class theory, on the other hand, holds that the pattern is always one of maintenance of the propertied class. James Madison suggests such an approach in his discussion of factions in No. X of *The Federalist:*

"The diversity in the faculties of men, from which the rights of property originate, is not less an insuperable obstacle to a uniformity of interests. The protection of these faculties is the first object of government. From the protection of different and unequal faculties of acquiring property, the possession of different degrees and kinds of property immediately results; and from the influence of these on the sentiments and views of the respective proprietors, ensues a division of the society into different interests and parties.

"The latent causes of faction are thus sown in the nature of man; and we see them everywhere brought into different degrees of activity, according to

---

[16] The liberal theory is sometimes called a *broker's* theory of the state, since the position of the government is analogous to that of a broker among his clients.

[17] From Charles and Mary Beard, *The Rise of American Civilization*, Vol. II, pp. 568-569. By permission of the Macmillan Company, publishers.

the different circumstances of civil society. . . . But the most common and durable source of factions has been the various and unequal distribution of property. Those who hold and those who are without property have ever formed distinct interests in society. Those who are creditors and those who are debtors fall under a like discrimination. A landed interest, a manufacturing interest, a mercantile interest, a moneyed interest, with many lesser interests, grow up of necessity in civilized nations, and divide them into different classes, actuated by different sentiments and views. The regulation of these various and interfering interests forms the principal task of modern legislation, and involves the spirit of party and faction in the necessary and ordinary operations of the government."

Madison believes a major problem of government to be the protection of minority rights, especially property rights, from the control of an opposing majority. Hence he desires not pure democracy, but a republic in which representatives govern, and he favors a large republic since cohesion of a majority faction in it will be more difficult.[18]

The Marxists present a class theory from the point of view of the propertyless. They argue that the state is, in effect, the executive arm of the dominant class. As class conflicts become more intense, the modern state assumes the guise of reconciler of class interests and sometimes makes temporary concessions to labor in order to avert more disastrous conflicts; but these concessions are withdrawn as soon as possible. Liberal democracy, with its various freedoms, is construed as the luxury of a period of rising and prosperous capitalism which could afford to retain the democratic political instruments it had found useful originally in overthrowing the landed class. But as the internal conflicts of a capitalist system become too great, and as these liberties become bases of action for the working class to extend its gains, the state loses its liberal democratic form. If there is no transition toward socialism the result is likely to be fascism in which the dominant class continues its rule by force without benefit of democratic liberties.

Issues between liberal and class analysis. The issue between the liberal and the class theory of the state is in part an empirical one to be resolved by examining the role of governments and government officials and of subjects' obedience in various countries. The liberal theory fastens attention upon the many features of state activity which serve all men alike (such as water supply, health service, education, and traffic regulation), as well as upon those serving only the subordinate groups (unemployment relief). The class theory fastens attention on the many features of state activity which serve the propertied class—protection of property, sterner penalties where property

[18] In his subsequent political career, nevertheless, Madison, as a leader in the Jeffersonian party, worked for the small farmers and property-holders with whose welfare the whole national interest was involved.

rights are violated, numerous laws aiding accumulation of wealth, the ways in which wealth allows manipulation of legal apparatus, the great proportion of taxes that fall on labor. It goes even further. It insists on an historical examination of the so-called common services and pro-labor measures, and apart from pointing to inadequacies (e.g., in health service, relief, etc.) it claims that most of these will be found to have arisen as *concessions* to the subordinate class to avert wider discontent and disturbance. Thus it claims that they are not to be reckoned as evidence of pro-labor attitudes on the part of the state. A concession is empirically testable as a measure beneficial to the subordinate class granted in a situation in which greater loss for the dominant class would have been the consequence of withholding it.[19]

Apart from these more directly verifiable differences, the liberal and class theories rest upon differences of economic theory and general social analysis. We shall have occasion to touch on a few of these problems in subsequent chapters.

COMMON ATTITUDES TO THE STATE

The theory of the state which one holds reflects not only ultimate goals but also attitudes toward immediate steps for social reorganization. The common attitude, for example, of assigning every troublesome problem to the state with such remarks as "The government ought to see to it that . . ." or "There ought to be a law . . ." clearly reflects an uncritical conception of the state as the general dispenser of good. Over against this view is the traditional conception of the state as an octopus extending its tentacles over an increasing domain of social life. Mill argued that interested individuals are usually able to do a job better than the government, and that even if not they ought to do it as a means to their own education and as a curb to the dangerous expansion of governmental power.[20] This is a classic statement of the octopus conception, and it still has numerous echoes. But both this attitude and the conception of the state as the general dispenser of good seem to conceive the state as a special entity set off from the people themselves. As such they view it with confidence or alarm, but do not examine realistically the diversity of its possible operations, sanctions, and influences, nor appraise concretely the detailed goods and evils which it can promote. When, furthermore, the internal character of government organization is considered, and the tremendous difference between different forms in re-

---

[19] The phenomenon of *reprivatization* under fascism in Germany and Italy (i.e., the return of government enterprises to private industry) is invoked by some as further evidence that concessions are withdrawn when the ruling class feels itself secure in so acting.

[20] *On Liberty,* Chapter V.

sponsiveness to the aims of the people at large, it is clear that evaluative judgments and attitudes with regard to the state should not be made to refer to "government" as such. On the one hand, they should be refined in terms of particular *kinds* of governmental organization and their possibilities for good. On the other hand, they should recognize the degree to which the fundamental policies of government may be controlled by the political activity of a wide-awake citizenry. Thus government can become a major instrument for social welfare rather than merely an object of dread or applause.

The analysis of the state thus leads to the same dual set of problems as the analysis of property. There is the problem of general goals or principles that government is to follow in making and carrying out decisions on questions of social policy, or that men are to follow in estimating the worth and achievements of government. And secondly there is the problem of the decision-system or form of organization employed and the extent to which it aids or hinders the development of such goals. In democratic theory, which we shall examine in the next chapter, both these problems are merged.

Limits of reconciliation and problems of coercion

Up to this point, in considering problems of conduct, emphasis has fallen upon securing agreement of the participants in any course of action and upon the reconciliation of conflicting aims. There is, however, a limit to possible agreement. An individual or group may be unready to surrender an aim which, despite all attempts to embrace it, is found inharmonious and incompatible with other, wider interests. At this point there arises the serious problem of coercion and the degrees and principles of its exercise.

The first attempt in such a case is to resort to *sanctions*. Here conciliatory procedures are replaced or supplemented by deterrent procedures. Threats of punishments are used in order to add incentives to restrain the desire in question. Sometimes such threats are necessary only in early stages, until a suitable habit has been formed. In such fashion the legal system supplements the educational system in securing necessary agreement in men's behavior. Bentham commented on the fact that rewards were seldom used to the same degree by the law although they might prove more successful in engendering approved desires than punishments in deterring disapproved ones.

OCCASIONS OF COERCION

In reward and punishment at least a foothold is found in the values and attitudes of the man on whom pressures are being exerted. Where no such foothold exists he is by definition immune to influence. Only direct coercion is possible. Santayana chooses a striking illustration of such a problem. Suppose a man announces his intention of committing suicide. You argue with him, but fail to find any values as a foothold to persuade him. He has no pleasures nor hopes, nor can you convince him that he has any. What is there left to discuss? *By definition,* nothing. It would be impertinence to argue with him further. You may turn to the bystander and attempt to point out what causes have brought the person to such a state. It is at this point that most of us might agree that coercion is justified, especially if there is a possibility of utilizing the knowledge of causes to bring about a subsequent alteration in the values.

Ultimate clash. When two participants in a clash of values find no common ground sufficient to act as the basis of agreement on a course of conduct, there are only two ways out of the situation. The two groups may agree to disagree and each go its own way—that is, remove the occasions of conflict. This is the principle underlying divorce for "incompatibility of temperament." The other possibility is that the dominant system coerces or eliminates the dissident one. This is the method implied in the treatment of treason. It may involve a long and bloody clash, as in war, to determine which is dominant. The American Civil War (which Seward called the irrepressible conflict), the recent civil war in Spain, and World War II are illustrations of such clashes of opposing value-systems.

It should be added that resort to such final steps—whether the pattern of divorce or of removal or annihilation—ought not to be hasty. The former pattern runs the risk of treating all *initial* disagreements as if they were *ultimate* disagreements; the latter is too dangerous, for a dominant group may be unwilling to consider even the possibility that it is not the best of all possible systems.

Claims for right of revolution. The recognition of the right to differ from the dominant existent system at any time has sometimes been expressed as a right to revolution. Jefferson thought of a little rebellion now and then as a good thing, and the right of revolution was so seriously regarded that in Philadelphia in 1805 an American citizen was arrested and indicted, principally because he had written and published statements "intending to condemn the principle of revolution."[21] Lincoln, in a speech to the House of Representatives on January 12, 1848, said: "Any people anywhere being inclined and having the power have the right to rise up and shake off the existing government, and form a new one that suits them better. This is a most valuable, a most sacred right—a right which we hope and believe is to liberate the world." Implicit in this approach is the assumption that when a whole people or its greater part in a given territory is ready to support a revolution, it is highly probable that the government is coercive and the

[21] *Freedom and the Modern World,* ed. H. M. Kallen, Coward McCann, Inc., 1928, p. 160.

channels of liberty are blocked. The right of revolution as defended by Jefferson and Lincoln is aimed against tyranny and carries with it a firm faith in the people.[22]

Minimizing coercion. In general the principle of minimizing coercion implies striving for a wider compatibility of aims, and when this is impossible, employing a lesser or more indirect form of coercion in preference to a greater or more direct form. Where a man must not be allowed to do something he still may be allowed to talk about it. Again, where education will produce a result it is a waste to resort to legislation. Coercion in its various forms ranks lowest in the scale.

All judgments of degree of coercion to be employed are exceedingly complex and highly dependent upon variable particular conditions and varieties of goals. It is therefore desirable to consider a number of concrete illustrations of the use of violence in modern society and the attitudes men have taken toward it.

COERCION MECHANISMS WITHIN A SOCIETY

In the internal functioning of our society, the issue of direct coercion appears at many points. There is, for example, the use of the death penalty. This has seemed to many to be an ineffective legal device and some states have accordingly abolished it. Again the whole use of an organized police force has been questioned. Most people today would probably agree on the need for such a force as a means. Even from the criminal's point of view, as the history of criminal law shows, an organized system is frequently a protection against spontaneous private violence and guarantees the opportunity of a fair trial. The problem of violence arises again within particular contexts of police activity. Should policemen be permitted to carry guns in the course of ordinary duty or should they usually be limited to sticks? This cannot be settled without observation of consequences. But the principle at least is clear. Where the lesser exertion of force will achieve the ends desired, it ought to be employed. Again the ideal direction of police development seems likewise clear: as much as possible police ought to be a humane security and emergency service squad.

Violence in labor disputes. Another important illustration of the problem of violence in our society arises in labor disputes. This is a domain which public policy leaves open to bargaining between the parties concerned, the laborer's need for a livelihood being the employer's chief weapon and the power to strike the employee's. In spite of the social dislocations strikes may give rise to, it is commonly agreed on the basis of historical experience that

[22] For analysis of such a faith see below, p. 299.

to take away or seriously to limit the right to strike is to enslave labor.[23] When a labor controversy becomes bitter, violence has been known to ensue. It is interesting, therefore, to note that labor has found by experience that violence in the strike situation is productive of more evil than good. The stimulation of violence by the use of spies has in fact been a standard technique for breaking a strike.[24] Accordingly well organized unions are careful to maintain the strictest self-discipline in strike situations, and even to withstand provocative assaults, using force only in clear self-defense.

WAR AND GENERAL ATTITUDES TOWARD VIOLENCE

The greatest problems of large-scale violence have, of course, occurred in the relations between societies and nations. In the absence of any effective technique for resolution of international problems, resort to war has been comparatively frequent and often cynical, and it has forced violence in the form of self-defense even upon peoples who ardently desired to avoid it. It is in the context of war that attitudes to violence may best be examined.

The glorification of violence. Some have tended to glorify violence and make it in itself the center of a system of values. Fascist theory has spoken of war as necessary for the rebirth of a nation, as a moral purge, and so forth. Now insofar as a readiness towards violence in an individual represents a reckless or daredevil spirit, the underlying impulse would, in an ideal form of life, be allowed some form of useful exercise. Santayana looks to sport as the gentler vehicle for whatever virtues the efforts of war may foster; James seeks in useful but rough social tasks to be carried out by organized youth the "moral equivalent" of war. A complex civilization always has a place for reckless spirits in its frontiers of enterprise. But the fascist glorification of violence has been a systematic fostering of opposition to the values of the traditional liberal spirit.

Absolute avoidance of violence. At the other extreme some have made a strict taboo out of their desire to avoid violence in any form. Yet even granting the pacifist value-judgment, that violence is itself an evil, does it follow that there are no conditions under which it may be right to employ it? Just because something is an evil if it occurs does not mean that it is always wrong when it occurs.[25] Pain is an evil, but in the context of surgical cure it can hardly be said to be wrong. In short the serious issue about violence is the question of its efficacy in securing the ends for which it is employed

---

[23] The situation is quite different when labor of its own accord refrains from striking, as by far the greatest part of American labor did during the war.

[24] See the reports of the La Follette Civil Liberties Committee, or the discussion of them in Leo Huberman's *The Labor Spy Racket*, Modern Age, 1937.

[25] For a fuller discussion of this point, see below, p. 433.

and the dangers to human values in its use. The pacifist contention seems to be that it can never be used as a means to produce a worthwhile total situation.

Is violence an effective means? It is commonly assumed that violence is an effective means and rational discourse a weak one. This belief should by no means be regarded as established. Violence alone is purely negative or destructive. It is a final way of stopping an activity by removing the actor, but is much less efficient in making people do something specific. It can suppress a movement or subdue a people only by eliminating its leaders, but if the movement is significantly grounded and sufficiently articulate or the country sufficiently roused to produce an endless stream of leaders the movement can ultimately withstand violence. It is easier to crush an army than to crush a whole people. That is why violence is employed in such a way as to inspire fear of further violence. Such fear operates widely as a sanction. And even where fear proves successful it has always seemed the better part of wisdom to a conqueror to try as rapidly as possible to build up beliefs, attitudes, values, in the conquered people on which his power may lean rather than to depend permanently on the sword alone.

Estimate of pacifism. The pacifist argument against the use of violence as a means even to a good end is that there is a contradiction in the use of an evil means to a good end. What sense is there in enslaving in order to free, in killing to let live? Again, violence recklessly employed becomes an habitual resort.

Opponents of pacifism have pointed out that this apparent contradiction cannot be judged *a priori*. Should not a dangerous lunatic at loose in a children's institution be shot if that is the only way to stop him from slaughter? Should Nazi brutality not have been resisted? Again, there is no contradiction in using regulations to achieve greater freedom, if they accomplish that end. The question of the efficacy of violence as the only means available in some situations must also be settled empirically.

Tolstoi presents such an argument against violence-as-means in his book *The Kingdom of God Is Within You*.[26] Violence, he says, knows how to treat counter-violence. It simply suppresses it. But non-resistance surprises and startles. At first it may seem like madness to be ready to go into the front lines if ordered, but to refuse to carry a gun. But the example spreads; suppression will have no effect upon it; and a rising tide of pacifism will end wars. The growth of pacifism has been great, and in World War II England set up special courts to examine conscientious objectors, and America made provision for them in its draft legislation. On the other hand, the growing importance of non-combatant services in war allows objectors to violence an increasing role, and makes them direct participants in total war.

[26] In Vol. 7 of Complete Works, New York, Crowell, 1898-1923.

Pacifism has thus been reduced to a purely personal protest of doubtful efficacy in a world in flames.

In general, a distinction should be drawn between instrumental pacifism which hopes to achieve peace on earth by its techniques, and absolute pacifism, which aims rather at a purity of the individual soul though the world perish. In the controversies about non-violence in India, for example, Gandhi's position tends to the latter, while Nehru's is clearly of the former sort.[27] Nehru accepts non-resistance as the best means by which a weak and impoverished people can gain freedom from an imperialist power well furnished with arms.

Analyses of war. The estimation of war and the possibility of eliminating it depends upon the analysis of war. There has been a common tendency to treat it as a chance illness of the body politic, which is to be expected occasionally, endured, and from which recovery is hoped. In recent years the awareness has grown that war is an integral part of the operations of our societies as organized at present, and that its elimination demands politico-economic structural changes against which powerful forces and traditions are entrenched. Hawtrey in his *Economic Aspects of Sovereignty* puts this strikingly.[28] War, he says, is to be regarded as an industry in contemporary societies. It has its plant equipment in the economic and technological organization of a country. With an eye to possible warfare, communications must be organized, railroads planned, factories built and kept in shape, skills maintained—even apart from a standing army—and popular attitudes built. The antagonisms of different countries, fundamentally economic, find their peace-time expression in the interplay of competitive international investments and the barometer of national prestige. War is simply a crucial phase of such strife when the other instruments fail and there is hope of success by its use. The Marxist analysis points to the further role of war as a continuation of the political struggles of classes within a country. In some cases the foreign war may also be a desperate episode in the fight of a dominant class to keep down a rising subordinate class, a favorable occasion for disarming and controlling it under a popular appeal to national unity.[29]

The analysis of war is thus part and parcel of the analysis of a society's operations, its internal conflicts and its external rivalries. It is, moreover, now established beyond doubt that peace is indivisible, and that war anywhere on the globe is everyone's danger, hence everyone's concern. It fol-

---

[27] For Gandhi's views see C. F. Andrews, *Mahatma Gandhi's Ideas*, Macmillan, 1930; for Nehru's, see his autobiography, *Toward Freedom*, John Day, 1941.

[28] R. G. Hawtrey, *Economic Aspects of Sovereignty*, Longmans, Green, 1930.

[29] The Marxian theory has also seen violence as likely to occur within countries in the struggle of classes, because of the desperate attempts of a ruling class to maintain a power which it no longer wields successfully. However, Marx recognized the possibility of a peaceful transition to socialism in the United States, England, and Holland.

lows that the elimination of war involves much more than merely passing a moral judgment on violence. It involves providing some remedies for the problems out of which war arises. This would include international organization to prevent or suppress outbreaks between nations, international economic co-operation to diminish rivalries and avoid depressions, and, within nations, popular governments through which the needs and will of the people may find ready expression.

Chapter 20 DEMOCRACY

The theory of democracy exhibits a profound and large-scale interrelation of means and ends, of instruments and values. Conceived by many simply as a political issue, a device by which decision may express the maximum agreement of the parties concerned, it turns out—when its assumptions have been rendered clear—to be a whole way of life, including ideals and principles, attitudes and techniques. Starting out as a method of increasing the satisfaction of human aims, it ends up by presenting a set of broad values which partially express but at the same time partially refashion the direction of men's strivings. It is the purpose of the present chapter to survey the ideals, principles, and attitudes that constitute democracy and to suggest that democracy in the widest sense represents the systematization of the effort to achieve liberty and freedom for men.

Democracy not just political theory. It is important to reiterate at the outset that democratic theory should not be too narrowly construed as merely a political technique. Politics itself has been too narrowly construed as the domain of the state, of its agencies, and of the devices their operation entails. The attempt to divide life into such separate fields as politics, economics, religion, education, makes semi-autonomous domains out of what are simply different phases of human activity. This separation is manifest in the isolation of democratic tendencies within the field of politics narrowly construed and its exclusion from other fields. The result is to discredit democratic theory because, bottled up in political life, it has failed to solve economic problems. The tendency to condemn democracy as a failure on the basis of experience is comparable to the condemnation of dental theory by a man who, visiting his dentist once a year and neglecting his teeth the rest of the time, is surprised at the evidence of decay.

In its widest sense politics is the study of types of decision-systems. The mass of decisions which constitute the activity of the state cannot be divorced from the decisions and pressures of other fields. So-called political decisions are of particular interest because of their large-scale effects, but they are no wider in scope than many decisions made in the course of industrial management, or in private negotiations of an international character.[1] The study

---

[1] See, for example, the *New York Times* editorial of Aug. 10, 1940, on *Patents and Defense,* in which international patent licenses are spoken of as "in effect private treaties, which have world-wide economic effects."

of democratic theory cannot therefore be limited to what has traditionally been called political democracy.

The ideals or principles of democracy have been expressed as *liberty, equality, fraternity,* and sometimes also as *individualism*. From the governmental point of view, their classic expression is *government of the people, by the people, for the people*. The attitudes of democracy are the states of character or virtues appropriate to the ideals, and the techniques should be specific organizational devices which will tend in the direction of democratic ideals, toward the development of democratic attitudes, and toward the achievement of democratic goals.

The ideals of democracy

LIBERTY

Liberty and the attitudes appropriate to it were discussed in detail in Chapters 17 and 18. Liberty in its widest sense was seen to point to the system of men's aims and the conditions required for their achievement. In this sense democracy itself may be viewed as the systematic cultivation of liberty and freedom in the relations of men. In its narrower sense, liberty is a constitutive ideal within the framework of democracy. On its negative side it delimits the areas in which a man may make his own decisions and specifies the areas in which he must make decisions as a member of a group, whether on an occupational, associational, local, or national basis. On its positive side, liberty is a guarantee that men will have the necessary conditions for achieving the typical goals of their society—such conditions as jobs or education.[2] As so construed, positive liberty, as we have seen, entails the provision of *security* as an integral part of the ideal. The frequent contemporary contrast—"men have to choose between liberty and security"—rests on a confused analysis of liberty.

EQUALITY

Equality is one of the most fundamental of democratic ideals. In fact it is basic to the existence of liberty, since liberty becomes a cruel jest if it is confined to a small group in the community. It is also basic to the meaning of fraternity and individualism. The democratic postulate of equality asserts that all men are equal. This formulation has given rise to considerable controversy. Surely, it is said, men's qualities and abilities differ. In what respect are they in fact equal?

[2] See the account of positive liberty above, p. 257 ff.

The meaning of human equality. The claim of men's equality may be asserted in either or both of two distinct senses. It may be offered as a factual matter; for example, all men are equal in resistance to a specific disease, in ability, in esthetic appreciation, in intelligence. Or the claim of equality may be an evaluative proposal; for example, all men should be fed the same amount of vitamins, be brought up in institutions, be given one vote.

As a factual claim in the theory of democracy, the equality of man has been suggested in a number of different senses. Thus in the greater part of the Christian tradition men are considered equal as souls before God. Or it may simply be said that every man has his own life to lead. Sometimes attention is turned to abilities, and it is claimed that differences in human achievement are by and large cultural and environmental products and that the range of differential "native" ability is not as wide as the range of achievement. Although differences have often been exaggerated, it is doubtful whether any claim of absolute equality in individual ability can withstand scientific scrutiny. On the other hand, in the case of racial, not individual comparison, this factual equality of ability appears more probable, the evidence so far presenting no adequate grounds for claims of superior native ability in one race as compared to another. In the case of individuals, again, our very inability to measure abilities completely and to classify men adequately is sometimes urged as a ground for assuming their equality. It is possible that a man whom we scorn today will turn out tomorrow, through some sudden liberation of his latent capacities, to be a man of positive genius. Hence it is wisest to regard all men as on an equal plane.

This last position almost merges with an evaluative approach since it appears to recommend equality of *treatment* in some respect. Such evaluative conceptions of equality need not assert an existence of equality of ability in fact. Every mother knows, as Tawney points out,[3] that her children are not equal, but does she therefore lavish her care on the strong and neglect the weak? Some people are born or grow up with good digestions, others with bad; is that a reason for giving good food to the former and bad to the latter? Widely varying bases may be offered for equality of treatment of men. There is the religious basis—the equality of men before God, mentioned above. There is the utilitarian basis—that every man is the best judge of his interests and that therefore the counting of each man's will as one is most likely to yield the greatest happiness of the greatest number.[4] There is the pragmatic justification of equal treatment—"that human nature is dynamic, that by such treatment men can actually be made more equal than they are, that such equality is desirable because it conditions co-operation, that some measure of co-operation is prerequisite to any human life at

[3] R. H. Tawney, *Equality*, Harcourt, Brace, 1931, p. 41.
[4] See below, pp. 447-48.

all. . . ."[5] There is a possible justification of equal treatment on egoistic grounds—that few of us can really get away with discrimination against others without in the long run suffering more ourselves from others' discrimination; hence it is best to treat others as equals. There is even a justification of equal treatment in some respects (equality of opportunity) on the ground that men are in fact of unequal ability. Since we have no initial measuring-rod, the only way in which the differences of ability among men may emerge in achievement, is to give all equal opportunity to show what they can do. And in addition to these grounds there remains the blunt fact that men will not be satisfied with inequalities for which they see no reason. Thus the unequal society remains unstable, breeding friction and dissent.

Application of the concept of equality. Further problems arise in the *application* of the concept of equality. Some of these are questions of principle, others of the domain in which application is to take place. Are we to use "absolute" equality or "proportionate" equality? Should rationing of gasoline, for example, provide exactly the same number of gallons per day to every car owner, or should it apportion the amount on a scale of need (business necessity, business convenience, pleasure), or on a scale of type, weight, and age of car? The latter alternative, by such proportionate distribution, might achieve numerically equal mileage for the different cars.[6] In political life, Aristotle points out,[7] men agree on awards according to *merit,* but, he adds, democrats identify merit with the status of a freeman, oligarchs with wealth, and supporters of aristocracy with excellence.

Values involved in application. Clearly, then, there is no simple rule which will provide a criterion for the type of equality to be sought. Every case requires evaluation in terms of the desired results. For example, there is wide agreement on the value of basic education for all children irrespective of wealth; in this context the rule would be absolute equality of opportunity at least in elementary and secondary education. In college education, the state of affairs for a long time was one of inequality; or—if the language of proportionate equality be desired—it was equal opportunity in proportion to wealth, that is, two persons of equal wealth had equal opportunity of securing a college education. As the scholarship system was extended and admissions were made on the basis of examination, equality of opportunity according to ability came into being. Today, where free public higher education is more widely extended, many believe that the aim should be a rule of absolute equality; namely, college education for all who are able and

---

[5] T. V. Smith, *The American Philosophy of Equality,* University of Chicago Press, 1927, p. ix.

[6] Examples in the context of distribution (taxes, piece-work payment, etc.) were considered in the discussion of property above, p. 273 ff.

[7] *Nicomachean Ethics,* V, 3.

willing to undertake it. It is clear from the above that the concept of proportionate equality may sometimes be used to cover what from the point of view of democratic theory constitutes genuine inequality. Great care must therefore be exercised in the use of the concept. Democracy does not lie in the mere use of the language of equality, but in the specific aims that are adopted.

Major types of inequality. Such an analysis points—as the comparable analysis of liberty likewise pointed—to the major types of discrimination against which the struggle for equality is directed. These are the fields in which men have had to struggle for equality of opportunity, and have in most cases still not achieved it—racial discrimination, discrimination on grounds of sex, religion, poverty, and political belief. In these respects the fight for equality is at the same time the fight for liberty for some portion of the human race. Whatever other role the concept of equality may play in democratic theory, in the minds of the mass of mankind it has meant the endeavor to remove these major inequalities. No difference of analysis in the concept should be permitted to obscure this fundamental historical core, if the aim is to represent accurately the hopes and strivings of men. Only as such battles are won does the positive conception of equality emerge: the provision of concrete and realizable opportunities for all alike.

Individualism implied in equality. Where equality in one form or another is accepted, individualism is already implied. To treat every man equally is to treat each as one individual. Individualism as an ideal of democracy means that the good of individual men is the goal of human activity, that no institution or social form has ends of its own beyond men—unless it be in terms of the lives of men to come. Individualism thus entails evaluating social institutions in terms of human welfare. The importance of this lesson, especially against attempts at tyranny and the demands for unwarranted sacrifice, has sometimes led theorists of democracy to regard the individual as an isolated atom and to give each individual *by himself* a veto over social policy. This is not a necessary nor desirable form for democratic individualism to take. To make every man *count* is not the same as to say that one man's vote determines every reckoning.

FRATERNITY

Fraternity likewise is implicit in equality. For equality gives every man a stake in what is to go on in society. Fraternity adds explicitly to the co-operative element. It represents a range of attitudes from mere recognition of others with accompanying tolerance, through sympathy and friendly interest, to active co-operation and the development of common goals for mutual striving.

Growth of the ideal of fraternity. The ideal of fraternity was developed early in the western tradition. It tended to be stated as a fact, not the mere biologic fact that we are all human beings (although this is no doubt the basis which makes fraternity among human beings possible) but as a cosmic or metaphysical fact. The Stoic cosmopolitan outlook saw every man as possessed of the divine fire, and the Christian doctrine rested the brotherhood of man on the fatherhood of God. Contemporary concepts of fraternity, apart from such bases, are formulated more as an ideal of what is desirable, necessary, and increasingly practicable. Throughout all the conflicts of nations and the growth of empires there has been some widening of the in-group and the establishment of common aims within it. Fraternity calls for the development of a whole-human ethic and the planning of well-being in terms not of one nation, however co-operative it may be in internal character, but of the two billion people of the globe. This entails the break-down of provincialism in outlook and the effective development of intercultural understanding and intercultural relations. The stimulus for such development comes increasingly from the material interdependence of the globe—the increasing rapidity of transportation, the mutual dependence of economic life, the need for common security against war and aggression. It was out of such bases, on a smaller scale, that national unities originally arose, and out of similar bases equally deep international unities may yet come one day to be created.

Governmental principles of democracy

GENERAL PRINCIPLES

In turning to the problem of government, it is important to construe the principles of democracy widely so as not to limit its techniques. It ought not, for example, to be identified with a simple system of voting.[8] On the other hand one must beware of stating democratic governmental principles in such a way as to allow appeals to "real" democracy or "higher" democracy which may in fact subvert democracy. Perhaps the best indication of the principles of democracy is to be found in the political ideas and ideals that have at one time or another played a part in its development.

Some historical ideas. The *Social Contract* idea was employed by Hobbes to provide a basis for the absolute state and to show the element of consent which men's desire for peace and order lends even to a tyrannical regime. In Locke and Rousseau it indicates the basic acceptance of an ordered so-

[8] Aristotle at one point identified it with the complete equality of drawing lots; he held that even voting for officials was not democracy but *aristocracy* since presumably people were voting for the *best* man!

ciety, but this is not without qualifications. For Locke the state must recognize "natural rights," especially property. For Rousseau the state rests on the *General Will* which is itself viewed as directed toward the common interest of men. In communistic and anarchistic theory there appears the ideal of the *Disappearance of the State*. In anarchistic theory this involves the smashing of the state apparatus accompanied by a spontaneous co-operativeness of men. In communist theory it appears as the "withering away" of the "workers' state" after it has supplanted the "bourgeois state" throughout the whole world; this withering away is due to growing co-operative habits as the competitive ways of capitalism become useless and dwindle.

Their reinterpretation. Whatever specific uses these various ideas may have in their own historical and social contexts, they seem capable of reinterpretation to embody the general principles of a democratic approach on matters of government. The idea of the Social Contract embodies the principle of a *basic common agreement*. The General Will points to the *widest participation of and responsibility to those interested in or affected by decisions*. The idea of the state disappearing may readily be seen as the idea of a *growing minimization of coercion*. If we add the conditions imposed by equality and liberty in the sphere of government, namely *elimination of discrimination* and the *provision of necessary conditions for men's efforts to achieve their goals*, we have a fairly rounded picture of what democratic governmental theory implies. It implies a group whose members share an interest in their common problems, and participate widely in the effort to live a common life. It also implies scope for a great variety of men's aims, and the fashioning of attitudes and objectives which will minimize the need for compulsion.

GOVERNMENT BY THE PEOPLE

The central problem of democratic governmental theory has always been that of securing extensive participation in governmental processes. In contemporary American life, some have urged that we are not a democracy and should not become such; we are a republic in which the people periodically elect those among them best fitted to rule. Once elected it is the job of those elected to rule in their own best fashion, not to be continually responsive to the multitude.

In ancient times, Socrates raised this question most sharply in his attack on Athenian democracy. When the question is one of ships to be built, he said, the Athenians leave it to ship-builders; when it is one of sculpture they leave it to sculptors. But when it is a question of what it is good to do, they seem to think anyone—tanner, farmer, lamp-maker—is capable of an expression of opinion. Thus the most important questions of public policy are decided by every Tom, Dick, and Harry. Socrates wanted these matters of the good to be decided by experts—the philosophers. He criticized both the Athenians for not following such a course, and contemporary philosophers for not taking such matters seriously.

The problem of leadership. The problem thus raised is that of the status of the expert in decisions of policy, and in a more general way of the whole character of leadership. Clearly the solution is influenced by one's theory of metaphysics and of knowledge. If the good is taken to be an absolute capable of being grasped by the specialized insight of a few, or even to be the will of some Deity ultimately revealed only to a few, leadership becomes authoritarian in character. The leader's business is to command in the light of his knowledge, and the rest of men have but to obey. From such a point of view the only remaining issues allowing some scope for democratic theory would be the procedures by which common men recognized who was the leader—e.g., by the cataleptic seizures which identify the Chukchee shamans, or by reliance on lot, or by listening to the voice of the people in a general election on the assumption that *vox populi vox Dei,* and so forth. Again there would be differences in the way in which such leadership would be checked and controlled. Aristotle in his *Politics* seems most worried about the corruptibility of men and uses democratic techniques to control exploitation of leadership for private gain. To Plato, on the other hand, knowledge of the good involves moral perfection, so that the real philosopher-king could not be corrupt.

Limitations on role of the expert. A democratic approach recognizes the expert on matters of fact, but even here insists that such technical knowledge be tested by its results. That is why construction experts are trusted in building bridges; but they do not decide how much is to be spent, and they may be asked to submit alternative designs for the layman's selection. On the other hand, experts in economics are not yet wholly relied upon even for the solution of technical problems. This is due to the state of the science itself and the fear that questions of value may be confused with matters of fact; sometimes perhaps because experts in the social sciences contradict one another and are felt to be aligned with different interests rather than to be working from a common basis of agreement. In short, even in its reliance on experts, a democratic approach treats them not as possessors of absolute truth, but as men who have mastered a publicly available field of accumulating knowledge.[9]

Democratic leadership. On such an approach intuition loses its absolute character. Democratic leadership is not private insight into the correct answers to social questions. It is the exercise of insight and imagination in conceiving of possible solutions and developing their applications and fore-

---

[9] See also the discussion of authority above, p. 80 ff.

seeing the changes they will require of and make in men's lives. It involves the ability to express such foresight in practicable plans that invite rather than shut out co-operative consideration and wide participation. The need for such consideration, as well as the importance of keeping open channels for new or rising leadership, gives added weight to the need for liberties of speech, writing, and assembly.[10]

On questions of value, democratic theory is suspicious of experts. For very frequently the man who tries to set other men's goals for them is in effect choosing what best suits his own goals. As Thrasymachus in Plato's *Republic* argues, even when the sheep grow fat it is not because the shepherd is looking out for *their* interests. Yet even in dealing with values, democratic leadership is not impossible. It may be that you see what I would want under altered conditions more clearly than I do myself. Democratic leadership on questions of value therefore takes the form not of your legislating my aims but of your giving me advice which I may test in my subsequent experience. Thus the goal proposed for me may really become incorporated as my own aim.[11] From the possibility of such leadership it follows that democracy is not simply a technique for discovering and mapping men's aims at any one time—and then working out a compromise of conflicting interests—but a dynamic process in which some men's goals may be satisfactorily altered in the development of a harmonious pattern. In short, democracy does not mean chaining men to existent interests at any time. It can instead operate as a technique of transition in social forms and social goals.

Wide dispersion of leadership. In a truly functioning democracy there will then be wide dispersion of leadership in the sense described above. There will also be a keen awareness of the importance of critically estimating general social policy. Given in addition the democratic guarantee of genuine freedom of expression for the minority and acceptance of majority rule for determining action, the resulting picture may well be described as self-government in the sense of *government by the people*. This, of course, is the literal meaning of the term "democracy." In his *Democracy and Social Change*,[12] Harry F. Ward objects to the description of such government by the people in the traditional terms of "government by consent of the governed." For this suggests control over the people. In a full democracy the people will not simply decide at intervals who is to rule them and then later express by re-election or rejection approval or disapproval of what was done. They will actually do the governing in the sense of deciding policy

---

[10] For a discussion of such liberties, see above, pp. 249, 255, 261.

[11] See the remarks on vocational guidance above, p. 242, and on the appeal from Philip drunk to Philip sober, p. 267.

[12] Modern Age, 1940.

and working out more refined mechanisms and techniques for expression of their will and for executing their decisions.

FAITH IN THE PEOPLE

This ideal of democratic government clearly rests on a *faith in the people*. Obviously this is a cornerstone of a democratic view. A man's attitude to the mass of the people is perhaps the best test for a democratic outlook. Those who hold an aristocratic view and believe that people need to be restrained or controlled will find a veto power over the people's will a necessary element of governmental structure.[13] This approach is at least as old as Plato, who compared the mass of the people to the bodily desires in a man going wildly in their own directions unless controlled by reason outside them. Fear of the people is a long-standing attitude in oligarchies, and it often takes the form of despising the people. In contemporary fascist theory we find an explicit contempt for the mass of men who are, we are assured, easy to fool by propagandist tricks.

Meaning of this faith. Faith in the people, as Rousseau realized, does not mean that even a unanimous vote on any occasion may not be wrong. Nor does it entail the Rousseau-like assumption of a natural man who shines out pure through the degradation that society often brings to people. It does not mean romanticizing the people. It may be simply the belief expressed by Lincoln that although all of the people can be fooled some of the time, and some of the people all of the time, you cannot fool all of the people all of the time, and that there will be increasing consolidation of the fruits of popular wisdom.

Bases for faith in the people. The bases of such faith are diverse. There is the recognition of the social causes of existing degradation and a vision of what men may increasingly become as social conditions are improved. This belief, which has sometimes been spoken of as a belief in the perfectibility of mankind or a faith in progress, need not point to perfection. It is enough to realize the wide gap between what exists and what is definitely achievable. Again, faith in the people finds empirical confirmation in the historical action of masses of men in crucial periods, in the endless initiative they exercised and their continuous capacity for co-operation. In our times particularly, we have had striking confirmation of the validity of this faith in the heroic struggles and endless self-sacrifice of the Spanish, Chinese, and Russian peoples. Even the occasional occurrence of a reign of terror is the

---

[13] See, for an example of this attitude, Irving Babbitt's *Democracy and Leadership*, Houghton Mifflin, 1925, Chapter VII. Babbitt contrasts the Jeffersonian attitude of which he disapproves with the opposite which he takes to be illustrated in Washington.

reaction to the pressure of counter-revolution driving men to despair. Tom Paine, writing his *Rights of Man* in the early years of the French Revolution, is much impressed with the moderation of the people. He analyzes various happenings to show their restraint under provocation. He expresses his faith forcibly: "When I contemplate the natural dignity of man, when I feel (for Nature has not been kind enough to me to blunt my feelings) for the honor and happiness of its character, I become irritated at the attempt to govern mankind by force and fraud, as if they were all knaves and fools, and can scarcely avoid disgust at those who are thus imposed upon."

Some find further cause for a belief in the people in the character of social circumstances. The particular organization of society today, it is urged, will constantly provoke and educate men. They will learn even by their sufferings. The rapidity of change will make it difficult for them to preserve in isolation attitudes by which their lack of unity and understanding is entrenched. They will come to see their lives as a whole, and beliefs that stand in the path of their improvement will be swept away. The very character of our industrial society involves increasing reliance on the mass of men, not on small groups, whether it be for industry or warfare. Even the processes of duping men today contribute unwittingly to their education and propaganda cannot hope constantly to enslave them.

Democratic attitudes

The ideals and principles of democracy which we have considered, in conjunction with the lessons of experience, determine the attitudes that may be recommended as congenial to democracy. Equality and fraternity involve co-operativeness and respect for others. The principles of democratic government point to rational co-operation in the solution of problems of social policy.

Comparison of attitudes of science and democracy. In this respect democracy is sometimes compared to science, in the attitudes that both require.[14] There is in both a general approach in terms of probability rather than necessity: no hypothesis, no proposal is ultimate and authoritative; it must be tested for the success of its operation; the divine right of kings with its assumption of absolute power is no more acceptable to democracy than self-evident unprovable assertions with their assumption of absolute truth are to science. This initial tentativeness involves no emotional intolerance to new ideas, but rather a positive receptivity. A scientific hypothesis is judged

[14] For a more complete outline of the relations of science and democracy, see Abraham Edel, "The Relations of Science and Democracy," *Journal of Philosophy*, Dec. 21, 1944.

by its scientific fruits in the progress of knowledge, a social policy by its practical fruits in achieving the aims of men. The criticism of assumptions in science is matched by the criticism of aims in democracy. The experimental outlook of science requires as its counterpart a serious attitude to ideas in society—they are to be regarded as maps for incipient action, not as cheap talk. The co-operative element in the growth of science ought to be matched by the co-operative discussion and comparison of various lines of social policy. The imaginative element in initiation of scientific ideas has as its democratic counterpart the exercise of initiative. In a democracy there is no excuse for having a good idea and not starting it off in some channel of co-operative consideration and action. Merely to say "Somebody ought to do such-and-such" is to reveal an attitude inimical to the extension of democracy. Finally, just as in science change in knowledge is expected and its consequences are carried through in other areas of knowledge, so in democracy there should be an attitude towards change as normal and an expectation that any change may have effects in areas other than the one in which it came about. It also demands co-operative assumption of the burdens entailed by such change.

This parallelism of the attitudes of democracy and science is perhaps no accidental one. In many respects—historically as well as logically—democracy may be viewed as the extension of scientific method and scientific attitudes to human life.

Applications of democracy

Political applications most familiar. The most familiar applications of the democratic approach lie, of course, in the domain of politics narrowly interpreted. Citizenship with its affirmative allegiance constitutes the basic common agreement. The widest participation and responsibility are attempted by the system of representative government with its techniques of universal adult suffrage, secret ballot, assemblies and senates or unicameral bodies, its regional organizations, referendum, recall, initiative, informal organizations like political parties, and a host of other devices whose testing and improvement ought to be a center of constant thought and experiment. Absence of discrimination should entail absence of restrictions on political activity (poll taxes, special requirements excluding Negroes, or informal limitations on women office-holders), absence of coercive pressures on political activity (e.g., threats of loss of jobs), expansion of facilities for factual information (equitable use of radio, an objective press, government research bureaus), and so forth. Positive aid to the achievement of men's goals is a function of the content of legislation and of maintenance by judiciary of various liberties. Minimizing coercion depends on the success of the educational system as well as on the positive satisfaction of men's needs.

This of course is only a bare outline of the directions in which democracy in government may move. In every case the actual test of its expansion would lie in whether the principles we have described would in fact be given increased scope and application. The test of growing democratization would thus be found in the lives and attitudes of men. Are they taking a more conscious share in government or are they becoming indifferent? What recourse have they against undesirable decisions? Are obstacles to their activity increasing or decreasing? Are liberties being extended or melting away?

Incomplete as even the best examples of democratic government have yet been (except perhaps in the smallest communities or in face-to-face groups), the directions towards which democratization should work are at least clear. But there are many fields of American life in which democratic experimentation has not been attempted. As a matter of fact a survey of our society would show that most fields are thoroughly imbued with an autocratic spirit reflecting an authoritarian decision-structure. This is probably derived from the dominance of the business-model.

Economic life still autocratic. The pattern of American economic life has been completely autocratic. As we have seen in the discussion of property,[15] controlling economic groups are responsible to no one in the formulation of most policies, however vital to public welfare. The chief limitations on economic autocracy have come from labor unions which exert pressure so that decisions may represent more adequately the interests of labor; occasionally these have been instrumental in stabilizing a whole industry. Consumer interests have not been represented at all except for the pressures that consumer organizations have exerted, and limited regulation by federal agencies. There have also been a few large-scale government enterprises aiming at the integrated solution of fundamental problems in a special area; among these the T.V.A. has been most widely hailed as an experiment in democracy.

The same autocratic structure that characterizes economic life at large is found in the inner operations of business. The owner or the managing group makes decisions with little or no responsibility to groups affected by them. Subordinates have no choice but to carry out orders, and those affected have rarely been able to do anything but suffer the consequences. Even major enterprises run by the government (such as the post office and a large part of the civil service) have taken the requirements of democracy to be fully satisfied by the fact that policies were set and administrative decisions made by government officials.

There are strict limits to which employee participation in control of indus-

[15] See above, p. 276.

try can be carried in present business enterprise.[16] It can remove grievances that arise from harsh management or misunderstanding, it can to some extent alleviate difficult conditions of labor, and it may sometimes stimulate employee initiative and improve employee morale. But experience has shown that it often strikes the reef of fundamental economic questions such as wages and hours of labor, and thus ultimately the relative shares of labor and capital in the benefits and products of industry. Thus the ultimate questions of economic democracy are not *techniques* of employer-employee-consumer relationship, but the ideals and principles to govern the distribution of wealth or property.

The difficulties encountered in even initial steps towards imparting democratic responsibility to economic enterprise and democratic attitudes to business operations have led many people to wonder whether our form of business is not essentially incompatible with democracy. They have asked whether the pressure for private profit is not inherently opposed to the achievement of social objectives, and whether the necessary competitiveness engendered by business habits is not the foe of the co-operativeness and mutuality so important in democratic attitudes. As sociologists have become more conscious of the pervasive role of business activity in fashioning the attitudes and outlook of our society these questions have become more critical.

Possible applications to education. Large domains such as education are likewise still predominantly autocratic in structure. Policy is set at the top and decisions handed down to be obeyed. There have been some attempts to make education a co-operative process in which the various interests involved (community at large, parents, teachers, students) should have some share in the formulation of policy and the direction, in varying degree, of administration. Such attempts are still in an early stage. The problem is not merely one of administrative techniques; it enters into the very classroom. Teacher attitudes have been dominantly authoritarian—"correct" information is handed out authoritatively to students. A democratic approach—whatever the detailed devices needed to achieve it—requires a reconstruction of the teaching situation so that students become active participants, not passive recipients. The classroom becomes a place where students and teacher, cognizant in common of specific problems, work out solutions with the teacher exercising a democratic leadership based on a head start in information and a higher trained imagination and critical power.

Morality, authoritarian and democratic. Morality likewise has worn the dominant authoritarian guise and been expressed as commands allowing

---

[16] For an account of an earnest early attempt in this direction see Mary Van Kleeck, *Miners and Management*, Russell Sage Foundation, 1934. For more recent experiments, see C. S. Golden and H. J. Ruttenberg, *The Dynamics of Industrial Democracy*, Harper, 1942.

only obedience or transgression. A democratic reinterpretation would see morals as lessons of experience in the solution of common human problems, to be refined and extended as all knowledge is, when there is a deepening understanding of problems and a growing elaboration of techniques. This special problem will be discussed in Part Five.

Questions of democracy may be raised in any field. Space-limitations as well as the specific character of the task forbid further consideration here of the detailed application of democratic principles. Clearly any domain of life, any type of organization could be examined from this point of view. What do democratic ideals and principles entail in the operation and functioning of clubs, trade unions, the family, radio, the cinema? Certainly, the form of democracy, that is, the organizational techniques, will be very different in intimate groups, in face-to-face groups, in large bodies, in groups sharing a large segment of life or only a specialized function, and so forth. In some cases democracy will appear as a formal organization, in others merely as specific attitudes in sharing and solving problems. But in every case it would involve clarification of the goals in the specific domain and their reorganization in terms of democratic ideals. The detailed examination of such questions would entail building up a whole social philosophy on democratic principles—a task beyond the scope of the present book. We have, nevertheless, seen its direction sufficiently to realize how democracy may be conceived as the *systematic* cultivation of liberty and freedom. Freedom, in turn, emerges as a co-operative social process making a system out of men's values and liberty as a set of arrangements by which these values are given adequate scope and hope of achievement.

Democracy and the future

In the years that preceded the outbreak of the war, there was considerable discussion of the shortcomings of democracy. Controversy about this question touched the foundations of democratic theory and it had a sense of urgency imparted by the growing encroachments of fascist power. The latter spread a shadow not merely over one country after another but even over the thoughts of men. Reflections on democracy were often phrased as a study of the crisis of democracy, and the question raised was how, if at all, democracy could survive. The war brought with it a more vigorous assertion of the faith in democracy. It is no longer a question of whether democracy is likely to survive, but a stern determination to maintain, extend, and purify it, so that the values it embodies may grow and flourish. Since the concrete fulfillment of this task should be a major effort of post-war reconstruction, it is important to look at the critiques that have been offered of democracy in our time and to estimate their lesson.

There are, of course, major critiques of democracy that proceed from a rejection of its values—for example, the Nietzschean glorification of power and strength and the attack on equality and kindliness as weakness[17]—but these do not here concern us. The analyses to which we refer aim at revealing either presumed defects discovered in democracy itself when it is put to the test, or, more often, the basic conditions on which it rests and which, as they are themselves shaken, threaten to bring down the edifice built upon them. It should be added that in our account of democratic theory we have been occupied largely with a clarification of the concept and have had little occasion to touch this fundamental question of the conditions of its existence.

BASIC CONDITIONS FOR ITS STABILITY

Some believe that the trouble lies in our unreadiness to adjust democratic techniques to changing conditions, or to devise new techniques. Inefficiency is even regarded by some as a necessary price which they may be ready to pay for democracy. Clearly this is not necessarily entailed by its structure; for it is permissible to alter specific techniques. Delegation of power in crises may be necessary, and is not undemocratic as such if sufficient safeguards are provided for subsequent responsibility. But we may suspect that democratic antipathy to unrestricted delegations of power has generally been guided by a fear that the power would not be used in the public interest. On the whole, the accusation that democracy is inefficient seems to arise from its unreadiness to sacrifice vital though perhaps less readily apparent interests. It is comparable to the doctor who hesitates to amputate a leg until there is thorough proof of necessity. Only on a superficial comparison is the quicker restoration to health by early amputation seen as greater efficiency. A well-functioning democracy provides a genuine sense of common enterprise and a greater readiness to make sacrifices which are necessitated by common purposes—both of which make for genuine efficiency. It is important to notice that even in a field in which democratic *techniques* may have only limited scope—such as the field of warfare—a democratic sense of common purpose has proved necessary for vigorous defense.

Search for moral and emotional bases. Some take the issue to be fundamentally a moral one. They imply that the basis of democracy is a mental outlook and find that the inroads which fascism made in the western world constituted a revolt against the dignity of man and the values of rationality. Archibald MacLeish states this view in *The Irresponsibles:* "Intellectuals in America and elsewhere—writers, scientists, the men of learning—have at-

---

[17] See below, p. 441.

tempted to ignore these questions. They have pretended to themselves that the burning of books, the exiling of artists, the invention of mythologies were merely incidents—after-thoughts—decorations: that the true crisis was the crisis of food, the crisis of arms, the crisis created by political forces, by economic collapse—that they had, and needed have, no truck with it. They have been wrong. These things are not incidents. They are not afterthoughts. They are the essential nature of the revolution of our age."[18]

Some [19] ascribe the difficulties democracy has faced to an inherent individualism, which, in the tradition of Rousseau, looks to the atomic individual for the source of moral obligation. They recommend a recasting of the concept of the individual so as to reveal binding obligations for him, and a more organic approach to the state.

Some again, finding in their analysis of democratic theory the need for a basic common agreement, a common effort to "make a go of it" and a basic agreement to abide by majority decision while advocating change of direction, see as a central danger the evaporation of such a common basis. Hence they blame class conflict, dispersive interests, human egoism, and any other apparent source of large-scale differences. They recommend the resort to any powerful cement which will hold men together, anything which will act as a centripetal force. Thus one group stresses religion as an indispensable basis of democracy and calls it the only sound foundation, neglectful of democracy's historically and logically divergent bases. Others look to nationalism to provide a powerful sentiment for unity. Many even are willing to welcome war, because it acts as a common stimulus to unify morale. Some try to make a faith out of democracy itself. Of the attempts to find some form of spiritual "cement," perhaps this last if carried out thoroughly, most exemplifies the spirit of democratic theory. For the democratic ideals of liberty and equality, when clarified, bring their devotees back to the concrete needs and aims of men. Men's needs are great enough and their plight is difficult enough to provide ample basis of unity for democratic energy.

RELATION OF DEMOCRACY AND CAPITALISM

Perhaps the largest number find the difficulty of democracy in the failure to satisfy men's concrete needs, that is, largely in the economic problems that confront modern societies. Concerning the analysis of these questions there are, however, several different views.

[18] From Archibald MacLeish, *The Irresponsibles,* p. 15. By permission of Duell, Sloan and Pearce, Inc., publishers.
[19] See, for example, Jacques Maritain, *Scholasticism and Politics.* Macmillan, 1940.

View that democracy depends on capitalism. One group—partisans of capitalism casting a longing eye on laissez-faire—finds democracy dependent on traditional economic freedom. They see democracy disappearing with the encroachment of the state on economic life. Accordingly they recommend a return to greater economic freedom, with the role of government limited to general regulation against excesses.

In Europe at large since the war, this view has little or no hold. In England the elections showed a widespread recognition that the role of government cannot be reduced to the confines envisaged in this return to the past. In America, on the other hand, the view has a wider following. It is sometimes propounded as a "fifth" freedom—freedom of enterprise—fundamental to all the rest. By and large, however, it represents the slogan of monopoly capital against government interference on behalf of labor, farmer, consumer, or small business. That it represents a fighting slogan rather than a clear analysis can be seen from the way in which it obliterates all distinction between fascism and socialism, and between socialism and the New Deal, and lumps them all together as "statism."

View that democracy is compatible with diverse economic systems. A second group lays primary stress on the accomplishment of democratic goals and finds this compatible with a variety of economic systems. It sees no contradiction in the notion of democratic socialism nor in that of democratic capitalism. Political democracy, it believes, can become a stable force representing the will of free peoples. Hence each people can judge from its own experience what kind of economic system it finds best, and choose it freely, whether capitalist, socialist, or any of a host of intermediate forms.

On an international scale, this view points to the bases that democracy requires—international co-operation for stable peace, increase of global productivity by the industrialization of undeveloped continents, a higher standard of living and freedom from want, and the extension of democratic political forms everywhere to release the energy and initiative of peoples. It hopes that just as capitalist America and Britain co-operated with the socialist Soviet Union during the war to achieve high production and military victory, so co-operation will continue for peace and international prosperity. Within the capitalist countries it believes that the extension of governmental activity in a democratic fashion can ensure production at high levels and counteract or obviate depressions, providing basic security and liberty for the mass of men without fundamental inroads upon capitalist institutions.

View that capitalism is incompatible with democracy. A third group—explicitly socialist or communist in its outlook—finds capitalism essentially incompatible with democracy and with those liberties that bring the wider satisfaction of men's aims. It rests its case on its analysis of the operations of our society and the controlling role of capitalist enterprise within it. Capitalist control, it finds, molds all phases of society to suit its needs. The ideals and principles and attitudes of democracy will thus remain idle dreams if they seek partial or isolated expression in one or another segment of society, whether it be education, co-operatives, or even the narrowly political sphere. These are bound to be ineffectual in any critical situation unless men face the problem of economic control and strive for a basic alteration in the system of business and property-holding. This point of view foresees increasing oppression supplanting democracy if capitalism is to continue, and recommends socialism as the desirable alternative. It asserts that socialism today would provide economic expansion more conducive to the widest development of democracy and the achievement of its ideals.

America and the future of democracy. The role of America in determining the future of democracy is a fundamental one. As the most powerful capitalist country and the one with the clearest tradition of political democracy it is precisely the place where the relation of capitalism and democracy will have its crucial test. It is important for Americans, therefore, to fashion a dynamic democratic philosophy appreciative of the past but not bound by its specific formulae, committed to expansion of human liberties, the removal of human bondage, and the growth of freedom in the whole globe.

Such a perspective, in its full historic vista, was suggested by Henry A. Wallace, in his famous speech of May 8, 1942:

"When the freedom-loving people march—when the farmers have an opportunity to buy land at reasonable prices and to sell the produce of their land through their own organizations, when workers have the opportunity to form unions and bargain through them collectively, and when the children of all the people have an opportunity to attend schools which teach them truths of the real world in which they live—when these opportunities are open to everyone, then the world moves straight ahead. . . .

"The march of freedom of the past 150 years has been a long-drawn-out people's revolution. In this Great Revolution of the people, there were the American Revolution of 1775, the French Revolution of 1792, the Latin-American revolutions of the Bolivarian era, the German Revolution of 1848, and the Russian Revolution of 1917. Each spoke for the common man in terms of blood on the battlefield. Some went to excess. But the significant thing is that the people groped their way to the light. More of them learned to think and work together. . . .

"The people in their millennial and revolutionary march toward manifesting here on earth the dignity that is in every human soul, hold as their credo the Four Freedoms enunciated by President Roosevelt in his message to Congress on January 6, 1941. These four freedoms are the very core of the revolution for which the United Nations have taken their stand. We who live in the United States may think there is nothing very revolutionary about freedom of religion, freedom of expression, and freedom from the fear of secret police. But when we begin to think about the significance of freedom from want for the average man, then we know that the revolution of the past 150 years has not been completed, either here in the United States or in any other nation in the world. We know that this revolution cannot stop until freedom from want has actually been attained. . . .

"Some have spoken of the 'American Century.' I say that the century on which we are entering—the century which will come into being after this war—can be and must be the century of the common man. Perhaps it will be America's opportunity to support the freedoms and duties by which the common man must live. Everywhere the common man must learn to build his own industries with his own hands in a practical fashion. Everywhere the common man must learn to increase his productivity so that he and his children can eventually pay to the world community all that they have received. No nation will have the God-given right to exploit other nations. Older nations will have the privilege to help younger nations get started on the path to industrialism, but there must be neither military nor economic imperialism.

"The methods of the nineteenth century will not work in the people's century which is now about to begin. India, China, and Latin America have a tremendous stake in the people's century. As their masses learn to read and write, and as they become productive mechanics, their standard of living will double and treble. Modern science, when devoted whole-heartedly to the general welfare, has in it potentialities of which we do not yet dream."

Part Five

THE DIRECTION OF HUMAN AFFAIRS

Chapter 21 MATERIALISM AND IDEALISM

Philosophic outlook basic to human affairs

The analysis of explanation in Part One, of method in Part Two, of man in Part Three, and of the process of harmonizing aims in Part Four has prepared us for an examination of different comprehensive *outlooks* on or perspectives of our world. By a philosophic outlook we mean more than a philosophic theory. It is a way of looking at the world, a set of attitudes guiding human life, a theory embodied in practice. A discussion of fundamental outlooks is therefore in one sense most general since it deals with systematic conceptions of the whole universe; and yet in another sense it is most specific and oriented to practice, since it provides foundations for an answer to the question "What should we do?"

Reflection on men's aims. A man is driven to clarify his outlook by reflection on his aims or goals. He may begin by itemizing the directions of his striving. He may list what he would like to achieve by way of material goods, bodily skills and satisfactions, intellectual activities and accomplishments, emotional depths and reactions. He may decide what character-traits on his own part and in others he admires, what types of social relations attract him, what esthetic and religious and philosophic experiences satisfy him. He may elaborate upon the kind of society in which he would want to live. When he has given us this catalogue of his values, we may note— as he himself often does—discrepancies and inconsistencies, not merely in the possibility of achieving certain values jointly, but even in holding them at the same time. Situations in which he finds himself will force choices upon him. In the process of working out the practical problems thus raised, he can build a pattern embracing criteria of judgment and decision, more dominant and less dominant values, more constant values and more transitory ones, pervasive attitudes and shifting attitudes, systems and hierarchies of ideals. The result will be a more or less coherent value-scheme discernible in his conduct and rendered explicit in his reflection.

Developing a world-perspective. In the sense that every man carries out such a process to some extent, every man may be said to have a philosophic outlook whether he realizes it or not. In carrying out such a process reflectively, profoundly, in the fullest sense philosophically, a man is led to conceive his life as a whole in relation to his contemporaries, to the past, to the future—in short to the cosmos. He finds it hard to stop short in the process we have described and simply say, "These are my values. I find myself holding them, acting on them, using them in reflection to justify my conduct. That is all I know, and all I need to know." Or, if he does say this, it also represents a philosophic reflection (implicit or explicit) on his relation to his world—an attitude elaborated in some forms of positivism.[1] More often, men have begun to ask, "Where do these values fit into the scheme of things? What is their source, their direction, their *status* in the world? Why do I find them impelling?"

From the point of view of such inquiry, the most fruitful philosophical distinction is between the *idealist* and the *materialist* perspective.[2] In the present part we shall, therefore, examine idealism and materialism first for their underlying concepts as philosophical theories, and then in subsequent chapters for the outlook they yield in such fields of men's lives as religion, art, morality, and society.

Idealist and materialist philosophies

When materialism and idealism are contrasted, a number of different ideas come to mind. In ordinary usage a materialist is a man who pursues certain "worldly" aims—in extreme form the money-grubber may be called a "crass materialist"—and an idealist is a man guided by lofty ideals or self-sacrificing motives, or at least a man who disdains the worldly. In historical writings and the discourse of social scientists, materialism has meant a stress on geographic-industrial-economic factors in explaining social change; idealism a stress on personal-religious-moral-intellectual factors.

In philosophy both materialism and idealism have meant definite ways of viewing the world and life as a whole. They have differed in their choice of fundamental methods for interpreting the world, in what they stress as fundamental in the world, and in their basic attitudes toward the conduct of human life. Materialism accepts scientific method as the most reliable way of giving an account of our world; idealism looks to some non-empirical method as a guide to a reality beyond the reach of science. Materialism in-

[1] See below, pp. 353, 428.
[2] The choice of the distinction to be stressed depends upon the type of interest that guides the inquiry. In the theory of science distinctions like *rationalism* and *empiricism* (see Chapters 6, 7) are most usual, though not necessarily exhaustive; similarly for the theory of mind, *naturalism, dualism,* and so forth (see Chapters 11, 14); for the theory of knowledge, *realism, subjectivism,* and so forth (see Chapters 8, 12); for a study of the relatedness of things, *monism* and *pluralism* (see Chapter 4). Some of these are themselves specialized forms of the distinction between materialism and idealism.

sists on the primacy of matter in the universe, idealism on the primacy of spirit. In human affairs materialism exhibits an attitude that is basically this-worldly, idealism an attitude that is either other-worldly or at least non-worldly.

Our study of idealism and materialism will show that, although each has a broad distinctive unity, each has likewise many divergent forms. There are some questions on which there is more agreement among some types of idealism and some types of materialism than among all within each group. Again there may be idealistic tendencies in some types of materialism, and materialistic tendencies in some types of idealism. Thus the supernaturalist may regard pantheism (although both are in the idealist tradition) as materialistic since it refuses to admit of disembodied spirits.

How far-reaching the opposition is between idealism and materialism can best be discerned by an examination of their central differences. We shall, accordingly, consider their respective interpretations of science, matter and change, spirit and the eternal, and the conduct of human life.

Interpretation of science

MATERIALISM AND THE HISTORY OF SCIENCE

In Part Two we considered the nature and reliability of scientific method in comparison with other ways of resolving doubt. Reliance upon this method is one of the characteristics of philosophical materialism. As a matter of fact, philosophical materialism may be viewed historically as an outlook developing alongside and to some extent out of the growing sciences. It appears in the Greek attempts to establish physics, culminating in the atomic theory of Democritus. Platonic idealism is at many points vehemently directed against Democritus' materialism. Scarcely had Galileo established the foundations of modern physics, when the 17th century witnessed the development of the physical materialism of Hobbes and a dominantly mechanistic drift in a great part of Cartesian dualism. With the development of Newtonian science came the conception of the world as a huge machine, operating with a machine-like apparatus of causality and determinism.[3] This *mechanical materialism*, as it is often called, is well-developed in the 18th century French materialists.[4] Much of late 19th century materialism got its inspiration from developments in biology, particularly the theory of evolu-

---

[3] See above, Chapter 3. For a brief historical presentation of this development, see J. H. Randall, Jr., *The Making of the Modern Mind*, rev. ed., Houghton Mifflin, 1940, Chapter XI.

[4] E.g., La Mettrie, Holbach.

tion.[5] The social and historical materialism of Marx and Engels rested more particularly on the development of the social sciences, especially the economic work of such men as Adam Smith, Ricardo, and, of course, Marx himself. Modern critical philosophies of science have freed the analysis of scientific method from complete reliance on physics, and physics itself has, as we have seen, broken from the world-machine idea. A modern philosophic materialism is not, therefore, bound to any one science, but is an expression of science come of age and confident of its method.

HISTORICAL RELATIONS OF IDEALISM AND SCIENCE

The historical relations of science and idealist philosophy are, on the other hand, extremely complicated. In some cases idealism itself derived strong inspiration from a specific science, e.g., Plato from mathematics or Berkeley from Lockean psychology. Philosophic idealism itself for a long time dominated the very analysis of science. For science was long regarded in the rationalist tradition as a logical system with fundamental premises grasped by intellectual insight. This conception, already full-grown in Aristotle's logic, enshrined a non-empirical procedure in the very heart of science. Intuition and, later, revelation were held to provide the premises for scientific elaboration. As the body of scientific knowledge grew, however, and the causal conception of the world gained in strength, the scope of non-empirical methods was narrowed to "fundamentals." The history of evolutionary theory illustrates such a development. Evolution was first fought as counter to revelation, but as the evolutionary theory became more widely accepted some assimilated it to religion, picturing the whole evolutionary process as an unfolding of God's original intention.

Although empiricism became more entrenched in the physical sciences, non-empirical methods remained at work in such less developed fields as social science, morals, and art. Here the imaginative sweep of philosophical idealism did much to prepare the ground for scientific work. The Hegelian insight into the relatedness of various elements of a culture is a notable example. It stimulated a search for integrated patterns of cultures which eventually became an important aspect of empirical social science.

Growing opposition of science and idealist philosophy. Even before this, however, as materialist philosophies made reliance on scientific method a central tenet, and claimed that such method would embrace the fields of human life and activity as well, philosophical idealism began to formulate its claims less as a theory of the nature of science than as a theory of the definite limitations of scientific method. Science, it was said, is secondary in

[5] E.g., in T. H. Huxley, or in Ernst Haeckel's very popular *The Riddle of the Universe*.

the kind of knowledge it gives; it deals with the quantitative, the analytical, the partial, the less real. Poetic insight, religious insight, feeling, imagination, introspection, philosophic criticism were all appealed to as methods to reach the truth which science could not give.[6]

Some such claim for a method superior to empirical science is generic to different types of idealist philosophy. To take a recent large-scale illustration, Oswald Spengler rested his method in *The Decline of the West* on the assumption that "the means whereby to identify dead forms is Mathematical Law. The means whereby to understand living forms is Analogy."[7] And in praising Goethe he tells us that Goethe hated mathematics; "For him, the world-as-mechanism stood opposed to the world-as-organism, dead nature to living nature, law to form. As naturalist, every line he wrote was meant to display the image of a thing-becoming, the 'impressed form' living and developing. Sympathy, observation, comparison, immediate and inward certainty, intellectual *flair*—these were the means whereby he was enabled to approach the secrets of the phenomenal world in motion."[8]

Hegel—the source of most modern philosophical idealism—took philosophy to be the supreme method of knowledge. Just as science provides the truth of common knowledge, so philosophy gives the truth of science. Hegel believed that history is the course of the World-Spirit attaining self-consciousness. The role of philosophic method is therefore to explain after the fact, and the realization it brings us is, in the last words of *The Philosophy of History,* "That the History of the World, with all the changing scenes which its annals present, is this process of development and realization of Spirit—this is the true *Theodicaea,* the justification of God in History. Only *this* insight can reconcile Spirit with the History of the World—viz. that what has happened, and is happening every day, is not only not 'without God,' but is essentially His Work."[9]

Matter and change

Matter and change are fundamental concepts in philosophical materialism. Their analysis is a very complicated question involving basic problems in the traditional field of metaphysics.

---

[6] For the criticism of the rationalist interpretation of science, see above, pp. 83-92; for intuition, etc., p. 77 ff.; for a superior philosophic method, p. 118 ff.; for introspective knowledge, p. 114 ff.

[7] Vol. 1, p. 4.

[8] From Oswald Spengler, *The Decline of the West,* translation by C. F. Atkinson, Vol. 1, p. 25. By permission of Alfred A. Knopf, Inc., publishers.

[9] Sibree translation, London, 1857.

MEANING OF MATTER

What do we mean ordinarily when we say that this piece of iron is matter? There are several possibilities which the long and complicated history of the concept has indicated.

Matter as existence. We might mean simply that it is an object existent in space and having a history in time. Clearly I would not need to know physics to use the term in such a way. Descartes, for instance, took extension to be the essence of body or matter. Hobbes included motion in its essence. This type of interpretation of matter equates it with the things in the world that are involved in the various goings-on or happenings we note.

Matter as physical elements. We might mean that this piece of iron would on investigation be found to be composed of matter. More strictly, then, we should say that this piece of iron is a form of matter or made up of matter. Matter thus becomes equated with the results of the physical analysis of things. This approach is found early in Greek philosophy. The Greek term for matter [10] meant originally *timber*. Hence to look for the matter of things was in effect to look for the building-materials of which they were constituted. Thales thought it was *water*, Anaximander spoke of it as an indeterminate *boundless*, while Anaximenes decided on *air* and attempted to explain how rarefaction and condensation would make air assume various forms of things as we know them. Empedocles thought there were four elements—earth, air, fire, and water—rather than a single one. Democritus took matter to be atoms, hard and indivisible, differing in shape and size, and by their various agglomerations in space building up the things we know. The history of modern chemistry is largely the story of the discovery of the various elements and compounds, the mapping of their properties, the analysis of their composition into different kinds of atoms, and the provision of a systematic basis for this knowledge in the periodic table. Atomic physics has carried out the analysis of atoms themselves, providing an electrical theory in which various kinds of atoms are seen as different organizations of various numbers of positively charged protons and negatively charged electrons. The analysis of these in turn, which is constantly being developed in scientific work today, yields an interpretation in terms of quanta of energy.

If we identify matter with the units employed in physical analysis, no description of it can be treated as final or absolute. Since no particular set of identifying marks can be more than tentative, it represents a confusion to say, as some have, that matter is disappearing from modern physics. All that can be meant is that some of the identifying marks used in the past are now no longer employed; new ones have developed to take their place.

---

[10] ὕλη (*hylē*), etymologically akin to the Latin *silva*.

Matter as materials. Matter has sometimes been used to refer to materials out of which the object under investigation is directly constituted. Thus paper and ink are the matter of this book, bricks the matter of a house, clay the matter of bricks, houses and men the matter of a city, and so forth. Aristotle generalized this way of analyzing an object or situation into a relative conception of matter. Matter is always the matter *of* some whole, and the whole consists of the matter shaped or ordered in a certain fashion or form or pattern. Matter and form are thus complementary notions. On this view anything can be conceived of as matter in some context, and Aristotle even sometimes thinks of premises as matter in the syllogism.

Prime matter or substratum. A fourth conception of matter has sometimes arisen by elaborating the relative conception of matter in physics. If clay is the matter of bricks, and various compounds are the matter of clay, and atoms the matter of these, and protons and electrons the matter of atoms, where does this end? An empirical approach would say that there are no *a priori* guarantees that it will end or, on the other hand, that it will prove endless. Only investigation can show where we end at any particular time, and whether an end beyond that is probable. But *any* conceivable end will be *describable,* and so the question "What is *its* matter?" can meaningfully be asked of it, though not necessarily answered. Some philosophers have felt uncomfortable at the thought of such a possible *infinite regress.* They have therefore sought a way to put a stop to the endless asking of this question, and found it by calling a halt in some *undescribed* and *indescribable* matter.

Hence there arose in ancient philosophy the suggestion of a prime matter, a sort of initial stuff having no properties but the fact that it is what everything determinate is made of. In this way it differs sharply from Democritus' atoms or the protons and electrons of modern physics, which are arrived at by physical analysis and possess definite properties. Locke, too, as we have seen,[11] resorted to the notion of matter as a something-I-know-not-what invoked to support qualities. If it did not exist, we should have to think of qualities as standing alone, and where iron rusts or wood burns or iron melts there would be no continuity. There would be simply disappearance of one set of qualities and appearance of another. The concept of matter as not being destroyed in such processes provides an underlying continuity. But it is such a formulation that gives rise to the problem of how matter about which we know nothing is related to the qualities which are the objects of our knowledge.

Idealist and materialist tendencies in the interpretation of matter. We have thus distinguished four different (though not necessarily conflicting) senses in which the term "matter" has been used: *existence, physical elements* as found in the results of physical investigation, *materials* in the relative sense,

[11] P. 148.

and *prime matter* or *substratum*. In the first sense the presence of matter is noted by some generic property of things like extension or motion; in the second by the techniques of the physical science of the day. In the third sense, since matter and form together constitute a mode of analyzing any situation, what would be taken to be matter depends on the interests and purposes guiding the inquiry. In the fourth sense, there is no empirical procedure for determining the presence of matter; prime matter is posited to fill some *need* in the analysis, such as the demand for continuity or the requirement for an underlying basis.

Of these conceptions of matter (and a more detailed historical examination would present additional ones) the third is a special usage compatible with almost any philosophy—most useful in ordinary life where processes of construction of one kind or another are constantly before us. Around the other conceptions, however, a continuous philosophical battle has been waged, and in this controversy it is possible to distinguish those tendencies which have led to philosophical idealism from those which lead to philosophical materialism. In the first two conceptions (matter as *existence* and matter as *physical elements*) the issue is that of the properties to be assigned to matter; materialists insist on such properties as would make matter self-sufficing, idealists on such as would render it inert, requiring some external force to set it in motion. In the fourth sense (matter as *substratum*) the issue becomes the very reality of matter. On the whole, acceptance of this Lockean conception tends ultimately to philosophical idealism, while a consistent materialism opposes the conception as a whole.

A comparison of the idealist and materialist treatments of matter may therefore best be carried out by considering the two major issues: (1) the relation of matter and change, centering on the alleged inertness of matter; and (2) the reality of matter, with special attention to those conceptions that render it illusory.

THE RELATION OF MATTER AND CHANGE

Expulsion of movement from matter in Greek philosophy. The issue of whether matter is inert or self-moving arose early in the history of Greek philosophy.[12] The first Greek philosophers had no trouble in conceiving the ultimate stuff as self-moving and full of activity. Parmenides, however, found Being or Reality to be one and unchanging, and his disciple Zeno, as we have seen,[13] gave ingenious arguments to prove that motion is impossible. It was Empedocles, in developing the theory of the four elements (earth, air,

---

[12] For an excellent analysis of this development, see George Boas, *The Major Traditions of European Philosophy,* Harper, 1929.
[13] See above, p. 119.

fire, and water), who first described them as inert and felt it necessary to add sources of movement—a unifying force and a separating force which he described, perhaps figuratively, as love and hate. This began the expulsion of self-movement from matter. Thereafter the source of movement was often said to lie in mind (Anaxagoras' view) or soul (Plato's) or the attraction of a first cause (Aristotle's) or the efficient agency of a Creator (Newton's). The frequent description of matter's essence as extension is an extreme formulation of such a development.

Matter not inert in materialist tradition. On the other hand, many philosophical materialists implicitly or explicitly opposed this view of matter as inert. The atoms of Democritus are in constant motion. Hobbes maintained that all that goes on in the world is matter in motion. La Mettrie objects specifically to taking extension as the essence of matter; matter has an active as well as a passive principle; there is power of self-movement in the substance of bodies. In modern physics the identification of a material object by use of the three dimensions of space was found insufficient, and gave way to the space-time relativity conception. With the breakdown of the sharp separation between matter and energy came the clearer realization that the separation of movement from matter had been a historical digression, not a philosophical necessity.

It is interesting to note that what was essentially a change in the mode of identifying matter forced by a growth in knowledge, was greeted from an idealist point of view as a dematerialization or spiritualization of matter. So fixed had the conception of matter as inert become that to think of it as ultimately electrical in character or as a form of energy made it seem ethereal. The true consequence of the liberalization of the concept of matter was exactly the opposite. It meant a reunion of matter and change and the end of a need to find a source of motion outside of matter.

A long development in the notion of movement or change itself pointed in the same direction. This development was largely a function of the growth of the sciences and the historical importance attached to physics. It is interesting to outline the development briefly at this point in our inquiry. Its outcome shows how intimately related in a materialist approach are the concepts of matter and change.

Aristotelian idea of change. In Aristotelian theory the idea of change or movement is a very generalized one: there is a change whenever an underlying substance first lacks a property and then possesses it. The types of change he recognizes are four in number, distinguished by the domains in which they occur. *Quantitative* change is illustrated by growth and diminution, whether biological or artificial. Alteration is *qualitative* change, such as a substance changing color. Motion is change of *position* and is most pervasive, being involved in all the others. Coming-into-being and passing-away are changes of *substance;* unlike the others they are instantaneous, since at any moment a bit of existence either is or is not of a definite sort. Other types of change may lead up to substantival change, but it does not itself cover an interval.

For Aristotle, all types of change are equally "real." He makes no attempt to reduce them to one another. In his physical theory qualitative change emerges as important. For the changes in the composition of things are ultimately traced to qualitative replacements. This rests on a definition of the four sublunar elements in qualitative terms, earth being the cool-dry stuff, water the cool-moist, air the hot-moist, and fire the hot-dry. Yet there is no attempt to assign any primacy to qualitative change. Similarly, while physics is described as the study of the properties that are not isolable from matter, namely movement and its kinds, there is no attempt to assign it any primacy among the sciences.

Reduction of change to physical motion in mechanistic materialism. In Democritean theory, which Aristotle constantly criticized, the fundamental elements of physics are atoms moving in space. All types of change are reduced to change of position. Quantitative change is adjunction and separation of atoms. Qualitative change and substantival change are illusory, since atoms and the void constitute all there is to reality. This glorification of physics, which Democritus pronounced, governed the materialist philosophies that centered around the early development of modern science. In Hobbes as in Galileo, all qualities but those of extension and motion are "subjective" phenomena, phenomena of mind, not of external nature. The world-machine is a world of physics, and when the mechanical materialists spoke of matter having movement in addition to extension as its essence, they meant ultimately motion in space.

Broader conception of change and matter in modern materialism. This materialist conception of change was liberalized with the growth of biological, psychological and social science, with data, methods and systematic results of their own. This removed the stigma of unreality from qualities other than physical. Data on various levels could be embraced, instead of being shunned as tainted with dualism. Such a changed attitude was evidenced in many forms. For example, evolutionary materialists spoke of fresh qualities of matter emerging in the process of evolution—the qualities of living matter, of conscious life, and so forth. The dialectical materialists, in their endeavor to establish a social science in terms of social groups and their properties, strongly opposed explanations which reduced social phenomena to physical or physiological terms.[14] In general, modern materialism finds no

---

[14] Dialectical materialism in general opposed mechanical materialism as reductionist. Following the Hegelian conception of dialectic it adhered to a law of the transformation of quantity into quality as a generalized statement that new qualities appear in processes of quantitative change which cannot be anticipated on a purely quantitative basis. For the analysis of reductionism, see above, pp. 179-83.

difficulty in speaking of the qualities of groups of atoms differing from the qualities of the atoms themselves, and allowing possibly independent sciences for various levels of groupings.[15] Thus biological phenomena (growth, reproduction), psychological phenomena (perceiving, remembering, feeling), and social phenomena (technological change, legal development, spread of a religion) can all be conceived without absurdity as dynamic organizational properties of matter. In this respect the growth of the sciences has brought about a naturalistic attitude which the initial emergence and glorification of physics had tended to destroy. Such an approach no longer expects to describe prayer or philosophical discourse as a pattern of atomic motion, although it keeps open the possibility of future unification of social and physical science.[16]

Both of the first two senses of matter described at the outset—matter as existence and matter as physical elements—have thus been broadened in modern materialism. Since all forms of change are conceived in terms of organizational properties of matter, matter as existence becomes equated with the total mass of things or happenings, events, goings-on which we observe in our world. In the second sense, which fastens attention on the analysis of things, the rapid progress of physics has left the specific defining properties of matter tentative, and thus committed it to the hands of physicists for continuous exploration.

IDEALIST ATTEMPTS TO DECLARE MATTER UNREAL

We turn now to the second issue concerning the nature of matter outlined above—the attempt to render it unreal or illusory. This derives from the fourth sense of matter—as prime matter or substratum. This view, separating matter and form, or matter and qualities, leaves to matter only the task of "embodying" form or "supporting" qualities. Matter thus becomes almost a nonentity. Since it has no identifiable form or describable qualities we cannot know it. On this basis, ancient idealism often proceeded to give matter an inferior and almost unreal status; modern subjective idealism often denies its existence altogether.

Matter in the Platonic tradition. In Platonic theory, as expounded in the *Timaeus,* "the mother and receptacle of all created and visible and in any way sensible things, is not to be termed earth, or air, or fire, or water, or any of their compounds or any of the elements from which these are derived, but is an invisible and formless being which receives all things and in some mysterious way partakes of the intelligible and is most incompre-

---

[15] E.g., Hyman Levy, *A Philosophy for a Modern Man,* Knopf, 1938.
[16] See above, Chapter 4.

hensible."[17] This matter is identified by Plato with space which provides a kind of home and location for the shadows of universals which we call things. Space itself has no properties, and is hardly real. Plato fashions the physical world out of mathematical forms applied to this material. In the mystical system of Plotinus, the greatest of the neo-Platonists, this formless conception of matter is taken over and coupled with the Aristotelian idea in which the distinction of matter and form is assimilated to that of potentiality and actuality. The result is a conception of matter as a kind of falling short of reality, bearing the same relation to the real that darkness does to light.

Subjective idealism questions existence of matter. Modern subjective idealism, as we have examined it in Berkeley's theory,[18] finds no merit in Locke's conception of an indescribable substratum supporting qualities. To believe in its existence is an unnecessary act of faith. Since qualities were described in terms of perception Berkeley finds sufficient support for them in the perceiving mind. Others, less ready to follow Berkeley all the way, are driven to a skeptical phenomenalism; we cannot know matter if it is indescribable, hence we cannot even know whether it exists. Mill defines matter as the permanent possibility of sensations. Thus it is not necessary to have a support for qualities; instead only a guarantee of continuity in psychological experience is needed. We have commented in a previous chapter on Russell's argument that the belief in material substance represents only the grammatical need of a subject in many languages.[19] Both Russell and others have suggested the treatment of things as constructs out of sensa or sense-data.

CRITIQUE OF LOCKE'S CONCEPTION OF MATTER AS SUBSTRATUM

The legitimacy of Locke's conception of matter as ultimate substratum is thus a serious question for philosophical materialism. Now we have suggested above that there is no way in which we can test empirically for the existence or presence of matter in Locke's sense of the term. Hence the only fruitful issue in a Lockean framework is whether matter is really required on scientific or logical grounds. If it turns out not to be required, this need not lead to Berkeleyan idealism. It can equally well mean that the definition of matter as prime matter or substratum is a useless one, and that the analysis which separated the qualities from matter was in the first place erroneous.

Physical science does not require this conception. Insofar as physical science is concerned the question becomes simply whether there is any need

---

[17] *Timaeus* 51 (Jowett translation).   [19] See above, p. 156.
[18] See above, p. 153.

to posit a relation of "underlying" such that a substratum will be required as underlying all qualities. Physical science does, it is true, take some properties or qualities and treat them as the basis for systematizing other qualities. Thus, as we have seen, Aristotle tried to systematize physics around the hot, the cold, the moist and the dry; Democritus around size, shape, number of elementary particles; modern physics at first around the properties of atoms, then of electrons and protons and their number, and so forth. The terms in which these selected elements are described are basic or underlying for that systematization. If therefore "underlying" means anything in the operations of physical science—and such usage is probably figurative at best—it refers to a relation *between qualities*. There is thus no scientific warrant for treating it as a relation between qualities and something that is not a quality.

The ground sought for the Lockean conception of matter as substratum must therefore be a philosophical or logical one—that the very idea of a quality requires that it *qualify* something which is not a quality. This raises a fundamental question of traditional metaphysics—the analysis of such categories as thing, quality, event, substance, and so forth—a task that lies beyond the scope of the present work. We may, however, offer a few indications of one path that a modern materialism might follow in meeting the problem.

Relativity of categories for describing existence. It might begin by regarding all such categories as simply ways of analyzing existence. Take, for example, the situation in which it is asserted that "this is red." Presumably red is a quality asserted of this; whereas to assert "this reddens" is to state a process or event in which this participates. But instead of saying "This is red" some have suggested that we might, if we wished, say "This reds," thus regarding the quality as "processive" in character. Some American Indian languages use such verbal forms to express what English regards as qualities. Conversely, events are often treated as adjectival, qualifying the things participating in them. Thus motion has traditionally been considered a quality or property of things. Even language reflects this, as when we speak of a rolling stone. Some philosophers have suggested analyzing all things into complexes of events.

The conclusion suggested from all this would be that existence may be described in terms of things and their properties or qualities, or in terms of things and the events they participate in, or in terms of events and their qualities, or in terms of qualities and their complexes, or in numerous other possible ways. Any description in one set of terms might be theoretically capable of translation into a description in any other set of terms. Abstractly, it would be indifferent which categories were used. In their application, however, some would yield more complicated modes of description, and thus turn out too cumbersome or impossible in practice. One set might fit one domain more efficiently, another set a second domain. Criteria of simplicity, practicability, convenience, and perhaps fruitfulness in engendering scientific developments, would be employed on this approach.

Locke's ultimate categories. On such a relativistic interpretation of categories, the Lockean conception of matter would in the first place be examined to see what categories it employed. All its definite discourse appears to be carried on in the language of qualities. This follows from the fact that knowledge is defined as an arrangement of ideas corresponding to or arising from qualities. There appears to be a further implicit definition of quality as adjectival. Hence this mode of description is compelled to assert an unknown x to which qualities are ascribed, since there can be no knowledge of what is not a quality. Thus Locke's categories for the description of existence turn out to be *describable quality* and *indescribable subject* (called matter). It is obvious that in such a mode of description the second part is merely a linguistic device to avoid the contradiction that arises when a quality which is defined as *of* something is prevented from having anything to which to attach itself by the identification of everything as a quality.

His categories preclude their application. When it comes to questions of application, Locke gives an empirical interpretation to the notion of quality in terms of sensation (or element of knowledge). He gives no empirical interpretation to matter. Hence there is still no problem of the relation of matter and quality. If matter means anything more it can only be a general name for existence about which qualities answer questions. Such an approach must not, however, be taken to draw a sharp distinction between existence as one thing and qualities as something else. The problem of the relation of matter and qualities arises only if an empirical interpretation is also given to matter, e.g., atoms or cells or the spatially extended. But once that is done there is no *general* question of the relation of quality to matter; rather there are many particular questions of the relation of specific qualities to specific combinations of matter, e.g., the relation of this color to this table, or the relation of color (psychologically described) to atoms. Such questions are empirical in character and are to be answered only by progressive scientific research—in this example by discovering the role of atoms in color-vision.

The Lockean conception of matter provides, therefore, neither a useful mode of identifying phases of existence nor fruitful categories for the extension of knowledge. It serves a purely limited purpose of avoiding contradiction in the other categories of Locke's metaphysics. The mysterious character that it imparts to matter is, therefore, not a ground for questioning the existence or reality of matter, but rather, on the theory of categories here outlined, for questioning the utility of Locke's other constructs.

First two meanings of "matter" more appropriate for materialism. Philosophical materialism, therefore, is led to a conception of matter in accordance with the first two meanings we described above—matter as existence in space and time, and matter as physical elements. The first allows matter to be described and analyzed by the categories and methods of all the sciences, without generating independent entities or substances for each; it also allows the sciences to look for empirical relations between qualities in different fields, such as the mental and the physical. And the second sense defines matter precisely in terms of those units that yield the most systematic physical description. Both these senses may be used side by side without confusion, and together they give the widest scope to the extension of knowledge.

MATERIALIST VIEW OF THE PRIMACY OF MATTER

On the basis of the above account of matter, we may see more clearly what philosophical materialism has meant by asserting the *primacy* of matter. It is not surprising that this assertion has had a complex career. To the mechanical materialists the primacy of matter has sometimes meant that all is illusory except the atoms moving in space. In the growth of science it has meant the primacy of physics and the belief that unification of sciences will rest on terms and laws of physics rather than any of the other sciences. The very notion of primacy or priority is comparative; it involves being ahead of something else, so that the meaning of an asserted primacy is often set by the context of a specific dispute. Thus the primacy of matter to mind in the context of historical inquiry means that the solar system including the earth and its terrestrial environment existed before there was thinking going on. In the context of biological and psychological inquiry the primacy of matter to mind may mean the discoverable dependence of mental phenomena on bodily phenomena. In the discussion of moral issues the primacy of matter has sometimes meant that impulse and desire are the basis upon which the order called reason is established rather than reason being an original and independent force. In social science it has often meant that explanation is more successful in terms of the conditions of existence than in terms of the ideas men propound. The unity underlying all these usages is largely one of analogy, but the context can always be rendered explicit enough to avoid confusion.

In most of these senses the assertion that matter is primary is not *a priori* but empirical. It either relies on the results of science or is a program for scientific inquiry, functioning as a general hypothesis. If the primacy of matter is taken to be an *a priori* principle, however, it can only refer to a definition constructed out of the first sense of matter as existence in space and time; it would mean that any inquiry presupposes existence, which guides the inquiry by giving us problems and materials on which hypotheses are to be tested and to which our results are to refer.

Spirit and the eternal

Spirit is the key notion in the various forms of philosophical idealism. It appears as soul—the individual soul with all its human functions—and as the creator and guide of the universe, in which case it is called God. Sometimes, instead of the conception of spirit as personal, we find a belief in a pervasive spiritual character of things. In all these cases there is intended some analogy to the human spirit, and the understanding of the latter is taken in most forms of idealism to be the key to an understanding of the universe.

Existence of phenomena of spirit not at issue. It is important to note that it is not the existence of phenomena of spirit or mind or will which is at issue between idealism and materialism; idealism does not affirm and materialism deny their existence. Rather both recognize the occurrence of vital, mental, and volitional phenomena, but differ about the way in which they are to be explained or interpreted.[20] Fundamental to the idealist tradition is the insistence on spirit as an immaterial entity (whether a substance or unity) which is in some sense efficacious in guiding the body and in ordering the material world, whether from without it or within it. Fundamental to the materialist tradition is the denial of this claim and the interpretation of spiritual phenomena as natural events within the world of matter.

The general agreement upon the phenomena of spirit has been obscured by the dominance of the idealist interpretation. Thus the idealist interpretation has frequently been taken to be part of the very definition of spirit. If to be an immaterial entity is included in the definition of spirit, the materialist can meaningfully raise the question of its existence.

The point is clarified by noting the discussion about the immortality of the soul in Plato's *Phaedo*. None of the participants would dream of denying that he has a soul (*psyche*); it would be almost equivalent to denying that he is alive. Would anyone nowadays deny that he has a mind? Any controversy would surely be concerned with its nature instead of its existence. It was only after the Christian tradition gave a definite form to the soul, so that its actual meaning generally came to be an immaterial immortal entity, that it became understandable for a man to deny its existence. A comparable position in the Platonic dialogue is expressed by calling the soul a harmony of the body's elements and by adding that the soul perishes instantaneously at death.

---

[20] In Part Three we have examined these interpretations in great detail. The soul theories, the dualistic theories, and the subjectivistic or mentalistic theories fall from our present point of view into the idealist tradition, while the mechanistic and naturalistic theories fall in the materialist tradition.

TYPES OF IDEALISM AND THE PRIMACY OF SPIRIT

Different features of the human spirit have been stressed in different idealist systems. Knowing and the attributes of thought, perceiving with retrospective memory and creative imagination, willing and the tumults of striving, purpose and the organization it gives to activity, have each been taken as the essential activity or the distinguishing mark of spirit. Without entering into detailed distinctions, the major types of idealism may be readily listed.

Major types. *Platonic idealism* identifies spirit with the knowing mind, to whose activity, culminating in intellectual vision, all other activity is instrumental. Ideas are the eternal unchanging objects of knowledge, the very structure of reality. All existence is a flux achieving a definite character only insofar as it embodies the Ideas.[21]

Mystical idealism takes as the mark of spirit the striving for unity. Its goal is that ecstatic state in which the sense of self is lost in union with the One or God.[22] In several contexts below we shall refer to Plotinus as an illustration of such a view.

Supernaturalistic idealism, which constitutes the dominant western religious tradition, conceives spirit as personality with its many attributes. It draws a sharp distinction between the natural or worldly and the supernatural or divine. In this respect it constitutes a clear illustration of philosophical dualism. Its account of the world is teleological, and the spiritual is identified with the presence of a purposive order.[23]

Subjective idealism, best illustrated in Berkeley's philosophy,[24] regards spirit essentially as a perceiver having perceptions or ideas (sensations, memory-images, etc.). These ideas are passive images which spirit itself creates, and their combination constitutes the world of things.

Objective idealism looks for spirit not merely in individual consciousness or perception but in the objective order of natural and social life. The pattern sought has its origin, however, in the analysis of the human spirit. In Hegelian idealism, for example, the analysis of reason or judgment provides the pattern by whose presence spirit is identified; this pattern is then applied to the whole realm of nature, man and history.[25] In Schopenhauer, on the other hand, willing or striving is the fundamental attribute of spirit, and reality is conceived as will.

---

[21] For a fuller statement, see Chapter 2.
[22] See also above, p. 141.
[23] For purpose or teleological theories, see above, Chapter 2.
[24] See above, pp. 151-54.
[25] See quotation from Hegel's *Philosophy of History* given above, p. 317.

Panpsychic idealism regards activity, movement, vitality as the characteristic of spirit. It regards everything as alive in this sense, treating all matter as imbued with spirit. Pantheism is its religious analogue.

These forms of idealism are not, of course, mutually exclusive. Mystical idealism, for example, may build on the foundations of Platonic idealism or of supernaturalism. Nor does the fact that they are all idealist in type prevent wide disagreements on many points—the character and destiny of spirit, personal immortality, the pattern of spirituality, and so forth. For example, in western religious supernaturalism cosmic purpose is fulfilled in the hereafter; in objective idealist philosophies it is being fulfilled in this life. Such differences may be of tremendous practical importance in the conduct of life. It may be illuminating to range the various types on a scale of increasing approximation to the border of materialism. Such a scale might start with supernaturalism and mysticism and end with objective idealism and panpsychism or pantheism, which, as we have noted,[26] is often considered materialistic because of its denial of disembodied spirit.

Primacy of spirit. The idealist assertion of the *primacy* of spirit may have different meanings according to the context of discourse. With reference to the temporal order of things in the universe, it would mean for the world at large something akin to a conception of God as creator of the universe; if asserted for man, it would mean the temporal priority of soul to body. Or primacy may be taken in the sense of mastery, and mean spirit's omnipotence in the world, and in the individual the dominance of soul over body. When logical primacy is intended it means that no adequate account can be given of anything in the natural world without ultimately revealing its dependence upon spirit. For example, idealists have sometimes held that to be real anything must be intelligible, and that nothing can be intelligible without being in some fashion the expression of intelligence; hence the reality of anything implies a mind that thinks and is thus dependent on spirit. In the Platonic theory the analysis of things leads to the eternal Ideas they embody; in the Berkeleyan version it leads logically to spirit as the creator of ideas whose association is what we call things.

Where primacy has the connotation of first in importance the primacy of spirit may mean the importance of the functions assigned to spirit (whether God or soul): its being the source of motion for a matter that is conceived to be inert, of perception and thought, of purpose and rationality in human life and in the universe, or even of all that men call existence. In the case of the individual spirit this primacy of spirit often means that the world is not alien to human spirit, that it is a creature or emanation or form of activity of the wider spirit to which the individual belongs as part; or else it may point to the contrast of eternal soul and temporal body. In the social studies it

[26] P. 315.

means explaining human conduct in terms of men's ideas and ideals rather than by reference to the material forces that operate upon them. In morals it means giving first place place to the phases of life which are chosen as characteristic of spirit.

IDEALIST AND MATERIALIST INTERPRETATIONS OF THE ETERNAL

Nothing is more typical of the many forms of idealistic theory than the emphasis on the eternal. The place it holds in the idealist interpretation of spirit is comparable to the stress on change in the materialist analysis of matter. Change is taken to be rooted in the bodily, the material, the temporal; the unchanging, the immaterial, and the timeless characterize spirit. Even where idealism describes matter as inert and attributes the source of movement to spirit, the movement itself is often either an unreal shadow of the eternal or else the attraction of the inferior material to the unchanging spiritual.

Meaning of "eternal" in the idealist tradition. The idea of the eternal covers a number of fairly distinct notions. The following are some of these.

(a) A process going on forever would be called eternal because it is *temporally unending*. Aristotle, for example, conceived of the motion of the heavenly bodies and also the generations of men as thus unending. Sometimes the term "infinite" is used with this meaning.

(b) An individual thing that continues to exist and whose central characteristics do not change through time may be considered eternal because it is *unchanging*. In this sense Aristotle thought of the earth as eternal, and many take the individual soul to be eternal.

(c) Some entities are thought of as eternal not because they continue to exist in time, but because they are *essentially non-temporal*. Thus universals were considered eternal by Plato. Laws of nature have often been taken to be eternal in this sense, because although the phenomena they "govern" are in time, they do not themselves have spatio-temporal existence.[27] The relation of this type of the eternal and the temporal is sometimes compared to that of a mathematical formula and its instances. The formula expresses the truth of a whole series of numbers (which may be eternal itself in the sense of endless). Figuratively we sometimes speak of the formula "generating" the series. So the eternal may "father" the temporal.

Even a truth describing a singular event may be regarded as eternal in the sense of unchangeable in time, since nothing happening in the future will alter the truth of the assertion about the past. In this sense "facts" are often regarded as eternal.[28]

[27] For a discussion of this view, see above, Chapter 4.
[28] See above, p. 130.

Since thinking involves language and language manipulates terms and terms have a universal reference, thinking is often taken in idealist theory to be a pre-eminent method of grasping the eternal.

Role of the eternal in idealist philosophy. Eternity, in one or another of its senses, is a central characteristic of spirit in the various forms of idealist theory. It characterizes the Platonic Ideas, the One of Plotinus and the mystics, the God of the western religious tradition, the Plan of the World in the objective idealists. The human spirit, itself conceived of as eternal, is also held to be striving for the eternal. In some theories this means that knowing is man's highest activity in which he grasps the eternal that is Truth; in others, as we noted above [29] it means a striving for timeless ecstatic union with the One or God. In Objective Idealism the role of the human spirit is to achieve a growing realization of its roots in the World-Spirit, which provides the meaning of life. In Supernaturalistic Idealism there is (in the western tradition) the promise to the soul of an eternal career beyond the confines of the present life. The central trend of philosophical idealism in relation to the human spirit is thus to ascribe it a cosmic role or an eternal destiny.

Materialist attitude toward the eternal. The materialist attitude toward the eternal is, of course, conditioned by its emphasis on the pervasiveness of change. Since time is a measure of change, there is no escape from the temporal as long as there is change. If eternity has any meaning it must represent some phase of the continuous process or change that characterizes the world. Clearly that phase is the relative constancy revealed at different points in change, without which even temporary stability, knowledge, and purpose would be impossible. The materialist analysis may be examined in each of the senses of the *eternal* distinguished above.

(a) The temporally unending would, for the materialist, be the most proper and legitimate sense of eternal. Whether anything is eternal in this sense could not be judged *a priori,* but requires to be established by evidence. If anything is thus unending it is more likely to be a continuous process than a single existent.

(b) It is highly improbable that an individual of any existent kind could continue to exist endlessly maintaining the characteristics central to it. Thus it is better not to think of things in this world as sharply fixed existents. Without ignoring their individuality we may view things as systems of forces maintaining a relative constancy and an only relatively stable equilibrium. We shall not be surprised to find points of disequilibrium making for change, as when water turns to steam, a flower to fruit, a body disintegrates or a nation collapses.[30] Materialists are thus prone to regard as an

---
[29] P. 141.
[30] Compare also above, pp. 322-23.

idealist mode of thought any consideration of existents *in isolation* as possessing an essence irrespective of their relations to the rest of the world.

(c) The eternity of universals is interpreted by philosophical materialism as a figurative way of describing the relative fixity of terms in discourse. A term is a device for noting recurrent elements in the temporal world about us. It does not designate a non-temporal entity. Similarly laws of nature tell us of uniformities or regularities in temporal existence, not of some eternal entities regulating existence.[31]

In general, the materialist's approach takes the non-temporal to refer to some abstracted phase of temporal process rather than to something utterly different and opposed to it. To lose the sense of time in some arresting thought or observation involves fastening attention upon the object apart from its relations to changes going on about it which constitute its temporal relations. This concentration abstracts from but does not transcend the temporal.

Similarly the eternity of truth can be given a temporal reference on a materialist interpretation. As we saw above, to call a statement true is to predict that it would be supported or verified in an endless testing of its consequences, actual or possible.[32]

The striving of the spirit for the eternal is taken on the materialist interpretation to represent man's striving for stability. Man finds himself in a shifting world, in an environment which he has not yet successfully mastered and of which he has only limited knowledge. The materialist approach seeks to analyze the hopes and fears to which this striving for the eternal gives expression and to provide a resolution for them in terms of man's life within this world.[33]

The conduct of human life

Difference in attitudes. The materialist looks upon things as forms of matter, relative equilibria exhibiting a rich variety of qualities. He expects change, and he expects to base his actions on knowledge acquired by empirical methods. His attitude to the conduct of life is therefore basically this-worldly. The idealist looks upon things as exhibiting some spiritual plan. That plan bears the stamp of eternity, and is the genuine reality of this world. Its revelation comes in some supra-empirical method. Change and the empirical methods by which it is charted are secondary. The idealist atti-

[31] Compare above, pp. 42-45.

[32] See the discussion of truth in Chapter 10, especially pp. 128-29.

[33] For this contrast of idealist and materialist attitudes, see their interpretation of religion in Chapter 22.

tude to the conduct of life is thus either directly other-worldly, the spirit moving in things of this world as a stranger in a hostile country, or at the very least non-worldly, trafficking with things only for their spiritual meaning, regarding them not as goods but as counters or symbols for the spiritual values they embody.

Outlook of particular men often composite. The outlook of particular men is often a composite of both idealism and materialism. Materialists will allow non-empirical methods in some areas of their lives, and often their hopes of the future course of events will become so fixed as to function in a manner comparable to an assumed eternal scheme of existence. Idealists must reckon to some extent with matter and its processes; especially in the modern world large areas of their lives often are guided predominantly by empirical studies of existence in a quite materialist fashion. Sometimes, in fact, their idealistic outlook is distinguishable only in a corner of their lives, separated from their regular conduct as sharply as many a business man's Sunday is separated from his weekday practices. In examining the contrast of outlooks we are not therefore marshaling all men into one of two distinct compartments, but indicating two distinct modes of viewing life.

WHERE IN LIFE IS PHILOSOPHIC OUTLOOK TO BE FOUND?

If we focus our attention on an individual and ask where we can find his idealist or materialist outlook, the question is by no means a simple one. We may, of course, look to his professed beliefs, not merely in formal philosophy, but also in religion, morality, and the explanations he gives of the conduct of men. But professed beliefs do not always have the direct influence in human affairs that might be expected, and in addition, we have distinguished between a theory and an outlook or theory embodied in attitudes and action. It is therefore appropriate to ask whether we can distinguish a man's outlook in the items of his conduct, in the motives that lie behind it, or in some other more general pattern.

Items of conduct. In theory there is no item of conduct which indicates uniquely one type of philosophic outlook. If we take extreme cases, the sensualist is usually this-worldly, while the ascetic is usually other-worldly or non-worldly; and this is more likely where we have consistent conduct of this sort, not merely isolated acts. However, sensualism may in some represent a desperate search for the flavor of eternity, while asceticism in others may represent dejected worldliness.

The theoretical possibility of these extremes, and in fact their occurrence, does not, however, preclude the possibility of making generalizations about outlook from conduct. It simply means that the generalizations will have to be empirical and historical in character. By and large, however, when we infer outlook from classes of actions we usually have in mind some reference to the kind of motives that accompany them.

Motives and values. If we focus attention on motives instead of behavior, the difficulties that we noted to some extent repeat themselves, but the results are more stable. We do find a *prima facie* catalogue of this-worldly and other-worldly or non-worldly goals: for example, wealth and fame, as contrasted with eternal salvation and strict adherence to duty. It is, of course, possible that in some love of fame may be a striving for vicarious immortality, while in others the picture of heaven may be stocked with worldly goods. Nor is it the case that devotion to duty as such, or a fine sense of what are ordinarily called spiritual values, are peculiar to idealism.

It follows that although motives and values may provide a good rough index of outlook, we cannot rest content with simply isolated motives or even sets of values. Outlooks represent a higher phase of unity in the life and conduct of individuals. They refer to patterns or organizations of values.

Patterns of value and patterns of justification. The motive or goal sought in performing an act provides us with some understanding of that behavior in terms of the values of the individual. It removes the contingency of the act, and puts it into a small system. The system is broadened considerably when the motive or isolated value is in turn seen as part of a wider pattern or organization of values. Outlooks are primarily qualities of such organizations rather than of single values.[34]

In the conduct of life we attempt to represent our value-patterns as patterns of justification of our action and of our motives. It is important therefore to examine the relation between the justification and that which it seeks to justify.

In the first place, there is often a greater agreement on concrete values among men than on the pattern of justification. For example, honesty is a virtue in many different ethical systems, ordained in one as the will of God, in another as the verdict of experience in producing harmonious relations of men, in a third as the mark of an ultimate love of man for man. Now the pattern of justification is far from irrelevant to concrete values held and to definite behavior. Just as two mathematical formulae may yield the same results within a given range and yet yield different results beyond it, so the patterns of justification whose quality is materialist and those whose quality is idealist may incline men in different directions beyond the range of common agreement.

This phenomenon is seen on a large scale in historical disputes over human institutions. For example, absolute monarchy was justified in the England of the Stuarts by the theory of the divine right of kings. Hobbes justi-

---

[34] For patterns of values as patterns of the self, see above, pp. 203-04; cf. below, pp. 436-40.

fied it in materialistic terms as the best way of maintaining peace and security.[35] Both would agree on general obedience to the monarch. But there would be points of possible disagreement. Thus on Hobbes' view it would not be the duty of a man sentenced to death to obey the king, since for him the basis for which he sought security was to be removed. Again, Hobbes could claim that if a king had been deposed and his supporters had done the best they could to restore him, they could make peace with the new ruler who had successfully maintained himself. More important than these, however, is the fact that the different justifications provide a different character for the very act of obedience on which both agree. The one is a surrender in terms of a divine plan, eternal and irrevocable. The other embodies a conditional attitude. It rests on what is changeable. Its appeal is ultimately to the experience of men, and future knowledge, gained by empirical means, may prove its own undoing. The difference in tone is not, therefore, merely a feeling element, but a definite potentiality of varying conduct under other conditions. On many occasions, historically, the shift in its mode of justification is the first breach in the fortifications of an entrenched institution.

Patterns of justification thus represent broader values in men's value-systems. The materialist and idealist outlook represent the very widest such patterns, embracing in their account attitudes to the cosmos as a whole, to fundamental methods, and to human life. As such they may provide a different tone to present action, even where the actual behavior is the same. They may point in different directions in rapidly changing conditions, even though they do not show exact paths. On the canvas of history they may be traced in the large scale movements of mankind. And in the areas of human life they appear as divergent interpretations of major fields of human activity. In the chapters that follow we shall examine the idealist and materialist interpretations of religion, art, and moral and social life.

[35] For Hobbes' general position, see above, p. 161.

Chapter 22   INTERPRETATION OF RELIGION

The phenomena of religion

Religion has been an important phase of human life in the history of mankind. No society has ever been reported in which men have not conceived of their welfare as being in some degree dependent upon supernatural or extraordinary powers. In the process of attaining security through control of or adjustment to such powers they have established different patterns of conduct, belief, and feeling. In some societies religion has been an isolated phase—a separate department of supernatural relations, requiring man's attention only upon given occasions. In others religion has been a mold in which almost all of life's activities have been shaped, so that from his earliest lisp to his last breath a man lives in the eyes of God, following all the details of God's plan for the righteous, feeling every striving as a command issuing from God or a yearning towards God, and greeting every turn of fortune as burden or blessing divinely ordained. Between these extremes lie most societies; study of them provides a brilliant display of the depth and breadth of human feeling, insight, and imagination.

Religion has been especially important in western culture, and our conception of it is likely to be fashioned in terms familiar to us. Most people in our culture regard themselves as belonging to one or another religious faith. They go to church, pray, try to regard their fellow-men as brothers. They feel that the world is being well taken care of by an all-powerful spiritual being whom they look upon as the Father. In their religious beliefs they find consolation for the death of near ones, and reassurance about their own destiny after death. When they have moral and spiritual problems there are definite persons in the framework of their religion to whom they owe respect and to whom they can go for authoritative and sympathetic advice. In all their efforts they are buttressed by a spiritual framework and all their sufferings are eased by a spiritual solace.

Religions have, however, taken quite different forms. In framing a more rounded conception we are, therefore, aided considerably by the variety of forms discovered by anthropological, sociological, and historical studies of religious phenomena in the Orient, in primitive societies, and in the changing phases of the western tradition itself. These studies of religious phenomena (a question independent of the truth of religious beliefs) provide wide comparative material and enable students of religion to analyze its central features.

USUAL FEATURES OF A RELIGION

It is commonly agreed today that religions generally contain one or more of the following features:

(1) An idea of the *supernatural*, as distinct from the natural. This ranges from the vaguer ideas of the "extraordinary," the "inspiring," the "awesome," the "holy," to explicit theological accounts of God and the attributes of divinity. The supernatural may be conceived personally, as God is in the western tradition, or as spirits are in *animism*, or impersonally as vibrant power or force acting in its own special way (e.g., the Polynesian idea of *mana*).

(2) Organized repeated and purposive behavior with respect to the supernatural. This is *ritual*. It covers the procedures of prayer, sacrifice, magic, and prescribed ceremonials at stated or special occasions. Anthropologists have found that the same ritual may have various meanings attached to it in different societies or periods, and the shift in meaning may often be clearly traced (e.g., the incorporation of pagan customs into Christian ritual). There is great variation between religions with respect to the amount of ritual and the degree of participation by religious laymen.

The general intent of ritual seems to be to influence the supernatural or adjust to it for man's welfare. There have been numerous theories concerning different types of ritual and their relation, but there is increasing agreement on regarding it as simply the application of ordinary human techniques to the domain of the extraordinary.[1] Thus in ordinary life men entreat, cajole, bargain, promise, reward, and offer expressions of gratitude; so too in religion we find not only prayer and all the familiar varieties of sacrifice, but also bribery and even threats. In ordinary life men use coercion on things and on people; so too in religion they use magic and witchcraft, and exercise of compulsion on the supernatural, to bring about desired results. Such rituals also provide release for a variety of human emotions. It is worth noting that the various types of physical behavior are not associated with specific meanings; thus speech may be either a compulsive formula of magic or a prayer or a promise of sacrifice.

(3) A specific class of *emotions* with regard to the supernatural. These take different forms such as feelings of awe or inspiration or of absolute dependence, a sense of the holy, a loss of the sense of self, an ecstasy of extreme possession of oneself by the spirit. Sometimes such responses are a

---

[1] See Ruth Benedict, "Religion," in Boas and others, *General Anthropology*, Heath, 1938; also Santayana, *Reason in Religion*, Scribner's, 1905.

standard part of religious expectation (as among revivalist sects and some American Indian tribes); sometimes they are an unusual but highly revered phenomenon (such as the visions of saints in the Christian tradition). In some religions, however, such experiences are almost wholly absent.

(4) A definite class of *beliefs* concerning the universe and men's place in it. This varies from unsystematized myths or formal cosmologies, such as the creation in *Genesis* or in Greek myths, to the systematic theologies of the western tradition which, as reasoned accounts, are definite types of philosophical systems. Such beliefs are not the rule in religions throughout the world, and the prevalent tendency to interpret religion as primarily a system of explanation is an historical function of western rationalism. Sometimes even where there are stories of creation they are not tied in any significant way to religion, any more than a scientific account of astronomical evolution need be. American Indian tales of creation frequently have this non-religious character; for example, a jokester may make the world as an accidental consequence of his pranks.

(5) A definite *ethical credo,* as in the ten commandments. This again is not found in all religions. The prevalent belief that without religious sanctions there can be no morality stems primarily from the western tradition. Moral rules often appear simply as rules of what is to be done, without being conceived by the people in question as related to their religion. Just as the Greek gods were themselves highly immoral—by Greek as well as modern standards—so in many primitive religions the gods may be entirely amoral, concerned for example with the offerings made to them rather than with the general good conduct of their suppliants.

(6) A special body of religious functionaries. This is a *priesthood*. It varies in type from independently functioning practitioners (shamans, diviners, etc.) to an organized craft (as in the western churches). An organized priesthood tends to develop a complex body of esoteric lore. The priesthood often becomes a powerful force in the life of a community.

RELIGION AS A SOCIAL FORM

As a social form religion has been studied in its interaction with other phases of the life of a society. Sometimes it provides sanctions regulating wide segments of men's conduct, as in the Christian teaching of a punishment in the next world, or among primitive tribes, the fear of contamination, which is a ground for avoiding relations with those who have broken a taboo. Sometimes its techniques serve as devices for secular use, as when in some societies a man places a magical charm on property to give pause to possible marauders. At its widest, religion becomes a mold for a great part of human activity. Thus ideals in every field may come to be conceived as religious duties: to have children is a religious duty among Catholics, to help one's fellow-men among Christians generally, to prove by economic success that one belongs to the saved among Calvinists, and so forth. Even where religion ceases to concern itself with everyday human affairs it may provide broad humanitarian ideals, or remain a cushion for softening hard blows of death and distress. Max Weber has shown the important role religion played in sharpening the attitudes of thrift, industry, individualism and what he calls rationalization that were constituents of the rise of capitalist enterprise.[2] The clash of religion and science, the conflict of religion and nationalism, the role of religion in social trends and similar interrelations with various phases of social activity are not phenomena to be understood by *a priori* deduction from a definition of religion, or even by an examination of a specific theology. They involve careful historical study of the functioning of churches and their ministers, of the effects of religious beliefs in the detailed attitudes and activities of men, even of the direction in which the material resources of churches (land, buildings, often considerable monetary wealth, legal privileges) are utilized.

Such, in brief outline, are the phenomena of religion. Philosophic problems arise not so much from their description as from their interpretation. What is the nature of religious belief, religious practice, and religious feeling? Are they in some fashion *cognitive,* bringing a knowledge of a spiritual order in our universe, alongside of and transcending the daily sensible world? If so, what is this spiritual order like, what is the role in it of the individual spirit, what avenues of insight, reason, feeling, are open for its inspection? What, in short, is the character of God and the individual soul, and how can we know about them? Or are religious phenomena simply culturally developed modes of expression, thought, and feeling, pointing to nothing but the source from which they issued—the fears and hopes and bewilderment of man in a world of nature he does not understand and cannot control? These alternatives indicate roughly the paths taken by the idealist and the materialist analyses of religion. In the remainder of this chapter we shall, therefore, consider the views of idealists and materialists on the existence of God, the individual soul and immortality, and the role of religion in human life.

Arguments on the existence of God

There have been many conceptions of God, modeled on diverse relationships found in the world. God has been conceived as impersonal force and as personal being; as one (monotheism) and as many (polythe-

[2] *The Protestant Ethic and the Spirit of Capitalism,* transl. by Talcott Parsons, Scribner, 1930. See also R. H. Tawney, *Religion and the Rise of Capitalism,* Harcourt, Brace, 1926.

ism); as transcendent to the world (deism), as wholly immersed throughout it (pantheism), and as in some sense in and apart from it (theism). The attributes assigned to God have likewise been diverse. God has been thought of as omnipotent and omniscient, as one of conflicting forces and as a growing power; as creator of the world and the source of its perfection, and as the very totality of the world; as guardian of values and as indifferent to values; as harsh judge, arbitrary ruler, kindly father, big brother. Most of these conceptions are found within the western religious and philosophical tradition, although their variety is considerably enriched by examination of Mohammedanism and various oriental and primitive religions.

Since philosophical idealism takes this world to be ultimately spiritual in character, it usually involves some conception of God. Even where it declines to draw a sharp distinction between the natural and the supernatural this is largely because the natural itself is regarded as ultimately revealing a spiritual design. Consideration of the various arguments that have attempted to establish the existence of God therefore reveals particularly the character of the idealist approach to the world at large. To some extent, however, it also exhibits the character of the materialist approach; for the latter is here concerned in each context with showing that the phenomena about which the controversy centers can be explained in naturalistic terms.

That the approach to the problem of God's existence has been varied might be anticipated from the conflict of methods upon which men have relied in the search for knowledge. There have been attempts to establish the existence of God on rational grounds, showing it as entailed or necessitated by other ideas which are accepted. There have been attempts to adduce empirical evidence, phenomena for which God's existence is offered as the sole or more intelligible hypothesis. There have been arguments based on moral grounds and promptings to belief on practical grounds. There have been intuitive approaches, pointing to a clear and unassailable idea in men's minds, and mystical approaches that disparaged argument in an appeal to the light of ecstasy. And there have even been some who concluded that no avenue of human awareness was sufficient to yield knowledge of God's existence, so that revelation alone saves men from what would otherwise be sheer ignorance of God.[3]

Such approaches have for the most part not been correlated with any specific religion. Several are likely to be found in each of the great religious traditions. Thus the conflict of rationalism and mysticism arises periodically in the development of Christian doctrine, and is also found in Mohammedan and Hebraic philosophy.

[3] In the Christian tradition, William of Occam is a good illustration of this view. He was led to it by his belief that human knowledge of existence came only from sensible experience.

COSMOLOGICAL AND TELEOLOGICAL ARGUMENTS

Spirit as "first cause" of the world. The conception of spirit as the cause of our world was developed early in Greek philosophy. Anaxagoras worked out the conception of an original state of the universe in which everything was thoroughly mixed together in an undifferentiated mass of being. Only mind (*nous*) was pure, and it set this whole into motion, and by the separation and combination that ensued the various things of this world were formed. Plato in his *Phaedo* has Socrates describe how he became dissatisfied with a mechanistic approach to physical phenomena and how excited he was when he heard of this conception of Anaxagoras'. "I said to myself: If mind is the disposer, mind will dispose all for the best, and put each particular in the best place; and I argued that if anyone desired to find out the cause of the generation or destruction or existence of anything, he must find out what state of being or doing or suffering was best for that thing, and therefore a man had only to consider the best for himself and others, and then he would also know the worse, since the same science comprehended both."[4] He was thoroughly disappointed to discover that Anaxagoras used mind chiefly to get the world started and thereafter relied largely on physical explanations.

This comment makes clear that there is really a variety of meanings of "first cause." The traditional first cause or *cosmological* arguments manifest this variety.

The first cause as temporally prior to the world. "First" is interpreted by some in a temporal sense. Since every event in nature has a cause and that event which was the cause itself has a cause, we have an endless series unless we come to a stop somewhere. Is it not reasonable to assume a starting-point in the causal series? Is it not then reasonable to assume that this starting-point is a spirit comparable to our own? Just as our own spirit sets in motion our own causal activity, so a greater spirit, which we may call God, is the starting-point of the causal series which constitutes the events of our world.

Critiques of this conception. Critiques of this argument, emanating from both materialist and idealist sources, find difficulty with this concept of a temporally first cause. If God as the first term in a causal series is part of the series, then since everything has a cause why may we not look further for the cause of God? If God has no cause, then the initial premise that everything has a cause is untrue and cannot be used as part of the proof of God's existence. If, on the other hand, God is outside the series of causes, then what is the type of causation involved in his being the first cause? Ordinarily

---

[4] *Phaedo* 97 (Jowett's translation).

a change implies existing material upon which a causal force, itself existing in nature, operates, making it assume a different form. But God's primary causation *from outside of nature*—whether of the whole world or part of it—would have to be something entirely different; hence no premises about what we mean by causation in nature help establish its existence.[5] This holds whether there was prior material for God to work on—in which case it was not the beginning of things but simply intervention at a definite point in the course of nature—or whether creation was *ex nihilo* and time created in the same act. Furthermore, many philosophers have claimed that the world as a whole is not a thing or event and that "cause" is a relationship *between things in this world*. Hence it would be a confusion of ideas to speak of a cause of the world.

Have matter and change always existed? Such problems, especially those engendered by the concept of a starting-point for time itself, have led many philosophers to prefer the alternative that there was no beginning in time and that matter and change were uncreated and have always existed. Aristotle, who was himself the founder of another type of first cause argument, held to this view, a fact which militated at first against his favorable acceptance in Catholic doctrine.

If both alternatives—a first cause in time and no first cause in time—were clearly worked out without ambiguity in the conceptions of causation, first, etc., the decision between them could not be *a priori*. Thomas Aquinas recognized this when he held that the belief in an uncreated and eternal universe was not philosophically unsound, and rested the case for the doctrine of creation on revelation. Empirical philosophies would regard the decision to lie in the province of the relevant sciences, that is, in astronomy, physics, geology, and biology. These sciences apparently find a temporal first cause conception an unnecessary addition to their theoretical equipment.

Aristotelian view of first cause as "final" cause. Another common meaning of first cause turns out ultimately to be teleological in character. Aristotle's identification of God as the Prime Mover, the unchanging eternal source of motion in the world, is such a conception. God is the *final* cause of movement in the sense of the purpose toward which all movement tends.

[5] Kant formulates this objection as follows: "If the supreme being should itself stand in this chain of conditions, it would be a member of the series, and like the lower members which it precedes, would call for further enquiry as to the still higher ground from which it follows. If, on the other hand, we propose to separate it from the chain, and to conceive it as a purely intelligible being, existing apart from the series of natural causes, by what bridge can reason contrive to pass over to it? For all laws governing the transition from effects to causes, all synthesis and extension of our knowledge, refer to nothing but possible experience, and therefore solely to objects of the sensible world, and apart from them can have no meaning whatsoever." (From N. Kemp Smith, *Immanuel Kant's Critique of Pure Reason*, pp. 518-519. By permission of the Macmillan Company, publishers.)

Since it is itself not in motion the Prime Mover operates not by efficient causation but by attraction. God arouses motion as the good stirs desire or as the object of thought stirs thinking.[6]

The sense in which causality is here employed may be suggested by looking at the language sometimes used in describing the relation of scientific laws to existence. Newton's law of gravitation is said to "govern" the movement of bodies, or the motion of bodies is said to "approximate" Newton's law. Clearly the law does not exert causal efficacy in the ordinary sense, nor do bodies strive to fit the formula. But something analogous to this seems to be implicit in Aristotle's description of the relation of God and the universe. God is almost the living rational nature of the universe which the things of this world are striving to express and conform to.

This view ultimately teleological. The argument for the existence of a God as thus conceived rests in Aristotle on his detailed analysis of motion or change, potentiality and its actualization, matter and form, and so forth. Some suggestion of the outlines of his system was offered in Chapter 2. Since its bent is ultimately teleological it is best here to consider the teleological argument for God's existence independently and in its own more traditional form.

Formulation of the design argument. The teleological or design argument states that there is an order discoverable in the universe, clearly manifest, for example, in the special adaptation of various types of life to natural conditions, and in the fitness of natural conditions to various types of life. All this cannot be accidental. To call it so is as absurd, some say, as to claim that a monkey sitting at a typewriter pressing the keys at random could turn out a Shakespearean play! There must therefore be purpose or design in things, for only thus can the existent order be explained. And this implies God as designer. Paley's watch analogy is directed towards the same point. In this famous analogy the theologian argued that just as discovery of a watch would lead us to infer a watch-maker, because of the fine co-ordination of its parts, so observation of the world and the wondrous ways in which its parts fit should lead us to infer a maker.

Question of the existence of such order. Objections to this argument take two forms. They question the existence of the order described; and they maintain that even an existent order does not require an explanation in terms of a designer. On the first point, the objector calls attention to the disorder, chaos, and waste which are found in a great part of nature. Even some of nature's finer instruments, such as the eye, do not, in spite of their utility, show the perfection of construction which an all-wise designer might have been expected to work out. So, at least, Helmholtz remarked, after his careful studies of vision.

---

[6] Aristotle, *Metaphysics,* Book XII, Chapter 7.

Does order presuppose purpose? On the second point the objector argues against the assumption that a complicated pattern cannot be accidental. After all, even a play by Shakespeare can be described as a definite combination of a limited number of letters and spaces; each set of alternative combinations is as probable as any other, if the monkey's movements are completely random. Therefore, according to the mathematical theory of probability, given indefinite time a Shakespeare play can turn up eventually. Thus, even if there were no positive explanatory theory, such as evolutionary theory, to give an account of discoverable order, chance could not be completely ruled out. Likewise, an argument from the suitability of the environment for man —that the physical and chemical properties of the environment are just right for the bodily needs of a complex, highly regulated mechanism—to something like purpose in cosmic and biologic evolution [7] simply begs the question. It conceives of man as if he were prior in existence and marvels to see him so well provided. If, on the other hand, we think of a long interacting development involving successful adjustment and elimination of the species not adjusted, there need be no surprise that man or any other creature as he exists today lives in an environment roughly suitable for his existence.

Evolution, not chance, the formidable opponent of design. The design argument cannot therefore rest on the *a priori* assumption that designing, an activity modeled on human purpose as observable in human works, is entailed wherever order is found. The hypothesis of design for whatever order is discoverable in the universe requires to be established by empirical evidence in competition with the chance theory and any other proposed solutions. In empirical investigation the design theory has suffered severely from the widespread acceptance of the theory of evolution, which gives an account confirmable by biologic and geologic evidence of the development and principles of development of animal forms. Accordingly today the theory which the design argument propounds has no status as a principle of biologic explanation. The feeling that the universe and life *must* have a purpose finds expression instead in the moral argument to be considered below.

Similar analysis of empirical arguments. The same kind of analysis that is applied to the design argument once it is regarded as a proposed explanation for discoverable phenomena in the world, may also be applied to what are generally called empirical arguments for the existence of God. These offer evidence in the occurrences of nature and human life which, it is asserted, only the hypothesis of a divine being or spiritual force can account for. Among such occurrences miracles have, of course, been the most prominent. A miracle is an event happening contrary to the expectations based on natural laws, so that it is interpreted as an intervention of God upon moral or human principles—to reward, punish, or effect some other objective, such

---

[7] E.g., L. J. Henderson, *The Fitness of the Environment*, Macmillan, 1913.

as display of powers. The argument based upon miracles is thus based in turn upon an interpretation of the world through moral or human categories. With the development of the sciences such interpretation has yielded largely to causal categories.

Nevertheless there have continued to be appeals to special types of phenomena as requiring the explanatory hypothesis of an existent God. William James, for example, as we have seen in considering his theory of meaning,[8] sought phenomena of intensely religious experience (as in conversion involving refashioning of one's life over-night) to support the conception of God as a reservoir of spiritual strength upon which men may draw to bring serenity into their lives. James' claims, however, suffer at the hands of psychological theories which offer an account of conversion and intense emotion in terms of the dynamics of personality. What is more, the same types of emotional experiences are found in non-religious contexts.

ONTOLOGICAL, INTUITIONAL AND MYSTICAL ARGUMENTS

Formulation of ontological argument. This argument begins by stating that the idea of God is the idea of a completely perfect being. Now such a perfect being would have diminished perfection (hence not be perfect) if it lacked the attribute of existence. Therefore, since the idea of God as a perfect being requires our conceiving him as existing, and since we do have this idea, it can only be concluded that God exists. This clearly begs the question, since all that could be concluded is that we have the idea of God existing. Hence if the argument is to be valid there must be some *further* tacit assumption about the nature of having ideas or of having ideas of perfect beings or of having the unique idea of the completely perfect being (perfection in *all* respects) which is God. Further inquiry shows at least two directions in which the ontological argument may be developed.

One possible basis in Platonic theory of ideas. It may derive its force from the Platonic type of theory of intellectual insight which we examined on several occasions above.[9] To have an idea of something is to be in direct intellectual contact with it, hence to know it. "I have an idea that . . ." actually implies knowing, and not, as in everyday usage now, "I guess that . . ." Hence to have an idea of God as a perfect being that exists means knowing that God, a perfect being, exists.

On this Platonic interpretation every object of the intellect is an Idea or perfect type. Hence the argument does not concern the unique idea of God. It could equally well be said that the idea of a perfect man implies our con-

---

[8] See above, p. 98. See James' *Varieties of Religious Experience,* Longmans, Green, 1903.
[9] See above, Chapters 2 and 6.

ceiving of a perfect man existing and hence that he exists. Clearly, however, this meaning of existence cannot be the same as the usual notion of spatio-temporal existence. It is rather the kind of reality that is eternal and unchanging which Plato claimed for his Ideas and the theological tradition similarly sought for God. It is the kind of reality that the medieval *realists* ascribed to universals or concepts as against the *nominalists,* who held that general terms were merely signs of existing singular things.[10]

Criticism of concept of existence involved. In modern philosophy there has been some attempt to speak of universals "subsisting" and particulars "existing." But even where universals are not conceived of in nominalist fashion as purely linguistic elements signifying groups of existents, they are more likely to be considered as referring to possibilities or ideals rather than as actualities or existences. When scientific results are stated under ideal conditions—the law of the lever for perfectly rigid bodies, for example [11]—it is not felt that a perfectly rigid body must somewhere exist. In fact it is believed that the ideal represents a *null class,* a class having no existent members. Our conception of the ideal may be formed by arranging a set of existents in such order as to exhibit an increasing or decreasing degree of a certain quality. The ideal will then be the theoretical limit of such a series. Its utility in stating formulae by which we can study such existents does not mean that it itself exists. Santayana has carried this idea to the opposite extreme of the ontological argument by suggesting that existence entails imperfection; an ideal, he holds, keeps its perfect character only by non-existence.[12]

Kant's criticism. Kant's critique of the ontological argument was based on an analysis of the idea of existence. He argued that existence was not an attribute that increased the content of the subject of which it was predicated. A hundred real thalers are not more in number than a hundred possible thalers, although they affect my financial position differently. Thus perfection is not diminished or increased by non-existence or existence. In similar fashion modern logic has drawn the distinction sharply between existence and meaning, so that the explication of the meaning of a term just as of an ideal leaves open the question whether it applies to anything in existence.

Alternative formulation of the argument by Descartes. The second way in which the ontological argument may be developed focuses attention on the problem of how we come to have the unique idea of a completely perfect being. How, it is asked, can we explain our having this idea if God is

---

[10] "It seems that in the vast network of the medieval polemic the *nominalists* (denying the reality of universals) in general represented scientific tendencies against the Platonizing mysticism of the *realists*." Frederigo Enriques, *The Historic Development of Logic,* translation by Jerome Rosenthal, Holt, 1929, p. 45.

[11] See above, p. 43.

[12] For his application of this idea to religion, see below, p. 359.

not the cause? Descartes states this view: "Thus, because we discover in our minds the idea of God, or of an all-perfect Being, we have a right to inquire into the source whence we derive it; and we will discover that the perfections it represents are so immense as to render it quite certain that we could only derive it from an all-perfect Being; that is, from a God really existing. For it is not only manifest by the natural light that nothing cannot be the cause of anything whatever, and that the more perfect cannot arise from the less perfect, so as to be thereby produced as by its efficient and total cause, but also that it is impossible we can have the idea or representation of anything whatever, unless there be somewhere, either in us or out of us, an original which comprises, in reality, all the perfections that are thus represented to us; but, as we do not in any way find in ourselves those absolute perfections of which we have the idea, we must conclude that they exist in some nature different from ours, that is, in God, or at least that they were once in him; and it most manifestly follows [from their infinity] that they are still there." [13]

Locke's derivation of the idea of God. Clearly Descartes' answer follows only if there is a clear and distinct idea of God, and if no psychological explanation can be given of the rise of this idea. Locke's explanation can serve to illustrate the critique of this Cartesian position. He takes the complex idea of God to be "made up of the simple ideas we receive from reflection: v.g., having, from what we experiment in ourselves, got the ideas of existence and duration, of knowledge and power, of pleasure and happiness, and of several other qualities and powers which it is better to have than to be without; when we frame an idea the most suitable we can to the Supreme Being, we enlarge every one of these with our idea of infinity; and so, putting them together, make our complex idea of God. For that the mind has such power of enlarging some of its ideas, received from sensation and reflection, has been already showed." [14] And infinity itself Locke takes to be a negative not a positive notion, being an idea of endless increase. Thus our idea of God is capable of being fashioned from the materials of ordinary experience.

Ready transition to intuitional and mystical approaches. There are no sharp lines between some types of ontological argument resting on the Platonic conception of knowing and a whole gradation of *intuitional* conceptions merging in turn with the claims of the *mystical* point of view. While it is clearly impossible to do full justice to such a tradition in a brief discussion, we may indicate its outlines by a few samples.

God as ultimate totality. In many philosophies there is a conception of God as the totality of the universe, the single ultimate substance, an idea somehow apprehended directly by a kind of intellectual intuition or framed

---

[13] Descartes, *The Principles of Philosophy*, Part I, §XVIII. See whole argument, §§XIV-XXII (Everyman edition). Compare also Descartes' *Meditations* III.

[14] *An Essay Concerning Human Understanding*, Book II, Chapter 23, §33.

by reason as a necessary presupposition of the finite character of particular things. For the finite is conceived as giving definite form to reality by limiting it or presenting some phase of it. The finite, then, is not self-existent and independent. It is rather a determination of something else which alone has complete reality and complete existence. This Spinoza calls substance and defines as "that which is in itself, and is conceived through itself: in other words, that of which a conception can be formed independently of any other conception." And he defines God as "a being absolutely infinite—that is, a substance consisting in infinite attributes, of which each expresses eternal and infinite essentiality."[15] All finite existence is thus in God and can only be understood as some modification of the one substance. This view of Spinoza's is sometimes described as a kind of pantheism.

In the idealist philosophers of the Hegelian school, attention is also called to the limited or conditioned character of existent things; they are not independent or self-existent but incomplete and dependent on one another. On the other hand, the completely self-existent is deemed to be the only fully real, the only genuine substance. Ordinary existents are fragments of it, pointing to it as a completion. God is then identified with the unified totality of the universe. The chief question then becomes the character to be assigned to this Absolute, e.g., whether it should be interpreted as rational or as will.

Direct experience of God. There is often, in the second place, an appeal to an indescribable feeling or experience, of which either some people or all people are said to be capable. The experience itself has a unique quality which validates the belief in a prime spiritual power in the universe. Such experience is talked about in the language of sensing, feeling, intuiting. Among the early Christian thinkers, for example, this emphasis is prominent in Tertullian, who uttered the famous remark "Credo quia impossibile" (I believe because it is impossible), and in Augustine who held that we must first believe in order that we may know. Many thinkers have held that we have a direct intuition of God's existence comparable to that which we have of our own existence.

In Bergson's philosophy, the creative force in evolution is spoken of as a vital impulse (l'élan vital) which is God in all existence. Access to God is through direct intuition which feels this drive within one. Most men are said to have this experience though only a few gain it in its deepest form.

Plato's approach to mysticism. Perhaps the most thorough-going approaches of this whole intuitionist group are the outright mystical ones. Plato was in many respects the father of this approach in the western tradition, in the sense that several strands in his system inspired its development. Mysticism appears in the early Christian thinkers and pre-eminently in the neo-Platonists of the third century A.D. It is found as a strong move-

[15] *Ethics,* Part I, Definitions (Elwes translation).

ment in the Catholic Church, constituting the Platonic tradition as against the more rationalistic Aristotelian tradition.

Because the mystic does not deny science or reason but claims to transcend them, Plato's strongly intellectualistic philosophy, although it held the real to be intelligible, could be fitted into the mystical framework as providing the introduction to the higher insight. Plato's own account of the way in which the soul attains to knowledge fits admirably with such tendencies. Thus in the *Republic* he describes the ascent of a man from a cavern, in which he sees only the shadows of figures of things, into the light of day. At first the man is dazed and cannot distinguish real objects, feeling more at home with shadows. Then he ventures to look at the heavenly bodies and the sky by night. Only at last can he look at the brilliance of the sun itself. So the soul travels from things that are in flux to the ideas that are eternal objects to the Good which is the source of all existence and all value.[16]

Plotinus' conception of pure unity. In the elaborate mysticism of the neo-Platonist Plotinus, the further path of the soul is more carefully charted. The soul is striving towards pure Unity, and this cannot be described in any of the categories of understanding. For the One is above intelligible experience just as the intelligible is above sensible experience. Hence mystical ecstasy is the only way in which, by union with it, the One can be reached. Plotinus thought that all men were capable of such vision, although few achieved it. He further added an account of the soul's original derivation from the One. The One overflows, as it were, and Reason is the first emanation. Reason in turn overflows, yielding Soul. And just as Reason is the system of Platonic ideas, so Soul is the World-Soul containing particular souls. The World-Soul overflowing yields the physical universe. The endeavor of the individual soul is to return to the source of its being over the path by which it had descended.

Critiques of intuitional and mystical approaches involve fundamental issues of method. Critiques of the intuitive and mystical approaches ultimately resolve themselves into critiques of the methods inherent in these approaches. Intuition has been criticized for its variability, for its dogmatic inaccessibility to co-operative verification, for its occasional irrationalism, and for its failure to understand its own legitimate but limited scope as imagination suggesting hypotheses for verification.[17]

MORAL AND PRAGMATIC ARGUMENTS

Moral argument rests on a theory of values. The moral argument for the existence of God rests on the belief that the fact of man's having values tells

[16] *Republic*, Book VII.
[17] For these criticisms, see above, Chapter 6.

us something ultimate about the character of our world. Values give our life its meaning. Values are not merely strivings of men. Values are somehow at home in the world, part of its very texture, and in sensing their own strivings men are learning profound truths about their world. They learn that the universe has a kind of spiritual force within it which makes human personality count and makes values meaningful. This value-supporting force is God. If there were no God, life would have no meaning. But men find life meaningful. Therefore there must be a God.

Kant's formulation of the argument. This type of argument has been stated in different ways. Kant, for example, treats it less as a proof than as the formulation of a principle or postulate in the moral life, or a demand of his moral theory.[18] Man's duty in life is to act according to the laws of a good will. The *summum bonum,* or highest good, is happiness proportionate to such virtue. And since Kant regards it a duty of man to endeavor to promote the *summum bonum,* he holds that the latter must be possible; for it cannot be a duty to do what is not possible. But in the world there is no guarantee of happiness proportionate to virtue; the moral law simply tells a man to do his duty, and since he is not the cause of the world and of nature but is dependent on it, he cannot by his own power bring about the harmony in question. Therefore the requisite guarantee must be found in the existence of a power distinct from nature. Kant points out that this moral necessity is subjective and connected with the consciousness of our duty, and constitutes a kind of rational faith.

Is a spiritual order required to account for values? Kant's argument lays bare the hopes that have inspired the moral argument and still make it in its more general form a widely accepted basis for the belief in God's existence. Belief on the basis of the moral argument turns out to be a call for help together with an assured feeling that help will come.

If we treat the argument as a hypothesis to explain the occurrence of values in the world, objections to the argument take the form of showing that other hypotheses not involving the appeal to the deity will explain the phenomena in question. The specific content of values is found to be highly variable in different societies. The differences can be explained in terms of social factors and social needs and traditions. But what about the fundamental fact of the insistent character of values that makes them often appear not merely as attracting but as constraining men? In short, can the sense of obligation be explained without reference to a deity? The critics of the moral argument claim that the feeling of obligation is to be explained as a natural phenomenon engendered in the growing child by the relations of group life, the application of sanctions and the development of such specific

[18] *Critique of Practical Reason,* First Part, Second Book, Chapter II, § 5.

attitudes as shame and guilt.[19] Hence the explanatory purposes of the moral argument can be satisfied otherwise.

The non-explanatory functions of the argument reduce themselves to a demand that the structure of the universe support men's values—his ideals of Truth, Beauty and Goodness. This, say the critics of the argument, tells us only about what *we* find important. But it is not necessary to found these values on a religious basis. Both in a mundane sense men have been moral without a belief in God, and in an exalted sense they can come to hold the highest ideals on a non-religious basis.[20]

James' pragmatic argument. William James' pragmatic argument for a belief in God shares many elements of the Kantian approach. Kant argued that reason was incapable of resolving such ultimate questions.[21] James was satisfied with the fact that the question of God's existence is one on which all the evidence is not in or likely soon to be in: this despite the fact that, as we have seen, he also advanced empirical arguments. Kant demanded God as a practical postulate of the moral consciousness. James urged a belief in God on pragmatic grounds, choosing the alternative which, he held, would most enrich our lives.[22] This "will to believe" in vital issues has been widely attacked as incompatible with men's devotion to truth. James, however, did not intend such will as a substitute for evidence, but only as a basis of choice in what he called "live options"—issues in which a man's conduct depended upon a choice for the making of which he was without a simple knowledge of the "truth" on evidence. Perhaps the best examples today of such "faiths" in James' sense are large-scale political philosophies which embody many hypotheses for which only historians of the 21st century will be able to muster conclusive evidence. The frequency with which the question of God's existence has became a live option has diminished as the role of religion as an integrating element in western culture has diminished. Many people have, accordingly, found it possible to resolve questions of their fundamental attitudes to life in non-religious terms.

AGNOSTICISM, POSITIVISM, ATHEISM

Various forms of agnosticism. In the frank this-worldliness of its appeal the pragmatic argument makes its decision without affirming a knowledge of God's existence. In this respect it approaches *agnosticism,* the view that we do not know whether there is a God. Agnosticism may be simply sus-

---

[19] See above, pp. 224-25; also below, p. 433.
[20] For illustration of some such views, see below, p. 434 ff. John Stuart Mill's picture of his father in his *Autobiography* is a case in point.
[21] See above, p. 120 ff.
[22] See above, pp. 98-99.

pension of decision, in the belief that the evidence is equally balanced or insufficient to reach a conclusion, and is likely to remain so. Or it may indicate a Spencerian belief in an Unknowable of which we can merely say that it lies beyond the knowledge that science and philosophy can give us in unifying experience. Again, it may rest on a philosophical skepticism which asserts that our knowledge is only of the phenomenal and so cannot penetrate to an underlying reality or even know whether there is such.

Not all agnosticism irreligious. Not all agnosticism of these types is irreligious. Some, on the contrary, has been made the basis of an outlook that employs the ideas of religion and feels itself relieved of the need for rational proof. Such views stress the consciousness of God or religious feeling, the subjective phenomena rather than the question of the existence of religious objects. Schleiermacher, for example, sought to found religion on inner experience and on man's ultimate dependence.[23] In approaches of this type feeling is often given an autonomous status and regarded as a way of approaching reality, so that religious feeling is at the same time religious reality. Such tendencies derive historically from the Kantian stress on the postulates of practical reason in realms which cannot be rationally comprehended.

Positivist attitudes. Positivism, which shares with materialism its stress on scientific method as the source of reliable knowledge, has held a position which varies from agnosticism to atheism. As against agnosticism, however, positivism shifts the emphasis from the impenetrable underlying reality to the course of phenomena. Comte, the founder of positivism as a definite philosophic movement, treated theological accounts as simply an early stage of the mental development of mankind in which men assigned to things about them and to the world the type of volition they found in themselves. In contemporary positivism phenomena are considered as all that there is. Scientific knowledge, though it is all that we can attain, is not a second-rate knowledge but all that knowledge really is. The concept of God is, therefore, considered almost meaningless or perhaps expressive of emotion, and questions concerning God's existence are never reached on the ground that they cannot be formulated as problems capable of scientific verification.[24] Some positivists, however, have described reality as sensations—all science being analyzed as a device for ordering sensations—and thus have seemed to give reality a subjective and spiritual character, opening the way to religion.

Atheism. Atheism, as the derivation of the term indicates, is the denial of the existence of God. Hence, as distinguished from the positivist approach, it finds the concept of God meaningful, but asserts that there is no evidence of the existence of anything corresponding to it. Propounders of atheism

---

[23] For an account of the trends here indicated, see D. C. Macintosh, *The Problem of Religious Knowledge*, Harper, 1940, Chapter 14, "Religious Agnosticism."

[24] Cf. A. J. Ayer, *Language, Truth and Logic*, London, 1936, pp. 174-175.

rest their case in part on the belief that the arguments for God's existence fail to establish its probability. More positively the view issues from a materialistic belief in the primacy of matter and an interpretation of spirit which rules out the existence of disembodied spirit. This, as we have seen, rests ultimately on a methodological approach involving acceptance of scientific method as a basic way of understanding the universe.[25]

Attitudes toward the soul and immortality

As we have seen above,[26] the phenomena of spirit are differently interpreted by the idealist and the materialist philosophies. The latter attempt to find a place for these phenomena among the activities of man as a natural being; the former either derive them from an individual's immaterial spirit or else take them to be expressive of the essential character of the cosmos. In the field of religion the issue is generally formulated as that of the existence of the soul and its properties. In the western tradition the property about which there is chief concern is immortality.

The existence of the soul. Arguments for the existence of the soul (as an immaterial spirit efficacious in the action of the individual) have closely paralleled those for God's existence, especially the cosmological and teleological forms. It is possible that the relationship is a reverse one and that the arguments for a soul provide the model for contentions on a larger scale concerning a world-spirit that is to the universe as the soul is to the body. Thus it is said that the body requires a prime unity to hold it together in life (as contrasted with the rapidity of disintegration on death) and similarly there must be something to account for the unity of experience. Spirit is assigned as the non-material first cause (sometimes temporally, sometimes as constant support or final cause) of the individual's life. The teleological approach appears in the argument that consciousness of purpose and the design discoverable in a man's activity cannot be explained in bodily terms and thus require a more controlling entity of a spiritual character. Materialist criticism of these arguments, as in the case of the analogous arguments concerning God's existence, seeks to translate such questions into questions of empirical physiology and psychology, and to show that answers have in part been

---

[25] It should be noted, however, that not all forms of materialism have been atheistic. The Epicureans, who adopted as a metaphysical basis the atomic theory of Democritus, believed that the gods either did not exist, or if they did, were huge masses of choice-quality atoms in some far-off space, unconcerned with man. Mechanical materialists found no room for God as an hypothesis within the mechanical framework of nature, but some accepted Deism which conceived God as transcendent to the world which he created and endowed with natural laws. Some tended toward agnosticism.

[26] P. 328; also Chapters 11, 14.

provided, so that a refuge in a non-natural interpretation of spiritual phenomena is scientifically unnecessary.[27]

Conceptions of immortality. Not all people who hold to a soul theory share the belief in immortality. Some allow merely a vague and shadowy lingering on for the spirit after death. Plato in his *Phaedo* takes pains to refute the view that the soul is like a cloak which may survive the wearer but in turn wears out after a while. In the western religious tradition the picture of the soul in a future abode reaping the reward of virtue or the punishment of wickedness for all eternity is a familiar one. Such immortality is personal or individual. There has, however, been a philosophic undercurrent which disparaged the finite character of the human spirit and set up as a goal its ultimate reabsorption into the infinite spirit from which it came.[28] Such escape from the "wheel of life" was suggested in some of the Greek religious cults and some of the ancient mystic philosophies. The idea is central to Buddhism.

Arguments for immortality. The arguments for immortality are continuous with those intended to prove the existence of the soul. To establish the existence of a spiritual entity providing a first cause and a purposive unity for the body does not, of course, prove immortality, but the inference intended is that a soul of this sort, not dependent on the body, could continue to exist independent of the body. Again, just as the concept of God was analyzed to establish existence in the ontological argument, the concept of the soul is invoked to prove immortality. The soul is by definition the unity which holds together body and experience. Therefore it is simple. But death is a disintegration which breaks a complex into parts. Now the purely simple is incapable of dissolution; therefore it must be eternal. Others appeal to intuitive grounds to establish the belief that the self whose essence is experienced immediately can never die. Or a mystical basis may be sought in terms of the soul's kinship with the eternal through thought and through feeling.

Kant applied the same type of reasoning to immortality as he did to God's existence. Immortality emerges as a postulate of his moral theory; moral consciousness turns out to require a genuine possibility of achieving the *summum bonum* (happiness proportionate to virtue) and Kant feels that this demands immortality. In less sophisticated fashion men have at various times argued that the soul is too noble a work to be so easily shattered as the body seems to be, that the universe cannot be so constructed that men must always leave off unfinished the tasks they undertake in life, and that the values men hold and work for in life are so great that they must have some real basis in a universe which, after all, allows them to exist.

Empirical arguments for immortality—in addition to empirical elements

[27] See Chapter 15.
[28] See above, pp. 349-50.

in the arguments stated above—come from those who discover in psychical research phenomena which they believe cannot be explained on a naturalistic basis. Criticism of such arguments has centered both on the validity of the research by which the occurrence of the phenomena is established and on the resort to a non-naturalistic hypothesis for their explanation as over-hasty.

Finally, the pragmatic argument for immortality points to the enrichment of life which, it claims, follows on a belief in immortality.

Materialist attitudes to immortality. Since philosophical materialism denies any perpetuation of the self apart from the body, materialist discussions of the topic have sometimes consisted of a search for substitutes. There is the vicarious immortality in offspring, or in the perpetuation in others of ideals with which a man has identified himself. There is the tenuous immortality that everything has in *having been,* that is, in occupying a place in the history of the world. There is perpetuation in the effect that a man's personality may have had in fashioning other persons and the course of events. There is a kind of eternity in devoting oneself to the vision of eternal things —the philosophic view of all time and all existence. There is even a flavor of eternity to be found in moving towards perfection, in approaching or achieving our goals. Yet all these are very meager substitutes for the traditional promise of personal eternity.

From the materialist's point of view the real issue in the problem of immortality is man's attitude to death during the course of his life, and the role of this attitude in shaping the direction of his activity. We noted above the argument for the belief in immortality on the pragmatic ground of the happiness it brought to life. Some men have felt that without a hope of immortality life is meaningless. Clearly this assumes that values cannot be found within the flux of existence. On this assumption, the probable result of disbelief is pessimism or cynicism.

On the other hand, in a mature philosophical materialism, values are taken to be functions of man's life in a natural world. Death is then a natural limitation of which one must take cognizance. Within this view there is room for differing attitudes, many of which have long found popular and poetic expression. The Bontoc Igorots of the Philippines say in the case of those who die old: "You were old and old people die. You are dead and now we shall place you in the earth. We too are old and soon we shall follow you." [29] There is the ancient Epicurean who said triumphantly "I have lived" at the end of each day. There is Swinburne's fervent gratitude that things do end:

> That no life lives forever;
> That dead men rise up never;
> That even the weariest river
> Winds somewhere safe to sea.[30]

[29] Quoted in Otto Klineberg, *Social Psychology,* Holt, 1940, p. 169.
[30] *The Garden of Proserpine.*

The tone of sadness in many materialist attitudes is not necessarily a consequence of the mere fact of death. Nor is it merely a function in the western tradition of the fact that the idealist religious philosophy has been dominant so that materialism when it appears often presents the picture of *robbing* men of an eternity already pledged to them. As Swinburne's lines indicate, the sadness reflects very directly on the quality of life. A life well led may take death in its stride, expecting it just as a flower may be expected to bloom and wither. A life lived without frustration, shared with others and secure in the knowledge that others will carry on, need not tie the sum of values to its own career. It need not be indifferent to death. There is room within it for the medical attitude toward death as an enemy and life as a battle with every fort to be held and every weapon forged; the stubborn fact of death can thus be transmuted into a collective campaign to extend life. But progress will not consist solely in lengthening life; it will consist also in enriching the life thus lengthened.

Idealist interpretation of the role of religion

Our survey of the many approaches to the problem of God and the soul shows the variety of philosophical bases on which men have sought to establish a spiritual structure for the universe. Some of these bases reflect an intellectual interest—to discover a source or cause for the universe, to reveal its organized perfection, to explain its order. Some, however, show a dominantly emotional interest—to ensure a secure footing for values in the cosmos. And others represent a turning away from the physical world into the hearts of men, to find there a deeper reality than the eye can see or even the intellect grasp. Running through them all, however, is the felt need to discern the spiritual order of the cosmos, and to bring man's life into closer and more satisfactory relation to it.

Various aspects of life have been given pre-eminence in this task. Hegel, for example, finds the fullest self-consciousness of spirit, the revelation of the Absolute to itself, in philosophy; religion only approximates it in representing ultimate truth imaginatively. As we shall see in the next chapter, others have assigned a major role to art. By and large, however, the accomplishment of those aims is seen in the idealist tradition as the task of religion.

The religious channels through which revelation of the spiritual power and governance of the world is taken to come are numerous and diverse. The revelation may come in the mystical ecstasy of the saint or the faith of his followers, the reasoning of theologians, the prayer of the faithful, the acceptance of religious teachings by ordinary men, the sense of sin, the feeling of dependence, the striving for the good, or any of innumerable ways in which consciousness of God's existence and presence may be attained. Whatever form it takes, the effect of religion, on the idealist interpretation, is to make a home of the universe. It imparts to men a sense of belonging, and this practical orientation of the self constitutes the core of the outlook. In the light of the God they discover, men see their own role in the spiritual universe, the plan of spirit insofar as they are part of it, and the attitudes appropriate to that plan. Theory and outlook are thus intimately related. In Chapter 24 we shall consider some illustrations of this perspective in the realm of human affairs.

The idealist interpretation of religion can thus be stated very simply; for it consists simply in the exposition of the truth of religion. The materialist interpretation, on the other hand, is necessarily more complicated. For it does not accept religious phenomena in their own terms, but seeks to provide an explanation for them.

Materialist interpretation of the role of religion

Philosophical materialism is led by its stress on the primacy of matter and the reliability of scientific method to deny that religious phenomena constitute any revelation of a fundamental spiritual order in the universe. It attempts instead to interpret these phenomena as purely human activities, expressive of entirely human qualities—ignorance, fear, desire, hope, devotion, and the whole range of human needs and feelings. These phenomena, embodied in social institutions, are subject to all the interrelations, pressures, and modifications of all social forms.

By and large, therefore, modern materialism is less concerned with arguments about God's existence and more concerned with the psychological, historical and social character of religion as a human institution. The result is a keener appreciation of its human bases. As illustration of two detailed materialist analyses of religion we may select Santayana's interpretation and the Marxian interpretation, the former because of its broad sympathy with religious values in spite of an avowed atheism, and the latter for its example of a socio-historical treatment.

SANTAYANA'S ANALYSIS OF RELIGION AND ITS VALUES

Santayana[31] expounds the role of religion as one major strand in what he calls the life of reason. The life of reason is the organization of human impulse to produce maximum fulfillment or satisfaction. This can best be done by channeling impulse within broad goals or ideals that do no vio-

---
[31] *Reason in Religion*, Scribner's, 1905.

lence to its nature. These goals are expressed in the domains of society, art, religion, and science. Religion is an attempt to lead the life of reason through the imagination rather than through reason itself. Few can achieve the latter; the former is therefore the closest approach the mass of men have made to the life of reason.

Religions as cultural expressions. Santayana regards religions, like languages, as cultural expressions. If properly viewed, religions should not be opposed to one another. They may be judged as better or worse according to their success in humanizing men and expressing men's needs and interests harmoniously. But they are not true or false any more than languages are true or false. Judaism, Christianity, and Mohammedanism have, according to Santayana, made the great mistake of ascribing exclusive existence to their gods. Greek religion seems to him to have been more frankly anthropomorphic. The Greek gods represented natural forces or human functions important for men's well-being. Zeus is the god of the sky, Apollo, the sun, Poseidon, the sea. Hera is goddess of child-birth, Aphrodite of love. Every activity can invoke its ideal patron. Apollo brings light and the arts, and heals. Even thieves can appeal to Hermes as their patron! Santayana's own preference for Catholicism is based not merely on its esthetic appeal and its all-embracing character, but on what he takes to be its polytheism: the divinities who actually function in the lives of its devotees are saints who can give an ideal character to specific and concrete interests.

The supernatural and the natural reinterpreted as the ideal and the existent. Santayana's interpretation of religion consists in a fundamental reinterpretation of the distinction between the natural and the supernatural. Since on a materialist approach there are no disembodied spirits, the distinction of *supernatural* and *natural* is translated into one of *ideal* and *existent*. The truly significant character of the gods is their ideal character. If the gods exist they cease to be gods and become merely powerful material forces like earthquakes and volcanoes. They may then be objects of fear but not of worship. To win men's worship gods must be ideals and not existents. Religion provides another world for men to live in; it is not a world into which men may pass after death, but a different mode of experiencing their present life.

It is important to note that Santayana is not offering his views merely as a recommendation to men. He believes that what the mass of religious men have in the course of history *found valuable* in religion has been its character as ideals and symbols by which they have organized their lives. With this he contrasts theological systems which, he believes, entirely misunderstand the basis of religious appeal.

Reinterpretation of heaven and hell. A good illustration of his approach is found in his treatment of myths. If heaven and hell existed, he says, they would be of no greater ideal interest than any other physical properties of substances, much as we might have to take their effects into our reckonings.

(Just as fire burns our fingers immediately and on the spot so it would be a fact of nature that to do certain things burns us some time later in hell.) As ideal objects, however, heaven and hell designate not existents but an imaginative dramatization of the tremendous importance of choice in human conduct. To say that present choice has the character of saving or damning us for all eternity is to express a profound moral truth: "The decisions we make from moment to moment, on which the ideal value of our life and character depends, actually constitute in a few years a decision which is irrevocable."[32] To yield to temptation in the myth and provide a happy ending by having all men saved eventually—even after millions of years in hell—would be untrue to the facts of the moral life.

Of course all this could be said in the prosaic language of psychology. But its power is greater expressed through the imagination. Religion, says Santayana, is just poetry intervening to guide human affairs, using symbols charged with human meaning and emotional suggestion rather than the transparent and deliberately colorless symbols of science. In similar fashion he estimates the rituals of religion, religious techniques, and religious virtues,[33] and religious hopes such as immortality, in terms of human needs and their satisfaction in this life.

Is belief a necessary element in religion? While Santayana has brilliantly explored the human side of religion, it may be questioned whether he has not underestimated the importance of actual belief in the objects of religion. Although values may be the kernel of religion, the existence of God seems required to provide assurance that these values are rooted deep in the structure of the universe. Santayana takes this belief in the actual existence of God to be the source of religious intolerance. It does introduce the view that other religions are false, and strengthens the authoritarian elements in religion. But, after all, intolerance springs from other sources as well. Inertia as such is characteristic not only of religion but of many other fields—even scientific fields like medicine. And intolerance characterizes most large-scale enterprises that have vested economic interests which are threatened by major change. Churches may fear novelty as monopolies fear competitive inventions. Such factors rather than belief itself make for intolerance.

It may likewise be doubted whether religion could long survive in a generation not brought up to literal belief in the existence of its objects. The various strands would too easily fall apart. Ritual that was purely an expressive vehicle for ideals might readily become secular; every movement that rouses men's emotions has tended to establish its own ceremonials. Again, in our day politics in the wide sense of social movements seems to

[32] "The Poetry of Christian Dogma," in *Interpretations of Poetry and Religion*, Scribner's, 1900, p. 102.
[33] For his estimate of the latter, see above, pp. 186-87.

be the center of deep emotions; social ideals with their own symbols may readily win the loyalties that religion has often held. In *A Common Faith*,[34] Dewey in fact suggests the adjective "religious" for broad social values which lift man out of his narrow self and summon his greatest energies. In this sense nationalism and communism have been called religions, and in some cases even militant atheism might be so construed. If religion were thus secularized and equated with social philosophy, the question of the existence of religious objects would be taken over by the sciences, and the imaginative elements by the arts. Only in some individuals might the sense of the past be able to hold these elements together in anything bearing even a lingering resemblance to traditional religion.

MARXIAN SOCIO-HISTORICAL ANALYSIS

Religion the "opium of the people." The Marxist estimate of religion[35] is based on the view that it is the "opium of the people." This reflects a definite analysis of its bases and history. Religion is taken to rest primarily on men's needs and fears—as indeed Santayana and many others also hold—and to reflect a kind of collective insecurity in the face of physical dangers and social distress. Man's increasing conquest over nature has weakened one base of religion, but its social base—the pervasive suffering and insecurity that come from class exploitation—still remains. Historically, the Marxists claim, religion has turned men's minds from the correction of present evils to the hope of future goods. It has condoned starvation in this life with the promise of "pie in the sky when you die." In short, religion has provided the very attitudes of resignation upon which class domination has safely rested. Marx and Engels somewhere pointedly remark that the mortgage of the clergy on the heavenly estates guarantees the mortgage of the nobles on the earthly estates of the peasants. This is intended as a historical summary of the direction of efforts on the part of the clergy in general.

Conditions of its decline. Lenin draws an interesting conclusion from such an analysis. He is inclined to the view that religion cannot be *argued* out of existence. Although he holds that Communism, being materialistic, is not compatible with a belief in the existence of God and the hereafter, Lenin is opposed to inscribing atheism in the platform of the Communist party. Work against religion should be carried on, he believes, by positive scientific education, by insisting that insofar as the state is concerned religion be regarded as an individual or private matter, and by unifying workers regardless of religious faith in economic struggles in the course of which

[34] Yale University Press, 1934.
[35] A clear formulation of this view is found in Lenin's *Religion*, International Publishers, 1935.

they will come to see the historical role of religion. He believes that elimination of concentrated wealth and power in many organized churches would cause religion to lose much of its economic and political force. With the advent of socialism and the release of economic productive energies social insecurity would disappear. Hence religion would wither away, especially with the increase of scientific knowledge that would ensue.

Views of Lenin and Santayana compared. It is interesting to compare the two views in their implications. In urging against a similar interpretation by Gorki, Lenin warns materialists against the kind of interpretation of religion that Santayana offers. Any attempt to save religion, he argues, bolsters it and so strengthens the attitudes it has stood for. Nevertheless both Lenin and Santayana are agreed on the fundamental bases of religion—need and fear. Santayana stresses physical and psychological insecurity; Lenin social insecurity and its causes. Santayana elaborates well some of the very features of religion which Lenin condemns. According to Santayana religion provides "another world to live in." [36] And so it takes man's efforts away from this one, Lenin would add. Santayana commends the role of religion in bringing consolation in the crises of life; one of the functions of prayer is to reconcile man to the inevitable. Lenin finds religion declaring too much of human misery to be inevitable, when men should be concerned about removing it. The difference lies in the fundamentally contemplative element in Santayana's philosophy—he is trying to fit a Platonic idealism into the framework of materialism—as contrasted with Lenin's insistence on uniting theory and ideals with social action.

Historical problems in the Marxian theory. Since a great part of the Marxist theory of religion rests on an account of its historical role, any estimate must be factual in character. Without going into detailed historical considerations it is important to distinguish two relatively separate questions. One concerns religious persons and the character of their activity, the other religious beliefs and their effects on men's attitudes.

In connection with this first problem it is, of course, true that the clergy of many religions have ministered to a dominant class; the Greek Orthodox Church in Tzarist Russia is a case in point. But it is equally the case that other religions (as reflected in the activity of clergy and devout laymen) have proved a rallying point for the oppressed—for example, in the Peasant Wars in Germany. Or they have rallied to a rising class, as did the Puritans in 17th century England. Again, in any great social crisis—as in the recent Spanish civil war—members of the same church were found on both sides.

To examine the second problem—the effect of religious beliefs on men's attitudes and activities—would be a much more elaborate task. Only de-

[36] *Op. cit.,* p. 6.

tailed investigation of the historical functioning of specific religious beliefs can decide whether they stirred men or lulled them and whether there has been a predominant tendency in one direction. Some discussion of this problem of religious attitudes will be found in Chapter 24.[37]

[37] Pp. 400-07. It is to be noted that Lenin concedes that there was a time in history when "the democratic and proletarian struggle took the form of *one religious* idea against another" but thinks that time has long been passed. (*Op. cit.*, pp. 45-46.)

Chapter 23   INTERPRETATION OF ART

The phenomena and problems of art

For many people today art rests on a pedestal. It is not a part of their ordinary life. It is something to behold with reverence—to look at in a museum, to listen to in concert-halls. It pertains to monuments and public buildings. In literature it is more familiar, but even here it means poetry and Shakespeare, and not the novels one gets from the corner lending-library. Nor is it usually thought of in connection with the movies. People will be ready to tell you what they like. But is it art? That is regarded as a question for an expert to decide.

We may leave to the social historian the task of explaining how it happened that among us art was driven into a corner, how it came to be regarded as collections of products for contemplation in one's leisure moments. From a philosophical point of view art has a much more significant role in human life. In the widest sense of the term, all deliberate fashioning or creating, all successful human activity may share in the character of art. And the appreciation of art, far from being a rare absorption, may be an element in all perception or apprehension of things done well.

Products and activities. In all societies things have been made. In connection with the production and preservation of food, the building of houses, the making of clothes, the care of children, the cure of disease, the propitiation of supernatural powers, all sorts of things come into existence through human activity. In pre-industrial society, these vary from crude digging sticks to the finely wrought Eskimo harpoon, the decorated blankets and baskets of the Hopi Indians, and the carved and painted totem poles by which west coast Indians celebrate their ancestry. There is no sharp line between things that are made well or admirably and things that win admiration for their beauty. Industrial societies have, of course, increased manyfold the opportunities for making things and altering the world about us.

Things are not the sole products of man's creative activity. Activities can themselves be patterned in intricate detail. The hands that make things can make motions of infinite variety—from well-planted blows to gestures and the measured movements in a Hindu dance. Sounds are patterned into language and into song. Bodily motions are given design in swimming, in dancing, in many a ritual and many a game.

When these activities are well done or their products done well, they invite *appreciation*. Appreciation has a wide scope. Its object is not limited to the works of men, but refers also natural surroundings: a sunset or a mountain seen in the distance has a definitely arresting quality. There can be appreciation of any kind of experience—intellectual, emotional, and volitional, as well as perceptual. This immediate appreciative quality is characterized as *esthetic*. This term is derived from the Greek word meaning to sense or perceive.

Esthetic and utilitarian phases. The esthetic phase of human experience is difficult to describe. It is a kind of sheer joy, whether in beholding the thing or act or in creating or doing.[1] It is often contrasted with the *utilitarian* phase, which is a sense of the use to which the thing or act is put, the results it will bring, whether food, prestige, or security from the wrath of the gods. The esthetic phase seems more immediate or terminal in character; it rarely points beyond or propels one, but it grips one and it may startle.

Although experience shows these two phases, things and patterns which are created cannot themselves be divided sharply into the utilitarian and the esthetic, or the useful and the artistic. Even musical patterns may have a utilitarian function and serve to facilitate rhythmic work or steady marching. Verbal patterns, like ornaments, sometimes have a magical intent; and religious paintings and effigies have a religious use as well as a religious content. Conversely, the esthetic element is often well-marked in craftsmanship. This has been especially true of handicrafts, but it is not necessarily so limited. Building is a useful craft, and at the same time architecture is one of the major arts. Nor is the architect's work divided into two compartments, one concerned with creating a useful structure, the other with creating a beautiful structure. Functional design is the artistic as well as the engineering goal of most modern architecture.

Specialized arts. Nevertheless some activities have come to be carried on primarily for ends that lie beyond themselves and so are specifically utilitarian. On the other hand, those products (both things and actions) which are created primarily for man's appreciation and enjoyment as such may be called esthetic. Concerned with these are the specialized arts of music, literature, painting, sculpture, and dancing, and their various combined forms such as acting, singing, opera, oratory. The movies constitute a recent important addition to the roster of arts.

The phenomena involved in the human pursuit of the arts invite careful scientific and philosophical scrutiny. No philosophical analysis of human

---

[1] The esthetic phase includes negative as well as positive elements: some things are esthetically displeasing, not merely neutral. Unless there is specific indication to the contrary, the positive reaction will be intended in the use of the term in what follows

values and their nature is complete which does not see the role and significance of art in the lives of men. There has by no means been general agreement on the nature of art. In fact the interpretation of art has proved historically to be a good criterion of philosophical attitudes, the type of analysis of art following closely the general type of analysis offered of the human spirit. Before comparing the idealist and materialist approaches we shall outline the kinds of problems with which the philosophy of art has on the whole concerned itself.

THE PROBLEM OF ESTHETIC QUALITY

One fundamental problem is, of course, the nature of the esthetic experience. Most persons who share the culture of the western tradition will agree that there is a definite quality in their experience of watching a sunset, listening to a Beethoven symphony, looking at a painting by El Greco. That there is such a quality found in experience is the starting-point of esthetic theory. It corresponds to the feeling in ethical theory that certain lines of conduct are right or that certain objects are good. Sometimes we refer to this esthetic quality as beauty.

Can esthetic quality be analyzed? Some theorists regard esthetic quality as simple and unanalyzable. They insist that it is immediately apprehended by the spectator, that he recognizes the quality, and finds it the same in varying situations with widely different materials. Its simplicity defies analysis; all we can do is to discover under what conditions it occurs and what concomitants it has. But the simplicity and unity of esthetic phenomena is stipulated at the very outset of inquiry.

Such an approach is valuable in imposing certain cautions. Esthetic quality must not be carelessly equated with any one of the factors that enter into esthetic appreciation. But we cannot carelessly accept the premise that it is single and unique. It may also, in advance, be taken to be a complex response, made up of many different qualities, and not necessarily always fully the same. There is still need for exploration of the phenomenon.

Thus far there has been no agreement among estheticians as to whether esthetic quality is a single quality or a cluster of disparate qualities with only a rough resemblance to each other. Certainly there is great variety in things that are esthetically pleasing. They may be simple colors and sounds, considered apart from the shapes or patterns they enter into, or very complex formal structures organized over a space (as a picture) or through a temporal span (as a musical composition), or words charged with meaning and themselves, in Samuel Alexander's apt phrase, "on fire."

Stress on different elements. There has been little agreement on the nature and analysis of esthetic quality, if indeed it be unitary. It is perhaps easy enough to distinguish the esthetic element from other elements of feeling, such as pleasures of novelty, of recognition, of association, in the same experience. But beyond that there have been differing theories concerning what may be a *generic* character to the many experiences of esthetic quality.

Some look to formal elements in the object which one experiences and try to show that a work of art or a natural scene is esthetically pleasing only when it achieves certain proportion, unity, integration, and so forth. Thus they analyze the geometric and color structures of great paintings, and treat music as a kind of "audible mathematics." Others find the common element to lie in the successful presentation of some content. The work has managed to tell us something or convey some significant emotion, whether it be the "representation of noble actions" (as Aristotle defined tragedy), or the full strength of grief, as in the second movement of Beethoven's *Eroica,* or the meaning of Christ, as in many a religious painting.[2]

Still others fasten attention on the appreciative observer, and seek a common element for esthetic quality in the effect produced upon him. Sometimes it is regarded as pleasure associated with utility. Thus Hume says a bronzed countenance is more beautiful than a pallid one because it suggests health, and he seeks to analyze the beauty of feminine form in terms of proportions fitted for child-bearing. Sometimes a more disinterested pleasure than association with utility is suggested as the common element in esthetic experience. It may be the joy of heightened awareness of our natural and human world, as when the artist shows us a familiar scene in a way we have never quite seen it before. Or it may be a feeling of "tension in equilibrium"—the poise of the *Discus Thrower*—or the sense of the "plot wound up" as in Greek tragedy. Paintings can also be analyzed in these terms, even with respect to their formal elements.

The question "What is esthetic quality or esthetic experience?" is thus the first problem to which we shall seek an answer in the interpretations given by idealist and materialist philosophies.

THE NATURE OF ART CREATION

The analysis of the work of art in terms of its creation is, of course, a second major problem. What is the nature of the process of artistic creation? What are the poet, the painter, the architect trying to do when they engage in their work?

The minimum description of their accomplishment is that they transform the raw materials on which they lay their hands. They start with things in

---

[2] See, for example, the analysis of the Avignon Pietà as an interpretation of the Christian Incarnation, given by T. M. Greene in his book *The Arts and the Art of Criticism*, Princeton University Press, 1940, pp. 285 ff.

one state and end with them in another state. This is a matter of simple observation. The marble is chiseled, the stones form a house, the canvas is covered with paint. Similarly in dancing or singing the body goes through definite motions, the voice issues in determinate sounds. But clearly much more takes place as well. Behind these physical transformations is the guiding power of the artist, selecting the original material, bringing his intent to bear in the changes that his hand or voice or body are fashioning.

Role of society. Behind the artist lies his society. It has spent centuries fashioning the materials he works with. It has made the raw materials of sound into the language of human relations, communicating ideas, emotions, and suggestions to action. It has made out of sounds an organized system of musically related tones, out of earth and stone and trees the clay and blocks and beams of the architect's structure. It provides the experiences that mold the artist's interests and fashion and give breadth to his personality. It provides the subject-matter of much of his work, and where he goes to his natural surroundings it supplies the perspective with which he scans his landscape. And it composes in the present and the future the audience to which he addresses himself.

Working thus in such materials and grounded in such a milieu, what is the artist attempting to do? Various theorists have debated whether he is engaged in representing something, expressing himself, or communicating a meaning. A fourth view, rejecting all these, holds the artist's essential task to be the manipulation of his materials to fashion esthetically pleasing and significant formal patterns. Each of these concepts requires examination; for they are not entirely clear, and they are certainly not all distinct.

Is art representative or expressive? Representation entails presenting the characteristics of a model in some medium. Such presentation does not imply photographic copying. Instead, art involves interpretation of the model, in the sense of selection among its characteristics. In this way the work may lead others to see things with a fresh view, born of the artist's insight.

Representation is, of course, a central element in most painting and sculpture. It can appear in other arts as well. Program music, for example, may depict some scene or set of events. In such a case representation involves translation into an entirely different medium. Those who regard art as essentially representational would even speak of music as representing the emotions it conveys. But if this is so, then the object of possible representation in art becomes indefinitely extended. The artist may copy his dreams and give free play to his imagination. He may aspire to exhibit what is not, or not yet. Representation thus loses its strict meaning. In this sense the term just serves to call attention to the existential core from which all art takes its rise.

The broadening of the concept of representation found in attempts to read it as the essence of art itself points to an expressive element that runs through all artistic creation. It is found in the basis of selection that representation itself involves. For the interpretation of the model expresses some principle or interest or plan of the artist. Even portrait-painting expresses the artist as well as representing the subject. It is therefore often held that art is primarily self-expression, that the artist's creative activity consists in giving existential form in one or another medium to his ideas, emotions or feelings, his attitudes, insights, experiences, strivings. The work of art is thus deemed to be charged with the artist's personality. Appreciation of a work of art accordingly involves grasping the content of the artist's expression. And since there are many conceptions of the self and its meanings, there are different interpretations of the expressed content of art and theories of its significance.[3]

Art creation as communication. The concept of art as communication, narrowly construed, entails that the artist consciously intends his work for others' contemplation, that he implants some message for others to extract. The artist does, in fact, sometimes choose his materials and adapt his methods in order that there may be ready understanding and widespread appeal. Some interpret in this way Beethoven's selection of a folk-theme to convey the brotherhood of man in his Ninth Symphony.

Although much art involves communication in this sense, and many people believe that more of it should, not all art-creation has this as an explicit element. Even apart from such artistic expressions as the solitary dance, or song improvisation in the bath, and deliberately obscure works like James Joyce's *Finnegans Wake,* many artists will report that in their actual creative work they grapple with a subject-matter that presents itself to them as real in its own terms, not as a vehicle reaching beyond to others. It might be said in some of these cases that the artist is his own audience; this need not be a paradox since we can distinguish between creation and appreciation in the act of creating. In other cases the work is a communication to a special élite or initiated few who will manage to understand it. In a fundamental sense, however, any expression is itself potential communication. For to understand an act of expression is, in a wider sense of communication, to have received a communication.

The basic issue between those who stress communication as central in art, and those who deny it, concerns the degree to which the artist should be conscious of his potential audience and social milieu. Should his decisions on subject-matter and form be influenced by the problems, interests, and probable level of comprehension of the community within which he functions? This becomes, in effect, the question of the social relations of art, to be considered below.

Stress on formal patterns. The view that the artist's essential task is the manipulation of his materials to fashion esthetically significant formal pat-

[3] These will appear below in the consideration of idealist and materialist interpretations of expression.

terns is not incompatible with the three conceptions we have just outlined. In fact, this view describes a *sine qua non* of all art. It embodies a concentration on the beauty that inheres in artistic forms, and which characterizes organizations of the various sensuous media, such as patterns of shapes, colors, or sounds. That the creation of beautiful structures is an essential element in art does not, however, make other aspects, especially content elements, nonessential. To insist that the making of significant formal patterns is the sole artistic aspect of the artist's task is simply a way of relieving the artist of responsibility for reckoning with the human meaning in his work. It is worth noting that even the creation of beauty in form may be an expressive act. Designs thought conceptually meaningless may be found to be symbolically expressive, just as children's finger painting, far from being random, embodies elaborate emotional outlets.

No ultimate conflict between these four conceptions. Clearly there is no need to choose between these various analyses of the process of artistic creation. Formal patterns in some degree belong to all art. Expression is likewise pervasive. In some of the arts, much of painting for example, the representative elements emerge more strongly; in most of literature the communicative; in some, as in music, the more directly expressive. The study of the process of artistic creation requires, however, more refined concepts, capable of more precise empirical interpretation, than these traditional ideas. The central question of the nature of the expressed content of art—what, in short, the artist is putting into his work in the process of creation—remains to be considered in the light of the idealist and materialist approaches.

THE CRITERIA OF ESTHETIC EVALUATION

A third major problem is the nature of esthetic evaluation. Works of art are judged, criticized, compared. Brahm's first symphony is generally considered more esthetically satisfying than the tune *Tipperary*. Shakespeare's *Hamlet* is considered to be a greater work than Eugene O'Neill's *Beyond the Horizon*. Some critics are said to have good taste, others poor taste.

Can there be dispute about tastes? What is meant by such judgments? Are they merely expressions of feeling, stating the likes and dislikes of the observer? Such an interpretation has been enshrined in the old dictum *de gustibus non disputandum* ("There is no disputing about tastes.") This enthrones possible arbitrariness; it need not produce actual arbitrariness since tastes may happen to agree. On the other hand, many theorists have argued for objective standards in the judgment of art. Clearly this implies either that beauty (or esthetic quality) is a discernible quality whose presence, absence, and degree any careful and well-equipped observer may note, or that men have similar constitutions whose development brings agreement in matters of taste.

Judgment of art multi-dimensional. The actual judgment of a particular work is multi-dimensional. It may be estimated for the quality of its content: its theme is petty or profound, its characters genuine or mere puppets. It may be appraised for its success or failure as an effort in expression: it speaks clearly in every detail or mumbles incoherently. Finally, it may be considered for its beauty and for the esthetic quality which inheres in its materials, its formal structure, and even in its character as successful expression. The detailed criteria employed vary, of course, in the different fields of art.

Great art. There is no ready procedure for "summing" the results of the evaluation of a work of art. Nevertheless the use of such terms as "great art" indicates a kind of synoptic judgment. In addition to excellence in the criteria just listed, great art is generally thought of as enduring. This points to a wide and constant appeal, and this in turn rests upon a concern with fundamental human themes, an insight into pervasive human needs, problems, and aspirations. Some types of esthetic theory speak of *truth* as characteristic of works of art. From this point of view great art would express fundamental truths. Whether this concept of esthetic truth may validly be employed depends upon the answer to the question raised above, the nature of expression and what is expressed. And this, as we have suggested, leads to problems of fundamental philosophical outlook. To the growing list of questions to be considered in the light of differing approaches we must, therefore, add "Is esthetic evaluation ultimately arbitrary?"

ETHICAL AND SOCIAL EVALUATION OF ART

The fourth set of problems, and the last with which we shall here be concerned, deals with the ethical and social evaluation of art and the artist. Such questions arise in the fundamental analysis of any human activity, for no activity constitutes a world by itself; it must make its home with the rest of a man's life and in the context of the lives of others.

Morality and the artist. To many the artist has often seemed a special kind of mortal, released from the ordinary obligations of mankind. This has been especially the case in our own commercial society in which artistic values have been isolated and the artist occasionally driven to a revolt which took the form of "Bohemianism." Questions of the personal ethics of the artist present no problem peculiar to art unless we conceive of him as having a "mission" to which everything else must not merely be subordinate, but actually ethically irrelevant. Apart from such a special view, the clash of ends, problems of sacrifice, means that thwart the end, and so forth, have the same nature in the artist's life as in any man's and require no special treatment.

Art for art's or life's sake? The problem of the social relations of art has been suggested in the discussion of the concept of communication. This has been a frequent battleground of extreme opinions. "Art for art's sake" has clashed with "Art for life's sake." Some artists have made a virtue of their isolation, others of their contributions to social welfare. And many artists, while keenly recognizing their social obligations, relate them only to themselves as citizens, not to themselves as artists.[4]

The objection to social significance as a major criterion in selecting content, vehicle, and techniques rests on the view that on such a criterion art is somehow being "used" for a purpose beyond itself, turned into propaganda, instead of following its own intrinsic goals. That such an approach misreads the nature of art can be seen from an attempt to apply it strictly. It would enjoin the architect, for example, to ignore the use of the building he was designing. Would it not, even, see the religious significance of many a famous painting as an extraneous element? It will be objected, however, that in these cases the social function of the building and the religious significance of the painting are internal parts of the content, not external uses. If that is the case, then there is no theoretical objection to any type of use, provided that it is digested by the artist and becomes part of the flesh and blood that create the work. What is being sought is good art, not forced creation.

The social role of the artist. The view that art flourishes when the artist as such has an integrated social role, rather than the position of a museum piece, has strong historical support. Drama in ancient Athens, religious art in medieval and early modern times are good examples. In the Soviet Union, under the stress of the German invasion, the output of art during the first year was enormous.[5] Most of these works devoted themselves to themes connected with the war, much of the musical and poetic composition dealing with the guerillas. A great social crisis produces great passions and summons all the resources of men. It is to be expected that this will find its way into the expressed content of art.

Such, in brief outline, are some of the major types of problems in the philosophic theory of art. In turning to the interpretations given in the

---

[4] Archibald MacLeish attacks this view in *The Irresponsibles*. The socially conscious poet, he says, even when he is ready to throw himself heart and soul into a social conflict (as some did in the case of the Spanish civil war) for the most part seizes a gun and rushes to battle. He does not usually think of using his art. The implication *is* that he regards his art as free from social responsibilities or social reference.

[5] Reported in *N. Y. Times,* June 22, 1942, p. 6.

idealist and materialist traditions we seek light on the four central questions that have appeared in our survey:

(1) What is the nature of the esthetic experience?
(2) What is the nature of the artist's expression in the process of art creation?
(3) What are the criteria of judgment and taste in esthetic evaluation?
(4) Has the artist any special ethical or social obligations?

Idealist interpretation

Art is frequently viewed as something springing from the spirit of man, as something unrelated to the ordinary natural world. It is treated as a product of inspiration, and the artist as one who, acquiring a special vision, is able to see through ordinary experience to some reality that underlies it.

This approach to art as an avenue to some higher realm of experience is found systematized and integrated in the great idealist philosophies. The essence of art, both in appreciation and in creation, is taken to be a kind of striving for ultimate reality; its success provides a special grasp of truth. Both these elements—the *conative* or striving and the *cognitive* or knowing—are intertwined in most idealist interpretations of art. Esthetic quality is the glimmer of reality in the domain of sense-experience, drawing the spirit toward the home for which it is yearning. Artistic creation is a process of fashioning natural materials so that reality may be more readily discerned. The true genius, as Schopenhauer puts it, understands nature's half-uttered speech and interprets her stammering so that we may comprehend more clearly what she wants to say.

PLATONIC APPROACHES

The role of art as appeasing and yet deepening man's hunger for the real is best seen in the Platonic tradition.[6] Plato, it will be recalled, disparaged the worldly flux of existence and took reality to lie in the eternal objects of knowledge, the Ideas, pre-eminent among which is the Idea of the Good. The beautiful is ultimately identical with the good, and the soul, striving for communion with the eternal, directs itself as a whole toward the good and the beautiful.

Plato's account in the "Symposium." Love, as the wise Diotima of Mantinea tells Socrates in the *Symposium,* is the desire for the everlasting possession of the good. It is not the love of the beautiful only, but the love of

---

[6] A fuller survey of this theory and the various ones discussed below will be found in Gilbert and Kuhn, *A History of Esthetics*, Macmillan, 1939.

generation and of "birth in beauty," since to mortals generation is a sort of eternity and immortality. In such pursuit men beget children and those who are creative in their souls conceive wisdom and virtue. Poets and all artists worthy to be called inventors are of this sort, and the greatest of them are concerned with the ordering of life, with temperance and justice, and with the eliciting of virtue in other souls. Homer, Hesiod, Lycurgus and Solon, created in their poems and laws the greatest of children.

The soul proceeding rightly in its pursuit of beauty starts with the beautiful forms of this world and comes gradually to recognize that beauty in every form is one and the same. Man comes to realize the superior character of beauty of mind over beauty of outward form, and contemplates the beauty of institutions and laws, then of the sciences, until at last he has the vision of a single science which is the science of beauty everywhere. He suddenly perceives "beauty absolute, separate, simple, and everlasting, which without diminution and without increase, or any change, is imparted to the ever-growing and perishing beauties of all other things . . . But what if man had eyes to see the true beauty—the divine beauty, I mean, pure and clear and unalloyed, not clogged with the pollutions of mortality and all the colors and vanities of human life—thither looking, and holding converse with the true beauty simple and divine? Remember how in that communion only, beholding beauty with the eye of the mind, he will be enabled to bring forth, not images of beauty, but realities (for he has hold not of an image but of a reality), and bringing forth and nourishing true virtue to become the friend of God and be immortal, if mortal man may. Would that be an ignoble life?"[7]

Plotinus on beauty. In the mystical neo-Platonic philosophy of Plotinus the approach was developed systematically. Plotinus outlined a detailed sequence of steps relating the individual soul to the prime One from which all things come and which is itself all beauty, truth, and goodness.[8] The longing of the soul which Plato described is interpreted as the yearning of the individual spirit for its home. Its apprehension of Beauty gives it glimmerings of the light from which it came and the peace it finds in intuition of beauty provides a foretaste of the joy in reunion with the One that it may achieve.

Plotinus believes that technical definitions of beauty miss this central point: the apprehension of beauty is a kind of loving recognition by the soul. With respect to art creation, it is a mistake to think that the artist is merely reproducing nature. The artist's spirit is going back to the Ideas from which Nature itself has come, and so a work of art may enrich what is being ostensibly copied. Similarly human beauty is not skin deep, but is

[7] *Symposium* 211-212 (Jowett translation).
[8] See above, p. 350.

due to the soul's life shining through the body. And in like fashion, nature has beauty because the objects of nature express directly the vision that the World-Soul has of the One. Both the creation of beauty and the vision of beauty aid the soul in fashioning itself to be fit for its homeward journey.

The early Christian tradition. This approach, developed in Plato and Plotinus, was very influential in the early Christian tradition. Instead of the Good or the One there was God. The endeavor of the soul was to attain communion with God through His manifestation in the sensible world. In Augustine, for example, the world becomes God's poem or His architectural accomplishment or His sculpture. The soul, impressed by the beauties of sight, is led to figures, measures, and numbers, thus to unity and, when the soul itself is sufficiently harmonious, to the beauty of God. The sensible materials serve as vehicles for reason to appear in their symmetry, measure, consonance, and so forth. And Augustine also has a ladder of beauty by which one may go from the senses to the divine.

The treatment of art in Plato's "Republic." A surprisingly different view of the relation between art and reality is to be found in Plato's *Republic*. In Book X the artist's work is described as imitative, with the result that the artist is thrice removed from the reality which the soul desires to know. In the first place there is, says Socrates using the example of a bed, the Idea or Form of bed, made by God. Then there is the bed made by the carpenter. Then there is the bed painted by the artist. What is more, the painter represents the thing as it appears, not as it is. Similarly the poet or tragedian represents the statesman who is already only a copy of the ideal, and represents him not as he is—for the poet knows little or nothing of statesmanship—but as he appears. The artist is thus not able to educate men to reality, but turns their minds to appearances. Furthermore, Plato is afraid that the poet and tragedian will arouse feelings of sympathy for the passions they are portraying and thus strengthen men's reactions to the non-rational side of life. Akin to this is the way in which Plato in various dialogues accuses arts such as rhetoric of pandering (like cookery) to men's appetites and feelings instead of feeding their minds so as to turn the soul to the eternal. Plato ridicules the man who listens to music for the sheer delight in the sound. True appreciation, he holds, is intellectual in character.

This disparaging view of the artist is quite different from the exalted account of the search for beauty in the *Symposium*. Perhaps the explanation of the discrepancy lies in the view of Socrates in the *Apology* that artists do their best work by a kind of divine inspiration without knowing what they are up to. Or perhaps it is because the *Republic,* planning an ideal state in which the influences that play on people are to be strictly regimented, cannot afford to give too independent a role to the artist.

SCHOPENHAUER'S ANALYSIS

Art provides a knowledge closer to reality. Schopenhauer [9] shares with Plato the view that the arts provide a type of knowledge, but he thinks it is a knowledge closer to reality, not further removed. Unlike Plato, he conceives reality itself as *Will,* a kind of blind striving or hunger. This Will, which is reality, finds its first expression in the Platonic Ideas, which include all the laws of nature, species of animals, and so forth. Individuals are fragments of the Will in objective form. An individual man's body, for example, is the objective form of his will of which he is aware through immediate intuition. The core of a man is thus blind striving which begets all the misery and frustration of life. Schopenhauer's well-known pessimism involves a sweeping condemnation of life.

The various studies in which men engage do not grasp the inmost character of reality. History merely follows the thread of events; natural science classifies the lowest grades of existence and notes the order of occurrences or the laws of change; mathematics treats of the forms in which the Ideas appear in human knowledge. All together they give us merely the connections and relations of phenomena. How then, Schopenhauer asks, do we attain knowledge of what is independent of all relations, really essential, and unchanging—in short the Ideas which directly objectify the ultimate will? His answer is that Art alone provides such insight. It reproduces the eternal Ideas grasped through pure contemplation in one or another medium. It springs from the knowledge of Ideas and aims to communicate this knowledge. It plucks its object out of the temporal flux and isolates it for contemplation. Genius consists in exceptional ability to engage in such Platonic contemplation.

In each of the arts Schopenhauer looks for the Idea which it reveals. Architecture exhibits gravity, cohesion, rigidity, hardness, which Schopenhauer calls the most inarticulate manifestations of Will or the bass notes of nature. The Ideas of plant, animal, and human life are revealed through landscape gardening and painting, painting of animals, and representation of human beauty in painting and sculpture. Poetry has still greater efficacy in exhibiting human life; it reveals the Ideas and communicates them by means of abstract conceptions to be enriched by the imagination of the hearer.

Music reveals the Will itself. Finally, Schopenhauer gives a special role to music. It speaks directly of the Will itself, not of the Ideas to which the other arts bring us. Schopenhauer attempts to show its richness by exhibit-

---

[9] Schopenhauer's treatment of art is to be found in Book III of *The World as Will and Idea.*

ing with it the full content of the other arts, from the bass notes which correspond to the materials of architecture through those representing the world of plants and animals, to the high singing of the melody representing the intellectual life and effort of men. Music never expresses these phenomena directly, but rather exhibits the inner nature of all phenomena which is the will. Music can touch all that goes on in the will and heart of man. It fits all the possible events of life without actually copying them. Such reflections lead Schopenhauer to assert that the world might as readily be called embodied music as embodied will.

Art both reveals discord and brings peace. Throughout the various arts Schopenhauer finds the discord which the striving of the Will brings. Even at the lowest level there is the conflict of gravity and rigidity which constitutes the esthetic material of architecture. And tragedy is regarded as the summit of poetry because it represents the terrible side of life, pain and the triumph of evil and the fall of the just, thus giving a significant view of the nature of the world and the inner strife of the Will. Art not merely gives man this insight into reality, but in doing so stills for the moment the clamor of his will. He is lifted suddenly out of the endless stream of willing and he observes without personal interest, seeing things insofar as they are Ideas, not insofar as they are motives for him. Thus comes the painless state of peace which is the highest good.

HEGELIAN THEORY

To the idealist treatment of art as expressing a yearning or striving for reality and as presenting an intimate revelation of phases of reality, the Hegelian theory of esthetics adds a third element. It assigns art a special historical role in a spiritual evolution.

Art and the Absolute. For Hegel, nature, history, and all its contents are essentially rational. Their rationality, which is their reality, is understood as a process of achieving self-consciousness on the part of the World-Spirit. (The latter Hegel also calls the Idea or Absolute.) [10] Art together with Religion and Philosophy constitute Absolute Mind in which the whole of reality is grasped as an organic unity. Art accomplishes this through use of sensuous form, Religion through the consciousness entailed in worship, and Philosophy through thought.

The Absolute appearing as beauty in the medium of sense, is called the Ideal. The physical and the animal world, however, lack the qualities required for genuine beauty. Man is the most beautiful animal form, express-

---

[10] The way in which this self-consciousness is achieved will be examined below, p. 421 ff. Hegel's theory of art is to be found in his *Philosophy of Fine Art* (English translation by F. P. B. Osmaston, London, 1920).

ing the rationality, the vitality, and the unity of the Absolute. But the Ideal appears best in men's works of art (Hegel refers to the fine arts) in which nature has been exalted, not merely represented, in its expression through the artist's mind.

Stages in the development of art. So far the role assigned to art has the generic traits of the idealist treatment. The unique Hegelian element appears when the historical development of art is revealed as a function of the growth of self-consciousness in the Idea. Hegel distinguishes three stages—symbolic, classical, and romantic. In each stage all the particular arts are found in one form or another, but not all serve equally well for the expression of the reigning spirit.

In the symbolic stage the Idea is grasped only abstractly or vaguely and thus sensuous representation of it is merely symbolic, with the meaning not fully embodied in the representation. As examples of this Hegel points to Hindu art, to Egyptian architecture, and to such literary forms as the fable. Architecture provides the best expression for the symbolic stage: mounds, tombs, columns, pyramids, and so forth hint at leading ideas. In this symbolic phase matter outweighs spirit; spirit rearranges matter, setting stone on stone, but cannot yet permeate the inert mass.

In the second stage the Idea is more concretely conceived as individual self-conscious spirit. Classical art utilizes the human body as an expression in which the meaning is perfectly embodied; for the human figure clearly represents the soul with its vitality and spiritual freedom. The gods are thus represented in statue form, and sculpture becomes the central art. In Greece architecture merely provides the house, while sculpture takes the lead in presenting meaning. In this stage matter and spirit are perfectly balanced.

In the third stage, as the development of the Idea reaches a point in which the inward spiritual aspect is stressed, art becomes romantic, striving to reveal in sensuous form the struggles and passions of the spirit. Its medium, which could convey adequately the freedom and equilibrium of the Greek spirit, is however unequal to this new task; spirit transcends the possibility of sensuous embodiment. Art goes on and grows, but the significant revelation of the Idea moves to the domain of religion. Classical art is thus the highest expression of art as such. Painting is the first of several arts in the romantic stage to express the change. It is not limited to nature, but may try to represent the emotions, ideas, and purposes of men. Thus it proves useful in religion. Music is freer still; the movement of the listener's soul and the movement of the music become almost identical. This, however, Hegel regards as emotional contagion rather than as rational communication. (When architecture in its Gothic forms becomes romantic in Hegel's sense, it is described as frozen music.) Poetry is the third art important in the romantic period. But it is also regarded by him as the universal art. It has flourished in various forms among all nations throughout all ages. Hegel finds that it has the clarity of sculpture, the temporal scope of music, and, since it deals with images, some of the qualities of space; in addition, it can tell the story of men. Of its forms, the epic reflects a whole people, the lyric personal feeling, the drama in its tragic form eternal forces in conflict through human beings.

IDEALIST ANSWERS TO THE FOUR PROBLEMS

The illustrations just given make clear the dominant idealist treatment of esthetic quality and of artistic production—the first two of the major questions we listed above. The content of art, what the artist expresses and the observer appreciates, is reality. The aspects of yearning or striving, of intuition or contemplation, of expression in act or in beholding are differentially selected or combined. But reality in all cases is spiritual and the artistic activity is the expression of spirit.

Criteria of judgment and of taste—the third of our central problems—are implicit in the idealist approach. Good art is art whose beauty reveals reality, whose content well expresses reality, whose effect on the observer is to awaken the mind to a readier grasp of reality. Great art is outstanding in its presentation of fundamental truths, whether they be universal truths (as for Plato or Schopenhauer) or a revelation of a special phase of the development of spirit (as in Hegel).

Finally, if we turn to the ethical and social relations of art, there are a number of quite distinct attitudes which are compatible with the idealist interpretation. Plato holds to an ultimate identification of the good and the beautiful so that what is not good cannot be fundamentally beautiful. He recognizes the tremendous influence of art on character, and therefore insists on careful regulation of the stories to be told the young and of styles of music to be heard by them in his ideal state. The judges of the moral fruits of art—and of taste for that matter—are to be those who have knowledge as distinct from belief, namely the wise or philosophic. As we have seen,[11] they are even to judge whether a man's pleasure is real or illusory.

As against this moralistic view of art, there is the "art for art's sake" theory. Although such a position may be held on naturalistic or materialistic grounds, it often expresses idealist attitudes. For art, in its pursuit of beauty, may be taken to be the special province of spirit, with ethical and social relations merely ancillary to it. Such an extreme position is illustrated in that popular romantic idealism which releases the artist, as one endowed with a special spiritual gift, from the ordinary moral ties and social obligations of men.

[11] See above, pp. 193-94.

It is quite possible, furthermore, that the general idealist approach, with its emphasis on insight into reality as a special content of art, lends an individualist tinge to the artist. For art becomes an affair between the artist and reality. His spirit is the one that gains the deeper insight and gives it expression; any responsibility he may owe is not essentially to his fellow-men, but to the World-Spirit or Reality which guides him.

Materialist interpretation

"NATURALIZING" ART

The central task of the materialist in analyzing art has been to "naturalize" it in the domain of human activities. This has involved exhibiting art in all its aspects—creation and appreciation and critical judgment—as a natural phenomenon, one phase of the manifold activities of men. Materialist philosophers have attempted this task in various ways, corresponding to the different types of materialist philosophy. These types, as we have seen,[12] are distinguished by their special stress on one or another science, and the more mature materialistic theories by a comprehensive inclusion of the perspectives of all the sciences. We may briefly survey materialistic theories of art as they appear in the mechanistic, the biological, and the psychological approach, and then from the fuller materialistic standpoint which embraces all these and includes also a social approach.

Mechanistic and biological approaches. Mechanical materialists take either of two paths. They may treat art as simply a phenomenon of imagination, and give imagination or fancy a physical interpretation as they do sensation and memory. This is the path taken by Hobbes. Or, finding no place for the artistic and esthetic in an account of the "objective" physical world, they may relegate esthetic phenomena to the semi-illusory status of the "subjective."

Biological approaches to art have sought its basis in impulses and instincts, sometimes generalized, sometimes specific. Some have studied art as an expression of the play impulse. Herbert Spencer, for example, regards play as artificial exercise of powers finding release in simulated actions. Games result from this exercise of the lower powers. The playful exercise of the higher powers yields esthetic production.[13] Reliance on a tendency to imitate as an explanation of art production is found in ancient times. Aristotle in his *Poetics* refers to such an instinct; imitation, he says, is natural

---

[12] See above, pp. 315-16, 322-23.
[13] For a critique of Spencer's views and other play theories of art, see C. J. Ducasse, *The Philosophy of Art,* MacVeagh, 1929, Chapter 7.

to man from childhood, and it is natural for all to delight in works of imitation.

Psychological materialist approach. Psychological theories of art, when they issue from a materialist point of view, have taken esthetic phenomena to be simply one class of psychological phenomena whose identity and relations might be systematically explored. Thus the artist's activity is seen as the expression of emotions, the communication of feeling, the imaginative expression of a wish, and so forth. Esthetic quality is analyzed in terms of psychological response. Such a materialist approach readily adopts the many analyses that have been made of the observer's reactions to art, and estimates their psychological authenticity. There is, for example, the Aristotelian account of emotional catharsis induced by observation of tragedy, in which pity and terror are raised to a high degree in the spectator and purged away. There is the phenomenon of empathy, sometimes described as feeling oneself into something and appreciating its situation. There are fine distinctions drawn between reactions in which one feels the stirring of desire, the impulse to action, the consciousness of learning, and, quite distinct from these, the repose and suspension of desire and will in a purely contemplative entertaining of perceptual objects. (Some have sought in these psychological terms to separate art from propaganda, didacticism, and so forth.) There is the description of beauty in terms of pleasurable effect on the observer. There are the differences of response to raw materials of art, such as specific colors, to patterns and structures, to ugly models beautifully represented, and so forth. A whole branch of psychology is revealed in such investigations—one whose problems cannot be cursorily dismissed by mere definition or individual introspection. And on this type of materialistic approach it is the results of such psychological investigation that would tell us the "nature" of art.

This psychological approach is also capable of eliciting standards of artistic judgment. Great art would be art successfully expressing fundamental and pervasive passions. Or, if the theorist were otherwise inclined, it would be art successfully expressing the unique, the "last fine shade" of feeling or perception. Beauty, indicating a special type of pleasure aroused, could be estimated by the degree of such feeling.

Transition to a more mature materialist approach. The psychological approach to both creation and appreciation of art grows into a more rounded materialist approach as psychology itself matures from a science of the subjective to a full study of man. Feelings and ideas cease to be treated as ultimate data of the science and become phases of the interactive life of men in a physical and social environment. Art secures a wider base and appreciation a broader scope in such an analysis, and the study of art no longer limits art's nature to the discoveries of a single science, but calls upon social as well as psychological sciences for its perspective. We may delineate the philosophical character of this broader approach by considering the major questions which were listed at the outset—the nature of esthetic quality and appreciation, the nature of the artist's activity, the standards of taste or esthetic judgment, and the ethical and social relations of art.

ANALYSIS OF APPRECIATION

The materialist treatment of appreciation follows two lines. One seeks a starting-point in a type or phase of experience. John Dewey, for example, in his *Art as Experience* treats esthetic quality as rounding out an experience into completeness and unity.[14] This would allow for an esthetic character not merely in perception but in almost all human activity. Santayana equates esthetic values with those inherent "in imagination, in instant intuition, in sense endowed with form," but thinks that "the rose's grace could more easily be plucked from its petals than the beauty of art from its subject, occasion, and use.[15] Various other conceptions have been recommended as starting-points along this line. The second approach uses social rather than psychological starting-points; beginning with culturally designated art products and culturally developed reactions to them its inquiry into appreciation needs no prior delineation in terms of a single central quality.

The object of appreciation. Such approaches to esthetic appreciation obviously allow a materialist theory to embrace any authenticated analyses of men's reactions to art and nature that an empirical psychology may discover. They permit the possibility of appreciation centering on any of the innumerable relationships into which an object or event may enter. Appreciation occurs in a definite span of time. Attention is focused during that time on a relatively delimited area. But the relationships of this limited spatio-temporal region which may be the center of awareness, the meanings supported by the attentive spectator, may vary from gross response to the most refined complexity. In this sense art appreciation like art creation may exhibit the range of men's capacities and the possible richness of human life. When a poem is being read appreciation may center on the music of the words, the rhythm, the stream of images, the structure of the theme, and even the panorama of all eternity in a compressed episode. And in each case observation may involve genuine appreciation with all the traditional attributes of unity, clarity, wholeness, poise of forces, arrested attention, or any other qualities of the object or the act that esthetic theory may prescribe.

Illustration from music. Music offers an interesting illustration of the va-

[14] Minton, Balch, 1934, Chapter III.
[15] *Reason in Art,* Scribner's, 1905, pp. 15-16.

riety of possible esthetic appreciation that may be found in the arts.[16] To some, listening to music is, in Santayana's words, "a drowsy revery relieved by nervous thrills."[17] To others it is an audible mathematics, appreciation centering on its structure. To many it is expressed feeling, but with passion stilled. Dewey calls attention to the way in which music expresses the shocks, instabilities, conflicts and resolutions, the stir and agitation of existence. Sound agitates directly, involving direct emotional expression. Parker points out that music is characterized by expression of emotion without representing the causes or objects of emotion.[18] And yet because it resounds through the whole body, it is most personal and intimate. For explanation of the concreteness of emotional content, Parker suggests the effects of rhythm, the arousing of emotions by association through analogy of music and the human voice with its familiar revelation of emotion, and the analogy between music and noises produced by nature and human activities. In addition we attach the concrete emotions of our own lives to the feeling provided by the music. Music provides a language for feelings which our ordinary vocabulary cannot express; what is more, by expressing our emotions in sound, it gives us a revelation of ourselves.

Possible variety of genuine appreciation. The variety of appreciation is an obvious consequence of the fact that a work of art, like any event in nature, is a complex phenomenon. Different features may invite selective responses on the part of the observer. Thus while one man's appreciation embraces several phases, another's may fasten on one or another feature. Each may constitute genuine appreciation. A materialist theory would not, as some idealist approaches might, select one phase as "essential" appreciation of the work of art *itself*, regarding the rest as "accidental appreciation." Thus it would not say that there is an "essence" of music which determines that "true" or "real" appreciation must be mathematical or structural, or that it must rest on emotional quality, and so forth. The only sense in which it might speak of "proper" or "correct" appreciation is where the work of art is construed as communication and the point at issue is the observer's grasp of the artist's intent.

ANALYSIS OF CREATION

This brings us to the second major problem—the nature of the artist's activity, and what it is that he "expresses," which the observer may "grasp" or "understand."

[16] For a discussion of this problem, see George Santayana, *op. cit.*, Chapter IV; John Dewey, *op. cit.*, pp. 236-239; De Witt H. Parker, *The Principles of Aesthetics*, Silver, Burdett, 1920, Chapter VIII.
[17] *Op. cit.*, p. 51.
[18] *Op. cit.*, p. 175.

Santayana's approach to art creation. Santayana's perspective in *Reason in Art* provides an excellent insight into the creation of art in its broader outlines. Art has its origins in human activity and the imprint it leaves in its surroundings—the manipulation of the hands, the noises of the throat, the movements of the body. All activity may become artistic as men become self-conscious about it and develop standards for it. Art is "spontaneous action made stable by success." The romantic picture has art arise from an idea or passion which strikes one in all its fullness and steers the body into expression. Santayana, on the other hand, sees artistic activity as a kind of groping which grows into consciousness with the activity itself. The activity, with its impulsive element, is primary; ideas and emotions become clear as the activity leaves well-marked traces in the body and its environment. This is the success which characterizes artistic activity—well-developed habits and well-fashioned objects. "Art is action which transcending the body makes the world a more congenial stimulus to the soul."[19] The objects molded—whether writings or sound-patterns or buildings or shoes or statues —have one or both of two roles. They may be useful or may give joy in contemplation or re-enactment. These roles constitute the industrial and liberal phases of art. Developed art is thus self-conscious activity fashioning the world as a more congenial place for men to live in.

Natural character of artistic activity. Clearly this type of approach allows for the greatest divergence in the content of art. It does not draw sharp distinctions between the fine arts and the arts not so designated. It does not treat certain activities as the privileged vehicles of the spirit. It does not require that the source of art be an agonized soul or a spirit drawn by an ideal. Artistic activity becomes a very natural thing in the world. It involves the task of molding the self and its environment to minister to human needs and actualize human values. The content of art is therefore as wide as the content of all values in men's lives and it may be explored in the widest scientific terms. The psychologist may, for example, trace the evolution of the work in the artist as it passes from private fantasy to socially acceptable materials communicated to an audience by means of acquired skill. And the sociologist may study art as a certain form of social production. Its character and function would vary depending on such factors as the social relations of the artist to patrons or public, the class structure of society which determines for whom art is produced, and the level of technology which affects the artist's mode of production.

The meaning of "expression" in art. In the light of these indications we may turn more specifically to the materialist's answer to the question of what is "expressed" by the artist and "understood" by one who appreciates the work of art. We may, however, distinguish two senses of expression and of

---

[19] *Op. cit.*, p. 15.

understanding in this context, just as there are two senses in which we understand a man's speech or conduct. One tells us what he intended to say or do, what the artist was consciously endeavoring to present. This is self-expression on his part; in this sense to understand the work of art gives us the artist's feelings, emotions, ideas, purposes. The other sense is that in which we say a man's art expresses his age or his society. To understand it means to know the milieu in which he lived and the play of causal forces of which the artist may have been only partially aware. Traditional dualism sharply separated these phases as the internal and the external or the purposive and the causal. Understanding in the first sense was a prerequisite to proper appreciation; understanding in the second sense provided scientific knowledge but added nothing to esthetic appreciation.

Content as revealed in appreciation. The breakdown of this sharp separation in a materialist approach has its consequences in the interpretation of art. Just as a man's actions may signify or express more of his personality than he is aware of, so the work of art may be understood and appreciated beyond the limits of the artist's conscious effort. What understanding is relevant to actual appreciation of a given work of art must be determined empirically. While the artist's purpose is usually important, there are some purposes (e.g., desire for prestige) which may on occasion prove irrelevant. On the other hand apparently remote questions, such as the physical properties of objects, may prove very relevant (as in the use of marble rather than porcelain to portray strife).

That the social history of the arts and of individual creation is only now beginning to receive wide attention is a function not merely of prevalent idealistic approaches to art but also of the lateness with which materialist philosophy came to rest on the social as compared to the physical and biological sciences. It is generally agreed that such study will contribute to the understanding of the causes and sources of art creation. It may also well be that it will add a new dimension—a socio-historical one—to actual appreciation. Certainly in architecture, literature, and painting scientific and historical knowledge may broaden the actual content and modify the quality of appreciation. Just as the purpose of a building is part of its architectural content, so the knowledge of the religious tradition is necessary to the fullest appreciation of medieval painting. To reduce its esthetic qualities to its formal patterns or immediate sensuous content robs it of appreciative elements most observers have found esthetically valuable. If religious elements can thus be part of artistic content, why not politico-economic elements, or historical elements of any variety? May not knowledge of the social context, aims, hopes and moods in the composer of a symphony provide a specificity and add a richness to feeling as well as furnish an intellectual understanding? This may prove esthetically relevant, just as is the understanding of formal musical structure to the lay hearer.

The content in creation. Thus, on a materialist approach to the concept of expression, the content of a work in the sense of what the artist deliberately put into it merges with its source or the background from which it grew. Art thus expresses the lives of men, their view of their natural surroundings, the complex relations among them, their hopes and fears and struggles, their feelings, emotions and values, the ideas and fantasies that rise among them. Free rein is given to the expression of the universal and of the highly individualized, of the substantial and of the fleeting or shadowy, and whatever else is begotten in the matrix of human life and activity.

STANDARDS OF ESTHETIC JUDGMENT

The relativity of tastes. On a materialist theory the standards of esthetic judgment and taste involve problems comparable to those that arise in a consideration of ethical values. There is certainly a relativity of tastes. It is found in the variety of traditions among different cultures—for example, western music and Chinese music. It is found within the history of a single culture, as the story of painting as well as of music clearly shows. Tradition and education play a substantial role in the fashioning of taste.

Limitations on relativity. Nevertheless the recognition of relativity does not mean that no criticism of taste is possible, or that every man's judgment of esthetic value is a private possession criticism of which constitutes esthetic trespass. For, in the first place, there are many technical questions in the various arts, and the judgment of taste if not simply an emotional expression is to some extent a judgment of the excellence with which certain aims have been achieved by certain techniques. In this alone there is plenty of scope for initial disagreement and eventual agreement after analysis. But even appreciation of qualities not involving dispute as to means may turn out to require training in distinction and apprehension of structure. Men appreciate music without a knowledge of its technical structure, but there seems to be general agreement that such knowledge brings greater appreciation. The greater weight of one judgment over another may thus serve, as authority does in science, as a prediction open to anyone to confirm by extended experience. Beyond that lies the prediction that further cultivation will result in a man's refining his taste. This is the appeal described above as "from Philip drunk to Philip sober." [20] A great part of that account of ethical advice may here be applied to esthetic judgment.

Interpretations of "ultimate" disagreement. It should be added that the type of position which rejects absolute judgments and also holds that initial disagreement need not imply ultimate disagreement, is not peculiar to the materialist approach. But the various theories of art do differ in their inter-

---

[20] See above, p. 267.

pretation of any ultimate disagreement. For the Platonic type of idealist one conflicting view must be wrong. For the idealist of the Hegelian type both conflicting views would be fragmentary judgments reconciled in the Absolute. For the materialist both would be evaluations expressing attitudes on the part of the respective critics, for which a causal explanation alone could be offered; choice between them would be a matter of evaluation on one's own standards.

In any given culture, the relativity of appreciation becomes limited by a set of assumptions or expectations concerning the role of art. Since these indicate what people look for, they implicitly define what correct appreciation will be and thus what will constitute the "essence" of a work of art. Thus the assumptions that art is an expression of the artist and that appreciation of a work of art involves understanding it are regulative in our dominant conception of art. In this sense a Verdi opera cannot be "properly" appreciated by one who does not know the plot and does not understand Italian. Correct appreciation becomes *full* appreciation of what is expressed, based on understanding. It is the response of the ideal observer who is sensitive (i.e., has the relevant habits and training) and who understands the work. The judgment of greatness in art is partly a judgment on the degree of beauty and success in expressiveness and partly a comment on content in relation to the critic's values. Often the latter refers to pervasive appeal of its content and the likelihood of its enduring through the years.

ETHICAL AND SOCIAL RELATIONS OF ART

The ethical and social relations of art—the last of our general types of problems—are not viewed uniformly by all forms of philosophical materialism. Even an art for art's sake theory is possible on a materialist interpretation; it would express an intense devotion to beauty and an egoistic ethics giving free and irresponsible scope to anything that won intense devotion. A developed materialism, however, inclines to a sense of social kinship. For the artist sees his work as revealing not only his values, but the common values of men and the special values of his culture; and this is done through a medium and technique socially derived from the traditions of his fellow-men. He is not in lone communion with the eternal or the Absolute. His source and his responsibility lie with his society; if he seeks inspiration, he goes to the aims and hopes and ideals of his fellow-men. Thus there is a general bias against the segregation of the artist from his society, and toward making art a widespread and integrated aspect of communal life.

Chapter 24 THE IDEALIST OUTLOOK ON HUMAN AFFAIRS

Just as philosophical idealism in general is a name for a common trend in a diversity of philosophical approaches, so many types of ethical and social theory may be characterized as idealist by their emphasis on the primacy of the spirit, the degree to which they rely on non-empirical methods, and the extent to which they involve a non-worldly outlook.

In human affairs the non-worldly outlook finds its clearest expression in an emphasis on the eternal. Just as in the domain of metaphysics, idealists have sometimes regarded time and change as merely the lengthened shadow of eternity, so in the domain of history change is viewed as development and development as merely the unfolding of an eternal plan, and in the domain of ethics change is disparaged.

This devotion to eternity is found in the theory of immortality, where the temporal world pales to insignificance before the light of the soul's eternal destiny. It is found in the ethics of duty, where the changing desires of the material world are crushed by the absoluteness of the moral law. It is found even in the apparent glorification of process in the Hegelian philosophy; for his process is not mere change, but the revelation of a fundamental logic of all history.

The idealist outlook on human affairs will be exhibited here by the study of several illustrations. The community of outlook emerges clearly in these different emphases. We shall examine six views: (1) Platonic ethical and social theory and the idealist strain in Aristotle's ethics; (2) Stoicism as a widespread and practical philosophy in ancient times, associated with a pantheistic metaphysics and thus often regarded as materialistically inclined; (3) the Christian outlook on good and evil, as the supernaturalistic idealism which has dominated the western religious tradition; (4) Kantian ethics as an ethics of stern duty and the starting-point of many tendencies in modern times; (5) Royce's philosophy of loyalty, as the ethical theory of the outstanding American philosophical idealist; (6) idealist approaches to the philosophy of history as setting human affairs in the context of a whole world-plan. We cannot, of course, deal here with the full content of each of these topics. Interest will be centered dominantly on the role that idealist philosophical elements play in the outlook on life and conduct.

Plato and Aristotle

PLATO'S ETHICAL AND SOCIAL THEORY

We are already familiar with Plato's general theory of ideas, his ultimate reliance on rational insight, his conception of the individual soul as striving towards the eternal, his attempt to prove the unreality of the bodily pleasures and the reality as well as superiority of the intellectual pleasures, and his double attitude toward art.[1] Plato's ethical and social theory is well-integrated with this general theory.

Plato's view of men as imprisoned souls. Plato's conception of the world as a system of eternal Ideas which existence imperfectly represents is reproduced in his ethical theory. The Idea of the good is the unified source of all values, all knowledge, and even all existence. Plato compares the good to the sun which enables things to grow and at the same time lights them up. He conceives of men as prisoners of the body, souls whose ultimate desire—when not perverted by bodily pressures—is that of reaching the highest knowledge in contemplation of the good. By communion with the eternal men free themselves of the body. The knowledge of the good brings complete understanding and consistent action; Plato follows Socrates in the view that no man can know the good and still not follow it. Hence when men fall short of the good in their conduct it is a sign of fundamental ignorance.

Most men do not know the good; their very pursuit of worldly aims attests to this. Most men would not prefer the life that Plato regards as ideal for the philosopher—to follow the life of the intellect with a group of kindred spirits, paying the least possible attention to bodily needs. Hence in his *Republic* he goes on to sketch the next best society which he deems good in the light of his theory of Ideas and his understanding of human nature.

The organization of Plato's ideal state. The *Republic* is written as a discussion concerning the nature of justice, in the broad sense of the right kind of life to lead. In the dialogue Thrasymachus argues for the egoist's position—that the right kind of life for a man to pursue is to follow his own desires regardless of others. He should endeavor to achieve a maximum of personal satisfaction by any means. Socrates sets out to show that the virtuous man is the really happy man, irrespective of his worldly fortunes. He constructs an ideal society because he hopes thereby to see justice writ large in the relations of men. Thus probing its essence on a large scale, he will find it more easily in the individual man.

---

[1] See above: for general theory, Chapter 2; reliance on insight, pp. 121-22, 346-47; the soul, p. 140; pleasures, pp. 193-94; art, pp. 373-75.

The fundamental principle with which the organization of the ideal society begins is that every man should do the work for which he is best fitted. This apparently obvious principle of division of labor as against the difficulties of everyone's being self-sufficient produces strange results under the guidance of Plato's idealism. It does not describe the way a *job* is carried out, as in a modern factory where, provided that they know the work, it does not matter who does which task. The principle of division of labor in Plato describes instead the way *men* are ordered. The assumption is that each by his nature has a definite role or function which he can best perform and he is fixed in that vocation. As a consequence Plato rejects a citizen-army in favor of a professional army. Three fundamental classes thus emerge. The lowest is that concerned with worldly tasks—workers, artisans, farmers, traders, and so forth. The class above is the army—the guardians of the state, not only of its territory against enemies without, but also of its structure within. The guardians are thus also the executive class of a society, including from a modern point of view the army, the whole administrative civil service, and also teachers and journalists and so forth. The highest class, chosen from this group, are the real guardians or rulers who decide public policy, legislate, and issue orders. The rest of the guardians may thus in the light of their role be called "auxiliaries."

The rulers are the custodians of the good of the society. They act not on opinion, but on knowledge of the good. They are the ones who have received genuine illumination. They are the true philosophers. Only when kings become philosophers or philosophers kings, says Plato, will his kind of society be possible.

Hierarchical conception of society. Plato thus associates a hierarchical conception of society with his theory of Ideas. In fact, in the *Republic,* the exposition of the theory of Ideas is introduced when he is trying to justify the proposition that the philosophers should be the rulers—a proposition which he expects his hearers to find ridiculous. The sharp distinction between opinion as concerned with the changing and knowledge as concerned with the eternal finds its social counterpart in the sharp distinction between the mass of the people who obey (for they do not really *know*) and the rulers who wield absolute power with a conviction of their knowledge. Democracy is thus condemned as the anarchic sway of opinion, in which every man's views are given equal status.

The rulers, keeping their eyes on the true good, regiment the whole society. In order to achieve unity and remove competing interests Plato abolishes the family among the guardians and auxiliaries, and substitutes a system of selective mating for eugenic breeding. Property likewise is in common among them, their needs being satisfied by public resources. Education is most carefully watched; there is strict censorship of the arts because of their influence, and even styles of music are prescribed. The sciences are so taught as to turn the mind from the realm of the senses to the mathematical and the intellectual, and finally to the philosophic. The guardians of the future are selected from among the most promising young people, who in virtue of their merit continue their education well on in life. We cannot here go into all the details of the Platonic ideal state, but the account may be recommended as perhaps the most thorough probing of the philosophic foundations of an authoritarian system in the history of ideas.

Virtues and the analysis of the soul. The virtues that emerge from Plato's search are wisdom, courage, temperance, and justice. The wisdom of the state is found in its rulers. Courage characterizes the whole guardian and auxiliary group, and is not merely valor but a readiness to stick to the principles of the state through thick and thin—the dye, so to speak, has permeated their whole being. Temperance is found in all classes but preeminently attaches to the lowest class; its essence is self-restraint in keeping out of others' places. Plato says there is perhaps little harm if one artisan tries to do another's work, but tremendous harm if members of the lowest class think they can try to rule. Justice is the ruling principle of the whole state, the assigning to each of his due, the role which he can best perform. Justice is thus the *typing* of men in society for the tasks of society, in the light of the good.

Similarly Plato conceives of the individual soul as consisting of three parts. There is the ruling reason, the spirited element or mettle, and the appetitive part. Plato compares the first to a man, the second to a lion, the third to a many-headed dragon. The task is to persuade the lion to aid the man in keeping the dragon of desire in check. The good man is one in whom the parts of the soul exercise their appropriate virtues. The reason of the highest part prevails; the spirit of the second part—the will—effectively and courageously obeys the dictates of reason; and the desires by keeping in order exhibit temperance. Justice or the right kind of life for a man is this integrated system in which each part of the soul plays its appropriate role. The highest part of the soul is thus enabled to achieve its contemplative functions and the true happiness of man is achieved.

The descent of man as of the state consists in power passing from the higher to the lower elements. With the second element in control honor and ambition replace wisdom as goals. Further deterioration makes wealth the aim, and we reach a business civilization. The pressure of the desires in the individual or of the lowest class in the state increases and a democracy of the self or of society results. Each desire considers itself as good as every other and entitled to equal expression, and every man's vote about what is good for the state is regarded as equal to any other man's. This liberty Plato regards as license. The very dogs and donkeys in the street get rights and refuse to get out of your way. Anarchy leads to dictatorship both in the soul and in society; as a result irrational repression is dominant and mutual fear and aggression prevail. The result is complete misery. Happiness lies at the other extreme in the order of the soul and the order of society under the rule of wisdom.

Role of Plato's theory in his day. Although Athens was a slave state it was comparatively democratic insofar as the body of free men was concerned. Within this group a struggle was going on in Socrates' time between the democrats or mass of the people and the oligarchs or wealthy few. The latter looked to Sparta for support. Much of Plato's social attitude was no doubt derived from Socrates, and many of Socrates' disciples played leading parts in the oligarchic movements. The attacks on the many as judges of the good in the Socratic dialogues, and the similarity between the regimented state of the Republic and Spartan procedures (Sparta is also mentioned as an illustration of the kind of state one step removed from the ideal) lead one to conclude that the Socratic and Platonic philosophy was indeed serviceable to the oligarchic faction. Socrates was in fact put to death by the restored democracy after an oligarchic revolution was overcome.[2]

THE IDEALIST STRAIN IN ARISTOTLE'S ETHICS

Aristotle's ethical and social theory as expressed in his *Nicomachean Ethics* and his *Politics* is a comprehensive system synthesizing logical, scientific, and metaphysical elements. One can find fused in it a broad naturalistic strain and a definitive idealistic strain. The former comes from his scientific, especially biological, interests, and his general desire to do justice to all phases of the natural world; the second is largely an evaluative element, with its metaphysical side derived from Platonic idealism. We shall outline here very briefly the general theory and then view the idealist side of his ethics in this setting.

His general ethical theory. Aristotle defines the good as the ultimate aim of man. Looking at the goals men pursue, he decides that the good is not to be identified with wealth, pleasure, or honor, but in general with happiness. Happiness is not a feeling, but a kind of living well; it is the functioning of the soul according to virtue, and since the soul is complex, according to the virtue of its highest parts. The good thus lies in activity or in actualizing the capacities of man. But what are the marks of virtue? Examining the various virtues men adhere to, Aristotle decides that the characteristic mark is action aiming at a *mean*. In discussing virtues as techniques of freedom and liberty, we have seen[3] that Aristotle analyzes virtues such as

---
[2] For a recent detailed study of Plato's theory in relation to his society, see A. D Winspear, *The Genesis of Plato's Thought*, The Dryden Press, 1940.

[3] See above, pp. 268-69.

courage and liberality by finding first the materials of human nature or social activity they embody (fear and confidence, giving and taking) and then the modes in which these materials can be given harmonious expression. Virtue lies between two vices (rashness and timidity, prodigality and miserliness), each of which consists in giving one-sided expression to one of its materials and repressing the other. Each virtue rests upon a habit of choice which embodies not an arithmetical mean, but the mean relative to person, time, place, and circumstance.

There is thus no precise rule for right conduct. Practical wisdom is required and this comes only as habits are established with practice. Aristotle thus pays considerable attention to education. The child at first imitates the man of practical wisdom and comes to regard certain lines of conduct as noble. Gradually when his habits of choice are already established he transcends his model and attains a consciousness of the good in which the reasons for his types of choice are grasped.

Rich as this account of Aristotle's is in insights for the theory of education, it remains largely formal until some content is inserted. This can happen in three ways: (a) Men of practical wisdom can be *pointed out*, so that we may form a conception of the good by concrete observation of their lives and conduct. (b) Specific types of character and habits of choice can be designated as *virtuous* so that we may analyze what materials of human nature and social activity they embody and how the notion of the mean functions concretely. (c) The contents of *human nature* may be specified antecedently so that we may work out the modes of conduct which will give it adequate expression. Consideration of Aristotle's theory in the light of such distinctions shows us his starting-points or assumptions. Apart from these we have only a well-developed framework for ethical and social theory which can be employed by diverse theories. Thus if the nature of the soul be taken as a striving for the perfect knowledge and the love of God, which alone will bring happiness, we can have a supernaturalistic ethics employing the whole Aristotelian framework.

How his formal account is given social content. Aristotle himself makes clear his assumptions in the specification of virtues (b) and of human nature (c). In both of these we can detect the role of his metaphysical theory. This theory, as we saw in Chapter 2, read existence in spiritual terms. It saw the world as a set of existents manifesting fixed natures. These natures, as resident ideals, governed the development and activity of existent things. Hence to those existents some activities were natural, others not. This was simply the treatment of the Platonic ideas or essences as *immanent* in things. This difference from the Platonic view is also found in Aristotle's ethical theory. Plato is readier to criticize existent forms and institutions because he regards all existence as an imperfect approximation to a transcendent ideal. Aristotle, believing in immanent natures, expects to find the natural types of conduct and institutions by looking at the regularities in existent institutions and practices, just as he finds the natures of animal species by examining individual specimens. And just as he has no theory of the evolution of species, so there is no belief that what is desirable or good for men has changed or will change. Forms of society vary, but the good is one and the same. Similarly it is the vicious nature that is fond of the changing, that likes now this, now that. The tastes of the good man are constant.[4]

It is not surprising therefore that the virtues and institutions Aristotle favors are those of his own time, place, and class. We cannot here enter into the details of his account. It ranges over the whole field of conduct. There are petty details such as the slow walk and deliberate speech of the high-minded man. There are searching analyses of the bases of law, such as the principles of justice and the nature of equity. There are studies of the intellectual virtues, of the psychology of moral conflict, and of the many social relations and exchanges that are grouped under friendship. While many of these analyses elaborate concepts capable of wide usage, the specific content nearly always reflects a very limited and local set of values. The concept of the mean itself in its application has an evaluative content, reflecting the general Greek idea of measure, of extremes being *hybris* or presumption challenging the Gods.[5] In its political reference, it appears in Aristotle as an opposition to rule by the very rich or the very poor. He regards both of these as dangerous elements in the state. He favors the mean as likely to maintain stability, that is to prevent continuous efforts toward change. This he identifies as *timocracy*, rule by the substantial citizens. This would include a large number of the citizens. Aristotle is wary of rule by one or a few, since he is fearful of human corruption.[6] In general he thinks the type of government best suited to a people varies with the composition of the people and with special circumstances.

Social role of the concept of nature. The concept of nature is employed by Aristotle in his *Politics* to justify the institutions of slavery, the family, the inferior position of women, and property. In his *Ethics,* he pointed out that although all men are rational, reason has a double side. In its active phase it thinks and rules. In its passive phase it understands or grasps and obeys. In free men the active side is dominant; in slaves and women, the passive side. Hence some men are by nature slaves, and women by nature belong under the mastery of men. Aristotle opposes Plato's abolition of the family: it is impracticable, it will not achieve the unity of feeling Plato

---

[4] *Nicomachean Ethics,* 1166a, 27 ff.

[5] Thus in Euripides' *Hyppolytus* even the vow of perpetual chastity is an affront to Aphrodite.

[6] Even Plato admitted late in life that although monarchy seemed to him capable of achieving the greatest good it could also achieve the greatest evil. Democracy, he thought, could accomplish least good, but also least evil.

sought in the state, but will dilute feeling (instead of every man thinking of others as brothers, he will think of brothers almost as strangers), and so forth. Similarly Plato's communism in property is opposed: without private property men will naturally cease exercising initiative and stop taking care of property. They will have little opportunity to exercise philanthropy, and so forth.

The idealist strain in Aristotle's metaphysics—his immanent teleology— thus comes to his aid in the defense of a middle class social conservatism. We must not assume, however, that the philosophical use of the notion of nature as such leads to conservatism. History shows that it may be the basis of the very opposite type of social attitude. Thus Rousseau took the nature of man to be guileless and simple: man is corrupted by the effects of civilization. It is only a step from the recognition that man is everywhere in chains to urge him to cast them off and give his nature free expression. Under a theory of natural rights the rising middle class in western Europe broke through feudal restrictions. The same doctrine in America was also used later to prevent government regulation of conditions and terms of labor. Whether the doctrine of nature in any of its various senses be used to maintain or to alter the ways of men, in either case it imparts an absolutism to the view. Men who argue from a knowledge of natures and essences are generally convinced of their insight, for they feel that they have grasped the reality of things.

Contemplation the highest value. In addition to the role of Aristotle's immanent teleology in his ethical and social theory, there is another idealist element in his very concept of the nature of man. For the most part, as we have seen,[7] his analysis of the human soul is a classification of the activities of a man—vegetative, motor-sensory, and rational. The feelings and dispositions which form the raw materials of many of his virtues are such as empirical psychology or even common-sense observation readily discovers. But in dealing with reason his account approximates Plato's. Man's reason, as the unique element in his nature, is his special function. Reason deals with the eternal and timeless in things, with that system of natures which is ultimately reckoned by Aristotle as God. The last book of the *Nicomachean Ethics* contains a panegyric of the highest good of man, the contemplation in which the individual transcends social relations. In fact, all moral virtues and social life appear almost as merely preparatory to this higher experience. Practical wisdom seems required only to make speculative wisdom possible.

Ultimately the life of the intellect is the keystone of the Aristotelian ethics. But it is not merely this respect for the intellect which reveals the Platonic element in Aristotle. For it is possible to value the intellect as an

---

[7] See above, pp. 168-69.

ability which has enabled man to attain his civilization, gives promise of more to come, and provides innumerable intrinsic joys—in fact, a central component of all happiness. But Aristotle, like Plato, disparages this instrumental function, just as manual labor is despised, and in Plato the experimental side of science is subordinated to the mathematical. The life of the intellect is a life of leisure. It is worth while for its own sake. For it is contact with the eternal and this is man's highest function.

Stoicism

State of Greek society at time of its rise. The Stoics arose as a philosophical sect in Hellenistic times about a century after the great war between Athens and Sparta. The school was founded by Zeno in Athens when the city-state civilization of the Greek cities was crumbling under the impact of external forces and internal dissensions. For the Greeks, participation in the city-community had been a co-ordinating element in their set of values, so that its break-down brought a certain moral pessimism. The material changes in their lives were tremendous. The seaport towns of Greece declined, as rivals rose on the Asia Minor coast battening on the trade towards the interior of Asia hitherto shut off by the enmity of Persia and the city-states. As the wealth of the Greek cities declined, internal dissension increased. Oligarchs and democrats, the rich and the poor, carried on a fierce class struggle.

Large-scale changes also took place in philosophy. Traditions of other lands seeped in and gave form to many tendencies. Mystery cults grew in number and popularity. In such material instability even Chance became worshiped as a goddess. Many philosophers accordingly turned away distrustfully from the shifting world. Self-sufficiency could not be found in the community, and in the world one could not even pin his hopes upon his own actions, for even the best laid plans could go astray. The only source of value lay in oneself, and so the dominant Hellenistic philosophies shared an individualist bent. The Epicureans looked to what a man *feels;* the Stoics turned to what he *is.* Character was the locus of their values.

Pantheism of the Stoics. The Stoics were fundamentally pantheistic in their outlook. They held that there is an active spirit or reason throughout matter, just as there is in man. This spirit is body and soul in one. The universe is thus God. In elaborating this view the Stoics drew considerably on the ancient Greek philosopher Heraclitus, who had held that all is in flux, that fire is the fundamental element, and that nevertheless there is an eternal *logos* or reason or order in the world. The Stoics combined all these in one and described the universe in all these terms. Man is a fragment of nature and so a fragment of spirit. At death he loses his finite character and is merged with the universal spirit. Since there is reason in the substance of the universe, stern determinism governs the whole process. The emphasis on *inherent* reason and determinism also made the Stoics staunch defenders of the view that the world as it is is thoroughly reasonable, hence good, and all that happens within it is for the best when seen on a worldview.

Conception of virtue and vice. Stoic ethical theory rested on this concept of an order in nature. A man's good lies in following his nature. This was interpreted in the spiritual sense of playing his role, not in the sense of giving free rein to impulse. The role itself is allotted by fate. The individual's task is to do it *fittingly*. Fitness is precisely the sense of the Greek word "aretē" or *virtue*. (Our term comes from the Latin *"vir*tus" which means "*man*liness" or the valorous character befitting a man who is to expect soldiering as a normal part of his activity.) And virtue became the pivotal notion of Stoic ethics. If you have *virtue* you have everything, and all your actions are right.

But virtue is no easy goal; there is no approximation to it, just as a rule allows no exceptions. One of the Stoics draws the comparison of a man under water. Provided his head is not above water, he will drown whether he be a few inches or many feet under. In the same way one cannot be partly virtuous. One has all or none of it. (This strictness of the earlier Stoics was somewhat relaxed by successive generations.) Virtue is the only good, vice the only evil. Everything else is indifferent. Under this "everything else" are comprised wealth, friends, family, indeed life itself. A Stoic sage never mourned the loss of a friend or a wife. In fact, a Stoic did not shrink from suicide in circumstances in which it was the exercise of virtue. Cato the Younger, whom Roman Stoics of the Empire greatly admired, killed himself by falling on his sword after the battle of Thapsus, when Caesar's mastery over the Roman Republic was assured. It was no disgrace to leave a world in which all he had stood for could no longer find a place.

Virtue appears thus as a sort of supreme fitness or excellence in action. When the Stoics described it in general terms they stressed the freedom and peace of mind that a man acquired by severing all ties of desire and attraction that bind him to the world. He engages in normal human life but his spirit does not become so tied to these loves and hopes as to be touched even by casualties. In this fashion he gains the self-sufficiency so stressed as the broad goal of men in Hellenistic ethics. The general trait of Stoic virtue was thus a far-reaching non-worldliness.

Guides for conduct. When the Stoics came to offer specific guides for conduct they were on the whole much too close to the actualities of existence to give an abstract set of rules, covering like a magic umbrella the whole of human nature. Instead they spoke as if a man's duties would grow naturally out of the role he had to play and the type of situation in which he found himself. Each role was held to prescribe its own excellence. To use Gilbert Murray's excellent example,[8] a messenger's duty is to deliver his parcel, and he has fulfilled his role in taking it to the assigned address, even if the person for whom it was intended is absent or no longer alive. We might add, even if it should prove to contain a bomb. Epictetus began as a slave. Marcus Aurelius was an emperor. Both were Stoics. Epictetus preached resignation, the lot of the slave. He might equally well, of course, have preached revolt, and if he found himself in a growing movement of liberation it would have been his duty to go on regardless of his own life. The senators of the early Roman Empire resisted their ruler in the name of the rights of their class and their people. Their resistance was unsuccessful and often they paid with their lives. This led to a Stoic fortitude in their assumption of a secondary place. Seneca earned his reputation for Stoicism by the show he put on in his letters, and by his death by suicide at the order of Nero. One example from his letters is illustrative. He writes that he has deliberately taken quarters over a public bath, where he studies daily, steeling his mind against the scraping and splashing, which he describes in full. Thus he hopes to achieve a mind independent of its surroundings.[9] When Vespasian exiled the philosophers from Rome he directed this edict mainly against the Stoics, who were daring to question the legitimacy of the armed force by which he had seized power.

A good example in classical times of the trust which a Stoic character inspired is that of Cato the Younger, who was sometimes regarded as a model by the later Roman Stoics. Plutarch tells how in one of the turbulent years before the accession of Caesar, when corruption was seething in Rome and electoral honesty seemed impossible, all candidates agreed to deposit a tremendous sum with Cato on the understanding that if he merely so much as affirmed that any of them had attempted bribery or any other kind of corruption, that one's share should be forfeit.[10] So, at least, Plutarch reports and regards it as a tribute to the character and dignity of the man, and to the respect which good character wins even among supposedly "corrupt" mankind.

The Stoic approach was of special importance in the elaboration of criteria of right conduct appropriate to different types of careers. They helped build up standards for a soldier, a patriot, a father, a husband, a philosopher, and so forth. Having at heart the concrete business of living rather than merely consistent speculation about it, they began a work necessary within a single culture and a single system of law—the elaboration of con-

[8] *The Stoic Philosophy,* Putnam's, 1915.
[9] *Epistles to Lucilius,* 56.
[10] *Plutarch's Lives,* Everyman's Library, Vol. 3, p. 62.

crete duties in definite types of situations. It is the same need that is faced in our society by the many agencies which meet problems like "What do the employer and employee owe to one another?" "Does the state owe food to all its citizens?" "What are the special responsibilities of a factory-owner, a landlord, a policeman?" "Should a teacher attempt to convey to the pupils his own convictions or those of his employers?" "What are a grown child's duties to his parents?"

No guide for clash of roles. If a part in life were as simple as wearing a character mask in an O'Neill play, or being a type such as the lover or harsh father in Terence's comedies, this kind of Stoic analysis would suffice us. But in reality we play many conflicting parts like the actor who is Hamlet on Monday, Romeo on Tuesday, Brutus on Wednesday, and Lear on Thursday. And even when not acting, he may yet be a perplexed avenger, lover, morbid philosopher, neglected parent, and partake in a dozen other careers. Nor does the elaboration of alternative roles tell him which to choose. Socrates thought it his duty as a citizen to die rather than escape from a death sentence he regarded as unjust; others with equal conviction might resist an unjust law.

The essential weakness in the Stoic formula is that it has no prescription for dealing with the clash of goals. This would require a conception of the common good as concrete as the picture of any man's role, and very much wider. It would have to rest on an analysis of trends and typical situations in the world of men and be oriented to the task of specific decision. The Stoics concentrated on mastery of the self regardless of what external circumstances might bring. In thus narrowing their conception of good to the goods of character they sacrificed the opportunity to fashion a set of common goals towards which men in a community might devote their efforts in an attempt to master their surroundings. This consequence followed from the individualist emphasis of Stoicism and fundamentally from its non-worldliness. Hence it provided at most a general attitude, though a very influential one. Among the positive contributions of Stoicism was a cosmopolitan outlook transcending local and accidental differences among mankind. Seneca, for example, derives this cosmopolitanism from the Stoic assumption that a spark of divine fire is inherent in the nature of every human being, and extends this to include even slaves. The conception that there is a single law of nature for all men also played a part in the development of the notion of natural law in Roman jurisprudence. But the stress on man brought in turn a cosmic narrowness. It was Cleanthes, second head of the Stoic school, who condemned Aristarchos of Samos for his declaration that the earth moved around the sun instead of the reverse. What a blow to morals it would be, he felt, if the hearth of the universe were moved from this earth!

The Christian outlook on good and evil

In a previous chapter we considered the tenets of the existence of God and the soul and the immortality of the soul, especially as they appear in the western religious tradition, and the types of philosophic grounds on which such beliefs have been held. From the point of view of the present chapter the problem is one of the attitudes in the conduct of life associated with a supernaturalistic idealism. How in the light of a positive acceptance of the Christian belief in God and the soul and immortality should a man live his life? What should he regard as good and what as evil, and how should he regard the good and the evil?

The Christian outlook on life, as it became embodied in the formal doctrines of medieval Catholicism, did not arise at one time. In its origins Christianity belonged to a period in which various types of religous mysticism in the Near East and throughout the Roman world competed for men's faith. Christianity was a social movement as well as a set of beliefs, and it triumphed through the appeal which its assurance of God's plan and man's immortality made to men, particularly the poor and the oppressed. Modern scholarship has shown how Christianity, starting with a basis of Hebraic religious tradition, absorbed elements from the various competing traditions and from the Greek philosophical schools.

In Christian theory as it developed, God's plan is known by revelation. It is found in the Bible, in the records of Christ's teachings, and the writings of the apostles. The assumption was made early in the development of Christianity that these embodied divine commands for the conduct of all of life. The specific injunctions for special situations were just a matter for interpretation. Moral recommendations were stated either as particular rules, precepts embodying divine commandment, or by reference to a general attitude with which conduct is to be imbued.

THE GOOD

In general, Christian theory takes man's good and his happiness to lie in doing the will of God. And God is taken to be good, so that the commands issued to man are themselves expressive of the good. For many theologians this goodness is not a matter of chance. When the question was pressed as to whether God, if almighty, might not interchange right and wrong (or for that matter render arithmetical rules false), the scholastic philosophers found a way out by insisting that God's goodness was not accidental but his very nature, as was also truth. God was asserting himself in whatever was good and true.[11]

Human life on this earth is, on this view, essentially a testing ground for the individual. The stakes are high—the eternal salvation or damnation of the soul. It is important to note, in this familiar conception of heaven and hell, that the conduct of this life is what determines future destiny. We need not enter here into the various opinions concerning the relative share of faith and works in contributing to salvation, nor the role of grace and the sufferings of Christ in compensating for original sin and making individual salvation possible. It is sufficient to recognize the central attitude involved—that by comparison to the fate of his eternal soul all other cares of man are trivial. The spiritual is the proper object of human devotion, and the desires and pleasures of this world are often explicitly branded as vain.

Opposition to worldliness. The result has often been a dominant anti-worldliness and anti-sensualism. The body and its drives—especially the sexual—are the source of temptation to sin and the loss of eternal good. Asceticism is an avenue to salvation. This has involved not only the condemnation of the worldly aims of wealth and ambition but even the disparagement of men's domestic and civic relations. The spiritual order stands totally opposed to the natural world. Such attitudes were given institutional form in the development of monastic orders.

Another result of this opposition of the spiritual and the natural has often been a stress on inwardness which makes the quality of spirit pre-eminent in ethical estimation. This has included reckoning evil desire as just as sinful as evil action. It is a stress on the spirit with which thought and action take place. Love is the central attribute of proper motivation. Primarily it is love of God, resting on faith in the spiritual order and trust in the divine support of an imperfect humanity. It is also a love of men as fellow-members in God's spiritual order.

Distinctive virtues. A number of distinctive virtues have characterized the outlook that results from this fundamental attitude,[12] particularly its medieval forms and those most akin to it. Obedience with unquestioning submission follows from the form of commandment in which morality as a whole is cast. Again, as Sidgwick says, "We might further derive from the general spirit of Christian unworldliness that repudiation of the secular modes of conflict, even in a righteous cause, which substituted a passive patience and endurance for the old pagan virtue of courage, in which the

---

[11] Some theologians took issue with this analysis (e.g., Duns Scotus as against Aquinas) and stressed the priority of will over intellect in the divine nature. This in effect gave morality ultimately an arbitrary or contingent character instead of a rational and absolute character.

[12] For a good, brief summary of these, as well as of Christian morality in general, see Henry Sidgwick, *Outlines of the History of Ethics*, 5th ed., Macmillan, 1906, Chapter 3.

active element was prominent."[13] This ethics of turning the other cheek in response to violence was expressive of a love that could conquer resentment. On a positive side this universal love found expression in benevolence and beneficence. Christian charity made the practical doing of good to others a form of divine service, as compared for example to the interchange of goods in a kind of mutually compensating friendship which characterizes Aristotle's theory. And all these activities of a good Christian are permeated with humility. This is more than an absence of pride. It is more than the natural concomitant of obedience and patience. Humility entails a rejection even of the feeling of personal merit; it constitutes a deep sense of the man's imperfection and his reliance on God.

Complexity and variety in the Christian tradition. This brief sketch of the attitudes whose possession marks a good life necessarily ignores variations over the centuries of development of Christian theory. It likewise omits differential elements in various sects and churches (especially after the Reformation). And it does not trace the practical consequences of these attitudes in different ages in the stands taken by Christian churches on matters of social policy. Such positions—as the opposition of the Catholic church to usury and its compromises in a growing commercialism, the present diversity of Catholic and various Protestant views on questions of birth control and censorship of movies, and many other important issues—do not come within the scope of our brief theoretical inquiry. Instead we turn from the account of the good in traditional Christian theory to the attitude taken toward the occurrence and nature of evil.

The vices. The type of character and outlook that the Christian tradition regards as evil requires little elaboration. The content of sin and the vices may readily be inferred from the virtues we have been discussing. Pride, Avarice, Anger, Gluttony, Unchastity appear in all lists of the seven "deadly sins." These are evils of character to be avoided by men. They are temptations to worldliness, tendencies to be struggled against.

More difficult problems are entailed in the analysis of evil in the sense of suffering and human misery. Here the central issue is the attitude men should adopt. How far should they resign themselves to such occurrences, how far should they spend time and effort in a struggle for the removal of as much misery as possible from human life? How far does such struggle entail the risk of worldliness?

THE PROBLEM OF EVIL

This question of attitude is at stake in the many theoretical disputes that center around the traditional "problem of evil." The problem is posed in

[13] *Op. cit.,* p. 120.

terms of the attributes of God. It arises because God is assigned omniscience, omnipotence, and goodness, and is likewise held to be the source of all existence. But how can there be evil in a universe which expresses the will of God who is omnipotent, omniscient, *and* good? This form of religious idealism is thus faced with the difficult task of resolving three apparently inconsistent beliefs: (a) God is good, (b) God is omnipotent and omniscient, and (c) there is evil in the world. If goodness is of God's essence and is coupled with omnipotence and omniscience, how can there be evil? If there is evil, and God is good, then God cannot be its cause; but if some other force is responsible, God's almightiness or wisdom is impaired. Finally, if in spite of the omnipotence and omniscience there is evil, how can God be good? [14]

There are only two alternative solutions within the framework of this problem. One is to introduce some fresh notion, such as an account of God's reasons for permitting evil in the world. The other alternative is to deny one of the three propositions. All four courses—a saving explanation, and the denial of each of (a), (b), and (c)—have been attempted.

Attempted solution in terms of original sin. The theory of original sin is an illustration of an attempt to keep all three propositions. In the beginning God gave man freedom of choice, and evil is a consequence of man's wrong choice. This, however, raises fresh problems. If freedom is absolute, God is no longer almighty—man can raise his proud spirit in the fashion of a Miltonesque Satan even while God crushes him; if freedom is not absolute, God is responsible for the kind of choice man makes. If that choice is unknown in advance to God, then omniscience is denied. Much ingenuity has been spent and numerous distinctions elaborated in defense of this type of solution; sometimes its ultimate resolution is said to lie beyond the finite understanding.

Attempted solution by denying reality of evil. Of the solutions that reject one of the three propositions, the denial of (c), the belief that there is evil in the world, has been most common in religious idealism. Such a solution implies a special conception of evil. It does not deny that there is human suffering or misery in the world—that is too patent for anyone to overlook—but it denies that these are evil. As Pope says in his *An Essay on Man:*

> All nature is but art, unknown to thee;
> All chance, direction which thou canst not see;
> All discord harmony not understood;
> All partial evil, universal good;

[14] John Stuart Mill says of his father, James Mill: "He found it impossible to believe that a world so full of evil was the work of an Author combining infinite power with perfect goodness and righteousness. His intellect spurned the subtleties by which men attempt to blind themselves to this open contradiction." (*Autobiography*, Chapter 2.)

And spite of pride, in erring reason's spite
One truth is clear: whatever is—is right.

Leibniz was equally convinced of the world's thorough goodness, when he thought of God, by nature good, choosing this as the best of all possible worlds.[15] And Browning's optimism in "God's in his heaven, all's right with the world," only echoes the chant of the faithful in sorrow, "The Lord giveth and the Lord taketh away; blessed be the name of the Lord."

Evil is thus defined implicitly as suffering without a good purpose, and the existence of such evil is denied. This approach is found in a restricted fashion in the Book of Job. Job's problem is not so much why there is suffering in the world as why good men who deserve rewards meet instead with suffering. If suffering fell only on the wicked, it would, presumably, be just punishment. Job is finally overcome by the grandeur of God's power and its creations. He is satisfied that his suffering served some good purpose, although man may be too puny to fathom divine intention. Yet the very existence of a wicked man deserving punishment would seem an evil demanding explanation if one accepts God's omnipotence and goodness.

Various other attempts have been made to dismiss evil. The view that suffering appears evil because we are considering merely a fragmentary portion of reality and not its full plan is common among philosophical idealists. The Stoics, for example, compared evil in life to phrases in a comedy, which appear ugly or uncouth in isolation, but play their part in the artistic character of the piece as a whole. Another attempt of a similar nature is to assign evil to matter's inertia—as the sculptor may blame the resistance of the marble—in the hope of giving it a purely negative character. This approach, however, threatens God's omnipotence. Christian Science theory simply declares evil illusory as inconsistent with the other properties of God, and is ready to carry its conviction to opposition to surgical treatment of bodily ailments.

Less sophisticated attempts to justify suffering arise from men's usual attitudes when they try to find some consolation for a misfortune. Perhaps "the loss of something makes us realize its worth"; we "learn to value what we have"; "Misfortune is also a great touchstone of character" and often serves to remold it. "The existence of evil is necessary for the enhancement of the appreciation of good,"—or for its recognition, or for its very achievement.

This type of claim, if made *a priori,* rests on a confusion of *meaning* and *existence.* It is true that we cannot know what good means unless we know

---

[15] See Voltaire's satire, in his *Candide,* on this position. Candide is taught the doctrine by his master Pangloss and faithfully believes it through a whole gamut of distressing and ridiculous situations.

what evil *means*.[16] But this does not imply that evil must *exist* for us to know the meaning of an existent good. It need have only a definition. We can define many things of which there are no actual examples, such as a fairy godfather with wings. As for the instrumental values of suffering and the demoralizing effects of a straight run of good, we may wonder whether these are not to be construed as lessons of experience for an economy of scarcity. Where a long run of happiness is to be construed as a run of luck it is well not to train people to accept it complacently but to be prepared for hardship. Such an attitude may linger, however, even where its basis has disappeared—as, for example, in the opposition to the use of partial anesthetics at child-birth on the ground that this type of suffering is the destined lot of women. In any case, even if we find that some good issues out of evil—and this is the fervent hope of men when evils befall them—it does not follow that further knowledge, much less than omniscience and omnipotence, may not find a way to achieve the same results without suffering.

Attempted solution by denying God's omnipotence. In the light of such problems and more especially because of the apparent callousness involved in denying the reality of evil, some philosophers have attempted instead to deny God's omnipotence. If God is not almighty, then he may be responsible for the good but not for the evil. Another power may bear the blame for this—the devil, for example. Or perhaps it is matter that dulls the spirit. The Persian religion (Zoroastrianism) tried a more positive dualistic course. There is a spirit of darkness as well as of light. Man's duty is to aid the spirit of light to overcome the spirit of darkness. The struggle between the forces of good and evil is conceived as a terrific one. Every ounce of strength and every good deed are requisite for the fray. However, the spirit of light is *sure* to win. Such are the irreconcilable desires for security of outcome on the one hand and the feeling of freedom in action on the other. And the security desired is not merely optimism, such as a college team's confidence in its coming victory, but a cosmic guarantee.

William James, following John Stuart Mill, also elaborated a conception of God in which omnipotence was eliminated. Condemning the theoretically well-ordered universe, he divided philosophers into tender-minded and tough-minded. The former wanted safety and order, the latter were ready to face unknown dangers. The one wanted pattern and determinism and a kindly cosmos; the other an open world with room for real struggle and consequently real success. Associating himself with the vigorous group because he thought that a completely ordered universe invited men to take a "moral holiday," James denied God's omnipotence and conceived of men as God's allies in the struggle to bring order out of chaos. With success God grows as well as man.

[16] For a discussion of a similar polarity, see the account of selfishness and unselfishness, pp. 204-05, above.

Attempted solution by putting God beyond good and evil. The last possibility within this framework is to reject the proposition that God is good. This does not make God evil but puts him beyond good and evil. The result is that good and evil are seen as consequences of some finite point of view. From an infinite point of view there is neither, just the set of natural events. Good becomes good *for* and evil evil *to* someone. Nor need there be a single absolute form of life which would reconcile all claims and be everyone's good. Spinoza held this view (though with a different interpretation of God) and because of it, more than perhaps anything else, was called an impious heretic. In a different fashion but with like result, Schopenhauer, who painted a thoroughly pessimistic picture of our world, treated the world will as without intelligence, purpose, or interest in goodness.

The fact that relatively few have taken the course of denying that goodness is predicable of God is itself significant. It reveals the essentially moral core of religious idealism—in fact of religion itself—in our tradition. To solve the problem of evil by taking away God's goodness would seem to most religious people in the western tradition equivalent to taking away the God they pray to and giving them instead an alien world-creator. In other religious traditions the proposition that God is good might seem less binding. For there are societies, for example in Africa, in which fear is the chief religious emotion, the spirits are conceived as powers to be placated, and the best one may hope from them is to be left alone.

Attempted solutions as fundamental attitudes to the conduct of life. These various solutions to the problem of evil are fundamentally recommendations of differing attitudes for the conduct of life. Broadly speaking, the denial of evil suggests resignation, the denial of God's omnipotence urges struggle, with the assurance of strong cosmic support, the denial of God's goodness prompts one to struggle entirely on one's own feet with a possible suggestion of pessimism.

While these attitudes give differing emotional tones to conduct they need not necessarily determine it fully. This is true even of extreme fatalism which believes every detail of life to be foreordained in line with some teleological scheme. Directly contrary attitudes are possible with such a view. For some, fatalism negates all striving. Success will not come from endeavor, but only from fate, and if it is preordained it will come even without effort. On the other hand, the belief in fatalism may provoke reckless daring and great venturesomeness. This is typified in the legend of the boy who went swimming in a river full of crocodiles to recover a hat that had blown away. He argued that had he been fated to die he would have died then in any case; no amount of care would have saved him. So long as he was destined to live, such an escapade could not be dangerous. Max Weber, in his *Protestant Ethic and the Spirit of Capitalism,* shows how the Calvinist belief in predestination (that it is preordained which souls are to be saved and which damned), instead of leading to inaction, was turned to yield initiative. For the further theory was added that every man had a calling, and success in the calling was evidence that he was among the elect.

In spite of the variety of conduct, in spite of the clash of attitudes within the Christian tradition, there is present throughout—except in those for whom religious concepts are a mere linguistic garb—a dominant non-worldliness, an orientation away from secular cares and the shifting basis of worldly aims, so that even worldly tendencies where they occur seek a non-worldly role and justification.

Kantian ethics

Kantian metaphysics has been called phenomenalist by some, idealist by others; but his ethical theory is clearly idealist. It is non-worldly to an extreme. It seeks to remove from morals the least taint of empirical method. And it draws a sharp contrast between Reason, which is not of this world but legislates for it, and desires, which are buffeted about by earthly forces. Kant provides the most influential example of an ethics of stern duty.

"The moral law within." Fundamentally Kant does not question common morality. His aim is rather to give it a solid foundation. Similarly in his metaphysical works he thought he was giving a solid foundation to mathematical and physical knowledge. "Two things," he says, in the conclusion of his *Critique of Practical Reason,* "fill the mind with ever new and increasing admiration and awe, the oftener and the more steadily we reflect on them: *the starry heavens above and the moral law within.* I have not to search for them and conjecture them as though they were veiled in darkness or were in the transcendent region beyond my horizon; I see them before me and connect them directly with the consciousness of my existence. . . . The former view of a countless multitude of worlds annihilates as it were my importance as an *animal creature,* which after it has been for a short time provided with vital power, one knows not how, must again give back the matter of which it was formed to the planet it inhabits (a mere speck in the universe). The second on the contrary infinitely elevates my worth as an *intelligence* by my personality, in which the moral law reveals to me a life independent on animality and even on the whole sensible world, at least so far as may be inferred from the destination assigned to my existence by this law, a destination not restricted to conditions and limits of this life, but reaching into the infinite." [17]

[17] *Kant's Theory of Ethics,* translation by T. K. Abbott, 2nd ed., Longmans, Green, 1879, pp. 376-77.

Kant opposes the empiricist tradition as represented by Hume, which made knowledge of nature merely an association of ideas, and moral feelings merely an association of the useful in the fulfillment of desires. At the same time he was discontented with the old procedure of establishing self-evident first principles for knowledge of nature and for morals. Thus he poses his work as directed against both *empiricism* with its probabilism and *rationalism* with its intuitive first principles. His own critical method consists in finding what *must* be the case to validate knowledge of nature and moral obligation. Just as the fall of a stone and the motion of a sling were resolved into elements and forces and treated mathematically with great success, so he hopes that the instances of the moral judgment of reason may be analyzable into elementary conceptions to produce comparably imposing results.[18]

The good will and the categorical imperative. Fundamentally Kant is arguing from a critical analysis of man's feeling of obligation. He finds that this has a "must" element, for which he seeks an account. Not the consequences of action—for these are a matter of chance—but the motives of action constitute the region in which moral worth is to be found. Yet how determine the proper motives? The answer is given by Kant in terms of the *good will*. "Nothing can possibly be conceived in the world, or even out of it, which can be called good without qualification, except a Good Will" is the opening sentence of his *Fundamental Principles of the Metaphysic of Morals*.[19]

The morality of an action therefore lies in its issuing from a good will. But what are the criteria of a good will? This problem for Kant is comparable to the Stoic search for the criteria of virtue. The Stoics offered an account in terms of an individual salvation of serenity secured by divorcing oneself from worldly ties. Kant's answer, as we shall see, bears a marked similarity despite a different formulation.

Since the good will is to provide the criterion for distinguishing motives that are moral from those that are not, it cannot be characterized by the content of the motives themselves, nor is it enough that the actions be the kind that duty would command. In addition to being *according to duty* action issuing from a good will must be *from a sense of duty*. Although it is a duty for people to seek happiness, Kant thinks that most people are not moral in seeking it—they act so because they like being happy and not because it is their duty to be so! Kant is usually suspicious of the morality of any action in which duty and interest coincide. To be moral the action must be done purely from a sense of duty and not constitute giving way

---

[18] This analogy comes from the conclusion of the *Critique of Practical Reason*. Kant does not expect mathematical precision in morals, but hopes for a process similar to that of chemistry.

[19] Abbott, *op. cit.*, p. 10.

to private interests, which Kant calls *subjective springs* of conduct as distinguished from objective moral law.

What Kant has in fact done is to reduce the moral reckoning to the abstract question of whether action issues from a sense of duty. For, once he has removed the consequences of the action and the motives that inspired it, there is nothing left in terms of which morality can be judged except the bare form of duty. With this removal of all specific content by which the individual and the circumstances of the action can be identified, all determination of morality can rest only on formal factors. The good will must act on universal law and the mark of its decisions must be that they hold for any man. Thus morality acquires the universal scope that Kant so admired in Newtonian physics.

From this analysis Kant formulates a principle which is to provide the "must" for human action: "I am never to act otherwise than so *that I could also will that my maxim should become a universal law.*" This he offers as a *categorical* imperative, a command without if's and but's, unlike the conditional or *hypothetical* commands of the form "If you want this, do that." Proper motivation, then, consists in acting only on a maxim which you can consistently universalize, upon which you are ready to have all men act. Take killing, for example. One could not sincerely will that all men should act with the motive of killing. Therefore it is wrong to kill. In this way a method is provided for generating absolutes.

That Kant regarded the results as absolute is well illustrated in his essay *On a Supposed Right to Tell Lies from Benevolent Motives.*[20] Here he insists that if you were questioned as to the whereabouts of a man by someone who wished to kill him, you had either to keep quiet or tell the truth, hoping (Kant suggests) that the intended victim would meanwhile have escaped. To circumvent the villain's designs by guiding him in the wrong direction while you call for aid is of course morally out of the question! The reasons Kant goes on to give are quite revealing. If you tell a lie and the victim has by chance gone in the direction in which you send the villain, the man's blood will be on your head because his death is a consequence of your lie. If you disobey the moral rule, all mischance lands at your door; if you obey it, all disaster is attributed to accident, and your hands are clean. Thus Kant's imperative simply generates individual salvation in a world in which there is no hope of controlling circumstances with any assurance of success. In these respects Kantian doctrine parallels the Stoic views that the spirit must be saved at any worldly cost.

Kant's absolutism estimated. The formal character of the categorical imperative is, however, really insufficient to determine specific rules of conduct. The test of a maxim's morality, as the statement of the categorical imperative itself shows, lies in whether a man can also will that his maxim

[20] *Ibid.*, pp. 431-37.

should become a universal law. The "can" presumably means "can will consistently." Now the consistency involved is not purely logical. A given man's willing thus would be consistent if it produced no internal clash among his various will-acts, present and future. But this is a contingent phenomenon that may not uniformly take the direction Kant seems to assume. Should X take advantage of Y's distress to gain profit? Only, says the categorical imperative, if he can consistently will a form of life in which everyone acted on that motive. Suppose X is not merely ready to do so, and to take his chances in such a world, but actually does so, that is, he behaves that way consistently without regret, admires such attitudes in others even when it involves action directed against himself, applauds great successes achieved in this way, educates his children in this fashion, and so forth. Then the act must, on Kantian grounds, be conceded as moral. And experience shows—much as we may regret it—that many people are in fact ready to treat this world as a battleground for individuals in which kindness is weakness. But if Kant's procedure for establishing the morality of conduct permits such a conclusion, how can that procedure determine the rules of right and wrong which he sets forth?

Kant does not entirely ignore this problem. Yet instead of seeing this as proof of an essential relativity in his theory, he introduces an *ad hoc* idea and begs the question by regarding such willing as perverse, and such a man as depraved.[21]

Other formulations of the imperative. In addition to his first formulation ("Act only on that maxim whereby thou canst at the same time will that it should become a universal law"), Kant stated the categorical imperative in two other ways. One, which has had a wide humanitarian influence, said: "So act as to treat humanity, whether in thine own person or in that of any other, in every case as an end withal, never as a means only." In spite of Kant's attempt to regard this as merely another formulation of his general categorical imperative, it clearly adds a special value. Thus it would not allow, as we saw the first formulation did, a complete and consistent egoism. This assertion of worth for every man has been regarded as a foremost expression of man's dignity in the cosmos. It bears an analogous position in his theory to cosmopolitanism in the Stoic doctrine. Their view was derived from the fact that there was reason in all existence; Kant's from the principle that rational nature is an end in itself.

The other reformulation of his imperative (expressed by Kant in a number of different ways) is: "Every rational being must so act as if he were by his maxims in every case a legislating member in the universal kingdom of ends." This becomes also the ideal of political theory for Kant: every man is a legislator in an ideal rational community, whether he be in the

[21] This problem is discussed in his essay *Of the Indwelling of the Bad Principle Along with the Good; or, On the Radical Evil in Human Nature.*

position of sovereign or of subject, for the laws of such a community express everyone's will.[22] At the same time this third formulation is given a transcendental character in Kantian ethics. Moral rules are orders which the rational self issues to itself, legislating in the realm of ends; it turns out to be a transcendental self legislating in a transcendental realm where it can ignore the disturbing influences of this world. But its rules are imperatives for us here and now. And they rule us not by stepping into the fray as forces, but as objects of our respect, continually drawing us away from the this-worldly conflict of desires and passions.

Inadequacy of his analysis of moral experience. It has generally been conceded by modern philosophers that Kantian ethics is an inadequate account of moral experience. Its stress on the completely formal does not provide a basis for application, except by smuggling in tacit assumptions about what men will in fact will or what everybody recognizes as necessary for social welfare. The stress on the sense of duty also does violence to men's moral feelings by the way in which it excludes humanitarian feelings as a basis of moral worth. Furthermore, once his particular moral rules are derived, Kant has little to say about the problems that rise in their clash. He does not develop a hierarchy of rules, and is certainly unwilling to abide by any empirical testing of how they function.

Some philosophers have sought to make Kant's categorical imperative more useful by emending it to read: "Act in such a way that you would be willing that anyone else *in the same circumstances* should act in the same way, even towards you." In this form it resembles the Golden Rule. While this does not meet the objection offered above of the thoroughly selfish man who is ready to let others be the same, it does offer a useful guide to conduct and is probably a less difficult alternative to operate with than a hierarchy of rules. Essentially it is a demand for a reasoned statement of the factors that justify conduct. It forces a man to find tenable grounds for any claim that he should be differentially treated. Further, in its references to *circumstances* it turns reason to the task of evaluating differences in experience and in conditions that may be the justifiable basis of different conduct. Hence it departs from the Kantian formalism in the direction of empiricism.

Royce's philosophy of loyalty

Quest of the eternal. "I believe in the eternal. I am in quest of the eternal. As to moral standards, in particular, I do not like that mere homesickness and spiritual estrangement, and that confusion of mind about moral

[22] The similarity of this view to Rousseau's conception of the general will is obvious.

ideals, which is nowadays too common.'I want to know the way that leads our human practical life homewards, even if that way prove to be infinitely long. I am discontented with mere discontent. I want, as well as I can, not merely to help you to revise some of your moral standards, but to help you to give to this revision some definitive form and tendency, some image and hint of finality." [23]

Nature of loyalty. This, in his own words, is the task that Royce sets himself. He finds a starting-point in the concept of loyalty and comes to believe that when loyalty is properly defined it constitutes the fulfillment of the whole moral law, rendering intelligible all such virtues as justice, charity, industry, wisdom, and spirituality. Loyalty itself is defined at the outset as *"the willing and practical and thoroughgoing devotion of a person to a cause."* [24]

Royce postpones consideration of the kind of cause to which a man should be loyal. He explores, instead, the nature of a man's relation to a cause. The cause is seen as outside the man or else as including the man, but not as merely an object of his affection. The loyal man serving his cause is not merely seeking his own private advantage but following something that is seen as objective and of value. It is not his alone, but may be served by others; common loyalty binds him to those others. In serving his cause the loyal man overcomes hesitancy, surrenders self-will, exercises self-control, and tends to achieve unity or stability in his life.

For Royce a man's duty is simply his own will brought to his clear self-consciousness and his good is simply the object of his deepest desire when he comes to know what it is. "Your duty is what you yourself will to do in so far as you clearly discover who you are, and what your place in the world is." [25] Royce maintains, however, that this discovery is not made by a ready introspection or following momentary caprice, nor by examining social standards but by a complex interplay of the inner and the outer in which both become clarified. For there is no ready-made self—you look within to find out what you want and what your duty is, but get no clear answer. You must therefore look without; but no sooner have you begun to model your conduct on the ways of the world than you reassert yourself, see your differences, and go back to yourself to discover your duty.

Loyalty to a cause alone breaks in on such a circular process. It grips you, exalts your self yet carries you out of yourself, intensifies your self-consciousness yet renders your will obedient. You develop unity of purpose, and the former hesitations melt away. Royce lavishes his eloquence upon this attitude of loyalty; in effect, his ultimate values—like the Stoics' virtue and

---

[23] From Josiah Royce, *The Philosophy of Loyalty*, pp. 10-11. By permission of The Macmillan Company, publishers.
[24] *Ibid.*, p. 16.
[25] *Ibid.*, p. 27.

Kant's good will—turn out to be the feelings and attitudes that he finds in loyal men.

Loyalty to loyalty. The crucial point comes when Royce turns to consider the problem of evaluating the causes to which loyalty is due. He sees that difficulties arise in life from the clash of loyalties. In the conflicts that arise men endanger and destroy not merely one another's well-being, but also one another's loyalties. This seems to Royce a supreme loss. Hence it suggests to him a criterion for the selection of causes. We should aim at increasing rather than diminishing loyalty in the world. *"In choosing and in serving the cause to which you are to be loyal, be, in any case, loyal to loyalty."* [26]

This, Royce decides, is a cause worthy of our loyalty. It is a cause which can unite rather than divide men, and all men are capable of loyalty. Men may constantly further the cause of loyalty in the very act of following the special causes to which they may be attached; in fact this wider cause will help reduce these others to a system. It is also a very practical cause, not a remote humanitarianism. For—and this shows how broadly loyalty is construed in Royce's ethical theory—all the usual virtues can be viewed as special forms of loyalty to loyalty. The virtue of telling the truth, for example, is an instance of loyalty to loyalty. To tell the truth on any occasion is to be loyal to the personal tie that arises in the special transaction between the men concerned in that discourse. Speaking the truth also furthers the general confidence of man in man and so extends loyalties. Similarly the whole alarm that arises from an act of dishonesty in business is due to the undermining of others' loyalties. Justice, too, is regarded by Royce as one aspect of loyalty—as decisiveness in the choice of a cause, faithfulness to it, and respect for the loyal ties of all other men. Other virtues can be analyzed in similar fashion. Royce does this and also considers many human relations specifically for the opportunities they offer for increased loyalties.

Man's place in the universe. Eventually Royce turns to the problem of man's place in the universe and discusses it in the light of his moral analysis. He begins by posing the question of the ultimate worth of loyalty. Any particular loyalty, he points out, may turn out not to be well-founded; for it is part of the loyal man's belief that his cause is good, apart from his service, and that particular good may turn out in the man's subsequent experience to be an illusory one. The same question may be raised about loyalty to loyalty. Is the fostering of loyalty among men ultimately a worth-while cause?

Royce goes on, however, to reverse the whole question. He has found loyalty to be the whole character of the moral life. He therefore asks instead, "What must be true about the universe if . . . loyalty itself is a genuine good, and not a merely inevitable human illusion?" [27] In this respect Royce,

[26] *Ibid.*, p. 121.
[27] *Ibid.*, p. 307.

like Kant, is trying to suggest what the world must be like to satisfy his analysis of moral consciousness, and thus to extract a metaphysics from ethics. The result is a kind of moral argument for the existence of God. For, as Royce points out,[28] loyalty involves "spiritual unity of life, which transcends the individual experience of any man. . . . For loyalty, as we have seen, is a service of causes that, from the human point of view, appear superpersonal. Loyalty holds these unities to be good. If loyalty is right, the real goodness of these causes is never completely manifested to any one man, or to any mere collection of men. Such goodness, then, if completely experienced at all, must be experienced upon some higher level of consciousness than any one human being ever reaches. If loyalty is right, social causes, social organizations, friendships, families, countries, yes, humanity, as you see, must have the sort of unity of consciousness which individual human persons fragmentarily get, but must have this unity upon a higher level than that of our ordinary human individuality. Some such view, I say, must be held if we are to regard loyalty as in the end anything more than a convenient illusion."

From this analysis Royce is able to reach a final definition of loyalty as "the will to manifest, so far as is possible, the Eternal, that is, the conscious and superhuman unity of life, in the form of the acts of an individual Self."[29] This leads him into a religious formulation of the real world as an Absolute that is alive and has the character of experience, that is interested in our personal destiny as moral beings.

Estimate of Royce's argument. In Royce's formulation there appears, however, to be a fundamental confusion in the very appeal to a metaphysical basis for loyalty to loyalty. The trouble is that Royce is unready at the outset to decide whether loyalty as an attitude is definitely good or whether its goodness is illusory. If such an attitude were definitely regarded as good, then clearly its spread would be good; hence loyalty as a cause would be good, and the goodness of loyalty to loyalty thus readily established. For although the goodness of loyalty to a cause is provisional until we are assured that the value of the attitude of loyalty is not marred by the character of its object, no such problem arises when the loyalty is to loyalty. If, on the other hand, we doubt the goodness of loyalty as an attitude to begin with, then the goodness of loyalty to loyalty is doubly doubtful. Hence the analysis of metaphysical conditions which would, if existent, support the value of loyalty to loyalty, can prove nothing if they are not independently established. But so far from demonstrating their existence independently Royce uses the fact that they would give value to loyalty as the ground for

---

[28] From Josiah Royce, *The Philosophy of Loyalty,* pp. 309-10. By permission of The Macmillan Company, publishers.

[29] *Ibid.,* p. 357.

belief in their reality. This circularity clearly fails to establish anything about loyalty or reality.

The solution to this problem lies, perhaps, in the recognition of the essential incompleteness of loyalty as the sum total of morality, that loyalty cannot truly and completely be a cause in the sense in which Royce urged it. So far from proving that there must be some things in the world worth being loyal to, the fact of loyalty invites the critical and independent examination of proposed goods. In doing this, we should not, however, gainsay the admirable qualities of character found in the attitudes of loyalty.

Estimate of loyalty as a value. Two questions remain in a purely ethical critique of Royce's assertion of loyalty as a fundamental value—the relation of loyalty to other values and the value of loyalty itself. From a historical point of view loyalty is only one of many possible broad values that have been used as central concepts in ethical theory. There is the *mean* of Aristotle and kindred concepts of *harmony,* the *object of a will universalized* of Kant, the *serene self-sufficiency* of Stoic theory, the *pleasurable* of the Epicureans, the *ecstatic* of mystic theories, and a host of other general attitudes. All of these might claim priority. And if Royce by a *tour de force* claimed that the harmonious man, for example, made harmony the particular cause to which he was loyal, the other might very well reply that any cause was only one means of securing harmony by concentration.

Royce's philosophy of loyalty, then, so far from providing finality, merely explores in intensive fashion the component values of the attitude of loyalty. What is more, even the value of loyalty is sometimes questioned. T. E. Lawrence says of a cause in the opening page of *Seven Pillars of Wisdom,*[30] "As time went by our need to fight for the ideal increased to an unquestioning possession, riding with spur and rein over our doubts. Willy-nilly it became a faith. We had sold ourselves into its slavery, manacled ourselves together in its chain-gang, bowed ourselves to serve its holiness with all our good and ill content. The mentality of ordinary human slaves is terrible—they have lost the world—and we had surrendered not body alone, but soul to the over-mastering greed of victory. By our own act we were drained of morality, of volition, of responsibility, like dead leaves in the wind."

The self and its ideals. The double character of loyalty—its exalting as well as its desiccating nature—springs from fundamental traits of human life. Idealist philosophers who have paid special attention to the analysis of the self, have called attention to the fact that the self is not an initially set core of determinate impulses, that self-expression does not mean selfishness, that the atomic individual, apart from social reference, is almost an abstraction, just as much as society or community without reference to individuals.

[30] From *Seven Pillars of Wisdom,* by T. E. Lawrence, copyright 1926 by Doubleday, Doran and Company, Inc.

They have thus shown that identification with ideals is a normal feature of selfhood, and that the choice lies in the type or range of the ideals and is not between ideals and no ideals. And in the stress on the unplumbed depths of the self they are aiming at what Royce does with the concept of loyalty to loyalty—preventing the self from attaching itself to specific ideals as ultimate or final. Self-expression or loyalty to loyalty as an ethical standard thus might serve to counter the possibly desiccating effect of a specific loyalty which has become unduly supreme.

One limitation of this type of approach lies in its failure to offer a mode of evaluation for specific values at specific times. Royce seems to treat choice among causes almost as secondary, provided that the general drive toward spreading loyalties is there. The expansionist emphasis in choosing causes which will expand loyalties, or in seeking continuous self-expression, is, like the comparable naturalistic notion of developing those capacities which will release fresh capacities, salutary against the formidable barriers of habit and routine. But it runs the risk of making fundamental values of mere number and variety. Both of these require qualification; it is not the case, for example, that *any* diversity is a value. As Santayana says, "The function of seeing double adds more to the variety than to the spice of life."[31]

Fundamentally, then, Royce's emphasis has been on only òne phase of the moral life. Specific moral criteria are required for causes. And although an ethical theory may not be able to furnish specific rules, it ought to provide the tools by which they may be established in concrete living.

Idealist interpretation of history

Idealist interpretations of history constitute perhaps the clearest large-scale illustration of the spiritual or non-worldly attitude in its application to human affairs. The term "idealist" is not always employed in this context in a purely philosophic sense. Sometimes it is used to designate the kind of writing of history in which emphasis falls on the moral motivation of men. There is, for example, the simplified political history in which the events of a period are the work of its kings or statesmen and these are divided into the good and the bad according to whether we approve or disapprove of their motives. Sometimes the term "idealist" indicates the kind of writing of history in which the dramatis personae are impersonal ideas sweeping through a country, or shaping currents of thought and action. Thus Protestantism battles Catholicism and Protection fights Free Trade.

Such approaches give a very partial picture of philosophical idealism in its application to history. It is true that it also stresses the moral element

---

[31] *Reason in Society,* Harper's, 1905, p. 63.

THE IDEALIST OUTLOOK ON HUMAN AFFAIRS 417

and talks in terms of ideas. But its essence is a more thoroughgoing, a more grandiose, at times a breath-taking conception of the character, unity, and sweep of the life of man. It aims at the revelation of the totality of history, and the provision of a framework into which men's moral strivings and ideas will fit together with all the other strands that make up human life and activity.

CENTRAL IDEAS OF THE IDEALIST SYNTHESIS

The central idea of the idealist synthesis is that history is the work of Spirit. This notion takes different forms depending on the conception of Spirit involved. In St. Augustine the process of history is, of course, the expression of God's creation and guidance of the world. In Vico, the history of mankind is the realization and manifestation of an eternal idea in the divine mind. In Hegel both nature and history are phases of the development of Spirit.

Since essential features of spirit on which idealist philosophic analysis has rested are unity and rationality, it is not surprising that the idealist interpretation of history assumes a unified pattern and logic operative in the manifold phenomena of history, modeled on the way in which mind operates in the individual's life. Unity is assumed in several respects.

The spirit of an age. Unity is taken to characterize the life of men in a given age. There is a kind of spirit of the age which states the period's inmost meaning. The many strands of that society—its politics, law, art, religion, science, philosophy, education, the character of its men—are viewed not as interacting and genuinely altering one another, but rather as manifesting a single plan or idea. Thus it becomes possible to speak of an age as a unit and to relate it to other units in a more comprehensive time scheme by considering the logical relation of their respective key ideas. We are familiar with such characterizations of epochs as the Hellenic Age and the Hellenistic Age, the Golden Age and the Silver Age of Latin culture, the Age of Individualism or of Collectivism, the Age of Innocence or of Decadence or of Reason; and men in different ages have been characterized as Savage, Barbarian, Civilized, and so forth.

Sometimes such appellations are loosely used; sometimes they are offered as scientific description. Munsterberg in an essay on *Psychology and History*[32] suggests that history studies the will-acts (or purposes in action) of men and that the widest systematization of an historical period may perhaps best be found not by attempting to discover laws in scientific fashion but by looking for the most general idea in terms of which men's will-acts may be appreciated; he offers as illustration the idea of *original sin* for

[32] In *Psychology and Life*, Houghton Mifflin, 1899.

medieval society. Oswald Spengler, in his *Decline of the West*,[33] characterizes each age by the season of the whole culture in which it falls—spring, summer, autumn, winter; or childhood, youth, manhood, and old age. Each of these has its special marks: e.g., for spring, rural settings, intuitional attitudes, myth; for summer, ripening consciousness, urban beginnings, critical tendencies; for autumn, enlightenment, belief in reason, zenith of mathematical thought; for winter, megalopolitan civilization, materialistic outlook. Into each type fit kindred developments in politics, architecture, music, and so forth.

The spirit of a people. Unity is often taken to be present in the life of a people over a succession of periods or ages. Each people or each nation is said to have a unique idea or spirit which determines the character of its culture. Thus, according to Matthew Arnold, the unique element in Hellenism was its intellectual strand, in Hebraism the moral strand.[34] In the idealist use of this notion of the spirit of a people or nation or culture the pattern issues from a kind of national or cultural soul. It is not interpreted in the naturalistic sense in which characteristic types or culture-patterns may develop by the social interplay of men in a continuous society.

Spengler provides a good illustration of this idealist use. He believes there have been distinct cultures in the history of man which are quite different in their fundamental type or idea; the cultures display similarities (or more properly analogies) with one another because they go through the same life cycle in their thousand-year span. The Greco-Roman culture had an Apollinian soul, the western culture a Faustian soul. The Apollinian soul centers on the finite, the definite; it lacks all idea of an inner development and finds expression in such forms as the human-like Olympian gods, the politically individual city-state, finite place, the mean in conduct. The Faustian soul strives for the infinite; it is introspective and finds expression in reflections, endless space, Galileian dynamics. Each independent historic culture expressed its special soul, although some were partially hindered in their fulfillment. Spengler considers spatial symbolism a prime symbolism of a culture: limited self-contained body typifies the Classical world-view, infinite three-dimensional space the western, the world as a cavern the Arabian; the inexorably prescribed path (the narrow groove), the Egyptian; landscape, the Chinese; limitless plane, the Russian. These are not bare symbols, but are given interpretation by analogy in the various fields of the culture.

In providing for separate souls for the various cultures, Spengler differs from the more traditional idealist view which looks for a single world-pattern. Hegel, for example, finds the unique character of a people to lie

---

[33] Translation by C. F. Atkinson, Knopf, 1928-9.
[34] Essay on *Hellenism and Hebraism*.

in the role it plays in the temporal scheme he offers for the development of the World-Spirit. Various nations are in turn vehicles for the Spirit in its unfolding, handing on the torch to the next people, and sinking out of the historical scene. A people thus has a unique character when it is on the scene where history is being made.

The conception of a national or cultural soul served a definite intellectual purpose in Europe after the French Revolution. It constituted a reaction against the rationalism embodied in the revolution and the readiness to break with the past and rely on reason. It condemned the view that civilization was merely an accretion which could be disregarded to reveal a natural man acting according to the light of reason. It denied that one could simply abolish institutions or write a code of reasonable law or reverse a trend by legislation. History, said the partisan of the Spirit of a People, cannot be overlooked; for the history of a people and the story of its institutions indicate the temper or soul of the people which will mold the future to its will. The total culture is an organism; it may be fed, but absorption and major growth must be left to its own accomplishment.

This approach was fruitful in the social sciences insofar as it gave them a historical orientation. It also called attention to the real factor of social habits and the inertial character of custom with which many a hasty proposal for change has failed to reckon. It provided a dominantly conservative bias in its idealization of the tendencies historically established, although it did allow for reading history to find an impending change of sweeping proportions.

Rational pattern of historical movement. The third sense in which philosophic idealists found unity in history is in the rational pattern of its movement. They see a logic in history which constitutes its driving force. This is not to be taken in a naturalistic sense as a discoverable order in historical succession, such as an empirical law relating periods. It is meant to be an explanation of the law, a veritable discovery of God in history, sometimes as pointing to God in and behind history. As Hegel says in the Introduction to *The Philosophy of History*,[35] "It was for a while the fashion to profess admiration for the wisdom of God, as displayed in animals, plants, and isolated occurrences. But, if it be allowed that Providence manifests itself in such objects and forms of existence, why not also in Universal History. This is deemed too great a matter to be thus regarded. But Divine Wisdom, i.e. Reason, is one and the same in the great as in the little; and we must not imagine God to be too weak to exercise his wisdom on the grand scale. Our intellectual striving aims at realizing the conviction that what was *intended* by eternal wisdom is actually *accomplished* in the domain of existent, active Spirit, as well as in that of mere Nature. Our mode of treating the subject is, in this aspect, a Theodicaea—a justification of the ways of

[35] Translation by J. Sibree, London, 1857.

God . . ." And Spengler, posing the problem of World-History, says: "There is an *organic logic,* an instinctive, dream-sure logic of all existence as opposed to the *logic of the inorganic,* the logic of understanding and of things understood—a logic of direction as against a logic of extension . . ."[36]

This sense of the unity of history has been the most prevalent one among philosophical idealists. In fact the specific unity of an age or a people has for the most part been derived from the terms required in the unfolding of such a logic. Thus, as we saw, Hegel characterized a people by their role in the stages of the world-process, and Spengler characterized an age by its season in the inevitable cycle of life of a culture. Such procedures are not inherently unscientific. They may involve investigations which are genuine attempts to confirm or disconfirm the theory. They become unscientific, however, if instead of testing there is merely presentation of favorable illustrations.

Varying accounts of logic of history. The idealist account of the logic of history and of the method by which it is established varies considerably. A few samples will indicate some of its range.[37]

St. Augustine saw the sin of Adam as breaking the unity of man. Thereafter there were two kinds of men, one sure of grace, the other destined for damnation. Mankind passed through several stages. Youth, from Adam to Abraham, found man predominantly attentive to physical wants and the development of languages and memory. Manhood, from Abraham to Christ, entailed the growth of reason and a sense of sin. Old age corresponded to the Christian era and was characterized as a reign of grace. Finally, when the city of God has its predestined number of inhabitants filled, judgment day will be here. The purpose of history will be accomplished in the future happiness of the elect. It is to be noted that in this supernaturalistic idealism the purpose of history is not being fulfilled in history itself, but lies beyond the process.

Vico's conception of historical process was a cyclical one. Society goes through three stages, designated as the Age of the Gods, the Age of Heroes, and the Age of Men. Then comes anarchy and dissolution and the cycle begins again. Each of the stages has its appropriate cultural forms; in politics, for example the succession is aristocracy, democracy, and monarchy. The present cycle (Vico wrote in the 18th century) is in the Age of Men; the Age of the Gods had reappeared in the Dark Ages after the fall of Rome, and the Age of Heroes had coincided with the Middle Ages. Although Vico thought that this cyclical development revealed God's plan, he did not take God to be the immediate cause of human action; God operated through human minds and the development of mind thus caused the development of history. Mind, itself, went from a stage in which feeling was predominant

[36] *Op. cit.,* Vol. I, p. 117. Spengler calls this the *Destiny-idea.*
[37] Spengler's picture discussed above is one such illustration.

THE IDEALIST OUTLOOK ON HUMAN AFFAIRS   421

to one of imaginative knowledge and then to one of understanding or conceptual knowledge.

Fichte, on the other hand, is thoroughly *a priori* in method. Since reality is spiritual through and through, temporal development must embody the process of spirit; this process is taken by Fichte to be the awakening and maturation of reason. Thus he says, "The philosopher follows the *a priori* thread of the world-plan which is clear to him without any history; and if he makes use of history, it is not to prove anything, since his theses are already proved independently of all history."[38] Fichte accordingly distinguishes epochs of instinctive reason, authoritarian reason, skepticism, conscious reason (as science), regnant reason (as art). He believed that in the first years of the 19th century—during his life-time—man had passed into the fourth epoch. The goal in this whole process is freedom in the sense of action fully self-conscious of its relations. The goal is ideal and unattainable but allows of indefinitely close approximation to it.

HEGEL'S PHILOSOPHY OF HISTORY

Hegel's is the most elaborate of the idealist philosophies of history. Hegel likewise starts from an analysis of the movement of reason, thereby establishing his well-known and much debated conception of *dialectic*. Our present concern, however, is not with this and the laws in which it was expressed, but with its application to history. Hegel considers the movement of history and the movement of reason to be identical since history is a thoroughly spiritual expression. In this he is in agreement with the old Platonic notion that the completely real is completely intelligible. Hegel expresses it by saying that the real is the rational. The essence of Spirit is taken by him to be Freedom, just as the essence of matter is gravity.[39] Matter is essentially composite, consisting of parts that exclude each other. Matter seeks unity. But Spirit has its center in itself. It is "self-contained existence." This is precisely what is meant by freedom; for freedom means independence in which existence depends on oneself. Such self-contained existence is another name for self-consciousness. Self-consciousness or Spirit knowing itself is a unity since the knowing and the object of knowledge are one. This point is important for Hegel since he was opposed to the view that reason is limited to the finite and thus can never know the ultimate unity of the universe.[40] Self-consciousness seemed to him to be precisely typical of the unity in question. In self-consciousness, therefore, Spirit knows itself, appreciates its own nature and

---

[38] Quoted in J. B. Bury, *The Idea of Progress*, Macmillan, 1932, p. 253.
[39] Hegel's exposition of the points that follow is to be found most clearly in the Introduction to *The Philosophy of History*.
[40] For such contention of the mystic, see above, pp. 77, note 1, 349-50.

manifests an energy enabling it to make itself *actually* what it is potentially. The exhibition of Spirit in the process of working out this knowledge is Universal History.

Hegel's outline of historical development. Hegel's outline of history travels through the Oriental world, the Greek world, the Roman world to the German world. The story is that of the growing self-consciousness of Spirit. In the Oriental world only one is free, and the ruler's freedom thus appears as despotism. The consciousness of freedom arose among the Greeks; among them and among the Romans only some were free. It was the German nations under Christian influence who first attained the consciousness that man, as man, is free. This consciousness first arose in religion, and is proceeding to interpenetrate and mold the constitution of society. In his discussion of each of the various historical worlds, Hegel traces the spirit of that age in the various fields of the culture, and within each world he distinguishes various phases.

The means of the World-Spirit for attaining its object are men's volitions, interests, and activities. Men carry on their activities unconscious of the purpose they are fulfilling. A consciousness of this necessity and at the same time a realization of it as his interest, constitute freedom for the individual.

Hegel's conception of the state. The object to be realized by these means is, of course, self-consciousness on the part of the World-Spirit. The crucial question is, however, the form which this assumes in the realm of reality. Merely to appeal to the freedom of man as such may suggest all sorts of ideals. But Hegel has something very definite to offer as the outcome of the historical development. This is what he calls "the moral Whole, the *State,* which is that form of reality in which the individual has and enjoys his freedom; but on the condition of his recognizing, believing in and willing that which is common to the Whole." Hegel adds that this does not intend the state as a means for securing a limited liberty for each. "Rather, we affirm, are Law, Morality, Government, and they alone, the positive reality and completion of Freedom. Freedom of a low and limited order is mere caprice, which finds its exercise in the sphere of particular and limited desires." And again, "The State is the Divine Idea as it exists on Earth."

To understand this aspect of Hegel's thought we must see how he regards the state in relation to the individual and to the social groups of which the individual is a part. The individual is not regarded by Hegel as an atomic core of spiritual being. Hegel stressed the way in which the individual's very being is constituted by his social relations. His very individuality comes not from within a private self but from identification with objectives socially furnished him. The family furnishes this to the child, and it also provides for the couple forming a family an ethical union of two persons. The many associations outside the family into which the individual enters Hegel calls civil society. This includes not only economic relationships but also public administration and public services. The state stands above all these. It is a supreme integration in which, if the state were ideal, everything would find its place and men's private interests would find themselves coinciding with the positive policies of the state. It is such an ideal of a rational system in which the state constitutes the real will of its citizens that Hegel believes history to be evolving.

This brief summary does not of course do justice to special features of Hegel's thought. It does not show the character of the dialectic (the specific logic that he found characteristic of the rational and the real); nor does it make clear his analysis of other specific fields. Nor shall we discuss at this point the tremendous influence that Hegel had or the extent to which his glorification of the state is a precursor of present fascist theory. The summary has, however, illustrated some of the general features of an idealist approach to history and it is to the consideration of a few questions these raise that we now turn. These may appropriately be considered from the point of view of an individual turning to this idealist outlook for attitudes with which he ought to face his world.

The individual and the logic of history. In the first place, he finds the Hegelian idealist drawing a distinction between the mere existent and the real. Momentary sensation and capricious or arbitrary conduct exist. But the more permanent, the directional in movement, the more extensively satisfying, the rational—these are what Hegel equated with the real. To equate something with the real means, for Hegel, primarily that it is the characteristic of Spirit; for Spirit is what this world is primarily. In Hegelian idealism, however, Spirit is not some separate cause underlying phenomena. The Idea or Absolute or World-Spirit is the world itself in its unity. Hence the discovery of the unity is the Absolute become self-conscious in men. In calling upon the individual to discover the direction of movement in his time the idealist calls upon the individual to become one with the deepest reality in the act of self-consciousness.

It is to be noted that the individual is not asked to fashion reality. Some men—like Alexander, Caesar, or Napoleon—become vehicles for the World-Spirit in the furtherance of its purpose. They may be conscious of their role or they may pursue some temporary aims little knowing the real tendency of their work. If they achieve the consciousness of their meaning they are genuinely free. Man's highest role is thus not to fashion history but to express it. If there is any fashioning to be done by the individual it is to fashion himself in line with the logic of events.

The relation of fact and value. But if this is the case, the individual is in effect being asked to consider the direction of movement to be good, and to use it as a standard for his conduct. At this point the idealist's claim has often been found vulnerable. It is said to involve a confusion of the descriptive and the evaluative. Even if history is in fact going in a certain direction, it may be asked, why should the individual jump on the bandwagon and call it good? The judgment of the value of the direction of movement is an entirely separate one.

If the assertion of historical movement in a certain direction is purely a descriptive one, a scientific prediction, simply extrapolating a curve part of which has been plotted, and if the assertion of value is a judgment of preference in the light of a standard brought by the individual to the act of evaluating, then the criticism is certainly just. The individual may accept or reject the verdict of history, and may struggle against it or perish if his struggle is hopeless. What the criticism brings out clearly, however, is that the assertion of historical direction is not on the idealist system purely a descriptive one, nor is the assertion of value purely an act of individual preference.

Insofar as the former is concerned, we have already seen that the philosophical idealist claims an absolute status for his account of reality, hence of the direction of movement, since he takes it to picture the unity of the world and a real necessity in history. These underlying premises may be criticized from a scientific or from a materialist point of view, but it must be recognized that they are not intended as merely empirical generalizations.

Insofar as the individual's judgments of value are concerned, the idealist is unready to treat them as individual preferences. Who are you to question the logic of the universe? This query is not impudence but a demand for an analysis of the individual. After all, the individual is a fragment of spirit and in discovering the logic of the World-Spirit he ought to recognize that he is finding the direction of his own deepest striving. In the Platonic dialogues Socrates refused to admit that a man could really know the good and not do it. Really to gaze on God's glory and not to recognize it as all that is good and as the object of the soul's deepest yearning is inconceivable to the religious man. A man might theoretically make the distinction, but only one who was blind would affirm it.

The criticism that Hegelian idealism confuses the descriptive and the evaluative is thus in one sense erroneous and yet in another fundamental. It is erroneous if it means that the mere separation of concepts will dissolve the Hegelian approach by convicting it of confusion. It is fundamental because it challenges the more basic premises of the Hegelian approach which deny the validity of such a distinction in the case of the logic of the universe.

The idealist approach thus directs the individual to find the will of God or the ultimate way of the universe, and to accept it, recognize its goodness and put himself in rapport with it. It is a call to the individual to recognize his profound kinship with the spiritual world of which he is a fragment and in which he is at home.

Chapter 25 THE MATERIALIST OUTLOOK ON HUMAN AFFAIRS

The major features of the materialist outlook—its reliance on scientific method, its recognition of the primacy of matter and its fundamental this-worldliness—are very apparent in its attitude toward human affairs. Materialism sees the universe at large as a flux of existence which needs no fashioning Deity or Universal Mind or all-embracing Purpose to explain it. It looks to nothing beyond the totality of the universe itself for its values and its explanations. Within the universe it has adopted as explanatory principles the best available results of science. It accepts an evolutionary account of the formation of the solar system; it looks to continuities of the organic with the inorganic to explain the origin of life, and to evolution in the animal kingdom to understand the rise of man. And, as we have already seen in Part Three, it treats mind and its works as functions of the body in its environment, physical and social. In human affairs, as against the idealist devotion to eternity, it stresses the need for a dynamic equilibrium in the midst of change.

Materialist interpretation of men's values

THE ANALYSIS OF THE GOOD

The materialist conception of the good is the outcome of a long tradition rooted in the practical aims of daily life and fed by philosophies of many sorts. Its central element is a search for man's good not in the transcendental dictates of a divinity nor in any absolute rules of reason but in the goals that arise within the activities of men. Materialist philosophies agree in interpreting "good" as referring to situations in which some individual or group at a definite place and for a definite period—or in special cases, if such exist, all men at all times everywhere—find something an object of value. The quality of value in such a situation is not something embedded in the structure of things themselves nor is it a cosmic property or spiritual aspect of the universe. It is a phenomenon of living beings, local and episodic in the sense of having a fixed reference to place and time.

Hobbes' physical description. The relation which consists in finding something to be of value or *good* has been described in various ways, stressing different aspects of the situation. Some philosophers describe the phenomenon in almost physical terms. Hobbes, for example, treats "good" as merely a name for the objects of appetite or desire; appetite or desire in turn is a name for endeavor towards something which causes it; and endeavor is the name for the small beginnings of motion within the body before they appear in visible actions.[1]

Use of subjectivist descriptions. The description of valuing in terms of "pleasure" and "pain" is a common one in materialistic ethical theory. Pleasures and pains are called mental or "subjective" phenomena, but regarded merely as functions of bodily states.[2] This view was, as we have seen, in part the result of the special role given by materialists to physics as the science discovering reality. In ancient times the pleasure-pain analysis of the good is found most fully developed in the Epicurean philosophy which also rested on a mechanistic materialism, having Democritus' theory as its physics. In modern times it has been very common among this-worldly ethical theories both materialist and semi-materialist. Its extensive use in Utilitarian ethics will be discussed in detail below. But the interpretation of good in terms of pleasure was only one of a variety of psychological analyses. Once Hobbes had imparted an empirical tone to English ethical theory alternatives to pleasure and desire were sought in the contents of consciousness. Reflective sentiments—such as the reactions of the disinterested spectator—sometimes replaced appetite or desire as the criterion of what was good. Hume founds his entire moral theory on the sentiments of approval and disapproval which men find themselves experiencing, and tries to outline the rules according to which these sentiments are guided. He concludes that the associations of these sentiments follow the steps of utility, men finding themselves approving what is useful or associated with the useful, and disapproving the opposite. In this light he analyzes many of the traditional virtues. Hume's ethics is thus thoroughly this-worldly.[3]

The subjectivist element clung to materialist ethics until the development of social science, and social psychology in particular, made it possible to deal with values as patterns of conduct and reflection. Prior to this the only "objective" description was the language of physics, or later of biology. This more recent development was, of course, part of the general liberalizing of the conception of matter indicated above.[4]

---

[1] Hobbes, *Leviathan,* Part I, Chapter 6. Cf. above, p. 161.

[2] This is a kind of *epiphenomenalist* approach; see above, pp. 157-58.

[3] In general the phenomenalism or positivism of the Humean type shares major features with materialism. In addition to the this-worldly bent of its ethics there is its complete reliance on empirical method.

[4] See above, pp. 322-23.

Variety of psychological and social descriptions. If we survey the varying descriptions of the phenomena of value which are compatible with a materialist outlook, we find the account of "good" cast in the language of each of the sciences. There is the psycho-biological language of "appetite," "impulse," "interest"; the subjective psychological language of "desire," "pleasure," "approval"; the psycho-physical language of "striving," "drive"; the socio-environmental language of "aims," "goals," "ends." These or any other terms may be employed which are found in scientific investigation of the phenomenon to be apt and fruitful modes of description. In fact, it is perhaps best to use them all, provided that each has an empirical content so that it may be separately identified; for this will make possible more precise studies of their relations. Thus "A values x" or "A finds x good" may mean any or all of "A likes x," "A wants or desires x," "A seeks x," "A is interested in x," "A is pleased by x," "A chooses x on various occasions," or even "A's conduct shows a pattern of activity which has x as a regular consequence in certain types of situations," or "x is the kind of object toward which A directs considerable energy," and a host of other possibilities. For most ethical discourse perhaps the ordinary language of goals or ends is most suitable.

The chief objection sometimes raised to such materialistic identifications of the good is that men frequently distinguish between what they like, desire, or aim at, and what they regard as good. Accordingly there have been many attempts to state criteria by which we may distinguish a man's ordinary desires or goals from those that constitute his account of the good. Traditional distinctions of this type are those between what a man wants at one moment and what he wants over a long period; what a man aims at now and what he aims at after reflection (Aristotle's distinction of the apparent and real good); goals uncritically held and those appraised in terms of their consequences (Dewey); an isolated objective and one that is harmonious with the rest of a man's objectives (Santayana's trend); a man's private desires and those desires that he wants to be universally held (Russell); a man's own desires and those which community tradition approves of (sociological tendency); and so forth.

Which is most fruitful an empirical question. Now there is no reason why materialist ethical theory should attach itself *a priori* to any one of these. Which one a particular man or group is using as a criterion in conduct is always a factual question to be investigated objectively; we find for the most part that a given individual (or group) does have certain desires or aims that are used to order or decide among other desires or aims. This set of aims may properly be called the man's (or group's) conception of the good. Which set it is *desirable* to use is of course a quite different question. To answer it involves a careful evaluation of the values embodied in each of the above proposals—long-range view, reflection, critical appraisal, impulsive action, harmony, universalization, tradition, and so forth. This means an estimate of the consequences of each for the achievement of men's aims; it permits us to combine them rather than arbitrarily select one. For the various concepts listed are not for the most part incompatible and appear to represent attempts to achieve a maximum of men's aims.

The meaning of ethical relativity. Such evaluation will, of course, be performed not by some mind without values but by men who have values. From a materialist point of view this relativity is inherent in the field of value-phenomena; to ask for a decision without at least tentative values to judge by is a meaningless question. It is often urged that such relativity makes it impossible fundamentally to criticize values and that what is taken to be good becomes simply a matter of taste, concerning which there can be only agreement or disagreement, not argument. An extreme form of this view is accepted in the theory advanced by some logical positivists that statements of value are meaningless, and have merely the status of expressions of feeling, such as a cry of pain or a word of command.[5] In its various forms, as Dewey has clearly pointed out,[6] such a view stems from an over-sharp separation of means and ends. Means are thrown aside as purely technical questions—how to get certain results—and ends are merely *held*. You have your feelings, desires, goals; and I have mine. They either coincide or differ. In the former case we agree, in the latter we disagree. Ethics becomes ultimately capricious.

Critique of arbitrary relativism. Such a description does of course represent *one* possible ethical arrangement for a particular group. *Its* principle of ordering desires and goals might be purely capricious and every desire considered immune from reflection or reconsideration. Such is not usually the case among men, nor were the logical positivists who presented this theory urging that such a principle of conduct be adopted; for a principle of this kind would tend toward discord and confusion. They advanced these views largely in reaction to the categorical imperatives of idealism and intuitionism, to absolute values thrust on all men whether they accepted them or not. They were therefore forcibly calling attention to the possibilities of ultimate differences which could not be rationally bridged and on which there would have to be either separate fields of action or else a clash.[7] But they spoke almost as if this genuine possibility, which need not arise unless both points of view are really incompatible, constituted the typical state of affairs.

In ethical inquiry differences of desire and feeling and aims are not necessarily contradictory any more than are differences in perception or even of belief in science. It is only when two wholly incompatible systems have been elaborated—or when there is a refusal to estimate beliefs—that we are faced

---

[5] E.g., A. J. Ayer, *Language, Truth, and Logic,* London, 1936, Chapter 6.

[6] *Theory of Valuation,* University of Chicago Press, 1939.

[7] See above, pp. 283-85, for a discussion of this problem and the issues of coercion involved.

with incompatible difference. To argue that ethics is capricious because of possible ultimate disagreement is almost like arguing that science is capricious because theoretically there might be differences in sense-perception. The community in sense-perception arises because of broad similarity among men in physical structure and functioning. Agreement on ethical values, less extensive though it be, has its definite causal conditions. This agreement is not lessened by the theoretical possibility that under other conditions it might not exist.

Materialist ethics does not entail arbitrary relativism. Materialist ethics does not therefore entail in its fundamental ethical relativism the view that ethical beliefs are purely matters of taste—unless this be a figurative, though misleading, way of saying that an act of valuing is a natural phenomenon and not an expression of some absolute spirit. And although there have been materialist philosophies in which individual caprice and conflict have been esteemed as values, most have not so regarded them. While allowing the possibility that clashes of value will occur where conflict cannot be avoided or minimized, they have sought to discover the conditions that give rise to such conflicts in order to eliminate their occurrence. Finally it is important to realize that such preference for genuine harmony and aversion to conflict is not itself regarded as an absolute value, but as a widely shared value fundamental to the achievement of other values. Preference for harmony has its own causes, but they are pervasive ones, operating to some degree in all men's lives where there are many values to be achieved under complex and changing conditions.

Why, it will be asked, should men try to achieve any of these values, if none are in some sense absolutely good? The materialist answer is that the reason men try to *achieve* values is because they *hold* values. For the resort to absolute worth philosophical materialism thus substitutes the causal analysis of why men have values.

WHY MEN HAVE VALUES

Having values a natural phenomenon. Fundamental to philosophical materialism is the view that a man's or a group's having a particular value is a definite phenomenon in the natural world which has its causal explanation just as does any other phenomenon. Any particular directional quality in men's activity and feeling rests upon or expresses a particular equilibrium of forces (with varying stability) and will endure only so long as the equilibrium endures or the forces have not spent themselves. Hence the question of why men have values is like the question of why there are sounds in the world—it entails an analysis of the conditions under which valuing arises.

Santayana's analysis of the natural basis of ideals. The fundamental facts on which the occurrence of men's values rests are impulse and change. Impulse is the bodily material out of which the phenomenon of value grows; change guarantees its complex character. In Santayana's dramatic language, "If man were a static or intelligible being, such as angels are thought to be, his life would have a single guiding interest, under which all other interests would be subsumed. His acts would explain themselves without looking beyond his given essence, and his soul would be like a musical composition, which once written out cannot grow different and once rendered can ask for nothing but, at most, to be rendered over again. In truth, however, man is an animal, a portion of the natural flux; and the consequence is that his nature has a moving center, his functions an external reference and his ideal a true ideality." [8]

In impulse and the friction of natural impulses—in their attempt to find expression, in their clash, and in their encounter with obstacles presented by environment—are generated values, strivings, and ideals. The study of human ideals in their scope and procession clearly reveals this relationship. Every ideal, says Santayana, has a natural basis and every natural impulse a possible ideal fulfillment.

Not all natural faculties do become the basis of ideals. Santayana somewhere cites breathing as an illustration of an impulse issuing in constant activity without generating special values. Yet even breathing does sometimes have special standards for its perfection. The way in which one should breathe is dictated for the man who would be a singer, who would be healthy, who would avoid snoring. There is also a clear joy in breathing deeply the fresh country air. If, finally, air involved a process of preparation similar to food, we might find a whole social superstructure with conflicting values, perhaps of asceticism and lavish breathing, in the casuistry of ethics.

Hunger and sexual impulse, however diverse their expression in varying ages and places, always require co-operation among human beings. To avoid conflict and achieve harmonious expression of various impulses, some organization or systematization is imperative. Our social institutions serve this purpose. Complex ideals such as love and honesty arise in this process, and help to organize the materials of impulse. Because of their importance they tend to become integrated as self-justifying values in human life.

The procession of values and ideals in a man's life expresses the constant change that is taking place within and about him. There are changes of feeling, mood, and interest. There is change that stems from new instrumentalities, emerging vistas of fresh possibilities, unexpected obstacles. There is change in response to the impact of other ways of other men. The biography

[8] From George Santayana, *Reason in Society*, p. 3. By permission of Charles Scribner's Sons, publishers.

of a man, the history of a people, the career of an ideal, all tell this same story.

The forces that kindle the light of ideals are spoken of by Santayana in terms which are largely, but not exclusively, biological. Love rests on the sexual impulse, but the extreme forms of romanticism rest on rigorous suppression of sexual impulse, which is a social phenomenon. Santayana resorts too readily to instincts in spite of his recognition of the plasticity of impulse; he takes values to arise too mechanically in certain situations expressing relationships of body and environment. But there is a keen realism in Santayana's constant view of man as an ideal-producing mechanism.

Dewey's instrumentalist analysis. Dewey's instrumentalist analysis of evaluation falls within a materialist tradition, broadly conceived. Men make evaluations because they have problems, and problem-situations grow out of one another in the efforts of men to solve them. The problem as it presents itself to men (and the mode of presentation is a function of experience) sets the terms of its solution. Goals or values are ends set up to organize and direct activity in the solution of problems—as a man may set up a target when he wishes to do some shooting, says Dewey. Ends would thus be evaluated by the success with which aiming at them resolves the tension of the situation. But this process of solving one problem generates fresh situations with fresh issues. The goals are never fixed or final, but the method of analyzing and reconstructing situations itself almost achieves the character of a constant value.

In approaching ethical problems Dewey definitely recognizes their social basis. He points out that two types of ethical issues arise. One is the situation created by the clash of desire and custom. This is the temptation situation, in which a man thinks a certain course of conduct right and proper, yet feels drawn elsewhere. The other type—the more crucial problem—is the clash of customs or habits themselves in particular situations. In such a case a man does not know what is the right thing to do, nor even sometimes what he wants to do. Dewey is concerned with the way in which ethical concepts function in resolving such problems. For questions of ends, means, standards, and obligations arise under such conditions. The virtues Dewey recommends are largely ones that will support the method of scientific inquiry in such processes.[9]

Marxian stress on socio-historical basis of values. The Marxian materialist approach has stressed the social basis of men's values: the problems on which the rise and fall of values depend are determined by the conflict of economic classes in a society. The importance of this approach lies in its insistence that biological, psychological, and even generalized social bases for values are not enough, that there must be a *historical* reference to the inter-

---

[9] See John Dewey and J. H. Tufts, *Ethics*, rev. ed., Holt, 1932, Part 2.

play of men and groups at a particular period in a particular background. The significance of this general contribution does not depend on the specific social mechanisms the theory involves; it can be maintained irrespective of an emphasis on economic factors. In a similar fashion the Freudian theories called attention to the need for close investigation of the individual's early experiences in order to explain his later reactions, a contribution which is not invalidated by any disagreement with specific mechanisms the Freudians postulate.

Value-phenomena to be scientifically explored. The answer which materialist ethics gives to the question of why men have values is thus a call for the widest possible scientific exploration of the phenomenon itself—an exploration including its physical, biological, psychological, and social bases, together with historical and personal determinants.

It is important to note that this analysis does not preclude the possibility that general or even universal values or ideals may exist. Whether such have existed is not an *a priori* question. The mere fact that certain needs have been universal (e.g., food) does not produce the *automatic* consequence that the value has been universal, although it makes it highly probable. For it is conceivable that in some cases eating should be treated as purely an instrumental activity, just as much of western moral theory sought to treat sexual activity. Again investigation is required to see whether food as such is regarded as a value or only *specific* foods. This carries the converse warning that apparently different values may turn out sometimes to be basically the same; the difference may lie in assumptions about the kind of means that are efficacious. The widest ideals like liberty and justice embrace great actual variety. Nevertheless underlying this variety there may be a broad similarity of structure in the situations in various ages and places which generate similar ideals. Marx and Engels, for example, suggested that the universality of the ideal of justice may be explained by the universality of men's striving against class exploitation. And Nietzsche took humanitarian values to represent a slave morality, the perennial cry of the weak against the strong.

RULES OF RIGHT AND OBLIGATION; VIRTUES AND VICES

Two approaches to ethical rules. Materialist ethics has tended to follow two courses with respect to rules of right and obligation, virtues and vices. One is simply to treat them as rules of conduct and types of character which a society has selected for special types of sanctioning or approval and disapproval, the modes of sanctioning being shame, praise, blame, the engendering of guilt-feelings and remorse. On this approach, essentially descriptive in character, obligations and virtues form a special segment of the class of customary conduct and their forms are to be explained historically as is the rise of customs generally.

A second approach has been more normative. It uses the values of the community in question or the philosopher's conception of good and tries to determine rules of obligation and states of character as right or wrong, virtuous or vicious, according as they tend to achieve or to thwart the achievement of the good. In general, materialist ethics treats rules of obligation and character as lessons of experience concerning the way in which the good may be achieved. They are therefore essentially *instrumental*. In Utilitarian theory for example right actions are to be selected in the light of what will achieve the greatest good of the greatest number; in Marxian theory existent rules reflect the historically developed instruments of the dominant class for attaining their objectives and maintaining their power.

Treating rules as essentially instrumental entails a readiness to modify established obligation and virtues under changing conditions. At a particularly critical time, such as the present, rules must be surveyed to see whether they and the type of character they entail are best for achieving what we take to be the good life. Should we become less individualistic and more co-operative? Should we grow more stoical and less attentive to personal comforts? Should we cultivate the habit of regarding change in institutions as just as normal as change in industrial techniques? Such a survey might issue in recommendations for altered virtues and amended rules.

Materialist interpretation of absolute element. The chief objection to such an instrumental interpretation of duty or obligation is that it neglects the categorical or absolute element which many people feel inheres in their judgments of right. This objection should not prove insuperable if a basis other than eternal truth can be found for that feeling. Such a basis may be found in psychological terms. The absolute element may, for example, represent force of habit, or a kind of character structure developed through early training. Vividness of conviction is a quality of feeling akin to the feeling of certainty in intuition; like it, it provides hypotheses rather than proofs.

Even in purely logical terms, a possible basis for the absolute element may be found on more careful inspection of the way moral rules function. Take for example the rule "Killing is wrong." The ordinary way of treating this as a lesson of experience is to translate it into "Most killings are wrong." This does not meet the objection raised that our feeling with regard to killing is stronger than that; yet to say absolutely that all killing is wrong forbids even cases of killing that seem necessary to avoid extreme evil (such as to save many lives that are threatened).[10] A different way of interpreting the rule—in terms of the process of evaluation—meets the difficulty and shows the source of the apparent absolute. Let "Killing is wrong" be taken to

---

[10] See the discussion of violence above, pp. 286-87.

mean "In the process of evaluating a situation the fact that there was a killing *always* means a diminution in value." This may be confirmed by experience for all but the most hardened killers, and at the same time the formulation does not guarantee that the result of evaluating the whole situation be negative. Some other great good might more than balance it. The rule that in *most* cases the evaluation of the total situation turns out to be negative is a separate lesson of experience. Thus Kant's inference from "Lying is absolutely wrong" to "You must not lie to save a life"[11] was not a valid one. It is comparable to inferring from "Subtracting 100 always *diminishes* a given finite quantity" that "Subtracting 100 in this particular case will yield a *negative* quantity." Clearly this does not follow if we start with 200.

TRUTHFULNESS AS AN ILLUSTRATION

Perhaps the best way of illustrating the materialist treatment of obligations and virtues will be to work out one case in more detail. Let us take the case of truthfulness, in order to contrast the materialist analysis with the Kantian which was discussed in the previous chapter.

Underlying needs and problems for this rule. The materialist analysis looks for the needs and problems within a society which lend value to the rule and virtue of truthfulness, and for those further values which in turn are supported or generated by such a rule. A number of such needs are readily discernible. There is first the fact that what others tell us sets up expectations on our part. If these expectations were as often disappointed as not it would bring a serious disorder in human affairs and make great caution necessary in our relations with others. Contrary to Kant's opinion, we can conceive of a man ready to face a society in which no man would believe his neighbor; but we can also readily conceive of innumerable ills that such a society would suffer. What Kant has demonstrated so admirably is that a liar could not gain very much if lying were the rule. Hence even from the point of view of a man addicted to lying for his own gain, the existence of the rule and the virtue of truthfulness are distinct advantages.

Needs of business. There are special fields in which a general regard for truth is an important matter. Men have, indeed, developed cynicism in politics, and do not expect a political party to live up to its pre-election platform. In business, too, the principle of *caveat emptor* (let the buyer look out) has long been dominant. Nevertheless the structure of business as a whole, with its complicated systems of inter-reliance and its need for speed in many operations could not afford the disturbing effects of the dislocation which would ensue if men did not on the whole live up to their agreements. The legal institution of contract helps enforce some contracts by the compensation it

---

[11] See above, p. 409.

gives to the promisee in many cases, and it is of great importance in determining the rules according to which agreements will be made. Now truth-telling is not identical with promising and contracting, but these require as a minimum that the assertions of one's intentions and of the future direction of one's energies be reliable. It is a great aid to industry, commerce, and especially to credit to have a man's word as good as his bond.

Needs of scientific knowledge. Another domain in which powerful currents are set going towards making truthfulness a virtue is that of science. Strong values are engendered by the fundamental battle of man with nature, and the role of knowledge in that endeavor is crucial. The respect for fact and the love of knowledge are often referred to as the love of truth. But science is a co-operative venture and communication is of its very essence. Hence falsehood in science is less pardonable than mistakes. We have here a whole nest of values with which the truth value is tied up and which support one another. For example, science demands objectivity; letting your desire for certain results make you see them or interfere with the experiments you perform is, in a scientist's credo, only one step away from tampering with your results. And science requires freedom, including the liberty fully to communicate results and their implications without fear of undue pressure. The values inherent in scientific exploration have frequently found expression in the ideal called "truth for truth's sake."

Value of habit. On the other hand, lying is a dangerous weapon. There is no guarantee that when it becomes habitual it may not be used outside the field in which it was developed. Deceitfulness may shade by degrees into cheating and other vices, and, especially if linked with desire for gain, become a major social evil. In similar fashion the habit of truthfulness shades into honesty, forthrightness, and a general uprightness in conduct.

Forms in which the virtue may be developed. Such considerations suggest that even if the maxim "Tell the truth" had not arisen as an ethical rule and truthfulness as a virtue, this value would be worth inculcating or developing.[12] As we have seen, such development might take several forms. Truthfulness might be taught simply as a lesson of experience, as some have tried to teach honesty ("Honesty is the best policy"). Or it might be taught as a positive element in all evaluation in which it arises. Thus truth-telling may be regarded as always worth while, even in situations where it is not controlling (e.g., a doctor's telling a patient that he is going to recover in order to give him the confidence which may enable him to recover); in such cases the lapse, though justified, may be regarded as a negative element in the total situation. Or in a third fashion, truth-telling and the truthful character may become goals or values in their own right.

---

[12] We might almost speak of a society "growing" a virtue spontaneously or by conscious cultivation.

Truth for truth's sake estimated. The ideal of truth for truth's sake mentioned above is an illustration of such a goal. That it has proved a powerful and self-justifying one to many scientists and philosophers is not to be doubted. The issue is whether it is to be increasingly cultivated or replaced by a variant ideal like truth for humanity's sake. This cannot be answered simply. Is the pursuance of the ideal of truth making scientists immune to humanitarian and social considerations? Are they becoming negligent of social responsibilities? Have scientists on the whole done better work under this ideal than under the pressure of social needs and humanitarian considerations? Perhaps the history of medical research in which the humanitarian element seems immediate could contribute to this study. If the ideal aids research it might be worth implanting and strengthening even at the cost of engendering occasional scientific callousness. Even under these conditions the development of the truth-for-truth's-sake ideal might be joined more closely with that of other ideals. This and a realization of its own relation to other human values would help to avoid scientific isolation.

Although more detailed treatment would be required to reach a careful decision in a given age, it is clear that a materialist ethics can without contradiction hold the pursuit of truth as a major human goal. This would entail not merely engendering and strengthening the attitude in scientists and future scientists, but developing the institutions and techniques of communication of truth throughout the society. It would mean widespread education, impartial agencies for dissemination of information, widespread critical discussion, and a readiness to allow these to continue regardless of their effects on the special interests of political, economic, religious, or professional groups.

Rules of personal morals really constitute social orientation. It should be apparent from our discussion that what appeared at first as a simple personal moral rule of right and wrong turns out to be a principle for the ordering of conduct, habits, character, and institutions. Judging it involves the whole conception of the good life; and when it is adopted consciously as a moral principle it becomes a powerful indication of the direction toward which social life must be oriented.

THE INDIVIDUAL'S POINT OF VIEW

In the light of the account given above what would be the general character of the individual's ethical task if he sought to guide his life in consonance with a materialist outlook?

It must be remembered that the individual does not live his life in isolation. The way in which he plans his life, as well as the way he lives it, is not entirely of his own making. His life is necessarily a co-operative venture, carried on amid family, friends, occupational associates, and a whole society of men. The individual provides the materials to be worked upon, and the initiative often lies with him; certainly the drive for adjustment lies within him. Although a materialist outlook does not regard his task as a solo one, it may still lodge responsibility with him. For materialist philosophies share the ideal of developing free men in the philosophic sense presented above.[13]

Task of clarifying values. The individual's first task will be to clarify his values. We have suggested several times that this is not a simple task which introspection alone can accomplish. This Socratic enterprise of knowing himself will entail observation of his feelings and reactions, analyses of the direction of his strivings and activity. He will develop the habit of having a set of hypotheses about himself and his values. This "science of himself" will never be reckoned as totally complete; its results will be subject to revision in the light of further experience.

Task of analyzing matrix of values. A second [14] task will be to form some idea of the forces that have fashioned his values and of the forces that support them. In a general way, a person does this in biological terms when he recognizes the difference in values associated with the energies of youth and the calm or even weariness of age. But a materialist ethics would bid a man look to biological, psychological, and social forces which have shaped him. Let him become cognizant of the specific way in which his language, his religion, his family life and the values of his parents, his specific contacts, friends, occupation, opportunities, wealth or poverty, education, socio-economic status and its associations, and numerous other factors have fashioned the direction of his action and the tone of his feelings. To do this and to interpret correctly the significance of these past materials, requires some acquaintance with the findings of the psychological, social, and historical sciences; this is the profoundly personal role that a good education may play in a man's life.

It is well to carry this causal analysis into present values. How many of a man's biases rest on his present security or lack of it, his associating with certain persons, his limiting his reading to definite sources, his following established routines? What—imaginatively—would be his response if these were altered in certain respects? What would he like his response to be? In this way he learns what ends, if any, have been peculiarly his in the past, have guided his path among alternative possibilities, and have kept other goals from becoming established as his own.

Sources of value change. The result of such self-study is not merely disinterested history. Nor, as many have feared, does discovering the cause of one's values mean losing them. To realize that had I been born and brought

---

[13] Chapter 18.

[14] The various tasks here described are not meant as temporally successive, but simply as distinguishable phases of the ethical process.

up in China my language would have been Chinese does not diminish my liking for English, nor its utility, nor my desire for communication. On the contrary, a person examining the causes of his values will find himself constantly taking sides. He will view causes as friends or enemies according as they shape or thwart the objects of his desire. But at the same time, he may find a sense of alternatives developing, a realization of the way in which other conditions might have, and might still engender, other values. And in his feelings of sympathy or antipathy, his sense of regret or relief, he will discover forces strengthening or unsettling his present values.

Three sources of value change may be distinguished in such a process. One is the discrepancy or conflict between existent values held conjointly; when we discover such contradictions, some must change to cohere with others. A second is a broadening of the horizon which may reveal fresh values that would bring a deeper satisfaction; these may not hitherto have come within the range of his striving, but on their appearance the individual recognizes their close kinship to untried regions of his self. The third is the change of outer circumstances which renders some values incapable of achievement; abstractly, they may remain goods, but they lose their status as objects of striving.

These sources of value change may be illustrated both from the career of interests in an individual's life and from his wider social values. Thus many a young man in World War II gave up a mode of life on which his heart was set to enlist in the armed forces in defense of wider human interests that moved him strongly. Again, new avenues of experience brought with them new interests in many realms—in human relations, in education, in work. And thirdly, in many cases economic changes or wounds received compelled the alteration of men's aims, irrespective of whether the old or the new brought greater satisfaction. Similarly, many social values were transformed profoundly during the war period. A narrow nationalism, for example, was weakened in all three ways. It had, in part, to yield because it was in conflict with the aim of victory; thus Americans learned to undergo certain privations in order to ship supplies to allied nations. In the second place, contact with other nations and their achievements broadened the horizon and revealed the values of a global outlook. And thirdly, the world political and economic situation has made a narrow nationalism unworkable no matter how much in the abstract some individuals may desire it.

Task of systematizing his values. These dynamic elements in the individual's life are by their very nature woven together; much more so in the kind of rapidly changing world in which we live. It follows that the process of analyzing the matrix of his values will lead a man imperceptibly into the normative task of systematizing his values in the light of the widest view of himself and the world that he can attain. In this process there should arise clearer distinctions between means and ends, between questions of fact —such as a man's abilities or how certain results may be achieved—and questions of value, between what depends on the individual and his immediate environment and what requires a wider national or even global foundation, between purely individual values and the vast majority of his values that qualify a man's interpersonal relationships. All this is done in the context of living—one does not stop living or acting in order to make a contemplative system of one's values—but as systematization advances, it may lead to alteration of whole areas or patterns of conduct. The redirection of one's values in such a process may be gradual and unnoticed, but where the tasks we have spoken of have been carried forward, it can be conscious, rapid, and even controlled.

Duration of this process. How far should an individual carry this systematization? There is no *a priori* end to the process of systematizing values and developing altered values. Some people and some societies consider a child's character set for life in its early years and by acting on this belief help to keep the child along the path it has chanced to tread. Some men will call a halt to their self-systematization when they are happy, without incorporating the desire for novel experience in their system. Some people will think in terms of years and once youth is over feel their ways fully molded. Others think that life begins at forty. Increased life expectancy in modern times may prove a factor in such evaluation. Experience has shown that the self may be in the making for a great part of life, but also that it can be fixed.

Dynamic rather than static security. Modern complexity and the need as well as the likelihood of continuous change make desirable the incorporation of change into one's system of values. This means organizing a growing system of values rather than a fixed one. A person thus aims at a *dynamic security* rather than a *static security*.[15] It would not lack stable elements, but these would be more generalized, more flexible, and capable of wider application. A system of values is ultimately a system of self-administration. Where an enterprise is small and its dealings uniform, it may be administered by rules. Where it grows, more complex rules prove too rigorous and generalized principles or methods have to be used. You can take care of diet by rules but the care of a child requires principles. Where the material is too complex for principles, administration may still be guided by general values, that is by broad outlook, entailing methods of analysis and expectancy of change.

[15] These terms are borrowed from René Demogue ("Analysis of Fundamental Notions," in *Modern French Legal Philosophy*, Boston Book Co., 1916), who applies them to systems of property, the static encouraging possession, the dynamic rapid transactions.

A world-outlook necessary. In extent again there is no *a priori* limit to the range of a system of values. Probably very few people consider only themselves, and even if they do in respect to values, they are compelled to go beyond in considering causal factors which will affect achievement of their values. A frontier farmer supporting himself entirely by his own efforts did not need to look far beyond his family, except for threatening dangers. Our modern society demands consideration of the whole country, with its diversity of interests, its sections, and its classes. It has become increasingly necessary to look at the whole earth and the trends of all its peoples. More and more individual value-systematization has come to require clear thought and firm choice on the basis of a world-wide scene. The task of choosing and working out the social destiny of mankind is increasingly forced upon men. This is a rare historical privilege, though full of suffering. It can be done actively or by default. In any case it is becoming necessary for the individual to have a world-outlook both in theory and practice.

Such tasks confronting the individual today cannot be settled by rule or even by principle. They require a mature systematic outlook and a clear conception of the nature of society and social values. We turn, therefore, to an examination of the materialist treatment of society.

Materialist treatment of society

INDIVIDUALISTIC FORMS

Philosophical materialists in common regard "society" as a name for men in their individual and group relations to one another, and not in any sense as indicating something super-individual. But there is no uniform materialist treatment of social values. In perhaps the greater part of the materialist tradition the emphasis has been individualistic, and social problems have been posed from the point of view of the individual and his goals. The good is a state of the individual, and the social question is: How can the individual manage his relations with others so as to achieve his ends? Only in the 19th and 20th centuries did the materialist tradition produce a more social approach cast in terms of social welfare, which came to recognize that the goals of the so-called atomic individual were themselves social products.

Power ethics. The types of individualistic goals on which outlooks on society have been built are themselves diverse. One philosophy recommends power, another seeks peace, a third pursues pleasure or the fulfillment of desire. In the first book of Plato's *Republic,* Thrasymachus presents a form of this-worldliness which, as we have seen,[16] constitutes the object of Plato's

---

[16] See above, p. 389.

continuous attack. It is the "crass materialism" which views every man as in perpetual struggle with all others to achieve his personal desires. The good is simply getting what you want; the right way to live is to acquire sufficient power over others to get what you want. The wise man is not fooled by conventions, moral rules, or laws. He violates them whenever it is profitable, and when he is in the seat of authority he makes them up to suit his needs. Justice (or right) is thus the interest of the stronger, established by the governing power in a community for its own benefit. The good life is the life of self-aggrandizement, and injustice with its instrumental use of others is the true wisdom and virtue.

Nietzsche in many respects provides a modern parallel. His glorification of power [17]—all life expresses the will to power on his theory—shares Thrasymachus' contempt for ordinary morality. Nietzsche attacks the whole of Hebraic-Christian morality, with its virtues of piety and humility, its unworldliness and its attitude to suffering, as the glorification of weakness, as making virtues out of necessity and impotence, as fashioning bonds for the free spirit. This phase of his philosophy, together with his contempt for the mass of mankind, was appealed to by the Nazis in their effort to find a philosophic ancestry for their doctrines. He looks to the development of the superman who will surpass man as man surpassed the ape. This element relieves his position from the individualism of Thrasymachus.

Peace or security ethics. In the second book of the *Republic,* Glaucon and Adeimantus, Plato's own brothers, urge another form of Thrasymachus' view. They agree that individual good lies in getting what the individual wants, but they do not think that stepping over others and violating morality and law is the best way to achieve this. Only a few could be successful in this way; for the vast majority of people there would be more harm than gain. Thus morality and law are devised as a compromise between doing injustice and suffering injustice, a compromise which will enable most men to achieve a substantial part of their desires. Morality is not intrinsically good; in fact most people teach their children to be virtuous by showing them that it pays. But it works on the whole. Only a person endowed with miraculous powers (an old story of a man who could become invisible is invoked) could afford to behave like the tyrant who is Thrasymachus' ideal.

This view of morality and law as a compromise to mediate between the grasping tendencies of men and their fear of harm at others' hands, is a common one in the modern world. For the traditional conception of man as naturally selfish leaves little other ground for development of ethics. The fountain-head of this view in modern philosophy is Hobbes. The state of

---

[17] Nietzsche is by no means a philosophical materialist; his ethics is, however, sometimes so regarded because of its stress on power, its opposition to traditional spirituality, and its use of evolutionary conceptions. His social outlook is to be found in the latter part of *The Will to Power.* See also *The Genealogy of Morals.*

nature as he describes it resembles the Thrasymachean position, and in agreement with Glaucon and Adeimantus he conceives of moral rules as instrumental for securing the order necessary to the achievement of men's desires. His own recommendation for maintaining peace is the instrument of absolute sovereignty. The major problem of this-worldly social philosophy after Hobbes was to develop a socially oriented ethics on his egoistic premises. How this was attempted in utilitarianism will be considered below.[18]

Pleasure ethics. That a man's aim is to secure a maximum of pleasure and a minimum of pain is a view of the good generally known as *hedonism*. In ancient times it is found in Epicurean theory. Epicurus did not believe that positive pleasure is attainable on a very large scale. Hence the best a man can do is to minimize desire and thus minimize the pain of frustration. Love of honor and glory are sources of distress to be avoided. A wise man will see fear of death, a potent cause of pain, as ungrounded; since the body is merely a mass of atoms, it has nothing to fear from the dissolution that ends all. Social life has as its aim protection from injury and injustice; politics is best avoided. Epicurus' hedonism was, then, not an active philosophy, but one of quietism. Its individualism reflected a period of increasing unrest in which the outcome of large-scale plans appeared a matter of chance. In modern philosophy, on the other hand, hedonism has been largely expansive in its mood, reaching its height of optimism in Bentham.[19]

SOCIALLY ORIENTED FORMS

A more socially oriented approach is characteristic of the most important modern forms of materialist ethics. In English utilitarianism and in historical materialism social and ethical theory are intimately intertwined and applications to conduct and social practice are rendered explicit.

The utilitarians were the intellectual wing of the middle class in the expansion of its political power in England during the early part of the 19th century. Jeremy Bentham and John Stuart Mill, the leading philosophical exponents of the school, dominated intellectual movements in England for a great part of the century. Much political, legal, and economic theory was expressed in terms of this school of thought.[20] The theory itself gave systematic intellectual expression to the type of life that the activity of the

[18] Pp. 445-46.
[19] For a brief account of the atmosphere in which Epicureanism as well as Stoicism arose, see above, p. 396; for Bentham, see below, p. 443 ff.
[20] For a thorough exposition of the growth of the school as a whole see Elie Halévy, *The Growth of Philosophical Radicalism,* translated by Mary Morris, Macmillan, 1928. On its economic side the group included Ricardo, following on the heels of Adam

middle class was fast developing. Much of common American formulation of social goals and personal ethics in relation to them still uses the language of utilitarian ethics.

To reckon utilitarian ethical theory as materialistic in its outlook is by no means to assert that the individual members of the school were philosophical materialists. Mill, for example, held to a type of phenomenalism, as evidenced in his famous definition of matter as "the permanent possibilities of sensation." The language of utilitarian ethics is that of subjectivism and phenomenalism. That, as we have observed, is quite common in earlier materialism.[21] But the impact of the theory in no way depended on the subjectivistic language it employed. And insofar as the content of the theory is concerned, no more sweeping this-worldliness is to be found anywhere in the domain of ethical and social analysis.

Historical materialism, on the other hand, is self-consciously materialistic, constituting a part of the philosophic approach known as dialectical materialism. Its founders—Karl Marx and Friedrich Engels—developed it in the course of their critique of capitalist society and their efforts to organize an international working-class movement. It first achieved wide public notice in the *Communist Manifesto* of 1848, and became thereafter the theoretical basis of various socialist movements. As a result it was developed in different ways; but the mainstream of its development is to be found in Lenin's writings. Lenin used it as a theoretical base for the founding of the Soviet Union and the construction of socialism, and it continues today to be the philosophy of communist movements throughout the world. Whereas utilitarianism is commonly regarded as an explicit philosophy of the growth of capitalism, historical materialism looks upon itself as the philosophy of the working class and eventually of the classless society.

ENGLISH UTILITARIANISM

Bentham's ethical position. Bentham states his fundamental position at the very beginning of *An Introduction to the Principles of Morals and Legislation:* "Nature has placed mankind under the governance of two sovereign masters, *pain* and *pleasure.* It is for them alone to point out what we ought to do, as well as to determine what we shall do. . . . By the principle of utility is meant that principle which approves or disapproves of every action whatsoever, according to the tendency which it appears to have to augment

---

Smith, and J. S. Mill, on its political side James Mill, on its legal, John Austin in addition to Bentham. Many elements in Herbert Spencer's ethics and politics make it possible to regard him as a subsequent extension of one wing of the school. Sidgwick is a later more academic representative.

[21] See above, p. 426.

or diminish the happiness of the party whose interest is in question: or, what is the same thing in other words, to promote or to oppose that happiness. . . . By utility is meant that property in any object whereby it tends to produce benefit, advantage, pleasure, good, or happiness (all this in the present case comes to the same thing) or (what comes again to the same thing) to prevent the happening of mischief, pain, evil, or unhappiness to the party whose interest is considered: if that party be the community in general, then the happiness of the community; if a particular individual, then the happiness of that individual."

Bentham opposes his principle of utility to all other theories. Some, he says, have adhered to a principle of asceticism, regarding many pleasures as evil. He holds, on the contrary, that any pleasure insofar as it is a pleasure to someone is good. Only insofar as it involves pain to others or subsequent pain or diminution of pleasure to the man himself is it to be regarded as evil. Others, he also points out, have adhered to a principle of caprice, offering the will of God (which *they* interpret) or their feelings of approval or their rules of reason, as the test of good or right conduct. He finds no reason to follow any of these rules unless they should claim they lead to the happiness of mankind. In the latter case he prefers to deal in terms of happiness directly.

His program for secularizing morality. How thorough and far-reaching was Bentham's program for secularizing morality is best seen in his treatment of detailed rules in his *Theory of Legislation*. For example, he holds that a son ought to choose his own bride, not have her chosen for him by his father, because, since the father has not so long a time to live, the duration of parental disappointment however extreme is normally less than the possible future dissatisfaction of the son. He approves of divorce under carefully formulated conditions. In a paper on sex which it appears he did not risk publishing [22] he attacks intolerance in respect to homosexuality. He grounds opposition to incest on the harm that would result from the opportunity for coercion by the males of a family in the face of permissible temptation. On questions of punishment he is opposed to revenge as a capricious basis and advocates an emphasis on deterrence instead. He works out detailed theorems for its application, the general rule being that the pain inflicted should be just enough to deter the criminal from repetition while the appearance of punishment should be as great as possible in order to impress and deter others. He would even, as we noted above, have created the appearance of capital punishment while shipping the criminal off to the colonies. He also devoted much time and money to advocating the Panopticon, a type of model prison. The details of his treatment of many practical

[22] Published by C. K. Ogden as an appendix to his edition of Bentham's *The Theory of Legislation*, Harcourt, Brace, 1931.

problems may be criticized for lack of judgment or foresight, but his intent is constantly to achieve an empirical estimation of pleasures and pains with due regard for varying conditions of sensibility.

Bentham's fundamental theory has often been criticized as a confusion of what men do with what men *ought* to do. If they pursue pleasure does that mean they ought to pursue it? If they pursue their own pleasure why *should* they pursue "the greatest happiness of the greatest number" which is his standard? These difficulties are not insoluble; though Bentham does not face them all explicitly, his whole approach provides an answer. *Ought* is defined as characterizing the kind of conduct that conforms to the principle of utility. Therefore it is meaningful to say that a man *ought* to pursue a certain course of conduct—whether it be a pleasurable course which he would pursue of his own accord or a course which now brings him pain—because of its probable effect on the sum of his pleasures in the long run. Bentham is constantly hammering at the idea that many of men's ethical wrongs are errors of calculation with regard to the future. Thus to tell a man that he *ought* to pursue pleasure is to draw him away from following capricious feelings (momentary attractions) to the more arduous but ultimately more satisfactory tasks revealed by moral arithmetic.

Similarly the group of men constituting the community will tend, if they make no mistakes in calculation of means, to adopt arrangements that yield the greatest available happiness of the majority. This will be the result of each willing his own happiness.

Transition from personal pleasure to greatest happiness of greatest number. But why ought an individual man to do what pains him but will contribute to the greater pleasure of the majority? Clearly Bentham is bound to the view that he ought to do so *only if acting for the interests of the majority in the long run is in his own best interest.* Bentham reckons with this in two ways. In his *Deontology* or treatise on personal obligations he attempts an empirical approach to what is after all an empirical matter and seeks to show that the usual virtues really pay a man in the long run. Doing others a good turn is like long-range investment in a savings bank. Interest accrues in many unexpected good turns; and in many unknown cases others refrain from action against you.[23] Apart from the monetary tone of many of his illustrations, Bentham is clearly interpreting virtues as obligations worth assuming for their utility in the long run.

The second way in which Bentham faces the problem of the individual finding his own interests in communal or majority interests is by what has

---

[23] Readers of Horatio Alger, Jr., success stories will recall the frequency with which old apparently worthless bonds or mining shares left by a father to his son who is the hero, blossom into wealth at crucial moments, such as when the mortgage is due or the villain is to be confounded.

aptly been called the principle of *artificial identification* of interests. Bentham in effect recommends a system of legal sanctions (punishments and rewards) so fashioned that the individual's interest *will* coincide with the common interest. This argument amounts to advice to the legislator. But why should the legislator follow such advice? James Mill's treatment of representative government shows that there can be techniques for making the legislator's private interests coincide with the majority interests—for example, shorten the term of Parliament so that he will have to seek re-election. In order to satisfy the electorate who are all concerned with their own individual interests, he will have to aim at the "greatest happiness of the greatest number" of them possible. This will help to develop this principle as a conscious criterion for all obligation.

John Stuart Mill, with a clearer eye on educational possibilities, recognizes the culturally conditioned character of pleasure seeking. Men can come by training to find pleasure in almost any type of activity, so that virtuous conduct is no less natural than vicious conduct. Men can thus come to find their pleasures in co-operative and mutually helpful conduct. Hence the artificial identification of interests in one generation might become the *natural identity* of interests in another when education has had time to operate.

The "felicific calculus." By what means are the pleasures and pains of men to be calculated? In fact how are we to tell what a man's pleasure is? Bentham gives the rules of calculation in verse—presumably so that they will be more readily recalled:

> *Intense, long, certain, speedy, fruitful, pure*—
> Such marks in *pleasures* and in *pains* endure.
> Such pleasures seek, if *private* be thy end;
> If it be *public*, wide let them *extend*.
> Such *pains* avoid, whichever be thy view;
> If pains *must* come, let them *extend* to few.

In his calculations, Bentham makes no qualitative distinctions in pleasures. Pleasures, he insists, differ in quantity, not in quality—pushpin is as good as poetry, if it provides the same quantity of pleasure. This claim has been frequently attacked as rating the ecstatic pig over the dissatisfied Socrates. The Benthamite may, of course, retort that the rational abilities which render Socrates capable of dissatisfaction render a man in the long run capable of much greater pleasure. John Stuart Mill departed, however, from this Benthamite position. He conceded that there are qualitative differences in pleasures, so that no quantity of the one equals any of the other in worth. Thus the pleasures of the intellect, of the feelings and imagination, and of the moral sentiments have a much higher value as pleasures than those of mere sensation: "Of two pleasures, if there be one to which all or almost all who have experience of both give a decided preference, irrespective of any feeling of moral obligation to prefer it, that is the more desirable pleasure."[24]

Two possible issues are involved in Bentham's position and Mill's departure: the commensurability of different pleasures felt by a single man, and the commensurability of different pleasures felt by different men. The first arises when I prefer pushpin to poetry, the second when I prefer pushpin and you prefer poetry and one of us must give way on a particular occasion.

On the question of pleasures felt by the same man, if Bentham's denial of qualitative difference in pleasure be taken to mean that pleasure is an extensive quality and that it can be reckoned just as lengths or weights can be, then he is certainly dealing in fictions or impractical hopes. If, however, he is asserting that pleasure is an intensive quality, that pleasures may be arranged in order of greater or less degree, as we "measure" temperature or intelligence, then he appears to be correct. For a choice between two pleasures involves just such a comparison; and any two pleasures, no matter how different, may conceivably come before a man in a situation in which he must choose between them. And if he is unable to choose, then so far as Bentham is concerned they are equal. The fact of consistent preferences confirms Bentham's statement once it is so interpreted.

Bentham's equalitarianism. The more important issue concerns *my* pushpin versus *your* poetry. Here Bentham's equalitarianism is clear and unequivocal. No man's pleasure, no matter in what he finds it, is to be ruled out on the ground that another man's vote for something else is of superior quality. Bentham indicates this more explicitly when he adds the fundamental proposition that every man is to count as one. The fact that A is richer or better educated or even more intelligent than B does not make his vote superior. The individual's vote is not to be restrained or interfered with. Bentham's ethics merely aids a man's moral arithmetic by helping him judge the effects of alternative courses of action on the achievement of his own future preferences and those of other men.

A man's equality with other men in Bentham's reckoning appears to have a twofold aspect. It means that there must be no moral condemnation of his vote if its effect on others is not evil; thus pushpin is as good as poetry for the man who is equally pleased by it. And it also means that his vote counts equally with anyone else's if the question is one for public decision. Even if he loses, no other man's vote has had greater weight. Mill's affirmation of qualities of pleasure seems to withdraw the immunity against moral condemnation, and its introduction of an aristocratic element at this point might jeopardize equality in the second sense.

In general, the question may be raised whether Bentham's equalitarianism is compatible with his pleasure theory. Suppose, for example, that some psy-

[24] *Utilitarianism*, Chapter 2.

chologist discovers that A's desire if satisfied yields him twice as many units of pleasure as B's would yield B. Why should not A's vote count as two? There are three possible ways of facing this situation.

(a) Treat the equality principle as equivalent to a denial that such psychological tests exist or are likely to be discovered. But while defending equality practically, this solution leaves a theoretical door open to future abandonment of equalitarianism.

(b) Accept any authenticated test, but claim as a lesson of experience that the dangers in its social application are so great that abandonment of the equality principle will introduce wide-scale caprice. Thus in the long run the available maximum of human happiness would be diminished rather than facilitated by aristocratic and oligarchic assumptions. Mill's approach, in *Liberty,* is along these lines; he allows a man to follow a course of conduct which is less valuable so long as it concerns him alone.

(c) Offer the principle that every man counts as one as an independent postulate. This might rest historically on the type of empirical investigation indicated in (b), but it would mean that equality had become a value in its own right. The consequence of this procedure would be that it leaves a theoretical door open to abandonment of the greatest pleasure principle; for it may happen under special circumstances that the total sum of pleasure under the equalitarian principle is less than under a principle of inequality.

Perhaps the most consistent outcome of Bentham's view that every man must judge his own pleasure, and its relative intensity, and that one man's pleasure is to count equally with another's, is to regard the subjective or introspective account of pleasure and pain as really irrelevant to the whole system. Bentham is in effect not basing ethics upon a man's feelings but on his vote: pleasure means aye, pain nay. When a man says he is pleased it amounts to what the Romans meant when they said "Senatui placuit" (it pleased the senate), for "the senate decreed" or what the regal phrase "It is our pleasure" intends. The whole utilitarian structure might thus be rewritten to use the language of men's choices and rejections instead of their pleasures and pains, the central goal becoming the maximum achievement of men's choices.

What this individualism meant in the theory of liberty we have already seen in examining Mill's theory.[25] It is worth tracing its consequences in other fields as well.

Utilitarian position in politics. In politics apart from questions of liberty it meant representative government with the widest representation. That entailed universal suffrage—but only in theory; it was not to be granted immediately—short-term parliaments, secret ballot, abolition of "rotten boroughs," and other reforms. In application it was carried only so far as was

[25] See Chapter 18 above, p. 245 ff.

necessary to give power to the middle class. John Stuart Mill later began to concern himself with the working class, but his father James Mill, the "executive director" of the Utilitarians, showed such faith in the middle class that he assumed all would be well for the lower classes too if the middle class were in control. In considering the desirable extent of the basis for government, he says:

"Another proposition may be stated, with a perfect confidence of the concurrence of all those men who have attentively considered the formation of opinions in the great body of society, or, indeed, the principles of human nature in general. It is, that the opinions of that class of the people who are below the middle rank are formed, and their minds directed, by that intelligent and virtuous rank who come the most immediately in contact with them, who are in the constant habit of intimate communication with them, to whom they fly for advice and assistance in all their numerous difficulties, upon whom they feel an immediate and daily dependence, in health and in sickness, in infancy and in old age; to whom their children look up as models for their imitation, whose opinions they hear daily repeated and account it their honor to adopt. There can be no doubt that the middle rank, which gives to science, to art, and to legislation itself their most distinguished ornaments, the chief source of all that has exalted and refined human nature, is that portion of the community of which, if the basis of representation were ever so far extended, the opinion would ultimately decide. Of the people beneath them a vast majority would be sure to be guided by their advice and example." [26]

Utilitarian position in law. In law Bentham applies the principle of utility directly. There are no fictions permitted, no natural rights, no conclusions that do not pose as probable ways in which the greatest happiness will be secured. Law operates by means of sanctions which will be exercised, the applications of pain and pleasure. Dominant emphasis has been on pain. The possible ends of law are subsistence, abundance, security, and equality. Subsistence may be left to men's efforts, since the motivation is sufficient; Bentham also seems to assume that the available means are sufficient. It is not part of the law's task to ensure abundance directly. Security is the primary aim. Equality must yield to security. It is no use redistributing income since equality will not last. It is sufficient merely to avoid excessive extremes. If men will only be secure in their possessions there is no end to the abundance their industry will produce. The benefits industry will bring, if its rewards are protected, will more than compensate for inequalities. The great end of government is to guarantee security, that is, to preserve property.

Bentham has no romantic illusions about the sacredness of property. It is entirely a creation of law, and without law it collapses. His insistence on

[26] James Mill, *Essay on Government*, X.

its protection is entirely a function of the utility he ascribes to it. He believes experience has amply proved that all the restrictions of government on the use of property serve only to encumber productivity. He calls for free play for men's energies and the removal of all hindrances. In this respect he was the voice of the commercial classes.

Utilitarian economic theory. Utilitarian economic theory up to Mill was simply the doctrine of laissez-faire. The economic machine is held to be self-adjusting. It operates in such a way that each man pursues his own interests in an enlightened way and the result is the interest of all. Halévy points to the marked divergence—almost amounting to contradiction—in the utilitarian conceptions of politics and of economics. In the former the aim is the *artificial identification* of interests. In the latter there is an assumed *natural identity* of interests. There was no *a priori* reason why government should not use legal sanctions to regulate economic affairs so as to ensure the greatest happiness of the greatest number. Bentham argued that as a lesson of experience it was inadvisable. He even defended abolition of usury restrictions, an experiment England later tried for some years and then abandoned. Mill's economic theory had a more transitional aspect. He recognized the social character of distribution, and was concerned with socialism and the future of the working class. But in Herbert Spencer the principle of natural identity of interest was even carried into politics, and all legislation disparaged. That government was therefore best that governed least.

Clearly utilitarian theory served the middle class well. Its governmental theory favored them. Its economic theory demanded a free hand for them. Its legal theory gave them the foundations of the protection of property and made them the carriers of community prosperity. It is interesting to note that the Utilarians ceased to be an effective school after the Reform Bill of 1832 secured the political rise of the middle class to equal partnership in the government of England and the Empire. The right wing of the school drew back; the left wing began to look towards socialism.

Both developments were quite compatible with utilitarian general principles, since the specific recommendations depended largely on the factual assumptions with which the theory was coupled. With altered factual premises far different systems of society might be recommended. Now since the theory had spoken with the voice of experience—empiricism was thoroughly ingrained in its structure—its supporters might have been expected to pay heed to the lessons of experience. Instead, as often happens in such historic developments when theory overshoots the mark for which supporters encouraged it, they gradually discarded the theory. Utilitarianism was in the vanguard of the political expansion of the industrial and commercial groups. Once they were established and the theory pointed to further advances, they sought justification in other theories or else made hallowed traditions out of the factual assumptions on which its outlook had rested.

The spread of this-worldliness. It was middle class *practice* that proved the effective mechanism for the spread of this-worldliness. The tremendous importance that industry and business as practiced under a capitalist structure have had in fashioning current attitudes and character is not to be underestimated. The rapid development of technology in producing an economy of potential abundance removed much of the basis for attitudes of resignation, and replaced them with an official optimism. Practical aims were given an explicitly dominant status. Wealth and its pleasures and powers became the dominant goals of men. In every field—art is an excellent illustration—the worth of a thing became identified with its price. Although men might claim that making money was only a means to the end of retiring to enjoy a life of culture—those at least who were in a position to do more than earn a meager living—the story of their lives shows that passions and ideal energies went into the business world, and the estate was left for others to administer.

The competitive attitudes that have become paramount with the rise of business have penetrated all fields of life, perhaps even the family. Egoistic traits produced by this civilization have become enshrined as human nature. The ideal of liberty served not merely to break the political restrictions of a previous age, but also to loosen older bonds of religion, kinship, patriotism, and cultural loyalties. Just as the hedonistic goal was the pursuit of pleasure, and where he found it a man's own concern, so the common note of the civilization sponsored by business enterprise has become the pursuit of wealth and where a man gets it (and even how he spends it) his own affair.

HISTORICAL MATERIALISM

A part of dialectical materialism. Marx and Engels regarded dialectical materialism, of which historical materialism constitutes the historical and social theory, as a development out of the whole history of materialism. Although our present concern is with their ethical and social theory, it may be noted that they developed philosophical materialism as a whole by focusing attention on the social sciences, as compared to mechanistic materialism which had concentrated on the physical sciences. From Hegel they took over a conception of dialectic, which itself represented a mixture of attitudes historically developed. Their exposition of dialectic tended to remain encumbered with Hegelian formulations, but its meaning emerges clearly in their actual application of its principles, especially to historical analysis. In practice, it involved several things. One is a habit of regarding existence as an unstable equilibrium, a complex of forces making for constant change. Another is an intense opposition to reductionism,[27] which brought an insistence on the occurrence of novel qualities and a recognition that all principles asserted by men are valid only within definite limits. The third is a sense of the zigzag upward course of the stream of events.[28] In addition they inherited Hegel's method of looking at a society as a whole and seeing the unifying elements among its various strands. But they did not look for an Hegelian spirit of the age. Instead, the unity of a society became in their theory a pattern actually hammered out by the interplay of groups of men pursuing their aims within a society. The analysis they advanced of such interplay constitutes an economic interpretation of history.

The primacy of mode of production. On the Marxian theory the fundamental features in determining the direction of events in a society are its forces of production and its mode of distribution of the products of labor. In an often quoted passage in the introduction to his *Critique of Political Economy,* Marx says: "The mode of production of the material means of existence conditions the whole process of social, political and intellectual life. It is not the consciousness of men that determines their existence, but, on the contrary, it is their social existence that determines their consciousness. At a certain stage of their development the material productive forces of society come into contradiction with the existing productive relationships, or, what is but a legal expression for these, with the property relationships within which they had moved before. From forms of development of the productive forces these relationships are transformed into their fetters. Then an epoch of social revolution opens. With the change in the economic foundation the whole vast superstructure is more or less rapidly transformed. In considering such revolutions it is necessary always to distinguish between the material revolution in the economic conditions of production, which can be determined with scientific accuracy, and the juridical, political, religious, esthetic or philosophic—in a word, ideological forms wherein men become conscious of this conflict and fight it out." [29]

History hitherto the history of class struggles. The form which these processes take is described in Marxian theory as the class struggle. The opening of the *Communist Manifesto* states this thesis:

"The history of all hitherto existing society is the history of class struggles.

"Freeman and slave, patrician and plebeian, lord and serf, guild-master

---

[27] For the tendency to reduce human and mental phenomena to purely physical phenomena, see above, p. 160 ff.

[28] These various strands here stated figuratively as attitudes were expressed as *laws of dialectic,* respectively the unity of opposites, the transformation of quantity into quality, and the negation of the negation.

[29] From *A Handbook of Marxism,* ed. by Emile Burns, p. 372. By permission of International Publishers.

and journeyman, in a word, oppressor and oppressed, stood in constant opposition to one another, carried on uninterrupted, now hidden, now open fight, a fight that each time ended, either in a revolutionary reconstitution of society at large, or in the common ruin of the contending classes. . . .

"Our epoch, the epoch of the bourgeoisie, possesses, however, this distinctive feature; it has simplified the class antagonisms. Society as a whole is more and more splitting up into two great hostile camps, into two great classes directly facing each other: Bourgeoisie and Proletariat."[30]

Classes are defined in the theory by the role that their members play in the processes of production. An examination of the processes of production and the way in which the products of labor are distributed reveals the points of control and power. Thus dominant classes appropriate whatever they can of the fruits of the subordinate classes' labor, leaving the latter merely subsistence and what concessions may occasionally be required for the maintenance of power. In the relation of master and slave this process is patent; in feudal relations it is barely disguised by the language of contract; in capital-labor relations it is so covered that a full-scale analysis of the economic system is required to confirm it. This Marx carried out in his *Capital*.

Marxian explanation of social change. The explanation of change in any phase of social life (government, law, religion, education, etc.) is to be found according to Marxian theory in terms of changes in the mode of production and the particular stage of the class struggle at the given time. The pattern of a society's culture is not created by the dominant class out of nothing; hence social explanation always begins with an existent system or in the middle of things. The pattern is fashioned by the gradual alteration of existent modes due to the pressures of a rising class. As this class takes power it remakes the face of society in its own image. This job has never been completed because the subordinate class develops its own tendencies in response to the development of productive forces within the society and to the course of the conflict. Constant readjustments in the various phases of the life of a society result from the struggle as it grows with increasing intensity. As long as the dominant class is able to maintain and increase productivity it may cling to its place, but when its vested rights come to hamper the development of the forces of production its day is drawing to an end. Violence ensues not because the subordinate class wants it but because the dominant class clings to power it can no longer successfully wield.

The development of capitalism. It is generally agreed by many non-Marxian as well as Marxian historians that the commercial middle class thus rose to power over the feudal landowners. It altered its religion in the process, it remade the political system, it broke with an older morality. According to the Marxian account it has continued to hold its power by virtue of the

[30] In *op. cit.*, pp. 22-23.

development of production which it organized in masterful fashion.[31] Schools, pulpits, press induce attitudes favorable to its control, and armies and police stand ready to enforce its power. But its very advance increases the depression of the laboring classes upon which it rests, and renders more difficult the position of the dominant class, revealing what Marxists regard as the central contradiction of capitalism—the incompatibility of its almost socialized system of production with its system of unplanned competitive distribution, its individual control and appropriation of the fruits of labor. Economic depressions, a cyclical phenomenon in the competitive economy, become increasingly severe and increasingly frequent. Technological change yields large-scale unemployment. There is collapse of weaker enterprise, growth of monopoly, increasing unification of industry and finance, and the emergence of a consolidated monopolistic ruling group instead of the more widely scattered group bound by looser ties of more general mutual interest. This involves shrinkage of the middle class and reduction of its lower groups to proletarian status. More drastic steps are required to maintain profits. In order to maintain and increase price levels there is contraction instead of expansion of production; there is suppression of technological advance, and even a cry against science itself; there is a depression of real wage levels; there is conflict between large national units in the world for material resources and fields of exploitation; and there is war with all its physical destruction. The class that ushered in great material progress thus becomes, by the direction of its efforts to hold its power, the greatest obstacle to the maintenance and expansion of that progress.

In this process, as Marxist theory describes it, the laboring class grows in strength through organization and obtains a clearer conception of its possible role. It comes to realize that many of the attitudes with which it is being indoctrinated are bulwarks of a system by which it is being exploited. As the laboring class breaks through these attitudes, and as the liberalism of prosperous days becomes a luxury in the face of declining profits, naked force and fear alone uphold the position of the dominant class.[32] Mean-

---

[31] It has itself undergone continuous change in virtue of shifts in its productive processes, e.g., from manufacture resting on organized handicraft production to machine industry. In fact a central feature of capitalist production is its constant revolutionizing of the means of production. Marx is able to treat such changes as part of the class struggle because he sees them as part of the process of exploiting labor or producing "surplus-value," i.e., that part of the value of the product which is created by labor but for which labor gets no return. For example, he says of machinery, "Like every other increase in the productiveness of labor, machinery is intended to cheapen commodities, and, by shortening that portion of the working-day in which the laborer works for himself, to lengthen the other portion that he gives, without an equivalent, to the capitalist. In short, it is a means for producing surplus-value." (*Capital*, Vol. I, Modern Library edition, p. 405.)

[32] This is the present-day Marxian description of fascism.

while the working class consciously grooms itself to take over power and to remold the face of society. When it does, new institutions will emerge, productive energy will be released, and a socialized society develop in which classes will disappear.

Controversies concerning classes and the class struggle. Numerous controversies have raged around the central ideas of Marxian theory. There are, for example, problems in the fundamental concepts of class, determinism, dialectic, and so forth. In the case of class, the issue has been in the first place whether the concept is more fruitfully defined in terms of conscious alignments into which men feel themselves to fall, or groupings determined on some objective basis (e.g., occupational, geographic, role in production, wealth) irrespective of men's feelings as to where they belong. Both Marxian theory and the social sciences generally have taken the latter course, treating men's feelings about their place as data to be explained rather than as explanatory factors. The primary issue has then become whether the economic divisions as used by the Marxian theory provide a more systematic account of social change than do other divisions. Some have questioned this stress on the economic factor as primary and offered instead pluralistic conceptions of the interplay of numerous factors within a society without assigning primacy to any. Such an outlook, for example, underlies Max Weber's work on the relation of religion and capitalism.[33]

Again, many have attacked the concept of the class struggle, especially where it concerns the antagonism of capital and labor. One issue here is whether there is an ultimate and irreconcilable conflict of interests, not whether employers and employees exhibit hostility toward one another. The view that there is no ultimate conflict rests ultimately on the theory that capitalism can remain an expanding productive force bringing increasing benefits to all sections of the community, workers as well as owners and investors. Henry Ford's policy in the early days of the automobile industry—raising of wages and lowering of prices, coupled with rationalized mass production—embodied this outlook. Such an outlook regards monopoly as an artificial growth, and in some cases looks to limited government operations to minimize the impact of depressions. The Marxists, on the other hand, hold monopoly to be an inevitable product of capitalism and see government itself as an instrument utilized by monopoly interests. The question whether there is an ultimate clash of the interests of capital and labor rather than merely occasional temporary conflicts can thus be answered only in terms of the total economic functioning of a society, and a prediction of its future trend in the light of world developments.[34]

[33] *The Protestant Ethic and the Spirit of Capitalism*, translated by Talcott Parsons, Scribner, 1930.

[34] For analysis of a similar problem in the theory of the state, see above, pp. 280-82.

The claim that socialism is inevitable. Serious problems are also raised by the idea of inevitability in the operations of human affairs, which is found in the Marxian theory of history. Especially because of its derivation from Hegelian philosophy,[35] it sometimes appears to assert a logic of history in the sense of an unfolding which is necessary and unalterable. In Marxian movements the notion of the inevitability of socialism has sometimes been teleologically colored. As such it has sometimes acted to give strength of purpose as well as a feeling of historical justification to revolutionary efforts. But it has equally well served to induce quietism on the assumption that economic developments would of themselves bring about the goal without any special effort. On the other hand, the mainstream of Marxist philosophy has specifically repudiated any teleological interpretation of the theory. By calling socialism inevitable Marxist philosophers mean simply that its attainment can be predicted on their analysis of the operations of society. For, they say, there will be increasing chaos as the mass of men find themselves frustrated by the control of the dominant class over production. Given the weight of their needs and the absence of any other practicable alternative, there will be a growing direction of men's efforts toward the achievement of socialism. In this sense inevitability carries no fatalistic implication. A crucial point in such analysis is the role of individuals and of intellectual clarity and moral strength in the progression the theory describes. On this point Marxian theorists have sometimes minimized the role of the individual. This may rest on the view that the relevant characteristics of men themselves are the outcome of social and economic influences, or, equally well, on a faith in the mass of men and the belief that they have sufficient resources of character, initiative and leadership, so that no particular individual is indispensable.[36]

Contributions to materialist ethics. In turning to the contributions of Marxian theory to the growth of materialist ethics, it is important to note that Marx regarded philosophy as itself a part of culture. Therefore he holds that philosophy, like education or religion, inevitably plays a part in the class struggle. This it does partly as a weapon serving to justify a class (for the dominant philosophy justifies the dominant class) and partly as a clarification to a class of its aims and their relations. Marx took his own philosophy to serve the latter role for the laboring class; he held it to be a product of the social conditions generated by the stage the class struggle had reached. The extent to which he carried a class interpretation of philosophical theory

---

[35] For Hegel's account of history, see above, pp. 421-24.

[36] For a fuller study of the central ideas of Marxism, see Howard Selsam, *What Is Philosophy?*, International Publishers, 1938; G. H. Sabine, *A History of Political Theory*, Holt, 1937, Chapters 32-33. *A Handbook of Marxism*, referred to above, provides a convenient collection of original materials. For a special study of Marxian ethical theory, see Howard Selsam, *Socialism and Ethics*, International Publishers, 1943.

can be seen from his criticism of utilitarianism; the reduction of everything to utility, he said, means treating every object, every person, every social relation for what it will bring. This is the reduction of everything to the relation of exploitation.[37] And that is what capitalism did to all social forms and human relations it found on the scene. As compared to feudalism it substituted naked exploitation for exploitation veiled by religious and political illusions.[38]

Although the Marxian theory of ethics is not formally elaborated and must be gathered from various concrete analyses and general social and historical discussions, its chief tenets may be easily discerned. Values are not reduced to a single element like pleasure, or describd in psychological terms like desire or appetite, but are regarded simply as goals of individuals or groups of men. Thus they are referred to in the language of ordinary life or of social description. It is sometimes thought that Marxian materialism treats all values as "really" economic in a fashion analogous to mechanical materialism treating all phenomena as "really" atomic. This is based on a confusion of reduction and causal explanation. Marx did not deny the genuine sincerity of non-economic motives; nor did he claim that a man in love was secretly hungering for gold. He advanced the hypothesis that the specific form of men's values in a given period could be explained as an historical function of the class they belonged to and the relation of classes during that and preceding periods.

Bentham and Mill had also pointed to causal bases for men's values. Bentham had recognized that what a man found pleasurable depended on factors such as health, strength, knowledge, inclination, moral and religious biases, habitual occupations, pecuniary circumstances, and a host of other influences. Mill contended in a general way that men could be brought up to find pleasure in almost any kind of activity. In comparison with utilitarianism, the causal theory which Marxian ethical theory offered laid far greater stress on specific social and historical causation.

According to the Marxian analysis not merely the things men hold good in a society but also the character traits they recommend (what they call virtues as against what they brand as vices), the rules of conduct they consider binding, are treated as functions of class aims and their perpetual conflict. Egoism is regarded not as a natural property of the self, but as a developed trait under a competitive capitalism, and one that will disappear when the conditions supporting it disappear. Thrift is a virtue in the early stages of capitalism where accumulation of capital is required. It ceases to be a virtue when investment funds are accumulated in immense quantity.

[37] "Marx on Bentham and Utilitarianism" (Appendix III in Sidney Hook, *From Hegel to Marx*, Reynal and Hitchcock, 1936), translated by Sidney Hook from Marx and Engel's *The German Ideology*.
[38] *Communist Manifesto*, in Burns, *op. cit.*, p. 25.

Chastity as an exclusively female virtue (coupled with a distinct standard for men) expresses proprietary attitudes of men—the owner controls the possession but has no responsibility to it—and would give way, with genuine economic freedom for women, to a single standard based on common respect. Respect for science is cultivated when business needs science, but yields to a disparagement even of scientific method when scientific advance becomes too rapid for business profits. Racial prejudice is an attitude fostered by the dominant class to keep the subordinate class divided.

The recognition of the changeability of men's character and attitudes is at least as old as Plato. But Marxian ethical theory made this changeability a central point of its position and because it included beliefs as to the causes of men's values it could frame a scheme which would envisage systematic large-scale changes in men's values, purposefully brought about by men themselves.

What the individual should do. When Marxian ethics turns to questions of what the individual *should* do, the problem becomes more difficult. Clearly a man's obligations depend on his fundamental values, and in Marxian terms these are usually a function of his class alignment. In a society at a given time there will be various groups of men. According to Marxian theory some of these groups take the stand of the dominant class, feel its obligations, impose its rules, and fight its battles. A second set of groups consists of self-conscious members of the subordinate class who feel its obligations, estimate rules of conduct by its aims, and fight the battles that will strengthen and organize it. A third or intermediate group consists of two parts. One segment consists of people who, although in one of the two classes by virtue of their objective position in the processes of production, do not understand the alignment of class forces. Their values will usually be those of the dominant class since all the weapons of social control and social conditioning are used to secure this state of affairs. To these people, Marxian theory believes, the advanced stages of class conflict will bring clarification. The remainder of the third group consists of remnants of former classes or subclasses now in process of disintegration, such as the lower middle class which is disappearing with the growth of monopolies and large economic units, or professional groups. To these, Marxian theory recommends that they abandon any hope of maintaining their present position and identify themselves with their prospective interests as members of the working class.

Human ethics and the classless society. In whatever class a man falls at present, according to Marxian theory, his moral system revolves about the central fact that there is class exploitation. In such a situation there is no such things as a classless morality. However, the morality of the working class—not the system of values and obligations to which workers may adhere in various countries, but that system which furthers their objective class interests—points to a classless morality. For the working class, if it assumes power, will end exploitation and therefore class morality itself. Hence if we wish to find a general doctrine of human goods and human morality in Marxian theory, we have to look to its conception of the classless society. But here its belief in the occurrence of novel qualities which are a function of concrete conditions has on the whole prevented it from offering detailed blue-prints of what it believes will eventually be the structure of human morality. Two broad features, however, distinguish it. It will operate on the general principle noted above, "From each according to his abilities, to each according to his needs." And the central struggle which the theory believes will replace the class struggle will be the fight to master the natural world.

The fact of abundance in a co-operative society that utilizes fully and expands its instruments of production will render many present moral rules obsolete, according to Marxian theory. Thus Engels says: "In a society in which the motive for stealing has been done away with, in which therefore at the very most only lunatics would ever steal, how the teacher of morals would be laughed at who tried solemnly to proclaim the eternal truth: Thou shalt not steal!"[39] The concrete experiences of the Soviet Union in the shift from a capitalist to a socialist economy enable us to fill in some of the outlines of Marxian ethics.[40] But the Soviet Union is, on its own theory, in a transitional stage, socialist and not yet communist, and therefore still far from the Marxian picture of the communist society.

Social values and the future

We have surveyed the general character of a materialist outlook on human affairs, and have examined two of the major movements which have embodied its this-worldly approach. We may now, in conclusion, note briefly the kinds of social values that we find in present-day materialist ethics. These values are widely shared by philosophers who take a naturalistic approach to the theory of man and an empirical approach to the theory of knowledge.

The meaning of individualism in a mature materialist ethics. A mature materialist outlook, in facing the world today, is not cynical or power-driven or devoted solely to personal pleasure. It is individualistic, but such individualism does not mean egoism, nor a disregard of the social nature of the self, nor free rein for every man to tread on any other. Its individualism lies in its aim of providing opportunities for the fullest development of the individual's capacities. Its individualism is inevitably world-wide in its scope.

---

[39] *Anti-Dühring*, translation by Emile Burns, International Publishers, p. 109.

[40] See, for example, Sidney and Beatrice Webb, *Soviet Communism: A New Civilization*, Scribner's, 1938; also Hewlett Johnson, *The Soviet Power*, Modern Age, 1942.

For under the conditions of man's life today, as the war has so dramatically shown, the well-being of any people is dependent on the well-being of all peoples. Fundamentals of morality are becoming indivisible in the sense in which it is now recognized that peace on this globe is indivisible. It will be increasingly difficult hereafter to think in purely local terms.

Attitude to change. Such a view expects constant change and development in the world and in man. It sees modern life as a critical period in the history of the globe, in which conscious beings—the most developed form of life which has ever existed—have within their grasp immensely widened powers of control and self-control. In that sense, mankind as a whole and the individual within society are on the verge of tremendously expanded freedom. The conditions for such development have been established by the growth and application of science. Changes in social organization and human ways are required to complete it. In bringing about such changes, in achieving their greater freedom, men can but rely on their own co-operative action. They may give thanks to men of the past and have faith in men of the future, but the source of change lies in the present and is guided by the wisdom or philosophy of the present.

Type of society envisaged. The society envisaged in such an approach is clearly a co-operative rather than a competitive one. It relies for the solution of social problems on the development of productivity and the conquest of the physical world so that conflicts are less likely to occur and do not have to be solved by restraints. It aims in the long run at a minimum of coercion and seeks adjustments through education, and where necessary through co-operative redirection of values. Its general virtues are modeled on pervasive conditions of life, not on the localized problems of a particular period. Objectivity, flexibility, initiative, awareness of the practical implications of theory and the theoretical implications of conduct, sympathy, co-operativeness—these are the traits it stresses for self-integrated men in a well-ordered society. Broadly, then, a mature materialist social philosophy envisages a democratic society of free men. Such an outlook brings a unique point of view to the consideration of democracy, the basis of its ideals and the conditions under which it may flourish. For it predicts that the richness and quality of life upon which men's hearts are set will emerge when the widest energies of individuals are given full scope for achieving the material prosperity and cultural development of all men throughout the world.

SUGGESTED READINGS

For historical data on philosophers or philosophies, see one of the standard histories of philosophy, such as
Fuller, B. A. G., *A History of Philosophy*
Höffding, Harald, *A History of Modern Philosophy*

Introduction

CHAPTER 1

Plato, *Apology; Republic,* Bk. 6
Aristotle, *Metaphysics,* Bk. I, chs. 1-2
Edman, Irwin, *Four Ways of Philosophy*
Selsam, Howard, *What is Philosophy?*
James, William, *Some Problems of Philosophy,* ch. 1
Hoernlé, R. F. A., *Idealism as a Philosophy,* ch. 1
Broad, C. D., *Scientific Thought,* Introduction

Part I

CHAPTER 2

The essence philosophies are best seen in the original writings of the ancient philosophers. For example:
Plato, *Republic,* sections 473-543
Aristotle, *Selections,* edited by W. D. Ross, nos. 21, 39, 53, 61

The most familiar teleological account of the cosmos is that found in the Bible:
The Book of Genesis (Old Testament)

For an interesting illustration of a teleological attitude in viewing the moment to moment happenings of life, see the selection from
Richard Mather's *Journal,* in Commager, H. S., and Nevins, A., *The Heritage of America,* pp. 34-40

Those interested in the history of teleology in the sciences will find it worth while to look into the use of purposive ideas in
Galen, *On the Natural Faculties*

For a general study of the historical conflict of science and the religious teleological appoach, see:
White, A. D., *A History of the Warfare of Science with Theology in Christendom*
Russell, Bertrand, *Religion and Science,* chs. 2-4

462   SUGGESTED READINGS

Illustrations of the teleological approach to history will be found under the idealist outlook on human affairs, ch. 24 below.

CHAPTERS 3-4

Most of the following works discuss several of the concepts of cause, law, necessity, determinism, system, and qualitative change. The listing is arranged under their points of special emphasis.

On cause and necessity:
  Hume, David, *Treatise on Human Nature*, Bk. I, Part 3
  Russell, Bertrand, "On the Notion of Cause" in *Mysticism and Logic*

On law, determinism, and probability:
  Reichenbach, Hans, *Atom and Cosmos*, ch. 18
  Russell, Bertrand, *Religion and Science*, ch. 6

On system and the nature of mathematics:
  Cohen, M. R., *Reason and Nature*, pp. 99-114
  Cohen, M. R., and Nagel, Ernest, *An Introduction to Logic and Scientific Method*, ch. 7
  Jourdain, P. E. B., *The Nature of Mathematics*

On qualitative novelty and the causes of qualitative change:
  Levy, Hyman, *A Philosophy for a Modern Man*, chs. 2-4

Part II

CHAPTER 5

On the nature of scientific method:
  Dewey, John, *How We Think*, rev. ed.
  Campbell, Norman, *What is Science?*
  Levy, Hyman, *The Universe of Science*, chs. 1-2
  Lenzen, V. F., *Procedures of Empirical Science*
  Schiller, F. C. S., "Hypothesis," in *Studies in the History and Methods of Science*, ed. by Charles Singer, Vol. II

CHAPTERS 6-10

On the history of science, and its intellectual, cultural, and social relations:
  Dampier, W. C. D., *A History of Science and its Relations with Philosophy and Religion* (third edition)
  Pledge, H. T., *Science Since 1500*
  Burtt, E. A., *Metaphysical Foundations of Modern Physical Science*
  Whitehead, A. N., *Science and the Modern World*
  Marvin, F. S. (ed.), *Science and Civilization*
  Bernal, J. D., *The Social Function of Science*
  Clark, G. N., *Science and Social Welfare in the Age of Newton*
  Merton, R. K., *Science, Technology and Society in Seventeenth Century England* (in *Osiris*, Vol. 4, pp. 360-632)

On the conflict of methods:
  Cohen, M. R., *Reason and Nature*, pp. 1-75
  Montague, W. P., *The Ways of Knowing*
  Bergson, Henri, *Introduction to Metaphysics*
  Descartes, René, *A Discourse on Method*
  James, William, "The Will to Believe" in *The Will to Believe; Pragmatism*, Lecture 2
  Peirce, C. S., "The Fixation of Belief" and "How to Make Our Ideas Clear" in *Chance, Love and Logic*, edited by M. R. Cohen, or *The Philosophy of Peirce*, by Justus Buchler.
  Locke, John, *An Essay Concerning Human Understanding*, Bk. I, ch. 2; Bk. II, chs. 1-9, 12; Bk. IV, chs. 1, 4, 5
  Berkeley, George, *Three Dialogues between Hylas and Philonous*, The first dialogue
  Lewis, C. I., *Mind and the World-Order*, chs. 2, 3
  Plato, *Theaetetus*
  Blanshard, Brand, *The Nature of Thought*, chs. 25-27

Part III

For a study of various theories:
  Morris, C. W., *Six Theories of Mind*
  Cohen, M. R., *Reason and Nature*, Bk. II, chs. 3-4

CHAPTER 11

On dualism and its various forms:
  Descartes, René, *Meditations*
  Locke, John, *An Essay Concerning Human Understanding*, discussions of substance and existence, especially Bk. II, ch. 23; Bk. IV, chs. 9-11
  Lovejoy, A. O., *The Revolt Against Dualism*
  McDougall, William, *Body and Mind*

CHAPTER 12

On mentalism and phenomenalism:
  Berkeley, George, *Principles of Human Knowledge*
  Hume, David, *A Treatise of Human Nature*, Bk. I
  Russell, Bertrand, *Religion and Science*, ch. 5
  Mach, Ernst, *The Analysis of Sensations*, ch. 1

CHAPTER 13

On mechanistic theories:
  Hobbes, Thomas, *Leviathan*, Bk. I
  LaMettrie, J. O. de, *Man A Machine*
  Loeb, Jacques, *The Mechanistic Conception of Life*
  Huxley, Aldous, *Brave New World*

CHAPTERS 14-15

On naturalistic approaches:
Aristotle, *De Anima*
Woodbridge, F. J. E., "The Nature of Man," in *Nature and Mind*
Dewey, John, *Experience and Nature*, ch. 7
Alexander, Samuel, *Space, Time and Deity*, Bk. 3, ch. 1
Krikorian, Y. H., "A Naturalistic View of Mind," in *Naturalism and the Human Spirit*, edited by Y. H. Krikorian
Mead, G. H., *Mind, Self and Society*

Part IV

CHAPTER 16

On means and ends:
Dewey, John, *Human Nature and Conduct*

CHAPTER 17

On freedom of the will:
Hume, David, *A Treatise of Human Nature*, Bk. II, Part 3
James, William, "The Dilemma of Determinism" and "Great Men and their Environment," in *The Will to Believe*
Taylor, A. E., *Elements of Metaphysics*, Bk. IV, ch. 4
Russell, Bertrand, *Religion and Science*, ch. 6
Spinoza, B., *Ethics*, fifth part

CHAPTERS 18-20

The theories of liberty, property, the state, war, and democracy are inextricably intertwined with the general problems of social philosophy. Perhaps the best approach to further study of these problems is to examine the various social philosophies, such as liberalism, socialism, communism. On the specific topics treated in the book, references to relevant works are given at various points in the footnotes and need not be repeated here. The number of books on these topics is legion, and the press of world problems today is constantly increasing their number. The following constitute merely a few suggestions.

Outlines of a positive theory of liberty will be found in
Laski, H. J., *Liberty in the Modern State* and *The Rise of Liberalism*
Laski's book on *The State in Theory and Practice* is a clear formulation of types of state theory.

For illustrative materials on problems of liberty in the United States:
Chafee, Zechariah, Jr., *Free Speech in the United States*
"Religious Freedom: A Debate," Justices Frankfurter and Stone, *New Republic*, June 24, 1940
Brooks, R. R. R., *Unions of their Own Choosing*

Good starting-points on the problems of equality and property will be found in
Tawney, R. H., *Equality*

SUGGESTED READINGS 465

Cohen, M. R., "Property and Sovereignty," in *Law and the Social Order*

There is an extended bibliography on democracy in its application to various fields by B. Y. Landis, appended to Ordway Tead's *The Case for Democracy*. For general reference see the *Encyclopedia of the Social Sciences*. For a philosophical treatment of historical approaches in political and economic theory, see

Sabine, G. H., *A History of Political Theory*
Bonar, James, *Philosophy and Political Economy*

Part V

CHAPTER 21

The contrast of the idealist tradition and the materialist-naturalist tradition is for the most part best studied in the various philosophers illustrative of types or development. Many of the following are classics in the field.

On the idealist tradition:

Plato, *Timaeus* (F. M. Cornford edition)
Gilson, Etienne, *Le Thomisme* (There is a good two-volume edition of selections from the works of Thomas Aquinas issued by Random House)
Berkeley, George, *Principles of Human Knowledge*
Hegel, G. W. F., *Selections* (Scribner's edition)
Schopenhauer, Arthur, *The World as Will and Idea*
Royce, Josiah, *The World and the Individual*

On the materialist-naturalist tradition:

Lucretius, *On the Nature of Things*
Hobbes, Thomas, *Leviathan*
Holbach, Baron d', *Système de la Nature*
Haeckel, Ernst, *The Riddle of the Universe*
Spencer, Herbert, *First Principles*
Engels, Frederick, *Anti-Dühring, Ludwig Feuerbach*
Santayana, George, *Reason in Science*
Dewey, John, *Experience and Nature*

Recent studies:

Barrett, Clifford (ed.), *Contemporary Idealism in America*
Krikorian, Y. H. (ed.), *Naturalism and the Human Spirit*

CHAPTER 22

On the phenomena of religion and their social relations:

Moore, G. F., *History of Religions*
Schneider, H. W., and Friess, H. L., *Religion in Various Cultures*
Benedict, R. F., "Religion," in Boas and Others, *General Anthropology*
Tawney, R. H., *Religion and the Rise of Capitalism*
Weber, Max, *Protestant Ethic and the Spirit of Capitalism*
White, A. D., *A History of the Warfare of Science with Theology in Christendom*

A convenient account of contemporary religious philosophies is to be found in

Burtt, E. A., *Types of Religious Philosophy*

On the existence of God:
> Mercier, Désiré, Cardinal, *A Manual of Modern Scholastic Philosophy*, Vol. II, "Natural Theology," Part I
> Pascal, Blaise, *Thoughts*
> James, William, *Varieties of Religious Experience;* "The Will to Believe" in *The Will to Believe*
> Hume, David, *Dialogues Concerning Natural Religion*
> Taylor, A. E., *The Faith of a Moralist*
> Macintosh, D. C., *The Problem of Religious Knowledge*

On immortality:
> Plato, *Phaedo*
> Lamont, Corliss, *The Illusion of Immortality*

Materialist-naturalist interpretations of religious phenomena:
> Dewey, John, *A Common Faith*
> Santayana, George, *Reason in Religion*
> Lenin, V. I., *Religion*

CHAPTER 23

For a historical study of the various theories of art:
> Gilbert, K. E., and Kuhn, Helmut, *A History of Esthetics*

Illustrations of interpretations in the idealist tradition:
> Plato, *Symposium*
> Schopenhauer, Arthur, *The World as Will and Idea*, Bk. III
> Hegel, G. W. F., *Philosophy of Fine Art*
> Greene, T. M., *The Arts and the Art of Criticism*

Illustrations of interpretations in the materialist-naturalist tradition:
> Aristotle, *Poetics*
> Santayana, George, *Reason in Art*
> Dewey, John, *Art as Experience*
> Prall, D. W., *Aesthetic Judgment*
> Siegmeister, Elie, *Music and Society*
> Kris, Ernst, "Approaches to Art," in *Psychoanalysis Today*, edited by Sandor Lorand, 1944 edition

CHAPTER 24

Plato and Aristotle:
> Plato, *Republic, Laws*
> Aristotle, *Nicomachean Ethics, Politics*

Stoicism:
> Epictetus, *Discourses*
> Marcus Aurelius, *Meditations*
> Murray, Gilbert, *The Stoic Philosophy*

The Christian outlook on good and evil:
> Mercier, Désiré, Cardinal, *A Manual of Modern Scholastic Philosophy*, Vol. II, "Natural Theology," Part III; "Ethics," Parts I, II
> Sidgwick, Henry, *Outlines of the History of Ethics*, ch. 3

For contrasting attitudes on the problem of evil:
  The Book of Job (Old Testament)
  Russell, Bertrand, "A Free Man's Worship" in *Mysticism and Logic*
  Spinoza, B., *Ethics*, appendix to Bk. I
  Mill, J. S., *Three Essays on Religion*

Kant's major ethical works are conveniently collected in
  Abbott, T. K., *Kant's Theory of Ethics*
This general ethical discussion should be supplemented with a study of his political essays. See the collection in
  Hastie, W., *Kant's Principles of Politics*

Royce's ethical views emerge clearly in
  Royce, Josiah, *The Philosophy of Loyalty* and *The Religious Aspect of Philosophy*

Idealist interpretation of history:
  Herder, J. G. von, *Ideas for the Philosophy of the History of Mankind*
  Vico, G. B., *Autobiography*
  Hegel, G. W. F., *Philosophy of History*
Descriptions of idealist interpretations of history will be found in
  Flint, Robert, *The Philosophy of History in France and Germany*, and *The Philosophy of History*
  Bury, J. B., *The Idea of Progress*

CHAPTER 25

Different strands are to be found in what may be broadly reckoned as the this-worldly materialist-naturalist tradition. The following are grouped according to types of approach.
  On Epicurean theory, see the materials in
  Oates, W. J. (ed.), *The Stoic and Epicurean Philosophers*

On power theory:
  Hobbes, Thomas, *Leviathan*
  Nietzsche, F. W., *The Will to Power*, Vol. II, Bk. 3, Pt. 3; *The Genealogy of Morals*. (For Nietzsche's inclusion in this context see above, p. 441, n. 17)
  Russell, Bertrand, *Power*

On utilitarian theory:
  Bentham, Jeremy, *Principles of Morals and Legislation, Theory of Legislation*
  Mill, J. S., *Utilitarianism, On Liberty*
  Halévy, Elie, *The Growth of Philosophical Radicalism*
  Sidgwick, Henry, *The Methods of Ethics*

On Marxian theory:
  Marx, Karl, and Engels, Frederick, *The Communist Manifesto*
  Engels, Frederick, *Anti-Dühring*, Pt. I, chs. 9-11, Pt. III
  Selsam, Howard, *Socialism and Ethics*
  Burns, Emile (ed.), *A Handbook of Marxism*

On anarchist and syndicalist theory:
: Kropotkin, Prince Peter, *Ethics, Mutual Aid*
: Proudhon, P. J., *What is Property?*
: Sorel, Georges, *Reflections on Violence*
: Russell, Bertrand, *Proposed Roads to Freedom*

On positivist theory:
: Ayer, A. J., *Language, Truth and Logic*, ch. 6
: Russell, Bertrand, *Religion and Science*, ch. 9
: Schlick, Moritz, *Problems of Ethics*
: Lévy-Bruhl, Lucien, *The Philosophy of Auguste Comte*, Bk. IV

On pragmatist theory:
: Dewey, John, and Tufts, J. H., *Ethics*, revised edition
: Dewey, John, *Freedom and Culture*

INDEX

Absolute, authority, 81; desires, 267; element in ethical rules, 409, 433-434; knowledge, 76 ff.; space, 121-22
Abstract, 118. (*See also* Idea, Ideal)
Abundance, 275, 459
Accident, 15, 16, 19
Activity, as mode of verification, 99-100; mind as, 168; human activities, 170 ff.
Adjustment, as vital phenomenon, 144
Agnosticism, 352
Alexander, Samuel (1859-1939), 366
Altruism, 204
Analytic statements, 45, 86
Anaxagoras (5th century, B.C.), 321, 342
Anaximander (6th century, B.C.), 318
Anaximenes (6th century, B.C.), 318
Animism, 338
Anthropomorphism, 37
Antinomies, 120 ff.
Apperception, 195
A priori statements, 85, 327, 421. (*See also* Axioms, Logical Principles)
Aquinas, Thomas (1227-1274), 343
Aristotle (384-322 B.C.), apparent and real good, 427; concept of change, 321-22; concept of the eternal, 331; contemplation, 395; distribution according to merit, 293; essence and nature, 13, 15 ff.; ethical theory, 392 ff.; first cause, 321, 343; mind, 168; physical theory, 325; political and social theory, 394-95; property, 258-59; space, 122-23; the state, 278; tragedy, 367, 381; voluntary and involuntary, 231; Zeno's paradoxes answered, 120
Arithmetic statements, 86
Art, 364 ff.; content of, 385-86; creation, 367 ff., 383-85; for art or life's sake, 372, 379; idealist interpretation of, 373 ff.; materialist interpretation of, 380 ff.; as representation, expression, or communication, 368-69; forms of, 365
Atheism, 353
Atomic theory, 2
Augustine (354-430), 349, 374, 417, 420
Aurelius, Marcus (121-180), 398

Authority, 80 ff.
Authoritarian attitudes, 82; contrasted with democratic, 302-04
Axioms, 85 ff.
Ayer, A. J. (1910-   ), 353, 428

Babbitt, Irving (1865-1933), 299
Bacon, Francis (1561-1626), 278
Beauty. *See* Esthetic quality
Behaviorism, 162 ff.
Bellamy, Edward (1850-1898), 278
Bentham, Jeremy (1748-1832), 78, 226, 443 ff.; *Deontology*, 445; equalitarianism, 448; legal theory, 231, 449-50; program for secularizing morality, 444
Bentley, A. F. (1870-   ), 280
Bergson, Henri (1859-1941), 118-19, 349
Berkeley, George (1685-1753), 112, 151-54
Beveridge plan, 227
Bill of Rights, 244
Biological factors, 238-40
Body, 137-39; and soul, 139 ff.; and mind, 145 ff.; Berkeley's interpretation of, 152. (*See also* Matter)
Bridgman, P. W. (1882-   ), 95, 100
Buckle, H. T. (1821-1862), 237
Buddhism, 355

Calvinism, 406
Capitalism, 273-74, 276, 281, 306-09, 450, 453-56. (*See also* Economic liberty)
Carnap, Rudolf (1891-   ), 90
Cartesian. *See* Descartes
Categorical imperative, 408-10
Categories, 325
Catholicism, 343, 350, 359, 400, 402
Causality, 28 ff., 180; estimate of, 32 ff.; final cause, 21; "first cause" argument, 342; in history, 34-35; of will, 218-19
Certainty. *See* Knowledge
Change, 317 ff.; Aristotle's analysis of, 321-22; has it always existed?, 343; and scientific laws, 43-44; teleological account of, 24
Character, 226, 232-34, 241-42, 247, 251-52, 406-07, 451, 460. (*See also* Self, Virtue)

469

Charity, 187
Choice, 217
Christian tradition, 3; on good and evil, 400 ff.; on human brotherhood, 295; on soul, 139 ff.
Civil liberties, 244, 255
Classes, 280-82, 288, 453-55
Classification, 18-19
Cleanthes (circ. 301-232 or 252 B.C.), 399
Coercion, 25, 232, 283 ff.
Cohen, M. R. (1880-   ), 280
Coherence, 126-27
Communism, 271, 275, 361, 443, 459
Communist Manifesto, 443
Comte, Auguste (1798-1857), 353
Conflict, of desires, 264 ff.; of classes, see Classes
Conscience, 99, 224-25
Consciousness. *See* Mental Phenomena
Consequences, logical, 56-57; testing by, 71-72, 95
Constitution, 106
Contemplation, 395
Contingency, 53, 57-58
Contradiction, principle of, 89, 91
Control, principles of property, 276
Convention, 86, 90-91
Correspondence, 109-11
Cosmological argument, 342 ff.
Critical philosophy, 3

Death, 137, 356-7. (*See also* Immortality)
Deduction, 38. (*See also* Logic)
Definition, 45, 86-87
Deism, 341
Democracy, 290-309
Democritus (b. circ. 460 B.C.), 2, 28, 161, 315, 318, 321, 325
Descartes, René (1596-1650), 25, 146-48, 158, 195, 318, 347
Design argument, 344
Determinism, 31-32, 221 ff. (*See also* Causality)
Dewey, John (1859-   ), 90, 212, 382, 427-28, 431
Dialectic, 451-52
Distribution, principles of, 273
Dogmatism, 17-18, 78
Driesch, Hans (1867-1941), 144
Dualism, 184, 314; of body and soul, 139; of body and mind, 145 ff.; of method, 159
Duress, 232
Duns Scotus (circ. 1274-1308), 401
Duty, 408, 412. (*See also* Values)
Dynamic, contrasted with static, 119, 439

Economic liberty, 252 ff., 258 ff.
Economic Bill of Rights, 259
Educational theory, 201-03; democracy in education, 303
Egoism, 204 ff.
Emotions, religious, 338; in ethical theory, 426-28
Empedocles (circ. 490-435 B.C.), 318-20
Empirical method, 73. (*See also* Scientific method)
Empirical statement, 45, 85
Empiricism, 314, 408. (*See also* Sense-perception)
Ends, 211 ff., 262. (*See also* Values)
Engels, Frederick (1820-1895), 361, 443, 459
Epictetus (b. circ. 60 A.D.), 398
Epicurus (341-270 B.C.), 442
Epiphenomenalism, 157, 184
Epistemology, 4. (*See also* Knowledge)
Equality, 291 ff., 448
Essence, 11 ff., 17
Esthetic quality, 365 ff., 379, 381-83
Esthetic evaluation, 370
Eternal, 14, 128, 141, 331-33, 338, 411-12
Ethics, nature of, 4; ethical advice, 267; ethical relativity, 428 ff. (*See also* Values)
Euclidean geometry, 87, 121
Evaluation, in art, 370 ff., 379, 381, 386-87; of means and ends, 213 ff.; of institutions, 269; of virtues, 268; instrumentalist analysis of, 431
Evil, problem of, 402 ff.
Evolution, 345
Existence, 13, 325, 347
Excluded middle, principle of, 89, 91
Experience, testing by, 93 ff.
Experiment, 71-72
Explanation, 11 ff., 179-83
Expression, in art, 384-85

Fact, 130, 423-24
Faith, in God, 401 (*see also* Will to Believe); in the people, 299 ff.
Fascism, 274, 276
Fatalism, 406-07. (*See also* Determinism)
Fault, 225 ff.
Feeling, as verification, 97, 99
Felicific calculus, 446
Fichte, J. G. (1762-1814), 196, 421
Feuerbach, Ludwig (1804-1872), 238
Final cause, 21, 343
First principles, 74, 77, 83 ff.
Formulating problems, 70
Four Freedoms, 259

INDEX

Fraternity, 294-95, 399, 410
Free will, 215, 217, 220 ff.
Freud, Sigmund (1856-1939), 20, 26, 57, 58

Galileo Galilei (1564-1642), 72, 315, 322
Gandhi, M. K. (1869-   ), 288
Generalization, 30, 34. (*See also* Law)
Geometric postulates, 87
Geulincx, Arnold (1624-1669), 147
God, in Christian doctrine, 23; in teleological explanation, 25; in Occasionalist theory, 147; in Berkeley's philosophy, 153; conception of, 340-41; as ultimate totality, 348; arguments on existence of, 340-54
Good, Christian outlook on, 400 ff.; materialist analysis of, 425 ff. (*See also* Values)
Government, by the people, 296 ff.; democratic, 295
Group-mind, 142, 185
Group-phenomena, 142-43. (*See also* Social molding)

Haeckel, Ernst (1834-1919), 316
Happiness, 392, 445, 460; *summum bonum*, 351. (*See also* Pleasure, Utilitarianism)
Hawtrey, R. G. (1879-   ), 288
Hebraism, 341, 418
Hedonism, 442. (*See also* Pleasure)
Hegel, G. W. F. (1770-1831), 196, 226, 278, 317; on religion, 357; on art, 377-79; philosophy of history, 419, 421 ff.; conception of the state, 422; on dialectic, 451-52
Helmholtz, Hermann (1821-1894), 344
Heredity, 239
Historical materialism, 452-59
History, of philosophy, 5-6; idealist interpretation of, 416-424; materistic interpretation, 452-56
Hobbes, Thomas (1588-1679), 161, 182, 218, 295, 315, 318, 321-22, 335-36, 380, 426, 442
Holbach, Baron d' (1723-1789), 315
Holt, E. B. (1873-   ), 145, 265-66
Human activities, classification of, 170 ff.
Hume, David (1711-1776), 37, 112, 154 ff., 195, 197, 367, 426
Huntington, Ellsworth (1876-   ), 238
Huxley, Aldous (1894-   ), 166
Huxley, T. H. (1825-1895), 157, 316
Hypothesis, 71, 79, 89

Idea, Platonic theory, 14; Berkeley's interpretation of, 151; Hegelian concept of, 423
Ideal, 13-14, 25, 43, 127, 347, 423, 430; ideals of democracy, 291 ff.
Idealism, central features, 314-15; major types, 329; Platonic, 315; subjective, 112, 151 ff., 324; Schopenhauer's theory of Will, 376; historical relation to science, 316 ff.; interpretation of art, 373 ff.; interpretation of history, 417 ff.; outlook on human affairs, 388 ff. (*See also* Plato, Berkeley, Hegel, Schopenhauer, Plotinus)
Identity, principle of, 89, 91; general theory of, 189-90; of individual man, 191 ff.
Identity theory, of body and mind, 158, 184
Imagination, 79, 359
Immanent, pattern, 16; goal, 21; teleology, 23
Immortality, 355-57
Indeterminacy, 47
Individual, 191 ff., 252; point of view, 423, 436 ff., 458
Individualism, 250, 294, 440 ff., 459
Induction, Mill's methods of, 36
Infinite, 120; regress, 83
Insight, 71, 79
Instinct theory, 240
Instrumentalism, analysis of evaluation, 431; on logical rules, 90. (*See also* Dewey)
Intelligence, 101; operational view, 102
Intention, 228
Interactionism, 146, 182
Intuition, 76-80, 118, 349-350
Intuitive induction, 15, 17
Irrationalism, 78

James, William (1842-1910), 93, 97, 127, 158, 346, 353, 405
Jefferson, Thomas (1743-1826), 259, 284
Jennings, H. S. (1868-   ), 159
Job, 404
Justice, 389, 432. (*See also* State, Law)

Kant, Immanuel (1724-1804), on percepts and concepts, 115; antinomies, 120 ff.; theory of space, 122; theory of self, 195 ff.; on first cause argument, 343; on ontological argument, 347; moral argument, 351; argument for immortality, 355; ethical theory, 407 ff.
Kepler, Johann (1571-1630), 25

INDEX

Knowledge, of whole world, 31; demand for absolute, 76-92; probable character of, 92; theories of sensation as, 108-117; criteria of, 129; limited to phenomena, 121, 155; of states of consciousness, 115; of mind, 154; of another's mental state, 178; of the self, 197-99; cognitive character of mental phenomena, 178-79. (*See also* Correspondence, Truth)

Krutch, J. W. (1893-   ), 165, 186, 233

Labor disputes, 285
LaMettrie, J. O. de (1709-1751), 162, 315, 321
Law, legal, 29, 225-28; of property, 270-71; theory of, 280, 449-50
Law, scientific, 3, 41-53, 57-60, 180-83
Leadership, 297-98
Legal terms, 106
Leibniz, G. W. (1646-1716), 404
Length, 100
Lenin, V. I. (1870-1924), 361-63, 443
Levels, 48-52, 59, 170-72, 181-83. (*See also* Qualities, novel)
Liberty, 215, 235-263, 291
Life. *See* Body, Mind, Soul; Quality, novel
Lincoln, Abraham (1809-1865), 284, 299
Locke, John (1632-1704), theory of sensation, 109 ff.; on interactionism, 148; Berkeley's critique of, 152; concept of matter, 319, 324 ff.; ultimate categories for describing existence, 326; derivation of idea of God, 348
Logic, 4, 56, 71, 93; logical necessity, 38, 45; logical principles, 88-91; alleged conflict with experience, 119-20
Logical positivism, 90, 95
Loyalty, 411 ff.
Loyola, Ignatius (1491-1556), 82

Mach, Ernst (1838-1916), 113
MacLeish, Archibald (1892-   ), 305, 372
Madison, James (1751-1836), 280-81
Malebranche, Nicolas (1638-1715), 147
Marx, Karl (1818-1883), 316, 361, 443, 452, 454, 456-57
Marxism, 281-82, 288, 361 ff., 431, 451-59
Materialism, central features, 314-15; mechanical, 315, 322; dialectical, 322, 451; historical, 443, 451 ff.; and the history of science, 315; conception of change, 322; interpretation of the eternal, 332-33; attitudes to death, 356; interpretation of religion, 358 ff.; interpretation of art, 380 ff.; treatment of society, 440 ff.; interpretation of values, 425 ff.; and democracy, 460

Mathematics, 85-88
Matrix of values, 437
Matter, 146, 152; meaning of, 318; relation to change, 320 ff.; idealist attempt to declare it unreal, 323; has it always existed?, 343; Hegel's view of, 421; J. S. Mill's definition of, 443
McDougall, William (1871-1938), 139, 144
Mead, G. H. (1863-1931), 199
Meaning, positivist theory of, 95
Means, 211 ff.
Mechanism, 28 ff., 160 ff., 182, 184, 315, 322, 380. (*See also* Causality, World-Machine)
Memory, 197
Mental Phenomena, 138, 158, 173 ff., 179 ff. (*See also* Sense-perception, Sense-data)
Metaphysics, 3, 317. (*See also* Idealism, Materialism, Dualism, Existence, Matter, Spirit)
Method, involved in conception of truth, 126-28; of philosophy, 125; of science, *see* Scientific Method
Mill, James (1773-1836), 443, 446, 449
Mill, J. S. (1806-1873), 36, 78, 245-257, 282, 443
Mind, body and mind, 145 ff.; Berkeley on, 153-54; Hume on, 154-55; mechanistic theories of, 157-165; naturalistic account of, 168 ff. (*See also* Mental Phenomena, Sense-perception, Will, Soul, Spirit, Self)
Miracles, 345
Mohammedanism, 341
Monism and pluralism compared, 63-64
Monotheism, 340
Moral argument, 351
Moral rules, 84 (*See also* Virtues, Truthfulness, Categorical imperative)
More, Thomas (1478-1535), 278
Motion, 119-20. (*See also* Change, Materialism, mechanical)
Münsterberg, Hugo (1863-1916), 417
Music, 376-78, 383
Mysticism, 329, 349, 374. (*See also* Plotinus)

Nature, of a thing, 16-18; living according to, 397; human, 239-241, 390-91, 393-95; is man naturally selfish?, 204 ff.; of man, Part III
Naturalism, 314; account of man, Chapter 14; theory of freedom, 229 ff.
Necessary condition, 35
Necessity, 30, 36-39, 44, 456

INDEX

Nehru, Jawaharlal (1889-), 288
Newton, Isaac (1642-1727), 25, 121, 315
Nietzsche, F. W. (1844-1900), 226, 441
Nirvana, 139
Nominal definition, 45
Nominalism, 347
Non-worldly, 334, 388
Noumenal, 195
Novelty. *See* Quality, novel
Null class, 347

Obedience, 82
Objective idealism, 329
Observation, 37, 71. (*See also* Sense-perception)
Occam, William of (c. 1300-1349), 341
Occasionalism, 147
Omnipotence, 403, 405
Ontological argument, 346 ff.
Operationalism, 95-96, 102-03
Opportunity, equality of, 293
Order, 2, 345
Organic, contrasted with mechanical, 144; logic, 420
Other-worldly, 334, 401
Outlook, 5-6, 313, 334, 388 ff., 425 ff., 440

Pacifism, 287
Paine, Thomas (1737-1809), 300
Paley, William (1743-1805), 344
Panpsychism, 330
Pantheism, 396
Parallelism, 148
Parmenides (b. circ. 539 B.C.), 320
Particulars, 12-13
Pater, Walter (1839-1894), 62, 233
Pavlov, I. P. (1849-1936), 223
Peirce, C. S. (1839-1914), 93, 127, 129, 131
Perfection. *See* Ideal, Ontological argument
Personal identity, 154
Personality, 197
Pessimism, 165
Phenomenalism, 154, 443. (*See also* Hume)
Philosophical systems, 1-3
Physical. *See* Body, Matter, Physics
Physics, 21, 25, 29-31, 43, 47, 59-60, 161, 163, 318, 322, 324-35. (*See also* Mechanism)
Piety, 186
Plato (427-347 B.C.), theory of ideas, 14-17, 346; idealism, 329; on art, 375; on the eternal, 331; ethical and social theory, 389-92; conception of matter, 323; approach to mysticism, 349; theory of pleasure, 193; theory of the soul, 140, 321, 389; on space, 121; *Phaedo*, 140, 328, 342, 355; *Republic*, 193, 350, 375, 389 ff.; *Symposium*, 373-74
Pleasure, Plato's theory, 193 ff.; Epicurean theory, 442; in materialist ethical theory, 426-27; Bentham on, 443-44
Plotinus (204-269), 350, 374
Pluralism and monism compared, 63-64, 314
Plurality of causes, 34, 36
Plutarch (circ. 46-120), 140, 398
Polarity, 116
Political liberty, 243, 254 ff., 260
Political theory, 290. (*See also* Democracy, State, Constitution)
Positivism, 113, 314, 353, 428
Post hoc ergo propter hoc, 35
Postulates. *See* First Principles
Pound, Roscoe (1870-), 226, 280
Power ethics, 440-41
Practical consequences, 93, 97
Practice, and verification, 97, 99; and theory, 5-7, 313-14, 334-35, 460. (*See also* Outlook)
Pragmatic argument for existence of God, 352
Pragmatism, 90, 93-94, 127. (*See also* James, Peirce, Dewey)
Praise, 224
Prayer, 338, 357
Prediction, 30, 51, 61-62
Preexistence, Plato on, 14
Primacy, 327, 330
Primary qualities. *See* Quality, primary
Prime mover, 343-44
Privacy, of sensation, 177
Probability, 46-48
Property, of a thing, 15; as legal institution, 270 ff.
Propositional function, 56, 87
Protagoras (481-411 B.C.), 125
Protestantism, 340, 402
Provocation, 232
Psychoanalysis, 241
Psychology, meaning of intelligence, 101-04; Locke's, 109-11; Behaviorism, 162-65; contemporary approaches to mind, 169; and relation of the sciences, 171-73, 181-85; study of the self, 199; psychological egoism, 204-07; psychological factors, 240-42; on moral ideas, 224-25
Punishment, 225 ff., 339
Purpose, 20-27

INDEX

Quality, novel, 60-63; primary and secondary, 111-12, 148; sense-data as qualities, 173-75; qualitative change, 321-23; as category, 325

Rationalism, 83, 314, 408
Rational pattern in history, 419
Realism, 314; medieval, 347
Reality, 13, 75, 104-05, 131-34
Reason, 121, 228, 266. (*See also* Logic)
Reduction, 180, 182, 322. (*See also* Materialism, mechanical)
Regularity, 30, 33 ff.
Religion, 337-363
Religious liberty, 256
Religious truth, 98
Responsibility, 225 ff.
Revelation, 343, 357
Revolution, right of, 284
Ricardo, David (1772-1823), 316, 442
Right, 432 ff.
Ritual, in religion, 338
Roosevelt, Franklin D. (1882-1945), 236, 259
Rousseau, J. J. (1712-1778), 295, 299, 395
Royce, Josiah (1855-1916), 411-16
Russell, Bertrand (1872-   ), 148, 156, 233, 427

Sanctions, 283 ff.
Santayana, George (1863-   ), 27, 157, 186-87, 264, 347, 358 ff., 384, 430
Schleiermacher, F. E. D. (1768-1834), 353
Schopenhauer, Arthur (1788-1860), 373, 376-77
Science, 3, 25-27, 69; critiques of, 118 ff.; relation of sciences, 171-72
Scientific method, Part II
Security, 29, 291, 439, 441
Self, problems of, 188 ff.; "real" self, 192 ff.; social character of, 198, 242; fixity and changeability of, 199 ff.; self-expression, 200 ff.; and values, 203; and ideals, 415-16
Self-evident propositions, 83 ff.
Seneca (4 B.C.-65 A.D.), 398-99
Sense-data, as corresponding to qualities, 109; as ultimate reality, 111-13; in scientific method, 113 ff.; as qualities of events, 173 ff.
Sense-perception, 16, 75, 95-96, 100, 108-117. (*See also* Sense-data, Mental phenomena)
Sidgwick, Henry (1838-1900), 401, 443
Sin, 224
Sinclair, Upton (1878-   ), 274
Skepticism, 124-25

Smith, Adam (1723-1790), 316, 442
Smith, T. V. (1890-   ), 292
Social evolution, 50
Social molding, 242 ff.
Social science, 105-07, 171-72, 185, 322-23
Socialism, 271, 275, 277, 459
Society, liberty and, 242-45; social institutions, 269-70; coercion mechanisms within, 285 ff.; materialist treatment of, 440 ff. (*See also* Group-phenomena, State, History)
Socrates (469-399 B.C.), 4, 200, 373, 389
Solipsism, 153
Soul, 139-45, 354-56
Space, 121-124, 324
Spencer, Herbert (1820-1903), 380, 450
Spengler, Oswald (1880-1936), 317, 418, 420
Speculative philosophy, 1-3
Spinoza, Baruch (1632-1677), 148, 158, 349
Spirit, 24, 328-31; of an age, 417; of a people, 418; Hegel's view of, 421; Berkeley's theory of, 153-54. (*See also* Soul)
Spirituality, 187
Standardization, 257-58
State, 105, 277-83, 422
Statement, a priori, 85, 327, 421; uninterpreted, 87; empirical, 45, 85
Static, contrasted with dynamic, 119, 439
Stoicism, 295, 396-99, 404
Subjective, *see* Idealism, subjective; of mental phenomena, 175; descriptions of "good," 426; subjectivism, 149-50, 314
Substance. *See* Body, Matter, Spirit, Soul
Substratum, 148, 319
Sufficient condition, 35
Supernatural, 329, 338, 359. (*See also* God)
Symbols, 176
System, 5, 53-65

Technocracy, 274
Technology, 238
Teleology, 23-27
Temporal precedence, in causality, 30, 32-34
Terms, 57, 59, 105-07, 180
Theism, 341
Theology. *See* God, Supernatural
Theory and practice, 5-7, 313-14, 334-35, 460. (*See also* Outlook, System, Knowledge)
This-worldliness, 333, 451
Thrasymachus (5th century, B.C.), 298, 440
Time, 119-22
Tolstoi, L. N. (1828-1910), 287

INDEX

Torts, 226
Transcendental, teleology, 23; self, 195
Truth, 75, 98, 114, 126-29, 331, 333
Truthfulness, 409, 413, 434-36

Uniformity, 42-3; of nature, 48 ff.
Unity. *See* Order, Monism, System, Mysticism
Universal, 12, 16
Unknowable, 155, 353
Utilitarianism, 292, 442-51. (*See also* Bentham, Mill, J. S.)

Values, current need for analysis of, 6; in epiphenomenalist theory, 158; in mechanistic theory, 165 ff.; naturalistic attitude to, 185 ff.; place in the self, 203; means and ends, 211 ff.; value content in legal concepts, 232; biological basis of, 239; Mill's positive values, 247; in interpretation of equality, 292; patterns of value and of justification, 335; is spiritual order presupposed by values?, 351; Aristotle's social values, 394; loyalty estimated, 415; relation to fact, 423-24; materialist interpretation of, 425-40
Verification, 72-73, 95-96
Vico, G. B. (1668-1744), 417, 420
Violence, 286 ff.
Virtues, 186, 268, 391, 397, 401-02, 432 ff.
Vitalism, 143-45
Voltaire (1694-1778), 404
Voluntary, 230 ff.

Wallace, H. A. (1888-   ), 308
Ward, H. F. (1878-   ), 298
Weber, Max (1864-1920), 340, 406, 455
Will, 217 ff., 376; will to believe, 98
Wisdom, love of, 1. (*See also* Theory)
Woodbridge, F. J. E. (1867-1940), 174
World-machine, 30-32
Worldliness, 401, 451

Zeno, the Eleatic (5th Century, B.C.), 119-20, 320
Zeno, the Stoic (circ. 350-258 B.C.), 396
Zoroastrianism, 405